# Minnesota State University, Mankato, 1868-2018:
## A Sesquicentennial History
### By William E. Lass

# Minnesota State University, Mankato 1868-2018:

# A Sesquicentennial History

By William E. Lass

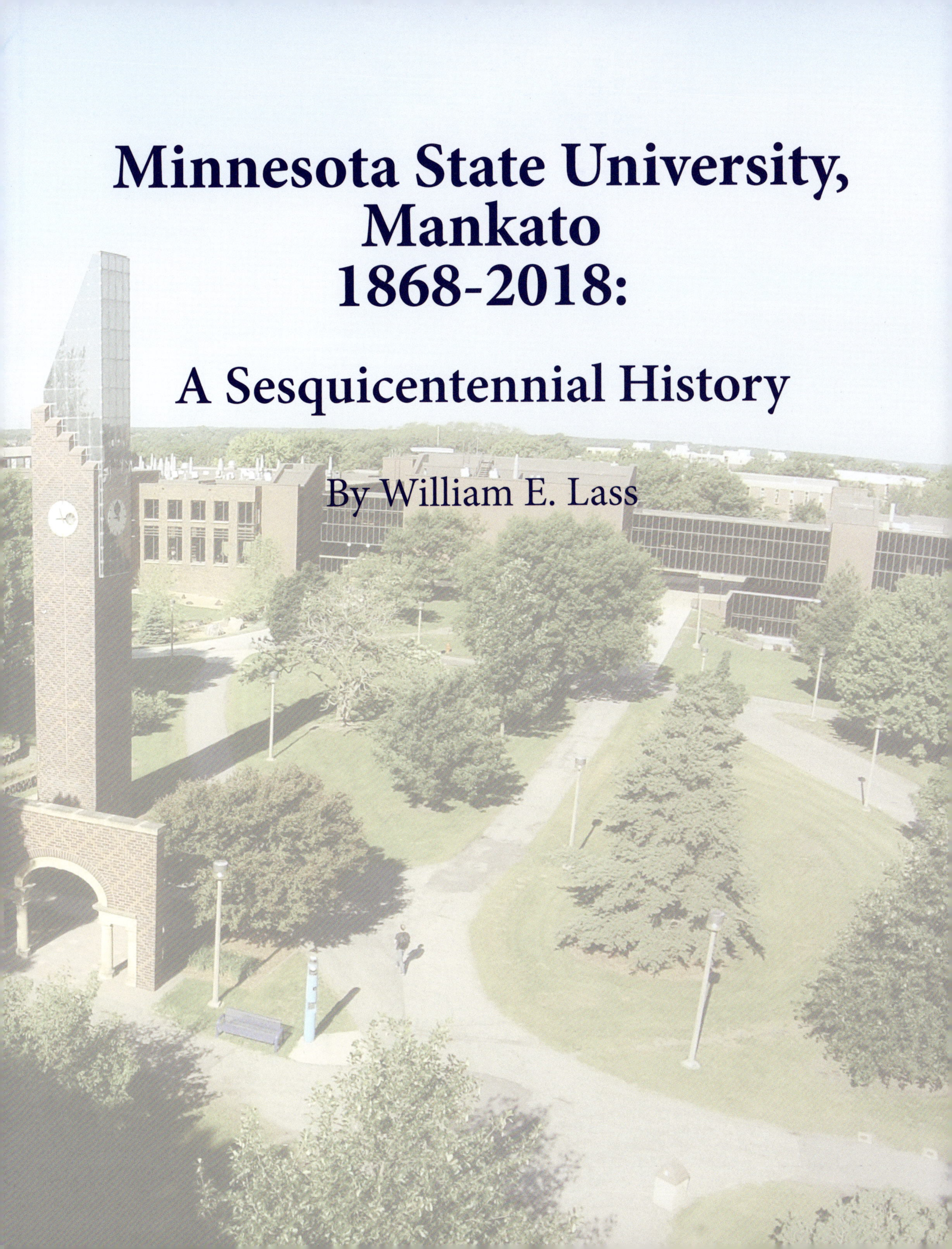

Designed and printed by Minnesota State University, Mankato Printing Services
Published by Minnesota State University, Mankato

Author: William E. Lass
Project editors: Daardi Sizemore Mixon and Sara Gilbert Frederick
Graphic Designer: Gail Connelly

Unless otherwise stated, all images provided by the University Archives at Minnesota State University, Mankato.

**Cataloging-in-Production Data available from the Library Congress**

ISBN: 978-0-9729134-6-1

**Printed in the United States of America**

# TABLE OF CONTENTS

Minnesota State University, Mankato, 1868-2018:
A Sesquicentennial History
By William E. Lass

# INTRODUCTION

The celebration of this university's 150th anniversary has been one of the highlights of my tenure as president at Minnesota State University, Mankato. I've especially enjoyed the process of preparing for this milestone occasion, as it affords us an opportunity to both honor our past and look toward our future.

This book does both.

Through his thorough research and clean, clear writing style, William E. Lass has honored our history in the most accurate and comprehensive way possible. He found new details, verified age-old stories and compiled the most complete history ever written about this institution. I thought I knew almost everything there was to know, but in this narrative, I've learned even more about Minnesota State Mankato and its history.

In crafting such a complete story of our past, Bill also helped shine a light on what we might expect in the future. Our history is fraught with challenges fought, from raising enough money to match the state appropriation for our founding to battling with the state legislature about offering graduate degrees. The lesson to take from those experiences is that perseverance pays off—and it will continue to do so. We are not done facing challenges. But our future depends on our ability to evolve as an institution, and we must be willing to work hard for the long haul to make that happen.

In these pages, you will read about the pioneers of higher education who invested much of their lives to the growth and development of this institution. Each of my predecessors as president has played an important role in our history, as have the many men and women who taught classes, kept the schedule, took care of students and tended the grounds. You will be introduced to people you may never have heard of before and learn more about some whose names are familiar.

You will also read about the physical campus and how it has changed over the past 150 years. The beautiful buildings we occupy today are the legacy of our founders, who operated classes in space rented from community members in 1868. They could not have imagined then the campus we inhabit today. In fact, the move from downtown to the rural farmland on Mankato's hilltop wouldn't have crossed their minds. Today, we just as likely can't imagine our almost 15,000 students existing at the bottom of the hill.

I encourage everyone to read this book with an ear tuned to the lessons of the past and an eye out for the possibilities of our future. There is much to learn about where we've been and what we've done— and how that has shaped our current standing as one of the top public institutions in Minnesota.

Bill Lass retired the same year I became president of Minnesota State Mankato. He has, however, remained a steady presence on campus. I am grateful for Bill's attention to detail, his insistence on accuracy and his nose for an interesting new story. I am also grateful for his extreme generosity: he asked for nothing but office supplies and staff support in return for writing this book. Bill, please take this as a personal thank you from me and from everyone at the University. You have done yeoman's work on this book, and we are deeply indebted to you for this.

This book is a wonderful read. Enjoy every minute of it.

# PREFACE

The academic institution that evolved into Minnesota State University, Mankato opened with its first classes on October 7, 1868, as the Mankato Normal School. In its century and a half long history, it has had four distinct organizational periods. The Mankato Normal School lasted until 1921 when it was replaced by Mankato Teachers College. The teachers college phase was succeeded in 1957 by Mankato State College, which, in turn, became Mankato State University in 1975. The current name —Minnesota State University, Mankato — was adopted in 1998.

The idea for this book was first suggested by Daardi Sizemore Mixon, archivist of Minnesota State University, Mankato. In her role of collecting, preserving and disseminating information about the institution's development, she has been affected by the lack of a general history that covers the entire scope of the institution's existence.

In writing this history I have tried to include coverage of the most significant developments in the institution's history. Short of having a marvelous time machine that somehow magically regurgitates everything about the past, any historian has to make decisions about inclusions and exclusions. Those seeking more information about any particular happening should consult the bibliography for preliminary guidance.

In the course of researching and writing history over the last 60 years, I have developed a certain philosophy of history. History is commonly defined as the study of the past. But, we should always remember that it is our past. Those people we are studying all lived in their own present. They had to deal with all of life's uncertainties. Somehow, through hindsight we can solve all their anxieties and problems very easily. I can well imagine a setting two centuries hence when history students will cover the solution to the war on terror in about an hour of classroom time at best.

History can be appreciated in various ways. Some adhere to the notion that knowledge of the past provides a perspective for the present and a guide to the future. Others find that entertainment is history's principal attraction. But anyone interested in life at some point will become interested in history. Our past, like our present, is sometimes tragic, sometimes pleasant, sometimes comical and sometimes even ludicrous.

The instructive value of history, the so-called "lessons of history," obviously varies from person to person. In this connection, I am reminded of the historian/philosopher Will Durant (1885-1981) who, with his wife Ariel, researched and wrote a multi-volume history of the world to 1815. When asked about the essence of what he had learned, Durant responded that he had gained a certain solace from studying history. He particularly noted that after contemplating the tragic lives of Marc Antony and Cleopatra, he better understood that his generation was not the first to have problems.

Those who see history as only a subject that is studied in school are the least likely to see that is has any practical value. But, if history is considered to be synonymous with experience, than it is obvious that everyone and everything has a history. Individuals, societies and nations are all influenced to a degree by their pasts. They have only to recognize that if you want to see where you are going you need to know where you have been.

The sesquicentennial presents a marvelous opportunity to consider the meaning of time in history. Gaining a better understanding of time perspective is a natural part of the aging process. Somehow the older people get, the past seems closer to their present. It is relatively easy to memorize dates, but it is much more difficult to really understand their meaning. I was reminded of time perspective, or lack thereof, when President Obama late in his second term talked to a kindergarten class. He must have suddenly realized a lot about time perspective when one of the students asked if he had fought in the Civil War. With regard to Minnesota State Mankato, the meaning of 150 years will be variously seen. Those older than about 70 will no doubt see it as a relatively short time, but those younger than 30 or so will be inclined to think of 1868 as being long, long ago.

The initial planning of this history was done by Robert Kent Clark, the vice president for University Advancement, Daardi Sizemore Mixon, university archivist, Sara Gilbert Frederick, director of content marketing in the university's Office of Integrated Marketing, Susan Taylor, director of development, College of Social and Behavioral Sciences and me, a professor emeritus of history. In our meeting of October 22, 2015, we first discussed the desirability of having a sesquicentennial history. After agreeing that such a history would be an appropriate contribution to the university's commemoration of its 150th anniversary, we established principles about its nature. The book was to be oversized to facilitate the display of appropriate illustrations. Further, we determined that short biographical sketches of selected individuals would be inserted at appropriate places in the text. Lastly, we concluded that the book should be documented with endnotes and a bibliography. Future historians, especially, should appreciate this feature. But the notes and bibliography should also serve as starting points for anyone seeking more information about any given aspect of the institution's history.

In this study I have generally used contemporary figures for dollar amounts such as salaries and construction costs. For example, I report that the normal school's first principal was paid $2,500 for his last year. Such a figure can be very misleading, because many readers do not have information about current values of historic dollars. Since the beginning of the Mankato Normal School, the value of the 1868 dollar or any other annual dollar has been affected by deflation or inflation. Thus, readers gain a better understanding of historic dollars if they know their current equivalencies. In some instances I have provided equivalent values in the text to illustrate the point about the impact of inflation or deflation. But doing so for every contemporary dollar would burden the text with unnecessary detail. Therefore, I compiled Appendix B, which shows the 2017 values of past dollars for 1868 and every five-year increment from 1870 to 2015. Those interested in the 1878 dollar, for instance, can do their own conversion by using the cited source for the historic value of the dollar.

# ACKNOWLEDGMENTS

Throughout the researching and writing of this history I have been assisted by a number of people. University Archivist Daardi Sizemore Mixon was especially significant. She not only originated the idea for the history but aided throughout the project. She read and commented on the manuscript, selected illustrations and wrote their captions, compiled the index and served as the liaison with the printer. Sara Gilbert Frederick edited the entire manuscript and made a number of helpful suggestions.

During many hours of research in University Archives, I was graciously assisted by Archives Technicians Mee Xiong and Anne Stenzel. They were vital in locating and copying source material and in meeting my sometimes tight deadlines. Their knowledge of various finding aids saved much time in pursuing sometimes obscure sources. Joan Roca, dean of Library Services, graciously and enthusiastically supported the project.

With respect to producing the history, I thank President Richard Davenport and Paul Allan, associate athletic director for communications. In addition to being continually interested in the preparation of this sesquicentennial history, Davenport wrote the introduction. Allan contributed significantly to the university's history by compiling Appendix A.

Other Minnesota State University, Mankato personnel who provided key information about selected aspects of the university's history were Steven Ardolf, chief engineer; Cheryl C. Azerbod, administrative assistant, Global Education; Cynthia L. Janney, director of Residential Life; Jerry Oman, research specialist, Institutional Research, Planning and Assessment; Todd Pfingston, director of Campus Recreation; Steven R. Smith, assistant vice president for Budget & Business Services; and Denise Thompson, assistant to the dean, College of Social and Behavioral Sciences.

Heather Harren, communications manager, Blue Earth County Historical Society, provided very useful information about Mankato's history. Jeff Iseminger, who is now retired from his position as Associate Vice President for University Advancement and Integrated Marketing, provided information about the origin of the university's tagline, "Big ideas. Real-world thinking."

Furthermore, I thank Lori Lahlum, professor of history at Minnesota State University, Mankato; Steve Potts, history instructor, Hibbing Community College; and Susan Taylor for discussing various aspects of the sesquicentennial history with me.

Customarily, acknowledgments deal with those who provided assistance in the research, writing and production phases of preparing a book. But, because of some unusual circumstances, I am indebted to some who helped in other ways. On August 9, 2017, I fell and severely injured my right leg. Following surgery, I was in a rehabilitation facility for five weeks. After I returned home I could not drive for another two months. During my incapacitation, Leslie McPhail Peterson, assistant to the library dean, graciously and enthusiastically tended to most of my affairs—including running numerous errands. My Skyline neighbors Don and Lori Waylett and Mary Dowd also generously assisted with a variety of household related tasks. The considerable assistance of Leslie, Don, Lori and Mary greatly facilitated my completion of this history.

My children, Barbara and Bill, have been my soul mates throughout the project. Our daily email exchanges and weekly telephone conversations oftentimes were concerned with aspects of my research and writing. Thus, they helped me plan for the next step.

# 1

# THE MANKATO NORMAL SCHOOL:
## BACKGROUND AND DEVELOPMENT TO 1880

On October 7, 1868, Principal George M. Gage presided over the opening of the Mankato Normal School in Mankato, Minnesota. At that time public normal schools were a relatively new innovation in American education. Like its predecessors, including Minnesota's first normal school at Winona, the Mankato school first experienced the travails of sparse enrollment and inadequate funding. In retrospect, the really troubled years ended in 1880, which marked the transition to increased enrollment, more state support and stability.

### Precedents of the Mankato Normal School

In the 1830s the state of Massachusetts pioneered major innovations in American education. Legislators led by Horace Mann and James G. Carter championed the advent of state-supported free public education for elementary students and the corollary development of normal schools. Leaders can be successful only if they have followers. As reformers of education, Mann and Carter lived in an age when many business leaders were dissatisfied with traditional educational practices. They were displeased with the Massachusetts system of district schools that varied greatly from locale to locale. Schools that were fortunate to have strong local financial support, excellent teachers and good buildings fared relatively well. But, according to Mann, Carter and other critics, a good school was an exception. Most schools lacked textbooks, had makeshift physical facilities and featured teachers who had no training in either subject matter or teaching. Mann, especially, objected to the traditional belief that teachers were born, not made. Teachers generally, he insisted, would benefit from training to continually acquire more knowledge and to learn effective ways of communicating with students.[1]

Reform of public education was a natural adjunct of Jacksonian Democracy, which emphasized the rights of the common people. At the time when states were abolishing property qualifications for manhood suffrage, it seemed only natural for them to make sweeping changes to benefit the masses in other ways. Consequently,

*Mankato Weekly Record*, October 10, 1868

education, prison reform and humane treatment for the insane all sprung from the same broad-based reform movement that challenged traditional practices.[2]

As members of the Massachusetts legislature, Carter and Mann were in good positions to promote school reform. Mainly because of Carter's initiative, the legislators took a major step in promoting public common schools in 1837 with the creation of a state board of public education. The bill creating the department was mainly shepherded through the legislature by Carter, who expected to be named its first secretary. But to his disappointment the governor appointed Mann, who held the position for 12 years.

Although Mann was only authorized to collect and disseminate information, he made the most of his limited authority. Through meetings with local groups and circulating questionnaires he compiled data to support his contention that public education in Massachusetts would be enhanced by secular schools that had a common curriculum and well-trained teachers.

Because of his well-circulated annual reports and his semi-monthly *Common School Journal*, Mann established a reputation as the nation's leading expert on public schools. His ideas, despite some opposition from those who thought secular education was godless, spread rather quickly to the other states.

Mann, Carter and the many other supporters of free public education realized

Mankato Normal School building, circa 1884

that it would swell enrollment and immediately create a sharp need for more teachers. The reformers were not satisfied with the customary practice of using teachers who had no professional training. They complained that most of the people who taught were deficient in both subject matter knowledge and teaching methodology. The obvious solution to this problem was to create special normal schools to train professional teachers. Only a year after forming the state education department, the Massachusetts legislation provided for state normal schools. Carter, who advocated school reforms before Mann, had first proposed public normal schools in 1826.

In an American context, the ideas of free universal public education and normal schools were new. But both were inspired by precedents in Prussia. A Prussian law of 1763, which was inspired by the educational reforms of Johann Julius Hecker and his mentor Hermann August Franke, instituted a system of state-supported primary schools. The Prussian System, as it came to be called, also developed normal schools, which were to train teachers in both the what and the how of teaching. By the end of the 18th century, Prussia had a system of six normal schools. Prussia borrowed the normal school idea from France, where the first normal school was established at Rheims in 1681. By the time normal schools were introduced in the United States, they had been established in most of the countries in northern and western Europe. But American reformers, who regarded the Prussian schools as the best, used them as their models.[3]

Several American educators had visited Prussian schools and written reports about them. A report by the French minister of education, Victor Cousin, had been translated into English and read by many Americans. Furthermore, American students who had studied in the German States brought information about the Prussian System home with them.[4]

These reports stimulated Mann to see European schools for himself. In 1843 he spent five months visiting schools at all levels, including elementary and normal schools in England, Ireland, Scotland as well as Prussia, Saxony and other German states. Mann was particularly smitten with Prussian schools because of their very knowledgeable teachers who demonstrated command of their subjects and a deep understanding of child psychology.

Massachusetts opened its first normal school in 1839 and by the end of the next year had started two more. The public normal school movement spread slowly. By 1850, after New York, Connecticut and Michigan had opened schools, there were six in the nation.[5]

Normal schools were not colleges and thus should not be considered higher education. Likewise, they did not offer college preparatory courses. Furthermore, when the first generation normal schools were started, high schools were rare. Thus, the later sequential pattern of grade schools, high schools and colleges did not exist. Normal schools, whose diplomas were terminal, were dedicated to preparing elementary school teachers.

The normal school curriculum was a combination of subject matter and teaching methodology. Students were expected to not only learn such conventional subjects as English, geography and spelling, but to also get experience in teaching them to elementary grade students. To facilitate what would later be called practice teaching, normal schools had two discrete parts—the normal and model departments. Typically, model school students were from the community in which the normal school was located, so the model department served as another local school. Staff of both parts were regarded as normal school faculty, but individuals had specific assignments to teach in either the normal or model department.

The purpose of normal schools was well-explained by David Clarke John, who served as the third principal of the Minnesota state normal school at Mankato. "The design of the Normal School," he wrote, "is not primarily to teach science or literature, but the *art of teaching, disciplining and governing pupils*." He explained that normal schools had to offer subject matter courses, "because pupils must learn what to teach before they can learn *how* to teach. Matter must precede method, just as language precedes grammar."[6]

The normal school name did not mean normal as used in such conventional senses as average or ordinary. Rather, normal was derived from one of the meanings of the Latin word norma, which meant standard as in the sense of a model. In the United States the only goal of normal schools was to train students for teaching in the elementary schools. Consequently, they had a rigidly structured curriculum suited to only that purpose.

By the time Congress formed the Minnesota Territory on March 4, 1849, provisions for free common school systems had spread throughout the northern states. Therefore, it was not too surprising that the first Minnesota territorial legislature passed a common school law. The "Act to establish and maintain Common Schools" authorized taxation for the creation of public schools. These schools were to be free for everyone aged five through 20.[7]

The development of Minnesota Territory was inhibited by the limited amount of land open for settlement. Only about 5,000 square miles in a delta-shaped area between the Mississippi and St. Croix rivers had been ceded by the indigenous Dakota and Ojibwe Indians. Consequently, the 1850 population not including Indians was only 6,077 people, who were concentrated in the St. Paul-Stillwater area. By January 1852, Ramsey County, with St. Paul as its main community, had eight school districts and Stillwater had one.[8]

Minnesota's territorial population boomed after major land cessions by the Dakota Indians. By the treaties of Traverse des Sioux and Mendota in 1851 the four Dakota bands sold most of southern and west central Minnesota to the United States. Once the ceded lands were opened to legal settlement in early 1853, Minnesota Territory experienced a population boom. Because of fertile, cheap land, a railroad extension to Rock Island, Illinois on the Mississippi River, and a booming national and regional economy, Minnesota's population nearly quadrupled from an estimated 40,000 in 1855 to almost 150,000 in 1857. The heaviest settlement was in the valleys of the Mississippi and Minnesota rivers south of St. Paul and in the Mississippi valley above St. Paul to Little Falls.[9]

The population surge caused an immediate and severe need for schools even before communities could arrange for public districts and local tax levies. Mankato, which was founded in February 1852, when approval of the Dakota treaties was pending, is an interesting case in point. Mankato's first school, which opened in 1853, was financed by subscriptions or payments by parents to a school fund. Mankato continued its subscription school pattern through 1855. Lafayette G. M. Fletcher taught the first public school of 37 students in 1856.[10]

Soon after Minnesota was admitted to the union on May 11, 1858, as the 32nd state, Governor Henry Hastings Sibley and state legislators acted to improve teacher preparation. Like Massachusetts lawmakers two decades earlier, they saw normal schools as the best way of training teachers for the elementary schools. The territorial legislature of 1851 had incorporated the University of Minnesota.[11] But, it was a paper institution until 1869 when its regents hired a president and faculty and started offering classes. Even if the state university had been operating in 1858, legislators, like those in other states, would not have regarded teaching preparation as part of its mission.[12]

The first advocacy of a Minnesota normal school was made by Dr. John D. Ford of Winona. Ford, a medical doctor, had moved from Connecticut to Winona in 1856. Like the thousands of other New Englanders who migrated to Minnesota before the Civil War, Ford brought knowledge of educational systems with him. As the main lobbyist for a state normal school, Ford worked with Winona area legislators including state senator Daniel Norton, whose political career was highlighted by his service as a United States senator from Minnesota, 1866-70. Naturally, Ford and area legislators wanted to locate Minnesota's first normal school in Winona. Although the concepts of Twin Cities Metropolitan area and outstate Minnesota did not exist in 1858, there was an acrimonious rivalry between Winona and the capital city of St. Paul, which was by far the state's largest community with approximately 10,000 residents. Winona's boosters, who aspired to make their city an important economic and cultural center, vigorously promoted through the city's two newspapers.[13]

The establishment of Minnesota normal schools had nearly unanimous support in the first state legislature. On July 11, 1858, Joseph Peckham, a representative from Cannon Falls, proposed a normal school bill in the House of Representatives. Peckham's bill, which was approved by a 45 to four vote in the House and unanimously in the Senate, was signed into law by Governor Henry Hastings Sibley on August 2.[14]

The Normal School Act of 1858 was a landmark achievement for Minnesota public education. It provided for three normal schools with the first to be created within five years of the act, the second within 10 years and the third within 15 years. Any community selected as a normal school site was required to donate $5,000 to the state, which would be matched by state funds. The law further specified that sites were to be determined by a six-man State Normal School Board appointed by the governor. In locating a specific school, the board was to "have due regard to healthfulness and beauty of situation, to accessibility and general convenience, to the wants of the common schools, and the wishes of donors who may make munificent donations, conditioned upon a particular location."[15]

Other than designating school sites, the State Normal School Board was authorized to contract for the erection of school buildings, appoint all faculty, prescribe the curriculum and admissions policy "and in general to adopt all needful rules for the governance of said schools."

Significantly, the Normal School Act also specified that the "general oversight and management of the prudential affairs" of each school was to be done by a prudential committee appointed annually by the State Normal School Board. One member of this three-person committee had to also be a member of the appointive board. The legislators apparently believed that school management and financial planning could be done better by a local prudential committee rather than the Normal School Board.

To further promote the cause of public education the Normal School Act specified that no tuition would be charged for any student who agreed to subsequently become a teacher in any Minnesota public school. The State Normal School Board was to determine a policy regarding the teaching obligations of normal school students.

The advent of Minnesota's Normal School Act was somewhat surprising. At that time the state economy had been devastated by the Panic of 1857. The panic, which was tripped off by the failure of the Ohio Life Insurance Company of New York, hit particularly hard on frontier areas such as Minnesota, where many businessmen were indebted to Eastern creditors. Prior to the start of the panic in the fall of 1857, Minnesota's seemingly robust economy was heavily dependent on land speculation. Ever-rising land values during a national boom led people into thinking that they would become prosperous simply by investing in land. But as the panic intensified when Eastern creditors demanded immediate loan repayments, Minnesota's economy collapsed. An estimated 20,000 people left Minnesota for such places as Kansas, Nebraska and the recently discovered Colorado gold strikes. Desperate state legislators passed an ill-advised railroad aid bill that burdened Minnesota with a public debt for more than two decades.[16]

The panic apparently delayed the formation of Minnesota's first normal school. But, after Governor Sibley named the members of the original State Normal School Board, it convened in the state capitol on August 16, 1859. Lieutenant Governor William Holcombe of Stillwater and Dr. John D. Ford

## MINNESOTA STATUTES 1858

23.]   EDUCATION.   353

STATE NORMAL SCHOOLS.

*See Ch. of 61 & 265 of ... ... ... 1866*

An Act to provide for the establishment of State Normal Schools.
[*Passed August 2, 1858.*]  c. 79

(30.) SEC. I. *Be it enacted by the legislature of the state of Minnesota:* There shall be established within five years after the passage of this act, an institution to educate and prepare teachers for teaching in the common schools of this state, to be called a state normal school. There shall be established within ten years after the passage of this act, a second state normal school, and within fifteen years a third: *provided,* there shall be no obligations to establish the first normal school until the sum of five thousand dollars is donated to the state in money and lands, or in money alone, for the erection of the necessary buildings, and for the support of the professors or teachers in such institution, but when such sum is donated for such purpose, a like sum of five thousand dollars shall be, and hereby is appropriated by the legislature on the order of the proper officers, and shall be paid out of any moneys in the treasury not otherwise appropriated by law, for the use and benefit of such institution.   State normal schools how to be established.

Minnesota Statutes 1858, Section 23.30

were chosen respectively as the board's president and secretary. The board took several major actions at its inaugural meeting. To implement part of the Normal School Act, it decided that the district of the first normal school would consist of judicial districts 3 and 5, the district of the second normal school would be judicial districts 1 and 2 and the district of the third normal school would be judicial districts 4 and 6.[17]

Following a resolution by Ford, the board agreed to locate the first normal school in Winona, which raised its required subscription of $5,000 and an additional $2,000 within a reported few hours. To help prepare for its opening, the board instructed Ford to solicit information from other states about the nature and operations of their normal schools. At that time there were normal schools in 10 other states. Only Massachusetts, with four normal schools, had more than one. The Winona Normal School gained the distinction of being the nation's 14th normal school and the first west of the Mississippi.

The Winona Normal School opened on September 3, 1860, with 20 students. It struggled to become established: It was closed from March 1862 to November 1864, because of financial and human shortages. State support was inadequate to fund operations and some faculty and male students had enlisted in the Union army. By the time the Winona Normal School graduated its first class on June 28, 1866, the legislature had provisionally approved the creation of the second and third state normal schools at Mankato and St. Cloud respectively.[18]

### Establishment of the Mankato Normal School

The principal advocate of a second normal to be located in Mankato was attorney Daniel Buck, who was elected to the Minnesota House of Representatives in 1865. Buck was a newcomer to Mankato when he was first elected to the state legislature. For eight years prior, he had lived and practiced law in South Bend, a village located about three miles southwest of downtown Mankato on the southernmost bend of the Minnesota River. South Bend was an aspiring rival of Mankato until 1868, when the St. Paul and Sioux City Railroad selected Mankato as the site of its district depot and did not prepare a stopping place in South Bend. But before this significant railroad decision, Buck obviously sensed that Mankato would develop as the principal city near

## MINNESOTA STATUTES 1866

37.]            STATE NORMAL SCHOOLS.           315

SEC. 2. There shall be established at Mankato, in this state, an institution to educate and prepare teachers for teaching in the common schools of this state, called the second state normal school. *Second state normal school at Mankato* 1869 - 16

SEC. 4. Whenever the sum of five thousand dollars in money, is donated to the state, for the erection of the necessary buildings, and the support of the professors or teachers in the second state normal school, a like sum of five thousand dollars is hereby appropriated for the use and benefit of such institution, and said sum shall be paid, on the order of the proper officer, out of any money in the treasury not otherwise appropriated, but no part of such named sum shall be drawn or paid, out of the treasury until after the first of April, 1867. *When five thousand dollars are donated for second normal school, the state shall furnish an equal sum.*

Minnesota Statutes 1866, Section 37.1

the elbow of the Minnesota River when he proposed to locate a normal school there.[19]

When he proposed a second normal school to the 1866 legislature, Buck and other normal school expansionists had to overcome recent setbacks to Minnesota's normal school movement. As part of its reaction to the Panic of 1857, the 1860 legislature had suspended the start of the second and third normal schools for five years. In 1865 the legislature extended the suspension for five more years.[20]

Fortunately for Buck and Mankato, the 1866 legislature was willing to negate these suspensions. A resurgence of frontier settlement following the temporary withdrawal caused by the Dakota-United States War of 1862, and the end of the Civil War made legislators more optimistic about the state's economic prospects. This rosy outlook and the combined lobbying efforts of Mankato and St. Cloud prompted the legislature to implement key parts of the 1858 Normal School Act.

The 1866 act authorized the establishment of the second state normal school at Mankato and the third state normal school at St. Cloud, provided each community contributed the required $5,000 within three years from the date of the act's passage. The Normal School Board was authorized to relocate the schools if the respective communities failed to meet the three-year deadline. But, once a community had made its $5,000 contribution, the board could not relocate its normal school to another community for at least 10 years. Otherwise, the act reiterated parts of the 1858 Normal School Act pertaining to the duties of the governing board and the role of local prudential committees. But to emphasize the close ties between normal schools and the common schools, the 1866 act specified that the state superintendent of public instruction would be an ex-officio member and secretary of the State Normal School Board. This stipulation had the practical effect of making the state superintendent of public instruction the board's chief administrator.[21]

Buck headed a subscription committee that included John G. Wise and William B. Griswold, the owners of Mankato's two newspapers.[22]

Buck extolled the need for and advantages of a Mankato normal school in the *Mankato Weekly Record* of September 1, 1866. He first contended that the normal school was a necessity, because of Minnesota's dire shortage of qualified school teachers. He insisted that 1,416 of the 1,888 teachers employed in the state's common schools were "utterly incompetent." He then asked rhetorically: "Can any good citizen but shudder at the statement?" As for benefits to Mankato, Buck insisted: "This Normal School will bring to our place a superior class of citizens. It will bring talent, wealth, business and a more elevated and refined society. It will raise the standard of intelligence and education and be a proud, enduring monument of the generosity and wisdom of our people." Despite such rhetoric, Mankatoans failed to raise the required $5,000 to match the state appropriation. In terms of 2016 equivalences the required $5,000 would have a value of about $81,800.

Buck and the other Mankatoans who wanted a normal school realized the importance of state-funded institutions to communities. With an eye to a distant future, they believed that cities with permanent, public facilities would continue to grow and prosper. In essence, they were motivated by the same urges that caused the people of St. Paul to prize their state capital location.

Faced with the prospect of losing the school site, Buck tried a new tactic in the 1867 legislature. He proposed that Mankato be authorized to raise the required $5,000 donation by selling bonds. The legislature and Governor William Marshall agreed. "An Act authorizing the trustees of the village of Mankato to issue bonds for the purpose of aiding in the establishment of the Second State Normal School" was approved on February 16, 1867.[23]

The bond approach worked. On June 24, 1868, when it was meeting at Winona, the State Normal School Board was notified that Mankato had satisfied the state's financial requirements for the second normal school. Accordingly, the board agreed to meet at Mankato on July 16 "for the purpose of taking initiatory steps to the organization of the Second State Normal School."[24]

At its Mankato meeting held in the Clifton House, the board accepted the $5,000 donation from municipal officials and appointed a prudential committee, which was to arrange for the prompt opening of the Mankato Normal School. The board named Buck as chairman of the Second State Normal School Prudential Committee, which also included James Brown and John B. Murphy. John

N. Hall, cashier of the First National Bank in Mankato, was named treasurer of the Prudential Committee and manager of the Mankato contribution.[25]

During the morning of their Mankato meeting, board members, some Mankato citizens and board guest William F. Phelps, principal of the Winona State Normal School, traveled about Mankato in horse-drawn carriages. In the words of the *Mankato Weekly Review*, they "visited the suburbs or our city." Actually, as they traveled from downtown toward today's Main Street hill, they covered only four blocks. Reportedly, they inspected several sites, but they were most intrigued by a triangular shaped block of about three acres uphill from South Fifth Street. This "Lines lot," owned by David Lines, was at the location of the present-day Old Main Village. Board members thought this site "opposite the centre of the town" was "a healthful and commanding position." Once they resumed their meeting they authorized the Mankato Prudential Committee to purchase the Lines lot for $2,000 provided it could be changed to a rectangular shape at a cost of no more than $500.

With the intention of opening the Mankato Normal School in the fall of 1868, the State Normal School Board at its August 4 meeting in St. Cloud appointed 34-year-old George M. Gage as its principal. A Maine native, Gage was then serving as principal of his home state's Farmington Normal School. Prior to his Farmington career, he had been an administrator and teacher in Massachusetts public schools after graduating from the Massachusetts State Normal School at Bridgewater in 1858. The Minnesota Normal School Board hired Gage on the recommendation of Principal William F. Phelps of the Winona Normal School and Mark H. Dunnell, state superintendent of public instruction.[26]

Dunnell, originally from Maine, had served as that state's superintendent of the common schools before moving to Minnesota soon after the end of the Civil War. After being named Minnesota's superintendent of public instruction in 1867, he actively recruited Maine normal school graduates to teach in Minnesota. Richard P. Mallett, the historian of Farmington Normal School, determined that Dunnell was responsible for luring 22 Farmington Normal School graduates to Minnesota. Mallett further concluded that Dunnell "prevailed upon" Gage to become principal of the Mankato Normal School. If Gage had any economic motivation, Dunnell did not have to be very persuasive, because Minnesota's pay scale was much higher than Maine's. For example, Dunnell was paid $2,500 annually and granted a $500 travel allowance as Minnesota state superintendent of public instruction. His Maine reimbursement for a comparable position was only $1,000.

Clifton House and Mankato Candy Kitchen, Mankato, Minnesota, 1914
Image courtesy of Blue Earth County Historical Society

## The Opening of the Mankato Normal School

When George M. Gage arrived in Mankato on Friday, August 28, 1868, he found it was rapidly transitioning out of its brief frontier stage. The original village was chartered as a city by an act of the Minnesota legislature on March 6, 1868. So, quite coincidentally the city and its normal school were started in the same year.[27]

In August 1868, Mankatoans were eagerly anticipating the arrival of the first railroad, which was being constructed from St. Paul through the Minnesota River valley. The St. Paul and Sioux City Railroad reached Mankato on October 3, only four days before the opening of the normal school. Prior to the railroad, Mankato had developed as an important steamboat port. It was the head of navigation for part of every steamboat season, because the Minnesota River's water volume was reduced by about half above the mouth of the tributary Blue Earth River in Mankato's present-day Sibley Park. Its steamboat legacy was one of the main reasons Mankato had developed as the largest community in its region.[28]

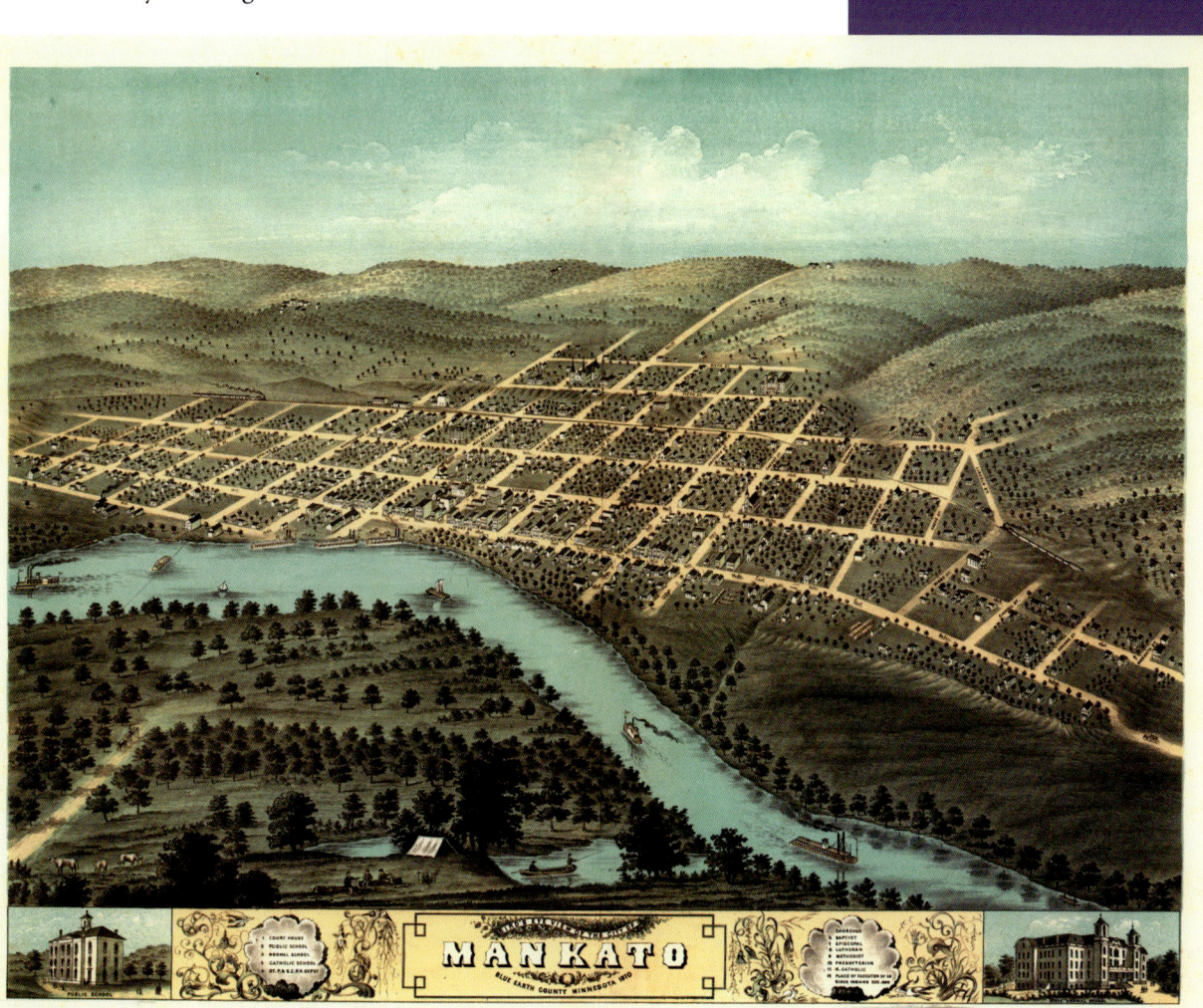

Bird's eye view of Mankato, Minnesota 1870. Image from Library of Congress, Geography and Map Division

George Gage,
circa 1900

The railroad helped jolt Mankato into a modern, mechanized age. It provided dependable, rapid, year-round transportation for those with convenient access to its line. But, since railroads had fixed routes, the use of horse-drawn vehicles persisted until the advent of the automobile age in the early 20th century. Consequently, inhabitants of Mankato's rural trade area as well as many city residents depended on horse-drawn buggies, wagons and other vehicles long after the beginning of the city's railroad age.

Newcomer Gage obviously noted that Mankato was an active, growing community. Its 1870 population of 3,482 residents was more than double the 1,558 reported 10 years earlier. He must also have noticed that the surrounding countryside was so new to settlement that it was only partially occupied. Only slightly more than a fifth of Blue Earth County's land area was being tilled in 1870. Most of the county's surface had its pre-settlement appearance with the northeastern part covered by a deciduous forest and the remainder by prairie except for the timbered valleys of the Blue Earth and Minnesota rivers.[29]

By the time Gage reached Mankato, most of Blue Earth County's cultivated land was reduced to stubble. Two small grains—wheat and oats—were the dominant crops. Wheat, the leading crop in terms of acreage, was popular in Minnesota's newly openly areas, because it was the main cash crop. Oats were in local demand as horse food. Only corn, the county's third ranking crop, would have been green and still growing when Gage set foot in Mankato.[30]

The 1870 census also showed that Blue Earth County had impressive numbers of domesticated animals with 4,023 horses, 4,730 milk cows, 6,690 sheep and 5,652 hogs. Gage would certainly have noticed that some of the horses and cows were in Mankato. Horses were kept for local transportation and family cows were the city's principal milk source. Keeping in-town livestock caused many residents to build a small barn adjacent to their house. With the advent of the automobile, many of these barns were converted to garages.

Mankato's increasing population in the 1860s had major ramifications for its school system. In 1867 the city consolidated several one-room schools when it completed building the 540-student capacity Union School on North Broad Street at a cost of $15,000. Despite a rather persistent local legend that the Union School was named after the Union (or North) of the Civil War, the school's name was derived from its organization where at least several districts were consolidated under one roof. Many of the first large city schools in the nation and Minnesota were union schools. Grade segregation was another significant characteristic of union schools. Each grade had its own room. Thus, in common parlance "graded school" and "union school" were synonymous. The Mankato Union School, which was dedicated on September 30, 1867, began with the aim of accommodating all elementary and high school grades. Mankato's first high school was started in the new Union School. But, in part, because of dropouts, it did not graduate its first class of nine students until 1876.[31]

Gage's first action in Mankato was to report to Daniel Buck, then a member State Normal School Board and president of the Mankato Normal Prudential Committee. It was probably Buck who advised Gage to immediately perform a service that would ingratiate himself with the community. Only three days after his arrival Gage began teaching a week-long "institute" for local teachers. Customarily, institutes (the equivalent of present-day workshops and seminars) were the most significant outreach activity by normal schools. They had been championed by Horace Mann, who thought there was a pressing need to

# Daniel Buck, Father of the Mankato Normal School

Daniel Buck (September 28, 1829-May 21, 1905) was born at Boonville in upstate New York of Yankee ancestry. After attending common schools, he studied law and was admitted to the bar. He moved to Minnesota in 1857 and practiced law in South Bend before relocating to nearby Mankato in 1865. During the aftermath of the United States-Dakota War of 1862, he became regionally well-known because he represented many clients who filed claims with the Sioux Claims Commission for property damage allegedly caused by marauding Dakotas. Perhaps because of his association with some grief-stricken survivors, Buck was extremely critical of the Dakotas and their culture. This stance, which was the common popular sentiment at that time, evidently endeared him to many contemporaries.

Buck, a lifelong Democratic, was elected to the Minnesota House of Representatives in 1865. Like many of his fellow legislators, Buck tried to enhance the economy of his own community. Consequently, he successfully campaigned to have Minnesota's second normal school established in Mankato. Buck had a deep interest in the school's success. While serving on both the Minnesota Normal School Board and the prudential committee of the Mankato school, he was active in every step of the school's founding. Buck's reputation as a local hero in creating the Mankato Normal School was especially strong during the institution's first half century. Consequently, the first women's dormitory, which was completed in 1913, was named

Daniel Buck,
circa 1900

in his honor as Daniel Buck Hall.

Buck was active in state politics and Mankato affairs during his long career. He was elected to the state Senate in 1878; in 1892, as the candidate of both the Democratic and People's (i.e. Populist) parties, he was elected as a Minnesota Supreme Court justice. He served on the court until forced to resign because of poor health in 1899.

In Mankato Buck was active in both civic and business affairs. He served on the Mankato School Board for five years and as city attorney for several years. Banking was his main business activity. He founded the Mankato National Bank and also served as vice-president of the Citizens' National Bank. In his long career of practicing law, Buck gained a reputation as a skillful and successful trial lawyer.

After resigning from the Supreme Court, Buck spent much of the remainder of his life writing his self-published *Indian Outbreaks* (1904). This undocumented history of the United States-Dakota War is pertinent today mainly for its point of view. As a Social Darwinist, Buck emphasized white superiority and denigrated the Dakotas and all other Indians, whom he saw as savages.

(*Mankato, Its First Fifty Years,* 188-90 [Photo on p. 189]; *Mankato Free Press*, 22 May 1905; William E. Lass, "Histories of the U. S.-Dakota War of 1862: A Review," *Minnesota History 63* (Summer 2012): 48; Hiram F. Stevens, ed., *History of the Bench and Bar of Minnesota*, vol. 1 (Minneapolis: Legal Publishing and Engraving Co., 1904), 134-136; *Minnesota Legislative Manual*, 1877, 71, 1879, 358, 1893, 322, 374, 467.)

Shaubut Building, circa 1868

continually train practicing teachers. Typically, institutes included coverage of both selected subject matter and teaching methodology. In Gage's case, his institute apparently was also intended to publicize the normal school in order to recruit students. Gage passed out copies of a circular about the imminent normal school at his institute and also distributed them at other regional institutes that were apparently offered by county school superintendents.[32]

Aside from the circular, the Mankato Normal School was well-publicized in Mankato's newspapers. John C. Wise, publisher of the *Mankato Review*, was particularly helpful in promoting the school.

In order to open the Mankato Normal School in the fall of 1868, Gage and the prudential committee had to find classroom space and hire a faculty. They agreed to rent for $350 a year the second or top story of a brick building under construction by merchant John J. Shaubut. But, fearing that postponing the normal school's opening would jeopardize its development, they arranged to start normal school classes on October 7, 1868, in the basement of the Methodist Episcopal Church.[33]

Because of limited space in the church, Gage met only with the normal department students there. He did not attempt to open the model department until after the normal department students were relocated on October 26 to the more spacious Shaubut Building, whose second floor of four rooms was 100 feet long and 20 feet wide. The Shaubut Building, which faced Front Street, was located at the corner of South Front and Main streets at the site of the present-day City Center Hotel. Since Shaubut used the building's first floor for his general merchandise business, he provided access to the upper story by an exterior stairway on the building's Main Street side. During the first day of classes in the Shaubut Building, the prudential committee rented a front room in the building for $100 annually. Evidently, this was for model department use.[34]

Gage used a very flexible admissions policy. He had 27 students the first day of the term, but admitted others whenever they appeared. The school had "upwards of 40" students when Gage moved it to the Shaubut Building. Once relocated, he organized a model department of two classes. In his November 20, 1868 report to the State Normal School Board, Gage noted that by then the entire school of 82 students consisted of 62 in the normal department (44 females and 18 males) and 20 in the model department (10 females and 10 males). Gage reported that a third of the normal department students were from Mankato and another third were from other places in Blue Earth County. Most of the remaining third was composed of students from the nearby counties of Martin, Le Sueur, Nicollet, Jackson and Faribault. Gage also observed that "the school has also numbered among its members one from each of the following named states, viz: Iowa, Pennsylvania, New Hampshire and Vermont." Obviously, those seeming out-of-state students were not lured to Mankato to attend the normal school. But, rather were members of families that had recently moved to the Mankato area.[35]

As principal, Gage's main duty was teaching. Early in the school's first term he did most of the teaching himself. But, during the term he hired four faculty members, who were all designated as "assistants." In Gage's estimation, the most important faculty member was Susie M. Dyer, who did not arrive in Mankato from her native Maine until late November. Dyer, a normal school graduate who had taught in Massachusetts, was assigned to teach the language and literature classes in the normal department. Emma H. Collins also taught in the normal department. The two other assistants—Charles A. Boston, a graduate of a Maine normal school, and Edna L. Montgomery—taught in the model department.[36]

When he first reported to the State Normal School Board, Gage was obviously satisfied with his early work in establishing the Mankato Normal School. But, since he was concerned with its "permanency and efficiency" he recommended the prompt construction of "a substantial, thoroughly built and well arranged edifice" and the creation of "the nucleus of a Library, and of a complete outfit of School Apparatus."

State of Minnesota.
[illegible] Normal School.
Mankato, Oct. 3, 1868.

Miss Susie M. Dyer
My Dear Friend.

I have the pleasure, with the consent of the Prudential Committee of the Second State Normal School of Minnesota, to offer you the position of Head Assistant in that Institution, of which I am to be Princ[illegible] at a yearly salary of $800. The first term of the school will open, as you see from the above "Calendar" in a few days, though on account of the unfinished condition of the rooms into which we are to go, and which, I may add, will be both pleasant and commodious, we shall not begin on the 6th. This place situated at the South bend of the Minnesota River, is growing very rapidly. It is now in direct connection with the East, by the way of the Minn. Valley R.R. to St. Paul. It will have a double con- [illegible] accept. [illegible] all rail route to St. [illegible] Mankato. the Minn. Valley R.R. [illegible] I hope to hear and that favorably from you when you shall have received this letter.

Very truly yours,
Geo. M. Gage.

Letter to Susie M. Dyer from George Gage, October 3, 1868

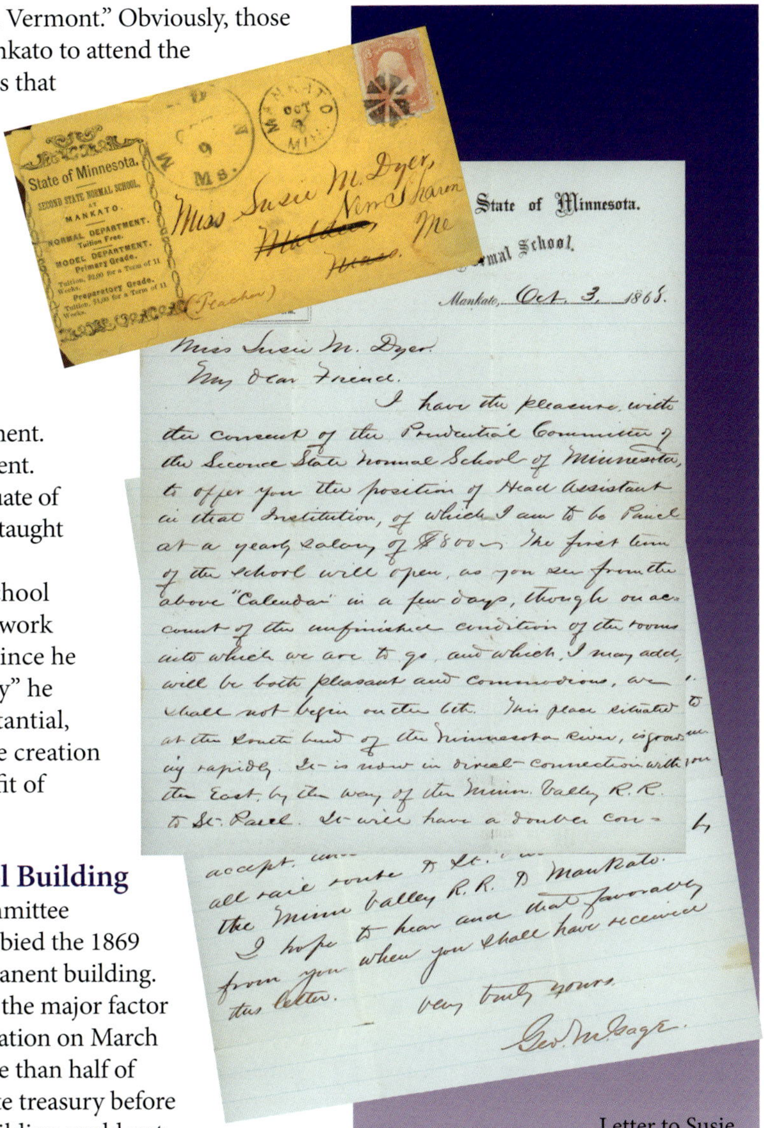

## Constructing the Mankato Normal School Building

The Mankato Normal School's Prudential Committee and the State Normal School Board successfully lobbied the 1869 legislature for an appropriation to construct a permanent building. The precedent of the Winona Normal building was the major factor in causing the legislature to approve a $30,000 allocation on March 5, 1869. Significantly, the act stipulated that no more than half of the appropriation could be withdrawn from the state treasury before April 1, 1870, and that the cost of the completed building could not exceed the total appropriation.[37]

On April 8, 1869, the State Normal School Board while meeting at Mankato authorized the Mankato Prudential Committee to plan the building's construction in accordance with the specifications prepared by architect William P. Boardman. The committee was instructed to advertise for bids in Mankato and St. Paul for two weeks.[38]

Subsequently, the Prudential Committee, chaired by Daniel Buck, received 25 proposals. But all of them exceeded the allocated $30,000. Consequently, the committee modified the building plan somewhat and advertised for new proposals. Only three were submitted—J. C. Hartman for $37,870, James and Wampler for $38,244 and Lewis J. Lewis for $37,600. Since Lewis, a Mankato building contractor, submitted the lowest bid, the committee signed a contract of $37,600 with him on May 3. The contract stipulated that the building, with the exceptions of finishing the basement and the library, laboratory

and museum facilities, was to be completed by July 3, 1870. The committee also selected William P. Boardman as the building's architect. His fee was to be no more than two percent of the total construction cost.[39]

In order to reimburse Lewis, the Prudential Committee decided to supplement the state appropriation with funds in its account. This still left a $2,700 deficiency, which the committee planned to request from the 1870 legislature. The *Mankato Weekly Record* of May 8, 1869, reported that the shortage "was guaranteed [sic] by the citizens of this city in case the Legislature refused to appropriate the deficiency."

Lewis' workers started basement excavation soon after the contract was signed. As they progressed, the Prudential Committee, Gage, architect Boardman, city officials and other community leaders planned an elaborate cornerstone laying ceremony to coincide with the beginning of stone work on the basement.[40]

The cornerstone laying ceremony, held on the evening of Tuesday, June 23, 1869, involved hundreds of people who assembled on South Front Street before starting a procession to the Normal School building site. The marchers, who stretched out for nearly four blocks, included Normal School faculty and students, Union School students and faculty, city officials including the mayor, businessmen, Normal Building construction workers, members of such fraternal orders as the International Order of Odd Fellows, the Good Templars and the Masons and townspeople. Their route up Normal Hill, as the rise toward South Fifth Street was then called, attracted hundreds of spectators. They and numerous horse-drawn carriages crowded both sides of the procession route.[41]

The contents of the tin cornerstone box included issues of contemporary Mankato newspapers, the 1869-70 Mankato Normal circular, about 20 cards of Mankato businesses, lists of the officers and members of the various fraternal orders, some photographs including one of the Shaubut Building and several coins including an 1864 bronze two-cent piece.[42]

After officers of the International Order of Odd Fellows presided during the placing of the box in an opening at the base of the building's rear wall, Gage, as the event's designated orator addressed his "Fellow Citizens." Speaking for about 20 minutes, Gage lauded the work of the Prudential Committee, Lewis' workmen and Minnesota's devotion to education. He concluded with: "Upon yonder corner-stone let this temple of learning rise, and let it tell to future generations that the settlers of this young and vigorous state were not unmindful of that which is the bulwark of free institutions, the common school."[43]

Lewis' crew rapidly constructed the exterior of the building after the cornerstone laying. By late January 1870, they had completed the exterior, laid floors and were starting to partition rooms.[44]

By then it was obvious that more state funding would be necessary to complete the interior. After considerable travail, the parsimonious legislature appropriated $12,500, which would enable the contractor to complete the interior work.[45]

Gage and the Mankato Prudential Committee, which managed the school's finances and acted as a school board, were planning on first using the new building at the opening of the Fall 1870 Term. But after a fire "badly damaged" the Shaubut Building's roof they moved the normal school students into the unfinished Normal School Building for the closing days of the spring 1870 term.[46]

When the building was used for the school's first graduation exercises on June 29, Gage and the Prudential Committee assumed it would be easily completed by the opening of the fall term.[47] But the finishing work was complicated by the accidental death of contractor Lewis. Shortly before midnight on Saturday, July 31, his shop and stable burned down. Searchers found Lewis' body under a dead horse. The *Mankato Weekly Record* of August 6, 1870, concluded that "it is one of the mysteries that will never be revealed how he met his fate."

In the aftermath of Lewis' demise, Daniel Buck was engaged to manage his business affairs that included completing building a church in Butternut Valley and a Mankato residence. Architect Boardman, who was to work under Buck's supervision, was designated to supervise the normal building completion.[48]

Gage was sincerely appreciative of the new building. When he reported to the Normal School

Board for the fiscal year ending November 30, 1870, Gage noted that "this edifice, so convenient, commodious, substantial, and pleasantly located, is a luxury which we think we know how to appreciate, and for which we are indeed thankful."[49]

Townspeople and visitors alike were impressed by the Mankato Normal School building, which loomed above the nearby downtown. Above the basement, its exterior walls were made of locally produced bricks. The main part of the building, which faced South Fifth Street, was 52 feet wide and 63 feet deep. The wings flanking it were recessed 10 feet from the front of the main building and then extended back 43 feet beyond the core building's rear wall. The portion of each wing abutting the central building was 30 feet wide. Beyond the building's rear wall each wing was 38 feet wide. This configuration left a spacious courtyard 52 feet wide x 43 feet deep between the wing extensions. The courtyard feature was designed to permit more natural light to enter the building.[50]

The building's most eye-catching feature was two towers, 11 feet square and 120 feet high at the front corners of the core building. Throughout, the building had spacious stories. The stone-walled basement was 12 feet high with only a quarter of it below ground level. The height dimensions of the first, second and third stories were respectively 12, 14 and 15 feet. There was a large attic topped by a mansard roof.

The building symbolized the seeming permanence of the Mankato Normal School. Until its completion, the school was not very visible. But the new building gave Mankatoans another source of pride for their city's material progress.

## Students, Faculty and Academic Program in the Gage Administration, 1868-1872

As the first principal of the Mankato Normal School, Gage was mainly responsible for developing its curriculum and class structure. Shortly before the school opened he prepared and circulated a leaflet about its course of study. Over the two years required to earn a diploma, students were required to complete courses in six categories— language, mathematics, physical and natural sciences, political economy and history, graphics and professional education. (See accompanying illustration for the courses in each category.)

The opportunity for introverted students to slip through the normal school without any personal contacts with their instructors did not exist. Anyone who applied for admission was interviewed and subjected to subject matter testing by the principal. This preliminary interview would enable Gage and succeeding principals to gain considerable insight into a student's potential as a teacher. Gage apparently did not reject anyone or require anyone to take remedial work.[51]

Entering students were assigned to the D class. As they progressed through the four terms in the two-year programs they were successively assigned to D, C, B and A classes. High attrition was one of the major characteristics of the fledgling Mankato Normal School student body. Only 10 of the 62 students who

## PROGRAMME.

A procession is to be formed opposite block 14 on Front street, consisting of the societies of Odd Fellows, and Good Templars, together with the Normal and Union Schools and Citizens. The lodges will meet at their respective lodge rooms and the schools at their respective school rooms, and at 3½ p. m. will meet in Block 14 Front street, and form into procession in the following order.

1st Marshall of the day.
2d Good Templars.
3d Public Schools.
4th Normal School.
5th Prudential committee and State Normal Board,
6th City Council and officers with officers fire department.
7th Order of Odd Fellows
8th Orator, Clergy and Architect.
9th Workmen on the building.

The procession will then move to the grounds where the exercises will be as follows.

1st Music by the Normal Scholars,
2d Prayer by———
3d Ceremony of laying corner stone by Noble Grand, S. F. Barney. of the I. O. of O. F.
4th Music.

The company will then repair to the grove and listen to an address by Prof. Geo. M. Gage. Thence the procession will form and return to block 14 and there be dismissed.

Normal School Cornerstone Ceremony Programme, 1869

were admitted to the fall 1868 term graduated at the end of the spring 1870 term. Gage was somewhat dissatisfied with student readiness for normal school courses. But, most dropouts were apparently caused by the virtual hand-to-mouth existence of many students. Minnesota's normal schools did not charge tuition, but out-of-town students had to have enough money to cover prevailing Mankato weekly rates of $3.50 to $4.00 for room and board.

Some enterprising students found ways of coping. William Dodsworth Willard recalled that his family lived at 122 State Street; they roomed and boarded "some Normal School boys," in exchange for their splitting wood and caring the family's livestock, which consisted of "at least two horses and a cow."[52]

Gage was concerned about student living costs. Even before classes opened in 1868, he deplored the lack of dormitories. He also acted as liaison between landlords and students who were seeking room and board by asking landlords to send him information about their available facilities and rates.[53]

Apparently, a number of normal school students dropped out in order to teach school. This was possible because of the split country school terms where districts operated during winter and summer terms. Winter terms usually started in early January and summer terms in late spring. Mark H. Dunnell, state superintendent of public instruction, reported that in 1869 the average statewide lengths of winter and summer terms were respectively 3.36 and 3.21 months. The 2,377 districts that reported employed a total of 3,775 teachers, of whom 2,620 were females and 1,155 males. The average monthly salary for males was $34.20, which was more than 50 percent more than the female compensation of $21.92.[54]

Normal school students were most likely to leave school after the fall term so they could teach in winter schools. All normal students were free in the summer because the early Mankato Normal did not offer summertime classes

Gage and his successors tried to accommodate dropouts by providing them with up-to-date progress reports. Such resumes provided county superintendents of school information about an individual's preparation for teaching. Furthermore, they facilitated re-enrollment at the normal school with re-entering students beginning at the point of their last class attendance.

Fortunately for the Mankato Normal School and all supporters of the state's normal system, its enrollment increased during Gage's administration. In the winter term of 1872, the normal department enrollment was 144—more than double the 62 of the school's enrollment for the fall 1868 term. During the same period, model department enrollment increased from 18 to "about 50."[55]

In his 1870 report to the Normal School Board Gage provided an excellent statistical profile of the 45 students admitted to the normal department for the fall 1870 term. Their average age was 18 years, 9 months. Twenty-four of them had taught school for an average of 37 weeks. All except one, who was born in Scotland, were natives of the United States. The top ranking birth states were New York (8), Wisconsin (8), Ohio (6) and Indiana and Massachusetts (4 each). Only one was Minnesota-born. In preparing a record for each student Gage noted that nine of them had knowledge of a language other than English. Five had studied Latin, two German and one each French and Welsh. The occupations of their parents or guardians accurately reflected the prevailing Mankato area society. Twenty-nine were farmers. The only other professions with more than one were mechanics (4), ministers (3), hotel keepers (2) and merchants (2). Gage did not explain the nature of mechanics. But, at that time, the word was used to describe any skilled laborers including carpenters and masons. Gage reported the students came from 14 different Minnesota counties. But, with 17 from Blue Earth, nine from Faribault and four from Waseca, it was evident that the Mankato Normal School had a limited reach.[56]

Although Mankato's newspapers extolled it, the Mankato Normal School was a small, struggling enterprise for its first 12 years. Gage found that it was difficult to maintain both students and faculty. The addition of Susie M. Dyer in late November 1868, increased the faculty including Gage to five. The faculty members, whom Gage usually recruited from the ranks of people he had known in Maine and Massachusetts, did not choose to become career normal school teachers. Dyer, Gage's most prized addition in 1868, left after three years when she married Mankato businessman and school leader

Lafayette G. M. Fletcher. By then only Gage remained from the original faculty.[57]

Gage himself gave up the struggle when he resigned in early June 1872, soon after the close of the school year. His appointment as superintendent of the St. Paul schools was a lateral move at best. His annual salary was $2,500, which was the same as his normal school reimbursement. But, his St. Paul position was more complex, because of the need to administer a school system that had far more employees than the Mankato Normal School.[58]

## Course of Study.
### Second State Normal School, Mankato.

| Language. | Mathematics | Physical and Nat. Sciences | Political Economy and History. | Graphics. | Professional.* |
|---|---|---|---|---|---|
| Spelling. | Number. | Natural Philosophy. | Government. | Penmanship. | Philosophy. |
| Phonetic, Alphabetic. | First Lessons. Properties. Oral Exercises | Geography. | Science, United States, Minnesota, Lectures on Government. | Principles, Practice. | Mental. Moral. |
| Words. | Arithmetic. | Mathematical, Physical, Political. | | Drawing. | Education. |
| Etymology. Definitions. | Intellectual, Written, | Chemistry. | History. | Isometric, Perspective Illustrative, Object. | Principles History. |
| Reading. | Geometry. | Botany. | United States, Lectures. | | School Laws of Minnesota. |
| Eng. Grammar. | Forms and Facts Demonstrations. | Zoology. | | | Practice. |
| First Lessons. Analysis. Parsing. | Applications. | Geology. | | | Sub-lectures, Discussions, Observations. Criticism, |
| Composition. | Algebra. | Astronomy. | | | |
| Practice, Criticism. | Elements, Applications, | | | | Teaching in |
| Literature. | Book-Keeping. | | | | Practice School, and in Sections. |
| English, American. | Surveying. | | | | |
| | Civil Engineering. | | | | |

GEORGE M. GAGE,
Principal.

*The whole work of the school is professional. We have only arranged that which is peculiarly so under this head.

1869 Course of Study

Julia Sears,
circa 1872

If Gage left Mankato because of dissatisfaction with his position, he never revealed it. His reports to the State Normal School Board were consistently decorous. His only public complaint was about the academic deficiencies of some normal school students. He never criticized such shortcomings as the poorly constructed normal building and inadequate funding.

## Julia A. Sears Administration, 1872-1873

On August 9, 1872, the *Mankato Weekly Union* reported that the State Normal School Board had hired Julia A. Sears to succeed Gage. The 32-year-old Sears had just completed her first year of teaching at Mankato Normal School. In the summer of 1871, Gage recruited her to join the Mankato Normal School faculty. Sears was a graduate of the Massachusetts normal school at Bridgewater. Later she taught public school in Boston and studied mathematics at the Massachusetts School of Technology. Gage apparently became acquainted with Sears when she was teaching mathematics at Maine's Farmington Normal School.[59]

During the 1871-72 school year Gage evidently regarded Sears as his first assistant. None of the faculty in Minnesota's three normal schools had formal designated rank. The principals were always identified as such and were oftentimes deferentially called "professors." All other faculty members were listed as assistants.

During her first year at the Mankato Normal School, Sears, apparently because of her teaching performance, came to be highly regarded by the Mankato Prudential Committee. So it was not too surprising that the prudential committee of Daniel Buck, chairman, state legislator Clark Keyser of Mankato, and Mankato banker John H. Ray thought she should succeed Gage as principal.[60]

The lines of authority between the local prudential committees and the State Normal School Board were not clear. It appears that in personnel matters a prudential committee could make recommendations that were subject to approval by the state board. Since about five weeks elapsed between Gage's resignation and the appointment of Sears as principal, the Normal School Board had plenty of time for contemplation. Late in 1872, when Sterling Yancey McMasters submitted the board's annual report to Governor Horace Austin, he noted that the board members had discussed whether or not to hire Sears or seek a male principal. Although McMasters, board president and an Episcopal minister, never provided any details of the board's decision, circumstantial evidence suggests that the board preferred a male principal, but deferred to the preference of the Mankato Prudential Committee. The board may have been influenced by Sears' willingness to accept an annual salary of $1,500—a thousand less than Gage had been paid for his last year.[61]

The Mankato Prudential Committee, which was in the best position to assess Sears' principalship, strongly endorsed her. In the report it submitted to the State Normal School Board on November 30, 1872, near the end of Sears' first term, the committee noted that "the employment of a lady as principal has more than realized our highest expectations." Expressing their desire to retain Sears, the committee members advised the board that "we should regret any change in the principalship of our school." They would have been well-advised to stop at that point. But, they undermined their own case with the judgment that ". . . where the principal is a female, it is quite important to have a male assistant teacher. Much of the heavier or physical work can better be done by a male than female teacher." In this regard, they noted that William F. Lyon, the teacher of penmanship, was providing "valuable assistance" and because of it was "doing much more than his contract really calls for."[62]

Sears was satisfied that the Mankato Normal School was progressing under her leadership. Near the end of her first term she reported to the Normal School Board that enrollment in the normal department was increasing and that "entire harmony and good feeling has existed between [prudential] committee, teachers and students. The term has been in all respects very pleasant, and we hope as *profitable* as pleasant." Sears then had six faculty members consisting of Lyon, Samuel Weigel, teacher of music, Calista Andrews, Carrie P. Townsend, Martha Seward, assistant instructors, and Ella Clark, model school teacher.[63]

Sears and the Mankato Prudential Committee were pleased with each other. But the winds of change soon undermined them. In his address to the 1873 legislature, Governor Horace Austin, a Republican from St. Peter and strong supporter of the normal school system, proposed reforming its administration. Austin agreed with some public criticism that the three-man prudential committees at Winona, Mankato and St. Cloud were too devoted to the interests of their own communities. Consequently, he recommended that the legislature assure that the normal school system be governed by a strong state normal school board. In recommending abolition of the prudential committees, Austin observed that "so long as the local boards exist, cases must occur where, from considerations of local matters, a bias will be given these schools calculated to render them subservient to local interests, to impair their general efficiency, and to make them more expensive to the State." Since he believed some local involvement was necessary, Austin recommended that the state normal school board include a resident director from Blue Earth, Stearns and Winona counties, whose county seats of Mankato, St. Cloud and Winona respectively were normal school locations.[64]

As the legislature considered Austin's recommendations, the *Mankato Weekly Review* denounced the abolition of the prudential committees as "a change, but not a reform." Editor John C. Wise thought the "success of the schools" . . . "is largely due to the efforts of the local boards."[65]

The Republican dominated legislature was not swayed by this local opinion. In its March 7, 1873, "An Act for the Regulation and Government of the State Normal Schools" the lawmakers enacted sweeping changes to the 1858 normal school law. Other than abolishing the prudential committees and providing for resident directors, the new law stipulated that "the state normal school board shall have the general supervision, management and control of the state normal schools . . ." This general authority included the power to establish admission policies, "courses of study," erection of buildings and "to appoint all professors and teachers in said schools" and to "fix their salaries." The law also specified that all gubernatorial appointments to the board had to be confirmed by the Senate.[66]

Despite the new law, Governor Austin wanted some continuity in state normal school board service. Therefore, in March, 1873, he appointed Daniel Buck as the resident director for Blue Earth County. But Buck soon resigned and was replaced by Mankato druggist George W. Austin.[67]

In a somewhat surprising move the governor also appointed George M. Gage to the normal school board. This move suggests that Gage had been displeased with the former prudential committee system and agreed with the governor that the state had the paramount interest in normal school education. To compound matters, Gage was elected board president at its June 3, 1873 meeting.[68] This made Gage the most important person in making personnel decisions for the three normal schools.

## The Normal School Board and Sears' Successor, Summer, 1873

With Gage presiding at its July 22 meeting, the normal board named the Mankato Normal School faculty for the 1873-74 academic year. They chose David Clarke John as principal at a salary of $2,500, a thousand more than Sears had been paid the preceding year.[69]

The 38-year-old John, a native of Pennsylvania, became a deacon and minister in the Methodist Episcopal Church graduating from Dickinson College (Carlisle, Pennsylvania) in 1859. In 1868-69 he taught natural science in the state normal school at Bloomsburg, Pennsylvania. Then he served for

David Clarke John,
circa 1873

four years as high school principal in Wilton, Pennsylvania. He chose to retain his religious identity during his Mankato normal school career by consistently using his title of "Reverend."[70]

The selection of a clergyman to head a public normal school was a perfectly logical move at that time. Clergymen were well-educated and generally interested in promoting better public education. Furthermore, some normal school officials—including Gage—believed normal faculty and students should lead moral lives. Evidently, they saw religion as a vital component in realizing that goal. As principal of the Mankato Normal School, Gage presided over chapel services for faculty and students, which included reading from the Bible, at the start of each day.

At its July 22 meeting the board also "elected" Julia A. Sears as "first assistant teacher at Mankato at a salary of $1,200." But their minutes noted that if Sears declined, the position should be offered to Cornelius W. G. Hyde, who had applied for the principal position. Board members apparently anticipated that Sears would not be pleased with a marked deduction from the $1,500 Resident Director Austin had offered to her in early June. Austin never explained his action because he missed the July 22 meeting. But, board members reasoned that he did not have unilateral authority to hire Sears at the same salary she had received as principal. So they offered her the same salary as the first assistant teachers at St. Cloud and Winona.[71]

Rather than informing Sears of their decision directly, the board decided that Austin should be the bearer of the bad news. Austin, accordingly, advised Sears of the board's decision in late July. Austin, as provided by the 1873 normal school law, was ex-officio treasurer of the Mankato Normal School. With respect to hiring faculty, the board, as stipulated in the new law, had exclusive appointive power. But, at its June 3 meeting newly elected President Gage appointed Austin to the Committee on the Employment of Teachers.[72]

Instead of responding to Austin, Sears notified Gage that she was not planning on accepting Austin's offer. Gage promptly informed Austin that Sears was not returning and the position of first assistant should go to Hyde. On August 9, Austin offered the position to Hyde, which seemingly settled the matter. But this was no sooner done than Austin received an offer from Sears to return for half a year. Gage's reaction to this proposal was to instruct Austin to inform Hyde that the position was "unsettled." In response, Austin told Sears to come to Mankato and informed Hyde that he was out. Sears naturally assumed that Austin had accepted her offer to return for half a year. But, Austin was not authorized to hire faculty on his own. The combination of Austin's assumption of power and Gage's equivocation resulted in both Sears and Hyde appearing in Mankato on September 1, the opening day of the school year, to claim the position of first assistant.[73]

By that time it was apparent that someone in authority had to make a decision. At its September 4 meeting the board decided that "Miss Sears, not having accepted the position tendered to her in the Normal School at Mankato, Mr. C. W. G. Hyde of Shakopee is entitled to the position, and the Board hereby order that he be given possession forthwith."[74] As far as the board was concerned that settled the matter. But, Austin, Gage, the normal board, incoming principal John, and Sears herself, did not anticipate a highly emotional reaction from some normal school students.

## The Sears Rebellion

On September 8, 40 normal school students, who were mostly from the A and B classes, told John that they intended to present a petition asking for the restoration of Sears. If that did not happen, they intended to withdraw from school. John responded that he would accept their petition if it was "respectful in tone" and they deferred acting until Resident Director Austin returned to Mankato from visiting his family in Chicago. John promised that he would present the petition to Austin and ask him to present it the board. But, John reported, "that very night some outside party took the matter in hand, and from some motive wholly inexplicable to me, advised the students to rebel . . . ."[75] According to the *Mankato Weekly Review*, this urging was done by some "older men and citizens of Mankato." But the rival *Mankato Weekly Record* claimed the students were influenced by "two or three bad advisors."[76]

It is impossible to establish the degree of collusion between the protesting students and townspeople. But, when the rebellious students first met with John they must have been aware that a number of prominent Mankatoans were preparing or had already prepared a petition demanding that the board name Sears as first assistant teacher. Normal students were in an excellent position to be privy to community affairs. Some of them lived with their Mankato parents and all others roomed and oftentimes boarded in private homes. The petition signed by 70 Mankato men, including Daniel Buck, was dated September 8. It was obviously initiated and circulated in the several days following the board's refusal to reinstate Sears.[77]

The existence of the petition probably inspired the students to harden their determination. John was dismayed when they boycotted chapel services prior to the start of classes on September 9. At that very time they were meeting in a nearby house. John's information was that they "all were pledged to stand by each other to the bitter end." John, who was predisposed to see things in black and white, reported that he felt it was necessary to exert a "strong hand." At the closing exercise on September 9, he announced the suspension of the 40 students with the caveat that any of them "could return by acknowledging his error, and promising obedience to all the regulations of the school in [the] future."[78]

Over the course of the next five days a few students returned, but John observed that "the rebellion seemed to be gaining strength; a spirit of defiance became more apparent every day." Consequently, after consulting with board president Gage, he gave the students a three-day ultimatum. By the time it expired on September 17, only nine students had returned. John promptly expelled the 31 diehards the next day.

The protesting students may have underestimated John's resolve and overestimated the support they would get from Mankato's petitioners. But, they were sincerely dedicated to what they thought was a noble cause. They obviously felt a special rapport with Sears. Generally, students have the strongest emotional ties to young instructors. They have certain shared experiences and attitudes that students would not have with much older teachers. Also, there is really no information about how Sears conducted herself with students. She may have been particularly adept in counseling students without resorting to conventional disciplinary techniques.

After the students were expelled, Austin presented the petition from Mankatoans to the Normal School Board, which considered it on October 23. Following some discussion, the board referred it to its Committee of Grievances, which was "instructed to prepare such a statement as in their judgment the interests of truth, justice and the Normal Schools demand."[79]

The Grievance Committee reported on December 4 at the next scheduled board meeting. After collecting and studying pertinent correspondence written by Austin, Gage, Sears and Hyde, which it included in its report, the committee concluded that it was "of the opinion that at this time to reinstate Miss Sears as requested is impractical." Its members also ruled that "they are convinced that the grave assumption in the petition that the Board has not acted in good faith is without foundation, but on the contrary the action and instruction of the Board has been clear and just." The report was a strong endorsement of the board's authority. But, the committee, without naming them, obliquely criticized Austin and Gage by noting: "The committee find no evidence of dishonesty or bad faith on the part of

**Normal School Matters.**

Since our last issue, Normal School matters have assumed a more serious and complicated condition. Last Tuesday morning, some forty odd scholars in the Normal department withdrew from the school, alleging dissatisfaction with the action of the State board in regard to teachers as the reason for their so doing. Prof. John suspended them from further connection with the school, unless they would acknowledge the error of their course. Some did so and returned, but about 36 remain out at the present time. The Normal department, in consequence has been reduced to about 45 scholars. We understand that the State board have taken steps to prevent the admission of the seceders into the Winona and St. Cloud schools and State University.

We had hoped that this matter might be conciliated and adjusted to the satisfaction of all parties, but now that hardly seems possible. The State board, acting upon the theory that the "King can do no harm," will not even admit a rehearing of the injustice done Miss Sears; and the scholars, sympathizing with that lady, and acting under a hasty impulse, in the mistaken idea that they were doing her a kindness, have complicated the matter beyond a reasonable possibility of satisfactory adjustment—at the same time doing themselves a great injury. In all probabilities the school will go on as if no difficulty had occurred, but we cannot but believe that its mission for good has been greatly impaired by a few evil disposed persons on the State board and outside of that body.

*Mankato Weekly Review,*
*16 September 1873*

those engaged in the transaction, yet are persuaded that if they had fully appreciated the bearing of their acts and confined their acts within the evident instruction of the Board, the difficulty would not have occurred." In other words, only the board had legal authority to hire normal school faculty.[80]

The *Mankato Union*, which supported the petitioners, observed that "it is not surprising that they [the Grievance Committee] should report the Board blameless. When Smith investigates Smith, the report is generally favorable to Smith."[81]

The Normal School Board and its supporters and the Mankatoans who wanted Sears reinstated could not find middle ground, because there was no middle ground. Board reinstatement of Sears would have been a capitulation to local interests, who obviously resented the strong state control legalized by the 1873 normal school law. Furthermore, when the board was considering the Mankato petition, it was concerned about the suspended students issue. If the board had ruled in Sears's favor, it would also have acceded to the key demand of the rebellious students. This would have been tantamount to admitting that the students should be readmitted, which would have severely undermined John's authority.

Once the Mankato appeal on behalf of Sears was resolved, the matter of the suspended students could be considered on its own merits. Newly elected state representative Silas Kenworthy took up their cause in the 1874 legislature. The 70-year-old lawmaker was a flour miller in Rapidan, a small village located about five miles south of downtown Mankato.[82] Kenworthy proposed that the House Education Committee consider taking action to reinstate the students. But the committee refused to get involved.

However, his effort, which was undoubtedly supported by many Mankatoans, was not in vain. On March 3, John recommended to Board President Henry Hastings Sibley that the students be reinstated. He professed to be "actuated by the kindest feelings toward these young ladies and gentlemen," who "would probably never have rebelled had they not been impelled to the rash act by one whom they deemed a competent loyal advisor." Fifteen days later Sibley informed John that he had polled the board, which favored reinstating the students provided they take a "pledge to obey in the future the regulations of the institution." Accordingly, John had a notice to that effect published in the *Mankato Review*.[83]

After leaving Mankato on September 23, 1873, Sears returned to her family's Fairhaven, Massachusetts home. In 1875 she was hired to teach mathematics at the newly formed Peabody Normal School (Nashville, Tennessee), which soon evolved into the Peabody College for Teachers, which, in turn became part of Vanderbilt University in 1979. During her 22 years at Peabody, Sears established a reputation as an excellent and popular teacher. She also worked for the cause of women's suffrage in Nashville. After retiring in 1907, she retired to her Fairhaven, Massachusetts home where she remained until her death on September 19, 1929.[84]

In an autobiographical account published eight years after her retirement, Sears recalled her Peabody years as her best lifetime experience. Evidently, she did not harbor such sentiments for the Mankato Normal School, which she did not even mention in the article.[85]

# THE REVIEW.

## MANKATO TUESDAY, MARCH 24, 1874

**The Expelled Normal School Pupils.**

EDITOR REVIEW :—DEAR SIR :—About two weeks ago, I requested the State Normal Board to consent to the restoration of the pupils expelled from this institution last September. Having received a favorable response from the President, Gen. H. H. Sibley, the entire correspondence is herewith presented for publication.

The expelled pupils can now return by simply signing the pledge usually signed by new pupils, and is is hoped that this will be promptly met by the spirit in which it is made. Yours, truly,
D. C. JOHN.

MANKATO, March 3d, 1874.
GEN. H. H. SIBLEY, Pres. State Normal Board:

DEAR SIR : The legislature having refused to interfere in behalf of the pupils expelled from this school, I think the time has come for the exercise of leniency, for the following reasons :

1. It is now definitely settled that Normal pupils cannot dictate who shall be their teachers nor combine to break up the school if their wishes are not gratified.

2d. So long as schemes were on foot to force their restoration by legislature enactment, I could not abate the penalty without seeming to do so under compulsion, and surrendering the authority they were expelled to maintain.

3p. The pupils would probably never have rebelled had they not been impelled to the rash act by one whom they deemed a competent legal adviser. While this does not release them from the consequence of their act, it does afford a reasonable ground for the exercise of leniency toward them.

4th. Actuated by the kindest feelings toward those young ladies and gentlemen who under the instigation of bad advice uncurred the extreme penalty of school government, and believing that their return at my invitation will no longer be attended with danger, I desire, if it meets the approval of the Board, to restore them upon the simple promise of obedience to the regulations of the school.

Please communicate with the other members of the Board and acquaint me with their decision as soon as you can conveniently. Your, very respectfully.
D. C. JOHN.

ST. PAUL, March 18th, 1874.
PROF. D. C. JOHN, Principal Normal School, Mankato, Minn.

DEAR SIR :—I have, as you suggested in you communication of 3d inst., communicated with the several members of the Normal School Board, with regard to the proposition to re-admit the students, who withdrew from the school, under their simple pledge to obey in the future the regulations of the institution. The last reply was received by me to day, and I am gratified to be able to announce to you, that the Board is a unit in favor of the measure as above stated. You are hereby authorized to make the fact known to the parties interested, in such manner as you may deem expedient.
Respectfully Yours,
H. H. SIBLEY, Prest.

*Mankato Weekly Review*, March 24, 1874

Joan Forssmark Pengilly provides much useful and accurate information about Sears, but unfortunately overstates her case by identifying Sears as "The First Female President of a Co-Educational Public Institution of Higher Learning." During her one year of leading the Mankato Normal School, Sears held the title of principal, not president. Furthermore, the Mankato Normal School, like all other normal schools in 1873, was not higher education. In identifying the Mankato Normal as higher education, Pengilly ignored her accepted definition of higher education, which was described as "any education above the high school grade."[86] The Mankato Normal did not require a high school diploma for admission during Sears's service and its course offerings overlapped with the standard high school curriculum.

The greatest contributor of Sears's lore was Alfred Leland Crabb, professor of education at Peabody, 1927-1949, and the author of three historical novels about Nashville during the Reconstruction Era. His supposedly historical article about Sears proves that he should have stayed in fiction. He did not document his article, perhaps because there was no way of proving invented dialogue and inaccurate claims about Sears's Mankato stint. His most egregious error was the claim that Sears was dismissed from the Mankato Normal School because townspeople were displeased by her alliance "with a few daring ladies and fewer super-daring gentlemen" in the women's suffrage cause. There is not a scintilla of evidence that supports this outlandish assertion.[87]

Understandably, Sears has figured prominently in the history and lore of the Mankato Normal School. As a unique event, the Sears Rebellion has been perpetuated and will no doubt be told and re-told as long as the institution endures. The whats of Sears and the rebellion are indisputable, the whys are another matter. Those who study history seem to have unbounded faith in their ability to determine the motives of their predecessors. Perhaps they are reluctant to admit there are some things they cannot ascertain. But it is perfectly natural that the reasons for some happenings cannot be established precisely.

With respect to the Sears Rebellion, even the most active participants never reached a consensus about why she was not retained as the Mankato Normal principal. Those who resorted to the simplistic explanation that Sears was replaced because she was a woman ignored her initial appointment as principal. She was a woman when she was named principal in 1872 and a woman when she was replaced the next year.

But, the governance of the Mankato Normal School changed. Sears initially became principal with the strong endorsement of the Mankato Normal Prudential Committee. During her one-year administration the committee was legislated out of existence and the authority of the State Normal School Board was sharply increased. Sears, who was seen as the Mankato candidate, was put in the position of being a pawn in the power struggle between local and state interests. Governor Austin and the legislature expected the Normal School Board to act as a strong state agency. Under those circumstances, it is perfectly understandable that the board would decide to appoint its own choice as Mankato Normal School principal.

Despite her short, ultimately unhappy Mankato Normal experience, Sears eventually had the satisfaction of having a distinguished teacher career. Gage and Austin, whose fumbling efforts led to Sears's removal from the Mankato Normal School, were much less fortunate.

On December 19, 1873, Gage wrote his letter of resignation from the Normal School Board to Governor Horace Austin. His official reason was that his position as superintendent of the St. Paul schools required his full time devotion. Some skeptics suspected the official reason was not the real reason. They noted his resignation came on the heels of the Grievance Committee's report, which portrayed him as an honest, but ineffective administrator. The *Mankato Review* attributed Gage's downfall to his association with Governor Austin by reporting that he "was virtuous, happy and popular before he commenced worshipping St. Peter's Governor."[88]

After being caught up in bitter personnel controversy, Gage, in 1874, left his position as St. Paul school superintendent. This ended his career as an educator. Thereafter, he worked mostly as a traveling salesman in Minnesota and adjoining areas. He moved to Portland, Oregon, in 1896, where he edited the *Pacific Monthly* magazine for about 13 years. After becoming seriously ill in late 1909, he relocated to his daughter's home in Sacramento, California. He died on April 13, 1910.[89]

Resident director Austin, like Gage, had a short board experience. As ex-officio Mankato Normal treasurer, he evidently kept public funds in his private bank account. The *Mankato Weekly Review* of March 24, 1874, reported that "an investigation of his Normal School business showed the fact his [Austin's] indebtedness to the State amounted to $2,053.14." Austin was able to repay $1,600, but had to give bondsmen security for the balance. Austin's bad fortune included the failure of his drug business and his discontinuance as resident director by Governor Cushman Kellogg Davis, a Republican who succeeded Horace Austin on January 7, 1874.

## Closure Attempt During the John Administration

David Clarke John served as the Mankato Normal School's principal from 1873 to 1880. His duties became much more routine after the Sears Rebellion crisis of his first year. During his tenure the school's main concerns other than the Sears Rebellion were coping with a closure threat, improving the building, and modifying academic policies.

In John's first year the fate of Minnesota's normal schools was debated in the state Senate between supporters of Republican governor Cushman Kellogg Davis and closure advocates led by Ignatius Donnelly from Dakota County. Davis agreed with his predecessor Horace Austin that if, as some critics insisted, the normal schools were too costly, the solution was to remedy their defects instead of abolishing the schools.

At the opening of the 1874 legislature, Donnelly proposed that the three normal schools be closed. He contended that they were not only too expensive, but unnecessary as well, because normal training could be offered by high schools. The proposal would have attracted much public attention on its own merits, but it was especially newsworthy because of Donnelly's fame.

Donnelly, who nearly two decades later became nationally famous as a Populist Party firebrand, was in the early stages of his third-party ventures. Donnelly began his long political career as an orthodox Republican. In 1859, when he was only 28 years old, he was elected Minnesota's lieutenant governor when Alexander Ramsey was the first Republican to win the state's governorship. Both Donnelly and Ramsey had unbounded ambition. They were easily re-elected in 1861, but neither of them finished their terms. In 1862 Donnelly was elected to the national House of Representatives and the next year Ramsey was selected as a United States senator by the state legislature.[90]

Donnelly served three consecutive terms before breaking with Ramsey shortly before the 1868 election. Since Ramsey was the acknowledged leader of Minnesota's Republicans, Donnelly's move against him backfired. After being defeated in his 1868 re-election attempt, Donnelly turned to lecturing before re-emerging in 1872 as a vocal supporter of the Liberal Republican Party.

After the Liberal Republicans failed to seriously challenge the re-election of President Ulysses S. Grant, Donnelly became active in the Grange. But, Donnelly believed this farm protest movement, which sought government regulation of railroads, was severely handicapped by its own charter which banned it from acting as a political party. Donnelly's solution was to spearhead the organization of the Anti-Monopoly Independent Party, which supported Granger aims. In 1873, Donnelly, as a candidate of the newly formed party, was elected to the state Senate.

As the most famous member of the 1874 legislature, Donnelly was expected to champion the anti-railroad crusade. So there was widespread shock when his first proposed reform was to abolish the normal schools.

Donnelly's main premise was that the normal schools, which were a pet project of spendthrift Republicans, placed an undue burden on Minnesota taxpayers. He tried to prove statistically that the state's normal schools were more costly than those in other states.

Donnelly's closure proposal caused an especially sharp reaction from the normal school localities. His vehemence and sometimes intemperate orations even provoked some personal attacks from normal school supporters.

Normal school defenders, including the extremely vocal Morton S. Wilkinson of Mankato, emphasized four main arguments: (1) The normal schools were a vital part of Minnesota's education system, because they could best serve the needs of common school teachers, which, in turn, would elevate rural education; (2) The state lacked authority to close the schools at Mankato and St. Cloud because the 1858 normal school law stipulated that in exchange for local monetary support the schools could not be moved for 10 years; (3) The normal schools were most beneficial to farmers, because an estimated 90 percent of normal school students were the children of farmers, and (4) Minnesota's normal school costs compared favorably to other states.

Wilkinson, a former United States senator, was the most prestigious opponent of Donnelly's bill. By wisely arguing that the normal schools benefitted the entire state, he avoided appearing to be a partisan voice for the Mankato Normal.

The alleged illegality of Donnelly's bill proved to be the most persuasive argument of normal school champions. The Senate Judiciary Committee, which was asked to investigate the legal foundation of the normal schools, concluded that the state lacked the authority to close them. This judgment doomed Donnelly's effort.[91]

Donnelly's bill to close the normal schools was neither the first nor the last suggestion to abolish them. But, as the most publicized, it coalesced support for the schools. The schools endured in large part because they were supported by the ruling Republican Party. But such leaders as Governor Davis apparently regarded saving the normal schools as a benefit to the University of Minnesota. If the normal schools had been closed, it is quite likely that there would have been a move to saddle the university with normal training. This was a role that neither the university or its key supporters wanted.

By the time Mankato and the other normals had weathered the closure crisis, John was absorbed in the more mundane issues of improving the building and academic programs.

## Building Repair During John's Administration

The Mankato Normal's building defects were first publicized by a board-appointed committee that inspected it in the fall of 1873. The committee reported that the building "was poorly constructed, the walls had been damaged, and the roof was so inadequately constructed that there was eminent [sic] danger of a calamity should there be a heavy fall of damp snow." Additionally, the committee, which was greatly concerned about school discipline, noted that the building's interior walls had been defaced. But, in an implied compliment to John's disciplinary actions, noted that lately defacement "had been carefully guarded against."[92]

In his first annual report dated November 30, 1873, John did not mention any defects in the building's construction. But, he reported that "our efforts to protect the walls from pencil depravity, and the floors from tobacco tessellation, have met with most gratifying success." John, who was easily exasperated by juvenile behavior, observed that overall discipline had improved from the early part of the fall term when the institution was plagued by the "twin pests of the school room, absence and tardiness."[93]

By the time he made his second annual report on November 30, 1874, John had decided to complain about the building's inadequacies. Cracks in the walls, apparently caused by settling, he reported, "have enlarged somewhat during the year." The roof was in the same "dangerous condition," which would force him to dismiss school if there was a heavy snowfall. John requested structural repairs, but, at least the wall and roof problems did not affect daily operations.[94]

The inadequate heating system was another matter. John insisted that the wood-burning furnaces, which had been extensively repaired, were poorly constructed and too small. Their "hot air flues," he reported, "are arranged with little regard to the law of atmospheric movements, and thus greatly diminish the amount of available heat." In very cold, windy weather, the top attainable temperature in some of the rooms was only 55. Therefore, John insisted the furnaces had to be replaced.

The board supported John's conclusion and recommended a special legislative appropriation to repair the Mankato building. Accordingly, Governor Cushman Kellogg Davis, in his January 9, 1875, message to the legislature, requested a special appropriation of $1,100 to $1,200 for Mankato Normal. But, the legislative appropriation of $10,000 was only for the standard salary and operating cost.[95]

Despite the lack of special funding for repairs, modest improvements in the Mankato building were made during the summer of 1875. Some of the walls, which had been discolored by furnace soot, were calcimined, the most severe breaks in walls were repaired, air circulation was improved and the furnaces were repaired. Significantly, the roof was reinforced with timbers, which removed the danger of it collapsing under the weight of heavy snow.[96]

But repairing the normal school proved to be akin to dealing with a moving target, because new problems emerged as the building aged. In his 1875 report, John noted that "the entire north wing is annually raised by frost, and the walks, floors, and door frames are considerably out of shape in consequence." Even though the furnaces had been repaired, the heating-air circulation system was still inadequate. Because the furnaces had to be operated at their utmost capacity, hot, dry air was pronounced by John to be "unfit for respiration."[97]

John's persistence, the board's support and a special $2,500 repairs appropriation by the 1877 legislature finally solved the Mankato Normal School's building woes. During the summer of 1877, resident director/ school treasurer Orrin Ormsby Pitcher supervised the installation of new furnaces and structural repairs. Pitcher worked with three contractors—the Henderson Furnace Company of Winona, Frank Barnard and Dennis Sullivan. The furnace company installed five new furnaces at a total cost of $1,075. Barnard had the carpentry contract for repairing cracked walls, rebuilding the stairways and cleaning the interior walls. Sullivan was engaged to repair the outside walls, which included improving adjacent drainage.[98]

John was finally happy with the building. In his report for the year ending September 1, 1877, he enthused that "the whole establishment now wears a neat, cosy [sic] appearance, which at once refines and stimulates to mental activity."[99]

Before the year was done, John was apparently relieved to find out that the normal school building could withstand a mild earthquake. About noon on Thursday, September 7, earthquake vibrations were felt in some parts of Mankato. They were reportedly strong enough to sway some items to and fro.[100] When the tremors hit, John was teaching in a third story room in the normal building. He wrote that his students became greatly alarmed and almost panicked when "the floor rose and fell three times in rapid succession."[101] John blocked the door to prevent the students from rushing to the nearest stairway where they were the most likely to fall and get injured. After they had calmed down, John ordered them to evacuate the building no faster than a brisk walk.

Interestingly, the shaking was not felt on the building's first floor and the edifice had no evident damage. But John assured skeptics who doubted the earthquake report that if they had been on the third floor of the normal building, they would be true believers.

## Academic Matters During John's Administration

With respect to academic matters, John's administration was characterized by continuity and change. As school administrator John was responsible for all academic matters from recruitment to graduation. His principal way of recruiting students was to issue an annual circular about a month before the start of the fall terms. These were usually advertised in Mankato newspapers and distributed to prospective enrollees. John's 1875 circular first notified potential applicants that the fall term would begin September 1 and end December 23. There were three board-specified admission requirements — pupils had to be at least 15 years old, take a subject matter examination and "pledge to teach two years in the public schools of the state or pay tuition at the rate of $16 per year." The circular also advised that "board can be secured for $3 per week. Students wishing to board themselves can rent rooms at very reasonable rates."[102]

During the opening days of the fall 1875 term, John and his faculty members examined 50 applicants for the D class and graded them on a scale of 10. Those who scored at least 6 were admitted to the D class. But, anyone below that was assigned to the E or preparatory class. This preparatory (i. e. remedial class), taught in the Model School, essentially reviewed common school subject matter. The five students who scored 8 or above could take a second, more rigorous exam, which gave them the opportunity to start in the C or B classes. Miss Alma J. Pattee of Stevens Point, Wisconsin, distinguished herself with a 9.6 score.[103]

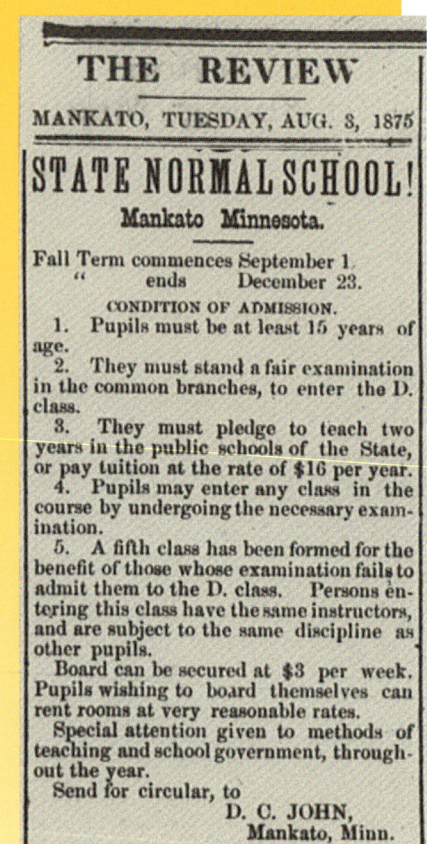

THE REVIEW

MANKATO, TUESDAY, AUG. 3, 1875

## STATE NORMAL SCHOOL!

### Mankato Minnesota.

Fall Term commences September 1.
" ends December 23.

CONDITION OF ADMISSION.

1. Pupils must be at least 15 years of age.
2. They must stand a fair examination in the common branches, to enter the D. class.
3. They must pledge to teach two years in the public schools of the State, or pay tuition at the rate of $16 per year.
4. Pupils may enter any class in the course by undergoing the necessary examination.
5. A fifth class has been formed for the benefit of those whose examination fails to admit them to the D. class. Persons entering this class have the same instructors, and are subject to the same discipline as other pupils.

Board can be secured at $3 per week. Pupils wishing to board themselves can rent rooms at very reasonable rates.

Special attention given to methods of teaching and school government, throughout the year.

Send for circular, to
D. C. JOHN,
Mankato, Minn.

*Mankato Weekly Review,*
August 3, 1875

John, who had some elitist tendencies, was not satisfied that pre-testing screened inadequately prepared students. He complained that "nearly all of our pupils come to us but poorly prepared to enter the lowest grade. Not one-tenth of them can remain long enough to complete the course, and the majority scarcely half that time."[104] As his thinking on the subject evolved, John became convinced that there should be stricter admission requirements. He observed that "under the present regulation it is questionable whether we have the right to reject any applicant not absolutely imbecile, who has reached the required age." John insisted that poorly prepared students forced the school to concentrate on subjects that should have been covered in the common schools.[105]

Since John's attitude coincided with public criticism of low normal school standards, the board approved reforms before the opening of the 1877-78 school year. It abolished the E class and added a third year to the course of study.

The E class, a particular object of John's scorn, was replaced by a Preparatory Class, which was to be a special department distinct from the normal and model departments. Those who failed to pass the entrance examinations could enroll in the preparatory class, but they had to pay tuition at a rate of $8.00 a term. Those who attended less than half a term were charged $0.50 a week.[106]

When it added a third year or "advanced course" to the course of study, the board also decided that only those pupils who completed it would be granted diplomas. Those who graduated after the two-year "Elementary Course" would be given certificates of attendance.

The Third Year component included the introduction of Latin. Board members and John believed that studying Latin was necessary to improve knowledge of many word origins in the English language.

After the addition of the Third Year, the revised course of study was:

During John's administration, the Mankato Normal greatly expanded its participation in teachers institutes. The initiative for this came from David Burt, Superintendent of the State Department of Public Instruction, who believed institutes were necessary to improve common school instruction. Burt was very concerned that only a small portion of the state's 3,896 common school teachers had attended normal schools. He also recognized that most common school teachers could not afford to live in a normal school city for an extended time. He reasoned that if the teachers could not go to school, the school should be taken to them.[107]

The State Normal School Board endorsed Burt's idea at its meeting of December 5, 1876. It resolved that for springtime institute work, each normal school was to "furnish the State Superintendent with [a] teaching force equal to the aggregate to the services of one teacher for six weeks." The allocation for fall teaching was decided jointly by each principal and resident director. Each normal school was to compensate institute instructors at regular salary rate, but the State Superintendent of Instruction had to "pay the necessary contingent expenses [i. e. travel and per diem]."

The three normal school principals strongly supported this institute expansion. They believed it would "not only be beneficial to the teachers rendering the service, but also a means of turning popular attention to the schools and of increasing the number of their students."

The Mankato Normal School launched an unprecedented institute program in 1877 by offering four two-week long institutes at Garden City,

Fairmont, Montevideo and Madelia. John, who taught in two of them, estimated that the four combined had an attendance of about 250 young teachers.[108] The next year Mankato Normal conducted two two-week institutes at Waseca and Windom and one-week institutes at Minnesota Falls and Le Sueur. John was satisfied that the institutes showed hundreds of participants "who would never go beyond the limits of their own county . . . a more excellent way" of teaching.[109]

Coincidently with the expanded institute program, the Mankato Normal began publicizing itself by circulating annual catalogs. In December 1877, the State Normal School Board authorized the schools to issue annual catalogs.[110] John accordingly compiled a catalog for the 1877-78 school year. This 24-page pamphlet was really a combination catalog-directory. In addition to providing information about the admissions policy and the courses of study, it listed by name the current faculty, all graduates from July 1870 through April 1877 and all students for the current academic year. John prepared two subsequent catalogs before leaving the Mankato Normal School after the 1879-80 academic year.

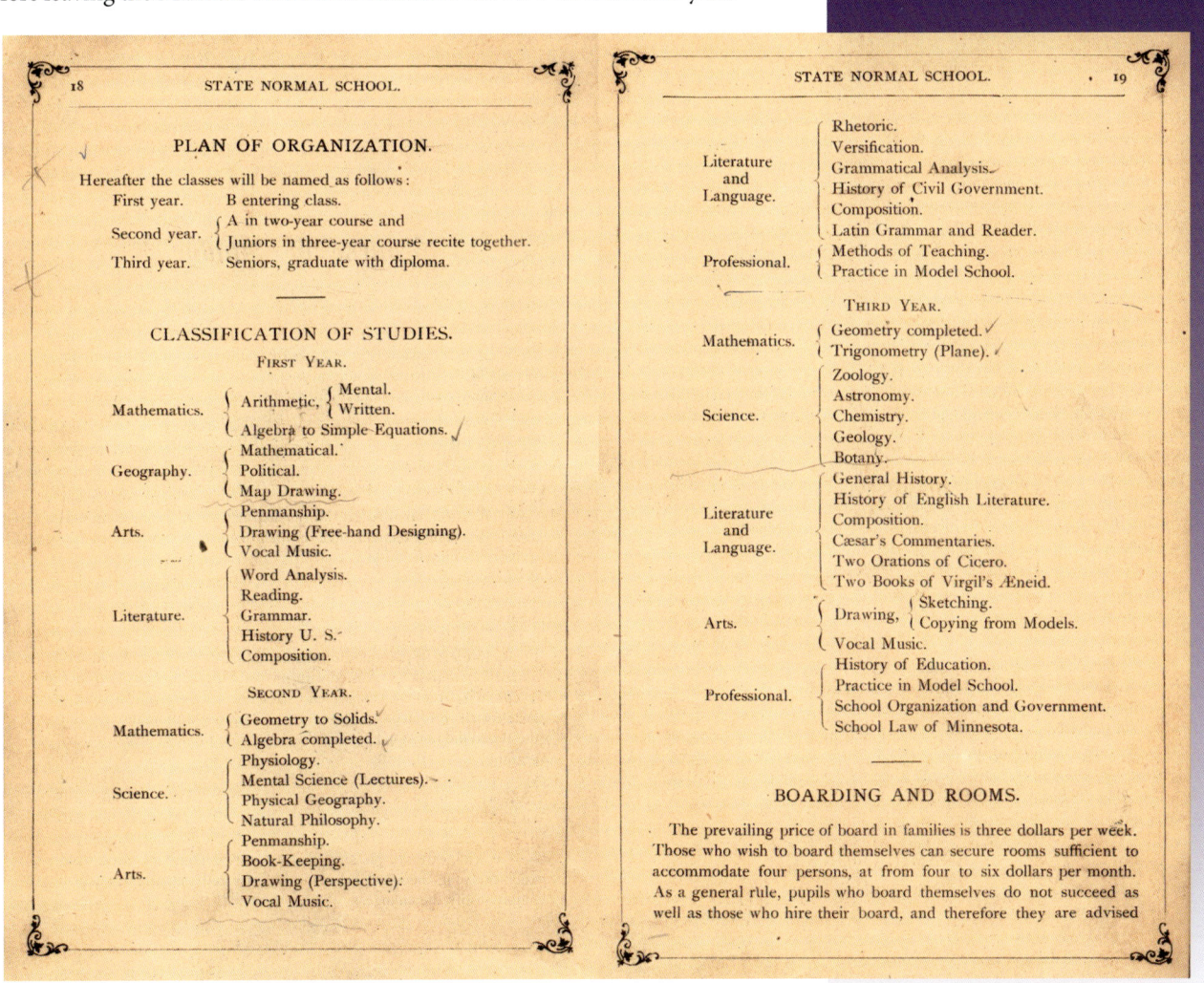

Course of Study, 1877-1878 Catalogue

## John's Resignation and Subsequent Career

John resigned from the Mankato Normal after the 1879-80 year to become president of Hamline College. His resignation was far from ordinary. He had originally resigned to accept the Hamline presidency after the 1875-76 school year. He was obviously ready for Hamline, but Hamline was not ready for him. After hiring John, the trustees of the Methodist-affiliated liberal arts college, which had been originally established in Red Wing, decided they did not have sufficient funding to relocate the institution to St. Paul and start offering classes on its new campus. So for the next four years both Hamline and the State Normal School Board accommodated John. Hamline retained its presidency for him until it was ready to enroll students at its St. Paul campus. The State Normal School Board, fully informed about John's desire to leave the Mankato Normal School, renewed his annual appointments.[111]

But anyone who expected John to be grateful must have been very disappointed. Ever the critic, he editorialized about his departure in the 1879-1880 *Mankato Normal Catalog*. He wrote: "After years of trial, and anxiety, of things pleasant and unpleasant, I now lay down the Principalship which I reluctantly and somewhat timidly accepted seven years ago. Measured by absolute results, I am not satisfied with the outcome of these best years of my life, but considering the difficulties which had to be overcome, I am not at all disheartened."[112]

John apparently thought better days were ahead at Hamline. But chronic funding shortages and sparse enrollment doomed his venture. After only three years, he resigned his presidency. Admittedly, Hamline College had problems, but historian David W. Johnson concluded John was the main villain. He noted that ". . . John, of serious demeanor and stern countenance, was neither skilled promoter nor effective solicitor." According to Johnson, John was handicapped by his normal school experience. John, he observed, "was more familiar with normal school methods than those of the liberal arts college, he tried but failed to introduce the former at Hamline to his ultimate discredit."[113]

After resigning from Hamline, John resumed his Methodist ministry career. Except for a three-year stint as president of Clark University in Atlanta, Georgia, 1893-1896, John worked mainly as a pastor and presiding elder in Wisconsin until he retired because of poor health in 1905. He died in St. Petersburg, Florida, on October 8, 1920.

John's passion was composing the lyrics and music for hymns. In a 36 year span he authored four hymnals — *The Guiding Star for Sunday Schools: A New Collection of Sunday School Songs...* (Philadelphia: Lee & Walker, 1872), *The Corona: A Treasury of Songs for Sunday Schools...*(Milwaukee: J. Flanner, 1893), *The Evangel A Collection of Hymns & Choruses Specially Adapted to Evangelistic Meetings...*(Chicago: F. H. Revell Co., [1895?], and *Songs Worth While: For Sunday Schools, Young People's Societies, Brotherhoods, Temperance Societies, Civic Clubs, Evangelists and All Others Who Are Laboring for the Kingdom of God and a Better Civilization* (Omaha: John & Edwards, 1908).[114]

# 2

# THE MANKATO NORMAL SCHOOL:
## GROWTH AND TRANSITION TO A TEACHERS COLLEGE, 1880-1921

From 1880 until 1921 when the legislature changed it and the other five Minnesota normal schools (in Winona, St. Cloud, Moorhead, Duluth and Bemidji) to teachers colleges, the Mankato normal experienced some fundamental changes. It enjoyed unprecedented stability because of the relatively long terms of Principal/President Edward Searing (1880-1898) and his successor President Charles H. Cooper. Sharply increased enrollment led to significant changes in the campus, including a major expansion of the normal building, the construction of a model school/gymnasium annex to the normal building and the creation and opening of the first women's dormitory. Increasing emphasis on improving academic standards caused programmatic changes to such a degree that by about 1910 Mankato and its sister schools were starting to resemble de facto colleges. Likewise, the advent of student organizations, publications and participation in interscholastic sports contributed to the emergence of a college-like atmosphere.

### Hiring of Edward Searing

On May 11, 1880, the Minnesota Normal School Board selected Edward Searing as David Clarke John's replacement. A native of Aurora, New York, the 45-year-old Searing had impressive academic credentials. He was schooled at Courtland Academy and Cazenovia Seminary (Methodist) in his home state. He then taught Latin at Cazenovia before moving to Bay City, Michigan, where he worked for a year as public school principal. After graduating from the University of Michigan in 1861, Searing was employed as a professor of Latin and Greek in Milton College (Milton, Wisconsin) 1861-73 and 1878-80.[1]

During his professorship at Milton, a private college, Searing became interested in public education. In 1873 he was elected Wisconsin's superintendent of public instruction. Re-elected in 1875, he served two two-year terms in Madison before returning to Milton. His Wisconsin state service gave Searing invaluable experience in dealing with Wisconsin's common schools, high schools and normal schools. Evidently, the Minnesota State Normal School Board regarded this aspect of Searing's career as his most important qualification.

Aside from his public school administrative work, Searing was a widely respected Latin scholar. In 1869, while teaching at Milton, his book *The First Six*

Edward Searing,
circa 1889

*Books of Virgil's Aeneid* was published. Searing confined himself to the first six of Virgil's 12 books, because, he explained that this portion, which covered the adventures of Aeneas from the time he left Troy until he arrived in Rome via Carthage, was the part usually read by students of Latin. Searing presented the Latin text of the books and added copious notes in English on words that could be variously interpreted. His publisher re-issued revised editions in 1874 and 1885. When Barnes released the last edition, it also published Searing's New York Normal College edition titled *Three Books of the Aeneid*.[2]

When the Minnesota Normal School Board began considering John's replacement, it tried to recruit Searing. At the request of board president Thomas Simpson, Searing visited the Mankato Normal School on April 15, 1880. But he never formally applied for its vacant principalship.[3]

At the board meeting of May 11, Orrin Ormsby Pitcher, resident director of the Mankato Normal, presented the credentials of seven applicants. He then informed the board that he had asked Searing if he would accept the position if the board offered it to him. Pitcher and the other board members were elated that Searing had said yes. So, without further discussion, they agreed to employ him.[4]

Searing was hired as the principal of the Mankato Normal School, but the Normal School Board soon changed his title and that of the Winona and St. Cloud normal school heads to president. Since the board did not make the change by a formal meeting action, it is impossible to determine exactly when the three principals became presidents. In the board minutes for its meetings of May 11 and December 7, 1880, the normal school leaders were identified as "principals." The board minutes of May 10, 1881, used both "principals" and "presidents." But, perhaps significantly, Searing and his Winona and St. Cloud peers were identified as "president" in the salary listing for each school.

## The Big Storm

When Searing first visited the Mankato Normal School, he professed to be "agreeably surprised at the size of the building, the convenient arrangement of rooms, and especially at the admirable condition of all portions of the building which had been in use."[5] Under these circumstances, he naturally anticipated a smooth transition to his first academic year.

Like many others in history, Searing was soon reminded that there was much wisdom in the immortal words of the Scottish poet Robert Burns: "The best laid schemes o' mice an[d] men gang aft agley."

On Saturday, June 5, 1880, the Mankato-Lake Crystal area was devastated by a straight-line windstorm, the greatest natural disaster in Mankato's short 28-year history. The mid-morning storm, which moved from the southwest, bore fierce winds, ominous dark clouds and heavy rain. The gale severely damaged numerous Mankato businesses and residences, uprooted hundreds of trees and even toppled such low-lying objects as rail fences and headstones in Glenwood Cemetery.[6]

But the Mankato normal building was hit especially hard. Its roof, which was blown loose, settled on the attic. Heavy roof beams broke through the attic and punched holes in the ceiling and walls of the third story. The building's towers were wrecked and parts of its chimneys were deposited on the steep hillside behind the building.

The storm itself was bad enough, but it occurred in an especially rainy, stormy season. In the week after it, Mankato had four heavy rains, whose waters poured down through the unroofed building. Consequently, there was severe water damage to walls and floors throughout the facility.[7]

Considering the extent of the damage, the normal school had an amazingly rapid recovery. Two days after the storm, Orrin Ormsby Pitcher went to St. Paul by railroad to meet with Governor John Sargent Pillsbury. The governor evidently told Pitcher to proceed with building repairs with the understanding that funding would have to be provided by the 1881 legislature. In his January 6, 1881, message to the legislature, Pillsbury informed the lawmakers that because a "terrible hurricane" had wrecked the Mankato Normal School's roof and threatened the building's future, he had authorized all necessary repairs. He recommended that the legislature appropriate repair costs. It obliged by an act of February 5, 1881, which appropriated up to $10,000.[8]

Immediately after meeting with Governor Pillsbury, Pitcher began arranging the repair of the normal school building. Within three weeks of the storm, workmen led by James A. James, a Mankato building contractor who had served a term in the Minnesota House of Representatives, had made considerable progress in enclosing the roof. When Searing arrived in Mankato on July 20, he found the roof was fully enclosed, but because little had been done with the interior, he said the building appeared to be only half-finished. Somehow, work crews arranged by Pitcher had the building looking like new when the fall term opened on August 23.[9]

Normal School building as remodeled after the storm, 1880

### Increased Enrollment in the Early Searing Administration

The Mankato Normal's enrollment more than doubled from 1880 to 1885. Total enrollment for the 1880-81 school year was 235, consisting of 120 in the normal department, 57 in the preparatory department and 58 in the model school. For 1884-85 the total enrollment was 577, with 326 in the normal department, 121 in the preparatory department and 130 in the model school.[10]

The enrollment surge to 1885 was spurred by statewide and local population growth, improved railroad service, an expanded institute program, an enrichment of the model school offerings and the willingness of the state to fund additional students and faculty.

From 1870 to 1880, Minnesota's population increased from 439,706 to 780,273. By 1890 it was 1,310,383. For the same three federal censuses, Blue Earth County's population was respectively 17,302, 22,889 and 29,210. Much of this increase was attributable to Mankato's growth from 3,482 in 1870 to 5,550 and 8,838 in 1880 and 1890.[11]

Easy access by railroad helped Mankato and its normal school. The town's original railroad—the St. Paul and Sioux City—provided the best routes for connecting with the state capital and southwestern Minnesota. The Winona and St. Peter was the main east-west route, and Mankato was connected with the Southern Minnesota line by branches to Albert Lea and Blue Earth. These lines, Searing claimed, made Mankato easily reachable "from all quarters." Furthermore, the railroads offered reduced fares to Mankato normal students at the beginning and end of terms if they presented an attendance certificate from Searing.[12] In Mankato, the railroad depots were within easy walking distance of the normal school. The extent of railroad passenger travel is well-indicated by the timetables published in Mankato's newspapers. On June 1, 1880, the *Mankato Weekly Review* reported that Mankato had 10 daily arrivals and departures.

### Institute Program Expansion

By 1881 the State of Minnesota, which was enjoying unprecedented revenue, was firmly committed to supporting the normal schools. Legislators were so pleased with the schools' institute program that they provided special funding for it. In an act of February 24, 1881, the legislature appropriated $8,000 for the year and each ensuing year for institute training conducted

# James Thompson McCleary: From Normal School to Congress

James Thompson McCleary (February 5, 1853-December 17, 1924) holds a unique distinction in the history of the Mankato Normal School and its successors. Of the hundreds of faculty members who retired or went elsewhere, he is the only one who left because he was elected to the United States Congress.

McCleary, who was born in Ingersoll, Ontario, Canada, was educated at his community's public schools and McGill University in Montreal. After college he moved to Wisconsin to teach and then served as the Pierce County school superintendent. As county superintendent he became very knowledgeable about common schools and the qualifications of their teachers.

McCleary's experience as a county school superintendent familiarized him with the role of institutes in teacher training. In 1881 he was hired as institute conductor by the Mankato Normal School.

In addition to coordinating the institute program, McCleary also taught classes in English, penmanship and civics. Teaching civics inspired him to write *Studies in Civics*, a text geared to the reading level of the upper elementary grades. First published in 1889, the book was slightly revised and re-issued six years later. It was a survey of city, county, state and federal governments with a certain emphasis on the constitution of the United States. McCleary dedicated it to his Mankato Normal students "Whose Questions Have Aided Me In Determining What Subjects To Treat And Whose Earnestness And Intelligence Have Made It A Pleasure To Be Their Teacher."

To supplement the 1895 edition, McCleary prepared *A Teacher' Manual to Accompany Studies in Civics*. His book was widely used as a text for at least three decades. The 1895 revision was followed by 1897, 1903, 1908, 1910, 1916

James Thompson McCleary

and 1918 editions. By writing *Studies in Civics*, McCleary gained the distinction of becoming the Mankato Normal School's first faculty author.

During his Mankato Normal years, McCleary became involved with the Minnesota Educational Association. He was the group's secretary in 1883 and president in 1891. This experience apparently helped launch his political career.

In 1892, McCleary, as the Republican candidate from Minnesota's second congressional district, was elected to Congress. Re-elected six times, he served from March 4, 1893 to March 3, 1897. During his congressional career, he staunchly advocated the orthodox Republican tenets of a high protective tariff and the gold standard. These positions served him well until 1906, when he was defeated in an eighth-term bid, because numerous southern Minnesota farmers had become convinced they would benefit from tariff reciprocity.

President Theodore Roosevelt appointed McCleary as second assistant postmaster general. He held the position from March 29, 1907-September 15, 1908. After leaving government service, he worked in New York City as the secretary of the American Iron and Steel Institute, 1911-1920. After retiring in 1920 because of poor health, he farmed for a time near Maiden Rock, Pierce County, Wisconsin. Following a sojourn to Mill Valley, California, he returned to Maiden Rock and died in a La Crosse, Wisconsin, hospital. His obituary, front-page news in the *Mankato Free Press*, highlighted his congressional career.

(*Biographical Directory of the United States Congress 1774-2005* (Washington: Government Printing Office, 2005), 1527; *Mankato: Its First Fifty Years*, 267-69, contains photo taken when he was in Congress; *Mankato Free Press*, 19 December 1924; J. T. McCleary, *Studies in Civics* (St. Paul: D. D. Merrill, 1889; rev. ed. New York: American Book Co., 1895; Bibliographical search in World Cat).

by the normal schools. Mankato and St. Cloud were each granted $3,000, with $2,000 going to the Winona Normal. The law specified that: "The State Normal School Board shall appoint one (1) teacher for each Normal School, especially qualified to give instruction in Teachers' Institutes. The salary of such teacher to be paid out of the money appropriated by this act."[13]

Searing and the board filled the Mankato Normal institute position in 1881 when James Thompson McCleary was added to the faculty. McCleary's position ranked next to Searing's. Searing's school year salary was $2,000 and McCleary's was originally $1,400. Normal schools did not have formal faculty ranks, but in the annual catalogs the faculty was evidently listed in order of significance and salary. McCleary always appeared just below Searing.[14]

## Facilities Improvements

When he started at the Mankato Normal, Searing was satisfied with its recently repaired building. But, within a year he was very upset about its ventilation, drainage and toilet inadequacies.

During the heating season, and especially during severe cold spells, the circulation system could not distribute fresh air into some of the classrooms. Because dry, dusty air impaired student health, some instructors opened windows to admit outside air. During cold weather this created another kind of discomfort. Searing's proposed solution was to remodel the ventilation system by enlarging and, in some instances, relocating air ducts.[15]

Poor drainage, which threatened to destroy the building's rear foundations, was complicated by its location at the base of steep Hanover Hill. Runoff and seepage from the hill's clayey soil, ran through and under the rear foundation into the basement. Searing complained that during particularly rainy times, water flooded the basement floor and threatened to extinguish the wood-burning furnaces. Such expedients as an open well in the basement and another outside the rear wall were not adequate to control this overflow. Periodically, the janitor had to hand pump water from both wells.

The small women and men's outhouses in back of the normal building were grossly inadequate as enrollment swelled after 1880. Both drained into cesspools that had to be pumped out periodically.

The building did have inside washrooms. Water used for drinking and washing was pumped from a cistern, which was fed by catchment water from the building's roof.

Extant photographs of the original Mankato Normal building were taken from the front. This is understandable because they were used to promote the school's best image. But, a photograph taken from the rear would have literally shown another side of the school. In addition to the outhouses, it would have shown immense wood piles during the heating season. Records kept by Orrin Ormsby Pitcher for the year ending December 1, 1880, show the school purchased 309 cords of wood. The largest single purchase was 161 cords, which was evidently delivered in a series of shipments. The usual cost of wood was approximately $2.25 per cord.[16]

Fortunately for the school, great quantities of wood were available from the timbered bottoms of the Minnesota and Blue Earth rivers. Additionally, sizeable tracts of the Big Woods, a deciduous forest, remained in that portion of Blue Earth County north of the Le Sueur River. During the coldest weather it would have been necessary to have at least several cords on hand. To appreciate the bulk of this amount of wood, one has only to recognize that a single cord of 128 cubic feet measured 8 feet long, 4 feet high and 4 feet deep.

In requesting ventilation, drainage and outhouses improvements for Mankato Normal, Searing's tactic was to provoke board support by making the Mankato Normal seem like a poor cousin compared to Winona and St. Cloud. Winona was the first of the schools to have interior plumbing and toilets, because the city of Winona had installed a sanitary sewer system. St. Cloud still had outside toilets, but after inspecting them, Searing concluded they were much more commodious and sanitary than Mankato's.

In both his 1881 and 1882 annual reports to the State Normal School Board, Searing complained vigorously about the ventilation, drainage and toilet problems. Subsequently, the board requested special repair funds from the legislature, which appropriated $7,500 on March 1, 1883.[17]

Following the appropriation, John H. Ray, a Mankato banker who was then serving as the Mankato Normal's resident director, developed an improvement plan for the normal building. The State Normal School Board approved it on June 5, 1883.[18]

In his next annual report to the board, Searing was happy to report that the necessary repairs and more were made during the summer of 1883. The circulation/heating problem was solved by installing "a thorough system of exhaust ventilation and the purchase of new and larger furnaces." These improvements, he noted, "resulted in better health and more satisfactory intellectual work with all" faculty and students.[19]

Satisfactory drainage was accomplished by installing a sewer 12 feet deep parallel to the rear of the building and then extending it some 20 rods to a shallow ravine located along present-day Glenwood Avenue. Primarily intended to drain excess runoff and ground water, the sewer also served as an outlet for the cistern, outside well and the urinals in the two outhouses.

Anticipating that the city of Mankato was within a few years of installing a sanitary sewer system, which would enable the school to install inside toilets, the outside toilets were not radically re-designed. The expedients of enlarging them and connecting their urinals to the sewer was deemed to be sufficient until sewer service would permit the installation of toilets in the basement.

Because the toilet changes cost much less than anticipated, the balance of the appropriation was used to erect a small house for the janitor and his family on the street bordering the rear grounds. This change freed up two large basement rooms, which were remodeled for Model School use.

## Advent of Telephone Service

In November 1883, soon after the circulation, drainage and toilet problems were remedied, Mankato Normal got its first telephone. Like many things in history, this first telephone was not accompanied by a bold pronouncement, but rather was revealed because telephone rent of $4.00 a month started appearing in the school's financial statements.[20]

The arrival of the telephone was yet another reminder of the rapid technological changes sweeping the nation. The founding and growth of Mankato Normal School coincided with the era that historians retrospectively labeled the Industrial Revolution. Variously called the "Age of Steel" and the "Railroad Age," this new period featured labor-saving machinery, mass-scale manufacturing, concentration of capital in cities, rapid transportation and communication, and urbanization.

During the Industrial Revolution, new technology spread amazingly fast, as evidenced by the popularization of the telephone. Only seven years elapsed between the time inventor Alexander Graham Bell demonstrated the first practical telephone at the Philadelphia Centennial Exposition in 1876 and the beginning of phone service in Mankato. In July 1883, the Erie Telegraph and Telephone Company began its Mankato operations with 63 subscribers. The Mankato experience typified what was happening in hundreds of other communities nationwide. Within a year Mankato's pioneer phone company was renamed to the Erie Telephone Company, which, in turn, within several years, was replaced by the Northwestern Telephone Exchange Company. Mankato Normal paid both companies $4.00 monthly.[21]

## Building Expansion

Searing realized that the growing Mankato Normal School always needed something that would cost money. He was grateful for the improvements made in 1883. But by the next year his priorities were an increased annual appropriation to fund the addition of at least three faculty members and "an additional building, or addition to the present one."[22]

In asking the governing board for more dollars and space, Searing admonished that "additional room is quite as much needed as additional income." He pointed out that the school was using all available space and did not have room for a natural history museum, laboratory, library, kindergarten and physical training. In an obvious reference to the Winona Normal, which Mankato's supporters consistently thought was the proverbial teacher's pet, Searing noted, "It is not necessary to go out of the State to find a Normal School well provided with all of these, or to see that these are proper adjuncts of such a school."

Searing reported that during a personal tour of "some Eastern institutions," he learned more about the importance of calisthenics to benefit student health and appearance. Furthermore, his tour gave him more insight into the importance of kindergarten education's place in normal model schools. He thought, "kindergarten is no less necessary in the Mankato school that at Winona, Oshkosh, Oswego and many other like schools east of us."

Expanding the building enough to accommodate a growing student body proved to be a rather long struggle. Since no appropriation had been secured by 1887, Searing got some relief by the abolition of the preparatory class. This year of remedial work, like the E class that preceded it, had never been popular with normal school presidents. The preparatory class rarely proved to be stepping stone to the regular three-year normal curriculum. Most of its underachieving students dropped out or failed to qualify for admission to the normal school. Searing's negative attitude toward the preparatory class was particularly evident when in 1885 he assigned two normal students to be its instructors. Since they were instructed by the most inexperienced people, it is hardly surprising that preparatory students collectively did not perform well. Finally, in June 1887, Searing with board permission abolished the preparatory class of 90 students in order to gain some much-needed space.[23]

This proved to be an ineffective stopgap remedy to the crowded normal building, because of increasing enrollment. Demand for attending Mankato Normal was so high that Searing found it was no longer necessary to use such recruiting techniques as distributing circulars at teacher's institutes. By 1888 he concluded that "every special method of inviting students was clearly unnecessary and unwise when more came unsolicited than could well be accommodated and instructed."

Unfortunately for the Mankato Normal School, Searing's 1888 $50,000 request for expansion funding coincided and conflicted with other normal board and legislative priorities, including the creation of the state's fourth normal school. In 1885 the Minnesota legislature authorized a normal school at Moorhead. This addition resulted from the rapid expansion of the agricultural frontier into the Red River valley and adjacent areas. Moorhead was a logical normal school site, because it was the region's largest community and an important railroad hub. The 1887 legislature appropriated $60,000 to construct a Moorhead Normal Building, which was completed in time for the opening of classes on August 29, 1888.[24]

Finally, the 1889 legislature appropriated $7,000 for building expansion and improvement at the Mankato Normal. Though far short of Searing's desired amount, the funding resulted in the first addition to the original Mankato Normal building. In 1889-90 the building was extended at only the basement and first floor levels to the rear of the right or south wing. This addition, which created two large classrooms and two cloakrooms for the model school, made the south wing's first floor approximately twice as large as its north counterpart. This expansion enabled Mankato Normal to enroll an unprecedented 239 model school students.[25]

Because building materials and labor were both relatively inexpensive,

Mankato Normal School Library, circa 1900

Mankato Normal was able to make other improvements with the balance of the legislative appropriation. Invaluable insight into these costs can be derived from the financial report of George H. Clark, resident director and treasurer of the Mankato Normal. In September, 1889, when the exterior walls to the addition were under construction, Clark paid $60.00 for 12,000 bricks. Anytime bricks could be obtained at a rate of two for a penny, money tended to go a long way. As for labor, Clark paid H. A. Hill a total of $53.25 for 35.5 working days. Clark's report and all other treasurer's reports always showed labor cost by the day rather than the hour. Presumably, all skilled laborers such as carpenters and masons and all unskilled laborers were then working 10-hour days.[26]

Other than the building addition during the 1889-90 school year, the Mankato Normal made other changes in its physical facilities. The space vacated by the model school classes, which were moved to the addition, was converted into the library. New hardwood floors were installed throughout most of the building and two ventilating fans powered by a steam engine were installed in the basement. Lastly, Searing was able to finally rid himself of the outside toilets problem when the City of Mankato extended its water and sanitary sewer systems to include the normal school. In the 1889-90 school catalog, Searing announced that the normal school would have water and sewer services by the opening of the fall 1890 term.[27]

The addition and other 1889-90 improvements prompted Searing to conclude that the year was "the most agreeable to both teachers and students during my connection with the school. The spacious, pleasant and well ventilated library has been especially appreciated."[28]

Although Searing appreciated the improvements, he was quick to remind that board that they did not solve Mankato Normal's urgent needs for more space and staff. He illustrated those shortcomings by citing the extraordinarily large C class. He contended that this class, which had average daily attendance of 100 students in one section, should be taught in three sections and the B class in two.

Searing's long-standing desire for a greatly enlarged building was fulfilled when the 1893 legislature on April 20 approved an appropriation of $50,000 "for enlarging, improving and furnishing the building and for building sidewalks and gutters about the grounds." [29]

Within a month of this action, Mankato architect Henry Gerlach completed a detailed expansion plan. Gerlach specified the addition of two wings at all levels of the original normal building. Each was to be 80 feet wide, which would increase the width of the building facing South Fifth Street to 272 feet. Both wings were to be 76 feet deep, which was 18 feet less than those of the original building.[30]

The project, which roughly doubled the building's size, was completed shortly before the start of the fall, 1894 term. Searing scheduled the building's dedication for Wednesday evening, August 15, to coincide with the annual meeting of the normal school's Alumni Association. Searing also invited past school principals Gage and John as well as Congressman McCleary. Gage appeared and in a

Normal School building after expansion, circa 1900

short talk reminisced about the school's start on October 7, 1868. Both John and McCleary sent regrets. Given the lack of outside dignitaries, the evening's principal address was presented by Mankato's James H. Baker, who was always identified by his Civil War rank of brigadier general as "General Baker." Baker, who ranked as one of Mankato's most prominent men, had served as United States Commissioner of Pensions for four years in the administration of President Ulysses S. Grant. Later he was elected as a Minnesota railroad commissioner. His private Mankato business included the formation of the *Mankato Daily Free Press*. Baker was followed by General Edmund M. Pope, another Civil War veteran, who was an important Mankato Normal booster during his service in the Minnesota Senate. The audience, consisting mostly of Mankato Normal alums and students, concluded by singing "America."[31]

During the time of the 1889-90 and 1893-94 building expansions the Mankato Normal was changed by the addition of electricity and manufactured gas—two very important manifestations of the Industrial Revolution.

A financial statement prepared by George H. Clark, the Mankato Normal treasurer, shows the Mankato Gas and Electric Company started providing service to the school in April 1889. Mankato's first generation of electricity occurred in February 1887, when an F. L. Waters opened an electric light plant. By this time the city's first gas works had been operating for nearly four years. Apparently, the gas service to the college was limited to laboratory use. Wood was the heating fuel until it was replaced by coal when a new free-standing heating plant was built in 1912. Mankato's first gas was manufactured by a coal-gasification process, which entailed extracting gas from burning coal. Contemporaries always referred to it as just "gas," which has led to the unfortunate common assumption that it was natural gas. But it was man-made or artificial gas. Until the advent of natural gas transported by pipelines, there were hundreds of coal-gasification plants nationwide. [32]

Due to such revolutionary technological advances as the telephone, electricity and artificial gas, the Mankato Normal school in the Searing administration was modernized as it was enlarged.

## Student Activities

During the Searing administration student cultural and athletic activities became more frequent and diverse. Most of what is known about them was first reported in monthly magazines produced by a student staff and supported by student subscriptions.

The first student publication, which bore the matter-of-fact title *The Student* was started in 1888. It was soon succeeded by *The Mankatonian*, whose first number was published in September 1891.[33]

Like its predecessor, *The Mankatonian* regularly featured a variety of items. Every issue had a least one boiler-plate syndicated article on some general interest item such as Egyptian pyramids, creative essays by normal students and snippets about campus happenings. Respectful, if not deferential in tone, the student reporters included coverage of the activities of Searing and the faculty. Until he resigned in 1892 to run for Congress, James Thompson McCleary was extolled with some regularity by both *The Student* and *The Mankatonian*. He was not only known as the school's most prominent author, but he was a strong supporter of student participation in extra-curricular activities.

The monthlies consistently provided much coverage of the various student

*The Student,* October 1890. This magazine was published from 1888-1891

*The Mankatonian*, October 1895. This magazine was published from 1891-1913.

clubs. The Literary Society was the school's most general purpose organization. Ostensibly, it was dedicated only to improving literary work and knowledge of parliamentary rules. But, in actual practice, it arranged musical performances, speech contests and even raised funds to start the first football team. A good sense of student interests can be derived by the oration topics in an April 22, 1892, contest featuring three normal school students and three Mankato High School students. Their titles were "Woman's Opportunities," "Battle of Waterloo," "Eulogy of Abraham Lincoln," "The Curse of Our Nation—Gambling," "The Old and New South," and "The Cry of the Laborer." Miss Fletcher, the high school student who spoke on Napoleon's downfall in the Battle of Waterloo, was criticized for addressing a topic that "did not offer the chance for originality." Nonetheless, the three judges decided the high schoolers won the contest.

Although the event was billed as an oratory contest, it included vocal and instrumental musical performances. Apparently, it did not conflict with any other activities. The normal assembly hall "prettily decorated with flags and flowers, was crowded in seat and isle [sic] with eager listeners . . ."[34]

The most active clubs included the Young Men's Christian Association (YMCA) and the Young Women's Christian Association (YWCA). Dedicated to the three-fold purpose of developing the body, mind and spirit, the organizations complemented the school's interest in promoting the Christian way of life.[35]

Throughout the Searing administration, the chapel service practice initiated by Gage was established school policy. Every annual catalog contained the following notice.

The school's purpose was not to promote the cause of organized religion *per se*. Rather, chapel services were held in the belief that religion was the most important factor in shaping moral living, a must for teachers who were seen as the role models for students. Insistence on moral living caused normal school administrators and teachers to regularly denounce the twin evils of liquor and tobacco.

Participation in sports was a natural adjunct for all those, including Searing, who held that the body was the temple of the mind. The idea that sound bodies contributed to the development of good minds was at least as old as Plato. In the context of this long philosophical background and a rapidly increasing public interest in spectator sports during the Industrial Revolution, it was only natural for interest in sports to pervade the nation's schools at all levels.

Football and baseball were Mankato Normal's first competitive sports. The November 1889 issue of *The Student* announced that a football team was now

"RELIGIOUS INFLUENCES. Students are expected to be present at the opening devotional exercises each morning, and to attend, on the Sabbath, the church of their choice. The various churches of the city are especially cordial in welcoming them to their services and Sunday schools. Besides this, flourishing branch organizations of the Young Men's and Young Women's Christian Associations exist in the school. These hold weekly afternoon meetings [and] have been well attended, and productive of much religious interest and profit. While no sectarian influence is found or allowed, the spirit and drift of the school are distinctively towards the Christian ideals of faith and conduct."[36]

1898-1899 Catalogue

fully organized and would play a game against the Mankato High School. Henry P. Cushing, the normal school's physical science teacher, was chosen to "instruct" the team. Unfettered by such inconvenient things as league rules, Mankato Normal did some unusual things. Cushing played as well as instructed. He was not only the team's strongest man, but played "with a spirit and energy that some would do well to emulate."[37] Cushing was not necessarily a behemoth. As a sign of the times, players who weighed 180 pounds were described as "giants."

The Mankato High School, dubbed "The Highs," was the commonest opponent of "The Normals" or "The Normalites." Their close proximity no doubt intensified their rivalry. In the fall of 1891 the high school was relocated from the Union School to its new building next to the Blue Earth County Courthouse. Located in the block bounded by South Fourth, South Fifth, Hickory and Jackson streets, the school was diagonally across South Fifth from the normal building.

The completion of the high school building was a landmark achievement in Mankato's educational history. Its dedication on the evening of September 18, 1891, featured such prominent educators as Cyrus Northrup, president of the University of Minnesota, Fred M. KIehle, state superintendent of public instruction and former president of the St. Cloud Normal School and Searing.[38]

In February, 1892, *The Mankatonian* reported a retrospective tally of the High-Normal competition. The Highs had won two baseball games and the Normals had prevailed in one baseball game and three football games. The contests, which attracted large followings from both schools, were unusual by today's standards. Rather than being a high-scoring game, football, in its pre-forward pass era, ordinarily featured defensive struggles with scores such as 6-0 or 10-6. On the other hand, such baseball scores as 34-19 suggest shoddy fielding and a dearth of good pitching.

The football and baseball competition helped create a school identity, which, in turn, intensified calls for distinctive school uniforms and colors. Originally, the football team donned white uniforms but *The Mankatonian* of November 1892 reported, "The Normal School has adopted school colors and a school call. The colors are gold and purple, and the call, — well here is: 'Mankato! For the Normal! Ho! Raco, Maco, Raco, Maco, Ho, Hi, Ho!'"[39]

Donned in colors symbolizing splendor and royalty, the "Normals" were ready to vanquish Mankato High and other foes. Before the end of the 1890s the normal

Normal School (left) and High School (right) buildings, circa 1912. Image courtesy of the Blue Earth County Historical Society

Mankato State Normal School football team, 1898

football team played games against Mankato and St. Peter community teams and widened its horizons by competing against Pillsbury Academy in Owatonna and Winona Normal. Convenient railroad access greatly facilitated scheduling road games. Mankato Normal's ultimate football road game was on Thanksgiving Day, 1898 against Winona Normal. *The Mankatonian* gleefully reported that Mankato won 11-6.[40]

Such team sports as football and baseball, which drew spectators naturally, attracted the most attention. However, tennis was a popular campus sport and many normal students exercised by cycling during Mankato's and the country's bicycle craze of the 1890s. In Blue Earth County the craze peaked in 1894 when most of its residents were reportedly "on wheels." Cycling helped popularize student jaunts to scenic Minneopa Falls, about five miles southwest of the normal school in present-day Minneopa Park. Cycling also improved rural transportation. For example, Fred O. True, a member of the normal school's first football team, peddled to his home 10 miles west of Winnebago on weekends. His estimated round-trip distance was more than 100 miles.[41]

## Faculty Expansion in the Searing Administration

Edward Searing led the Mankato Normal School for 19 full years and part of another. In his first year, counting himself, the Mankato Normal faculty had

Mankato State Normal School faculty and class of 1889

nine members. For 1897-1898, Searing's last complete academic year, there were 30 faculty members. The faculty listings (on next page) were as shown in the annual catalogs. The normal department faculty was listed before the model/practice department. Within each group members were listed according to a combination of their levels of responsibility and years of school service.

The approximate tripling of the faculty during the Searing administration was caused by sharply increased enrollment in both the normal and model departments. The model department was usually called the practice department by the end of the Searing administration. In 1880-81 the school's total enrollment was 235 with 120 in the normal department, 57 in the preparatory department (i. e. remedial) and 58 in the practice school. The preparatory department, which had a peak enrollment of 130 in 1885-86, was discontinued after the next school year.[42]

The abolition of the preparatory department caused a short-lived decline in overall enrollment. In 1891-92 the combined normal/practice school enrollment exceeded 600 for the first time. For 1897-98 the enrollment boomed to 677 in the normal department and 503 in the practice school. This then-record enrollment was stimulated by the advent of an experimental four-quarter year in which the summer session was on a par with the fall, winter and spring terms. The four-quarter year was discontinued after one more year, because the legislature chose to discontinue funding it.[43]

Other than becoming much larger, faculty evolution during the Searing administration featured more faculty members with earned college degrees, relatively rapid turnover and static salaries.

In 1880-81 Searing and A. F. Bechdolt, both of whom had master's degrees, were the only college graduates on the faculty. The pattern of employing more degree holders is well-illustrated by the 1895 additions of Stuart H. Rowe, Agnes H. Ford and Josephine Holt.

Rowe, a native of New Haven, Connecticut, holds the unique Mankato Normal distinction as the first faculty member with a doctor's degree. After graduating from Yale University, he studied in Germany where he earned a Ph.D. at the University of Jena. Searing described Rowe, who was employed to direct the practice school, as possessing "good judgment, high scholarship and excellent acquaintance with the best modern thought and methods in the pedagogical world" with "a due admixture of suavity and vigor."[44]

Ford, a classical languages graduate from the University of Syracuse (New York), had taught Greek and Latin in the Pueblo (Colorado) High School before joining the Mankato Normal. Searing thought she had the promise of "equaling her sisters as an accomplished instructor." Her two sisters, also Syracuse graduates, taught at Moorhead (Minnesota) Normal School and the Iowa Agricultural College in Ames.

Josephine Holt, a University of Wisconsin graduate, was employed to teach music and reading. Searing regarded her appointment as a "fortunate one."

In addition to exemplifying the trend toward a better-educated faculty, Rowe, Ford and Holt also demonstrated the relatively short tenures of most Mankato Normal faculty. Rowe left after three years to accept a much more lucrative position in his hometown. Rowe and Ford had married each other in June 1897, so she went with him. Holt's last year was 1901-1902.[45]

Several factors contributed to the high faculty turnover. Generally, new faculty members were young people who left the Mankato Normal to pursue college education. Young female instructors often quit teaching because they got married. Searing complained that the school lost some of its ablest faculty because Minnesota's normal school salaries, especially as compared to eastern institutions, were not competitive. The frequency of faculty members who lasted for only a year suggests that some of them were not retained. All faculty—including Searing—were on one-year appointments, which were formally approved by the state normal board. But with the exception of the presidents, the board acted on a list submitted and endorsed by each normal president. So, if Searing wanted to end someone's service, he had only to not list them on his recommendations to the board. There is no record of Searing ever deciding to discontinue someone's service. But during his relatively long presidency, he must have made some non-retention decisions.

Faculty salaries tended to be relatively static during the Searing administration. There were no such things as annual increases for experience. But, some adjustments were made for very

## MANKATO NORMAL SCHOOL FACULTY, 1880-1881

(Years of service shown parenthetically)

**Edward Searing,** A. M., Principal, Mental Science, School Economy and Latin. $2,000. (1880-1898)

**Helen M. Phillips,** Mathematics and English Literature. $1,200. (1873-1904)

**Defransa A. Swann,** Drawing, Theory and Practice of Teaching. $1,000. (1873-1913)

**A. M. Bechdolt,** A. M., Natural Science. $1,000. (1880-1885)

**Anna McCutcheon,** Geography, Grammar and U. S. History. $800. (1879-1883)

**Grace Pitcher,** Vocal Music and Teacher Preparatory Class. (1880-1882)

**Andrew Carson,** Penmanship and Book-Keeping. $1,000. (1880-1881)

**Agnes Green,** Critic Teacher, Model School, Intermediate Department (Grades 4-6). $500. (1880-1881)

**Emma Ingram,** Critic Teacher, Model School, Primary Department (Grades 1-3). $500. (1880-1881)[47]

## MANKATO NORMAL SCHOOL FACULTY, 1897-1898

(Years of service shown parenthetically)

**Edward Searing,** President, History of Education and School Economy. $2,500. (1880-1898)

**Charles F. Koehler,** Psychology, Civics and Social Science. $1,600. (1892-1902)

**Stuart H. Rowe,** Pedagogy and Director of Practice School. $1,800. (1895-1898)

**Ulysses O. Cox,** Biology, and Secretary of the Faculty. $1,600. (1891-1905)

**Fred L. Holtz,** Physical Science. $1,000. (1894-1907)

**Peter A. Yoder.** Physical Science. (1897-1898)

**Helen M. Phillips,** Higher Mathematics. $1,300. (1873-1904)

**Defransa A. Swann,** Geography and Methods in Geography. $1,100. (1873-1913)

**Achsa Parker,** History, Rhetoric and Literature. $1,000. (1889-1903)

**Agnes F. Rowe,** (nee Ford). Latin Language. $800. (1895-1898)

**Orithia Josephine Holt,** Music and Reading. $900. (1895-1902)

**Gertrude Darling,** English Grammar and Methods in Language. $900. (1893-1899)

**Jessie Spencer,** Drawing. $900. (1896-1904)

**Alice V. Robbins,** Arithmetic and Methods in Arithmetic. $900. (1894-1937)

**Sophie M. Pendergast,** Assistant in English and History. $900. (1897-1900)

**Charles J. Dyke,** History and Mathematics. (1897-1898)

**Carl J. Ulrich.** Assistant in Biology. $600. (1897-1900)

**Harry J. Orsborn,** Assistant in Geography and Mathematics. $450. (1897-1899)

**Francis L Milnor,** Assistant in English Grammar. (1897-1898)

**Estella Spencer,** Assistant in Drawing. (1897-1898)

**Carolyn M. Robbins,** Principal Grammar Department*, Practice School. $1,200. (1888-1919)

**Estelle M. Darrah,** Methods and Prin., Intermediate Dept.*, Practice School. (1897-1898)

**Minnie S. Parry.,** Assistant Principal Intermediate Dept., Practice School. (1890-1893, 1897-1932)

**Mariette Louise Johnson,** (nee Pierce). Principal Primary Dept.,* Practice School. $1,000. (1896-1900)

**Margaret T. Barr,** Director of Kindergarten. $800. (1894-1898)

**Grace B. Clark,** Assistant Grammar Department, Practice School. (1897-1901)

**Daisy Sheehan,** Assistant Intermediate Department, Practice School. (1895-1899)

**Cora A. N. Carney,** Assistant in Music and Primary Department. $450. (1895-1902)

**Alice Williams,** Assistant in Kindergarten. $270. (1896-1935)

**Alice N. Farr,** Librarian. (1897-1924)[48]

*Primary Dept. was grades 1-3; Intermediate Dept. was grades 4-6 and Grammar Dept. was grades 7-8.

experienced faculty members such as Helen M. Phillips and Defransa A. Swann, the only teachers to serve throughout the Searing administration. For 1880-81 Phillips and Swann were each paid $1,000. Their 1897-98 salaries were respectively $1,300 and $1,100.

A prolonged nationwide deflationary run was the principal reason faculty salaries did not regularly change from year to year. During the 19 inclusive years, 1880-1898, deflation of three to four percent occurred in five years and there was no deflation or inflation in 14 years. In terms of the 2017 dollar, the 1880 and 1898 dollars respectively had values of $25.36 and $29.42. So even if salaries remained the same throughout the period wage earners experienced increased buying power.[46]

## Evolving Courses of Study

Throughout his administration Searing was a strong advocate of upgrading normal school academic standards, expanding the courses of study and changing the traditional normal school role of preparing common school teachers to include serving a post-high school clientele.

To improve student subject-matter education, Searing and his Winona and St. Cloud peers advocated lengthening the school year. Searing had inherited a system of a two-term academic year. For example, the 1880-1881 academic year had fall and spring terms, which respectively extended from August 25-December 23, 1880 and January 3-April 15, 1881.[49]

On May 10, 1882, the three normal school presidents—Searing, Irwin Shepherd (Winona) and Jerome Allen (St. Cloud) asked that the Normal School Board extend the academic year to at least 38 weeks. The board complied by establishing a three-term format for 1882-83 with a fall term (September 4-November 8 or 9, winter term (November 14-March 8 with a holiday vacation December21-January 3) and a spring term (March 13-May 20.) This calendar established the three-term year precedent, which subsequently became the usual pattern for the Mankato Normal School. [50]

The extended year accommodated revised courses of study. For the 1884-85 academic year, Mankato Normal offered both an Elementary Course and an Advanced Course. The subject matter classes in the three-year Elementary Course were essentially the same as those that had been adopted in 1877 with a first-year C Class, a second-year B Class and a third-year A Class.[51]

The Advanced Course was a five-year program. Its first two years had the same subjects as the C and B classes of the Elementary Course and its third year—the Junior Class — had the same curriculum as the elementary A class. The fourth year, designated the "Senior Class," emphasized Latin, Geology, English Literature, Astronomy and Practice Teaching. The fifth-year "Professional Course" concentrated on teaching methods and practice teaching.

The Preparatory Department for students who needed remedial work to qualify for admission was not considered part of either the Elementary Course or the Advanced Course.

The following enrollment statistics for 1885-86 illustrate the usual annual enrollment pattern with relatively small enrollments in the upper classes and large enrollments in B and C classes and Preparatory Department.

Seniors      13
Juniors      15
A Class      10
B Class      89
C Class    205
Preparatory Dept. 130[52]

The most striking aspect of these enrollment statistics is the sharp decline after the C and B classes. This attrition does not necessarily mean that large numbers of students had failed academically. Most of those in the C Class never intended to advance or graduate. They were usually experienced teachers who were trying to upgrade their credentials in order to qualify for a better teaching certificate. In other instances, they did not have enough money to pursue anything more than short-term enrollments. The same factors apply to the B Class.[53]

Biographical information on Mankato Normal graduates suggest that even most of those who

## NORMAL GRADE,—ELEMENTARY COURSE.

### C CLASS.

| FALL TERM. | WINTER TERM. | SPRING TERM. |
|---|---|---|
| Arithmetic. | Arithmetic. | Physical Geography. |
| Geography. | Geography. | Grammatical Analysis. |
| Grammar and Composition. | Grammar and Composition. | U. S. History. |
| Voice Culture. | Voice Culture. | Voice Culture. |
| | Penmanship. | |

### B CLASS.

| FALL TERM. | WINTER TERM. | SPRING TERM. |
|---|---|---|
| Algebra. | Algebra. | Civil Government. |
| Physiology and Hygiene. | Rhetoric and Composition. | General History. |
| Botany. | Book-Keeping. | Methods of Teaching. |
| Methods of Teaching. | Methods of Teaching. | |

Drawing during second year.

### A CLASS.

| FALL TERM. | WINTER TERM. | SPRING TERM. |
|---|---|---|
| Geometry. | English Literature. | Geometry. |
| Zoology. | Physics. | Psychology. |
| Physics. | Chemistry. | School Economy. |
| Practice Teaching. | Practice Teaching. | Practice Teaching. |

Rhetorical exercises throughout the course. Vocal Music during First and Second years.

24

MANKATO NORMAL SCHOOL.

Elementary Course – Course of Study – 1884-1885 Catalogue

## ADVANCED COURSE.

### B AND C CLASSES.

SAME SUBJECTS AS FIRST TWO YEARS OF ELEMENTARY COURSE.

### JUNIOR CLASS.

| FALL TERM. | WINTER TERM. | SPRING TERM. |
|---|---|---|
| Latin. | Latin. | Latin. |
| Geometry. | Physics. | Geometry. |
| Physics. | Chemistry. | Psychology. |
| Zoology. | | Practice Teaching. |

Drawing during second year.

### SENIOR CLASS.

| FALL TERM. | WINTER TERM. | SPRING TERM. |
|---|---|---|
| Latin. | Latin. | Latin. |
| Geology. | English Literature. | Astronomy. |
| Practice Teaching. | Practice Teaching. | School Economy. |
| | | Practice Teaching. |

### PROFESSIONAL COURSE.

| FALL TERM. | WINTER TERM. | SPRING TERM. |
|---|---|---|
| Methods of Teaching. | Methods of Teaching. | Methods of Teaching. |
| Reviews. | History of Education. | Psychology. |
| Practice Teaching. | Reviews. | School Economy. |
| | Practice Teaching. | Practice Teaching. |

Rhetorical exercises throughout the course. Vocal Music during First and Second years.

25

MANKATO NORMAL SCHOOL.

Advanced Course – Course of Study – 1884-1885 Catalogue

completed either the elementary or advanced course did not do so by attending for either three or five consecutive years. In 1887 Mankato Normal had 34 graduates—25 in the elementary course and nine in the advanced course. Twenty-seven of them had teaching experience before graduation.[54]

Minnesota's teacher certification law did not require normal school, college or university graduation in order to qualify for teaching. County superintendents of schools were empowered to issue First Grade, Second Grade and Third Grade certificates. The First Grade Certificate was a county certificate limited to two years. The Second Grade Certificate was a county certificate limited to one year, and the Third Grade Certificate was a six-month district certificate. County superintendents could renew all certificates indefinitely. But, the certificate system gave superintendents a mighty cudgel if they chose to compel erstwhile teachers to get more education. The certification system obviously caused many teachers to improve their credentials by either short-term enrollments or participating in teachers' institutes.[55]

Searing regularly complained that the state's certification policy did not recognize normal school diplomas. Finally, in 1891 the legislature, at the insistence of the Normal School Board, authorized certification for normal school graduates. The law validated normal diplomas by providing they would serve as First Grade Certificates for two years. After that, if the supervisors of any teacher certified satisfactory performance, the Elementary Course diploma was recognized as a state certificate for five years and the Advanced Course diploma qualified one for a lifetime certificate. The act significantly enhanced the status of Minnesota's then four normal schools.[56]

On April 26, 1895, the Normal School Board approved two new courses of study for high school graduates. Both the one-year Elementary Course and the two-year Advanced Course consisted of schooling in the teaching methodology of various subjects, educational psychology and practice teaching. The Advanced Course included more training in psychology, history of education, science of education and ethics.[57]

These programs for high school graduates were an important landmark in the evolution of normal school education. For the first time the Minnesota normal schools assumed the posture that they were a higher level than high schools. This development was in response to the rapid growth of Minnesota high schools, which caused the normal schools to re-assess their place in state public education.

When the Mankato Normal School was started in 1868, Minnesota had only a few high schools. Most of these schools, as in the instance of Mankato, were departments in union schools. The feeble impact of high schools was evident. In 1877 Minnesota high schools had a total of only 117 graduates.[58]

The lack of high schools alarmed William Watts Folwell, the first president of the University of Minnesota. Folwell, who assumed his duties in 1869, believed a statewide system of good high schools was vital to the university's development. Such high schools, Folwell insisted, would insure that the university could draw its students from qualified high school graduates and enable it to discontinue preparatory classes.[59]

Folwell's long campaign to stimulate high school development was rewarded in 1878 when the legislature approved the state's first comprehensive high school law. The act provided state financial aid for high schools and the creation of a state High School Board, consisting of the superintendent of public instruction, the university president and a third member to be appointed by the governor. The law provided that any high school that met High School Board academic standards would receive an annual payment of $400.

The law had an immediate, significant impact on high school development. For the 1882-83 school year the state granted $400 each to 38 high schools. In 1890 there were 64 high schools with a total enrollment of 3,665. The 1898 totals were 100 high schools with 11,503 students.[60]

As Folwell intended, the 1878 law created a system that enabled the University of Minnesota to attract high school graduates. But the law also had the unintended effect of altering the nature of the normal schools. Many high school graduates from southern Minnesota chose to attend an institution closer to home rather than to relocate to the state university in Minneapolis. In 1899, for example, 38 of the 53 Mankato Normal graduates had earned high school diplomas.[61] Although Mankato and

# ALMA D. WAGEN:
# FROM NORMAL SCHOOL TO MOUNTAIN TOPS (LITERALLY).

Alma D. Wagen (November 5, 1878-December 7, 1967), a Mankato native and Mankato Normal School graduate, gained fame as a mountain climbing guide in the Pacific Northwest. Her zeal for climbing was evident in her youth when she regularly climbed windmills in the neighborhood of her grandparents' farm.

After graduating from Mankato High School in 1897, Wagen enrolled at the Mankato Normal School and graduated two years later. She then taught in Duluth and North Mankato before studying at the University of Minnesota. She was awarded a Bachelor of Arts degree from the University's College of Science, Literature and the Arts on June 13, 1907.

Once she completed her university degree, Wagen moved to Tacoma, Washington, where she was employed as a mathematics teacher in Stadium High School. She began mountain climbing after she joined the Mountaineers, a club devoted to mountaineering and arduous backcountry treks. Her first notable venture was to hike across the Olympic Mountains from Port Angeles to the Pacific Ocean and to ascend and explore many of its peaks.

In the summer of 1915, Wagen was a member of a party that climbed to the top of Mount Rainier. At 14,417 feet, Rainier is the highest peak in the Cascade Range and the second highest in the contiguous United States. Wagen and her colleagues also circumnavigated the mountain at a snow and ice-covered elevation far above the tree line. This experience led to a yet more strenuous trek the following year when Wagen and colleagues did a 240-mile journey that included ascents of mounts Saint Helens, Adams and Hood in the Cascades. Wagen had a near-death experience when she was badly injured by a falling rock. Unable to walk, she was taken down the mountain by being lashed to the body of one of her companions, who acted as a human toboggan.

Wagen is especially remembered for becoming the National Park Service's first female mountain climbing guide. Her opportunity was created by the

Alma Wagen, Guide in Rainier National Park, 1919. Image courtesy of the University of Washington Libraries, Special Collections, UW14003.

manpower needs of World War I when many male guides were serving in American military forces. Faced with a shortage of guides, the Mount Rainier National Park superintendent hired Wagen to lead tours, including some to Mount Rainier's summit.

By 1920, when she led the John D. Rockefeller, Jr. party up Mount Rainier, Wagen was widely recognized by her experienced peers as an outstanding guide. Except for some work at Yosemite National Park in the spring of 1922, she worked at Mount Rainier for the remainder of her mountain climbing days.

The most-publicized photograph of Wagen as a guide shows her bedecked in a Tyrolean hat adorned with a single, long pheasant tail feather. Apparently, this was the look she preferred and the one that seemed to impress tourists.

Evidently, Wagen retired from both mountain climbing and teaching in about 1927 when she married Dr. Horace J. Whitacre and became Alma D. Whitacre. Until his death in 1950, she was very active in medical auxiliaries. She was a charter member and one-time president of the Washington State Medical Auxiliary who also served the National Medical Auxiliary as a vice president.

After her husband's death, she moved to Claremont, California, where she lived for the rest of her life. She was survived by two stepsons—Dr. G. Marshall Whitacre and Horace J. Whitacre.

(Alma D. Wagen records, Minnesota State University, Mankato Archives; *The Mankatonian*, April, 1899, 9; September, 1899, 10; Alma D. Wagen records, University of Minnesota Archives; University of Minnesota, *General Alumni Catalogue* (1916), 105; *Tacoma News Tribune*, 09 December 1967, .2; Jason D. Martin, "Pretty Girls & Windmills," accessible online at: http://www.alpenglow.org/nwmj/04/041_Guides.html; "High School Math Teacher Alma Wagen Whitacre: Pioneering Mountain Climber and National Parks Guide," http://chalkboard-champions.blogspot.com/2014/05/high-school-math-teacher-alma-wagen; "Two Woman Who Changed the Face of Mountain Climbing in the Northwest," http://mtn.tpl.lib.wa.us/climbs/climbing/people/wagen.asp.

the three other normal schools did not qualify as legal post-secondary education, they had actually evolved to a level above high schools.

As the courses of study became more advanced, Searing worked to improve the library and the museum, the school's main learning resources. In his 1896 report, Searing complained that the library of no "more than 1,500 volumes of miscellaneous books" was the school's "weakest feature." Considering the age and size of the school, he thought the library should have 10,000 volumes.[62]

The museum, located in the old third floor assembly room, was intended to support science teaching. Searing reported that it contained "a respectable collection of mounted quadrupeds and birds of the state and a good collection of minerals, in addition to the largest collection of fishes (preserved in alcohol) to be found in this section of the Union." But these objects were not suitably arranged and displayed, because the museum lacked display cases.

## Mankato Normal School Profile in 1898

For the 1897-98 academic year the Mankato Normal School had a total enrollment of 1,180 students with 677 in the normal department and 503 in the practice school. The Mankato Normal was the largest of Minnesota's four normal schools. Total enrollment at Winona, St. Cloud and Moorhead respectively was 830, 660 and 382.[63]

Females, as they had throughout Mankato Normal's history, dominated the normal department. There were 541 compared to 136 males.

Mankato's enrollment represented 43 Minnesota counties and nine other states. Blue Earth County, the leader for every year, produced 286 students. The adjacent counties of Le Sueur (36), Nicollet (22), Waseca (20) and Brown (16) had the next ranking enrollments. Ten students came from Hennepin County (Minneapolis) and five from Ramsey County (St. Paul). Searing contended that the Blue Earth County statistics belied the school's actual geographic drawing power, because many students, sometimes accompanied by their families, established Mankato residencies.

There were 37 out-of-state students, including 17 from Iowa and 13 from South Dakota. One or two were from Colorado, Indiana, Missouri, Nebraska, Tennessee and Wisconsin.

Searing was satisfied that the school was a major contributor to Minnesota's public education system. But, he admonished that it needed building expansions. Specifically, he recommended a second-story addition to the space that had been added to the rear of the building in 1889-90. This, he thought, would facilitate a much-needed library growth. Additionally, he believed that the practice school needed more space. Both of these suggestions were carried to fruition by Searing's successor—Charles H. Cooper.

## Searing's Death, Funeral, and Legacy

Edward Searing died suddenly on Saturday, October 22, 1898, in St. Paul, where he was attending a meeting of the normal school presidents and other public school officials. Searing, who reached the capital two days before, was reportedly vigorous throughout the meetings. The only premonition that he did not feel well was his decision on Friday evening to retire early to his Windsor Hotel room. The next morning at 6:30 a.m. he asked one of his colleagues to summon a doctor. Soon after the doctor arrived, Searing became dizzy and laid down. Within minutes he lapsed into unconsciousness and died.[64]

Searing's passing shocked the normal school staff and students and the Mankato community. His funeral of Tuesday, October 25 was a grand affair. At 2:00 that afternoon the normal faculty and students filed two-by-two down Normal Hill to the Presbyterian Church, where Searing's body lay in state. The six pall bearers were three former resident directors—Orrin Ormsby Pitcher, John H. Ray, George T. Barr, current resident director George H. Clark and two senior faculty members—Charles F. Koehler and Ulysses O. Cox.

The services in the crowded church featured speeches by Dean Pattee of Minneapolis, president of the State Normal Board, William F. Phelps, a former principal of the Winona Normal School, whose friendship with Searing dated to their New York days, and Reverend Lee W. Beattie, who spoke on behalf of the citizens of Mankato. They remembered Searing as a scholar, a compassionate teacher and efficient administrator who loved his school and worked harmoniously with its faculty and students.

As a special tribute to Searing, the staff of *The Mankatonian* devoted the entire November 1898, issue to his life and funeral. This "Memorial Number" included tributes by faculty and student committees. The faculty committee's statement was probably written by Charles F. Koehler, who was the first listed of its six members. The statement included the observation that Searing had never had any "serious friction" with the faculty. "This happy state of affairs must be attributed in large measure to the wise management and genial, hopeful disposition of our leader."

At its meeting of December 7, 1898, the Normal School Board appointed a three-man committee to prepare "a suitable memorial of the life and labors of the late Edward Searing." The committee's statement was included in the minutes of its December 22, 1898, meeting. Titled "IN MEMORIAM. EDWARD SEARING," it capsulized his life and contributions to the Mankato Normal School. Searing was extolled "as a scholar, he was accurate, learned and full; in his specialties as a teacher, concise, lucid and apt; and as an executive officer, able, energetic, firm and efficient." The committee's final judgment was that Searing's "influence over the Mankato normal school will be felt for many years to come."

To perpetuate Searing's legacy, faculty, students and alumni contributed enough funds to have a bronze Searing bust sculpted in New York City by Isabel Moore Kimball. An Iowa-born artist, Kimball was then in the early stages of her celebrated career. Working under the supervision of Herbert Adams, one of the country's most prestigious sculptors, Kimball completed the Searing bust in the summer of 1899.[65]

The bust was formally unveiled at ceremonies in the normal school's Assembly Hall on October 25, 1899, the first anniversary of Searing's funeral. Speaking to a crowd of faculty, students, alumni and other school supporters,

1897-1898 *Mankatonian* staff. Front, l to r: Harry D. Horton, Ruth Drake, Alice V. Robbins, Emma Firestone, Paul Callaghan. Middle: Myrtle E. Holmes, Royal C. Burnett, William S. Lindsley, Edyth Thompson. Back: Otto A. Drews, Nellie L. Tyler, Lottie Roberts, William J. Janssen

President Cooper credited Searing with creating high student and faculty morale and solidifying the school's reputation. The Searing bust was displayed in the school's main building except for an interregnum after fire destroyed the building on February 5, 1922. It was moved to Searing Hall, the men's dormitory that was completed in 1952. The bust disappeared, apparently because of theft, when the entire lower campus was sold and vacated in the fall of 1979.

## The Transition to Charles H. Cooper

On December 7, 1898, the State Normal Board held a special meeting in St. Paul to select new presidents for the Mankato and Winona normal schools. Its first order of business was to hear presentations from the Mankato and Winona delegations.

Mankato's group consisted of Lewis P. Hunt, founder of the *Mankato Free Press* and Mankato's postmaster, William Norton Plymat, a Mankato lawyer, Edmund M. Pope, a Mankato merchant and former state senator, and three Mankato Normal School students. In a 40-minute presentation, these spokespeople, recommended Charles F. Koehler as Searing's replacement.[66]

Koehler had been on the Mankato Normal faculty since 1892, when he was named to succeed James McCleary Thompson as institute director. Koehler, who was also assigned to teach civics and physiology, had most recently been the principal of the normal department of Baldwin University in Ohio. At the Mankato Normal, he consistently ranked next to Searing in terms of both salary and status. Evidently, he acted as the faculty's leader in the hiatus between Searing and Cooper.[67]

The Mankato group failed to persuade the board. After the names and credentials of all candidates had been submitted, the board, by a formal ballot, unanimously elected Charles H[ermance] Cooper, a 43 year old history instructor and librarian at Carleton College, Northfield, Minnesota. For his one-year term, which was to begin January 1, 1899, Cooper was to be paid $2,500.[68]

Cooper was born on June 16, 1855, in La Crosse, Wisconsin. Years later, he recalled being raised in a "simple-living, hard-working, God-fearing household."[69] After his father died when Cooper was 10 years old, his mother took in boarders and worked as a seamstress to provide for her only child. Before he started teaching in a country school when he was 17, Cooper had some elementary schooling and worked for two years as a surveyor.

Before his 18th birthday, Cooper started attending Dartmouth College (Hanover, New Hampshire). He supported himself through part-time teaching and working on a farm and in a hotel. After graduating with a Bachelor of Arts degree, he was named the sub-master of the Abbott School in Washington, D. C. A year later he became the principal of the Hitchcock Free High School in Bromfield, Massachusetts. In 1880, Cooper completed a Master of Arts degree at Dartmouth and then tutored Greek and history there until 1883, when he was appointed librarian and history teacher at Carleton. During his 18-year Carleton career, Cooper was recognized for developing the library and playing a leading role in developing the curriculum.[70]

In part, because of Koehler's support, Cooper got off to a rousing start at the Mankato Normal School. When Koehler announced Cooper's election to faculty and students at a chapel session, he stated "that all the teachers are united in their resolve to be loyal to the new president, and in the wish to assist him in every possible way."[71]

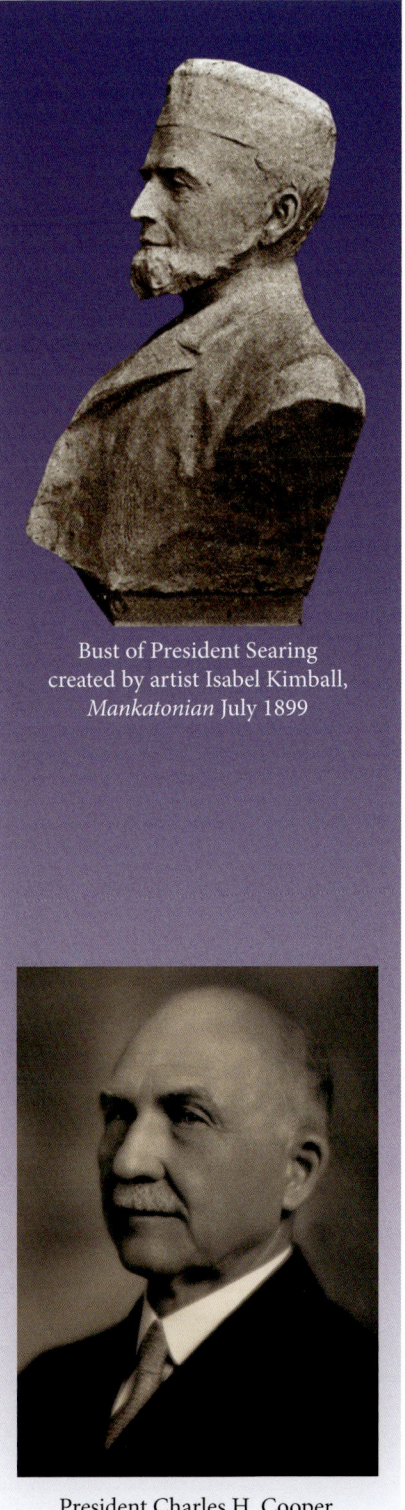

Bust of President Searing created by artist Isabel Kimball, *Mankatonian* July 1899

President Charles H. Cooper, circa 1924

When Cooper visited the school on December 16, 1898, Koehler arranged a special reception. All students from kindergarten through the most advanced normal enrollees and the faculty were assembled in the chapel. After the "usual devotional exercises," Koehler introduced Cooper, who was greeted with "deafening" applause. The tactful Cooper assured the audience of his deep interest in normal school education, his admiration of Searing and his determination to adhere to policies that were those of an evolutionist, not a revolutionist.

## Status and Prospects of the Mankato Normal School During the Early Cooper Years

Soon after Cooper began his presidential duties on January 1, 1899, he demonstrated a willingness and resolve to change the school. In his relations with faculty, students and the governing board, he championed progressive changes designed to improve academic standards and expand the campus. Those who dealt with him found that Cooper, while sincere and gracious, was remarkably persistent. Over time he earned a reputation as a principled advocate who strove to better the school and its reputation. True to his determination to be an evolutionist, Cooper's standard message was that he was merely building on the Searing legacy.

With respect to academics, Cooper inherited the traditional great disparity between the numbers of enrollees and graduates. In 1900, Alexander T. Ankeny, president of the Normal School Board, estimated that from their respective beginnings, Minnesota's four normal schools had graduated four to five thousand teachers and "given a partial instruction to twice as many more."[72] Cooper, in presenting a statistically precise report for the Mankato Normal School, showed that for the period 1868-1902 inclusive, there were only 1,402 graduates out of an aggregate enrollment of 8,460.[73]

With the aim of improving its success rate, the board abolished the C class in 1899. This class, which was the consistently largest in all schools, was notorious for attracting temporary students. One of Cooper's first actions was to identify and drop 70 students, whose unsatisfactory performance demonstrated that they lacked either the ability or zeal to complete a course of study. Cooper reported, "this weeding process was anything but pleasant, but the teachers supported me fully in it. It is the unanimous opinion of the teachers that the influence upon the school has been most helpful."[74]

The board's decision to eliminate the C class, the legislature's refusal to continue funding the four-term year beyond two years and Cooper's decision to drop students had the cumulative effect of temporarily decreasing enrollment. For the academic year 1898-99, the last for the four-year term and the C class, Mankato Normal had an enrollment of 1,329 consisting of 801 in the normal department and 528 in the model school. For 1901-02, the first after Cooper's student trimming, the total enrollment of 660 included 334 in the normal department and 326 in the model school.[75]

Pursuant to Searing's initiative, Cooper advocated campus expansion. Among other things he thought there was an "urgent need for facilities" that would contribute to the "systematic physical development" of students. He noted, "stooping, one-sided, undeveloped figures, flat chests, bad complexions, dull eyes, and awkward gaits are altogether too common." The addition of a gymnasium and a well-qualified instructor, he admonished, would do more good "for these young people, and through them for the children of Minnesota, than any other investment of money that I can think of."[76]

When the Cooper administration began, the Normal School Board was in the process of starting the state's fifth normal school. The 1895 legislature authorized the school at Duluth, but did not make a $75,000 construction appropriation for it until four years later. The school was expected to open in 1901, but in February of that year the nearly completed building was mostly destroyed by fire. This setback was the principal reason the school was not opened until September 2, 1902.[77]

Creating the Duluth Normal School was prompted by the development of an iron mining frontier in northeastern Minnesota. When the school opened, the Mesabi Range boom was about a decade old. Its development of large, open-pit mines not only spurred a sharp population increase but also contributed significantly to Duluth's development as an iron-exporting port. As the emerging metropolis of northeastern Minnesota, Duluth was the most logical site for the expansion of the normal school system.

## Normal School Campus Expansion During the Cooper Administration

During the normal school phase of Cooper's administration the main building was modified somewhat and a practice school/gymnasium building, a women's dormitory and a central heating plant were constructed.

The principal change to the main building was remodeling the annex that had been built in 1889-90 into the library. Cooper, a voracious reader, had a deep interest in improving the library, which, he saw, as a vital component of student education. He started agitating with the board for a better library in 1903, but the legislature did not make the necessary appropriation until three years later.[78]

Preparing the new library involved both construction and heating apparatus contracts. On June 18, 1906, the normal school board awarded the construction contract of $9,227 to Otto Neitge, who undercut two Mankato rivals. Neitge's remodeling of the annex to the rear of the school's south wing entailed removing interior walls, adding about six feet of brick work to the exterior walls and installing a new roof. This resulted in a library space about 50 feet wide and 60 feet long with a high vaulted ceiling. The heating apparatus contract was awarded to low bidder C. M. Masters of Mankato. He was awarded $1,588 for doing this work.[79]

Work on the library, which was started in the summer of 1906, proceeded quite rapidly. Cooper arranged its opening and formal dedication on April 13, 1907. Cooper, his wife, resident director John C. Wise, Jr. and librarian Alice N. Farr greeted nearly 200 townspeople at the Saturday evening reception. Several faculty members attended to the punch bowls. Entertainment was provided by an orchestra and to add some color the library was adorned with daffodils and palm branches.[80]

Cooper was very pleased with this accomplishment. He reported to the board that the "beautiful and spacious library . . . has not only given the students light and air and beauty, while at work with the books, but has also solved the long-standing problem of a supervised study room for the students."[81]

Library, 1915 *Mankatonian* (yearbook)

## Construction of the Practice School/Gymnasium Building

Cooper's desire for a practice school/gymnasium building was fulfilled when the 1907 legislature funded new practice schools at the Mankato, Winona and Moorhead campuses. The Mankato appropriation of $65,000 became available August 1, 1907.[82]

By the end of July 1908, Cooper reported that the four-story brick building, which was 188 feet long and 70 feet wide, was nearing completion. It included a full basement, first and second story rooms for the practice department and above it a gymnasium, which was 80-by-43 feet. Furnished with galleries and a basketball floor, the gymnasium was near locker rooms and what Cooper described as "baths." The gymnasium, Cooper concluded, fulfilled all "the needs for the simple work of a normal school in which the students are mainly women."[83] The building, constructed to the south of the main building, was connected to it by a second story enclosed walkway about 15 feet long.

The practice school/gymnasium building, which was completed by early January, 1909, was dedicated on Saturday evening, February 6, 1909. Proclaiming it to be a "red letter day," Cooper hosted a delegation of political dignitaries led by Lieutenant Governor Adolph Olson Eberhart of Mankato. The seven state legislators who attended included Senator Frank Clague of Lamberton, a lawyer and 1886 graduate of the Mankato Normal School.[84]

Eberhart and the legislators had a busy schedule. In the afternoon they took a guided tour of the new building and watched two basketball games by unspecified teams. After being treated to dinner at the downtown Elks Club, they returned to the building for the evening ceremonies. The attending crowd of 600 guests completely filled the gymnasium galleries and spilled over onto the floor.

The prolonged dedication exercises included folk dances by 40 normal school female students, a performance by the school's gymnastics classes and songs by the glee club. Eberhart, who presided during the actual dedication, lauded the normal school's progress and related that he had supported the effort to obtain state funding for the building. Remarks by all of the legislators were highlighted by Clague, who fondly reminisced about his normal school days and association with President Searing.

Cooper noted that the new building not only provided excellent facilities, but that its opening freed up space in the main building's first floor. This enabled Cooper to move his office from the second floor to a much more visible first floor room near the central front door. In connection with that shift, he had a storeroom and large, fireproof walk-in vault built near his office. The vault, which was about 12 feet long, 6 feet wide and 8 feet high, was evidently installed to safeguard vital records such as student transcripts.[85]

## The First Women's Dormitory

When Cooper proposed a women's dormitory in 1910, the Mankato Normal School was in the unique position of being the only one of the five schools that lacked such a facility. Duluth, the newest school in the system, had

Gymnasium, 1915 *Mankatonian* (yearbook)

two. But much of the rationale for that development was that Duluth Normal had been started as an all women's institution. However, the St. Cloud and Moorhead schools also had two women's dorms and Winona had one. Over the years the Normal School Board had decided that those schools had more pressing needs than Mankato, because they were not close enough to housing in private homes. Finally, the board supported the addition of a dormitory to the Mankato campus because Cooper insisted that it would not only improve living conditions for some students, but would also boost enrollment. Reportedly, many parents in the Mankato vicinity were sending their daughters to other state normal schools, because they could provide dormitory living.[86]

Building the Mankato campus dormitory involved two appropriations — one for site acquisition and the other for construction. With a legislative appropriation of up to $30,000, resident director John C. Wise, Jr., negotiated for sites near the school. In the summer of 1911, he arranged the purchase of 11 adjoining lots about three blocks southward of the campus between South Fourth and Warren streets.[87]

Planning for the building was done by the state architect, who was an agent for the state Board of Control. The Board of Control, modeled after similar agencies in Iowa and Wisconsin, was created by the 1901 legislature at the instigation of Governor Samuel R. Van Sant. Van Sant's original intention was to create a salaried board to supervise the fiscal affairs of the state's prisons and such specialized institutions as the State School for the Deaf. The idea of centralizing state financing was so appealing to the legislature that it decided to place the normal schools and the University of Minnesota under the Board of Control. Legislators were apparently motivated by the desire to limit appropriations requests to a single state board, which would free them from the lobbying of the normal schools and all other state institutions. Allied with this was the legislative belief that a Board of Control would improve fiscal responsibility and reduce state expenditures.[88]

The Normal School Board and the University of Minnesota, extremely covetous of their traditional prerogatives, strenuously objected to being

Practice School/Gymnasium building shown to the right of the Normal School building, 1908

placed under the Board of Control. Their complaints were heeded by the 1905 legislature, which significantly changed the Board of Control's authority. Henceforth, the board's authority over the normal schools and the university was reduced to developing specifications and supervising the construction of new buildings.

In late April 1912, Cooper received the plans prepared by the state architect from the Board of Control. They specified a three-story building in the Maryland Colonial style, 162.5 feet long and 36.75 feet wide.[89]

On May 6, 1912, the Board of Control opened bids for the general construction, heating and plumbing, and electrical wiring contracts. Erick Carlstrom of Mankato, with a low bid of $48,000, was awarded the general construction contract.[90]

The construction was started by Carlstrom in June 1912. George Pass, Sr., a Mankato architect who superintended the construction, was reportedly at the site every day during the nearly yearlong building period.[91]

On February 18, 1913, when it was evident that the dormitory would be ready for summer school occupants, it was christened by Cooper and Wise. Rather than hold formal dedication ceremonies, they simply announced that they had decided to name it Daniel Buck Hall in honor of "The Father of the Mankato Normal School." Evidently, there was some sentiment to name it after Edward Searing. For some reason, Cooper and Wise felt compelled to announce that the school's second dormitory when it was built would be named Edward Searing Hall.[92]

In a bit of a Freudian slip, the *Mankato Daily Free Press* of Friday, June 13, 1913, announced that Buck Hall would "welcome its first inmates" three days hence with the opening of summer school.

Buck Hall was reported to be a very attractive but highly functional structure. Finished with a red brick exterior, it featured wide porches and panel windows with green shutters on its first and second floors. The third floor had dormer windows.[93]

The kitchen and a 120-seat capacity dining room were located in the basement. The "complete and modern" kitchen was equipped with a "motor potato peeler, a dishwasher and every convenience for cooking." An ice-box with a capacity of a ton of ice had three compartments— vegetables, eggs and dairy products and meats. The

Daniel Buck Hall, circa 1920

boiler of the steam-heated building was at one end of the basement.

The first floor featured a large living room equipped with baby grand piano, a waiting room for visitors, quarters for the dean of women and the dorm matron and some student rooms. Most of the double occupancy student rooms were located on the second and third levels. Each was equipped with two single beds, a dresser, several chairs, a library table and two small closets. Other than student rooms, the third story had an infirmary with its own kitchen and servants' quarters. There were two toilets on each floor. Servicing the building was facilitated by a freight elevator and dumb waiter.

Cooper thought the completion of Buck Hall was an important "forward step" in the school's development. Other than providing housing for 85 young women, it offered meal service to 50 more. Beyond the convenience to its occupants, Cooper anticipated the dormitory would lead to "a more refined social life in the school, not only to those who live there but among all students."[94]

As Buck Hall was being planned, a new $20,000 boiler house was built to the rear of the main building. This facility fueled by coal, provided a central steam-heating system for both the main building and the practice school/gymnasium building. Cooper reported that this "modern and efficient plant" would enhance the environment of both buildings. In 1913 further improvements were made in the heating system by installing automatic heat controls and new air vents in both the main and practice school/gymnasium building.[95]

## The Mankato Normal School Student Body During Cooper's Administration

The collective face of normal students changed dramatically during Cooper's years. The attraction of more high school graduates and the corresponding decline in the number of experienced country schoolteachers during the regular school year made the student body younger. In 1911, Cooper recalled that: "Grey-haired women were not uncommon 10 years ago; there are none now." They had been replaced by high school graduates and young students from graded schools. In comparing old and young students, Cooper judged: "These young students have less of independence and a less vigorous grasp than the best of the older ones, but they are quicker and more adaptable" to new conditions.[96]

A second major change was the sharp disparity between female and male students. For the year 1910-1911, in which the normal department's enrollment was 961, women outnumbered men by about 11 to one. Cooper observed that this ratio had prevailed for the last several years. The gap between men and women students widened yet more after 1911. The 1916 Senior Class had 168 women and only 7 men.[97]

Daniel Buck Hall, 1915 *Mankatonian* (yearbook)

Living room at Daniel Buck Hall, 1915 *Mankatonian* (yearbook)

Dormitory room at Daniel Buck Hall, 1915 *Mankatonian* (yearbook)

Apparently, the sharp decline of men was caused by the accumulated effects of the Industrial Revolution. Rather than prepare to become teachers at relatively low salaries, males sought other outlets. Those who wanted professional white collar employment were drawn to colleges or universities. Many others chose not to prepare for teaching, because factory jobs in the rapidly growing Twin Cities and elsewhere offered higher pay.

The decline of male students brought changes to student activities. This was most evident in football, where a school needed at least 22 men for a starting 11 and a scrimmage squad. After two decades of fielding teams, the Mankato Normal did not have a football team in 1910-11. The sport was revived the next year and then dropped.[98]

Afterwards, women's basketball became the school's most popular sport. There was a men's team that usually played in a city league. But, because of their vastly superior numbers, women had a number of intramural teams in addition to their varsity team.[99]

Over the years, *The Mankatonian* often published comments about school spirit— or lack thereof. Apparently, student disinterest led to the discontinuation of the monthly in 1913. The next year, the *Senior Annual M. S. N.,* was published. It and the subsequent yearbooks contained some of the material that formerly appeared in *The Mankatonian,* but their principal value is as a source for student and faculty photographs.

There were numerous opportunities for student participation in various clubs and societies. The YMCA and the YWCA were particularly active in sponsoring programs with guest speakers. The Searing Society and the Phillips Society were the leading literary groups. The Debating Society, the Dramatic Club and the glee clubs attracted a number of students. As a sign of changing times, a Country Life Club was formed in 1915 when the Cooper administration was actively promoting rural school education.[100]

Evidently, the best attended programs were the compulsory chapel services presided over by Cooper. Although the services regularly had a reading from the Bible, they also had featured faculty presentations on current events or their travels.[101]

## Faculty and Staff Development

During the normal school phase of his administration, Cooper experienced numerous faculty and staff changes. These were caused, in part by rising enrollments and curriculum modifications. Mankato Normal had difficulty retaining faculty. Some were promoted into administrative positions at other educational institutions and others took new teaching jobs because of better pay. Like Searing, Cooper frequently complained that Minnesota teacher salaries, especially as compared to eastern states, were not competitive. Some faculty members left Mankato Normal to obtain more education.

In 1899-1900, Cooper's first full academic year, Mankato Normal had 24 faculty members counting librarian Alice N. Farr. Eleven of them had earned degrees with one Ph.D., three masters and seven bachelors. There were exactly twice as many in the normal department than the model department. Salaries ranged from a high of $1,800 for Eugene W. Bohannon, model school director and instructor of psychology and pedagogy, to a low of $315 for Alice Williams, a kindergarten assistant.[102]

After three years at Mankato Normal, Bohannon resigned in 1901 when he was named president of the new Duluth Normal School. Subsequently, he had a long, distinguished career at Duluth Normal and its successor, the Duluth State Teachers College. Bohannon retired on January 1, 1938. He died in Duluth on May 9, 1955, when he was 89 years old.[103]

In 1902 Charles F. Koehler, a faculty leader since he replaced McCleary a decade earlier, resigned to accept the presidency of the new Northern Normal and Industrial School in Aberdeen, South Dakota. During his three-year tenure, Koehler was reportedly liked by the faculty and students. But, he ran afoul of a tight-fisted board of regents, who did not trust him to adhere to their budgetary restraints. When he was forced out in 1905, the regents gave him the opportunity of continuing to teach at the school, which he declined.[104]

Practice school administrating was one of Cooper's high priorities. In 1901 he hired Dr. John A. Hancock as Bohannon's replacement. Like his predecessor, Hancock also taught psychology and pedagogy. After 11 years, Cooper decided this assignment was too demanding. While praising Hancock for his energy, Cooper concluded the model school needed more effective organization. Consequently, in 1911 he employed Manfred W. Deputy to direct the model school and teach pedagogy. Hancock continued teaching psychology at the normal school and teachers college until 1933.[105]

Cooper, who had nothing but praise for Deputy, was impressed by his background in education. The 44-year-old Deputy, born on an Indiana farm, attended rural schools before completing a two-year course at Southern

Women's basketball, 1911

YWCA officers,
1915 *Mankatonian* (yearbook)

Indiana Normal. Later he earned B. A. and M. A. degrees from the University of Indiana. He took some graduate work at Columbia University. When he arrived at Mankato Normal, Deputy had experience as a rural school teacher, high school principal, city and county superintendent of schools and two years of teaching pedagogy and directing the elementary school at Eastern State Normal in Charleston, Illinois.[106]

Much to Cooper's regret, Deputy resigned from Mankato Normal after five years, when he moved to the Kansas City, Missouri, public school system as director of teachers' training. In the spring of 1919 he returned to Minnesota when he was named the president of the newly formed Bemidji Normal School, the sixth and last in the state system. Deputy was the Bemidji State president until December 31, 1937, when he retired.[107]

Cooper found that replacing Deputy was complicated. He first hired Mr. E. G. Quigley, who resigned to accept a position with the Los Angeles, California, schools before he was barely "warm in his seat." Cooper was not able to replace Quigley with Fowler D. Brooks until the beginning of the spring 1917 term. Brooks, "young in years," Cooper reported, was zealous with an attractive personality. Cooper thought he was an "excellent find."[108]

Science education was also a high Cooper priority. In 1907 Fred L. Holtz, teacher of biological science, resigned to accept a position in the Brooklyn (New York) Training School. Cooper reported that Holtz had given Mankato Normal "13 years of the most efficient service."[109]

The next year Marvin A. Nichols was hired as Holtz's replacement. Nichols, who taught chemistry and physics, shared the science instruction with Chessley Justin Posey, instructor of physical science and nature study.[110]

When Posey left the school in 1911, Cooper was extremely concerned about the potential loss of nature study. Nature study, which among other things, was concerned with such environmental issues as the impact of agriculture upon the land, was then being promoted nationwide by the Country Life Movement. Dominated by Progressive Era reformers, who decried the disastrous impact of the Industrial Revolution on the natural environment, the Country Life Movement promoted an idyllic view of rural living.[111]

Country Life Movement promoters saw the country school as the principal agency for not only making agriculture more efficient and productive, but also as the way of introducing environmental practices that were harmonious with nature. Obviously, the most practical way of instilling country schools with this new mission was to educate their teachers, which was then being done principally in normal schools. Normal school educators, who traditionally believed one of their aims was to improve society, were naturally drawn to the Country Life Movement and nature study.

Cooper in 1911 was able to hire the highly qualified Gilbert H. Trafton to teach nature study with a certain emphasis on vocational agriculture. A 37-year-old bachelor, Trafton had earned a Master of Arts degree from Wesleyan University in Connecticut and a master of science from Columbia University in New York City. He had also studied at Cornell University in Ithaca, New York. An experienced teacher, he had spent three years at a normal school in Randolph, Vermont, and just prior to joining Mankato Normal eight years in the Passaic, New Jersey, schools. Active in the Nature Study Society, Trafton had developed a particular interest in agriculture.[112]

The Country Life Movement, which was especially active 1900-1920, promoted vocational training for all aspects of rural life. If boys who had been raised on farms would benefit from instruction in agriculture, then logically farm girls would profit from formal training in such domestic arts as cooking and sewing. Cooper believed that the addition of cooking and sewing classes as electives to the Mankato Normal curriculum would provide useful, practical training for some students. In 1905, Mary Louise Clark became the school's first sewing instructor and four years later Mary L. Oberlin was added as the first cooking instructor. Usually they were identified by the subjects they taught, but infrequently they were described as being in Home Economics.[113]

During his normal school time Cooper lost only two faculty members because of retirement. Helen M. Phillips, who had taught mathematics since 1873, retired in 1904. Defransa A. Swann, who started the same year as Phillips retired in 1913 after becoming the institution's first 40-year faculty member. Swann initially taught a variety of courses including penmanship, but after about the mid-1890s was devoted to geography. Swann, who was in her mid-60s when she retired, was then a generation older than most of the faculty, who were in the early stages of their teaching careers.[114]

Cooper replaced Swann with George J Miller, a graduate of Western Michigan Normal in Ypsilanti and the University of Michigan. The 35-year-old geographer had served as teacher, principal and superintendent and taken graduate work at the University of Chicago before joining Mankato Normal. Cooper, impressed by Miller's credentials, expected him "to become one of the very strongest men in the school." This proved to be an accurate judgment.

Due in large part to more liberal state funding, Cooper as compared to Searing, was able to augment the school's support staff. He added a halftime dean of women, increased clerical support and expanded janitorial services.

By 1910, when approximately 90 percent of the students were women, Cooper appointed Almeda May Janney Dean of Women. Janney, who joined the faculty two years earlier as an assistant in English and history, had demonstrated a special aptitude for counseling women students. Before there was a Dean of Women, all female faculty members worked with a group of students. However, Cooper recognized that "only a few women are really qualified to do this work well, and if it is to be done it needs time and energy that a fully employed teacher should not be asked to give to it." When Janney was appointed dean, she was relieved of teaching English, but continued as a halftime history teacher. After Buck Hall was opened in 1913, Janney was assigned living quarters in it.[115]

Cooper thought Janney did outstanding work as Dean of Women. But, like so many of her young colleagues, she chose to seek further education. In 1914 she resigned to enroll in Columbia University.

Cooper immediately replaced Janney with Georgia Louise Field, who had earned Master of Arts and Ph.D. degrees in English from the University of Colorado and served for a year as an assistant to the Dean of Women. Before going to Colorado, Field, a Massachusetts native, had graduated Phi Beta Kappa from Smith College (Northampton, Massachusetts). During her four years as Dean of Women and halftime English instructor, Field, while living in Buck Hall, organized student groups and from them developed a dean's council. The hall occupants praised her willingness to devote much time to

Gilbert H. Trafton,
1914 *MSN Annual* (yearbook)

them and to inspire them by dint of character. Like her predecessor, Field left Mankato Normal after four years. She was succeeded by Alice D. Goss, who served in the position, 1918-1921.[116]

Historically, the principals/presidents of Mankato Normal had both administrative and teaching duties; Gage, Sears and John all taught fulltime. Searing did likewise until late in his administration, when his Latin instruction was assigned to another teacher and he was reduced to part-time teaching. Cooper taught part-time and in his presidential role also performed registrar, placement and counseling duties. In the spring of each year, placement alone demanded much time. Area superintendents who were seeking new faculty depended on Cooper to make recommendations and act as liaison in any hiring process.

When Cooper began in 1899, his only clerical assistant was Agnes C. Glotzbach, who had started under Searing the previous year. Officially designated as the school secretary and purchasing agent, Glotzbach also served as the textbook librarian. The textbook librarian duties, which entailed administering the rental of texts to students, was handled as an office rather than a library function. Glotzbach, after what Cooper described as "10 years of excellent service" resigned in 1908.[117]

Belle Colby Carrington, Glotzbach's replacement, became, after Cooper, the face of the campus. Carrington, who had a 12-month appointment, was personally known to most of the students and evidently was the first person they contacted about any matters relating to transcripts and preparing credentials. By 1918, when she was officially listed as "secretary and purchasing agent," Carrington was assisted by a "president's secretary," who worked year-round and two clerks, who had 11-month appointments.[118]

The physical plant expansion created a need for a larger custodial staff. For the 1918-1919 year, Henry S. Holman, "head janitor and engineer," supervised four other janitors who also had 12-month appointments. "Daddy" Holman, as the students affectionately called him, had by then been with the school for nearly three decades. A Civil War veteran, Holman was well-known for relating war experiences to students. Holman probably had more campus presence than anyone else, since he and his family lived in campus housing provided by the school.[119]

For 1919-1920, its last full year as Mankato Normal, the school had 34 faculty members—20 in the normal department and 14 in the training school. Ten of the normal department members had master's degrees, six bachelor's degrees and four had not graduated from college. The training school had three master's and four bachelor's. The other seven had not earned a degree. Typically, these non-graduates had earned a normal school diploma.[120]

The training school faculty had increased faster than the normal department faculty, because of the addition of ninth graders. This addition caused the seventh, eighth and ninth grades be classified as junior high. The name "training school" had evolved over time. The original name of model school was variously called the practice school by the late 1890s. But, by about 1910, elementary school was the preferred name. But the start of the ninth grade made the name training school more appropriate.

The 1919-1920 catalog faculty listing did not include librarian Alice N. Farr, who was in the faculty listing of the 1899-1900 catalog. Cooper apparently decided that someone who did not have a classroom assignment should not be considered faculty. In the 1919-1920 catalog, Farr was listed in an unlabeled category after the training school faculty. The five others in that group were

Blanche Vinton, assistant librarian; Belle Colby Carrington, secretary and purchasing agent; Jennie La Rue, school nurse; Etta Coulter Green, manager of Daniel Buck Hall; and Henry S. Holman, head janitor and engineer.

During Cooper's normal school years, faculty salaries increased numerically but did not keep pace with inflation. For the academic year 1897-1898, Dr. Stuart F. Rose at $1,800 was the highest paid faculty member. For 1920-1921, John A. Hancock, George J. Miller, Marvin A. Nichols, Gustav S. Petterson (Sociology) and Gilbert H. Trafton all were paid the top highest nine-month salary of $2,700. Additionally, they were each compensated $400 for teaching a five-week summer session. The lowest salary for the normal department faculty was $1,400 for Martha E. Bain, sewing and textiles instructor.[121]

Belle Colby Carrington, a 12-month employee who earned $1,800, was the highest paid administrative staff member. For the same period, Henry S. Holman earned $1,200 and was provided with a rent-free house.

From the beginning of Cooper's administration until 1917 the value of money was basically static. But, for 1917-1920 inclusive, which included the period of the nation's participation in World War I, inflation reached unprecedented levels. The annual percentage increases for 1917, 1918, 1919 and 1920 were respectively 17.8, 17.3, 15.2 and 15.6.[122]

This staggering increase in the cost of living prompted the normal school board to express its appreciation for the "loyal services of the teachers" in the normal school system. Furthermore, the board assured the faculties that it would seek salary increases.[123]

## The Campaign for Teacher College Status

As the last president of the Mankato Normal School and the first president of Mankato State Teachers College, Cooper actively participated in the transition. In 1899, his first year, the governing board drastically changed the academic programs. It first ended the three-year elementary course. The C class was discontinued effective at the end of the 1898-1899 year. A and B class students currently enrolled were permitted to complete the course if they remained continually in school and graduated no later than June 1901, the deadline for the end of A and B classes.[124]

In its 1901 reforms, the board reiterated its important distinction of 1895 between those students with less than a high school education and high school graduates. Those who had not graduated from high school or, for that matter, had never attended high school, could enroll in a five-year (15 terms) course with the years identified successively as First Year, Second Year, Third Year, Junior Year and Senior Year. The course had both English and Latin tracks. They were very similar except students in the Latin course had a required five terms of Latin mainly in lieu of history and literature. The five-year course included the usual high school subjects, which were presumably taught at a high school level.[125]

Administrative staff Belle Colby Carrington (left) and Ida Conkling (right), circa 1915

High school graduates could enroll in a one-year Elementary Graduate Course, a two-year Advanced Graduate Course or a two-year Kindergarten Training Course. All three courses were devoted to professional education training with the emphasis on educational psychology, history of education, teaching methodologies and practice teaching.[126]

Serving both high school graduates and non-graduates was a logical approach in the first decade of the twentieth century. But, conditions changed very dramatically with the proliferation of high schools and high school graduates. In his report for the 1910-1911 academic year, Cooper observed that the school's most "startling" recent development was the sharp increase in advanced course enrollment and the commensurate decline in the pre-high school graduation courses. During the four years before the start of the 1910-1911 year, the percentage of students in the advanced courses had increased from 31 to 61 percent. This trend accelerated during the year. Sixty-three percent of the June 1911 graduates earned an advanced diploma and only 37 percent the elementary course diploma.[127]

With the very recent past as their guide, Cooper, the other normal school presidents and the governing board, recognized that the Minnesota normal schools, like those in other states, had evolved into institutions at a level above high schools. Furthermore, they were convinced that the high school movement would continue to accelerate and it was just a matter of time before normal schools could not draw on pre-high school graduates. The obvious solution was to convert the normal schools into teachers colleges.

Minnesota normal school educators were well aware of the advent of teachers colleges in other states. The first Midwestern normal school to teachers college conversion occurred in 1899 with the school at Ypsilanti, Michigan. By 1910 two Ohio normal schools, two Illinois normal schools and Iowa's lone normal school at Cedar Rapids had become teachers colleges.[128]

These precedents and their own situation prompted Minnesota's normal school presidents and the governing board to seek teachers college status. Such a change would need legislative approval, because all of the then five normal schools had been authorized by the legislature.

By 1912 the Minnesota Normal School Board was convinced that the five schools should become teachers colleges. At its June 19 meeting, the board asked Cooper and the other presidents to prepare a bill for presentation to the 1913 legislature. The draft delivered by the presidents on August 13 stipulated that the "normal school board shall have authority to grant the degree, Bachelor of Education . . . ." While endorsing the aim, the board believed its request to the legislature would stand a much better chance of succeeding if it was supported by the University of Minnesota and the state's private colleges. Consequently, the board decided to ask for a special meeting with representatives of the university, the colleges and the high school board.[129]

Carl G. Schultz, board secretary and state superintendent of public instruction, arranged an evening meeting held in the state capitol on October 2, 1912. Ell Torrance, president of the normal school board, presided at the well-attended event. The five normal school presidents and most of the board members were present. The University of Minnesota was represented by President George E. Vincent and the deans of the arts, education and agriculture colleges as well as John Lind, president of the board of regents and former Minnesota governor. The presidents of Carleton College, Gustavus Adolphus College, Macalester College and St. Olaf College participated as did the dean of Hamline University. The High School Board participants included its president and two of its school inspectors.[130]

Reportedly, all participants expressed their views. However, the tone was set by Vincent, his deans and Lind, who opined that the normal schools were not qualified to become teachers colleges. There was some tension when Jed L. Washburn, the resident director of Duluth Normal, accused Vincent of being jealous of the university's position as Minnesota's only public degree granting institution. While professing "to have no desire to be so understood," Vincent responded that "the proposed course ending with a degree would lower the standard set for a bachelor's degree in the state." Lengthy articles in the *Minneapolis Morning Tribune* and the *Mankato Daily Review* emphasized the disagreement.[131]

Speaking on behalf of the denominational college representatives and the Hamline dean, President Thomas M. Hodgman of Macalester said that they did not believe "that there was grave danger in the proposal of lowering the standard of the bachelor's degree." But, he meaningfully expressed his personal opinion that he thought the issue should be decided by the state's public institutions.[132]

Faced with the university's opposition, Washburn moved "to defer any further consideration of the question until the next regular meeting of the Board."[133] The board members concurred. Subsequently, the board decided that because of the university's opposition there was no point in asking the legislature to change the normal schools to teachers colleges.

The 1912 setback left Mankato Normal and its four sister institutions in a quandary. They had evolved beyond the early normal college era when the schools did not enroll any high school graduates. But, as the number of high school graduates increased, the normal schools achieved a post-high school level. The University of Minnesota's admission policy recognized this. Advanced course normal school graduates who enrolled at the university were given credit for a year's work in the four-year course. The university's College of Education had a more liberal policy. It gave credit for a year and a half to normal graduates of the five-year course.[134]

The board asked Cooper and his peers—Eugene W. Bohannon (Duluth), Guy E. Maxwell (Winona), Waite A.

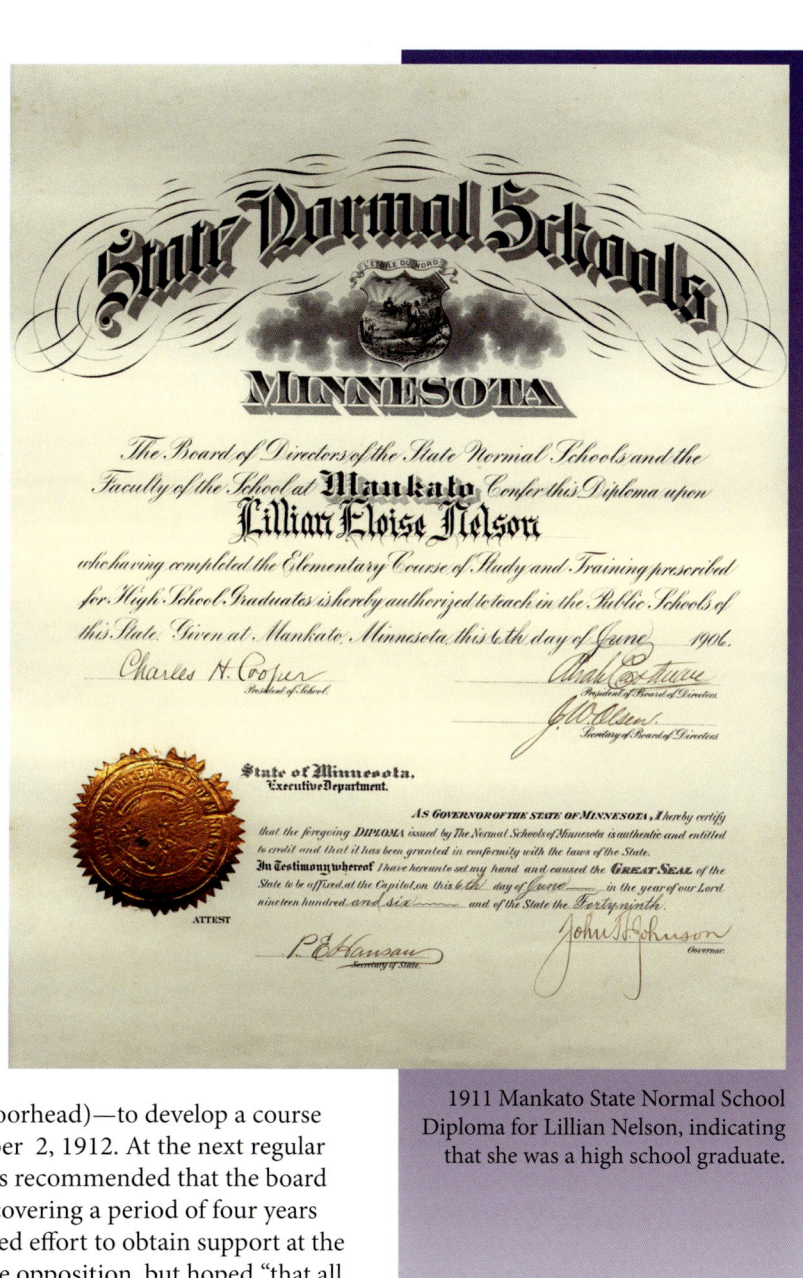

1911 Mankato State Normal School Diploma for Lillian Nelson, indicating that she was a high school graduate.

Shoemaker (St. Cloud) and Frank E. Weld (Moorhead)—to develop a course of action after the disastrous meeting of October 2, 1912. At the next regular board meeting on November 30, the presidents recommended that the board authorize them "to propose a course of study covering a period of four years beyond high school."[135] With regard to the failed effort to obtain support at the October 2 meeting, the presidents regretted the opposition, but hoped "that all institutions of learning in our state will co-operate with the normal schools to promote the efficiency of work in the field of elementary education."[136]

The presidents and the board accepted the premise that the normal school mission was to train elementary school teachers. But, they also recognized that nearly all of their regular year students were high school graduates. Accordingly, the board on November 9, 1915, approved high school graduation or equivalent schooling as an admission requirement for the regular courses of study at the Mankato and Winona schools. This stipulation did not pertain to summer session enrollees.[137]

Once its admission policy required high school graduation for regular year students, Mankato Normal replaced the five-year course with a standard two-year course. The First, Second and Third years of the five-year course, which were deemed to be high school level, were eliminated. The new two-year course had only juniors and seniors. This change caused the University of Minnesota's School of Education to admit normal graduates as juniors.[138]

This move was prompted by the proliferation of high schools. For the academic year 1915-1916, Carl G. Schultz, superintendent of the State Department of Public Instruction, reported a new high of 230 high schools. Additionally, an estimated 50 graded schools offered complete high school courses.[139]

The growth of consolidated country graded schools was then starting to revolutionize rural education. At the urging of Governor Adolph Olson Eberhart the 1911 legislature approved the state's first significant school consolidation law. The measure, supported by educators, provided state aid for constructing buildings and school support. The very popular act had an immediate effect. By 1916 Minnesota had 170 consolidated districts compared to only nine five years earlier.[140]

Any consolidated school with at least four teachers was recognized as a state graded school. In 1915-1916 the graded schools statewide had 6,866 high school students. This development meant the normal schools had a new, important source of potential post-high school students.[141]

The sudden emergence of rural graded schools was greatly facilitated by the advent of the automobile age. In 1900 there were 8,000 motor vehicle registrations nationwide. In 1910 there were 468,500 registrations; five years later 2,490,900. In Minnesota, from 1915 to 1920, motor vehicle registration increased from nearly 94,000 to more than 324,000.[142]

Motor vehicles, which rapidly transformed all aspects of American society, helped make education at all levels more attainable. Their unprecedented speed and mobility enabled many country students to attend consolidated schools, which offered a more diverse curriculum than the traditional one-room schools. Furthermore, for those who aspired to attend college or a normal school, they provided convenient links to either their ultimate destination or a railroad depot. With respect to the normal schools themselves, it is not at all coincidental that their rural education programs were feasible because of automobiles. By the World War I era, the Mankato Normal found it was relatively easy to place practice teachers in rural schools or to have rural elementary students transported to the campus school.

As Minnesota's normal schools were adjusting to serve post-high school student bodies, they increased their publicity efforts. In June 1915, the presidents and board decided to launch a quarterly journal, which would feature normal school activities. The first issue of *Minnesota State Normal Schools Quarterly Journal* was published by the board in October 1915. Aside from a number of informative articles, it imparted the message that normal schools were dedicated to innovative programs that would improve elementary education in the state.[143]

## Effects of World War I

Business as usual for Minnesota and its normal schools ended abruptly when the United States entered World War I on April 6, 1917. The congressional decision to support the Allies (dominated by Great Britain and France) and to oppose the Central Powers (led by Germany and Austria-Hungary) was justified by unrestricted German submarine warfare against neutral shipping.

During the war, which ended with Germany's surrender on November 11, 1918 (Armistice Day), the United States mobilized its armed forces and home front. The armed forces included 118,497 Minnesota men. Minnesota's battlefield casualties totaled 1,432 and 2,175 died of disease.[144]

The most unique aspect of Minnesota's participation in the "Great War," as World War I was usually called by contemporaries was the Commission of Public Safety. The commission, established on April 16, 1917, only 10 days after the United States declared war, was promoted by conservative Governor Joseph A. A. Burnquist and ultra-zealous legislators. Ostensibly, it was intended to coordinate wartime activities with the Council of National Defense, which was responsible for mobilizing industries and resources for national security. The Minnesota commission was especially empowered to control any act inconsistent with the federal and state constitutions.[145]

If it had been judiciously administered, the Commission of Public Safety would not have become the accuser, judge and jury in matters of civil liberties. Its supporters, rapt with war hysteria, felt compelled to control all "un-American" groups and people. Wartime emotions have a unique way of removing all shades of gray and creating a them and us mentality. The commission's fears of seditious activities were fueled by the presence of numerous German-Americans and the rise of the socialistic Nonpartisan League.

The 1910 federal census showed that 71 percent of the 2,075,708 Minnesota residents were either foreign-born or had at least one foreign-born parent. Slightly more than a fourth of the foreign-born/ foreign-born parentage were Germans. The natural tendency to suspect them was exacerbated when New Ulm city officials refused to cooperate with the Brown County draft board.

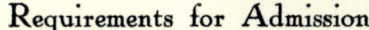

### Requirements for Admission

The school requires for admission to the standard course a diploma from an accredited high school of Minnesota or other states, or evidence of an equivalent training. Official records should be presented when application for admission is made; a convenient blank is to be found in this catalogue.

1917-1918 Catalogue

The Commission of Public Safety became a power unto itself. With a director for each county, it had a home guard force of 10,281 uniformed men. They were supported by some 600 plain-clothes officers. With this constabulary, the commission pursued its principal aim of causing Minnesotans to conform to proper wartime conduct.

The commission's goal of Americanization effected education. It reasoned that the best way of curtailing un-American conduct was to educate people in American tradition though schools at all levels.

Carl G. Schultz, superintendent of the Minnesota Department of Education, stoked interest in education and the war by pronouncing that "illiteracy is perhaps the greatest enemy of democracy and no means or efforts should be spared to remove this evil."[146] Schultz thought the best solution for illiteracy was adult education in evening schools.

Schultz saw the existing schools from elementary though university as vital to the war effort. He thought they were the best means of organizing such wartime activities as bond drives and patriotic rallies. The rallies would not only encourage proper American conduct, but would also promote food and fuel conservation and volunteerism to such organizations as the Red Cross.[147]

To mobilize support for the war, nearly 600 educators "pledged themselves and the schools of the state to the support of the government in the Great War in defense of democracy."[148] At a conference held on October 12 and 13, 1917, at the University of Minnesota's agriculture campus in St. Paul, the educators divided themselves into four groups to consider ways of supporting the war effort. Three of the groups were composed of elementary and secondary school officials. The fourth, composed of normal school and University of Minnesota representatives, was classified as "higher education."

The higher education group, led by Dr. Marion L. Burton, president of the University of Minnesota, unqualifiedly supported the war effort. They agreed that each institution should appoint a committee, which would urge faculty and students to purchase Liberty Bonds. Additionally, they endorsed the validity of the draft and encouraged programs dedicated to conserving essential foods including wheat, fats, meat and sugar. Significantly, they recommended that "every institution of higher education in the state should see to it that the issues of the war are repeatedly presented to the students in order to foster a sound patriotism among them."[149]

Evidently, educators at all levels were influenced by Commission of

FRONT STREET LOOKING NORTH FROM CHERRY STREET, MANKATO, MINN.

Postcard, Front Street looking north from Cherry Street, Mankato, Minnesota, circa 1920. Image courtesy of the Blue Earth County Historical Society

Public Safety presenters. Among other things, the commission recommended and the educators concurred that all German language books be banned and that the commission publish and circulate lists of both acceptable and unacceptable textbooks.[150]

Like all of its sister institutions, Mankato Normal enthusiastically supported the war effort. Faculty and students purchased Liberty Bonds and War Savings Stamps, contributed to Red Cross fund drives and urged compliance with the federal government's goals of producing and saving food. Ell Torrance, Normal School Board president, Civil War veteran and Grand Army of the Republic official, thought the normal schools played an essential role in the Americanization process. They prepared the teachers who would "Americanize" schoolchildren.[151]

For his part, Cooper was primarily concerned with the war's disruptive effects. He especially deplored Mankato Normal's enrollment decline. For the academic year 1917-1918, the normal department had 732 students, which was 139 less than the previous year. For 1918-1919 the enrollment fell to 656.[152]

The already rather sparse pre-war male enrollment dropped precipitously. At one point in 1917-1918, the normal department had only one male student. Men left school primarily because of military service. A number of female students also withdrew, because of job opportunities in war-related businesses and industries.[153]

The war also drastically affected the golden anniversary of the school's founding. Cooper had initially planned a major commemoration. But, preoccupied with wartime concerns, he limited the anniversary to a modest ceremony. On the evening of June 4, 1918, Cooper commemorated the school's founding by hosting a library reception for the graduating class and some alums. The program featured a presentation by Mrs. Lafayette G. M. Fletcher, who as Susie M. Dyer, was on Gage's original faculty. She wrote and read "Early Days in the Mankato State Normal School," a reminiscent account of her experiences during the school's first two years.[154]

By early fall 1918, Mankato Normal's people and the rest of the nation anticipated an imminent close of the war. Allied armies, including the America Expeditionary Force, were pushing a major offensive on the Western Front. But American society was soon threatened by the 1918 influenza outbreak, a worldwide pandemic that had already ravaged much of Europe, Asia and Africa.

After the first Minnesota flu cases occurred in mid-September, the contagion spread rapidly. By October 12, Minneapolis, which was hit particularly hard, reported 1,538 cases; outside of the Twin Cities, Minnesota had an additional 2,538.[155]

Combatting flu was a cooperative effort of the Minnesota Health Board, United States Public Health Service and the American Red Cross. Officials of those organizations knew that the disease was very contagious and that it mainly affected young adults. Consequently, the commonest recommended preventive measure was to curtail large public assemblages. Closures could be decreed by either the state health board or city health departments. A flurry of closures was triggered by an October 11 mandate from the Minneapolis Health Department. It ordered the immediate, indefinite closure of "all schools, churches, theaters, motion picture shows, dance halls and pool and billiard halls . . . ."[156]

By the end of the next week, Mankato reported 157 new influenza cases. This prompted the Minnesota Health Board to close the city's public schools as well as Mankato Normal's training department.[157]

Evidently, the state health board deferred acting on the normal department, because "there have been very few cases of the influenza among the attendants at the school and careful oversight by a competent trained nurse has made the likelihood of spread of the disease from the school as a center but very small."[158] But, after re-evaluating the situation, the Minnesota Health Board ordered all state normal schools closed effective Monday, October 28.

Cooper reported that Mankato Normal was closed for three weeks "and the work of many students was badly broken by illness."[159] On November 12, when the epidemic was still raging, the governing board decided that the closure time "shall not be required to be made up by the students either by depriving them of their holidays or prolonging the subsequent terms of the schools."[160]

Fortunately, Mankato Normal got through the epidemic without any loss of life. But statewide it was a major disaster. By mid-November there were a reported 75,110 cases. The state's death toll was 7,521 in 1918 and 2,579 the next year.[161]

## STATE NORMAL SCHOOL HAS BEEN ORDERED CLOSED

### Such Was the Action Taken by the Health Board This Morning

By order of the Board of Health, the Mankato State Normal School has been closed until further notice. There have been very few cases of the influenza among the attendants at the school and careful oversight by a competent trained nurse has made the likelihood of spread of the disease from the school as a center but very small.

The judgement of the health officers, however was that all the schools of the city should be closed, and their judgement must necessarily control.

The training department of the school has been closed the past week but the Normal department was permitted to continue.

*Mankato Weekly Review,*
*26 October 1918*

## Achievement of Teachers College Status

World War I temporarily disrupted Minnesota's public education system, but pre-war educational trends continued throughout the war and accelerated soon after its end. Faced with what it regarded as a crisis in public education, the Minnesota Department of Education convened a meeting of the six normal school presidents and the University of Minnesota's dean of the College of Education. On January 26, 1920, the Department of Education advised the normal presidents and university dean that the state demand for teachers exceeded the supply by at least 300 and more than 1,800 teachers did not have appropriate training for the positions they held. The board's determination to certify only qualified teachers would obviously exacerbate the teacher shortage. Apparently, the presidents and the dean agreed with the board's conclusions.[162]

The Department of Education also noted that the number of high schools and high school students was continuing to increase. In 1916-17 Minnesota had 230 high schools with a total enrollment of 45,928. For 1919-20 the totals were 240 and 49,060.[163]

Armed with the information about the teacher shortage and the development of high schools, the normal presidents recommended that their schools be converted into teachers colleges. In response the Normal School Board at its January 25, 1921, meeting resolved "that the State Normal Schools and the State Normal School Board be designated hereafter as State Teachers' Colleges and the State Teachers' College Board respectively; and that said Board be authorized to award appropriate degrees for the completion of the four years courses in said schools . . . ." The board promptly appointed a three-man committee to prepare and present appropriate legislation to the legislature, which was then in session.[164]

Converting the normal schools into teachers colleges proved to be a routine matter. Everyone concerned evidently believed that it should be done. The bill breezed through the Senate by a vote of 39 to 0 and the House strongly favored it. On April 13, 1921, Governor Jacob A. O. Preus signed "An act to redesignate the state normal schools and the normal school board, and to enable that board to award appropriate degrees."[165]

The act, which took effect on its signing date, first provided that: "The six educational institutions in this state heretofore designated as state normal schools shall hereafter be designated as state teachers colleges as follows: the 'Winona State Teachers College', the 'Mankato State Teachers College', the 'St. Cloud State Teachers College', the 'Duluth State Teachers College', the 'Moorhead State Teachers College', the 'Bemidji State Teachers College', respectively." The law also specified that the newly named "state teachers college board shall have authority to award appropriate degrees to persons who complete the prescribed four-year curriculum [sic] of studies in the state teachers college."

The act represented the first significant step in creating a new state higher education system. Obviously, everyone concerned, including the act's key advocates, realized the six former normal schools would have to make major program changes before they were really teachers colleges in ways other than their names. That realization presented Cooper with his next great challenge.

# 3

# MANKATO STATE TEACHERS COLLEGE, 1921-1946

The first quarter-century of the Mankato State Teachers College was a very eventful period highlighted by the major fire of 1922, which destroyed the main building, the Great Depression and World War II. During those trying times the college had two presidents—Charles H. Cooper, 1921-1930, and Frank D. McElroy, 1930-1946. Although they had to cope with crises, Cooper and McElroy spent most of their time dealing with business-as-usual matters including curriculum development, faculty professionalization, administrative reorganization and campus expansion.

## Institutional Status in 1921

The re-designation from normal school to teachers college amounted to a license to change. Board members and school presidents realized that they had to make sweeping curricular changes before the six schools would be actual teachers colleges in ways other than their names.

At its outset, the Mankato State Teachers College was a modest venture. For its first full academic year, 1921-1922, the school had nine "officers of administration" headed by Cooper. The others were Mattie Cook Ellis, dean of women; Floss Ann Turner, resident teacher, Cooper Hall; Belle Colby Carrington, secretary and accountant; Alice N. Farr, librarian; Winnifred Diment, assistant librarian; Etta Coulter Green, manager of halls; Mollie Mae Rose R.N., school nurse; and Henry S. Holman, superintendent of buildings. Four of them—Cooper, Ellis (history), Turner (training teacher, intermediate grades) and Green (home economics) also taught.[1]

Including the four administrators who taught part-time, there were 34 faculty members including 21 in the College Department and 13 in the Training School. By way of academic training, 10 members of the College Department had master's degrees, seven bachelor's degrees and the four who had not completed college had earned diplomas. The training school faculty consisted of three with master's degrees, five with bachelor's degrees and five with no degrees. Typically, those who had not graduated from college had earned normal school diplomas.

Initially, Mankato State Teachers College continued the two-year normal school course. Its "juniors" and "seniors" concentrated in one of five options—kindergarten-primary, primary, intermediate, junior high school and rural. Generally, the same subject matter courses were required in all of these programs. But each was distinguished by the type of its practice teaching requirement.[2]

The two-year course was a minimum requirement for most students who sought teacher certification. But selected students could be certified to teach in rural schools for two years after completing only one year of college classes. They had to be high school graduates who had demonstrated teaching competency and practice taught for six weeks in "good rural schools associated with the College."[3] Those rural teachers who completed this year-long program could

## RURAL

The work in this department is designed to give special preparation to rural teachers, supervisors, and directors of high school training departments. It parallels the regular course both in entrance requirements and value of diploma granted at its completion.

| Junior Year | Senior Year |
|---|---|
| Introduction to Teaching | Hygiene and Sanitation |
| *Intermediate Arithmetic | Nature Study |
| *Geography 1 | Agriculture (2) |
| *Grammar and Composition | Rural Sociology |
| *American History, Introductory | Music |
| Course | Rural Methods, Advanced Course |
| *Reading | Children's Literature |
| *Rural Methods | Public School Art |
| *Practice Teaching | Practice Teaching (1) |
| Contemporary History | Elective |
| Rural School Cooking and Sewing | |
| Elementary Handwork (½) | |
| Writing (½) | |

*Required for first grade certificate. A first grade certificate is granted on the satisfactory completion of the junior year of this course of study.

8

Description of rural education curriculum, 1921-1922 Catalog

be re-certified for two-year periods if they applied to the college president and presented evidence of satisfactory teaching.

The year-long rural schools program was deemed necessary because of the continuing need to replenish the supply of rural teachers. The various state superintendents of public instruction regarded rural schools as Minnesota's major public education problem. For the academic year 1915-1916, Superintendent Carl G. Schultz reported 215,427 of Minnesota's 434,299 public schools elementary students were enrolled in rural schools. Surveys showed that approximately 70 percent of the rural students did not take any post-elementary education. Furthermore, thousands of them quit school before completing the elementary program. For the preceding year only 5,532 rural elementary students had finished the eighth grade.[4]

The rural elementary enrollment of 1915-1916 was distributed among 7,409 schools of which 6,517 qualified for state aid. Most were one-room schools where one teacher was responsible for all eight grades. As Cooper had noted from the beginning of his presidency in 1900, normal school graduates preferred teaching in town and city elementary schools rather than country schools.

The one-room country school presented some unique challenges that repelled many young women. The relative isolation of rural schools was compounded by the anti-education attitudes of some students and their parents. It was not at all uncommon for parents to keep working-age boys home to do farm work. Furthermore, rural teachers often had to deal with stingy and sometimes puritanical district school boards. Under these circumstances there was an understandable very high turnover rate in rural teaching positions.

Rural school demand for teachers was so high that it could not be fulfilled by the state's normal schools. Consequently, the state department of education with the blessing of the normal schools, sponsored a unique program of rural teacher preparation departments in high schools. For the 1920-1921 academic year Minnesota had 243 high schools with a total enrollment of 52,788. Ninety-four of them had teacher training departments. Each received $1,600 in state aid. Statewide the departments were staffed by 98 teachers, so nearly all were one-teacher departments. Admission to the teaching training programs was restricted to top-achieving seniors, which limited enrollment. The statewide average for the 94 departments was only 10 students. During their year of training the students did several weeks of practice teaching in a nearby rural school. Despite their small enrollments the high school training departments contributed significantly in preparing rural teachers. Collectively, they supplied 38 percent of Minnesota's rural teachers.[5]

Mankato and its sister institutions recognized high school trained teachers as potentially good college students. Therefore, they tried to recruit them for their two-year programs. As an inducement they offered such people full year's credit on their two-year courses.[6]

In describing the one- and two-year curriculums that the Mankato State Teachers College offered in its first year, Cooper felt obligated to explain the institution's main purpose was to offer a future four-year degree program. He wrote: "The four-year curriculum, authorized by the last legislature, leads to the degree of Bachelor of Arts in Education. It is designed to prepare for administrative and supervisory positions in elementary education, and for junior high school positions. At present the resources of the institution do not permit it to offer the full curriculum; but they do permit it to offer certain courses beyond the two-year curriculum. The institution urges those who are interested in the four-year curriculum to avail themselves of this opportunity to make advanced credits; it plans to offer the full curriculum when there is sufficient demand."[7]

About six weeks after it became a teachers college, Mankato State's campus was expanded somewhat with the opening of Cooper Hall, the institution's second women's dormitory. After the completion of Buck Hall, Cooper had agitated for more dormitory housing. In February 1919, when it appeared the legislature was willing to fund state building projects, the Normal School Board decided to request $100,000 for each of three women's dormitories for the Mankato, Winona and Bemidji campuses.[8]

Soon after the legislature on April 25, 1919, appropriated $100,000 for the Mankato dormitory, Cooper, resident board director John C. Wise and board officers began planning with the State Board of Control. They decided that the new dorm should be, like Buck Hall, constructed in the Maryland Colonial style. They also planned that the dormitory should face Ramsey Street and lay perpendicularly to Buck Hall.[9]

Most of the exterior construction on the dormitory was done in 1920 before winter's onset. During the winter and the spring of 1920-1921 workmen rushed to have the building's two lowest floors ready for summer school. Somewhat to the planners' surprise, there was not enough funding to do the inside work on the third story.[10]

As the building was being readied, the faculty petitioned to have it named Cooper Hall in honor of their president. Evidently, Wise, who presented the petition to the governing board, did nothing to dissuade the petitioners. Consequently, the

Cooper Hall, circa 1950

faculty was probably not even aware that when Buck Hall was dedicated, Wise and Cooper had agreed that the second dormitory should be named Searing Hall. After he signed the faculty petition, Wise presented it to the board, which on April 26, 1921, officially named the new dormitory Cooper Hall.

Cooper was pleased that the dormitory's lowest two floors were ready for occupancy at the start of summer school on June 13, 1921. The hall's completed portion accommodated 42 coeds compared to 85 for Buck Hall.[11]

Each room in Buck and Cooper halls, which was shared by two coeds, was equipped with two couch beds, a dresser, a study table, two chairs, a rocker and one large rug. Occupants, who had to take care of their rooms, were required to furnish their own linen, towels and soap.[12]

In 1921-1922 room and board weekly charges for most of the dorm rooms was $5.50. But third floor Buck Hall students had a slightly discounted charge of $5.25 and those who had corner rooms with two full windows paid $5.75. Board was much costlier than rooming. Non-dorm female students were charged $4.50 weekly (payable in advance) for boarding in Buck Hall.

Combined, the two dormitories provided only a relatively small portion of the housing needs for female students. Because they were less expensive than living in private homes, dorm rooms were in demand. Dorm occupancy was available only to those students who planned on full-year attendance and applied early. Rooms were assigned in order of the application dates.

Those students who lived in private homes usually paid $6 to $8 weekly for room and board. The charge for rooms without board was $10 to $16 per month. The college exerted some control over this private housing market by maintaining an official list of approved housing. Students were advised that they had to live in homes on the approved list. Any exceptions had to be approved by the dean of women.

The rationale for this policy was that "the social and moral welfare of women students is under direct supervision of the dean of women." The dean personally inspected all homes on the approved list to ascertain that they had suitable accommodations including a parlor for visitors and did not have male tenants.[13]

Because of a sharp enrollment increase for 1921-1922, the demand for student housing reached unprecedented levels. The college department enrollment of 1,368 was nearly 400 more than the prior year and slightly more than double that of 1918-1919.[14]

The college students were drawn from 61 Minnesota counties and 10 states other than Minnesota. Student demographics featured the institution's traditional heavy reliance on Blue Earth and nearby counties. Blue Earth was home to 255 students, followed respectively by Brown, Faribault and Le Sueur with 67, 56 and 49. With the exception of Hennepin County (Minneapolis) with 41 students, all other counties with at least 20 students were located in southwestern and south central Minnesota. The total student enrollment from that part of the state north of the latitude of the Twin Cities was no more than a dozen.[15]

The 34 out-of-state students were mainly from bordering Iowa (15), Wisconsin (6), North Dakota (4) and South Dakota (3). One each was from Illinois, Kansas, Missouri, Montana, Texas and Washington.

## The Great Fire

For nearly half of Mankato State Teachers College's first full year, it seemed to Cooper that the school's main future issue was readying a four-year curriculum preparatory to offering degree programs. But, the burning and destruction of the main building on Sunday, February 5, 1922, dramatically re-shuffled the college's priorities.

Like many calamities, the fire came without warning. About nine in the morning head custodian Henry S. Holman and his family, who lived in a college-provided house behind the main building, noticed smoke coming out of a basement room under the manual arts shop. Edith Holman, Henry's daughter, promptly telephoned Maurice J. Nelson, the manual arts instructor.[16]

When he reached the scene, Nelson was soon joined by Cooper, who had hurried over from his nearby Ramsey Street home close to the dormitories. Their initial reaction was that the fire was not very serious. So Nelson entered the shop by breaking a window and removed most of the tools. Cooper, meanwhile, had been joined by secretary and accountant Belle Colby Carrington. They entered the front part of the building and apparently removed some current records from their offices. Many people, including some eyewitnesses, assumed that Cooper and Carrington were intent on saving vital student transcripts. But, they would have had no reason to do so, because those and other old school records were housed in a large fireproof vault. History instructor Albert B. Morris, who entered the building about the same time, removed the Searing bust, the most significant symbol of the institution's tradition.

These brief forays were no sooner done than the building erupted in flames. The fire, which originated in a room where waste paper was kept, was much stronger than the first eyewitnesses assumed. Once the fire entered the heating flues it literally exploded. By 10 o'clock much of the roof had collapsed and all of the windows had been blown out.

In the meantime, Mankato's volunteer firemen, joined by those from North Mankato, rushed to the scene. They quickly strung out hoses from South Fifth Street hydrants in front of the building while apparently thinking they still had a chance to quell the flames. But, much to their dismay, they found that the water pressure was so weak that spray could not reach the flame tops. So, like the hundreds of spectators who were attracted to the scene, the firemen stood by as the building was reduced to a hollow shell in less than two hours.

No one ever claimed that high water pressure would have saved the building. But the State Teachers College Board implied as much when it condemned the city's lack of preparedness and demanded an upgrade of municipal water conduits.  But, considering the conflagration's explosive spread, it is unlikely that the firemen could have saved the building with fully pressurized hoses. Once they realized the main building was doomed, firemen and some spectators quickly erected asbestos panels between the main building and the nearby training school building. Consequently, except for some relatively minor smoke damage, the training school building was unaffected by the disaster.

Crowd watches as the Mankato State Teachers College building burns in the February 5, 1922 fire.

However, the college-owned house of head custodian Henry S. Holman in back of the main building was so badly damaged that it had to be razed. Since this rent-free residence was part of Holman's compensation, the governing board increased his salary by $50 a month effective February 1, 1922.[17]

Except for those items stored in the vault or salvaged by Nelson, Cooper, Carrington, Morris and several other faculty members, the building's contents, including the library, museum, science laboratories and faculty office holdings, were all destroyed. The only part of the approximate 20,000-volume library that was saved was about 800 checked-out books. Cooper, who had championed the quadrupling of library holdings during his administration, deeply felt the library's misfortune. The museum, which featured Minnesota birds, mammals, fish and geologic specimens, had been an important teaching aid and source of pride since late in the Searing administration. The loss of the science labs was a major drawback when classes were resumed in several unequipped sites. Except for the salvaging of a few typewriters, the contents of all faculty offices were destroyed. George J Miller and Gilbert Trafton, the faculty's most productive scholars, both lost book manuscripts. Since persistence is one of an author's key traits, they both rewrote their studies.[18]

After the fire was over and the jagged exterior wall remnants that reared as high as three stories had been leveled by firemen, Cooper, Carrington and some faculty members determined that the vault's contents had survived. That finding was publicized and was common knowledge in the immediate post-fire days. But somehow over the years, the traditional belief was that everything in the building had been destroyed. For example, 36 years after the fire, this erroneous lore was perpetuated by an article in the *College Reporter*. Readers were assured that the fire had destroyed "all the past records, catalogs, etc."[19] College officials in 1958, including President Clarence L. Crawford, his administrative assistant

Not much of the building remained after the February 5, 1922 fire.

Gretchen S. Morris, and the registrar's office staff, all knew that this statement was patently false, because they were using the vault to store current and retrospective vital records. However, the existence of the vault and its contents was generally unknown in the college community.

The vault's contents were not systematically inventoried until after the Valley Campus was officially closed on November 1, 1979. Since that event coincided with the organization of university archives, the institution's first archivist determined that the vault's contents at the time of the fire included all student records since the normal school's founding in 1868, a file of catalogs since the first one issued in 1878, files of *The Student* and *The Mankatonian*, and other significant records, such as the minutes of the normal school's Prudential Committee, 1868-1873. The fire was certainly a major disaster. But, it would have been far worse if Cooper had not had the foresight to have a vault constructed.

The ashes had not even cooled before Cooper, townspeople and the State Teachers College Board began coping with the immediate need of continuing winter quarter classes and the longer range priority of reconstructing the building. At 3 p.m. the day of the fire, Cooper met with some 100 Mankatoans at an unspecified downtown location to discuss accommodations for continuing classes. They were almost overwhelmed with invitations. The downtown Baptist, Episcopal, Methodist and Presbyterian churches all offered rooms. The North Mankato school wanted to make classroom space available, as did the Mankato school district. Other offers came from Bethany Lutheran College, Loyola School and several mens' clubs, including the Masons and the International Order of Odd Fellows (I. O. O. F.)[20]

Cooper explained to the group that the college needed at least 15 rooms to continue its full schedule. For the winter 1922 term the college was using its then customary schedule of seven 50-minute class times beginning in the morning at 8, 9, 10 and 11 and in the afternoon at 1:30, 2:30 and 3:30.

With only 10 minutes scheduled between most of the class times, Cooper decided it was preferable to conduct classes in a relatively small area. So he chose to use the four churches, Odd Fellows Hall, the Training School/Gymnasium Building and the basement of Cooper Hall. The Mankato public library, located about a block north of the Presbyterian Church, accommodated the college library and the administrative officers including Cooper, Carrington and her accounting assistants were placed in a rented house at 218 South Broad Street, the second place north of the Presbyterian Church.

The initial downtown campus was relatively compact with all five sites being located along Broad and Second streets. The First Presbyterian Church is at the intersection of Broad and Hickory. The Baptist Church at 415 South Broad Street has been converted into the Devine Towers apartment complex. St. John's Episcopal Church at the intersection of Warren and South Broad was gutted by fire on December 6, 1922, and its replacement was built on the same site. On Second Street the Odd Fellows Hall stood at the Jackson Street intersection and the Methodist Church at the southeast corner of Second and Cherry has been replaced by the Centenary United Methodist Church.

The first downtown campus was modified somewhat for the Fall 1922 term when the college decided to use rooms in the Union School at 201 North Broad Street rather than the Episcopal Church. This move had the effect of extending the length of the scattered classrooms space to about half a mile. The records are silent on how students made it from one end to the other in the 10 minutes between classes. But it is probably safe to assume that the various teachers adjusted by shortening their classes on both ends.

Until classes were resumed at the start of the Fall 1923 term in the partially completed new main building, the teachers college got by with makeshift accommodations for part of the winter 1922 Term and the four full terms of spring 1922, fall 1922, winter 1923 and spring 1923. The 1922 and 1923 summer schools were held in the Mankato High School and the Training School/Gymnasium Building. With the exception of the partial winter 1922 term, Cooper prepared printed class schedules.[21]

Naturally, there was great student anxiety about the school's future immediately after the fire. But, Cooper moved quickly to re-assure students that their educations would not be discontinued or even interrupted for a long time. He informed students and faculty by phone and word-of-mouth to meet with him in the Presbyterian Church auditorium at 9 a.m. the day after the fire. At the meeting he informed them that classes would be resumed on Tuesday, the next day, and that they should report to the church's auditorium for their scheduling information. The next morning Cooper was on hand to inform students and faculty of their classroom locations.[22]

The training school/gymnasium building was not structurally damaged by the fire. But Ben E. Bangerter, the Mankato fire chief, forbade its use until he and his men had inspected it thoroughly and razed the potentially dangerous shell of the burned-out main building. They completed both tasks on Monday, February 6, which enabled the training school to resume the next day.[23]

Six days after the fire, the *Mankato Free Press* featured a story titled "Teachers' College Work Progressing Very Fine." According to Cooper the temporary housing arrangements were not only successful, but also "served to cement a closer relationship between students and the faculty than ever before." The paper's conclusion was that "work is going forward without loss of time or quality. Materials have begun to arrive for departments where they are necessary and no student of the Mankato college will suffer in the least from inferior work."[24]

Cooper was determined to show the students, faculty and community that the fire would not prevent scheduled activities. On Monday evening, the day after the blaze, the college's men's basketball team played against the Loyola Stars (apparently an alumni team) in the Loyola gym. A "big crowd" was treated to a game featuring close guarding with the "Peddies" prevailing by scoring three baskets, one more than the Loyola team. The article's writer could not resist the temptation to report that "Phoenixlike, Mankato Teachers' College rose out of the ashes . . . ." The Mankato Teachers College athletic teams were known as the Pedagogues, but sports stories oftentimes described them as simply "Peddies," "Peds" and "Teachers."[25]

The spring 1922, class schedule provides a good description of the scattered "campus." With 17 classes, the Methodist Church was the most-used site. There were also 13 classes in the Presbyterian Church, 10 in the Baptist Church, nine in Odd Fellows Hall, eight in the Training School/Gymnasium, seven in the Episcopal Church and two in the basement of Cooper Hall.

Mankato State Teachers College, Class of Summer 1922. Students and faculty are in front of the training school/gymnasium building. The remains of main building have been removed.

The two Cooper Hall classes were sewing and shop. After one term, sewing was moved to the Presbyterian Church, but Nelson's industrial arts classes remained in Cooper Hall until April 1924, when all classes were finally consolidated in the fully completed new building.[26]

Neither Cooper nor the *Mankato Free Press* ever publicized that the state was paying rent for its off-campus facilities. Consequently, the public was left with the impression that the churches, the Odd Fellows Club and the Mankato school district had simply donated their space gratis. There is no record of the total rent paid from February 1922 through the summer of 1923. But, governing board records show that it paid $70 monthly rent for the house used as the administration building. Furthermore, it budgeted a rental total of $3,450 for the three-month period March, April and May, 1923 and $1,500 for using the Mankato high school in the summer of 1923.[27]

During the first hectic week after the fire, Cooper's most urgent need was to resume classes, but he also began planning with board members to reconstruct the main building. Once he was aware of the disaster's extent, Cooper promptly notified the board's 10 members. Two of them—James H. McConnell (St. Paul) and Clarence L. Atwood (St. Cloud)—hurried to Mankato Sunday night. Both participated in Cooper's Monday morning meeting with students and faculty.[28]

In addressing the group, McConnell, who was then as state superintendent of public instruction an ex-officio board member, was particularly reassuring about the board's support for continuing classes and reconstructing the main building. As a longtime Mankatoan, he was well known to Cooper, most faculty members and many townspeople.

McConnell had moved to Mankato in 1904 when he was appointed superintendent of schools. He left that position five years later when he was employed to teach history and government at the Mankato Normal School. After a decade on the faculty he was named state superintendent of instruction by Governor Joseph A. A. Burnquist.[29]

## Teachers' College Work Progressing Very Fine

### Trial of Temporary Housing Quarters Has Proved Quite Successful

One weeks' trial of temporary housing quarters for the Mankato State Teachers' college has proven successful in every way and has served to cement a closer relationship between students and faculty than ever before, according to a statement made today by President C. H. Cooper. Student morale is at the peak at this time and there is a spirit of cooperation tending to make the best of all improvised conditions since the disastrous fire last Sunday which robbed students of their school home.

President Cooper expressed himself as very much pleased with the spirit shown by his students in face of the calamity of week ago. They have shown a great deal of self reliance in acclimating themselves to the new conditions and have adapted themselves quickly to the new order of events.

Work is going forward without loss of time or quality. Materials have begun to arrive for departments where they are necessary and no student of the Mankato college will suffer in the least from inferior work.

*Mankato Free Press* 11 February 1922

After four more board members arrived on the Monday noon trains, the board held an emergency meeting with Cooper that afternoon in the Masonic Temple. The meeting also included C. R. Butler, the spokesman for the Mankato Citizens Committee that had been formed to aid the college, and E. F. Nelson of the state architect's office. In addition to representing the community, Butler was substituting for Isaac N. Tompkins, the resident Mankato board director who could not attend because he was seriously ill.[30]

After getting Cooper's report about his college's loss, the board unanimously agreed on plans to continue classes and to rebuild the main building. The members first resolved that the board's officers ask the State Board of Control to determine the loss amount preparatory to requesting that the state treasurer transfer that sum from the State Insurance Fund for the purpose of "rebuilding and restoring the property damaged." Secondly, the board authorized Cooper and resident director Tompkins to arrange for all temporary accommodations needed to continue college operations. Lastly, the board decided to hire Mankato contractor J. B. Carlstrom to prepare an estimate of the college's loss.[31]

By the time the board met next at St. Paul on February 15, its members had been made aware that the State Insurance Fund was much too small to cover the entire Mankato State Teachers College loss. After consulting with state architect Clarence H. Johnston, the board knew that the estimated cost or reconstructing the Mankato State building would be more than $500,000. Board members initially assumed that expense would be covered by the State Insurance Fund. With the exception of the state prison at Stillwater, the state self-insured all its buildings. The legislature had created an insurance fund in 1913, but had only sparingly funded it. Immediately after the Mankato State fire, the fund amounted to $255,462.18. State law required the legislature to appropriate any additional funds needed to reconstruct a state building.[32]

Board members knew that they could use the insurance fund, but they also knew that no additional appropriation could be made until the legislature's 1923 session. So throughout the board's planning with Johnston,

Architectural rendering of new Mankato State Teachers College building. 1923 *Katonian*

its members realized that Mankato State's new building would have to be constructed in stages. When he met with the board on February 15, 1922, Johnston presented preliminary building plans. At that and later meetings, he conceptualized that the destroyed building would be reconstructed in four phases: south wing, central core (the so-called T section), auditorium (behind the T section) and north wing. Consequently, the board and the State Board of Control decided to construct the south wing and T section first with insurance fund money. Building on the other two sections could not be started until the legislature appropriated additional funding.[33]

With the aim of starting partial rebuilding in 1922, the board on March 16 appointed a four-member committee, which included resident director Tompkins, to work with Johnston on finalizing reconstruction plans. On June 20 Tompkins reported that Johnston expected to have the plans ready to receive bids on the south wing and central sections by July 15. Accordingly, after the competitive bidding procedure, the J. R. Nelsen Company of Mankato was awarded the general construction contracts. Mankato's Cuddy Plumbing & Heating Company got the contract for heating, plumbing and ventilating. The electric lighting contract went to the Langford Electric Company of Minneapolis and A. A. Zimmerman (Mankato) obtained the roofing and sheet metal contract. The Nelsen Company began working on September 20, 1922.[34]

Meanwhile, the board moved to resolve its grievances with the City of Mankato. On April 11, it proclaimed that the water pressure during the fire was "wholly inadequate." Therefore, it requested and recommended "that the City Council of the City of Mankato take immediate steps to have new and sufficient water mains connected and laid on Fifth Street . . . to furnish an ample supply of water and pressure for fire protection purposes at the location named in this resolution."[35]

While the board was planning to request additional funding for its Mankato project from the legislature, it was surprised by a new crisis in the teachers college system. On Sunday, December 3, 1922, a fire at Winona State completely destroyed its main building and heating plant and ruined the roof of its library building. Attempts to quell the blaze resulted in water damage to many library

Construction of new building. 1923 *Katonian*

Front entrance of Old Main, late 1960s. The "M" engravings and the Dunce and Scholar corbels can be seen above the third floor windows.

The dunce, holding a tablet with 2+2=5.

The scholar, with a quill and tablet.

books, which had to be salvaged.[36]

Because of the Winona crisis, the board increased its building appropriations request to the legislature. The lawmakers acted promptly to fund rebuilding on the Mankato and Winona campuses. On March 13, 1923, Governor Jacob A. O. Preus approved the measure that appropriated a total of $1,287,000 for the two colleges. Mankato State's portion of $655,100 consisted of $233,000 to the state treasury to restore the amount it had advanced out of the State Insurance Fund, $362,000 to complete the building and $60,000 to equip it.[37]

By the time Mankato State acquired the additional state funding, the Nelsen Company had completed the exterior walls of both the south wing and central core sections.[38]

The legislative appropriation removed any uncertainty about completing the building in a timely manner. The Nelsen Company and most of the other original contractors were engaged to finish the project. The only change for the last two sections was the replacement of A. A. Zimmerman as the roofing and sheet metal contractor by the Schwickert Hardware Company of Mankato.[39]

The Nelsen Company, which had to its credit such Mankato buildings as Mankato State's training school/gymnasium, Good Counsel Academy, Bethany Lutheran College and the Mankato Commercial College, was equipped to work rapidly. Its on-site labor saving machinery consisted of a large steam shovel, a stone crusher, three concrete mixers and an electric saw. The steam shovel greatly facilitated the removal of the old building's foundation, which was then ground and used as a component in making concrete. In addition to the thousands of bricks and tons of local Kasota stone used in the construction, the company used an estimated 17,000 board feet of lumber for supporting the concrete work on the south and central portions. This was later removed and re-used on the last two sections. The construction scene, where workers were notified of shift times by an electric horn, presented an interesting admixture of new and old technologies. Deliveries of building materials to the site reportedly kept two trucks and many horse-drawn wagons "busy every day."

With Mankato architect Albert Schippel serving as project supervisor for the State Board of Control, building construction was accelerated after the state appropriation. Cooper was pleased with the opening of the south and central sections on September 1, 1923, in time for fall classes. But, this occupation of one-half of the building proved to be a mixed blessing, because of the noisy construction on the auditorium and north wing portions. The auditorium, to the rear of the central core, was completed in January 1924 and the entire building, except for some interior finishing, was declared to be finished three months later.[40]

Cooper and all others involved in the project agreed that the new brick and Kasota stone structure was a vast improvement over its predecessor. It was fireproof and esthetically pleasing. Basically, it was a three-story building, but there was a small fourth story above the building's front center. This "tower" section featured two copper domed towers that accented the building's broad central entrance. The base of each tower, inline with the top of the third story, featured a large M etched from Kasota stone. The letters, which were noticeable from Fifth Street, symbolized Mankato State Teachers College.

While the meaning of the letters was self-evident, the building's main front entrance had the odd and mysterious feature of two corbels placed just above the third-story windows. Carved from Kasota stone, each corbel, which has remained in its original position, featured what a contemporary newspaper reporter identified as a "grotesque" figure. This judgment is understandable. From ground level, any bare-eyed observer would have been able to see the gargoyle-like faces, but not discern that they were actually representations of the dunce and the scholar. The dunce, who appeared to be drowsing, was holding a tablet on which the addition of 2 and 2 totaled 5. In contrast, the bright-eyed scholar, equipped with a quill and tablet, was apparently writing something momentous.[41]

Other than the newspaper comment about the grotesque images, no one else associated with the building's dedication mentioned the corbels. But, in 1939, Anders Anderson, a curious Mankato artist, etched the two images from photographs he had obtained from the Breen Stone and Marble Company, the installer of the corbels.[42]

Over the years it is unlikely that any more than a handful of the thousands of people who went through the main entrance ever noticed the corbels. Likewise, their planners obviously wanted to remain anonymous. So, the origin of the dunce and the scholar representations became a campus mystery. But, it is clear that the carvings were not casually installed. Cooper, state architect Carlstrom and the building contractor must have been involved in their planning and installation. But none of them apparently ever explained the symbolic meaning of the images. So like many art objects, their meaning is in the eye of the beholder. Perhaps the dunce represented the uneducable who were doomed to a life of ignorance and the scholar symbolized those who benefitted from education.

The new building's most striking interior feature was a second-floor 818-seat auditorium, which Cooper and others proclaimed to be an acoustical marvel. As the subsequent location of numerous assembly programs and public events, it became a key in developing a college culture.

Cooper arranged a rather elaborate public ceremony to mark the building's completion. On the afternoon of April 8, 1924, the auditorium was filled to hear Cooper and four other speakers extol the college's accomplishments. Stage guests included the other five state teachers college presidents, members of the governing board and three legislators. The event was sort of a homecoming for former Mankato Normal faculty members James H. McConnell, Eugene W. Bohannon, president of Duluth State Teachers College, and Manfred W. Deputy, president of Bemidji State Teachers College.

Cooper presided and gave the opening talk. In his customary gracious manner, he first thanked the faculty and students for their forbearance during the crisis. In praising general contractor Nelsen, Cooper noted that the new building was exactly what the college needed. Because of its fine construction, he observed: "The splendid structure has the strength of the pyramids of old and should stand against fire and other elements for a thousand years."[43]

The other speakers—McConnell, Melvin F. Haggerty, dean of the College of Education at the University of Minnesota, Julius Borras, president of both St. Olaf College and the State Board of Education, and Judge Ell Torrance of Minneapolis, who had served as president of the State Normal School Board, 1907-1920—all stressed the importance of Mankato State in carrying out Minnesota's educational mission.

The 1922 fire and the rapid construction of a new main building were the most newsworthy events in the lower campus phase of Minnesota State University, Mankato's history. The building served the institution for 57 years after the fire. In 1979, when the valley campus was vacated, there were still faculty members who had become aware of the fire because they had become acquainted with people who had experienced it. Therefore, it was perfectly natural for the fire to become deeply embedded in the institution's oral tradition. Naturally, some aspects were magnified in the numerous retellings. As long as 40 years after the fire, it seemed that any library deficiency was explained away as: "We used to have that book, but it was destroyed in the fire."

## Development of the Degree Program

The Minnesota legislature's authorization of six teachers colleges that were empowered to offer a bachelor's degree is a classic case of putting the cart before the horse. In 1921 the newly formed colleges were not ready to offer degree programs and there was no noticeable student demand for them.

After the teachers colleges were created, Cooper and the other five presidents were far more eager to develop a four-year curriculum than the governing board. Their sharp differences were evident at the board meeting of January 10, 1922. Cooper, speaking for the presidents, "presented resolutions asking the Board to provide for the introduction, in all of the colleges, of a four year course, and the granting of a degree . . . ." In the ensuing prolonged discussion, board members expressed two major reservations—the main purpose of the colleges should be teacher preparation for rural schools, which did not require degree-holding teachers, and "the limited teaching force and equipment now available in the different schools." These shortcomings, in the board's judgment, showed that the colleges were not ready to offer degree programs. Consequently, as a sop to the presidents the board authorized them "to insert in the forthcoming catalogs an announcement that the four-year course of study leading to the degree, 'Bachelor of Arts in Education,' will be offered when the demand therefor [sic] and the resources of the Colleges may justify it."[44]

After the board's rejection, the presidents took a very long pause of more than three years. Finally, on March 26, 1925, Cooper—again acting as spokesman for his peers—presented a four-year course of study to the board and recommended its adoption. The board's response was to defer action to its next meeting.[45]

On May 5, 1925, Cooper, with the endorsement of the other presidents, proposed a "provisional" four-year course to the board. The board's first reaction was to approve a four-year course in elementary education that would lead to a "Bachelor of Education" degree. But the board qualified that permission by stipulating: "That the four-year course shall be undertaken in any college only as the demand for such course is apparent and as the facilities of the College may permit without loss to the work of the two-year course . . . ." The board next approved a "Temporary Four Year Curriculum," which required course work in five categories—Education, Science and Mathematics, Geography and Social Science, Language and Literature and Arts and Expression.[46]

Lastly, for the first time in the history of the teachers colleges and their preceding normal schools, the term "quarter hours" was used. A student had to complete 192 quarter hours to earn a degree. This total resulted from 12 quarters of courses at the regular student load of 16 credits per term. Prior to the beginning of the quarter-hour system, the schools had all used the standard high school system of requiring the completion of designated courses identified as units.

After it became a teachers college, Mankato State continued the normal school practice of assigning letter grades A, B, C, D and E. In this system E denoted failure. Beginning with students who entered after the 1925-1926 school year, the college used a 3.0 grade point average system. It was concisely described in the 1926-1927 catalog: "For each quarter-hour of credit of A quality, a student will be given three honor points; of B quality, two honor points; of C quality, one honor point. For D quality no honor points will be given, and for each quarter-hour of work of E quality, one honor point will be deducted." In order to graduate or obtain teacher certification a student had to have a minimum 1.0 grade point average.[47]

The *Mankato State Teachers College Catalog* for 1925-1926 was published before the board's action, so Cooper could not use his best way of advertising the degree. But he did advise certain students of this development. At least one of them, Valentine H. Aurit of Mankato, decided to pursue the degree program, which was open to anyone who had completed the two-year course requirements. Aurit, the 20-year-old grandson of a German immigrant farmer, holds the unique distinction of being the first degree graduate of the Mankato college. In the commencement exercises of June 2, 1927, he was awarded his Bachelor of Education degree.

This distinction made him a campus celebrity. The uniqueness of his feat was demonstrated during the next several years. No one earned a degree during the 1927-28 year and two were awarded the next year. For the academic year 1929-30 there were three degree earners compared with 236 who completed the two-year course.[48]

Three years after he graduated, Aurit was sought out by the yearbook's editors, who asked him to write a memoir of his Mankato State Teachers College experience. His brief comments provide some useful insight into college life from a student perspective.

## Development of the Four-Year Course Program

The board's provisional four-year program, which it had adopted on May 5, 1925, was superseded by a permanent one after four years. In 1928, when the presidents and board members were considering the final degree program, they made a significant change in the teachers colleges' mission.  Originally the colleges continued the normal school goal of preparing teachers for elementary schools.

But at the instigation of James H. McConnell, the board on December 4, 1928, agreed that the education of high school teachers should be included in the four-year program's purpose. The board described the scope of the program thusly: "Four year courses may be offered for the preparation of teachers in one or more of the following fields: (a) Elementary Schools; (b) Junior High Schools; (c) Senior or Four Year High Schools; (d) Junior-Senior High School organizations; (e) Special Subject Fields—Music, Fine Arts, Physical Education, Industrial Arts, Commercial Subjects, Home Economics or Special Classes for Defectives." [50]

The board agreed on the precise nature of the Bachelor of Education degree program on May 10, 1929. The 192-quarter credits program had three major components—constants (i. e. general education), majors and minors and electives. The 24 constant courses of 4-credit hours each, which totaled exactly half of the degree requirements, were required of all students. The constant courses consisted of nine in Education, five in English, four in Science, four in Social Sciences, one in Mathematics and one in Physical Education. After the constants each student had to complete two majors of at least 20 credits each and a minor of at least 12 credits. Electives consisted of courses other than constants, majors and minors that were needed to complete 192 credit hours.[51]

Majors and minors were available in the general fields of Education, English, Social Science, Science, Mathematics and Foreign Language and the special fields of Music, Fine Arts, Industrial Arts and Physical Education.

With its action of May 10, 1929, the board significantly agreed that the eight-year-old colleges could at last offer permanent four-year programs. So, on paper, at least, the colleges had programs that could fulfill the promise of their status as institutions of higher learning.  But, it took approximately a decade at the Mankato State Teachers College before the number of four-year degree graduates roughly equaled those who completed the two-year diploma program. For the academic year 1938-39, the college granted 106 degrees and 116 diplomas.[52]

## The End of the Cooper Era

The establishment of the permanent four-year program was the capstone experience of President Cooper's long career. On April 8, 1930, his resignation letter was read at a meeting of the State Teachers College Board. Cooper wrote, in part: "At the end of the College year, I shall have reached the age of seventy-five years. Recognizing the fact that men of that age are expected to retire from positions of leadership and special responsibility, I hereby withdraw my name from your consideration in the election of a President for the Mankato Teachers College."[53]

In addition to profusely thanking Cooper for his long, distinguished presidential career, the

## The First Degree Student

When I first came to Teachers College in the Fall of 1924, the new building was still under construction, and it was only with much difficulty that classes were held in the midst of disorder and noise. There was an enrollment of about five hundred of which only about twenty were men.

I remember well how I went out for football and climbed the steep hill behind the college every night for practice. I was well rewarded for that sacrifice for in spite of some great competition (twenty men reported) I made the second team.

Valentine Aurit,
1927 *Katonian*

I struggled, just as hundreds of other students have struggled through the first and second year, and then decided to complete the work prescribed by the state board, for a degree of Bachelor of Education. I happened to be the only one, and incidentally, the first one, to be granted a degree from the Mankato State Teachers College.

To organize that graduating class was a big task. No one could be found in it who was honest enough to collect the dues and when I was unanimously elected as treasurer, all the members of the class were broke. I finally collected all the money, but instead of using it to buy a memorial to leave to the college I bought some crackers and milk, and Mr. Petterson, the faculty advisor for the class, joined it in a banquet.

I was one of the first members of the Coterie club. I helped to organize it, and watched it grow with a small society with little or no influence in college to a large club, with much responsibility.

I have always valued my Degree from the Mankato State Teachers College very highly. It has been accepted and respected wherever I have gone. At the present time I am teaching mechanical drawing, with a first grade Indiana State High School license, in the Horace Mann School, which is one of the most successful schools in the world famous Gary School System.

I attribute my success in my three years of teaching experience to the splendid combination of scientific theories, and their practical application in education, which I received in the Mankato State Teachers College.

VAL H. AURIT
Gary, Indiana
(Copied verbatim from The 1930 *Katonian*, 108.)

Explanatory comments: The dues Aurit mentioned were donated by members of each graduating class and were used to purchase a class gift for the college. This practice dated to the Searing administration. Aurit's "Mr. Petterson" was Gustav S. Petterson, the college's sociology instructor, who joined the faculty in 1913. The Coterie Club of student and faculty men dedicated to promoting good fellowship among its members and sponsoring programs on contemporary issues. (*Mankato State Teachers College Catalog*, 1926-1927, 27). Aurit had a long career in the Gary, Indiana school system. He died in Coral Gables, Florida on April 22, 1987.[49]

board designated him "president emeritus" and appointed him to the Mankato State Teachers College faculty at an annual salary of $2,400. His duties were to be determined by his successor. When the board decided on Cooper's emeritus reimbursement, it also decided that all of the six presidents in the system would be paid $5,500 for their 12-month appointments.

Cooper was a widower by the time he resigned. On February 10, 1929, his wife died suddenly of a heart attack. The former Caroline Wheeler, one of the first graduates of Wellesley College (Holyoke, Massachusetts), married Cooper in 1883 when he was teaching at Dartmouth College. At the Mankato Normal/Teachers College she graciously complemented her husband's role. Over the course of three decades faculty and students alike tended to regard them as the institution's father and mother figures. They actively participated in the school's social and cultural affairs and after World War I were particularly well-known for presiding at the annual Washington's Birthday Ball (sometimes called the Colonial Ball.)[54]

Like her husband, Caroline Cooper was deeply involved in community affairs. She and Mr. Cooper actively participated in Presbyterian Church affairs. For a time, she served as president of the church's missionary society. At various times she was also the president of the Art History Club and the Mankato chapters of the Daughters of the American Revolution and Association of University Women. The *Mankato Free Press* obituary eulogized: "Mrs. Cooper's charm of personality, quaint humor and cultural background, made her a valued member of the community, who will be much missed in home, church and club circles."

Cooper had informed the faculty of his decision to resign before the board received his letter. They and a number of former faculty members, like Cooper's fellow presidents and numerous alumni, seized on the development to show their appreciation for his role in developing the college.

The faculty honored Cooper at a farewell dinner in Daniel Buck Hall on May 12. The organizers sent invitations to all current and former faculty who had served with Cooper. Miss Alice V. Robbins, a mathematics instructor and senior faculty member who had started at the normal school in 1894, presided over the affair. The program featured a talk by Manfred W. Deputy, president of Bemidji State Teachers College, who had directed Mankato State's training school, 1911-1916. Deputy was reported to have "voiced the general feeling when he spoke in glowing terms of the scholarship, culture, high ideals, uprightness and kindliness which make President Cooper a man to whom his associates delight to pay loyal and loving tribute."[55]

History instructor Albert B. Morris presented Cooper two gifts from the faculty—a reading lamp and cash for the purchase of an easy chair. Cooper's response was reported to be "in keeping with his happy faculty of always saying just the right thing."

*School Spirit,* the weekly student newspaper, solicited reactions from college presidents who had worked with Cooper in various capacities. Under the caption "College Presidents Pay Tribute to President Cooper's Great Work," the paper published tributes from three of Cooper's Minnesota peers—Manfred W. Deputy (Bemidji State), Guy E. Maxwell (Winona State) and George A. Selke (St. Cloud State). The Minnesota presidents were particularly familiar with Cooper's role in improving the state's teachers colleges. But some of the out-of-state presidents, such as Charles McKenny of Western Michigan, praised another dimension of Cooper. McKenny thought that Cooper had "made a distinct contribution to the history of the teachers college movement" when he served as secretary of the National Council of Normal School Presidents and Principals.[56]

After retiring, Cooper as "president emeritus" served on the Mankato State faculty until his death on September 12, 1934. His duties included heading the Placement Bureau and teaching either a government or history class during most terms. In 1931 President McElroy established a Bureau of Recommendations, which he soon renamed the Placement Bureau. Its main function was to collect and maintain information on candidates for faculty positions.[57]

Cooper's sudden death of a heart attack shocked the campus and the community. He was apparently in good health and had worked at the college until a few hours before he expired. His tendency to regard the faculty as an extended family was evident in his funeral arrangements. His six active pallbearers—Albert B.

Morris, Carlyn P. Blakeslee, George J Miller, Marvin A. Nichols, Gustav S. Petterson and Otto Welton Snarr—were all recruited by him to join the Mankato State faculty. Two of his other recruits, music instructor Alexis Parlova and Gilbert H. Trafton, along with President McElroy, served as honorary pallbearers.[58]

Snarr led the way in organizing a final tribute to Cooper. As the editor of *School Progress,* a journal published four times a year since its inception in 1919, Snarr devoted the entire January 1935, "Memorial Issue" to Cooper's career. Snarr's personal contribution was the essay "President Cooper—The Truly Educated Man." Harriet M. Beale, an English instructor, wrote on "The Early Life of Mr. Cooper." Anna M. Wiecking, a Mankato Normal School graduate who was then Mankato State's elementary school principal, authored "Educational Changes During President Cooper's Administration," and Alice V. Robbins penned "Messages From Distant Friends," a collection of tributes she had solicited from former faculty, alumni and educators who had worked with Cooper. This *School Progress* issue remains as the best single source of information about Cooper.

## The Beginning of the McElroy Presidency

On August 18, 1930, the State Teachers College Board unanimously elected Frank D. McElroy (pronounced mac-el-roy) president of the Mankato State Teachers College. His appointment was effective at the beginning of the next month at an annual salary of $5,500, the same as all other Minnesota teachers college presidents.[59]

The board was obviously impressed with McElroy's experience in public education. The 52-year-old educator was born on February 28, 1878, in Putnam County, Indiana. He lived there for 20 years before moving to Terre Haute, Indiana, to attend its state normal school part-time and teach at a local school. In 1906, two years after completing his normal school course, he earned his bachelor's degree from Wabash College. Subsequently, he was employed as a school principal in Crawfordsville and Hammond, Indiana, and as an assistant superintendent in Rockford, Illinois and Akron, Ohio.[60]

During the Indiana phase of his career, McElroy actively participated in educational matters. He was state commissioner for vocational and agricultural education for two years and also served on the state's textbook commission and an advisory committee to the Indiana education commissioner.

From 1925 to 1929 he was the personnel supervisor for the Cleveland, Ohio school system. While thus employed he earned a master's degree from Western Reserve University in 1926.

McElroy resigned from his Cleveland position to work on a Ph.D. degree at Ohio State University. He was proceeding with his degree work when he was hired to lead Mankato State Teachers College. At that time the *Mankato Free Press* reported he would complete his doctorate in September 1930. But he did not do so until 1939 when he gained the distinction of becoming the first president of the Mankato Normal School/Teachers College to have earned a doctoral degree.

## Campus Expansion during the McElroy Administration

Approximately two-thirds of McElroy's administration coincided with the Great Depression that had been tripped off by the Wall Street stock market crash in October 1929. But, despite the hard times, the Mankato State Teachers College was enlarged significantly. The major construction projects were an athletic field and an adjacent field house. These additions led to the landscaping of Hanover Hill, which loomed above the new facilities and the partial remodeling of the training school building.

Planning for an on-campus athletic field was started late in the Cooper administration. Cooper and Blakeslee, who then coached all sports, as well as the athletes and students, were all displeased with the inconvenience of using Lewis Field. About a mile from campus, the field was located on Hubbell Avenue three blocks east of Sibley Park. Lewis Field, which appears on a Mankato map published in a 1910, was also used by the Mankato High School and the YMCA.[61]

In 1928 Cooper persuaded the State Teachers College Board to request a $70,000 legislative appropriation to acquire land bordering the south edge of the campus. In its education appropriations act of April 23, 1929, the legislature fully funded the requested amount.[62]

The proposed athletic field site—between the main building/training school/heating plant cluster and Glenwood Avenue—had some vacant lots as well as 10 houses. From September 14-December 30, 1929, the state purchased the land by seventeen transactions at a total cost of $65,571. With the exception of a two-story brick block building at the corner of Glenwood and South Fifth and four adjacent frame houses, the northern, eastern, southern and western boundaries of the acquired land were respectively the campus buildings, Hanover Hill, Glenwood Avenue and Fifth Street. The problems in acquiring the athletic field tract caused college and state officials to recognize that the institution was literally hemmed in by geography and residential development. With steep Hanover Hill to its rear and a residential area to its front, any more campus growth seemed to be impossible.[63]

After the land was obtained, the governing board moved to the next phase of requesting the legislature to approve funding for grading and improving the field, which entailed razing the purchased homes. On April 25, 1931, the lawmakers appropriated $20,000 for that purpose.[64]

Writers of the student newspaper *School Spirit* were elated by the development. They profusely thanked Gustaf Widell, a Mankato contractor, who was then serving as a state senator, for his key role in shepherding the appropriation through the legislation. As the paper saw it, "our ugly duckling is headed for swanhood—in other and more explicit terms, the junk heap beside the training school is to become a full grown athletic field."[65]

Once the appropriation had been made, McElroy proceeded with planning the athletic field. By early May 1931, he announced that the plans had been completed. They called for the construction of a lighted football field surrounded by a quarter-mile cinder track; the entire facility was to be enclosed with steel cyclone fencing. Lack of space on the campus and Glenwood Avenue sides of the field meant the roofed, concrete stands had to be placed near the western end zone along South Fifth Street.[66]

Initially, McElroy hoped that the field would be ready by late in the 1931 football season. But construction was delayed by the need to level the field by bringing in dirt to fill some low places and the re-routing of Glenwood Creek into an underground conduit.

The inaugural use of the field was a football game between the Peds and Stout Institute of Menominee, Wisconsin, on September 24, 1932. Many spectators must have been disappointed in the defensive struggle that ended in a scoreless tie. But the day's big story was the lighted field, not the game.

The floodlights, which were funded "by the aid of various organizations and individuals connected with the school" were proclaimed to be "superior to any field using floodlights in this section of the state including the Gustavus Adolphus field." There were five light towers on either side of the field. Each of the 10 towers had a cluster of four lights. The lights also made night tennis possible on the new court adjacent to the field.[67]

*School Progress*, January 1935

President Frank D. McElroy,
circa 1940

The track surrounding the football field was first used in the spring of 1933. The season's first scheduled event was a dual meet between the Peds and Gustavus Adolphus.[68]

The athletic field was dedicated on October 6, 1933 as part of homecoming, which also featured a football game between the Peds and Bemidji State and a dance in the college library. Governor Floyd B. Olson, the state's first Farmer-Labor Party chief executive, participated in the dedication ceremony and congratulated the college for its latest accomplishment.[69]

The athletic field was a boon to such sports as football and outdoor track. But basketball and the other indoor sports were handicapped by the small gym in the training school building. McElroy, who wanted to promote both varsity and intramural athletics, sought community assistance to improve indoor facilities by remodeling and adding to the training school building. With that goal in mind, selected community leaders organized a committee whose goal was to seek state funding. The committee that led lobbying efforts with legislators included bankers William Dodsworth Willard and Fred Buscher. Other members were Dr. Frank A. Baker, resident State Teachers College Board member for Blue Earth County, state Senator Val Imm, C. Nachbar, a former Mankato State student and president of the Mankato Chamber of Commerce, Edward Nyguist, the chamber's secretary, and J. A. Callahan, publisher of the *Mankato Free Press*.[70]

During its initial meetings the committee decided to seek state funding for a new physical education building rather than asking to enlarge and remodel the training school building. With the support of the State Teachers College Board, the group successfully lobbied the 1937 state legislature.

On April 24, 1937, the legislature in its appropriations act for educational institutions designated $240,000 "to construct an additional building" on the Mankato State campus. Planning of the building was to be done by the state Commission of Administration and Finance in consultation with the State Teachers College Board. The commission, which had been created by the 1925 legislature, succeeded the State Board of Control as the construction supervisor of all state buildings except those of the University of Minnesota.[71]

Foss and Company, an architectural and engineering firm, was engaged by the Commission of Administration and Finance to design the field house. Before the State Teachers College Board meeting of September 14, 1937, E. R. Boyd of the Foss firm had visited the campus for two days to inspect and survey the proposed building site between the training school and Hanover Hill. The building was to face the athletic field and Glenwood Avenue and to incorporate the college heating plant. When Boyd and M. O. Foss presented their preliminary building sketch to the board, they evidently pointed out a potentially major problem with the site. They proposed to place the west end of the new facility about 47 feet from the training school, which meant that its east end, 232 feet distant, would be within a few feet of a 40-foot-high dirt cliff that was the lower edge of Hanover Hill. Board members agreed that the site was the only one available on campus land. But, they also recognized the threat of soil erosion from the cliff, which was privately owned by various parties.[72]

As Foss and Company was evaluating the field house site, McElroy and resident board director Frank A. Baker wanted to expand the campus to hilltop land near Buck and Cooper halls. They secured a 90-day option on a 54-acre tract bounded by present-day Highland Avenue, Val Imm Drive, Ellis Avenue

## Gilbert H. Trafton: Scientist

Gilbert H. Trafton (January 9, 1874-October 31, 1943), who taught nature study and its successor biology at the Mankato State Normal School and Mankato State Teachers College, 1911-1943, became nationally famed because of his prolific writing. Over a span of four decades he wrote 11 books and co-authored 10 more.

Gilbert H. Trafton,
1936 *Katonian*

Trafton began writing before Cooper recruited him for the Mankato Normal School faculty in 1911. A native of South Elliott, Maine, and a holder of masters' degrees from Wesleyan University in Connecticut and Columbia University (New York City), Trafton wrote *Laboratory and Field Exercises in Physical Geography* (Boston: Ginn & Co., 1905) and co-authored *Methods of Attracting Birds* (Boston: Houghton Mifflin Co., 1910) while teaching science in the Passaic, New Jersey, school system.

Cooper was particularly interested in hiring Trafton because the Mankato Normal School was then starting to place more emphasis on rural education, including scientific agriculture. As a graduate student Trafton had studied and written on the environmental interrelationships of agriculture and nature. When Trafton joined the Mankato Normal faculty, Cooper noted: "He is highly commended by many men of high authority and promises to be a valuable acquisition to the practical scientific workers of Minnesota."

After one year, Cooper observed that Trafton was "an enthusiastic and practical teacher and is developing much enthusiasm for his work among the students." That judgment was seconded by a feature article on Trafton in *M. S. N. Annual 1916*, the senior yearbook. The student writer commended Trafton for putting "zeal and energy into his work" and for using "an unlimited store of interesting methods and devices for teaching, not only his own subject, but anything related to it. It is not at all unusual to see Mr. Trafton come to class with a complete garden cultivator outfit, a bee-hive, a dozen bird houses, and a trap nest, under his arms."

Trafton obviously saw research and writing as an essential tool in extending education beyond his classes. Most of his books were elementary and secondary level texts. All were commercially published and thus assured of wide circulation. Some of them went through several editions, which indicates there was a consistent school demand for them.

Trafton's authored and co-authored textbooks could best be classified as "general science" in elementary schools. But he also wrote about more specialized topics including ornithology and astronomy. *His Bird Friends: A Complete Book for Americans* (Boston: Houghton Mifflin Co., 1916) had particular appeal for lay audiences.

His amazing productivity over his career evidences Trafton's commitment to writing. His first book was published in 1905 and in 1942 with Victor C. Smith (Department of General Science, Ramsey Junior High School, Minneapolis) as lead author, he co-wrote his last three books—*Exploring Science, Enjoying Science and Using Science*. They were published commercially by Lippincott.

Trafton did not work in an environment where writing was an institutional expectation of faculty members. Consequently, he researched and wrote without benefit of financial support, reduced teaching loads or salary increases. Over the years, he must have scheduled his writing in the same way one would follow a class or work schedule.

Because of his declining health, Trafton retired at the end of the 1942-1943 academic year. After his death in Mankato on October 31, 1943, his Teachers College colleagues perpetuated his memory. This tradition helped cause the new science building on the Highland Campus to be named in his honor. (Trafton, Gilbert H., World Cat Discovery bibliographical search; Cooper, Charles H., Annual reports for 1911-1912 and 1912-1913, Minnesota State University, Mankato Archives; *M. S. N. Annual 1916*; *Mankato Free Press*, 01 November 1943, 5; Trafton, Gilbert H. file, Minnesota State University, Mankato Archives.)

and Haynes Avenue. This parcel would have extended to the north end of the vee formed by Highland Avenue and Val Imm Drive. Its only overlapping with the current Highland Campus would have been the Wiecking Hall site and its adjoining parking lots.[73]

McElroy and Baker thought the land, which was then owned by the American State Bank, would be a good site to develop two athletic fields — one for men and the other for women. If this was done, they believed the existing campus field could be used as a practice facility.

But McElroy's vision for the college's future extended far beyond additional athletic fields. He was already considering the possibility of relocating the entire campus to the hilltop. He complained that the severely cramped valley campus could be expanded only at the great expense of acquiring adjacent residential areas. Therefore, McElroy opined that perhaps the entire campus should be relocated to the hilltop. The *Mankato Free Press* quoted him as having said: "If there is any way of disposing of the present property I will be glad to see it done as soon as possible."

The McElroy-Baker hilltop campus scheme was undone by the age-old problem of insufficient funding. Any additional land purchase would have to have been done out of the $240,000 appropriated by the last legislature. But the board had a more pressing priority.

When the board re-visited the field house site question several months later it decided that it was necessary for the college to acquire Hanover Hill and grade it down to remove the erosion threat. Therefore, McElroy and resident director Baker were instructed to proceed with purchasing the seven lots on the Hanover Hill slope. In a series of transactions ranging from May 10 to November 10, 1937, the state purchased the lots at a total cost of $3,311.43.[74]

After completing the building plans, Boyd and Foss spent two days on campus in late January 1938, to confer with McElroy and athletic department faculty about the building's interior layout. At that time, the designers expected their plans to be completed by March 1, which would enable the competitive bidding for the construction project to begin soon after. The State Teachers College Board approved the final plans and specifications on March 8, 1938.[75]

During the design stage, it became evident that the state appropriation would cover only approximately half of the building's projected cost. McElroy and the Mankato committee decided to apply for a Public Works Administration (PWA) matching grant. The initial PWA grant, which was made in August 1938, was for $199,514. But during the field house construction it was supplemented somewhat, which brought the total PWA funding to $211,886.94. When completed, the field house and its furnishings cost a total of $451,886.94.[76]

The PWA, one of the many so-called alphabet agencies created during President Franklin D. Roosevelt's New Deal Program should not be confused with the Works Project Administration (WPA). Both were designed to

New athletic field, 1933 *Katonian*

stimulate the economy. But, the PWA's realm was large construction projects such as public buildings and dams, whereas the WPA's main purpose was to provide employment for manual laborers as well as such white collar types as teachers and artists. Since the PWA was popularly lampooned to stand for "poppa's working again," many people erroneously associated it with such small scale WPA projects as laying municipal sidewalks.

Once he knew construction would be commenced in late October 1938, McElroy arranged an elaborate groundbreaking ceremony. It was held on October 7 to coincide with the 70th anniversary of the normal school's opening classes.[77]

The ceremony began at 4 p.m. Friday on the future building's site, which was then the training school's playground. The college band, followed by the choir bedecked in purple and gold robes and the student body, marched from their assembly point on South Fifth Street in front of the main building to the site via the athletic field.

McElroy presided at the program, replete with a symbolic groundbreaking, which featured short talks by Otto Welton Snarr on behalf of the faculty, Adeline Schaus, alumni association president, Wayne Anderson, senior class president, Kenneth M. Krost, a state representative when the initial appropriation was made and C. A. Nachbar, a member of the local committee that led the effort to obtain the PWA grant.

Platform guests included state senator Val Imm, state representative George Champlin and several members of the local building committee. The commemoration of the 70th anniversary included introducing Mrs. Lafayette G. M. Fletcher, nee Susie Dyer, who was a member of the first normal school faculty and Dr. M. B. Wood, an 1868 student. Both were presented with flowers.

The event was well-publicized. Earle Sly, on behalf of Paramount News, took a motion picture, which was projected to be shown in about 800 movie theaters throughout the Midwest. KYSM, the college's radio station, recorded the proceedings and broadcasted them that evening.

The Standard Construction Company of Minneapolis was the building's general contractor and the Preston Construction Company had the excavation contract. Preston employees equipped with a power shovel and a fleet of dump trucks began leveling the building site the week after the dedication. To assure that the site would not be affected by erosion from Hanover Hill the company removed the dirt cliff at the base of the hill and graded down the slope up to the hill's crest. This entailed removing 100,000 cubic yards of dirt. The October 17 *Free Press* reported that Preston was making rapid progress by operating the shovel 14 hours a day. Preston's trucks "with their loads of dirt are seen on city streets continually these days as they make their hauls" . . . "to outlying sections of the city."[78]

Once the site was prepared the general contractor proceeded rapidly with preparing the foundation and the connecting tunnel to the training school building. By mid-December 1938, the western portion of the foundation had been completed. The building's plans specified a foundation that was to be 266 feet long and 182 feet wide. Furthermore, the concrete tunnel was ready to be covered. Work was being expedited by a concrete heater, which enabled construction to continue throughout the winter.[79]

About July 19, 1939, S. J. Silverson, the PWA's resident supervisor, estimated the building would be completed before December 6, 1939, the expiration date of the PWA grant. By then it was evident that some additional funding was necessary to stabilize the Hanover Hill slope. Recent heavy rains, which had cut gullies on the hillside, washed tons of dirt against the building's east end.[80]

This situation caused the college to apply for a $6,000 grant from the State Legislative Emergency Fund. Since this fund was supported by the federal government's Works Project Administration, the ensuing hillside stabilization was identified as a WPA project. The institution received the funding in late September 1939, when the goal was to work on the hillside the following summer.[81]

When hillside stabilization, the last phase of the building project, was pending, the physical education building was completed and dedicated. The building was first opened to the public for a January 25, 1940, basketball game, but the last interior work was not finished until the next month.[82]

As the last details were being finished, a faculty committee chaired by geographer George J Miller was planning for dedication ceremonies in March. But since Governor Harold E. Stassen, who had agreed to be the featured speaker, developed scheduling problems, the ceremony was delayed until Tuesday evening, April 16. The committee arranged to have student guides lead visitor tours of the building the afternoon preceding the dedication.

In his keynote address, Stassen stressed the importance of public higher education to society. After Thor Knudson, president of the Standard Construction Company, formally presented the building, Senator Val Imm commented on the legislative funding process. McElroy introduced and thanked platform guests, including the members of the State Teachers College Board. Entertainment was provided by the college choir directed by Elias J. Halling and the college band led by Alexis Parlova.[83]

The physical education building provided the college with what was hailed as a state-of-the-art facility. The main floor featured a varsity basketball court and two smaller ones for physical education classes and intramural games. The varsity court was large enough to be converted into two for intramural games or classes, so at times four courts were available. The large court arena had a normal seating capacity of 1,480, which could be expanded by adding temporary seats to about 2,000. Additionally, the main floor had two classrooms, four activity rooms for such things as dancing and calisthenics, locker rooms, restrooms and showers. The front exit from this level led to a long sundeck overlooking the athletic field.[84]

The basement level below the main deck housed a 70-yard-long indoor track and space for such field events as pole vaulting, high jumping, long jumping (then called broad jumping) as well as archery, golf practice and baseball practice. A 40-by 90-foot recreation room had table tennis and shuffle board activities. Other space was devoted to two handball courts, two squash courts, a faculty men's locker room, locker rooms for physical education classes, an equipment storage room, and a warming room for ice skaters who used the athletic field rink. As a reflection of the times in which smoking was customarily advertised as a macho activity, the basement had a smoking room for the building's custodians.

The level above the basketball courts, which appeared to be third story when viewed from the athletic field, housed physical education faculty offices and the school nurse's office. Associated with the school nurse there was a waiting room, examination room, medical storage room and day infirmary. Lastly, there was a large classroom, the so-called "little theater," which was equipped with opaque windows and used for instruction involving movies.

In retrospect, the reception of the physical education building may seem to have been somewhat overblown. But the people who planned it, constructed it and used it naturally judged it in the milieu of their times. Generally, the Depression era was a time of economic stagnation when most people eked out livings and looked forward to better times. To them it seemed like the traditional American goal of material progress had been derailed. Thus, symbolically the new building showed that determined people could realize their dreams and plan for a prosperous future.

The physical education building proved to be the highlight of McElroy's administration. On the occasion of McElroy's retirement, history professor Theodore L. Nydahl, who had joined the faculty in 1928, concluded that "as long as the physical education building stands, it will give silent but solid testimony to the driving energy of President McElroy."[85]

Soon after the building was dedicated, the appearance of the campus was drastically changed by the Hanover Hill stabilization project. In 1940 about two dozen WPA laborers were engaged to terrace the hillside. Using hundreds of tons of Kasota Stone, they erected 15 terrace levels. Facing uphill the terraced area was shaped like an inverted vee. The lowermost terrace, which was about 100 yards long, ran from near the rear of the southernmost part of the main building and around most of the north side and east end of the physical education building to a point opposite the northeastern corner of the track that ran around the athletic field. The topmost terrace was approximately 20 yards long. The narrow terraces were usually six to 10 feet wide.  The terrace walls, which were generally four to six feet high were simply erected by stacking stone blocks, as much as a foot thick, and relying on gravity to hold it in place. The terracing project, which was reported to be about half completed by December 6, 1940, was projected to be continued during the winter as conditions allowed.[86]

Evidently terrace construction was completed in 1941. But, the entire slope project was not finished until the next year. In January 1942, Mankato State received a $19,845 WPA grant for various building and grounds improvements. Part of it was used to erect a retaining wall along the base of the terracing, The stone wall, which was reinforced with concrete, was about 2.5 feet high and 10 inches wide. The easiest way of getting a hilltop view of the campus was to use the standard mountain climbing technique of ascending and descending gradually by following the circuitous path formed by the terraces. But some agile, impatient sorts with good leg joints hurried directly down by jumping from the tops of the terrace walls.[87]

The terraced Hanover Hill was one of Mankato's most unusual landmarks. Until the lower campus was phased out in 1979 the radically landscaped hill stood in sharp contrast to the city's timbered slopes. But nature has reasserted itself. Over the years the terrace trail has become obscured and in places blocked by the tree and brush growth. There is so much vegetation today that the terracing is not visible at all when the leaves are out and is even mostly obscured when the trees and dense brush are bare.

## Student Activities, 1921-1941

From the beginning of the Mankato State Teachers College until the nation's entry into World War II, student activities featured publications and a variety of cultural activities relating to clubs, music and drama performances as well as men's intercollegiate sports and women's intramural sports.

Throughout the period a student staff annually produced a yearbook variously titled *The Katonian* or *Katonian*. Considering the two-year disruption caused by the great fire, compiling the 1923 and 1924 yearbooks was an especially noteworthy accomplishment.

Boosterish in nature, the yearbooks promoted camaraderie. Typically, each issue described the college's clubs, administration, faculty and fine arts productions and summarized the year's happenings in both men and women's sports. Because they were profusely illustrated with contemporary photographs, the yearbooks are significant sources of information about the campus facilities, students and faculty.

School identity was also stimulated by a weekly student newspaper. The first issue of *Among Ourselves*, headlined "T. C. TO HAVE A SCHOOL PUBLICATION", was issued on Tuesday, March 23, 1926. Noting that the paper was "to serve the interest of all the school," its staff urged students to support

Valley Gym with Training School in background, 1939

Larry Buendorf helps Mankato defeat Moorhead in the Valley Gym, 1959

Hurdling practice on indoor track, 1958

the effort, which was initially financed by the advertisements of various Mankato businesses. But the paper struggled. By October 19, 1926, only six issues (with none during the summer) had been issued. However, the staff announced its determination to enlarge the format and produce 20 issues during the academic year. But this was feasible only if students would pay an annual 50-cent subscription. Evidently lack of support doomed *Among Ourselves*, whose last issue was published on April 2, 1927.[88]

Nearly two years elapsed before another aspiring student staff began producing *School Spirit* on March 7, 1929. Its name reflected a long-standing institutional issue. The student producers of *The Mankatonian* during the turn of the century era were regularly concerned about school spirit or lack thereof. Beginning with the May 25, 1933, issue, *School Spirit* was renamed to the *College Spirit*. The paper's editorial policy was proclaimed to be:

"A. To promote an ideal college spirit among the students; to inculate [sic] the doctrine of 'Honest Play' in all activities of life.

B. To encourage student thought about the serious matters of college life.

C. To encourage clean sportsmanship in all college sports.

D. To encourage good scholarship; to endeavor to show the necessity for diligent study and for real thinking.

E. To provide a medium of communication for students and teachers — share and share alike.

F. To establish and maintain faith in the present and future of the Mankato State Teachers College; to bring home in the student the importance to him of a cultural-professional education and to aid the student in understanding the work of the teachers in directing student initiative."[89]

The last issue of *College Spirit* appeared on June 4, 1935. When the student newspaper was resumed the following fall it had been renamed to the *College Reporter*. In explaining the change, the paper's staff, with Harold Ronnenberg as editor-in-chief, proclaimed "COLLEGE SPIRIT GIVES UP GHOST AS EDITORS REVEAL NEW EPITHET." They wrote: "The 'College Spirit' is dead; it gave up its ghost this summer. It was then that the editors, haunted by the name 'Spirit' which is a better term for a motor boat than for a newspaper, decided to break with tradition by re-christening it the 'College Reporter.' Since that time the editors have enjoyed comparative peace of minds, for the 'Spirit' no longer lurks behind trees and lamp posts to haunt them. It is dead and buried."

In addition to Ronnenberg, the *Reporter's* initial staff members were George Jorgensen, associate editor, Margaret Kemp, managing editor, Ruth Wheelock, news editor, Ruby Jorgensen, copy editor, Helen Lamm, feature editor, Richard

Boehm, sports editor, James Gladhill, assistant sports editor, and Jerry Lamm, business manager. Byron B. Williams, an English instructor, was the editorial adviser and Gustav S. Petterson, a sociology instructor, was the business adviser.[90]

During the 1920s, when Mankato State was adapting to its new status as a college, more student organizations were formed. The YWCA was the principal club dating to the normal school era. Interest in women's participation in the political process, which was spurred by the acceptance of the Women's Suffrage Amendment (the Nineteenth Amendment)

Aerial view showing Main Building (left), Training School, Valley Gym (with terracing behind), and track and field, circa 1951

to the U.S. Constitution on August 18, 1920, led to the formation of a college chapter of the League of Women Voters in October, 1926. The club explained that "the purpose of the league is to train women in the use of the vote and to make them desire to use it."[91]

Two co-educational religious clubs—the Lutheran Club and the Newman Club (Roman Catholic)—reflected the dominant religious culture of southern Minnesota.

Each of the four training school departments had a club for student teachers. The clubs for the kindergarten, primary, intermediate and junior high school departments were respectively the K. K. X. (Kappa Kappa Xi sorority), Makata, M. G. O. and A. I. A. G. The last two were identified only by their initials. The A. I. A. G. members apparently took a particular delight in keeping their full name secret. The caption of the group's picture in the 1927 *Katonian* stated: "A. I. A. G.! What does it mean? This question is asked repeatedly, but it speaks well for the members of the organization, that the secret has never been divulged."[92]

The training school clubs proved to be short-lived because of school reorganization. In 1931-1932 the kindergarten, primary and intermediate were merged into an "elementary school" and the junior high department was designated as the junior high school.[93]

There were three glee clubs—two for women and the other for men. The Cecelian Club, which was the advanced women's glee club, had 75 members in the 1926-27 academic year. Its principal all-school activity was to sing at

## George J Miller: Geographer

George J Miller (February 7, 1880-July 23, 1973), who taught geography at the Mankato State Normal School and Mankato State Teachers College, 1913-1948, gained a national reputation as a teacher, editor and author.

A native of Sturgis, Michigan, Miller graduated from the Michigan State Normal School at Ypsilanti in June 1900. After eight years of public school teaching, he returned to school and earned B.S. and M.S. degrees from the University of Chicago. While he was teaching classes in Chicago's College of Education, Miller came to the attention of Charles H. Cooper, who customarily recruited university students for his normal school faculty.

Caption: George J Miller, circa 1940s

In 1913 Cooper hired Miller to replace the retiring Defransa Swann, the normal school's first geography instructor. Cooper was anticipating the transition to a teachers college and was striving to upgrade the faculty. After Miller's first year at Mankato Normal, Cooper observed: "He is thoroughly trained, has had long and successful experience, and understands the problems and work of a normal school."

Early in his Mankato career Miller became involved in promoting geography education. In 1914 he started the National Council for Geography Teachers, which evolved into the National Council for Geography Education (NCGE). Miller was its secretary from 1916 to 1929, vice-president in 1929 and president the next year. Additionally, he edited the *Journal of Geography,* 1920-1949, and was its assistant editor for two more years. Miller was granted the NCGE's distinguished service award in 1938. In 1975, two years after his death, the organization honored his memory by naming the award after him.

While teaching and championing geography education, Miller saw publication as a key way of disseminating information for teachers. From 1934-1937, he edited four books, which consisted of reprinted articles from the *Journal of Geography.* Issued as the Geographic Education Series, the books *Geography: How to Teach It* (1934), *Human Geography Studies: The United States* (1935), *Life in Asia* (1936) and *Activities in Geography* (1937) each contained about 30 reprinted articles. All four were published by McKnight & McKnight, Bloomington, Illinois.

Miller's particular teaching and writing interest was North American geography. In 1928 he co-authored with Almon E. Parkins, a geography teacher at George Peabody College for Teachers, Nashville, Tennessee, as junior author, the college text *Geography of North America.* It was commercially published by John Wiley & Sons of New York City. Wiley issued a second edition of this popular book in 1934. The third edition (1954) was authored by Miller, Parkins and Bert Hudgins of Wayne University.

Because he regarded firsthand observations as vital to an understanding of landscapes, Miller traveled widely in the United States and Canada. During these extended trips he took hundreds of pictures of the various terrains and recorded observations in his diaries. In 1931, when he was a visiting professor at the University of London, Miller traveled through much of Europe.

Miller resigned from Mankato State Teachers College in 1948 to accept a teaching position at the University of Indiana (Bloomington). He retired from it in 1951.

Two years after Miller's first wife died in 1956 he married E. Joan Miller, a geography lecturer at the University of Indiana. Soon thereafter the Millers moved to Normal, Illinois, because Mrs. Miller (Dr. E. Joan) had been added to the Illinois State University faculty. George Miller lived in Normal for the rest of his life. Because of Miller's long, satisfying experience with the Mankato State Normal School and Mankato State Teachers College, E. Joan Miller donated his extensive personal and professional records to the Minnesota State University, Mankato Archives.

Miller's baptismal name was George J Miller. Consequently, the J is not an abbreviation for a middle name and should not be punctuated with a period. Evidently Miller chose not to insist on the use of his original name during his professional career. On the title pages of his books and in Mankato State catalogs his name was consistently shown as George J. Miller.

(George J Miller Collection, Mankato State University, Mankato Archives; Charles H. Cooper, "Annual Report," 1913-1914, Minnesota State University, Mankato Archives; World Cat Discovery bibliographical search and *Mankato State Teachers College Catalog,* 1942.)

graduation exercises. The second women's glee club, the Euterpean Club (named after the Greek muse of music) was formed in the fall of 1926 to provide an opportunity for coeds who were not members of the Cecelian Club.[94]

The Country Life Club, consisting of rural students, promoted a better understanding of rural problems and lifestyles. Throughout the year it sponsored presentations about country life. Outside of athletics, the Coterie Club, formed in 1924, was the only exclusive men's club. Other than promoting good fellowship, it maintained an employment bureau and supported intercollegiate athletics. By 1930 the M Club of athletes who had earned letters had taken over the Coterie Club's functions.[95]

The most significant new student activities development in the 1930s was the advent of the student council. Organized in the fall of 1931, the council developed into the All-College Association, which promoted student participation in institutional governance.[96]

The rise of intercollegiate men's athletics was an important development for the new teachers college. Cooper revived men's football and basketball for the 1922-1923 year by hiring Hugh Jameson as the college's lone coach. Jameson stayed for only two years. He was succeeded in 1924 by Carlyn P. Blakeslee. A Pennsylvania native and graduate of that state's Edinboro Normal School, Blakeslee moved to Mankato in 1919 to coach Mankato High School teams. After three years in that position, Blakeslee worked two more as the coach of the Fort Dodge, Iowa, High School and the basketball coach of the city's junior college. In 1924 he returned to Mankato to coach the college's varsity teams and teach physical education. This marked the start of his illustrious 37-year coaching career.[97]

In 1922 Jameson started football inauspiciously with only 14 men—only five of whom had high school experience. The squad played games against Rochester Junior College, Parker College (Winnebago, Minnesota), Pillsbury Academy (Owatonna) and the high schools from Rochester, Owatonna and Blue Earth. The basketball team played nine games including one against Winona State Teachers College and two against area high schools.[98]

In 1923-1924, Mankato State, as a member of the newly formed Minnesota Junior College Conference, started competing in intercollegiate athletics. The conference, originally consisting of the Bemidji, Mankato, St. Cloud and Winona teachers colleges and the Ely, Eveleth, Hibbing, Itasca (Grand Rapids), Rochester and Virginia junior colleges, came to be colloquially known as the "Little Ten". This moniker was retained after the newly formed Duluth Junior College joined the conference as the eleventh member in 1927. Consequently, the name henceforth did not represent the actual conference composition. But, such inconsistency is hardly novel in higher

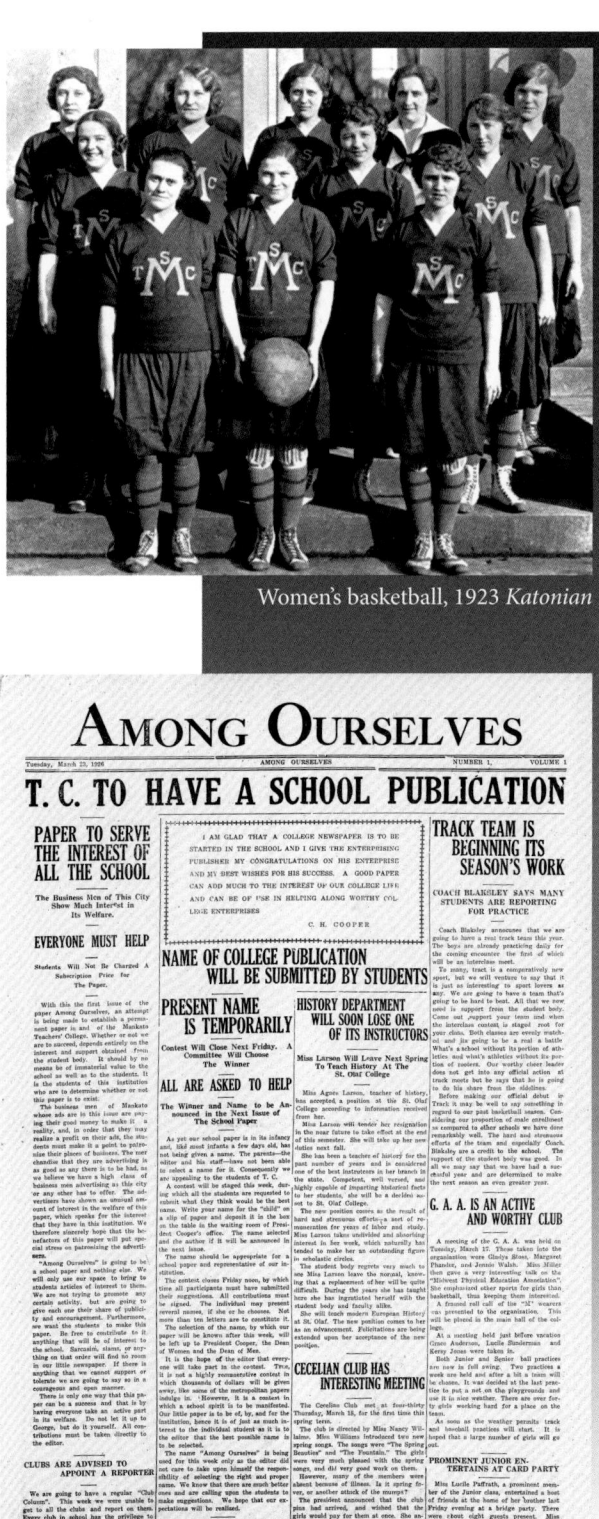

Women's basketball, 1923 *Katonian*

*Among Ourselves*, 23 March 1926

education. Today's Big Ten Conference has 14 members and the Big 12 has 10.[99]

The conference membership of four state teachers colleges and seven junior colleges was a tacit recognition that all of the schools competed at a junior college level. Prior to the beginning and subsequent growth of the four-year degree program, the teachers colleges and junior colleges were comparable with respect to academic programs and student ages.

Conference football and basketball competition was divided into southern (Mankato, Winona, and St. Cloud teachers colleges and Rochester Junior College) and northern (Bemidji Teachers College and the Duluth, Ely, Eveleth, Hibbing, Itasca, and Virginia junior colleges) divisions. All conference games were within the respective divisions. Apparently this division arrangement was caused by the desire to reduce travel expenses and to cope with the inconvenience of extended road trips.

Conference competition was changed somewhat by the addition of track as the third major sport in 1925. Customarily, teams competed in their own divisions. But in 1928, for the first time, the conference decided to conclude the season with an all-conference track meet. The event was held at Hamline College in St. Paul, a convenient approximate central location.[100]

Mankato State Teachers College stayed in the Little Ten Conference until 1932 when it and the other five Minnesota teachers colleges formed the Northern Teachers College Conference. Mankato State's first conference football game was played on September 30 against the Duluth State Teachers College on Mankato's new athletic field. Evidently, the new conference and the new athletic field spurred student and community interest in intercollegiate competition. During the 1932-1933 basketball season, Blakeslee arranged to have Mankato's home games played in the downtown National Guard Armory to attract the crowds that would not fit in the training school's small gym.[101]

During its brief Little Ten era, Mankato State started its first M Club and its first homecoming. The M Club, was formed in the fall of 1924. Membership in it was soon recognized as a major mark of distinction. A combination of M Club activities and the school's 60th anniversary of its first classes caused the celebration of Mankato State's first homecoming on Friday and Saturday, October 26-27, 1928. This was a joyous event marked by the return of many alums, a downtown parade of student-prepared floats and a 13-0 football victory over Rochester Junior College.[102]

Football, basketball and track were the only major sports during the Little Ten Conference period. But Blakeslee started both gymnastics and tennis in the 1929-1930 year. Neither of them engaged in conference competition.[103]

Until homecoming 1935 the Mankato State Teachers College athletic teams were usually identified as the Peds or such variants as Pedagogues or Teachers. But beginning late in the 1926 football season they were oftentimes referred as The Orange, Orangemen or Orange Peds, which related to the evolution of school colors.[104]

The official purple and gold school colors were announced

*College Reporter*, 3 September 1935

in the *Mankatonian* of November 1892. Over the years the use of those colors was perpetuated until the 1926 change to burnt orange and navy blue. The new colors were used for more than athletic team uniforms. The menu of "The Second Annual Home Coming Alumni Dinner of the Mankato State Teachers College. October 26, 1929" featured a logo of burnt orange and navy blue colors.[105]

An article titled "Sport Forecast" by Dick Boehm in the *College Spirit* of October 11, 1934, claimed the origin of the burnt orange and navy blue colors "dates back to the time

The Mask and Dagger Club put on theatrical performances each year, 1934

when the old colors were purple and gold. The 'M' club [sic.] voted to change the colors to Burnt Orange [sic.] and Blue [sic.] because of the conflict with Winona (purple and white) and the hard duplication of a true gold color."[106]

Continued use of burnt orange and navy blue caused confusion over the official colors. Albert Nemic, an alum who returned to campus in the spring of 1935, reported seeing students "clad in official orange and purple uniforms of the college."[107]

Nemic erroneously reported one color from each of two versions being used at that time. The athletic teams used burnt orange and navy blue, but the band and glee clubs continued to use purple and gold.

Both color versions were continued into the World War II years. The *College Reporter* of March 26, 1943, in a "10 second quiz" feature queried: "What are the school colors of Mankato State?
A  Purple and gold.
A. Burnt orange and navy blue.
Some student should write an editorial advocating the adoption of one set to be used exclusively . . . ."

Evidently no aspiring student took up the challenge. On December 11, 1947, the *College Reporter* published a scathing editorial titled "Who Wears Purple, Gold?" The writer pointed out that the college's band and choir dressed in purple and gold uniforms, but the football and the basketball teams and the cheerleaders wore "black, orange, white or whatever color they may happen to decide on." The complainer was particularly exasperated because athletic events featured the school song, which opened with "Hail to our colors, the purple and the gold . . ." The editorialist concluded that: "If purple and gold are the school colors, purple and gold should appear on every uniform the school buys. If they aren't, TC should stop hailing them, and find a song which would be appropriate to the colors worn. Visitors at games must think that we students are either desperate for a song or else color blind."

The editorial failed to provoke the athletic teams to use the official school colors, so the dual color schemes were continued. Since purple and gold were

Student Council, 1935

the official colors, athletic teams were sometimes identified as the purple and gold even though they wore burnt orange and navy blue uniforms.[108]

Fortunately, the Minnesota State University, Mankato Archives has acquired some artifacts that illustrate the burnt orange and navy blue colors. They consist of a pair of track shorts, a sleeveless track shirt and an M letter that belonged to Don Frerichs, Mankato State's first All-American in track, who competed 1952-54. These articles are orange fringed with navy blue.[109]

Soon after Frerichs completed his college competition, Mankato State changed its athletic team colors to purple and gold in 1955. The *College Reporter* of November 17, 1955, featured a picture of two varsity basketball players. One was wearing the "new" home warmup outfit and the other was dressed in the "new game uniform." Both were "all white with purple and gold numerals and trim."[110]

After the Northern Teachers College Conference was formed the Peds nickname seemed out of place, if not effete, compared with such conference rivals as the Beavers (Bemidji), Bulldogs (Duluth) and Dragons (Moorhead). Consequently, on November 1, 1935, the eve of the homecoming football game against the St. Cloud Teachers College Huskies, the Peds were officially renamed to Indians. The campus homecoming ceremony was called a "pow wow" and the subsequent assemblage on downtown Front Street was a "war dance".[111] Such stereotyping, which was then in vogue nationally, was only a preview of the later homecoming tradition of choosing an Indian "princess." The homecoming princess and other campus traditions developed that utilized faux ceremonies and costumes inspired by stereotypical imagery of Native Americans in Hollywood.

During Mankato State's teachers college era only male athletes participated in intercollegiate completion. But, the college also promoted an extensive intramural athletic program for female students, the overwhelming majority of the student body.

The intramural program was a natural offshoot of the required physical education courses. All first-year students had to take a physical education course each of their three terms. Two of the courses involved participating in a team activity, which was intended to enhance social life. The third course was concerned with the teaching methodologies of elementary school physical activities. Since most of the students were preparing to become elementary teachers, it was essential that they were knowledgeable about certain sports and how to teach them to young students.[112]

The women's program started modestly in 1922, when its only sports were basketball and soccer. But by 1924, when the Girls Athletic Association (GAA) was

formed, the college added training
and participation in baseball,
hiking, ice skating, tennis, track
and volleyball. Adelaide Miller, the
physical education director and
coach of all women's sports, 1923-
1927, was succeeded by Helen A.
Pendergast.[113]

Teams represented the
two classes and various clubs.
The most featured competition
was between the "juniors" and
"seniors," the very imprecise
definition of the first- and second-
year students in the two-year
elementary program.

"M" Club, 1935 *Katonian*

A year-long schedule for the various sports entailed using both
campus and off-campus facilities. The gymnasium in the laboratory school
accommodated basketball and volleyball. The most convenient tennis courts
were located just east of the women's dormitories. The fairgrounds two miles
north of downtown Mankato, Lewis Field and Sibley Park were used for both
practicing and engaging in baseball, soccer and field hockey. Transportation to
and from these fields was provided by trucks.

The GAA, which was governed by a student board, was renamed the WAA
(Women's Athletic Association) in 1927. The association awarded points to
athletes based on their degrees of participation. For example, any member of
a first team was awarded 100 points for a season's participation. Rewards were
given for various achievement levels. The highest award was a purple M (the
equivalent of a letter in men's athletics), which required 600 points. In 1925
the Mankato State association became a member of the Athletic Conference
of American College Women. This affiliation allowed students to transfer their
points totals to any member school.[114]

## Administrative and Academic Developments in
## the McElroy Administration

McElroy's administrative reforms and development of a better trained
faculty, combined with new state laws and the quest for accreditation of the
four-year program by the North Central Association of Colleges and Schools,
significantly changed the Mankato State Teachers College.

The administrative staff McElroy inherited from Cooper consisted
of a dean of women, training school director, office manager/accountant,
librarian, assistant librarian, halls and cafeteria manager, school nurse and
superintendent of buildings.

Sara Norris, who was named dean of women in 1930, was also an English
instructor. After earning a B.A. from Oxford College for Women (Oxford,
Ohio) and a M.A. from the University of Wisconsin, she had completed further
graduate work at Wisconsin. Additionally, she had been the acting dean of
women at Oxford College for a year.[115]

Otto Welton Snarr, training school director, had joined the Mankato
Normal School faculty in 1920. After attending a normal school, he earned a

B.A. from West Virginia University in 1917 and a master's degree two years later from the University of Chicago.

Office manager/accountant Ethel Anne DeVaney was a holdover from the Cooper administration. In 1925 Cooper hired her to replace Belle Colby Carrington, who had retired.

Librarian Emma Wiecking had held the position since 1924. A Mankato native, she earned a diploma from the Mankato State Normal School in 1914. She obtained her library training at the Library School of the New York Public Library and while completing her master's at Columbia University. In 1922 she was named assistant librarian at Mankato State Teachers College.

The assistant librarian Phyllis Bentley joined the Mankato State faculty in 1930 after completing her bachelor's degree and library training at the University of Wisconsin. Ethel M. Cochran, the manager of halls and cafeteria, had earned a diploma from Valley City State University (North Dakota) and had taught home economics for a decade before starting at Mankato State in 1926. Helen E. Boyce, an R.N., completed her B.S. at the University of Minnesota in 1928 and started at Mankato State the same year. Tom Farmer, the superintendent of buildings, had assumed his Mankato State position in 1928.

In his first year, McElroy, in recognition of the increasing number of male students, appointed Maurice J. Nelson to the newly created position of dean of men. Nelson, who had taught manual arts at the Mankato normal school/teachers college since 1918, had been a manual training student at the Mankato State Normal School in 1912-1913. Subsequently, he earned a diploma from Stout Institute (Menominee, Wisconsin) and taught for four years in public schools.[116]

McElroy's main step in streamlining college administration was to remove the registrar's function from the president's office, where it had resided since the start of the normal school. In 1932 he chose history instructor Albert B. Morris to direct the newly created office of Personnel and Registrar. Morris was assisted by Georgia P. Bekke, who had previously done the registrar duties when she served as the president's secretary. "Personnel" referred to students. Historically, the institution, in addition to compiling transcripts, had prepared written evaluations on the personality and teaching potential of students. Initially, it appeared to McElroy that the personnel activity was a natural adjunct of registrar duties.[117]

Morris had been hired by Cooper for the Mankato Normal School faculty in 1919. After earning a bachelor's degree from Kansas Wesleyan University in 1911, he completed a master's at the University of Chicago five years later. Before joining Mankato State he had also taught in high school for one year and had been employed as a superintendent.

1957 Homecoming court float, with Princess Barbara Kubicek on the back, in the homecoming parade. All students are wearing costumes for the parade.

After only a year, McElroy separated the registrar and personnel duties by creating a separate Personnel Office and naming Miles E. Hawk to direct it. Hawk, who had joined the Mankato State faculty in 1931, held bachelor's (1906) and master's (1909) degrees from Ohio Northern and a M.A. in Education from Harvard. He had taught for 18 years in elementary and secondary schools and had served as high school principal for two years.[118]

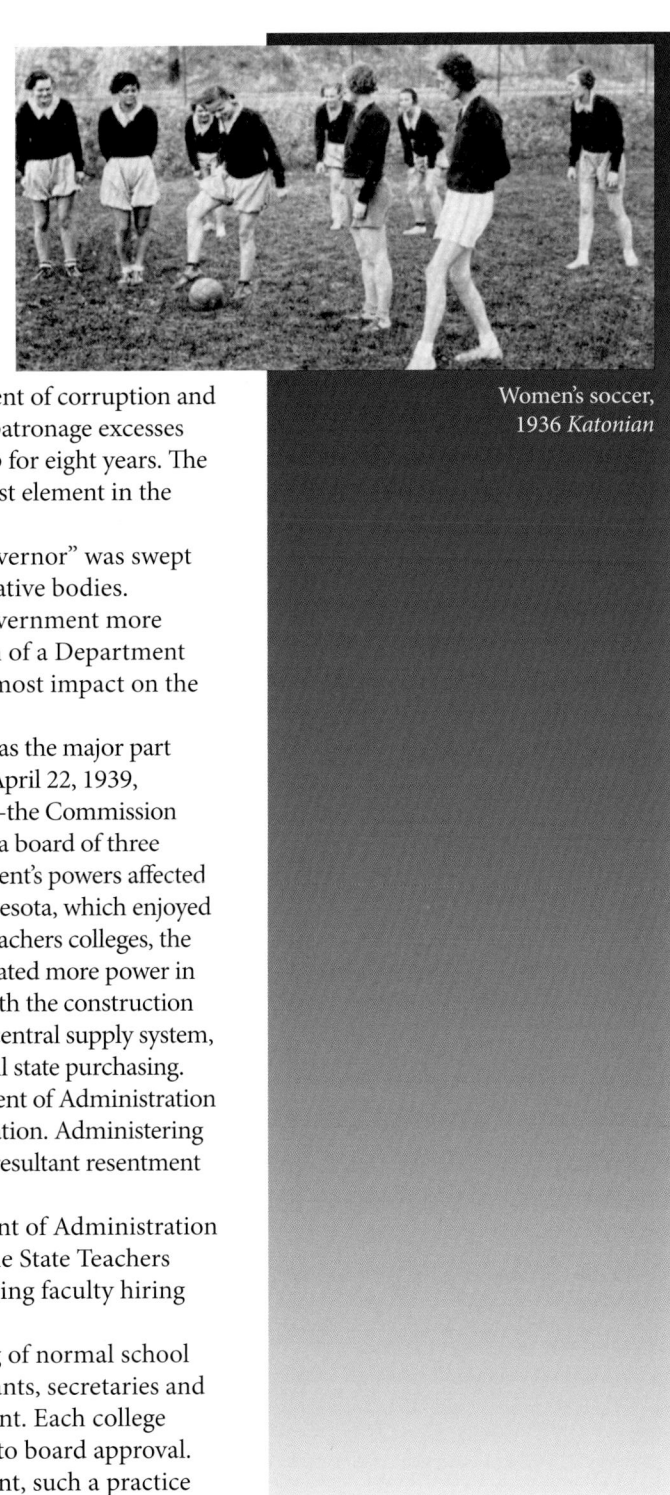

Women's soccer, 1936 *Katonian*

The administrative nature of Mankato State and the other state teachers colleges was changed profoundly by 1939 state legislation. In 1938 Republican Harold E. Stassen ran for governor on the pledge to rid state government of corruption and Communism. His alleged corruption related mainly to the patronage excesses of the Farmer-Labor Party, which had held the governorship for eight years. The Communist issue was fueled by the presence of a Communist element in the Farmer-Labor Party and its advocacy of socialism.[119]

The 31-year old Stassen, oftentimes called the "boy governor" was swept into power along with Republican majorities in both legislative bodies. Consequently, his suggested reforms, intended to make government more accountable and efficient, were easily enacted. The creation of a Department of Administration and a state civil service system had the most impact on the state teachers colleges and other state agencies.

The authorization of the Department of Administration was the major part of an act to reorganize state government. The law, passed on April 22, 1939, granted the department more authority than its predecessor—the Commission of Administration and Finance, which had been managed by a board of three commissioners. Headed by a single director the new department's powers affected all state agencies with the exception of the University of Minnesota, which enjoyed a unique constitutional immunity. With respect to the state teachers colleges, the establishment of the Department of Administration concentrated more power in St. Paul. Among other things, the department was charged with the construction and maintenance of all state buildings, the management of a central supply system, the supervision of rigid accounting and the management of all state purchasing. All college equipment purchases had to conform to Department of Administration procedures with respect to competitive bidding and authorization. Administering these procedures naturally caused more paperwork with the resultant resentment of "red tape" by campus authorities.[120]

As the watchdog of state appropriations, the Department of Administration epitomized the centralization of fiscal control. However, the State Teachers College Board retained control of academic matters including faculty hiring and the development of programs.

Prior to the start of state civil service in 1939 the hiring of normal school and teachers college support personnel including accountants, secretaries and custodians was done in the same way as faculty employment. Each college president had the authority to appoint individuals subject to board approval. Since position qualifications were determined by a president, such a practice was potentially a spoils system in which hiring decisions could have been based on personal or political favoritism.

Civil service was first established on a limited basis by the federal government's Pendleton Act of 1883. Its aim was to insure that the hiring

## The President Speaks

# Provincialism Obscures Broad View of Education

Since 1922 this college has been in a sate of transition from a two-year to a four-year school. It has been concerned with all of the problems of staff, students, curriculum, public relations, and finances. So many problems of that type have been foremost in our attention that it seems to me we have failed to look beyond the immediate environment to see what is going on in the rest of the educational world — in other words, we are provincial. I think it is now time to widen our horizon, both geographically and professionally speaking, and consider our actual and possible national relationships. The one really effective membership we have in a national organization is that of the American Association of Teachers Colleges where we have maintained a good rating for a number of years. Our possible national relationships include memberships in the North Central Association of Colleges and Secondary Schools, the American Council on Education, and the numerous learned societies.

It seems apparent that our next significant step would be to ask for a critical survey by the North Central Association where our shortcomings would be pointed out to us and where we would be enabled to make improvement in light of those criticisms. It seems apparent, also, that we should affiliate ourselves with the American Council on Education which is a splendid cooperative enterprise that has under its control the studies supported by grants from educational foundations.

Graduate schools of large universities where our students will go for advanced training should be contacted. We should get acquainted with them and they with us in order to establish an effective basis of cooperation.

Let us give attention to external affairs. Let us broaden our horizon.

Frank D. McElroy
President

President McElroy had a regular column in the *College Reporter* where he shared his thoughts about education and MSTC. *College Reporter* 18 November 1938

of public employees was based on the principles of equal opportunity and proof that applicants were qualified for each type of position.[121]

The State Civil Service Act of 1939 was an amazingly detailed law. Its text of nearly 28 printed pages described the nature of the new agency and its policies and procedures.[122]

Technically, the law regarded all state employees as civil servants, but distinguished between unclassified and classified employees. Unclassified employees, who did not have to take competitive qualifying examinations and who did not have designated civil service ranks, included "teachers, research assistants, student employees on less than half-time pay basis, presidents, deans, and administrative officers in the teachers' colleges; but this subdivision shall not be construed to include the custodial, clerical, or maintenance employees, or any administrative officers, or clerical workers performing duties in connection with the business administration of such institutions." To comply with the University of Minnesota's distinctive legal status the unclassified also included: "Regents of the University of Minnesota and the employees and persons under the jurisdiction of the Regents of the University of Minnesota."

Most of the act was concerned with classified service policies including stipulations for position classifications, competitive examinations, preparation of certified lists of qualified candidates, probationary appointments, transfers and order of layoffs. The law soon had a practical effect on the Mankato State Teachers College. For the first time in college history the catalog for 1944-1945 had separate "Instructional Personnel" and "Classified Personnel" staff categories.[123]

McElroy's aims to upgrade faculty academic credentials, permit more faculty involvement in college governance and support the beginning of sabbatical leave and tenure policies were deeply influenced by his desire to have the four-year program accredited by the North Central Association of Colleges and Secondary Schools. The association included a much larger region than its name suggests. It served Arkansas, Arizona, Colorado, Illinois, Indiana, Iowa, Kansas, Michigan, Minnesota, Missouri, Nebraska, New Mexico, North Dakota, Ohio, Oklahoma, South Dakota, West Virginia, Wisconsin and Wyoming.[124]

Gaining North Central Association accreditation of Minnesota's teachers colleges four-year programs was a major concern of the State Teachers College Board. The board recognized that unaccredited institutions were regarded as sub-par and that their students who attempted to transfer would not be accepted by accredited colleges and universities. But the board and the college presidents also knew that there was no point in applying for accreditation until the colleges had taken certain self-improvement steps. They realized that North Central Association guidelines recommended faculty involvement in school governance, faculty with strong academic credentials from graduate schools instead of a background in public school teaching, tenure and sabbatical leave policies, and the establishment of faculty ranks based on a combination of training and experience.

When he assessed his first year's faculty, McElroy recognized its shortcomings relative to North Central standards. The 1930-1931 faculty had a College Department (including McElroy) of 26 members and a Training School of 17. With respect to academic training, 13 of the College Department faculty had master's degrees. Twelve had bachelors degrees and one had not earned a degree.[125]

As McElroy first contemplated applying for accreditation in February 1932, he realized that adding more terminal degree holders to the faculty would have to be done gradually. However, changes in faculty organization that would place more emphasis on subject matter groupings and give the faculty more voice in college governance could be accomplished without more funding. McElroy inherited the normal school system in which all faculty members were identified as instructors and customarily listed as staff. His practice was to meet with the faculty at least once a month. The idea of organizing the faculty into divisions was first discussed at these faculty meetings.[126]

After much contemplation and planning by committees, the new division plan went into effect in the fall of 1938. This reorganization, the first in the history of the normal school/teachers college, resulted in five academic divisions: Fine and Applied Arts, Health and Physical Education, Language and Literature, Science and Mathematics and Social Studies. Teachers of education courses were placed in the Division of Professional Courses within the Unit of Professional Education, which also had a Division of Laboratory Schools.[127]

The Fine and Applied Arts Division consisted of Art, Industrial Education and Music Education. During its first year, the Health and Physical Education Division listed 35 physical education courses and three health courses. The composition of the Language and Literature Division was English, Speech, French and Spanish. The sub-units of the Science and Mathematics Division were Biology, General Science, Chemistry, Geography, Mathematics and Physics. Economics, History, Political Science and Sociology comprised the Social Studies Division. After only one year Geography was transferred from Science and Mathematics to Social Studies.

The division organization of Mankato State coincided with the development of an inter-faculty organization that would be concerned with the welfare of all faculty members of the six Minnesota teachers colleges. The idea of forming the Inter-Faculty Organization (IFO) was originated in a conversation between Herbert A. Clugston, professor of psychology at St. Cloud State, Lee O. Garber, principal of the College High School at Mankato State and President Herbert F. Sorenson of the Duluth State Teachers College. At a meeting in Colorado during the summer of 1938, they agreed that such an organization would be desirable in order to consider matters that were of concern to all faculty in the Minnesota Teachers College system.[128]

Subsequently, Clugston organized a meeting of one delegate from each of the six colleges during the Minnesota Education Association's convention in late October 1938. The delegates agreed to form an inter-faculty organization and to begin planning the organization's aims. Garber, the Mankato representative, reported to the Mankato State faculty at its staff meeting of February 8, 1939, that the organization's purpose was to "work for the welfare" of the six faculties in order to secure "progressive" legislation regarding salaries and tenure.[129]

Led by Clugston, delegates chosen by their respective faculty organized the first IFO conference that met in St. Cloud on May 12-13, 1939. The organization held its second inter-faculty conference at Mankato on April 26 and 27, 1940. The planners anticipated that 150-200 instructors from the six colleges would participate.[130]

After the Mankato meeting the IFO agreed to hold biennial conferences. The third conference was held in Bemidji May 22-23, 1942. Sessions were devoted to the conference theme: "Reorientation in Teachers Education Demanded by the Present World Crisis."[131]

Because of wartime gasoline rationing, which necessarily restricted travel, the 1944 conference

# Dr. Fair Heads Faculty Group

Dr. Eugene Fair, assistant professor of history, has been elected president of the Mankato State Faculty association. Miss Hilda Beug, associate professor of education, is vice president; and Miss Evon Ryan, assistant professor of education, is secretary-treasurer. Other executive members are Miss Grace Armstrong, acting director of professional education, and Dr. G. M. Wissink, professor of physics.

This association is an affiliate of the inter-faculty organization of the six teachers colleges of Minnesota, whose purpose is to promote favorable legislation for teacher education.

It was established in 1938 with joint faculty conferences being held in 1939, 1940, and 1942. Because of travel restrictions, the conference for this year was cancelled and the Inter-Faculty Policies committee will take its place. Miss Armstrong and Dr. Wissink have been named as representatives to this committee.

*College Reporter* 17 March 1944

was cancelled. But the IFO's governing committee—with Gerrit M. Wissink, professor of physics, and Grace Armstrong, associate professor of education, representing Mankato State—completed writing a "Constitution of the Inter-Faculty Organization of the Minnesota State Teachers Colleges."[132]

The IFO significantly changed administration-faculty relations. The two delegates from each of the six colleges elected a president, vice-president, secretary and treasurer from their group. The governing board and presidents willingly consented to the IFO president's participation in board meetings. Typically, they relied on the IFO president to provide guidance in deciding faculty salary adjustments and other personnel matters.

Soon after the Mankato reorganization and the formation of the Inter-Faculty Organization, the State Teachers College Board began considering the start of tenure and sabbatical leave policies. On December 12, 1939, only four months before a North Central Association accreditation team was scheduled to visit the Mankato campus, the board, on the recommendation of its Personnel and Classification Committee, approved tenure and sabbatical leave policies. Both policies were to go into effect on July 1, 1940.[133]

The tenure policy first stipulated that tenure would be granted to "instructors and employees who, in the opinion of the president, department head, and resident director, have served and performed their duties successfully for a period of three years." The policy's most immediate effect was to "blanket in" all teachers and employees who had been in their positions for three years. Lastly, the policy outlined a procedure for the dismissal of tenured employees.

The key provision of the sabbatical leave policy was that faculty "who have taught or administered successfully for at least six years, may, with the recommendation of the president and resident director and the approval of the Board be granted a full year's leave of absence with half pay for advanced study, professional writing, or approved travel." The policy further stipulated that any leave recipient had to teach a full year after returning from leave and that no more than five percent of the faculty could be on leave simultaneously.

The policies partially ameliorated the concerns of the two-man North Central Association accrediting team that visited the Mankato State campus March 5-6, 1940. In their report, the examiners—Charles H. Oldfather, dean of the College of Arts and Sciences, University of Nebraska, and Orval R. Latham, president of Iowa State Teachers College (Cedar Falls)—enumerated and described Mankato State's "Elements of Strength" and "Points of Weakness."[134]

Oldfather and Latham concluded Mankato State's strong points were its advantageous location, a vigorous, progressive administration, a clearly enunciated institutional purpose that was supported by the faculty, an "outstanding" general education program, an "adequate" library, a well-organized and efficient counseling program and the physical plant facilities.

The first weakness identified by Oldfather and Latham was the "low" professional training of the faculty. They were particularly concerned that only six of the 43 college faculty members had earned doctor's degrees. But they softened this criticism somewhat by noting that McElroy's inclusion would make seven and that the faculty McElroy inherited in 1930 did not have any members with a doctorate.

Oldfather and Latham also criticized the absence of an academic dean, a key figure in curriculum development, as well as the lack of a faculty ranking system and the "thoroughly unsound" system of electing division heads annually. They thought the short terms of governing board members undermined "stability and continuity" in policy development. Some of their harshest criticism was of the recently created Department of Administration. They were clearly unimpressed by the situation in which the college's educational program was under "the control of one governmental agency while the financial program is controlled by another."

Lastly, they observed that "the future expansion of the site is limited as to possibilities except at great cost."

Overall, the Oldfather-Latham report was favorable. At its early April 1940 meeting the North Central Association accredited Mankato State Teachers College. The State Teachers College Board was pleased with this development and the simultaneous accreditation of Winona State Teachers College. But the teachers college system suffered a setback during the academic year 1941-42, when the North Central Association, after a critical report by Oldfather and Latham, refused to accredit St. Cloud Teachers College.[135]

In the aftermath of the North Central report Mankato State instituted a faculty ranking system beginning with the 1941-42 academic year. The 57 ranked faculty members consisted of 14 professors, nine associate professors, 16 assistant professors and 18 instructors. In assigning ranks, longevity at Mankato State was apparently more important than academic training. Such men as George J Miller, Albert B. Morris, Maurice J. Nelson, Gustav S. Petterson and Gilbert H. Trafton, all of whom had started in the late normal school era and did not have doctor's degrees, were ranked as professors. But on the other extreme, Leonard A. Ford, who had earned a Ph.D., but had only two years service at Mankato State, was ranked as an "instructor in chemistry and mathematics."[136]

## Effects of the Great Depression

On September 1, 1930, Frank D. McElroy's first day as the Mankato State Teachers College president, the nation's economy was reeling from the shock of the recent stock market crash. For eight consecutive years beginning with 1922, the New York stock exchange as measured by the Dow Jones Industrial Average had gained about 20 percent annually and reached a high of 381.2 on September 3, 1929. These spectacular gains caused millions of people to take out loans so they could invest in the market, whose value seemed destined for inevitable rises.[137]

But debtor investors, especially, were shocked and in most cases ruined financially by the stock market crash of October 1929, highlighted by the losses of October 24 (Black Thursday), 28 (Black Monday) and 29 (Black Tuesday). The 11 percent drop on Black Thursday was mostly remedied when New York City's major banks rushed in to buy stocks. But the incident unnerved many stockholders who sold on the following Monday and Tuesday, when the market dropped 13 and 12 percent respectively. Realizing that the market would not recover in the foreseeable future, creditors demanded repayment of their loans. This action not only created a new debtor class but discouraged further lending, which caused businesses to curtail operations and capital to become dearer.

In retrospect, the October 1929 crash, was identified as the start of the Great Depression. Widespread hopes for a relatively rapid recovery were devastated by the continuous worsening of the stock market, which by the end of 1931 had lost about 80 percent of its pre-crash value.

Other economic indicators also demonstrated the deepening depression. For 1930 the country had a deflation rate of -2.7 percent. This increased sharply the next two years with deflation of -8.9 and -10.3 percent respectively.[138] During this deflationary run the national unemployment rate increased from 8.7 percent in 1930 to a depression era low of 23.6 percent two years later.[139]

On a daily basis, producers were primarily concerned with declining commodity prices. For example, at the end of 1929 No.1 Northern wheat was selling for $1.23 a bushel on the Mankato market. Exactly two years later it stood at $0.61. For the same period the price of yellow shelled corn fell from $0.61 to $0.32 per bushel. Since agriculture was Minnesota's ranking industry, the sharp decline in farm produce prices had ripple effects that detrimentally affected all aspects of the state's economy.[140]

As incomes were being reduced consumers became aware that because of deflation, what little money they possessed had more purchasing power. This is well illustrated by the price of flour. On December 31, 1929, a 49-pound bag of Mother Hubbard flour retailed for $2.20 in Mankato. Two years later it sold for $1.45. In terms of 2017 equivalencies, the 1929 dollar had a value of about $14.25 and the dollar for 1933, the most deflated of the depression years, was worth $18.90.[141]

As state revenue, which was derived mainly from property taxes and certain excise taxes, declined during the deepening depression, the State Teachers College Board acknowledged that it would have to reduce college budgets. At its meeting of April 25,1932, the board resolved: "That this Board recognizes the widespread economic depression throughout the state and nation, the necessity for rigid economy in the expenditures and the necessity for limiting, except in cases of emergency, the acquisition of grounds, buildings, and equipment other than those already contracted for, or for which appropriation has already been made, and the need for restricting any increases in salaries or expenditures for other activities until such time as present economic depression shall have passed."[142]

In issuing this policy statement, the board evidently assumed that faculty salaries would be frozen. Consequently, they maintained faculty salaries for the 1932-1933 academic year at the previous year's rate. But the board members soon learned that Farmer-Labor Governor Floyd B. Olson, a candidate for re-election in 1932, had other ideas.

Targeting all public employee salaries, Olson sent instructions to all state agencies, including the State Teachers College Board. He requested that all state college faculty members and other employees forego half of their June salary if they received more than $100 monthly and one-quarter of it if their monthly salary was less than $100. The board on June 10, 1932, approved the reductions, but recognized that with respect to the faculties they would effect only summer session teachers and those compensated on a 12-month basis. Furthermore, the board reduced all previously approved 1932-1933 salaries by 1/24 (4.17 %).[143]

But, in the judgment of the governor and the board, the reductions approved in 1932 did not go far enough. Consequently, when it considered 1933-1934 salaries the board slashed them 20 percent from the original previous year's base. The impact of this reduction is well-illustrated in the nine-month salaries of George J Miller and Gilbert H. Trafton, the top Mankato State faculty wage earners. Miller's $3,600 salary was cut to $2,880 and Trafton's $3,300 reimbursement was reduced to $2,640.[144]

The cuts proved to be relatively short-lived as the economy improved slightly. Without offering any rationale, the board began increasing faculty salaries in 1935. Consequently, for the 1937-1938 academic year, the salaries of Miller, Trafton and all other faculty members were fully restored to their pre-cut amounts.[145]

Depression conditions also caused the state to re-examine the free tuition policy of the teachers colleges that had been in place since their inceptions as normal schools. Since the original policy had been established by law, only the legislature could change it. By an act approved on April 17, 1933, the legislature enacted tuition specifications. It authorized the State Teachers College Board to begin charging tuition commencing September 1, 1933. The law allowed the board to charge Minnesota residents "not less than $5.00 nor more than $15.00 during each of the first six quarters" and "not less than $10.00 nor more than $20.00 for each quarter thereafter." The act regarded a summer session as a quarter. Non-resident students were required to pay an additional $5.00 per quarter.[146]

On May 1, 1933, the board decided that beginning with the fall 1933 quarter, resident tuition would be $10.00 per quarter. Non-residents were required to pay $15.00. Although they were not part of the law, the board also provided that tuition would "include the use of textbooks where such books are now owned and controlled by the college" and that the tuition proceeds would be devoted to maintenance, repairs, betterments and equipment purchasing.[147]

The new resident tuition charges of $30 for the three-quarter 1933-1934 academic year increased the total cost of attending Mankato State by approximately 15 percent. The occupants of Buck and Cooper halls paid $60 quarterly for room and board. Private home rates for other students were comparable. Additionally, all students paid a quarterly fee of $9.50 that covered textbook rental, attendance at all cultural and athletic events and student health services. Thus, the academic year charges for a dormitory resident totaled $238.50. At first glance these seem like modest costs, but their total was the equivalent of about $4362.17 in 2017 dollars.[148]

During the depression there were several student relief programs consisting of Mankato State's Student Loan Fund and two federally sponsored student work-study programs. The Student Loan Fund, which amounted to $2,300 in 1935, was established by donations from the graduating classes of 1916, 1917 and 1918 and a $1,000 bequest from Josephine H. Bowden, who taught English at Mankato State from 1911 to 1927. The college used the fund to make short-term loans of $10 to $75 to students "who have shown good scholarship."[149]

Federal funding for student work-study programs was an essential part of President Franklin D. Roosevelt's New Deal program. Roosevelt, believed that the depression could be ended only by a massive infusion of federal funding and instituting such reforms as a national social security system.

The New Deal's first relief action to benefit college students was the Civil Works Administration (CWA), which Roosevelt created by an executive order in 1933. Placed within the Federal Emergency Relief Administration (FERA), the CWA made block grants to states, which were required to contribute some matching funds. The State of Minnesota distributed a designated sum to the State Teachers College Board, which in turn made allocations to the respective colleges.[150]

The CWA program was started at Mankato State in December, 1933, but because of Christmas vacation its first full month of operation was January, 1934. For the period December, 1933 through May 1934, Mankato State employed 106 student CWA workers. They worked a total of 7,164 hours and were reimbursed $3,950.81 or $0.55 per hour. Federal funding covered 60 percent of the program's cost and the state contributed the remainder.[151]

The CWA work force comprised nearly a tenth of the student body, whose enrollment as of January 27, 1933, was 1,156. The commonest CWA assignment was assisting instructors, which involved 36 students. The only other classifications that had more than six students were janitorial work, assisting in library, clerking, typing and repairing furniture/equipment.

The CWA was discontinued in 1935 when the FERA, which was intended to provide only short-term relief, was replaced by the WPA. In order to continue college work study and other relief for young people, Roosevelt, again by executive order, created the National Youth Administration (NYA). The NYA, which was operated until 1939 as part of the WPA before being transferred to another agency, was discontinued in 1943.[152]

Extant Mankato State records suggest that the NYA did not have as much impact as the CWA. In the winter quarter of the 1937-1938 academic year, Mankato State employed 126 (67 freshmen, 28 sophomores, 14 juniors and 17 seniors) NYA students. Their total compensation was $924.50. Individual payments ranged from a low of $5 to a high of $18 with most in the $7 to $8 range.[153]

Although such New Deal programs as the PWA and WPA provided some economic relief, the Great Depression was not ended until after the United States entered World War II. In 1942, the first full year of American involvement, the national unemployment rate was only 4.7 percent. Wartime mobilization helped the economy, but it caused new problems for Mankato State Teachers College.

## World War II Developments

World War II was started in Europe when Germany invaded Poland on September 1, 1939. Two days later Great Britain and France declared war on Germany. The United States, which had pursued an isolationist neutrality policy throughout the 1930s, reacted with the Neutrality Act of November 4, 1939. While reaffirming neutrality, it significantly authorized arms sales on a cash and carry basis.

Americans became increasingly concerned about the United States being drawn into the war as German armies waged successful offensives against British and French forces on the Western Front. Consequently, on September 16, 1940, Congress approved the Selective Service Act, which established the first peacetime draft in American history. In a move clearly aimed at the United

## To Students And Faculty

Dr. Frank D. McElroy, president of the college, announced Monday the position the Mankato State Teachers college would take in the present emergency conflict.

"Since schools are essential to defense, it is our obligation to carry on as in the past until such time as it becomes apparent to national leaders that we can contribute more to the national good in some other line.

"The leaders of this institution are urging all students and staff members to carry on in any duty assigned without loss of time or energy, and to be ready to make any sacrifice or perform any service that will promote the successful termination of our international conflict."

President McElroy's response to Pearl Harbor. *College Reporter*, 12 December 1941

States, the Fascist nations of Germany, Italy and Japan allied themselves by the Tripartite Pact. Signed in Berlin about a week and a half after the passage of the American draft law, the Triple Alliance increased the likelihood of a Pacific war between the United States and Japan.

The United States abandoned its neutrality policy when Congress passed the Lend-Lease Act on March 11, 1941. The law authorized the president to provide military aid on credit to any country whose defense was deemed vital to the security of the United States. The act was originally intended to aid Great Britain and France, but was extended to the Union of Soviet Socialist Republics (USSR) after Germany invaded it on June 22, 1941.

After a German army began occupying Paris on June 14, 1941, President Roosevelt agreed to an unprecedented degree of cooperation with Great Britain. On August 14, 1941, after Germany established an occupation zone in France, Roosevelt and Great Britain's Prime Minister Winston Churchill agreed to the Atlantic Charter. By this pact the United States and Great Britain pledged to support democratic countries and oppose aggression.

Meanwhile, Japan, which had imperial aspirations in the Far East, became alarmed at the apparently increasing American threat. Believing that the United States could devastate their country's economy simply by blocking the importation of oil, Japanese leaders decided their only chance of prevailing was to go on the offensive.

The surprise Japanese aerial attack on American naval forces at Pearl Harbor, Hawaii, on Sunday, December 7, 1941, was brilliantly executed and caused heavy U.S. losses. But, its unintended effect was to stimulate American determination and morale. The United States declared war on Japan the next day. On December 11, Germany and Italy declared war on the United States, which reciprocated the same day.

The Triple Alliance, generally called the Axis Powers during the war because of the Berlin-Rome axis, was initially on the offensive. But, its success was relatively short-lived. The turning point in the Pacific was the naval battle off Midway Atoll on June 4-7, 1942. In this engagement American forces notably destroyed four Japanese aircraft carriers. With no capacity to rebuild them, Japan had to go on the defensive against America's island hopping offensive. After Great Britain successfully withstood German aid bombardment, American and British forces on July 10, 1943, invaded Sicily, the large Mediterranean island just south of the Italian boot. Their subsequent invasion of the mainland later in the month took Italy out of the war.

After the collapse of Italy's Fascist government, the Allies planned an offensive against occupied France. Named and extensively broadcasted in advance, D-Day (generically, military lingo for the day an event will occur), the invasion from southern England was launched on June 6, 1944. Unable to resist Allied advances on both their Western and Eastern fronts, Germany surrendered on May 7, 1945, which the victors declared V-E Day (Victory in Europe Day).

The Pacific War was ended earlier than anticipated because of President Harry Truman's decision to use the recently developed atomic bomb against Japan. Japan surrendered on August 14, 1945 (V-J Day or Victory in Japan Day), only eight days after an American airplane dropped an atomic bomb on the city of Hiroshima and five days after a second atomic bomb devastated the city of Nagasaki.[154]

Throughout the military phases of World War II the Roosevelt administration also emphasized the "Home Front." Americans were constantly reminded that the war involved all elements of society and that civilians as well as the armed forces were expected to contribute to the war effort. All governmental levels—federal, state, county and municipal—encouraged the purchasing of war bonds. The bond program involved school children who were exhorted to buy a weekly savings stamp for a quarter. A completed stamp book could be redeemed for a $25 savings bond.

Other than the bond drives, civilians were involved by wartime rationing of gasoline, sugar, meat and other food products. Some of the sacrifices civilians were expected to make included the lack of consumer goods. There was no automobile manufacturing during the war, because vehicle factories were converted to the production of tanks and other armored vehicles. Even such common household items as pots and pans were in short supply, because kitchen appliance factories were generally converted to the production of ammunition.[155]

The various home front programs and policies created an atmosphere in which civilians generally felt they had a personal stake in the war. The seeming totality of the war effort affected all elements of society including Mankato State Teachers College, which rapidly adjusted to a wartime environment.

Although wartime mobilization boomed the state and nation's economies, Mankato State did not share in this prosperity. Actually, the war created an enrollment crisis that was worse than the preceding depression era. The wartime enrollment slump was precipitated by the combined effects of building up the armed forces and the luring of young women into defense-related jobs that paid better than teaching positions.

Like all states, Minnesota contributed heavily to the buildup of the nation's armed forces. The 304,100 Minnesotans who had military experience represented more than 10 percent of the state's population of 2,792,300 that was reported in the 1940 federal census. This degree of participation meant that all Minnesotans had a personal stake in the war because they had a relative, neighbor or acquaintance who was on military duty. During the war, 209,500 Minnesotans served in the army and army air corps, 79,300 in the navy, 11,800 in the Marine Corps and 3,500 in the coast guard. Army/army air corps casualties totaled 4,399 died in combat or because of wounds, 382 died in prison camps and 32 were classified as missing. Of Minnesota's navy servicemen, 1,444 died in combat or because of wounds, 30 died in prison camps and 22 were categorized as missing.[156]

The wartime history of Mankato State Teachers College and its five sister institutions was dominated by enrollment decline. For the last full pre-war academic year, which extended from aummer aession I 1940, through spring 1941, Mankato State had a total enrollment of 1,479. The combined enrollment for the two summer sessions was 777 and the total for the fall, winter and spring terms was 702. For 1942-43, the first fulltime war year, the total enrollment of 1,051 consisted of 769 in the summer sessions and 282 in the fall, winter and spring terms combined. In the second full war year, 1943-44, the total enrollment of 1,039 included 236 in the fall, winter and spring terms and 803 in the summer sessions. The 236 was the lowest nine-month enrollment since 1883-84.[157]

Other than peaking during the summer sessions, the wartime enrollment featured a spectacular decline of male students. For Fall 1941, the enrollment was 236 men and 438 women. The statistics for Fall 1945, were 46 men and 314 women.

The enrollment sag affected all education programs and policies. Low enrollment aggravated the existing shortage of rural teachers. The enrollment crisis furthermore meant that Mankato State and the other Minnesota teachers colleges were overstaffed. But correctly presuming a postwar enrollment surge, the governing board decided that rather than dismissing faculty it would employ them in ways other than teaching regular on-campus classes. Additionally, the dearth of men caused drastic adjustments in the intercollegiate athletic program, an integral part of the college's social life.

To allay the rural teacher shortage, McElroy started an accelerated course for the 1942-43 academic year. The calendar was contracted by starting the fall term on August 31 and eliminating all vacations except Christmas. Offering regular courses in four quarters throughout the year enabled four-year degree students to complete their work in three years and two-year diploma students to

# College Will Put in Call 'Hedy Lamarr'--Urgent

Is Mankato State in need of a **Hedy Lamarr**? "No," chorus the 361 TC coeds who find competition keen enough already. "Yes," says **Miss Sara Alexander**, who supervises the sale of war stamps in the bookroom. "We could use her war bond sales ability here."

War stamps are on sale at the college bookroom every day during bookroom hours. So far this year, **Miss Alexander** reports, purchase of the stamps by college students has been very small; elementary students in the training school have been far better customers.

Lack of sufficient advertising may be one reason for the small sale, **Miss Alexander** believes. She suggests that war stamps be sold in the hall one day a week (here's a chance for the local Hedys to do their part), that blackboard notices urging the sale of stamps be placed in classrooms, and that signs and slogans in the corridor be changed periodically.

## Coming Events

**Tonight . . .**
Football game at Bemidji.
**Saturday, October 3 . . .**
All-college women's tea at the city YWCA from 2-4 p. m.
**Monday, October 5 . . .**
Primary election for Homecoming princess.
**Wednesday, October 7 . . .**
Walter P. Morgan, president of State Teachers College in McComb, Illinois.
**At 7 p. m. . . .**
Columbus Day broadcast over the College Radio Hour, KYSM.

The *College Reporter* regularly included articles and advertisements for war stamp and bond purchases. *College Reporter*, 2 October 1942

finish in a year and two quarters.[158]

The college's traditional on-campus course offerings were supplemented by the start of off-campus extension courses and participation in the federal government's program of training naval air cadets.

At the governing board's meeting of December 8, 1942, McElroy, speaking on behalf of himself and the other five teachers college presidents, proposed that the board authorize the teaching of off-campus extension courses. The board was intrigued by this then-novel idea of exporting education to an off-campus clientele. But it did not act on the proposal, because it was not clear that it had the authority to do so. Consequently, the issue was presented to the next legislature, which by an act of April 20, 1943, authorized the teachers colleges to offer extension courses.[159]

During the 1943 summer sessions, Mankato State offered a total of six extension courses in Freeborn, Mower, Jackson, Rice, Scott and Yellow Medicine counties. A subsequent board report showed that 137 students combined completed these courses. Thus, the extension enrollment accounted for approximately eight percent of the 1,039 students enrolled for the 1943-1944 academic year. The success of the off-campus program encouraged Mankato and its sister institutions to greatly expand It in the postwar era.[160]

The ground training of naval air cadets was the college's major effort to expand its non-traditional offerings. This program, which lasted from January, 1943 to August 3, 1944, had two important precedents.

The federal government first turned to colleges as sites for ground training for pilots after the passage of the Civil Aeronautics Act in 1939. Since the United States had a shortage of civilian pilots, the act authorized the development of the Civilian Pilot Training Program (CPTP). Like other college programs nationwide, the Mankato State Teachers College CPTP, which was started in September 1939, was designed to offer ground training for its own students who wanted to become civilian aviators. Throughout its brief history, which lasted until July 1942, Mankato State offered seven training sessions, which had a total enrollment of 146 students. The fourth through the seventh sessions included some non-Mankato State students.[161]

The CPTP program was succeeded by the War Training Service (WTS) program, because after the advent of World War II the country's most pressing need was for military pilots. This program, which lasted at Mankato State from July 1942 until January 1943, trained both army and navy air cadets. Participants were required to enlist in either the army or navy reserves and thus were not classified as being on active duty. Mankato State's WTS program featured eight-week sessions with 240 instructional hours during each session. With 30 hours of classroom time weekly, the trainees had little time for other activities.[162]

The WTS program provided the model for its successor—the ground training of naval air cadets. The navy decided its best option for pilot ground training was to contract with former WTS institutions, including Mankato State. During its approximate year-and-a-half duration, the naval air cadets ground training program consisted of a succession of eight-week sessions with a class of new cadets arriving every eight weeks. Like the preceding WTS program, each session had a total of 240 instructional hours with the emphasis on mathematics, physics, navigation, air regulations, physical training, aircraft identification and meteorology. Compared to the college's regular enrollment, participation in the naval air training program was relatively heavy. Slightly more than 400 trainees completed the elementary training course and 372 were taught in the secondary course. For statistical purposes, they were not considered to be regular Mankato State students and thus were not included in the college's enrollment.[163]

All naval air cadets were on active duty, dressed in uniforms and adhered to the dictates of military discipline. Generally, they were quite segregated from the student body. Cooper Hall was designated for their exclusive housing use and the third floor of the main building was reserved for their classrooms. Their on-campus presence featured marching in formation between the dormitory and their classrooms.

The naval training program on college campuses proved to be short-lived. The Navy phased it out in August, 1944, in favor of conducting its own training at Navy air stations with its own pilots as instructors.[164]

For Mankato State, the program did provide much needed relief for its awkward overstaffing problem. Thirteen different faculty members, or more than a quarter of the total faculty, were involved in the naval training program. Much of the technical instruction was done by Gerrit M. Wissink, professor of physics, who taught aircraft engine operation and aerial and celestial navigation, and Leonard A. Ford, assistant professor of chemistry, who instructed aircraft operation and servicing. Eugene Fair, Jr., who taught history at Mankato State, 1935-1945, was the aerial navigation instructor. Biologist Mark M. Keith and J. N. Hook of English taught civil air regulations. Music instructor Alexis Parlova taught military science and discipline. Coach Carlyn P. Blakeslee, who had served on the Western Front during World War I, taught infantry drill and, along with football coach James R. Clark, Earle S. Wigley, training school administrator and former varsity athlete, and Maurice Nelson taught physical education. Miles E. Hawk, professor of education, taught aerial physics. Anson Van Eaton, a political scientist, taught aerial mathematics and Thomas A. Hart of English taught radio code.[165]

The striking shortage of male students during the war devastated the intercollegiate athletic program. In the spring of 1942 the track team participated in only two events—including the conference meet at Bemidji. The undermanned baseball team played only four games against nearby Gustavus Adolphus. The basketball schedule was reduced in the days after the Pearl Harbor attack, the darkest period of the war when Japan had the upper hand. The fall 1942, football schedule was reduced to six games. Mankato State and St. Cloud State, which tied for the conference title, did not play each other. As a patriotic gesture to support the federal government's gasoline rationing program, they decided not to schedule a playoff game.[166]

Despite the cutbacks, 1942 proved to be the most active for intercollegiate sports. Football was cancelled for 1943, 1944 and 1945, which forced the college to schedule homecomings as a winter event observed in connection with an intramural basketball game.[167]

Unlike Cooper, who during World War I minimized the 50th anniversary of the institution's founding, McElroy and some faculty members chose to emphasize the 75th anniversary of their school's start despite the persistent wartime crisis. Their interest in local history may have been spurred by wartime patriotism, which glorified the nation's unique history as the world's largest democracy.

On August 23, 1943, when the 75th birthday of the school's opening on October 7, 1868, was fast approaching, E. Raymond Hughes, a Mankato lawyer who was then serving as Blue Earth County's resident director, asked the State Teachers College Board to financially support celebration events. The board responded by approving the expenditure of up to $800 for the resident director, president and staff to plan the anniversary observance.[168]

Apparently the appropriation was used primarily to fund a series of talks during the week of the anniversary. On Wednesday, October 6, Dr. Arthur E. Morgan, famed as a civil engineer, author, environmentalist, educator and government official, spoke on the "The Place of the Community in the Future of Minnesota." Morgan's many accomplishments were highlighted by his presidency of Antioch College, 1919-1936, and his service as first chairman of the Tennessee Valley Authority, 1933-1938. During World War II he was mainly involved in Quaker relief activities in Finland and other countries. His evening presentation in the college auditorium was preceded by a banquet hosted by the Mankato Chamber of Commerce for the college faculty and distinguished guests.[169]

The next morning Otto Welton Snarr, president of Moorhead State Teachers College, presented "History of the Mankato State Teachers College." His talk was based on his own Mankato State experiences, research on the early normal school history and his doctoral dissertation. As director of professional education at Mankato State, 1920-1941, Snarr ranked next to presidents Cooper and McElroy in importance; his interest in the history of Mankato State caused him to supervise NYA work study students, who compiled information about the early normal school era. Snarr's University of Chicago doctoral dissertation, "The Education of Teachers in the Middle States: An Historical Study of Professional Education of Public School Teachers as a State Function," made him a leading scholar about normal schools and teachers colleges.[170]

On Thursday evening, October 7, Will Durant, the commemoration's featured presenter, talked on "The Coming Peace." At that time Durant was best known nationally and internationally for writing The *Story of Philosophy* (1926). His popular book, which reportedly had sold two million copies by 1943, introduced much of the lay public to the salient aspects of western philosophy. Its popularity made Durant financially independent, which enabled him to embark on his life-long project of writing in association with his wife Ariel the 11-volume *The Story of Civilization*.[171]

The series was closed on Friday evening, October 8, by William Lydgate, editor of the Gallup Poll, whose address was titled "Can We Trust the Common Man?" Lydgate, whose experience as a journalist, including writing for *Fortune* and *Time* magazines, joined George Gallup in 1935 when the Gallup Poll was formed as a service to newspapers.[172]

The talks were a significant community outreach effort by the college. All were open to the public and throughout their presentations, McElroy arranged student-guided campus tours.

Other than the four talks, the commemoration was marked by two efforts to write about the institution's history. Dr. J. N. Hook, a University of Illinois Ph.D. who had joined the Mankato State faculty as an English instructor in 1941, wrote a series of six articles for the *Mankato Free Press*. Relying almost entirely on Mankato newspapers, Hook reported on the formation and early years of the normal school, the school at the turn of the century and a very general review of the first 75 years.[173]

Lengthy portions of Hook's articles were incorporated verbatim into "The First Seventy-Five Years: An Informal History of Mankato State Teachers College" that was published in the January 1944 issue of *School Progress*. This survey of about 8,000 words was apparently designated informal because it was undocumented. Except for those portions copied without attribution from Hook's articles, it was also written anonymously. Judging by its contents, the history was based primarily on newspaper articles, school catalogs and faculty reminiscences. Despite its limitations, the history was the most complete one done during Mankato State's first 75 years.

## The McElroy Legacy

The twin crises of the Great Depression and World War II threatened to make McElroy's administration the dark age in the entire history of Mankato State. But amazingly, there was a sharp increase in the faculty's size from 1930 to 1946. For the academic year 1945-1946 there were 44 faculty members in the college's six divisions with nine in Fine and Applied Arts, nine in Health and Physical

## The College Reporter

### Do Cadets Burn Midnight Oil?

From left to right are aviation cadets Richard Larson, Henry Klemke, and Roger Koercher studying navigation.

## Formulae Confuse Studious Naviators

### By Cadet John Halaska

"SRM equals DRM, MRM equals miles of relative movement. EP equals WS, oh darn, I'm tired—wonder what my girl back home is doing? Gee I'll bet the gang is having fun. I wonder what we'll do tomorrow in gym class? Just think, tomorrow is Saturday and we get liberty."

Thoughts like these mosey through the heads of the cadets each evening as they observe their scheduled study hour. At this time of the day, you will always find cadets in various attires and positions bent over their books, attempting to determine the why's, wherefore's and how come's of a particular lesson.

These men, who upon completion of their training, will become naval officers. They are taking courses, which in the future, will be used in their everyday life as civilians.

Included in these courses are navigation, to enable the pilot to know at all the times his exact location; meteorology, to predict the weather; communications, to be able to take and send code blinker and semaphore; engines, to know just what makes his engine operate, how it operates, and just what to do if it stops operating; civil air regulations, to know the rules of the skyways; and recognition, to be able to recognize instantly planes, destroyers, battleships, cruisers, etc.

After all of these subjects are covered, or at least looked into, the cadet retires so that he may reserve enough energy to carry him through the activities of the morrow.

## Cadets Pick Page Name

"Slipstream" is the name that has been chosen for this page. It is derived from the flight of a plane. The definition given by Webster is: "The stream of air driven aft by the propeller, having a velocity greater than the surrounding air."

The name was chosen because of its significance. The stream of air is the news, the propeller signifies the editor and his staff. The phrase, "having a greater velocity than the surrounding air," tells the story that the articles have the power to stand out in any competition. (You name it.)

### To A Cadet

## For Future Use

Fall . . . the fresh, crisp air . . . the smell of damp leaves . . . the silver of frost on adjoining roofs . . . the flaming red and yellow maple beacons . . . late blooming flowers—cannas, asters, marigolds—reds, and purples, and yellows . . . a patch of green entangled in dead grass . . . the scratch of bare tree limbs against the screens . . . a harvest moon . . . little kids shuffling through the leaves, big kids waiting 'til dark to try the same thing . . . a foggy morning . . . hikes and weinies and bonfires . . . the smell of leaves burning . . . the blackness of freshly plowed fields . . . even lines of shocked corn . . . the tang of new-mown hay . . . the northern forest fires . . . storm windows to wash . . . yards to rake . . . early twilight . . . hazy dawn . . . Fall . . .

### The Slipstream

**CADET STAFF**

Editor.................Cadet John Halaska
Assistant-editor ...........................
...................Cadet Milton L. Reynolds
Photographer ...............................
..................Cadet Richard Larson
Student assistant..........................
..................Charlotte Mitchell
Adviser.............Lieutenant Banks

# The Slipstream

Number 2        MANKATO, MINNESOTA        October 8, 1943

## Meet The Cadets

### by Cadet Milton L. Reynolds

The first cadet to be interviewed is not a relative of John L. Sullivan, but just plain **Paul Sullivan** of Hibbing. "The Iron Ore Capital of the World," it says here in small print.

While attending high school he was outstanding in basketball. He was one of the best guards the mines could produce. His quick judgment and dead-eye shooting has been displayed many times in the Mankato State gym.

Even during his childhood, he was interested in planes and this interest continued until his enlistment in the Navy V-5 program.

His girl friend back home is attending Hibbing Junior college majoring in nursing education. She intends to aid John by joining the Red Cross upon completion of her training.

Meet Cadet **Harold (Lewy) Benson**. He comes from the state of Minneapolis. To him there isn't a state of Minnesota, just the state that Minneapolis is located in.

After finishing high school, Lewy saw a future in welding. He took a nine months course in welding at Smith Chemical Gas company in Minneapolis. He intended to take the navy examination for welding but abandoned the idea and worked as a receiving clerk in the Central and Hanover bank.

Whenever a dance is held for the cadets, you can see him in the midst of it having fun. In the event that you doubt his marching abilities, you can see these displayed before Daniel Buck hall, any time between reveille and taps.

Writing up Lewy Benson and not his inseparable pal, **Robert W. Johnson**, is like attempting to get gasoline without stamps. (Or can you?)

In any case, here he is. As historical facts have it, Bobby has known Lewy since they were knee high to a grasshopper. They both joined the Navy V-5, and now we have them here at Mankato State, brother Benson and brother Johnson.

However, we must get on with this interview of R. W. Johnson. Upon graduating from high school, he traveled to Los Angeles and worked as inspector in the Douglas Aircraft corporation. Inspector, in this case, meaning a member of the receiving department of small parts used in planes.

Bobby worked in the Douglas plant until his enlistment, whereupon he returned to his home in Minneapolis to await his call to duty.

The last cadet for the week is **Jay Schulenburg** from Wells. According to Jay, the distance from Mankato to Wells may be covered in 15 minutes, if you run.

While in high school, Jay wanted to be a big business man like his brothers. Besides having this interest in business, he was a letterman in basketball and starred in track.

His interest in business carried through until his completion of high school when he entered the grocery business to work for his brothers. This was his occupation until his enlistment in the navy.

Included in his hobbies are photography and hunting. However, since the war has stopped these activities, Joey has concentrated upon flying and upon earning his wings.

## State Receives More Cadets

A new group of naval aviation cadets arrived at Mankato September 30. These members of the sixth and seventh battalions at St. Olaf college, Northfield, became members of the 44D group elementary at this base.

Immediately upon their arrival they received the primary instructions of the Mankato base.

Ground school classes for the new group began October 1.

## Barracks Bugler Looks At Life

Some day I'm gonna murder the bugler,
Some day they're gonna find him dead ,
**But first I'll murder the other pup,
The guy who wakes the bugler up
And spend the rest of my life in bed.**

There's no doubt about it—being a bugler in the navy is one of the most unpopular jobs on the books. His job lasts from taps 'til reveille. Every time the cadets have to assemble, it's the bugler who lets them know. He tells them when to get up and when to go to bed; when to eat, and when to go to classes; when to assemble for inspection and when to turn off the lights.

But what about the bugler? Who tells him all these things? It's the unlucky cadet on the dog watch who wakes the bugler before the crack of dawn. The rest of the time he's on his own.

In the first five minutes that elapse after the bugle call, all the kinks that were supposedly straightened out over night, are put back by a session of calisthenics. At the completion of this five minute period of joint-creaking, comes the thirty minute period of comparative rest when all you have to do is: shine your shoes, wash and shave, make your bunk, sweep the deck, and, of course, get dressed for inspection. When you're almost done with this, the bugler blows the chow call and the cadets race down the stairs to the dining hall like a pack of hungry wolves.

While you're swallowing your last mouthful of coffee the bugler sounds off again. This time it's school call!

The cadets muster while the platoon leader takes roll call to see that some cadet hasn't gotten lost in the shuffle.

After a morning of flying for some and academics for others, it's chow time and the bugler has to beat the rest of the cadets up to the barracks to blow chow call.

After noon chow, cadets have 45 minutes in which to read (the literature ranges from comics to classics, from love letters to family letters). Per usual, the bugler breaks this up. It's the school call, and classes for the afternoon begin.

Coming back from classes the cadets immediately answer the last chow call for the day.

It's 1900 when the land sailor starts to march. For one long hour we march to the strains of "Hut, two, three four." After completing this new foot-sweller, we have study until (and here we go again) the bugler sounds the call to quarters. We have fifteen minutes in which to prepare ourselves for sleep.

We call it rugged. This is the time we want to talk and write letters, but the bugler sounds off and we go to bed knowing that tomorrow we will have at least a couple of hours' liberty.

"The Slipstream" was a section of the *College Reporter* dedicated to cadet news.
*College Reporter* 8 October 1943.

1868

# 75th ANNIVERSARY

**Schedule of Events:**

**WEDNESDAY, OCTOBER 6**

Chamber of Commerce Dinner, Saulpaugh Hotel

Address, "The Place of the Community in the Future of Minnesota," Dr. A. E. Morgan, former chairman TVA and president of Antioch college

*8:15 P. M., College Auditorium*

**THURSDAY, OCTOBER 7**

Address, "History of Mankato State Teachers College", Dr. O. W. Snarr, President, Moorhead State Teachers College

*10:00 A. M., College Auditorium*

Address, "The Coming Peace", Dr. Will Durant, philosopher and author

*8:15 P. M., College Auditorium*

*Public Reception, College Auditorium*

**FRIDAY, OCTOBER 8**

Address, "Can We Trust the Common Man?", Dr. William Lydgate, Editor, The Gallup Poll

*8:15 P. M., College Auditorium*

Mankato
State Teachers College
**OCTOBER 6-7-8**

1943

75th Anniversary schedule
of events poster, 1943

Education, seven in Language and Literature, eight in Professional Education, four in Science and Mathematics and seven in Social Studies. With regard to academic training, nine had earned doctorates, 24 master's, 10 bachelor's and one a diploma.[174]

The 1945-1946 faculty improved markedly since 1930-1931, McElroy's first year. Then, there were 26 faculty members in the College Department. Their collective academic training was 13 master's, 12 bachelor's and one without a degree.[175]

The faculty grew because the governing board and the legislature were willing to recognize that staffing a teachers college should be based primarily on programmatic needs rather than the credit hours generated. The 1930-1931 and 1945-1946 enrollments were roughly comparable. For the academic year 1930-1931, which started with summer school, the college enrolled 934 different students. The 1945-1946 enrollment was 1,085, which included 135 extension students.[176]

Other than expanding the faculty, the curriculum and the physical plant, McElroy quietly changed the school's culture. Unlike Searing and Cooper, the principal shapers of the normal school culture, McElroy de-emphasized the role of organized religion in a public institution. Without any grand pronouncement he quietly discontinued chapel services and instead promoted convocation presentations by noted speakers and performing artists.

After retiring in 1946 when he was 68 years old, McElroy continued living in Mankato. Active in the Presbyterian Church, he also participated in several fraternal clubs and unsuccessfully ran for the Mankato City Council in 1952. He died on December 7, 1954.[177]

# 4

# THE CRAWFORD PRESIDENCY: ENROLLMENT BOOM AND DEVELOPMENT OF TWIN CAMPUSES, 1946-1965

At its St. Paul meeting of March 5, 1946, the Minnesota State Teachers College Board interviewed five finalists for the presidency of Mankato State Teachers College. They had been selected from "a number of available prospects." The interviewees included Clarence L. Crawford, superintendent of the Council Bluffs, Iowa, schools and Theodore L. Nydahl, professor of history and head of the Division of Social Studies at Mankato State Teachers College. Nydahl, a Minnesota native who earned his undergraduate degree from Augsburg College and his Ph.D. from the University of Minnesota, began teaching at Mankato State in 1928. The board unanimously elected Crawford, apparently because of his extensive background in public education.[1]

Crawford was born in Nuckolls County, Nebraska, on December 13, 1902. He graduated from Cotner College (Lincoln, Nebraska) in 1925 and three years later earned a master's degree from the University of Nebraska-Lincoln. He completed his Ph.D. degree at the University of Michigan in 1936. Crawford's varied experience included public high school teaching, serving as the superintendent of three public schools and directing research for the Michigan State Department of Education. Immediately prior to being selected to head Mankato State, he had been the Council Bluffs superintendent for six years.

Crawford served as president of Mankato State until he resigned in 1965. During his administration the college was rapidly transformed from a small school with about a thousand students to a very large one with an enrollment of more than 13,000 students.[2]

President Clarence L. Crawford, circa 1960

## The Enrollment Boom

Traditionally, Americans have glorified bigness. This was especially true of anything that could be quantified statistically. A numerical increase, be it of area, population, gross national production or number of participants, was seen as irrefutable proof of improvement and achievement. In Crawford's time it was much easier to measure the number of students than it was to determine improvements in the institution's academic achievements. Consequently, new, record-breaking enrollments provided the grist for most of the college's publicity. This affected the public perception of Mankato State, which to thousands of Minnesotans was primarily regarded as a rapidly growing place.

The emphasis on Mankato State's growth was underscored by impressive statistics. The head count enrollment (i. e. number of different individuals) of 1,017 for the 1945-46 academic year nearly doubled to 2,185 five years later. By 1955-56 the figure stood at 4,967, which zoomed to 9,187 for the 1961-62 academic year. In 1964-65, Crawford's last, the college had 13,378 students.[3]

Much of Mankato State's spectacular growth was caused by national and state developments. The pool of potential college students was increased by state population growth from 2,792,300 in 1940 to 3,806,103 three decades later. Furthermore, during that period Minnesota made the transition from being a rural to an urban state as measured by the number of residents who lived in places with a population of at least 5,000. Because of their more varied economy based on numerous professional specialties, urban areas increased the demand for college-educated workers.[4]

Mankato State's enrollment boom coincided with and benefitted from a rapid expansion of the national economy. During the 1950s and 1960s economic growth as measured by the Gross Domestic Product (GDP) calculation averaged more than four percent annually. This robust growth translated into higher employment and a more prosperous society, which helped make college affordable to thousands of families.[5]

Enrollment in the country's institutions of higher learning intensified in the quarter-century following

## Mankato State Reports

Enrollment increases at Mankato State College have been striking in recent years. The following charts indicate this progress. Figures are for the year 1958-1959 (where total figures for the year are used, the Spring Quarter figures are estimated) and for the period immediately after World War II, the year 1947-1948.

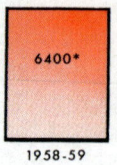

**MORE STUDENTS**

1762* — 1947-48

6400* — 1958-59

*Total for twelve months

**RAPID GROWTH**

Enrollment increases at Mankato compared to those in the State and in the entire country.

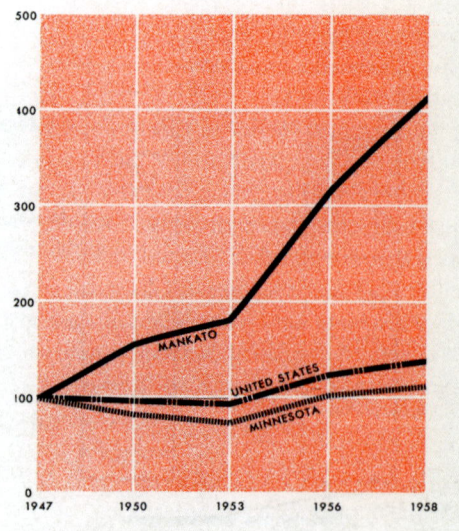

Fall Quarter 1947: 100
Sources: *Enrollment Reports For Upper Midwest Association of Collegiate Registrars* and annual enrollment reports in *Higher Education*.

School Progress, 1959

the end of World War II. In 1946 the nation's total enrollment of degree seekers stood at 2,078,000. By 1970 it had nearly quadrupled to 7,920,000.[6]

Part of this enrollment surge was caused by the federal government's financial aid of military veterans. In early 1944 Congress began considering ways of rewarding World War II veterans. On June 22, 1944, only 16 days after D-Day, Congress approved the Servicemen's Readjustment Act, which came to be popularly known as the G.I. Bill. After the passage of the Veterans' Adjustment Act of 1952, the original bill was generally identified as the World War II G.I. Bill to distinguish it from the second act, which was colloquially named the Korean War G.I. Bill.[7]

Among other benefits, which included support for home loans and unemployment compensation, both bills included an education component. The original G.I. Bill covered all college tuition, fees, books and supplies in addition to a monthly stipend of $75. The overall effect of the G.I. bills was to bring an infusion of students and money into the nation's institutions of higher learning. The G.I. bills are regularly hailed for their positive effects on millions of individual lives as well as the nation's economy and society. By 1965 an estimated 1.2 million veterans had benefitted from the higher education stipulations of the G.I. bills. At Mankato State, the highest proportion of G.I. enrollment occurred soon after World War II. For the winter term 1946-47, the G.I. enrollment of 414 represented slightly more than one-fourth of the student body.

Aside from state and national factors, an essential part of Mankato State's enrollment boom was caused by regional and municipal characteristics and college policies. The community of Mankato enjoyed unique geographic advantages. Within years of the city's founding in 1852, it emerged as the main municipality in an extensive hinterland. This feature is recognizable to the present day. Without a larger rival to its immediate south, Mankato's economic influence extends into northern Iowa. Sioux Falls, South Dakota, is the first city to the southwest that is larger than Mankato. To the northeast there is no place larger than Mankato until the Twin Cities Metropolitan Area and on the east one has to travel to Rochester to reach a place larger than Mankato. Before the 1967 opening of Southwest State University at Marshall, a hundred miles from Mankato, Mankato State did not have a public four-year college rival in southwestern Minnesota. Thus, Mankato's location left Mankato State unrivaled in attracting students to a degree granting public institution of higher learning.[8]

It is difficult to determine the cause-and-effect relationships between Mankato State and the City of Mankato. Obviously, more students benefitted the city's economy and were a major factor in its population growth. But, the growing city influenced many students to attend college there. The 1940 federal census reported Mankato had a population of 15,654. That figure was nearly doubled by 1970 when Mankato had 30,895 residents. Among other things Mankato's growth stimulated business, which, in turn, provided employment opportunities to hundreds of college students who needed to work part-time to defray their expenses.[9]

It is unlikely that any students were attracted to Mankato State solely because of the city's reputation for its lively social scene. But Mankato's social and cultural attractions may have been part of the reason some students decided to attend Mankato State.

There is much to be said for growth begetting growth. Students being attracted to Mankato State is somewhat analogous to the movement of European immigrants to the United States. Many who moved were influenced by their predecessors who lauded the opportunities presented in their new land. It would be impossible to determine the number of students who chose to attend Mankato State because of word-of-mouth recommendations, but is quite likely that many of them were influenced by relatives and acquaintances who preceded them. As Mankato State produced hundreds of new graduates, it was also generating potential recruitment agents. Part of their message probably emphasized that Mankato State was a bargain compared to attending a private college or the University of Minnesota, which was located in a relatively high-cost major urban area.

Lastly, Mankato State grew rapidly because Crawford emphasized growth and developed policies to encourage more of it. The first enrollment increase after World War II caused the campus to be very crowded. Obviously, the long range solution was to expand the physical plant. But that involved getting

The location of the City of Mankato has impacted the growth of the university over the years.

state appropriations and construction, which combined often ranged over two biennia. Thus, Crawford's first step in accommodating the burgeoning enrollment was to use existing space more efficiently, which was done by expanding class schedules. For the Fall 1946 term, all 50-minute class periods were scheduled to start at 8 a.m., 9 a.m., 10 a.m., 11 a.m., 1 p.m., 2 p.m. and 3 p.m. Noon and 4 p.m. classes were added in Fall 1949 and night classes in winter 1950-51. A night class covered the equivalent of the day classes scheduled during a week. So, for example, a 3-credit night class had to have two-and-a-half hours of instructional time.[10]

Crawford was also a strong promoter of off-campus classes, which were usually held in the classrooms of cooperating area high schools. Offering off-campus night classes throughout an area that extended to the southwest corner of the state required Mankato State to acquire a fleet of vehicles. The extended campus classes, as they came to be called, had the effect of expanding enrollment without the necessity of using the crowded college campus.

Coping with the enrollment explosion dominated all Crawford era planning. The initial reaction of Crawford, the governing board and the legislature was to expand the Valley Campus. But by late 1957 state officials recognized that despite the recent expansion of the campus to the downtown side of South Fifth Street, the Valley Campus had reached its limits. Therefore, they decided to expand to a Highland Campus location approximately a mile from the Valley Campus. At that time it appeared that Mankato State would permanently rely on two campuses.

The need to enlarge Mankato State physically was the first and most obvious outcome of the enrollment revolution. But larger enrollments created a more complex student body that wanted a regional college with a variety of offerings rather than a sole mission of preparing teachers. Consequently, the curriculum was enriched by the addition of numerous specialized courses and the increasing popularity of the Bachelor of Arts degree that did not have a required professional education component and the start of a graduate program in 1953. Moreover, new directions were undertaken with the organization of the Business Education Division in 1949 and the Nursing Division in 1953.

The addition of more new courses and programs and the need to teach more general education classes led to a rapid expansion of the faculty. This, in turn, made the old division system outmoded and led to a major reorganization of Mankato State's academic units near the end of Crawford's administration.

Lastly, more students, more courses, more faculty and new programs created the need for more administrators and the employment of more classified staff. By the close of Crawford's administration it was obvious that the burgeoning enrollment had profoundly affected the nature of the curriculum, the faculty, the administration and the support staff.

## Overview of Valley Campus Changes

During Crawford's time the most pressing Valley Campus needs were more student housing, more classrooms and more library space. The housing needs caused the creation of an off-campus facility for married students, the use of such expedients as temporarily housing students in one of the field house's basketball courts, the enlargement of coed housing and the construction of Searing Hall primarily for male students. The building of Nichols Hall on the block between the main building and the Blue Earth County courthouse solved the short term needs for more classroom space. Library enlargement was a two-step process. The first phase was the expansion of the library in the main building. But, this proved to be inadequate. Consequently, Lincoln Library, which was opened in 1958, was built on South Fifth Street opposite the Administration Building and campus training school building.

## Barracks Housing for Married Students

A partial solution to Mankato State's student housing shortage was provided by an off-campus complex of re-furbished surplus army barracks. Locally known as "The Barracks" after its opening in 1947, the facility was located on a tract of land that measured 188 by 264 feet (approximately 1.14 acres) just east across Dickinson Street from St. Joseph's Hospital, the predecessor of today's Mayo Clinic Health System Hospital in Mankato's hilltop area. This site on the north side of present-day Anderson Drive was mainly owned by the Mankato School District.[11]

According to local tradition Crawford first proposed this unique project. But, there is irrefutable evidence that the idea of using government surplus barracks for married student housing was originated by the State Teachers College Board late in the McElroy administration.[12]

At its meeting of March 5, 1945, the board noted that: "With the recent return of large numbers of veterans and the resulting increases in enrollments at the teachers colleges, a problem of housing students, particularly those who are married, has been created." Prior to the meeting, some board members had investigated the possibility of obtaining surplus federal government barracks from wartime prisoner-of-war camps, remodeling them and installing them on state teachers college campuses. They had also solicited opinions from the state attorney general about the legal issues involved in such transfers. McElroy's contribution to the lengthy discussion was to urge the board to act quickly while surplus barracks were still available.[13]

Despite McElroy's admonishment, two years elapsed before the board again discussed the surplus housing situation. But, fortuitously, on March 8, 1947, board president Warren H. Stewart was able to report that surplus buildings were "in use at St. Cloud, Moorhead and Winona. The Mankato College has procured some which are not in use at this time."[14]

Distribution of the surplus barracks for the Minnesota region was administered by the Chicago regional office of the U.S. Housing Authority The buildings purchased by the state for Mankato State's use were moved from the former German prisoner-of-war camp at Algona, Iowa.

While the State Teachers College Board and other state officials were arranging the transfer of the buildings, Mankato State had to find a site for them that would desirably be relatively close to the Valley Campus. Miles E. Hawk, who was then serving as Mankato State's director of student personnel and professor of education, chaired the site committee that negotiated with the Mankato school board and several private parties for land on which the barracks were erected. For those who followed South Fifth, Main and Dickinson streets, it was about 1.4 miles from the Valley Campus to The Barracks. But pedestrians usually used a convenient shortcut by hiking up and down the two-stage concrete stairway on the Pearl Street right-of-way. This rather steep path, which had been constructed sometime before 1931, ran from close to the rear northeast corner of the college's main building to the top of the hill overlooking the campus and the city. It was apparently constructed to provide a closer link between the Mankato High School and Hilltop Field at the site of present-day C. D. Alexander Park.[15]

The 12 barracks, each of which was 100 feet long and 20 feet wide, assigned to Mankato State had to be partitioned into apartment units before they could be used for married student housing. This remodeling provided space for 39 families with 27 two-bedroom apartments and 12 one-bedroom

Barracks housing for veterans, 1948

Joe Stepka and daughter Kathie in barracks housing, circa 1957.

apartments. The barracks project was completed shortly before the opening of the Fall 1947 term.[16]

All apartments were unfurnished except for a natural gas stove and space heater. Each unit had a shower but not a bathtub. So bathing babies had to be done in the kitchen sinks.

The barracks apartments, which in 1955 rented for $20 a month for two-bedroom units and $18 for one-bedroom, were generally reserved for military veterans during their 17-year history. But, during the early 1950s, when there was a lull in veterans' demand, some units were rented to other married students. Because The Barracks housing cost much less than privately owned Mankato apartments, there was a heavy demand for it. Consequently, the college maintained a waiting list, which was originally administered by Maurice Nelson, the dean of men, until he retired in 1959.

Most of what is known about life in The Barracks was due to Marcia Baer, who worked at Mankato State from October 1987 to March 2003, as an information officer for Printing Services in the University Advancement Division. She solicited and compiled reminiscences and photographs of 80 families that lived there. Their stories comprise the bulk of Baer's book, *Those Barracks Babies.*

Certain common themes ran through the reminiscences of the former occupants who were mostly 18 to 22 years old when they lived in The Barracks. With a seemingly high birth rate, The Barracks had many babies and young children. This feature caused residents to sometimes use the alternate name of "Rabbit Villa." Many barracks dwellers commented on having to cope with Minnesota's boreal winters. With only space heaters, no basements and thin walls, the apartments were usually very chilly. Snuggling up to space heaters was similar to the traditional rural use of wood-fueled heating stoves where people had hot fronts and cool backs. Some barracks residents tried to insulate their dwellings by piling snow against the outside walls. The lack of garages combined with automobiles equipped with manual chokes made starting cars a bit of an adventure.

Yet despite the housing's shortcomings, former residents invariably fondly recalled their life there as the good old days. They especially extolled the community's affordability and camaraderie.

In 1957 the Mankato school district notified Mankato State that it wanted its land back. But somehow the Crawford administration delayed until 1964, when The Barracks project was closed. Ten of the buildings were razed and their lumber was salvaged. The other two were sold to private parties.[17]

## The First Men's Dormitory

Because the overwhelming majority of Mankato State students were women until after World War II, there was no need for a men's dormitory. But, as several hundred veterans enrolled in each of the immediate postwar years, it was evident that the college needed a men's dormitory. Crawford urged it and the board included it in its request to the 1949 legislature.

The legislature responded by appropriating $700,000 for "constructing and equipping" the facility and another $60,000 to purchase its site. Nearly two months after the April 25 appropriation, the State Teachers College Board considered obtaining land for the dormitory. Director Howard Williams of Mankato reported to the board that the recommended dormitory site was the lower part of the steep hill that ran down from the city's Highland Park section to Glenwood Avenue. Glenwood formed the southern boundary of the land obtained for Mankato State in 1929 prior to the construction of the athletic field. Williams identified 50 lots in five different additions or sub-divisions of the city that needed to be acquired for the dormitory. Apparently, Williams knew that some of the property owners would not sell voluntarily. So he persuaded the board to approve his resolution that if necessary the board obtain the support of the attorney general when legal proceedings proved to be necessary.[18]

The required ground was acquired quite rapidly. Bids for the dorm construction were opened in June 1950 and building was started the next month. The Eric A. Carlstrom Company of Mankato was awarded the general construction contract and the architectural firm of Ernest H. Schmidt and Company was selected as the building's designer. Other significant contracts were made with Mankato Electric, F. J. Cuddy Plumbing and Heating and the graders Brown and Leguil.[19]

In preparing the site, Brown and Leguil levelled several acres just above the bottom of the hill. They found that it was necessary to remove hundreds of tons of dirt. The effect of their work was to leave a vertical bank about 60 feet high on the uphill side of the dormitory building and another sharp bank about 30 feet high adjacent to Glenwood Avenue.

The Schmidt Company designed a three-part building with the lowest portion paralleling Glenwood. The other long part extended diagonally toward the high bank. It and the Glenwood side unit were connected by a short third phase above the lower or western end of Glenwood Avenue. The completed three-story brick building trimmed with Kasota stone resembled a stylized vee with a squared bottom.

Construction on the men's dormitory proceeded very rapidly. The building was ready for occupancy at the opening of the Fall 1952 term and was dedicated as Searing Hall on October 11, 1952, as part of the homecoming observance.

With Crawford presiding at the dedication ceremonies, Dr. Dean

Searing Center after completion of 1957 addition overlooking Glenwood Avenue and MSTC athletic field.

Searing Center with residents
playing volleyball out front, 1968

Schweickhard, state commissioner of education, was the featured speaker. He was uniquely qualified to talk about Mankato State's progress. He was born and raised in Mankato and graduated from the Mankato Normal School in 1912. Subsequently, he earned a B.A. from the University of Wisconsin, a M.A. from the University of Minnesota and a Doctor of Education degree from Hamline University. He was appointed state education commissioner in 1943. Among other things, Schweickhard emphasized the key role of Edward Searing in the institution's development.[20]

Crawford, board member Williams and the homecoming visitors who toured Searing Hall were very pleased with it. The building featured 128-double rooms and was fully occupied for its first term. Additionally, there were two guest rooms and three apartments. The dorm's director had a ground-floor apartment and there were second- and third-story apartments with attached kitchenettes on the second and third floors.

Each of the regular dorm rooms had twin beds as well as two desks, a bookcase, an easy chair and wash basin. Each floor featured a tiled bathroom equipped with five showers and storage space for luggage.

Although it was hailed for meeting one of the college's major needs, Searing Hall soon proved to be inadequate for the college's male student housing needs. Therefore, only three years after it was dedicated, the board, at Crawford's instigation, authorized its enlargement.

Significantly, the addition to Searing Hall did not require a specific legislative appropriation. In 1955 the legislature authorized the State Teachers College Board to fund dormitory construction by issuing bonds. This process also involved final approval by the State Investment Board.[21]

In late winter 1956, the State Investment Board approved the issuance of state teachers college bonds to the extent of $3,100,000. The State Teachers College Board promptly announced that bids on the projected $840,000 Searing Hall expansion would be advertised within the next 30 to 45 days. The dormitory addition was to be a six-story building north of the Searing Hall section that paralleled Glenwood Avenue. Its western end was to be connected to the original hall.[22]

The State Teachers College Board awarded the various contracts on April 23, 1956. The George Carlstrom Construction Company of Mankato won the general construction contract. The mechanical, electrical, and elevator contracts were awarded respectively to Durenberger Plumbing and Heating of Mankato, Mankato Electric Company and the R and O Elevator Company of Minneapolis.[23]

Construction on the new Searing wing proceeded rapidly. Carlstom began pouring concrete footings and laying the foundation in early June. The new wing was projected to have a housing capacity of 300 students or about 50 more than the existing Searing Hall. The crowded Searing dorm residents were elated by the news that Carlstrom started laying bricks on September 17. This news augured well for the opening of the new wing by fall 1957.[24]

Despite a five-week workers' strike that began in early summer 1957, the contractors completed the wing's sleeping accommodations by the opening of the fall term. Although Searing Hall was generally a men's dormitory, the lower two floors of the six-story addition were devoted to women's housing. But, the opening of the new first floor cafeteria was delayed until fall 1958. By that time the steep bank between the addition and Glenwood Avenue had been graded and sodded.[25]

In fall of 1959, the Mankato State College Building Naming Committee recommended that Searing Hall be renamed to Searing Center. At that time the committee consisting of Ira H. Johnson, chairman and campus planner, Dave Peterson, Student Senate appointee, Marlyn Pixley, Student Senate appointee, Franklin Rogers, editor, *Mankato Free Press*, Morgan I. Thomas, Faculty Association president, Andrew R. Een, secretary, Alumni Association and Gretchen S. Morris, treasurer, Alumni Association, was considering names for all new college buildings. The Searing Center name became official on November 20, 1959, when it was approved by the State College Board.[26]

Cooper Center, 1958

## Expanding the Women's Dormitories

Crawford, who preferred that all freshman coeds live in college dorms, recognized that Buck and Cooper halls were too small and moreover needed some refurbishment. In 1946 the top floor of Cooper, which had been unfinished for a quarter century, was finally completed. Five years later, a legislative appropriation of $8,000 enabled the college to convert the dorm's outmoded coal-burning heating system to natural gas.[27]

Then in 1953 the legislature authorized a major expansion of existing dorms by appropriating $500,000. Later in the year Ernest Schmidt and Company of Mankato, the architectural firm chosen to design the changes, announced its plans. First, Cooper Hall would be extended about 30 feet toward South Fourth Street. Then the hall's other end (the right side when viewed from Ramsey Street) would be extended about 125 feet toward Ramsey Street. It would connect with Buck Hall and extend about 20 feet beyond it. This four-story extension was sometimes colloquially called Center Hall by dorm residents.[28]

Cooper Center roommates wearing freshman beanies setting up their room during Freshman Week 1959.

These additions not only increased dorm capacity, but also improved food service. Since the opening of Cooper Hall in 1921, which did not have its own dining hall, its residents had to use the facility on Buck Hall's ground floor. The inconvenience of having to go outside for meals, especially during inclement weather, was a significant shortcoming of Cooper Hall life.

The remodeled complex retained the dining room in the Buck Hall section but expanded it into Center Hall to create a large commons area. Construction on

Move in day at Crawford Center, 1958

the two extensions was started in the spring of 1954. The enlarged, renovated and united dorms were ready by the opening of the fall 1955 term.[29]

The builders skillfully matched the red brick walls of the two additions to those of the original Cooper Hall. Anyone just glancing at the walls of the three sections could easily conclude they were erected in the same year. But, there were telltale architectural differences. When viewed from the Ramsey Street side only the original Cooper Hall had top-story dormer windows. Furthermore, the long addition to Cooper Hall that connected with Buck Hall was flat-topped, whereas the original hall portion as well as its short addition had a gabled roof.

Prior to the additions, Buck and Cooper halls combined housed about 225-250 coeds. But the new complex provided room for an additional 176 occupants. Center Hall and the Cooper Hall extension toward South Fourth Street added respectively 68 and 20 double occupancy rooms. Significantly, the new food service was able to cater to as many as 650 diners. In keeping with college tradition, non-dorm students, including males, could get their lunches, dinners and weekend meals in the coed dorm.

After the joining of Buck and Cooper halls, it was more difficult to distinguish them with their traditional distinctive names. Therefore, in 1959 the State College Board, acting on the recommendation of the Mankato State College Building Naming Committee, re-christened the complex to Cooper Center. In dropping any reference to Buck Hall, the committee wanted to establish the precedent of naming all dormitories after Mankato State presidents.[30]

While temporarily helpful, the expansion of coed housing was soon inadequate. Further enrollment increases created more demand, which were partially met in 1957 when the lower two floors of the Searing Hall addition were devoted to coed housing. But there was no long range solution for the housing shortage until dorms were built on the Highland Campus.

## Nichols Hall

Nichols Hall, whose first and larger phase was completed in 1953, temporarily fulfilled the college's need for more classroom space. The genesis of a new classroom building dated to the wartime McElroy administration. On June 20, 1944, the State Teachers College Board proposed the construction of a Science and Applied Arts Building at Mankato State. At that time, it appeared there was an opportunity to place the building adjacent to the existing campus. When the field house was being constructed, McElroy was convinced that the college was destined to be forever hemmed in by a steep hill to its rear and development to its front. But that situation was changed when the Mankato High School in the northeastern part of the block between Mankato State's Administration Building and the Blue Earth County Courthouse burned down.

After that disaster of July 19, 1941, the Mankato school district, which owned the entire block on which the high school stood, decided not to rebuild on that site.[31]

The 1945 legislature did not fund the proposed Mankato State classroom building. But two years later the lawmakers took their first step in starting the building process by appropriating $100,000 for additional Mankato State land.[32]

In the summer of 1947, for $100,000 the state purchased from the Mankato school district the block between South Fourth and South Fifth streets, which was bounded by Hickory Street on the courthouse side and Jackson Street on the opposite side. Inconveniently, over the years the school district had permitted two apartment buildings and eight houses to be built on the block. In early summer 1947, an estimated 27 families lived in them.[33]

Crawford wanted to have these dwellings renovated and converted into housing for about 200 students—with preference for veterans—by September 1. Consequently, during the first week of July the state served 30-day eviction notices on the block's residents. But as the notices expired in early August some of the residents had refused to vacate, because they had not been able to find other housing. Unfortunately for the college's image, some of those who clung to their homes were veterans, who were supported by the local American Legion.[34]

But, since the state was determined to evict all residents, it exerted its considerable power. At the urging of the State Teachers College Board, the attorney general appointed Mankato attorney Arthur Ogle as a special assistant to force the residents out. Ogle renewed some of the original eviction notices to a November 1 deadline, which caused some of the occupants to move.[35]

However, on that date "approximately nine families" had refused to move, and three of them had hired Mankato attorney Robert Reagan to represent them against the state. In response, E. Raymond Hughes, resident board director, while averring that the board "did not want to cause any hardship," announced that the attorney general would seek eviction notices on November 11. Reagan rejoined: "We don't want to cause any trouble but we just want the state and college to be reasonable in their demands."

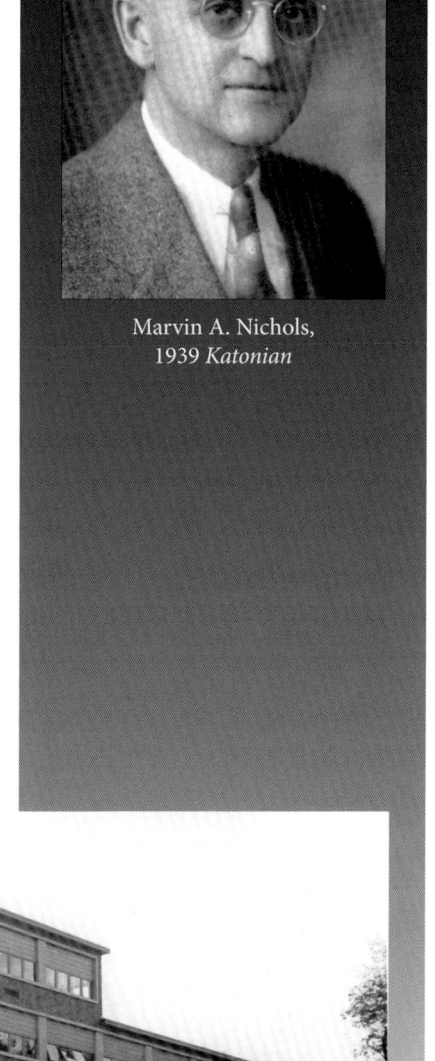

Marvin A. Nichols,
1939 *Katonian*

Nichols Hall, view from corner of South 4th and E. Hickory Streets, circa 1953

Chemistry laboratory in Nichols Hall, circa 1953

As the stalemate continued with the families who lived on the South Fourth Street half of the block, the state proceeded with grading the upper half, which had been occupied by the high school and its grounds. The bulldozed land was to be used for a college parking lot and physical education activities.[36]

Because of resistance from the apartment and house occupants, Crawford was not able to convert their dwellings into student housing for the opening of the fall 1947 term. As events transpired, with the exception of the four-story Avoca apartment building at the corner of South Fourth and Jackson streets, all of the other buildings on the block purchased from the high school were razed while Mankato State was seeking funding for the new classroom building.

The 1949 legislature appropriated $800,000 "for constructing and equipping" the building. But the start of construction was delayed when planners found that this amount would cover only about two-thirds of the estimated cost. Consequently, Senator Val Imm led the successful effort to obtain a deficiency appropriation of $450,000 from the 1951 legislature.[37]

The building was designed by the Minneapolis architectural firm of McEnary and Krafft. After a competitive bidding process, the Minnesota Department of Administration awarded the general construction contract to the Fred O. Watson Company of Minneapolis. Two Mankato firms—Cuddy Plumbing and Heating and Draper Electric also got contracts and the Lee Hoff Manufacturing Company of St. Paul was engaged to install the elevators. But, for some unspecified reason, the R & O Elevator Company of Minneapolis was employed to build the dumbwaiter.[38]

Construction proceeded rapidly after the groundbreaking in June 1951. The building was open for fall 1952 classes, but some interior finishing work remained to be done. With 78,000 feet of floor space, the facility had 125 rooms including classrooms, laboratories and faculty offices.[39]

The new three-part structure had some unusual features, because it had to be adapted to the slope that descended from South Fifth Street to South Fourth Street. It was mostly a four-story building with some split level features. The portion facing South Fifth Street, which extended half way across the block from the northeast corner, had two stories on its street side and four on the opposite side. The longest part opposite the courthouse connected the South Fifth Street and South Fourth Street sections. The portion facing South Fifth Street was about 30 feet longer than its South Fourth Street counterpart.

The building housed sciences, home

Home Economics food laboratory, circa 1960

economics, business education, industrial arts, music and art. It had separate chemistry, physics and biology laboratories and a biology solarium. Music, which had been cramped in its former Administration Building space, enjoyed the seeming luxury of private piano rooms and a large rehearsal room for the college band. Added space enabled Home Economics to use several model kitchens. The college's garage, which serviced all institutional vehicles, was located at the lowest level on the South Fifth Street side.

What proved to be the first phase of Nichols Hall was dedicated on June 26, 1953. After Earl L. Berg, commissioner of administration, presented the keys to the building to Howard Williams, resident board member for Blue Earth County, the program included various speakers. Val Imm represented the legislature and Charles H. Russsell, publisher of the *Mankato Free Press*, spoke about the benefits of the enlarged campus to the community. Gerrit M. Wissink, the former professor of physics who had been recently named dean of instruction, represented the faculty. Don Heinzman, editor of the *College Reporter*, spoke on behalf of the student body. All of the remarks were in keeping with the optimism of the cornerstone's inscription: "Bringing greater educational opportunities to the generations of college students of the state of Minnesota."[40]

Within a few years Crawford and the State College Board decided the building needed to be enlarged to meet the demands of ever-increasing enrollment. Accordingly, the legislature in 1957 appropriated $1,337,000 for its "completion and extension."[41]

Like any other state college appropriation this one had to be administered by the Department of Administration. After the state architect's office within the department completed building plans, competitive construction bids were advertised.

In early November 1958, the Department of Administration announced the awarding of the construction, plumbing and heating, and electrical contracts. The Eric A. Carlstrom Construction Company of Mankato was awarded the general construction contract. Other contracts were made with Wright Plumbing and Heating of Marshall and the All-City Electric Company of Willmar. The total for all contracts was $1,088,668, well under the appropriated amount.[42]

Extending and completing the building entailed adding two sections on the Jackson Street side of the block. The lower one was a five-story classroom building, which was located between the Avoca House and the uppermost lecture building, whose South Fifth Street front faced the Administration Building. The classroom building was designed for small classrooms, chemistry and physics laboratories and faculty offices. Its stories from the ground up were designated as Level A, Level B, Level C, Level D and Level

Aerial view of Nichols, circa 1960s. Original building is on left, 1960 addition is on the right.

E. The two-story lecture building was designed to accommodate large general education classes. Its main facility was a 250-seat auditorium, which slanted down from its main entrance off South Fifth Street. It was supplemented by four 80-seat classrooms.

Although the classroom and lecture buildings were joined, each had distinctive features. The tall, massive brick classroom building was accented with pieces of Kasota stone. But, the low lecture building was finished with vertical slabs of the stone.

Good progress in 1959 raised hope that both new sections would be ready for spring 1960 classes. But, because of some unanticipated delays, the Chemistry and Physics departments were unable to start moving into the classroom building until the summer of 1960. It and the lecture building were first used for classes and other activities beginning with the Fall 1960 term.

Although the classroom and lecture sections were referred to as "buildings" during their construction, they were actually sections of a five-part building. The original three sections were all connected by interior hallways. But the last two, while connected with each other by an inside hallway, stood somewhat apart from the first phase structures. Consequently, the lecture building was connected with the older South Fifth Street side by an elevated, enclosed pedestrian causeway. On the South Fourth Street side there was a ground level gap about six feet long between the classroom building and the section to its north. The completed building enclosed a grass-covered courtyard, which was very visible from the gap between the two South Fifth Street sections.

From its inception until December 18, 1967, the building was known by its functional name—the Science and Arts Building. It was officially renamed Nichols Hall by the State College Board, which accepted the recommendation of the Mankato State Committee on Naming College Buildings.[43]

The new name was selected in honor of Marvin A. Nichols, a chemistry instructor who had served on the Mankato normal/teachers college faculty for three decades, 1908-1938. Nichols was well remembered on campus, in part because of a tragic accident in the college's chemistry laboratory. On September 9, 1938, while Nichols was preparing to give a class demonstration on the dilution of nitric acid, a gallon glass container of the fluid slipped from his grasp and shattered on the stone-topped laboratory table. The acid spilled onto Nichols' legs and feet. Because he was wearing what were described as "perforated" shoes, Nichols' feet suffered the most damage.[44]

Nichols promptly instructed Robert Heidel, his student assistant, to perform emergency aid. The first step was to rinse the affected parts with cold water. Heidel then applied ammonia hydroxide, a neutralizing agent. Dr. H. Bradley Troost, who rushed to the campus, administered more first aid before committing Nichols to St. Joseph's Hospital.

Just after the accident, Nichols' colleagues assumed his injuries were not serious. But, Nichols, who was apparently suffering from a toxic reaction to his burns, declined rapidly. Blood transfusions failed to remedy his condition and he died in the hospital five days after the accident.[45]

Nichols, who was 55 at the time of his death, had been hired by President Cooper to teach hygiene, chemistry and physics in the normal school. A graduate of the DeKalb Normal School (Illinois), he earned a bachelor's degree from the University of Illinois and did graduate work there and at the University of Minnesota.[46]

## Lincoln Library

By 1954 Mankato State had outgrown its library space in the Administration Building. Therefore, Crawford asked the governing board's Committee on Building Needs to support the construction of a library building. Acting on the committee's recommendation, the State Teachers College Board agreed to ask the legislature for $1 million to acquire land for the library and to construct it.[47]

After the 1955 legislature appropriated $950,000 ($150,000 for land acquisition and $800,000 for construction), the Crawford administration, the state architect and the Department of Administration decided to locate the library across South Fifth Street from the Administration Building and the campus school. This site was then occupied by several Victorian style boarding homes, which had to be removed after the 400 block of South Fifth Street was purchased.[48]

Library construction, which commenced in late spring 1957, was delayed for five weeks by the same workers' strike that affected the building of the Searing Hall addition. But by late July concrete pouring for the first floor was slated to be done soon. By the opening of the Fall 1957 term, the building's steel girder frame was erected. At that time the college administration was anticipating that the library would be completed the following spring.[49]

Lincoln Library with college marching band, 1964

However, the building was not finished until the third week of August 1958. Plans to have it ready for the opening of classes on September 18 were frustrated by picketing from the local sheet metal workers union. Sympathetic to the union's demands, workers of the Ben Deike Moving Company of Mankato, which had been hired to move all library books and audiovisual materials from the Administration Building, refused to cross the picket line. Consequently, the library, whose holdings included about 62,000 books, was not ready until the third day of classes.[50]

The three-story building, finished with reddish-colored brick and Kasota stone, had four levels, including the full-sized basement. For most of the rear side the basement was at ground level. Measuring 176 feet long and 78 feet feet wide, the library provided nearly 55,000 feet of floor space. The three floors that were entirely above ground housed open stacks of books, a reserve room, a reference room, a cataloging room, library science classrooms and faculty offices. Part of the upper story was initially unoccupied because the library was built with expansion space.

The basement was used exclusively for the college's audiovisual department, headed by Edward R. McMahon, who had joined the faculty in 1954. While this department was in the library, it was not part of the library for administrative purposes. Other than housing audiovisual equipment and staff, the walkout basement also featured a receiving/shipping room accessible from backside doors.

Quite coincidentally, the library's first year was also the last year for head librarian Emma Wiecking, who had joined the college staff as the assistant librarian in 1922. Two years later, when head librarian Alice N. Farr retired after 27 years of service, Wiecking was named to replace her. Although Wiecking retained the title of librarian until she retired, her status was changed in 1952 when Crawford named Donald B. Youel to the newly created position of director of library services. Youel, who also chaired the Division of Language and Literature, evidently managed the library's budget and served as the liaison to the president. Consequently, Wiecking's responsibilities were apparently confined to staff coordination and supervision.[51]

In 1959 Ernest A. Thomas, whose most recent position was library director of Southwestern State College in Weatherford, Oklahoma, was hired as Wiecking's replacement. He and Youel had adjacent first-floor library offices. Usually, those who wanted to propose some library initiative would consult with both Youel and Thomas.

Abraham Lincoln statue, 1960

This rather awkward administrative arrangement was discontinued after Thomas died suddenly of a heart attack on August 5, 1961. In late winter 1962, Jack O'Bar, Thomas' replacement at Southwestern State College, was hired to succeed Thomas at Mankato State. In the course of negotiating with Crawford, O'Bar indicated that he wanted the library to be an independent department, whose head would have direct access to the president. This, he insisted, would be consistent with national trends in higher education. Crawford acquiesced and eliminated Youel's director of library services position.[52]

During its construction, the library was generally called simply the "new library." But in its first term it was officially named the Lincoln Library by the State College Board, which approved the recommendation of the Mankato State College Building Naming Committee. The committee explained that: "Since 'Old Abe,' presented to the college in 1925 by several graduating classes, has become a traditional symbol of the college, and since it was felt that the new library would be a more appropriate setting for this statue [than its location in the Administration Building's first floor hallway], it is hereby recommended that the new library be named Lincoln Library, carrying with it both the tradition of Lincoln, the man, and 'Old Abe', the beloved symbol of the college."[53]

After the sale and closing of the Valley Campus in 1979, the Lincoln Statue was moved to the Centennial Student Union building. Today it stands in the union building's first floor north hallway near the entry to food services.

## The Transition from Teachers College to State College

Mankato State's 36-year teachers college era ended in 1957 when the legislature renamed Mankato State and its four sister institutions at Bemidji, Moorhead, St. Cloud and Winona as state colleges. That achievement capped a campaign that had been started nearly two decades earlier.

Agitation for the change from teachers colleges to state colleges was started in Duluth. On November 5, 1938, a dozen secondary and college-level educational leaders met with the State Teachers College Board at a special meeting held in the president's office of the Duluth State Teachers College.[54]

A. I. Jedlicka, the Proctor superintendent of schools and chairman of the Duluth College Committee, was the group's principal spokesman. Speaking for the committee, which had studied the higher education situation in Duluth and the nearby iron mining district, Jedlicka first traced the region's discontent with the limited role of the Duluth State Teachers College to 1924. At that time some Duluthians were dissatisfied because the local teachers college was restricted to training elementary school teachers. Desiring more options, Duluth first formed a junior college and later arranged for a University of Minnesota extension center. But these additions did not satisfy Duluth's aim of getting a four-year college that offered more than teacher training.

By the mid-1930s those interested in reforming Duluth's higher education system decided their best option was for the teachers college to become a branch of the University of Minnesota. But the university's regents, who did not want to decentralize their system, refused to support Duluth's quest. Consequently, the university's administration and regents opposed the 1937 attempt by Duluth area legislators to convert the Duluth Teachers College into a branch of the University of Minnesota. Without university support the proposed legislation failed.

After that rejection the Duluth College Committee decided its only option was to get the State Teachers College Board to support the conversion of the Duluth Teachers College to the Duluth State College. Jedlicka informed the board that: "The plan is to take the Duluth State Teachers College, add the necessary buildings, provide the necessary curricula, enlarge the teaching force, and provide within the institution the training not only for teachers but training for degrees in the arts and sciences, and preparatory courses in pre-law, pre-engineering, pre-medics, etc. . . ."

Jedlicka and the other Duluth College Committee advocates who spoke after him emphasized the advantages of a Duluth state college. They related that their area had many potential college students who were interested in fields other than teaching. Such students, they insisted, should not be forced to attend the University of Minnesota in Minneapolis. The expense of living away from home would mean that many of them could not afford to get a college education.

The State Teachers College Board was sympathetic to Duluth's plight, but other than commiserate it could not do anything. Only the legislature was empowered to change a teachers college to a state college and appropriate funds for any related expenses.

Consequently, the board listened to the Duluth College Committee spokespeople but took no action to support their goal. In responding to the committee, board president Benjamin Drake stated: "You understand that additional legislative enactment is needed. The Board has no power, as the law now stands, to put this proposal into effect unless and until legal enactment is put into effect. Use your own judgment as to campaigning among legislators in order to have the necessary legislation."

Charles E. Sattgast, president of Bemidji State, opined that the Duluth committee was on the right track, because there was an ongoing national movement to convert teachers colleges to state colleges. All of Ohio's former teachers colleges, he noted, had already been converted. Furthermore, Sattgast thought the Minnesota teachers colleges should take steps to improve themselves before requesting the legislature to make them state colleges. He suggested that the colleges apply for accreditation by the North Central Association of Colleges and Secondary Schools, add liberal arts courses and change their degree from Bachelor of Education to Bachelor of Science. But, he also warned that Minnesota's private colleges would likely oppose any change of the teachers colleges to state colleges.

Drake believed that the University of Minnesota would also oppose anything that would lead to increased appropriations for the teachers college system. Regarding the university, he declared: "That they want everything. Only within the last two years have we overcome our timidity to ask for more funds. We hold no hostility to the University, but we represent the teachers colleges, and I don't think that any sense of loyalty demands that we sit around and see a disproportionate share go to the University. We have been getting the crumbs that fall from the appropriation table."

Although the board acknowledged that it was powerless to address Duluth's concerns, it was inspired to pursue some of Sattgast's recommendations. It tried to bolster the accreditation applications for the teachers colleges by instituting system-wide sabbatical leave and tenure policies. Furthermore, acting on a unanimous recommendation of the six teachers college presidents it authorized on September 23, 1939, the replacement of the Bachelor of Education degree with the Bachelor of Science.[55]

The cosmetic name change was apparently intended to give students and the public the impression that the teachers colleges had somehow morphed into a more elevated status. But the B. E. and B. S. degree requirements were identical except for some minor adjustments in their general education components. They were both education degrees with stipulated professional education courses that led to teacher certification.[56]

Subsequently, McElroy informed faculty and students that the change conformed with current nationwide practices. At the end of the Fall 1939 term, five Mankato State graduates became their school's first to earn a B. S.[57]

After their 1938 failure, Duluth citizens revived their effort to improve their city's higher education system during World War II. On July 6, 1944, a group of them met with the State Teachers College Board in Duluth. They believed Duluth's higher education offerings would be improved by merging the Duluth State Teachers College and the Duluth Junior College. Board president Warren H. Stewart of St. Cloud informed them that the board did not have any authority over any junior college and thus could not be of any help.[58]

But Stewart also told them that there would be strong opposition to changing the purpose and offerings of the Duluth State Teachers College. In particular, he cited the report of an interim education committee to the 1941 legislature. Stewart said he had testified before the committee about the desirability of expanding the function of the teachers colleges and was "amazed and considerably shocked" when its final report accused the teachers colleges of "invading the field of the University and the other colleges of the state." According to Stewart, the report contended that teachers colleges should not even be permitted to train high school teachers. Restricting them to preparing only elementary school teachers would, of course, force them to regress to their pre-1928 status.

During the discussion following Stewart's comments, both the board members and Duluth representatives considered the advisability or trying to change the Duluth teachers college before the end of the war. Furthermore, the participants were somewhat heartened with the information that St. Cloud State was now offering a business course. They saw this action as an effective way of expanding beyond teacher training.

Board consideration of the colleges changing their missions lapsed until May 14, 1945, when its members requested that the college presidents study nationwide trends in teachers colleges. On August 27, McElroy, as spokesperson for the presidents, reported to the board. In reviewing Minnesota's educational history, McElroy noted that the state had lagged behind other regions in converting its normal schools into teachers colleges. This pattern had been continued by Minnesota's laggardness in expanding its teacher college curriculum to include the opportunity for a non-teaching degree despite encouragement from accrediting associations.[59]

But, McElroy seemed pleased to report that during the last few years Minnesota's "lay public" was demanding "a broadening of the [teachers colleges] functions." He encouraged the board to seek legislature support to accomplish this aim.

However, the strongest advocacy of change continued to come from Duluth. On August 12, 1946, another Duluth delegation, which included Jedlicka of the 1938 committee, appeared before the board. The Duluth superintendent of schools, a representative of the Federated Trades and Labor Assembly of Duluth and the chairwoman of the Citizens Committee on Public Education were also members of this group.[60]

Buoyed by a recent enrollment rise, caused in part by returning veterans, the delegation first reiterated its case for a college that was authorized to grant a degree in fields other than teacher training. It insisted that Duluth had unique needs because of its isolation from the University of Minnesota, the state's only public higher education institution that offered training outside of education. Therefore, it asked the board to authorize a Bachelor of Arts degree for the Duluth State Teachers College. This prompted Clarence R. Smith, the resident board director from Beltrami County, to claim that the Bemidji area was as bad off as Duluth. Then E. Raymond Hughes, the resident board member from Blue Earth County, demanded that any consideration of authorizing the teachers colleges at Duluth and Bemidji to offer B. A. degrees should be extended to all six teachers colleges. Hughes was strongly supported by Senator Val Imm, who apparently had been invited to the meeting because of his sympathy for changing the state teachers colleges to state colleges. Hughes prevailed. The board unanimously authorized all of the teachers colleges to offer Bachelor of Arts degrees. Presumably, this would prove that the teachers colleges were more than their name implied and influence the legislature to rename them to state colleges.

Mankato State's first B. A. degree was awarded to Charles E. Lampright of Mankato, who had majored in history and science, at the end of the spring 1947 term. He was the only B. A. in a graduating class of 90 that included 36 B. S. recipients and 53 graduates of the two-year diploma program.[61]

Soon after the 1947 legislature convened on January 7, Val Imm introduced a Senate bill to rename the teachers colleges to state colleges. But that move was too moderate for Duluth's educational reformers, who sought legislative approval for the Duluth State Teachers College to become a branch of the University of Minnesota.[62]

During the session Imm received about two dozen supporting letters. Most of them were from Mankato State students, who emphasized that they could not fulfill their desire for training in fields other than teaching training at the existing teachers college.[63]

A letter from Dorothy B. Magnus, a graduate of the Winona State Teachers College, was the most comprehensive appeal for the proposed name change. She wrote: "I am heartily in favor of the bill for a number of reasons:

First — The trend toward a broader offering in colleges like ours has been clearly seen in such states as Michigan, Illinois, Arizona.

Second — More high school students will be demanding local opportunities to continue their education in the year immediately ahead. Even now the private colleges are closing registration for next year.

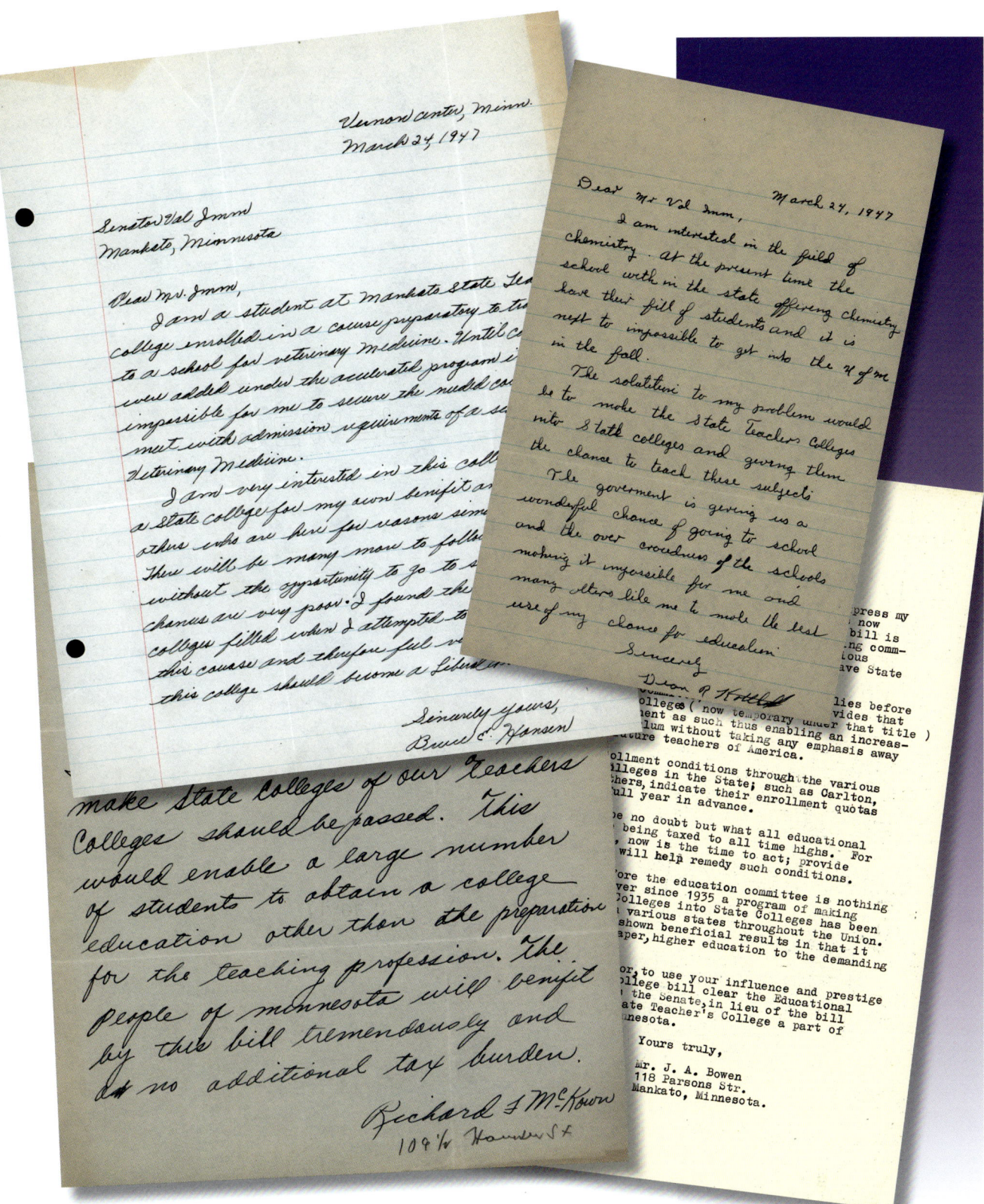

Examples of letters received by Senator Val Imm in support of the change to State College, 1947.

*School Progress* promoting the Business program, 1951

Third — A broadening of the offering will tend to strengthen our teacher education function with a resulting improved output. Fourth — Many students leaving high school have not decided on a vocation. They are inclined to avoid a teachers college because it offers only one curriculum—that of teacher training.

Fifth — For many reasons these same students are obliged to attend college at home or not at all. They deserve a general education program within their financial reach.

Sixth — The increased enrollments, which a broadened offering permits, allows for a greater selection of candidates for and the improvement of the teaching profession."[64]

Interestingly, Imm initiated the name change effort without any support from the State Teachers College Board. On February 19, 1947, board president Warren H. Stewart informed Imm that he thought the bill was premature. Stewart was satisfied that the board had done enough for the time being when it approved the Bachelor of Arts degree. He preferred that the name change be sought two to four years hence, when the board and presidents had more information about enrollment trends. But, if Imm persisted, Stewart wrote that he would "be glad" to supply any information from the board that may be helpful. Imm responded that he thought "that this is the opportune time to make an effort to get state teachers colleges on a permanent basis in the liberal arts field."[65]

As the bill was pending in the legislature, Stewart was converted to Imm's viewpoint. When he attended a hearing by the Senate Education Committee, Stewart was dismayed by the opinion of most of its members that the name change would diminish the colleges' traditional emphasis on teacher training. This realization caused him to explain to committee chairman A. L. Almen that even if they were re-designated state colleges, the institutions would still be primarily devoted to teacher training. But Stewart also insisted that the colleges should be able to also offer training in fields other than education.[66]

When he thanked Stewart for his support, Imm informed him that the Senate Education Committee had refused to endorse the bill and the House Education Committee had reached the same decision. But, Imm informed Stewart that: "I shall introduce it again two years from now and perhaps it will have a better chance next time."[67]

Imm became yet more optimistic near the end of the session. On April 25, he wrote to Ruth M. Schellberg, assistant professor of physical education at Mankato State Teachers College, that he thought "sufficient ground work has been laid to insure passage of the bill two years hence, when I shall introduce it again and press for its adoption."[68]

Although the legislature failed to rename the teachers colleges it did make a major change in their system when it passed an act that made the former Duluth State Teachers College a branch of the University of Minnesota. It is clear that the impetus for the change came from Duluth rather than the university's administration and regents. Apparently the lawmakers were convinced that the Duluth area had pressing unique needs, but the other teachers colleges should live with the status quo.[69]

On August 30, 1948, the State Teachers College Board decided to ask the

1949 legislature to rename the teachers colleges to state colleges. Board members concluded that such a change would not only be consistent with the nationwide trend, but would serve the needs of students who wanted options other than teacher training.[70]

Before the legislature convened, the board received a strong objection from Walter E. Englund, executive secretary of the Minnesota Education Association (MEA). On October 6, 1948, Englund informed board president Arthur M. Clure that the MEA's executive board strongly opposed the deletion of "the word 'teacher' from the official name of the State Teachers Colleges." Englund further admonished: "Teacher training institutions that do well their appointed task of preparing instructors for youth are performing a service in the public good. They should bear their title, with the word teacher included, proudly and with distinction."[71]

In responding to Englund, Clure emphasized that the proposed change from teachers colleges to state colleges would actually improve the teaching profession. It would, he believed, lead to expanded facilities and course offerings that would benefit all students.

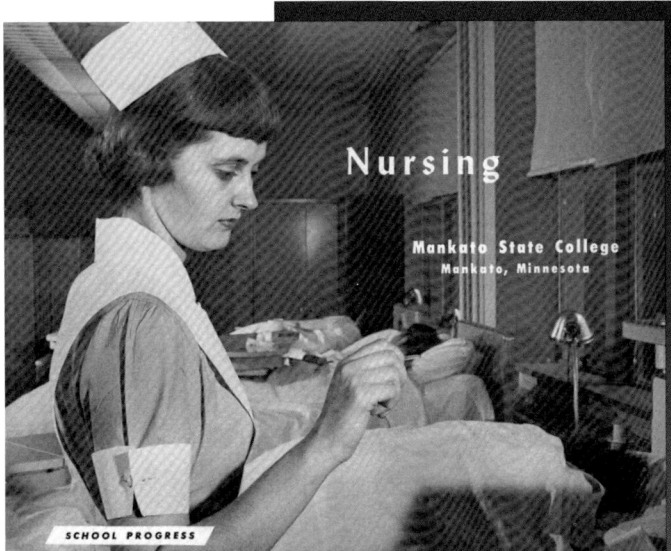

*School Progress* promoting the Nursing program, 1958

Apparently Clure failed to persuade Englund, so when the State Teachers College Board proposed the name change to the legislature it was handicapped by MEA opposition. Despite the support of the board, the 1949 name change bill met the same fate as the 1947 effort. It died in committee, because the House and Senate education committees decided not to support it.[72]

After their 1949 experience the board and Imm, the legislature's main name change advocate, decided to bide their time until conditions improved. By the time they tried again in 1957 there was little opposition to the name change. On April 20, 1957, the legislature "re-designated" the state teachers colleges to state colleges.[73]

In approving the change legislators tacitly acknowledged that the nature of the teachers colleges had been changed in recent years by the advent of new programs, increasing enrollment, greatly enlarged faculties and academic offerings and a much larger proportion of degree earners.

With regard to Mankato State since the attempted 1949 name change, the institution had formed a Division of Business to meet demands for business graduates and had added a nursing training program in 1953. Within a year the nursing program evolved into the Division of Nursing, which had seven faculty members including Clara May Miller, who was described as its "chairman." Moreover, the college started a Master of Science degree program after the 1953 legislature authorized the offering of a post-graduate program.[74]

With respect to enrollment, all of the five teachers colleges had grown, which gave them more public visibility and created more demand for non-teaching studies. In Mankato State's case, its enrollment of 4,967 for the 1955-1956 academic year was nearly triple that of 1947-1948.[75]

The enrollment spurt caused a great enlargement of the faculty. Mankato State had 161 faculty members for the 1956-1957 academic year. In McElroy's last year, 1945-1946, there were only 26. The significantly larger faculty reflected additions to the curriculum. For example, in 1946-1947 the Division of Science

Greek Fraternities and Sororities, 1964

Freshman week picnic, circa 1955

Snow Week King Bruce Williams and
Queen Kathy Suel,
1956 *Katonian*

and Mathematics had only four faculty members—one each for biology, chemistry, mathematics and physics. La Roy Zell, the biologist, had sole responsibility for the 10 undergraduate biology courses. In 1956-1957 the division had 17 faculty and offered 20 undergraduate and two graduate biology courses. During the same period the number of faculty members in the Division of Language and Literature grew from seven to 25 and the number of English courses increased from 20 undergraduate to 30 undergraduate and one graduate.[76]

The changing nature of the Mankato Teachers College in the decade before it became Mankato State College is well-illustrated by graduation data. At its June 3, 1946, commencement Mankato State had 57 graduates. Forty-eight of them had completed the two-year diploma course for rural school teachers and the other nine were granted B. S. degrees. On June 1, 1956, Mankato State graduated 193 students consisting of four who earned a Master of Science degree, 121 who earned a B. S., 35 who earned a B. A. and 33 who were awarded diplomas for completing the two-year rural teaching program. The decline of diploma graduates from 84 percent of the graduates to 17 percent and the corresponding sharp increase of B. A. graduates was strong proof that the college had evolved beyond its teachers college status.[77]

Mankato State's decline in rural education students was an effect of a fundamental shift from country schools to town- or city-based consolidated schools. Data for Blue Earth County is illustrative of this statewide trend. In 1950 Blue Earth County had 100 rural school districts. Only 11 remained by 1960, because the pace of school consolidation had rapidly accelerated. The county's last two rural schools were consolidated in 1970.[78] Rapid country school consolidation caused the discontinuation of the diploma program, which by the late 1950s had been expanded to a three-year requirement. On December 1, 1960, Mankato State graduated its last two diploma earners.[79]

The change of status from teachers college to state college was welcome news on the Mankato campus. There was some light-hearted carping about the need to change the stationery and the outdated "TC" sweatshirts that still had a lot of wear in them. In the college, the change from TC to MSC occurred rapidly.[80] But the community was another matter. As long as five years after the name change it was not at all uncommon for some Mankatoans to refer to the college as TC.

## Origin of the Split Campus

By 1956, its last full year as a state teachers college, Mankato State was facing an expansion crisis. Crawford and the board had identified the institution's highest priority needs as completion and extension of the Science and Arts Building, enlargement of the Valley Field House, construction of a new laboratory school and land acquisition. Accordingly, the 1957 legislature appropriated $1,337,000 for the Science and Arts project, $455,500 for Valley Field House "completion," $1,470,000 for a laboratory school and $380,000 for land acquisition.[81]

Planning to enlarge the Science and Arts Building was easy, because the state already owned land adjacent to the building's first phase. But the proposed addition to the campus field house was complicated. The physical education faculty and Crawford wanted to enlarge the building to provide room for an indoor swimming pool and more exercise space. The matters of building the laboratory school and acquiring land were obviously intertwined, because there was no space for a new building on the existing campus. Furthermore, any newly acquired land would have to be sufficient to facilitate anticipated long-term college growth.

In late July 1957, Richard Hammel, the architect selected by the Department of Administration to plan all state colleges construction, conferred with a Mankato State building committee about pending construction and land acquisition issues. Evidently, he disagreed with the committee and Crawford about the feasibility of enlarging the field house and purchasing land adjacent to the college.[82]

New Mankato State College sign on North 5th Street in front of main building, circa 1957. Note the incorrect founding date on the sign. It should be 1868.

Subsequently, Hammel decided that the intercession of a higher power was necessary. He asked Arthur Naftalin, the commissioner of administration, to arrange an on-campus public meeting with Crawford and a group of Mankato businessmen. Naftalin presided at the September 12 two-and-a-half-hour session in the Administration Building's main auditorium before an audience of about 150 people. Also in attendance were the members of the Legislative Building Commission appointed by Governor Orville Freeman and Roy C. Prentiss, executive secretary of the State College Board.[83]

The two main issues considered at the meeting were the re-location of the laboratory school and the acquisition of land for college expansion. There was general agreement that it would be advisable to construct the new campus school at a site outside of the city limits.

But the question of future campus expansion proved to be very contentious. The businessmen insisted that all future academic building sites should be located by enlarging the current campus. They proposed to do this by acquiring land on both sides of Glenwood Avenue between Hanover and Division streets. This area had only narrow strips of flat terrain on both sides of Glenwood. Consequently, contractor Sumner Carlstrom recommended enlarging that section by removing parts of the adjacent hillsides. He urged that the excavated dirt be used to elevate the base of Glenwood Avenue and adjacent parts of the existing campus and some abutting tracts that would have to be purchased. After this raise it would be necessary to connect South Fifth and Division streets by a 1,500-foot-long tunnel under the newly elevated area. He estimated that the removal of a million yards of dirt at a cost of $200,000 would add 15 to 17 acres to the 23-acre campus. The cost of the tunnel, he claimed, would be $300,000.

Hammel was appalled by such a radical proposal that would only modestly expand the existing 23-acre campus. He claimed that the excavation and tunnel projects would actually cost 10 times as much as Carlstrom's estimate. Casting himself as a long-range planner, Hammel envisioned Mankato State as having an enrollment of 8,000 to 10,000 within 10 to 15 years. Such an institution, he advised, would need an additional 87 acres. Hammel insisted that 200 acres of rural land could be acquired for only $500 to $1,000 per acre.

Abandoning his role as a supposedly neutral presider, Naftalin not only agreed with Hammel, but lectured Carlstrom and his business colleagues about their short-sightedness in insisting on a small, costly campus addition. The restricted valley campus desired by the businessmen, Naftalin insisted, would mean that Mankato State's enrollment would be permanently capped at 5,000 to 6,000. Expressing a grander view for the college's future, Naftalin said: "Who knows but in 10 or 15 years they may be building another university in this state. . . . I'm not offering this as tempting bait, but you're certainly not going to put a university on this hill [existing campus and elevated area suggested by Carlstrom], but you might put it outside the city someplace."

Even though Hammel and Naftalin were opposed to any expansion of the present campus, they had to concede that the appropriations bill stipulated the enlargement of the existing field house. So they agreed to an accommodation with the businessmen, who wanted to keep the present and future campus close to downtown. They would plan to add space to the field house. But they would investigate acquiring rural land for campus expansion, including the construction of a new laboratory school.

The meeting had very important implications for Mankato State's future. It was the first time the notion of a "split campus" was broached. It also served notice that the Department of Administration was determined to fulfill its role as the state's planning agency.

After the meeting, Hammel proceeded with the routine process of planning an addition to the field house. But all the construction bids exceeded the appropriated amount and there was no prospect of increasing it.[84]

This situation caused Naftalin, William E. Stevenson, assistant commissioner of administration, and Hammel to revert to their preconceived notion that any expansion of athletic facilities should be accomplished by constructing new facilities on a new campus. After consulting with Naftalin on September 25, 1957, Hammel, Crawford, Stevenson and Prentiss agreed that the state should acquire 171.5 acres of land in the Dolph Heights area about a mile south-southeast of the Valley Campus. After Naftalin accepted this recommendation, he decided that any plan to restrict all new building construction to the new campus should be endorsed by the State College Board.[85]

Consequently, he met with the board on September 26, 1958. After endorsing Hammel's conclusion about the problem of expanding the existing field house, Naftalin recommended that any board decision should be based on Mankato State's long-range planning rather than its immediate needs.[86]

Naftalin's advice prompted S. J. Kryzsko (Winona), the board president, to request that the board determine whether it wanted to pursue expansion of the existing field house or plan for a new facility on the new highland campus. Mankato banker Fred Buscher, the resident director for Blue Earth County, agreed with Crawford that the college had an immediate need for improved athletic facilities. Therefore, he moved "that the Board request the Commissioner of Administration to proceed with the drawing of new plans for a facility on the present site within the funds available." The motion failed, because no one seconded it. Naftalin and the board obviously recognized that upper campus development was essential to assure the college's future growth.

Director Roland Muller of Windom then moved the abandonment of plans to expand the valley field house and to construct a new facility on the "upper campus." His motion passed unanimously.

So the die was cast. Henceforth, all new facilities would be built on the Highland Campus, with the exception of completing the science and arts building on the Valley Campus. Interestingly, this momentous change had been initiated by the Department of Administration rather than the Crawford administration or the State College Board.

After the Wilson Campus School (the present Wiecking Building) and the first dormitories were opened on the Highland Campus in the fall of 1959, the State College Board requested that the land on which they stood be annexed to the City of Mankato.[87]

## Val Imm: State Legislator

Val Imm (August 28, 1893-June 10, 1981), who represented the Mankato area in the Minnesota legislature for more than four decades, earned a reputation as a particular friend of Mankato State. At the time of his death he was credited with having been the main reason for the state funding of nearly $20-million worth of campus buildings. Additionally, he was instrumental in the 1957 status change from teachers college to state college and in the early to mid-1960s, spearheaded the campaign to have Mankato State designated a university.

Imm was born in Granton, Wisconsin, and lived there until age 16, when his family moved to Kearney, Nebraska. He completed high school in Kearney before attending and graduating from Kearney State Normal School. He taught in Nebraska rural schools before moving to Rockford, Minnesota, to engage in general merchandising. From 1915-1926 he operated a general store in Jordan, Minnesota. During that time he also served in the nation's World War I armed forces. In 1926 he moved to Mankato where he bought his father's and brother's interest in the weekly *Mankato News*. Henceforth, he worked as a newspaper publisher.

Imm entered politics in 1930 when he was elected to a two-year term on the Mankato city council. He was elected to the Minnesota House of Representatives as the Blue Earth County representative on November 8, 1932. After one two-year term in the House, Imm was elected to the state senate where he served until 1967. During his legislative service Imm caucused with the Conservatives in the non-partisan legislature. Although legislators did not have a formal party designation, it was publicly known that the Conservatives were Republicans and the Liberals came from the Farmer-Labor and Democratic parties, which merged as the Democratic-Farmer-Labor Party in 1944. Although Conservatives were ostensibly fiscal watchdogs, Imm and his colleagues were strong supporters of public education and measures that benefitted their constituencies.

Val Imm,
circa 1957

During Imm's early Senate experience, he played a vital role in obtaining state funding for the Valley Campus field house. From then on, he championed the funding of all land acquisition and new buildings on the Valley Campus and the new Highland Campus. Imm was especially effective during his last decade of Senate service when, thanks to the seniority system, he chaired the Senate Finance Committee. His position gave him much power in the shaping of final appropriations bills.

Imm's forte was not impassioned floor speeches, but rather bargaining in committees. His congenial personality made him particularly effective in that setting. Imm personally attributed some of his political support to the public assumption that he was of Scandinavian ethnicity. He was actually of German ethnicity. But since many people believed he was descended from Scandinavians he did not correct them, because he knew that being regarded as Scandinavian was a political advantage in Minnesota.

In 1964, near the end of Imm's legislative career, his role in building Mankato State was recognized when the City of Mankato at Crawford's urging named the newly constructed Val Imm Drive in his honor. Appropriately, the street was designed and constructed as the main link between the Valley and Highland campuses that Imm had done so much to develop.

Imm's political career was ended when he was defeated in his 1966 re-election bid for state senator. He and his wife Gertrude continued to live in Mankato until the summer of 1979, when they moved to Dallas, Texas, the home of their daughter Valerie.

(*Mankato Free Press*, 23 June 1979, 11; 12 June 1981, 8; Imm, Val Papers, Southern Minnesota Historical Center, Minnesota State University, Mankato; "Imm, Val," "Minnesota Legislative Reference Library: Legislators Past & Present," online source, access by title.)

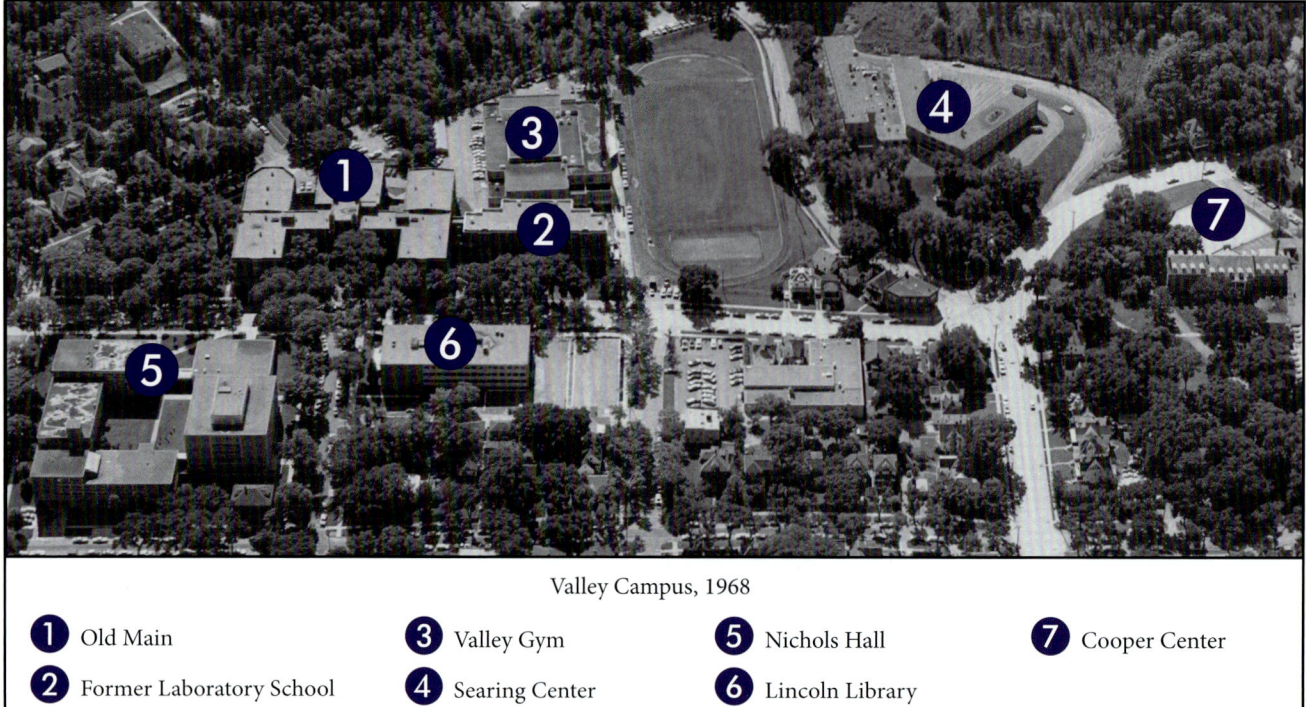

Valley Campus, 1968

**1** Old Main     **3** Valley Gym     **5** Nichols Hall     **7** Cooper Center

**2** Former Laboratory School     **4** Searing Center     **6** Lincoln Library

## Highland Campus Building

From 1959-1965, the last seven years of the Crawford Administration, the face of Mankato State College was changed dramatically by an unprecedented construction boom on the new Highland Campus. The completed buildings consisted of a laboratory school, three dormitory complexes, a physical education complex that included an outdoor stadium, two classroom buildings and a utilities plant.

## Laboratory School

The Crawford administration began planning the design of the new laboratory or campus school soon after the State College Board decided that Mankato State should develop a hilltop campus on recently acquired land in Dolph Heights. On December 4, 1957, two architects from the firm of Nagel-Graffunder presented preliminary plans to college officials, campus school faculty members and Richard Hammel, the consulting architect for the State College Board. The presenters, who had a detailed floor plan and a model, solicited additional suggestions from the audience. But, "on the whole, those attending were well pleased with the entire arrangement and expressed very little criticism."[88]

Subsequently, the Department of Administration went through the competitive bidding process. When the bids were opened on July 17, 1958, it was revealed that the low bidder for the general construction contract was Madson & Sons.[89]

The building's design expedited rapid construction. Its exterior walls of Kasota stone could be constructed much faster than those that required methodical bricklaying. Furthermore, the one-story building did not have a basement with the exception of the space required for its heating plant. By mid-

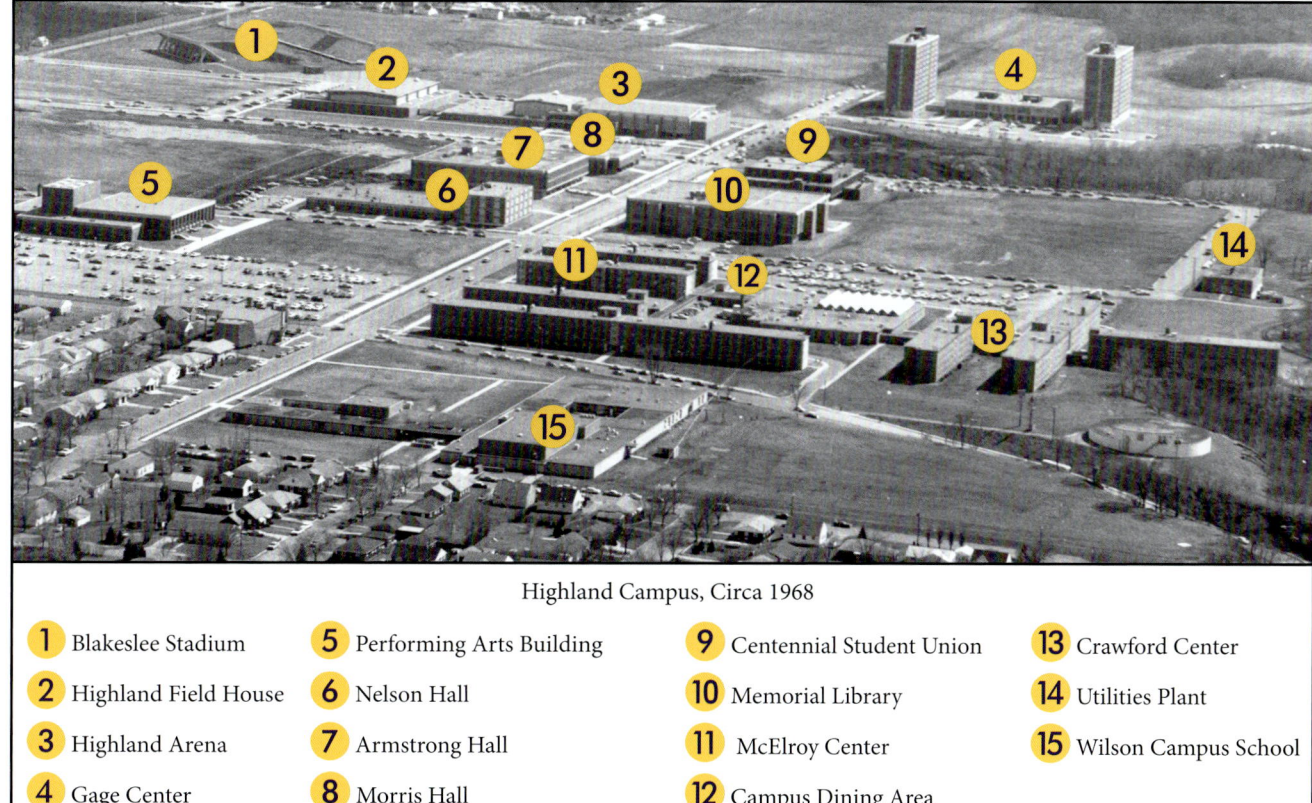

Highland Campus, Circa 1968

1 Blakeslee Stadium
2 Highland Field House
3 Highland Arena
4 Gage Center
5 Performing Arts Building
6 Nelson Hall
7 Armstrong Hall
8 Morris Hall
9 Centennial Student Union
10 Memorial Library
11 McElroy Center
12 Campus Dining Area
13 Crawford Center
14 Utilities Plant
15 Wilson Campus School

June, 1959, the building was done with the exception of some interior finishing work. So the work was on schedule for opening that fall.[90]

On Sunday, November 8, 1959, the campus school faculty hosted an open house for Mankato State students and faculty and the public. At that time the school was planning to use 41 elementary student teachers for the next term. Initially, the campus school had grades kindergarten through nine, the same as its Valley Campus predecessor. But the college intended to expand the school beyond the junior high level by adding high school classes.[91]

The campus school was built with the aim of being a model for the most modern schools. Its central office was equipped with a public address system and television monitor, which connected with every classroom. Esthetically, the school featured two vegetated courtyards that could be viewed through windows that extended down to floor level. The classrooms were furnished with brightly colored plastic chairs that helped create feelings of warmth and hospitality. The 325-seat auditorium made all-school assemblies possible. Even the boiler room in the partial basement was designed to be a learning experience. It could be viewed from above through a glass wall.[92]

When it was only a few months old, the campus school by action of the State College Board was officially named the Wilson Campus School. The college building naming committee recommended using the surname of Thomas Woodrow Wilson, the 28th president of the United States, because other Mankato schools such as Jefferson, Roosevelt and Washington had been named after presidents and the

Aerial view of Wilson Campus school with dormitory construction in background

Wilson Campus School was also serving the community. The inclusion of the word "campus" was "to designate" [the school's] "fundamental purpose in the teacher education program of the college."[93]

The completion of the Wilson Campus School enabled the Crawford administration to convert the valley laboratory school into a college classroom building. The only remodeling of note was to change several of the rooms into faculty offices by erecting cubicles. Other than being equipped with chairs for adults, the classrooms were not altered. As former homerooms for specified grades each of them featured a small bookcase of grade level books. For some reason the campus school authorities abandoned the old books rather than move them to the Wilson Campus School. Fortunately, these little room libraries were saved when the Valley Campus was closed and are now in Minnesota State Mankato's University Archives.

## Dormitories

Most of the buildings constructed on the Highland Campus during Crawford's administration were dormitories, which consisted of the Crawford Center, McElroy Center and Gage Center.

On June 30, 1958, the State College Board accepted bids on a new "600-bed dormitory" to be constructed on the Highland Campus. Although the board described the facility as a single unit, it actually had four parts. The largest section appeared to be a single, very long building.  But its southern and northern halves were designated respectively as the A and B wings. The C wing was built east of and parallel to the B wing. The fourth unit was a dining services building that was constructed adjacent to the south end of the C wing. The contracts awarded by the board contained only a total amount for all the units. Thus, it is not possible to determine the specific cost of the dining services building.[94]

In all instances the board awarded contracts to the lowest bidders. The George Carlstrom Construction Company of Mankato won the general construction contract.  The mechanical contract went to Cuddy Plumbing and Heating of Mankato and the electrical contract was awarded to the Mankato Electric Company. The project's grand total cost was $1,904,175.

Before deciding on the final contracts the board discussed a proposal from director Fred Buscher, a Mankato banker, who wanted the buildings finished with local Kasota stone rather than brick. Buscher conceded that the stone would cost about $46,000 more than brick, but he thought it was important to support a local industry. His fellow directors were not persuaded. With only Buscher dissenting, they rejected the stone amendment.

Carlstrom broke ground on the dormitory project in July 1958.  Construction proceeded very rapidly, in part because the project minimized excavation. Only the dining services section had a full basement. The dormitory wings had just enough basement space to provide facilities for heat conversion equipment. By mid-January 1959, the dormitory project was reported to be about 40 percent complete and was anticipated to be ready by the opening of the Fall 1959 term.[95]

That assumption proved to be too optimistic. Classes were scheduled to start on Thursday, September 17. But Crawford was forced to delay the first instructional day until the following Monday, when the A and B wings were finally ready for occupants. Although they were opened, Crawford reported that among other things "mirrors were still lacking on the bathroom walls, study lights were not yet in their rooms, [and] the desk tops were not yet completed." Some of these problems, including inoperative elevators, were still unresolved as late as November 10.[96]

But the C wing and the dining services structure had far more serious issues than the A and B wings. Construction on the C wing was so delayed that it was not ready until sometime between November 10, 1959 and February 8, 1960.

The greatest aggravation was the lack of food services. Because completion of the dining facilities was significantly delayed, it was necessary to transport the new dorm residents to the lower campus for their regular meals. This situation was improved gradually. By the time the food services section was dedicated on Sunday, January 31, 1960, breakfasts and the evening meals were being served in the new facility, but dormitory residents were still being transported to the lower campus for their noon meals. Crawford anticipated that three daily meals would not be available on the Highland Campus until September 1960.

According to building plans, the first three Crawford Center wings had a total capacity of 600 students. Each four-story wing had 25 double occupancy rooms on each floor. But, in actual practice, the dormitory occupancy sometimes exceeded its scheduled capacity, because three students shared a room.

The fourth or D wing of the Crawford Center was completed and opened for the Fall 1962 term. Its size and shape were identical to the C wing. Its total estimated cost of $568,000 consisted of $480,000 for construction, $28,000 for design and supervision, $45,000 for equipment and $15,000 for contingencies.[97] The D wing was the seventh 200-person-capacity dormitory

Crawford Center, 1960

on the Highland Campus. The year before its completion the first three wings of the adjoining McElroy Center had been completed and opened.

While the first phase of the initial dormitory project was still incomplete, the State College Board, acting on the recommendation of Mankato State's naming committee, decided to name it the Crawford Center. At its same November 20, 1959, meeting the board also decided to name the second recently approved 600-bed residence hall the McElroy Center in honor of Crawford's predecessor.[98]

On July 10, 1959, when the completion of the first three Crawford Center wings appeared to be imminent, the State College Board approved preliminary plans for another 600-bed dormitory complex. Its estimated cost, to be financed by the sale of revenue bonds, was $2,659,395.[99]

Subsequently, the board, after completing the competitive bidding process, awarded the various construction contracts for what became the E, F and G wings of the McElroy Center on October 24, 1959. The George E. Carlstrom Company of Mankato was awarded the general construction contract. The other two contracts went to R-W Electric of Mankato and Cuddy Plumbing and Heating of Mankato. In addition to these construction costs the board allowed $127,000 for design and supervision, $134,000 for equipment and $70,686 for contingencies.[100]

Before accepting the bids, the board again considered a proposal from Buscher and representatives of Mankato's stone industry to face the buildings with Kasota stone rather than brick. And again they rejected it, because stone was more costly.

The McElroy wings were built on the model of the original Crawford Center wings. McElroy E and F were, like Crawford A and B, one long four-story structure divided by midpoint doors-hallway. Wing G looked like a duplicate of Crawford C. When McElroy E, F and G were opened for the Fall

Aerial view of Crawford Center (bottom), Carkoski Commons (middle), and McElroy E, F, and G (top), 1961

1961 term, they doubled the Highland Campus's dormitory capacity.[101]

When enrollment projections for the Fall 1963 term indicated that the Highland Campus's seven dormitory wings could not satisfy the increasing demand, the State College Board decided to add two wings to the McElroy Center. In late July 1963, the board awarded construction contracts to the low bidders. The George E. Carlstrom Construction Company was awarded the general construction contract. Schwickert Plumbing and Heating of Mankato was chosen as the mechanical contractor and the electric contract went to R-W Electric. The

Construction of Gage A Tower, 1964

project's architect was the Ernest H. Schmidt Company of Mankato.[102]

Construction on the two wings, which were designated as H and I, was underway by the opening of the Fall 1963 term. The following July they were reported "to be ready for fall occupancy."[103]

That prediction proved to be half right. The wings were not ready, but were occupied nonetheless. Residents were permitted to move in for the Fall 1964 term even though the installation of plumbing, floor tiles and general furnishing had not been completed. Although some progress was made in the term's first month, Crawford reported on October 23 that he did not expect the laundry rooms, lounges and corridor tiling to be completed until Christmas vacation.[104]

With the completion of McElroy H and I the college had dormitory space for 2,800 students on the Highland Campus. But the actual occupancy for the Fall 1964 term was 2,850, because 50 rooms were used to accommodate three students rather than the usual two. This situation increased anticipation about the pending opening of a new 600-bed, 13-story dormitory the following year.[105]

When the last two McElroy wings were being constructed the State College Board approved the building of a third dormitory complex. To preserve ground space they decided the new facility would be twin 12-story towers with a connecting food services building.

With the intention of treating the two towers as separate projects the board awarded contracts for the first, or A, tower on June 15, 1964. Sheehy Construction Company of St. Paul, with the low bid got the general construction contract. The electrical contract went to Mankato Electric and the mechanical contract was awarded to Cuddy Plumbing and Heating of Mankato.

Gage Center dormitory room, circa 1984

The total of $2,265,957 was under the board's budgeted amount.[106] The Sheehy Company's construction proceeded rapidly. After only slightly more than 10 weeks it completed the tower's shell and anticipated starting interior work about December 1. The company and college were very optimistic that the structure would be ready for occupancy by the beginning of the Fall 1965 term.[107] As the building's interior were being finished, the *College Reporter* extolled its unprecedented luxurious feature of room telephones. Each of the rooms, which were mostly double occupancy, had its own phone, which cost each occupant $3 monthly. The rooms were equipped with single beds, individual desks, a closet, sink, medicine cabinet and drawer space "that make most off-campus students green with envy." Each floor had a smoker-lounge area and a utility room equipped with a washing machine, dryer, hot plate, sink and typing tables. The building was equipped with two high speed elevators that reportedly covered its height in "only seconds."[108]

On August 2, 1965, when the completion of the A tower was only a few weeks away, the board awarded contracts for the construction of its twin tower and food services building expansion. The total cost of $2,356,000 consisted of a general construction contract to the Sheehy Company, a mechanical contract to Cuddy Plumbing and Heating and an electrical contract to Hoffman Electric of Minneapolis. With a specified completion deadline of the start of the Fall 1966 term, the companies had about six months less than the A tower's builders.[109]

Moving rapidly, the Sheehy Company by October was making excellent progress in erecting the tower's frame. By that time the board had accepted the recommendation of the college's building naming committee and designated the two towers and connecting food services section Gage Center. Naming the complex in honor of George M. Gage, the normal school's first principal, was particularly apt, because he was the pioneer advocate of dormitory facilities.[110]

Gage B, west of Gage A, was a twin of its predecessor. It had space for 600 double occupancy residents on 12 floors. The ground floor was devoted to a lounge area equipped with television sets, activity and meeting areas, vending machines, a kitchenette and music practice rooms.

The completion of Gage Center in 1965-66 added 1,200 dormitory residents, which brought the campus total to 4,000. If tentative plans had been carried out there would have been an additional 1,200. Only two months after accepting the bids for Gage A, the board decided to plan for building another two-tower dormitory complex on the Mankato campus. It was intended to be a duplicate of the Gage towers with respect to size and shape. The board proposed to cover three-fourths of its cost by issuing revenue bonds and to request the legislature to appropriate the remainder.[111]

The ambitious plan, which would have added significantly to the Mankato campus, was derailed by Mankato State's university ambitions. In May 1965, the board decided not to proceed with the Gage Center clone. Members were concerned that if Mankato State became a university outside of State College Board jurisdiction, the board could be saddled with costly dormitory obligations.[112]

Some who contemplate history insist that there are no ifs in the past. But, they have to recognize that there were alternatives. And one of them was the possibility that Mankato State's Highland Campus might have featured four high-rise dormitories.

## Sports and Physical Education Facilities

By the opening of the Fall 1960 term, when the only buildings in use on the Highland Campus were the Wilson Campus School and the first three Crawford dormitory wings and their adjacent food services building, the State College Board had advertised for bids on sports and physical education facilities. The new structures were to be a sports complex about two blocks long and an outdoor stadium on the south side of the campus. The sports complex was to have three discrete parts—a gymnasium on the west, a central building

Gage Center, circa 1980

Aerial view of Highland Campus physical education facilities, 1962. Blakeslee Stadium (bottom) and Highland Arena (top left) and Highland Field House under construction.

Carlyn P. (C.P.) Blakeslee,
1961 *Katonian*

that would have a swimming pool and offices for intercollegiate coaches and physical education faculty and a field house with an indoor track on the east. The stadium was to be located southeast across the street from the field house.[113]

The opening of bids on October 13, 1960, revealed that the Eric A. Carlstrom Construction Company of Mankato was the low bidder for the general construction of all four structures. Cuddy Plumbing and Heating Company bid for the largest plumbing, heating, automatic controls and thermal insulation contract. The low bidders for other plumbing and heating contracts were the Harris Plumbing and Heating Company of St. Paul, Weidner Plumbing and Heating of St. Cloud, Vono Pipe Covering of St. Paul and Axel Newman Plumbing and Heating. All-City Electric of Willmar submitted the low bid for the electrical work in all of the structures. The total of all bids was $2,123,488, which was within the appropriations made by the 1957 and 1959 legislatures.[114]

At the opening of the Fall 1961 term, Crawford reported that good progress was being made on the physical education facilities. He thought they would all be completed in another year. In describing the structures, he mentioned that the gymnasium-auditorium would have a seating capacity of 7,000 for cultural events such as commencement exercises when all of its floor space was used and that the swimming pool and the field house would each have room for 500 spectators.[115]

Crawford's expectation proved to be too optimistic. By Fall 1962, only the north section of the stadium was ready for its first football game, which was held on September 22. All of the other facilities, including the office/classroom area between the swimming pool and the field house, had been nearly enclosed. The south half of the stadium was not completed until the next year. The stadium and its football field gained the unique distinction of being named before they were completed. On May 9, 1961, when he spoke at Carlyn P. Blakelee's retirement banquet, Crawford announced that the Highland Campus field and stadium would be named after Blakeslee to recognize his long and distinguished service to Mankato State.[116]

During the 1962-63 academic year there was widespread hope that the completed gymnasium-auditorium would be available for at least part of the basketball season. But a series of delays, including a labor dispute, postponed the opening of all athletic facilities until the Fall 1963 term.[117]

Completing Blakeslee Stadium involved the letting of three contracts. MacGill and Vogelsang of Mankato was awarded the general construction contract. The mechanical and electrical contracts went respectively to Cuddy Plumbing and Heating and Brown Electric Company of Waseca. The finishing of Blakeslee Stadium brought its seating capacity to 6,500.[118]

## Classroom Buildings

During the Crawford administration the classroom buildings that were later named Nelson Hall and Armstrong Hall were completed on the Highland Campus. Bids for Nelson Hall, which was originally named the Industrial Arts Building, were opened in October 1960. The George E. Carlstrom Company made the lowest bid for the general construction contract. Two other Mankato companies, Mankato Electric and Schwickert Plumbing and Heating, submitted the lowest electrical and mechanical work bids. The total for all three contracts was sharply below the state-allocated $900,000.[119]

Originally, Crawford anticipated that the building would be completed for the winter term of the 1961-62 academic year. But it was not ready for classes until the Fall 1962 term. It was built primarily for the industrial arts and mathematics departments. But when it opened, some of its space was used for two sections each of the general education requirement in geography, history, political science and sociology. Offering the general education courses made it theoretically possible that some students could have all their classes on the Highland Campus.[120]

The Industrial Arts Building was designed and constructed to accommodate both shops and classrooms. Consequently, it had two distinct parts. Its long, narrow easternmost part was a one-story shop facility. Its four-story classroom part was separated from the shop part by a corridor between its north and south exits. Although the shop section and the lowest floor of the classroom portion were both classified as the ground floor, the bottom classroom level was placed five feet below the shop level. The second level of the classroom section, which is five feet above the ground floor, is considered to be the second floor. It is topped by floors three and four. The building's rather unique design reflects its dual nature.[121]

Like the physical education facilities, the Industrial Arts Building was constructed of brick trimmed with Kasota stone. Its placement along Maywood Avenue shows that the college had not yet developed an overall Highland Campus design. With a north entry next to the avenue and no access on the west, the building appeared to be an outlier unrelated to any other development.

By the time the Industrial Arts Building was opened, another but much

Nelson Hall, 1962

Maurice J. Nelson,
1958

larger classroom building was being constructed adjacent to it. The building that officially became Armstrong Hall in 1967 was originally usually known as the English-Education Building. From its inception it was projected to be a massive edifice. The 1961 legislative appropriation for Mankato State included $2,040,000 for a "general classroom building." But by then, the Crawford administration had decided that it would be used by all professional education units in addition to the English, journalism and foreign languages departments.[122]

The general contractor, the George Carlstrom Construction Company, made enough progress in 1963 to make completion by the opening of the Fall 1964 term seem likely. But the Carlstrom firm and Cuddy Plumbing and Heating, the mechanical contractor, and Brown Electric of Waseca, the electrical contractor, were all slowed by a worker's strike. Consequently, the building's first, second and third floors were not completed by the opening of the term, but they were opened anyway. The original contracts did not include finishing the basement, which had only a gravel floor.[123]

On October 23, 1964, a month after the fall term's first class day, Crawford reported to the State College Board that: "The new Classroom Building, likewise, was moved into without completion and there have been numerous instances of interruptions caused by the presence of workmen during class hours." In enumerating specific problems, Crawford mentioned the shortage of stairwell handrails, doors, wiring, flooring and telephones. He hoped that these problems would be solved by Thanksgiving.[124]

Although these problems were aggravating, they were solvable and did not detract from the overall good impression of the building. Once its exterior had been constructed, the campus and city communities were awed by the massive structure. Its second and third floors overhung the ground floor on all sides by about 16 feet each. The ground floor was finished with Kasota stone and the levels above it were faced with brick and some Kasota stone accenting. The exterior feature that provoked the most attention was the window boxes, which consisted of thick Kasota stone slabs that jutted out about two feet from the four sides of all windows. Their purpose was to make the air conditioning more effective by blocking out much of the direct sunlight. But, many observers thought they looked like gun ports in a seeming fortress-like structure.[125]

The building's interior design was unique. The only second and third story rooms that had windows were the faculty offices that rimmed all four sides. The classrooms were located in two inner cores. The outmost ones were separated from the office rows by a narrow hallway and from the innermost block of rooms by a wide hallway designed to absorb the heavy student traffic. The first, second and third floors combined were reported to have 65 classrooms and 125 offices.[126]

Students and faculty adjusted quickly to the windowless classrooms, which were immune from such outside noises as lawnmowers and motorcycles. But they soon found that their "climate-controlled" building had an inadequate air circulation system. Ostensibly, circulation was achieved in each classroom by the air entering in narrow slits through the ceiling tiles and exiting through a louvered portion of the hallway door.

Automotive engineering students work on cars in Nelson Hall, 1976

But the system proved to be inefficient and there were many complaints about temperature variances from room to room. For example, Garold H. McCullock, an English major from St. Louis Park, complained that "each room has a different temperature. Personal experience dictates my wearing a coat in some rooms and simply wearing a T-shirt in others."[127]

The original construction names for the first two Highland Campus classrooms were used until December 18, 1967, when the State College Board gave them permanent names. Acting on the recommendation of the college's Committee on Naming College Buildings, the board named the first classroom building Nelson Hall and the second one Armstrong Hall.[128]

Nelson Hall recognized the long service of Maurice J. Nelson, who joined the faculty of the Mankato Normal School as an industrial arts instructor in 1918. After attending the Mankato State Normal School in 1912-1913, Nelson earned a diploma from Stout Institute at Menominee, Wisconsin. In 1930 President Frank D. McElroy named him dean of men, a new part-time position. Nelson's long service, which ended with his retirement in 1959, spanned Mankato State's teachers college phase and short parts of the normal school and college phases.[129]

Grace Armstrong, the namesake of Armstrong Hall, started teaching education courses at the Mankato Teachers College in 1927. She earned her bachelor's and master's degrees from the University of Minnesota and did additional graduate work there and at Columbia University. Although she served for a time as the associate director of professional education, she was primarily remembered for her long classroom service. By the time Armstrong retired in 1963 she was the longest serving member of the Division of Professional Education.[130]

The opening of Armstrong Hall in 1964 was a landmark achievement in Highland Campus development. Once it was in use, the college's class offerings were about equally divided between the Valley and Highland campuses. This feature underscored the explosive growth of the Highland Campus, which changed the face of Mankato State College in an amazingly short time period.

The advent of Armstrong Hall classes was mainly responsible for improved free inter-campus bus transportation. In the fall of 1964 Administrative Dean Gerrit

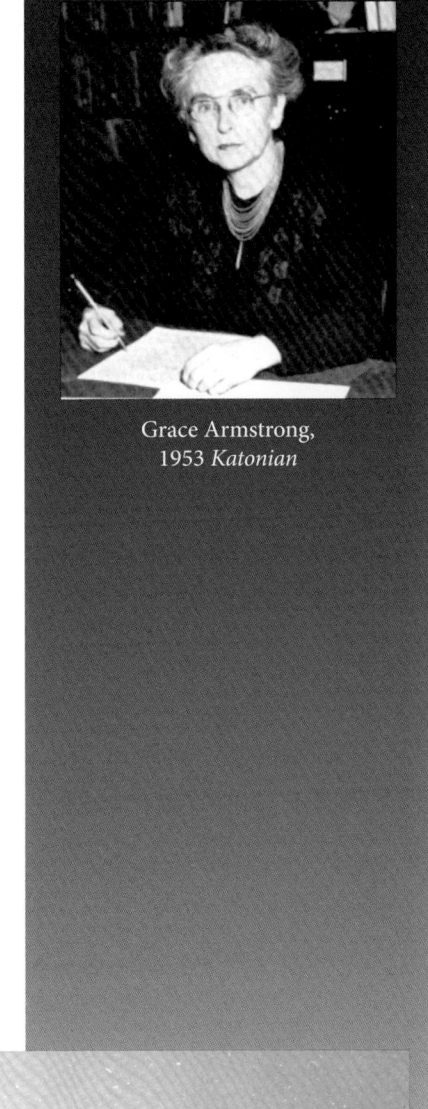

Grace Armstrong,
1953 *Katonian*

Armstrong Hall, 1966

Inter-campus bus service dropping students on Lower Campus

M. Wissink reported that "'we are running buses on a nip-and-tuck schedule." On weekdays a bus left the South Fifth Street stop by the Administration Building every four minutes from 7:00 to 9:00 a.m., the busiest time of each day. Departure times ranged from that to every 10 minutes during the afternoon hours. Evening intervals were set at 20 minutes. The annual bus service cost the college $48,000.[131]

The rather hectic bus service with stops at the Administration Building, Cooper Center, the Crawford and McElroy dormitory complexes, the Industrial Arts Building and the Wilson Campus School typified the college's fast pace. With hundreds of students being shuttled between the two campuses, the institution exuded robust activity. Students of that time no doubt vividly remember the loud sound of bus engines and the lingering smell of diesel fuel fumes.

## Utilities Plant

The first heating facility for the Highland Campus was a boiler room in the Wilson Campus School. It was used to heat the building and nearby dormitories. But it did not have the capacity to heat an expanding campus that included the physical education/athletics complex and a classroom building. Consequently, in October 1960, when bids were let on the physical education facilities and the classroom building, they were also opened on a new, free-standing utilities building. This plant was subsequently built on the western edge of the campus about a block south of Crawford D.[132]

The four bids totaling more than a half million dollars for constructing the utilities plant and related tunnels were opened on October 21. Kulseth Brothers Construction Company of Mankato proposed to build the plant for $72,630. The lowest bids for the electrical and mechanical works were respectively bid by the Mankato Electric Company and the H. R. Nichols Company of St. Paul. Usually the general construction costs for new campus buildings exceeded the electrical and mechanical expenditures combined. But, the utilities building was unique, because it featured a massive boiler, which had a 15,000-gallon capacity. The boiler, fueled by natural gas, produced steam heat, which was dispersed through pipes in concreted tunnels that were seven feet high and five feet wide. The George E. Carlstrom Company bid $167,740 to construct the tunnels that also housed electrical conduits.

The original utilities plant, which was completed in 1962, was soon outmoded. As soon as the English-Education Building and the first high rise dormitory were authorized, it was apparent that the plant and the tunnel system would have to be expanded. In 1964 the Eric Carlstrom Construction Company completed most of the work on a $300,000 contract for enlarging the utilities plant. When the expanded plant was outfitted with a second boiler with the same capacity of the first one, the Wilson Campus School boiler was removed and used to replace a Valley Campus boiler. As the Carlstrom Company was completing the plant addition, the Ben Neitge Construction Company of Mankato was working on a $147,650 contract to install additional tunnels, water mains and storm and sanitary sewers. Its work was scheduled to be completed by September 30, 1964. But it and the Carlstrom contract were not completed until early 1965. In 1966, a third 15,000-gallon boiler was added to the utilities plant.[133]

## Evolution of Central Administration

During Crawford's administration the constant enrollment and faculty growth caused Crawford and the board to make the central administration larger and more diversified. In 1946-1947, Crawford's first year, the administrative staff, other than Crawford, consisted of Albert B. Morris, dean of instruction and registrar, Ralph R. Reeder, director of professional education, placement, and laboratory schools, Grace Armstrong, assistant director of professional education, Miles E. Hawk, director of student personnel, Maurice J. Nelson, dean of men, Sara Norris, dean of women, Emma Wiecking, head librarian, Phyllis Bentley, assistant librarian, Johanna Weblemoe, health service, Anna Wiecking, principal of college elementary school, Morris H. Nelson, principal of college junior high school, Earle J. Wigley, director of veterans guidance center, Ethel M. Cochran, director of halls and cafeteria, Georgia Bekke, assistant registrar, Ethel Anne DeVaney, accountant and office manager, Gretchen S. Morris, secretary to the president and Tom Farmer, building and grounds.[134]

Although the 1940 North Central accreditation report identified the lack of an academic dean as a major shortcoming, that problem was not even partially addressed until 1946. Then Albert B. Morris, the college's original registrar, was made "dean of instruction and registrar." Presumably, Morris split his time between the two functions. He served in that position for three years. But, starting in the academic year 1949-1950, he was only the dean of instruction. Newcomer Lawrence D. Edmonson was named registrar.

When Morris retired after the 1954-1955 year he was replaced by Gerrit M. Wissink, a physics professor who had joined the faculty in 1935. Wissink held the position for four years until he was named administrative dean, a new position created to supervise buildings and grounds on what was by then a two-campus college.[135]

Crawford and the board named Milton J. Hassel to replace Wissink in academic affairs. Hassel, who had joined the administration in 1957 as the director of special services, was given the new title of "academic dean."

Hassel's promotion was the beginning of a short period of very rapid turnover in the academic dean position. During his last six years, Crawford was assisted by four different academic deans.

Hassel resigned in 1961 when he was named president of Kearney State College in Nebraska. In July 1961, he was replaced by Bevington Reed, a 46-year-old Texas native, who had most recently served as the academic dean of Sul Ross State College, Alpine, Texas. But Reed, who was direct, efficient and capable, soon caught the attention of the State College Board. In May 1964, the board hired him effective July 1, 1964, to replace the recently deceased Roy Prentiss, the board's original executive director.[136]

Meredith Freeman, who had entered the administration as the director of special services, was

## Gretchen S. Morris: Administrative Assistant

During the Crawford era Gretchen S. Morris (October 2, 1901- February 27, 1986) ranked next to the president as Mankato State's most influential campus official. As Crawford's administrative assistant, she arranged his agenda and determined who could meet with him. Furthermore, she was involved in the development of administrative actions and policies.

A native of Grant County, South Dakota, Morris was born to Bertha Matilda and John Schad. The family regarded the village of Summit in adjoining Roberts County as their hometown. Morris attended the state normal school in Aberdeen, South Dakota, and married Ed R. Morris on December 21, 1923. The Morrises moved to Appleton, Minnesota, where Gretchen worked for five years as the school superintendent's secretary, 1937-1942.

Morris started working for the Mankato State Teachers College in 1942 as an account clerk in the business office. She remained in that position for four years before being appointed as secretary to the president. After five years as Crawford's secretary, Morris was designated as administrative assistant to the president.

While working fulltime, Morris continued her education. She completed an undergraduate degree at Mankato State Teachers College in 1949. Two years later she was awarded a Master of Arts degree by the University of Michigan. Her thesis title was "The Development of a Faculty Handbook for the Mankato State Teachers College, Mankato, Minnesota." After completing her master's, Morris taught office methods in the college's business education program.

Morris' reputation as the campus power broker resulted from her efficient management

Gretchen S. Morris, 1963

of the president's office. She courteously screened requests from anyone who wanted to meet with the president. No one, including the division heads, who were regarded as campus oligarchs, casually bypassed her and dropped in on Crawford. Furthermore, she independently made decisions about some new proposals.

Aside from her regular office duties, Morris served on several committees—including the important Allocations Committee that made decisions about student-related activities such as the funding of the college newspaper. Morris also led the way in forming the Alumni Association and served as its first secretary. During the prolonged campaign to achieve university status, she did most of the justification research.

Morris continued in her position after Crawford resigned in 1965. She worked with acting president Melvin G. Scarlett during the 1965-1966 academic year and with President James F. Nickerson from July 1, 1966 until she resigned in early November, 1969.

After retiring Morris moved to Englewood, Florida, where she lived for the rest of her life. She briefly returned to campus to participate in spring quarter commencement ceremonies on May 29, 1976, when she was recognized as the recipient of the Distinguished Alumni Achievement Award. An announcement of the award included the statement: "Mrs. Morris became known as a high level policy maker for Dr. Crawford; her OK on proposals was viewed as absolutely essential before any administrative action was taken. She was a tireless worker on behalf of the college.... Few people in the college's history have been viewed as making a longer or more lasting contribution to MSU."

(Morris, Gretchen S. file, University Archives.)

selected as acting academic dean for the 1964-1965 year. But, in mid-March 1965 he was replaced by Melvin G. Scarlett, who had most recently served as the dean of Hastings College (Nebraska). Scarlett, 44 years old when he joined Mankato State, held a doctorate in education from Oklahoma State University. He also had considerable college teaching experience in English, speech and journalism.[137]

For 1964-1965, Crawford's last year, Mankato State had 31 "officers of administration" positions including the president, academic dean and administrative dean. The others were:

- Gretchen S. Morris, assistant to the president
- Edwin M. Boyne, dean of the School of Graduate Studies
- John A. Johnson, dean of the School of Education
- Benjamin A. Buck, assistant dean of the School of Education
- Theodore L. Nydahl, dean of the School of Arts and Science
- Elias J. Halling, assistant dean of the School of Arts and Science
- Morgan I. Thomas, dean of the School of Business
- Bess Ellison, chair of the Division of Nursing
- Roy B. Moore, chair of the Division of Health and Physical Education
- Jack O'Bar, head librarian
- Norbert K. Baumgart, dean of students
- Marie Bruce, associate dean of students
- Chester A. Carkowski, assistant dean of students
- Andrew R. Een, registrar
- Donald F. Jorgensen, assistant registrar
- Claire E. Faust, principal of the college campus school
- William H. Dawe, director of student teaching
- Dan M. Duffy, director of student housing
- Leonard A. Ford, coordinator of special programs
- Donald L. Henderson, director of computer services
- Arden E. Hesla, director of field services
- John B. Hodapp, director of athletics
- John L. Hodowanic, director of informational services
- Ira H. Johnson, director of campus planning
- Edward R. McMahon, director of audio-visual services
- Darwin A. Slocum, director of placement
- Donald B. Youel, director of college publications
- Melvin A. Ziehl, business manager[138]

## College Reorganization

When Crawford became president he inherited the division organization for academic programs, which had been in place since 1938. Since he had a penchant for controlling things, Crawford assumed the authority to name division heads rather than continue the original practice of having them elected by division faculty.[139]

Over the years as faculty numbers swelled the divisions became increasingly large and unwieldy. Finally, calls from faculty members, whose advanced training was in a specific discipline such as chemistry as opposed to science and mathematics, led to a major reorganization. In 1964 the divisions were replaced by schools that included departments.

During its 16-year history the division organization was expanded. In 1949 the "Division of Business Education" was added to the original divisions of Fine and Applied Arts, Health and Physical Education, Language and Literature, Science and Mathematics and Social Studies. Business education courses had originally been in the Division of Social Studies. The same year the Unit of Professional Education was reorganized to the Division of Professional Education and Psychology. The Division of Nursing first appeared in the 1955-1956 catalog.[140]

The tenure of the division heads, whom Crawford seemingly regarded as his informal cabinet, was remarkably stable. Throughout the division period of Crawford's presidency, Elias J. Halling was the only head of the Division of Fine and Applied Arts. The same was true for Leonard A. Ford with the Division of Science and Mathematics. Theodore L. Nydahl headed the Social Studies Division except for three years when he was on leave. Starting in 1947 Donald B. Youel was the only leader of the Language and Literature Division. Duane McCracken, Mankato State College's first business teacher, led the Division of Business Education from 1949 until his retirement in 1960. He was replaced by Ernest I. Thomas. Harry Meyering, the first head of the Division of Professional Education and Psychology, was replaced by John A. Johnson in 1957. From 1953 to the end of the division era, Roy B. Moore headed the Health and Physical Education Division.[141]

By the early 1960s the divisions were large enough to cause the recognition of subject matter sections. For example, in 1963-1964, the last year for divisions, the Division of Science and Mathematics had 55 faculty members. There were 15 each in biology and mathematics, 13 in chemistry and 12 in physics.[142]

In some instances the sections acted as de facto departments with leaders who chaired section meetings. Although hiring new faculty, which was almost an annual occurrence for every section after about 1955, was the purview of the division head, it oftentimes involved section leaders and selected faculty members. Any such involvement was by invitation of the division heads, who found it was not physically possible to screen applications without some assistance. At that time the college did not have any funding to bring candidates to campus for interviews. Consequently, after finalists for a position had been determined, the division head contacted references and conducted telephone interviews.

The reorganization to schools and departments for most academic units, which was considered by numerous faculty committee meetings, was approved by the administration and the Mankato State Faculty Association. It established the schools of Arts and Science, Business, Education and Graduate Studies and retained the Division of Health and Physical Education and the Division of Nursing.[143]

The School of Arts and Science, with 203 members, included slightly more than half of all faculty. Its departments were art, biological sciences, chemistry, English, foreign languages (French, German, Russian and Spanish), geography, history, journalism, library science, mathematics and astronomy, music, philosophy, physics, political science, sociology and speech. Its largest departments were English and music, which were respectively staffed by 32 and 24 faculty. The smallest departments were journalism and philosophy with one each. The school was administered by Crawford appointees Dean Theodore L. Nydahl and Assistant Dean Elias J. Halling.[144]

The School of Business, led by Dean Morgan I. Thomas, had four departments — accounting, business administration, business education and economics.

The administrators of the School of Education were John A. Johnson, dean, and Benjamin A. Buck, assistant dean. Its departments were audio-visual education, campus school, elementary education, secondary and foundation education, educational psychology, home economics, industrial arts, psychology and special education.

Most of the departments in today's Minnesota State University, Mankato were originally established by the 1964 reorganization. Soon after they were created, each department chose an elected chairperson. But, only the tenured members were authorized to vote.

Dean Edwin M. Boyne administered the School of Graduate Studies, which offered both the Master of Science and Master of Arts degrees. Members of the graduate faculty were selected on the basis of their academic training. All faculty who held terminal degrees automatically received permanent appointments to the graduate faculty. But in some instances, those with less than a terminal degree who had unique specialties were added to the graduate faculty to teach a designated course.[145]

Roy B. Moore continued to head the Division of Health and Physical Education after college reorganization. The tenured faculty chose Clem W. Thompson as the chairman of the 23-member Health Education Department, which included five varsity coaches—Rometo "Rummy" Macias, wrestling and golf, William Morris, basketball, Earl "Bud" Myers, track and cross country, Jean

McCarthy, baseball and James Robert "Bob" Otto, football. Ruth M. Schellberg, the only full professor in Women's Physical Education, was chosen to chair the four-member department.

Bess Ellison continued to lead the Division of Nursing, which had six instructors including Ellison and five acting instructors. The division, which offered a Bachelor of Science degree in nursing, had clinical experience arrangements with Immanuel Hospital, Mankato (no longer in existence, but then located at the southwest corner of South Fourth and Washington streets), St. Joseph's Hospital, Mankato (the present Mayo Health System Hospital), The Children's Hospital, St. Paul, St. Peter State Hospital and Blue Earth County Nursing Service (public health).

## Civil Defense: A Cold War Reaction

Like all other parts of American society, Mankato State was affected by the Cold War between the United States and its western European allies and the Union of Soviet Socialist Republics (USSR).

The World War II alliance of convenience between the United States and the Soviet Union was shattered soon after war's end. Pursuing its aim of internationalizing communism, the Soviets established a political-military zone across eastern Europe. This action caused great alarm in Western Europe which prompted Winston Churchill, Great Britain's wartime prime minister, to warn of Soviet aggression. In his famous iron curtain address delivered at Westminster College in Fulton, Missouri, on March 5, 1946, Churchill condemned Soviet action by observing: "From Stettin in the Baltic to Trieste in the Adriatic, an iron curtain has descended across the continent."[146]

Accordingly, the United States during the administration of President Harry S. Truman took steps to thwart anticipated Soviet aggression. On March 12, 1947, Truman announced the Truman Doctrine, which provided for aid to Greece and Turkey in order to prevent the establishment of Soviet puppet governments. Then, on April 3, 1948, Truman approved the more comprehensive Marshall Plan, which stipulated that the United States would fund economic aid for Western European countries.[147]

The Cold War, which was pronounced to be over by President George H. W. Bush on Christmas Day, 1991, featured hot spells and cold spells. Such events as the testing of the first Soviet atomic bomb in 1949 and the Cuban Missile Crisis of 1962 intensified concern over the outbreak of a "hot" war. Conversely, the threat of a nuclear war eased, for example, by the acceptance of the Nuclear Non-Proliferation Treaty by the Soviet Union, United Kingdom, and United States and other countries in 1970.

But despite events that temporarily eased tension, the Cold War was somewhat akin to a chronic headache. It was always there.

Obviously, civil defense measures that affected Minnesota and Mankato State reflected federal policy. President Truman created the Federal Civil Defense Administration (FCDA) by executive order on December 1, 1950. It was made an official federal agency by the Federal Civil Defense Act of January 12, 1951. In 1958 President Dwight D. Eisenhower, Truman's successor, created the Office of Civil and Defense Mobilization by merging the FCDA and the Office of Defense Mobilization.[148]

Within days after Truman's executive order the FCDA began coordinating defense programs with officials in all states. To facilitate FCDA-Minnesota coordination, the 1951 legislature created the State Civil Defense Agency.[149]

The Cold War took a more ominous turn when the United States and the USSR developed hydrogen bombs. The United States developed its first H-Bomb in 1952 and the USSR responded the following year. Reportedly, a single H-Bomb had the destructive force of a thousand of the two atomic bombs the United States used against Japan late in World War II.

After the development of H-bombs, federal defense officials assumed the greatest Soviet threat would come from long range bombers that would target America's major metropolitan areas. Defensive strategies included the establishment of an elaborate radar station warning system and the evacuation of cities.

In keeping with federal directives, Hubert A. Schon, Minnesota's civil defense director, held a series of annual operation alerts beginning in 1954. An operation alert exercise, which called for the evacuation of the Twin Cities, was predicated on the assumption that the initial Soviet attack would

United States Civil defense logo, undated

## MSTC Anticipates Civil Defense Alert

Although no additional word has been received from the state capitol, "Operation Alert" is still anticipated for July 20 or 21, according to business manager M. A. Ziehl.

"Operation Alert" is a civil defense exercise in which Mankato State Teachers college will be turned into an emergency state capitol. Gov. Orville Freeman will move his office staff to Mankato and set up operations here. The test evacuation will probably include the state's constitutional officers such as the auditor, treasurer, and secretary of state.

It is anticipated that no classes will be interrupted, as only a few rooms will be used by the governor and his staff. In event of a real attack, Mankato would become the capitol city of the state and MSTC would become the capitol building as in the mock attack.

*College Reporter* 12 July 1956

devastate the cores of Minneapolis and St. Paul. During the first operation alert, the state civil defense director estimated that Minneapolis alone would have 67,000 casualties.

The 1956 operation alert was of particular significance to Mankato and Mankato State. It was predicated on the assumption that an evacuation of the metropolitan area would force state officials to move the capital from St. Paul to Mankato.[150]

In planning for the 1956 operation alert state officials announced on April 5 that Mankato was the designated state emergency capital. In May state civil defense personnel visited Mankato State to determine locations for the governor's office and other state constitutional officers including the auditor, treasurer and secretary of state. They decided to place the governor's office in the president's office of Mankato State. This decision immediately made that office, the first room on the left inside the main or central entrance of the Administration Building, one of the state's most noteworthy sites. The other state offices were to be located in nearby rooms. During the same visit the civil defense officials decided to use Washington Elementary School, near St. Joseph's Hospital, as their headquarters during the practice alert. They also scheduled the two-day exercise for Friday and Saturday, July 20-21, which minimized the disruption of Mankato State's summer classes.

For some unapparent reason, Governor Orville Freeman decided that contingency office arrangements would suffice and that he and other state officials did not have to physically move into their designated college space. Instead, Freeman, accompanied by state civil defense director Colonel Hubert A. Schon, flew by helicopter to Washington Elementary School on the operation's second day.[151]

Most of the operation entailed establishing a communications center in the Washington Elementary School. Schon was satisfied that it provided an efficient means of coordinating activities with district defense offices statewide. He also concluded that locating the emergency state capital at Mankato improved state civil defense. Anoka, a northwest Minneapolis suburb that was used the year before, was deemed to be too close to the assumed primary destruction zone.

On May 3-5, 1960, Minnesota used Mankato as headquarters for an operation alert that was larger and more complicated than the 1956 one. The scenario for the alert, which was deliberately scheduled on the workdays of Tuesday, Wednesday and Thursday, was that the Twin Cities, Duluth, Sioux Falls, South Dakota and two North Dakota sites had all been destroyed by airplane-delivered nuclear bombs. The main purpose of the alert was to determine how rapidly and efficiently Mankato could become the emergency state capital and communications center after the bombs were dropped at a specified time on Tuesday.[152]

The Mankato activities, which involved about 400 people, were concentrated in Mankato State's Administration Building and the National Guard Armory on downtown North Second Street. Governor Freeman, who was then in the last year of his second term, and other state officials established a provisional state government in the Administration Building. State civil defense director Schon and his support personnel converted the armory into a communications center from which they determined the bombing casualties and coordinated the evacuation of urban populaces. Owatonna was designated as the central registration point for Twin Cities evacuees and civil defense personnel in cooperation with the state highway patrol managed coordination of the mock evacuation over designated routes out of the Twin Cities.

Minnesota's civil defense strategy shifted to a new strategy after the 1960 operation alert. National and state officials decided that any Soviet nuclear bombs would be delivered by intercontinental ballistic missiles (ICBMs) rather than conventional bombers. The proper response to such devices, which would have massive fallout areas, they decided, was to emphasize home protection.[153]

Therefore, every county's civil defense director urged homeowners to prepare basement fallout shelters. In 1966 Blue Earth County's civil defense director distributed copies of a 24-page pamphlet titled Fallout Protection for Homes with Basements to all households in the county. Published by the federal Office of Civil Defense with the Department of Defense it briefly described and illustrated various ways of erecting basement fallout shelters. Those who wanted more construction details for various fallout models were advised and invited to submit a tear-off postage-paid form.

At least several years before the manual's distribution, every community had identified specified public buildings as fallout shelters. At Mankato State the shelters were the basements of large buildings including the Administration Building on the Valley Campus and the Crawford and McElroy dormitory complexes on the Highland Campus. Each facility was identified by an exterior sign showing the civil defense logo of a blue circle surrounding a white triangle. The red letters "CD" filled up most of the space within the triangle. The establishment of the civil defense shelters at Mankato State and other state colleges was authorized by the State College Board on January 11, 1963. This process, which was encouraged by the governor, entailed the colleges' administrations contracting with civilian defense officials to designate shelters and store "certain materials."[154]

Presumably any private or public fallout shelters would have to be used for days or even weeks before an all-clear was issued. Therefore, it would be vital that shelter occupants have emergency rations on hand. Homeowners were advised to stockpile appropriate canned foods and potable water. But, to support public shelters, the government's plan was to distribute surplus army C-rations.

Although there was a pervasive urgency about civil defense preparations, actual implementations were typically slow to develop. The major delivery of emergency fallout rations to Mankato did not occur until December 18, 1968, when eight semi-truck loads of rations were delivered to Mankato State. The rations were not identified to the public, but they were surplus army C-rations. The *Free Press* article about the delivery mentioned only that the rations were stored as some unspecified campus site. But the specific storage site was the unfinished basement of Morris Hall, a newly constructed classroom building. Since on-campus space was dear, the sand-floored basement was the only available space for hundreds of boxes.[155]

The 40-pound C-ration boxes made of heavy cardboard and sealed with metal bands were so sturdy that they were stacked on wooden pallets from floor to ceiling.

Strangely, the location of the C-rations was never publicized on campus or in the Mankato community. Except for such people as campus planner Ira Johnson and some Morris Hall occupants, no one seemed to know about them. It would seem that if the rations were to be accessed in the event of a nuclear emergency, their location should have been publicized. But, despite their concern of keeping the public on edge about the Soviet threat, civil defense officials never carried out their planning to the point of actually holding maneuvers during which the public would be directed to shelters and emergency food caches.

Likewise, when the rations were delivered those who were aware of them seemed to believe that they would last in perpetuity. But, like most things, they had a limited shelf life.

The original C-ration or Type C ration was first developed for American troops in 1938. During World War II it was used in situations where troops had to prepare their own food because hot mess hall meals were not available.[156]

The C-ration for one meal (breakfast, lunch and dinner were all the same) consisted of three cans—a 12-ounce meat ration, a "bread" ration (actually crackers) and "dessert" items. The usual meat ration was some variety of stew or hash. Dessert included a packet of instant coffee, orange drink powder and hard candy.

Since the Mankato State C-rations were out-of-sight and out-of-mind they were ignored for about a decade until the meat rations deteriorated. Like any canned meat product, a C-ration meat container developed gas as it aged. Typically, the result was a corroded can whose contents soon spoiled and reeked accordingly.

Hard candy proved to be the only salvageable part of Mankato State's C-rations. For some reason that is not clear, great quantities of it ended up in Memorial Library. For about a decade beginning in the late 1970s, Leona Meyers, the library's secretary, kept a jar of the hard candy on her desk as treats for passersby.

In the meantime, Cold War tensions highlighted by the international Nuclear Non-Proliferation Treaty had been eased. Minnesota and Mankato State responded accordingly. In 1969 the state Civil Defense Department, which was by then primarily concerned with natural disasters, became part of the Minnesota Department of Public Safety. During the 1970s fallout shelters throughout the state were abandoned.[157]

## The University of Southern Minnesota Campaign

Mankato State had been a college for only three years when its students began agitating for university status in 1960. Early advocates, who realized such a change would require legislative approval, were given a voice by the *College Reporter*. On June 21, 1960, the paper urged people to ask a visiting delegation of Republican-endorsed legislative candidates: "What do you plan to do about establishing a University of Southern Minnesota, Mankato?" Apparently, the newspaper did not originate the name, but merely reiterated the one that had been talked about.[158]

The possibility of Mankato State becoming a university was first mentioned on September 12, 1957, by State Commissioner of Administration Arthur Naftalin. During a Mankato public meeting to consider the prospects of Mankato State College, Naftalin urged the opening of a second campus. He thought this would permit the college to realize its great growth potential due to Mankato's strategic location. In that context he commented "who knows but in 10 or 15 years they may be building another university in this state . . . ."[159] While hardly a stirring call for immediate action, Naftalin's remark was enough to spur local sentiment in favor of establishing the University of Southern Minnesota.

The impetus and rationale for university status was the college's rapid growth. On December 3, 1960, when he met with Mankato area legislators, Crawford emphasized that the institution had more students than the three smallest—Bemidji, Moorhead and Winona—combined. Citing on-campus fall 1960 enrollment statistics, Crawford reported Mankato State's enrollment as 4,935 compared to respectively 1,545, 1,542 and 1,305 for Bemidji, Moorhead and Winona. St. Cloud, with an enrollment of 3,445, had been the largest school traditionally, but after 1950 was outstripped by Mankato. Crawford complained that the three smallest colleges were being given preferential treatment, because their student share of building support exceeded their enrollment. On the other hand, Mankato was underfunded with building appropriations for only 3,690 students or 885 less than its enrollment. Without elaborating, Crawford was reported to have pointed out "the need for considering the transition of the college to university status with its own governing board." Apparently, only then would Mankato State be funded at the level it deserved.[160]

The University of Southern Minnesota cause was given a positive jolt by Alex Smetka, mayor of Rochester, Minnesota, and Mankato State Teachers College alum. In delivering the winter term commencement address on March 3, 1961, Smetka expressed the hope that "Mankato State College would soon be known as the University of Southern Minnesota." The audience responded with "enthusiastic applause."[161]

Smetka's presentation helped stimulate student politicians to endorse university status. In their April 1961, campaigns for the election of student senators and student body president, the Progressive Party and the rival United Party both included university status planks in their platforms. The Progressive Party's recommendation read: "The Progressive Party feels that due to the tremendous progress in all areas of college functions, we urge university status." The United Party wanted to: "Stimulate interest in the state legislature for the purpose of transforming Mankato State College to the University of Southern Minnesota."[162]

According to the *College Reporter,* one of the principal reasons students supported university status was because they believed it would lead to Mankato State's switch to a more prestigious athletic conference. When the Minnesota State Teachers College Conference was formed in 1932, all six of its original members were relatively small institutions. But, by the time the conference was renamed to the Minnesota State College Conference in 1957, Mankato State's enrollment dwarfed the three smallest colleges (Bemidji, Moorhead and Winona) and was about a fifth larger than St. Cloud. The addition of the Michigan College of Mining and Technology in 1960 (renamed to Michigan Technological University in 1964) caused the conference to be renamed to Northern States College Conference.

By the time the University of Southern Minnesota question was advanced, Mankato State students thought that the Northern States College Conference was not competitive enough for their large college. Their sentiment was for Mankato State to join the North Central Conference, which consisted of the University of North Dakota, North Dakota State University, South Dakota State University, University of South Dakota, Augustana College (Sioux Falls, South Dakota), Morningside College (Sioux City, Iowa) and Iowa State Teachers College (now the University of Northern Iowa.) The advantages of this move, according to an unspecified Mankato State coach, would be "that it would be good for the school in the long run, providing a much better athletic program as well as a better reputation."[163] It was generally assumed that the State College Board favored the current conference. So, in order for Mankato State to join North Central, it would be necessary for it to have university status with its own regents.[164]

Mankato State's student political parties kept advocacy of the University of Southern Minnesota alive in 1962. But this had no more practical effect than preaching to the converted. Everyone realized that there could only be such a university if and when it was authorized by the legislature.[165]

State Senator Val Imm, the long-standing champion of Mankato State's building needs, was certainly attuned to the sentiment for a University of Southern Minnesota. Shortly before Christmas 1962, when the convening of the 1963 legislature was only about two weeks away, Imm announced that he would sponsor legislation to convert Mankato State College into a university.[166]

Imm's critics reacted sharply even before the suggested bill had been written. They did not have to wait for details, because they opposed the very idea of making Mankato State a university independent of both the University of Minnesota and the State College Board.

Major opposition came from Norman Nelson, a member of the State College Board, Paul A. Thuet, Senate minority leader, and O. Meredith Wilson, University of Minnesota president. Nelson of Moorhead, who also served on the legislature's Liaison Committee on Higher Education, labeled Imm's proposal as a "form of secession." Apparently he was referring to secession from the state college system. But his opposition was also based on decisions made by the liaison committee. The first "opposed creating any new institutions of higher learning that would have self-governing status." The second was that the University of Minnesota should remain as the only institution authorized to offer professional and post-graduate programs.[167]

Thuet of St. Paul was quoted as having said that Imm's proposal, which called for a new university with its own board of regents, would be "expensive and unnecessary." A better solution, he opined would be to make "Mankato State a branch of the University of Minnesota." Thuet was no doubt influenced by the precedent of Duluth State Teachers College.

Wilson, who had also served on the liaison committee, defended its resolution against creating a second Minnesota public university. He thought another university might be added in the future, but "'for the moment it is enough to say that we have not yet seen reason for us to change our position.'"

The University of Minnesota *Daily* thought that Imm's proposal "'would be of dubious benefit to either Mankato or the State.'" Because it "would take a great deal of money to set up another good Minnesota university," the *Daily* supported the notion that Mankato State be made a branch of the University of Minnesota. It observed: "'Certainly the Duluth Campus has prospered under that system.'"[168]

Probably because he anticipated opposition from the State College Board, Imm had not consulted with it prior to making his public announcement about university status for Mankato State. This oversight apparently offended board member Charles F. Mourin of Virginia, Minnesota. At the board's meeting of December 17, 1962, he stated "that he had heard rumors to the effect that separate university status would be sought for the Mankato State College." Board member F. Kelton Gage, a Mankato attorney, acknowledged "that there was a great deal of discussion in Mankato on this issue but that this did not originate primarily with college personnel." Gage went on to assure the board that he would continue to work for the continuation of the board's five-college system.[169]

About the time Imm introduced his bill, Gage "publicly announced that advocating university status for MSC is not the business of the college."[170] Gage's admonishment that the college could not act as its own self-promoter had the effect of creating a shadow game mentality. It enabled the Crawford administration to appear to be nothing more than a mere spectator to a public movement.

Before the University of Southern Minnesota bill was introduced in both the Senate and House of Representatives on February 13, 1963, Imm and his chief ally, Representative Roy Schulz, Blue Earth County Conservative, recruited co-sponsors. Imm's Senate co-sponsors were Walter Frazer, Conservative from Mountain Lake, and Michael McGuire, a Montgomery Liberal. Schulz was joined by Fred Cina, Aurora Liberal, Lyle Farmer, St. Paul Liberal and Mankato State alum, Roy Dunn, Pelican Rapids Conservative and C. A. "Gus" Johnson, a Mankato Independent.[171]

The highly detailed 15-page bill first specified that "Mankato State College, located at Mankato, Minnesota, shall hereafter be known as 'The University of Southern Minnesota' and under that name shall have all the rights, privileges, powers, and duties which are defined hereinafter." The objectives of the proposed university were to "offer courses in Agriculture, Business Administration, Education, Engineering, Fine Arts and Liberal Arts, Medical Technology, Nursing and Pharmacy; and to offer such other courses of instruction as the University determines; provided no professional courses culminating in degrees in Law, Medicine, Dentistry may be offered by such University."[172]

The University of Southern Minnesota was to be governed by a seven-member "Board of Trustees . . . appointed by the Governor, by and with the advice and consent of the Senate." . . . . "All the rights and duties vested by law in the State College Board, as they formerly applied to Mankato State College relating to the operation, management, control and maintenance of Mankato State College" were to be transferred to the board of trustees.

Most of the bill was an elaboration of the board's duties and powers. These included such usual items as the appointment of the administration and faculty and the bonding authority to construct new buildings.

In a memorandum he prepared for an unspecified Senate committee, Imm insisted that the proposed biennial allocation, which was listed on the last page of the bill, would not be costly. He reported that the existing Mankato State College had a recommended budget of $12,612,158 for fiscal years 1964 and 1965. The creation of the University of Southern Minnesota would require only $250,000 more each year. Imm calculated that only about three-fourths of that amount would have to be appropriated, because the institution would have estimated revenues of more than $3,000,000.[173]

Exuding bravado, Imm and Schulz, at least in their public pronouncements, believed their bill had a good chance of being passed. They thought it should have considerable appeal because of its bipartisan sponsorship, which included a representative from the Twin Cities and two from northern Minnesota. Furthermore, they seemed to have been counting on a certain resentment of the University of Minnesota, which was seen by some as being too large and dominant.[174]

As the bill was under consideration by the House and Senate education committees, its pros and cons became better defined. Most of the supporters emphasized the desirability of having an engineering school on the Mankato campus and of enhancing the business curriculum. They were invariably positive and never attempted to justify the University of Southern Minnesota by criticizing the University of Minnesota.[175]

Those who favored the bill were elated with the results of a "Minnesota Poll" conducted by the *Minneapolis Star and Tribune*. The newspaper polled a cross-section of 600 people who were informed and asked: "'The state of Minnesota gives financial support to the University of Minnesota and to five state colleges. Now it's been suggested that university education should be made available closer to home for students in southwestern Minnesota, and that the state college at Mankato be expanded to become a new state university. Are you in favor of, or against, establishing a new state university at Mankato?'"[176]

Sixty-nine percent (men, 63 percent; women, 73 percent) were in favor, 18 percent were against (men, 22 percent; women, 14 percent), 12 percent had no opinion and 1 percent had other answers. Not surprisingly, the strongest support was from southern Minnesota where 76 percent were in favor. The favorable ratings for the Twin Cities and northern Minnesota were respectively 71 percent and 60 percent.

The *College Reporter* regularly covered the bill's consideration by the legislature. Throughout the bill's hearings the *Reporter* never published any submissions from the college administration and faculty. Apparently none was submitted, because the Crawford administration was refraining from overtly supporting the creation of the University of Southern Minnesota.

Some legislative skeptics of the proposed University of Southern Minnesota wondered if the state needed another engineering school beside the University of Minnesota's Institute of Technology. Senator Harold R. Popp posed that question to O. Meredith Wilson, the university's president. Wilson, in turn, had the institute's Dean Athelstan Spilhaus and Associate Dean Frank Verbrugge consider that and other related questions. Spilhaus and Verbrugge concluded that the institute could accommodate approximately 800 additional students and "that development of duplicate facilities would constitute a needless dissipation of the resources of the State of Minnesota." They also estimated that it would cost approximately $11,000,000 to duplicate the university's Institute of Technology. To assure that some legislators saw the determinations by Spilhaus and Verbrugge, the University of Minnesota's Alumni Association reported them in its Alumni Legislative Newsletter.[177]

Meanwhile, the University of Southern Minnesota bill was being considered by the legislature. Most of the action was in the Senate where Imm, Franz and McGuire introduced the bill on February 13, 1963, when it was read for the first time. On April 6 it was submitted to the Senate Education Committee, which referred it to the Senate Finance Committee. After approving two significant amendments, the Finance Committee passed the bill by a 10 to seven vote and referred it back to the Education Committee on April 19. The first amendment changed the name of the proposed university to Minnesota State University. McGuire, who suggested the name change, explained that the new name suggested that the proposed institution would have a statewide scope, whereas the original name made it appear to be too regional and hence provincial. McGuire also proposed the second amendment, which reduced the additional biennial appropriation from $500,000 to $100,000.[178]

When the session ended on May 23 the bill was awaiting a Senate floor vote and was under consideration by a House committee. Imm and his supporters seemed to be satisfied with the bill's progress, because it was never voted down.

Although he had maintained an outward public indifference during the bill's consideration, Crawford was privately very concerned about possible university status. After the 1963 session was over he wrote to Imm: "You certainly went much farther so far as the University Bill was concerned than anyone had any right to hope for when the session opened. You have established a very firm base on which to begin new and successful operations two years from now."[179]

Crawford seemed to assume that nothing would happen on the university drive front until the 1965 legislative session. But, he had not reckoned with opposition from Governor Karl Rolvaag. Furthermore, he had not anticipated that the State College Board, which was clearly irked by the effort to convert Mankato State College into a university, would assert itself.

When he spoke to the Association of Minnesota Colleges meeting in St. Paul on November 8, 1963, Rolvaag expressed opinions on graduate work and higher education governance that were seen as opposition to university status for Mankato State. He believed that only the University of Minnesota should offer graduate work and he thought Minnesota already had too many boards. Imm reacted by claiming that the governor was intent on blocking university status for Mankato State. Nonetheless, Imm insisted that Minnesota needed a second university and that he would continue working for that goal.[180]

Students for Status co-chairs Jeri Deveraux and Mark Korting pin each other with "Me for U" buttons, 1965 *Katonian*

In the meantime the State College Board had projected itself into the Mankato State university status issue. At its September 19, 1964, meeting in Moorhead, board member Norman Nelson "noted that there has been a great deal of discussion of the move to secure university status for Mankato State College, "and he suggested" that the State College Board should inform itself on this matter." Nelson went on to recommend that "at an early meeting of the Board the administration of Mankato State College and its staff should make a presentation to the Board." Crawford responded "that this could be done, but that the Mankato people would have to begin from the beginning to build up a presentation, since this matter has not been discussed at the college." The Board agreed that Mankato State's presentation should be done at its next scheduled meeting on November 16, 1964.[181]

The board's action forced Mankato State to become its own advocate for university status rather than pretending that it had no active interest in the political movement to create the state's second public university. Crawford's first move was to involve the faculty. On October 6 he met with "about 165 faculty members and several interested spectators" in the Administration Building's main auditorium. Crawford most dramatic utterance was "I predict that the 1965 legislature will give University status to Mankato State College." In justifying university status he noted that "Minnesota is one of the slowest states nationally in establishing more than one-state supported university." For examples, he specifically cited the neighboring states of North Dakota, South Dakota, Iowa and Wisconsin, which in recent years had created more than one university. Crawford cautioned that even if Mankato State was granted university status, it would have to grow into the role by expanding degree programs and improving the library.[182]

Subsequent to his faculty meeting, Crawford had his administrative assistant Gretchen Morris work with John Hodowanic, the college's public relations director, to prepare a written justification for university status. Additionally, he conferred with faculty association leaders, who agreed to assist in making the university status case before the board. Morris became the administration's principal source for keeping the *College Reporter* informed about developments.[183]

The university status possibility, which had been popular with alumni and students since its inception, created an unprecedented degree of enthusiastic support during the fall of 1964. What the *College Reporter* called "university fever" was grandly displayed at the 1964 homecoming. The alumni association's executive board decided to launch a fundraising campaign to support university status. The parade, dedicated to university status, featured a Searing Center float labelled 'Dawn of U Status.' During the halftime ceremonies of the football game, emcee John Coumbe introduced the college's band as "the Mankato State University marching band." This announcement elicited a "spontaneous cheer from the crowd." Crawford delighted the alumni banquet crowd by proclaiming: "The trend toward university status is in the air and it is inevitable."[184]

On the heels of homecoming a group of students organized Students for Status, a committee devoted to making Mankato State a university. The 20-person committee lead by Mark Korting, a junior from Mankato, Jeri Devereaux, a junior from Cottonwood, James Zwickey, a junior from Lake Crystal and Lynne Bloomstrand, a junior from St. Paul, held its organizational meeting on October 27. Students for Status aimed to promote university status through student meetings and demonstrations and press releases. To boost student participation, Students for Status also ordered buttons inscribed with "Me for U" and "University of Southern Minnesota." It intended to have them ready for sale within a few weeks. In calling for the University of Southern Minnesota, Students for Status indicated that it preferred Imm's original name rather than the change to Minnesota State University approved by a 1963 legislative committee.[185]

After its initial meeting, Students for Status held weekly meetings with the aim of informing students and getting more of them involved in its cause. The committee's publicity also included the issuance of five thousand "Me for U" buttons, which went on sale November 12 from booths in the Administration Building on the Valley Campus and the Education-English Building (later renamed to Armstrong Hall) on the Highland Campus. Additionally, seven members of the Students for Status Committee handed out buttons at the corner of Hennepin and Seventh in downtown Minneapolis. Devereaux said this action was to "show our Twin Cities friends that Mankato State students are behind this effort and that it is not simply a drive by the Mankato Chamber of Commerce as some have charged."[186] Simultaneously, the committee announced plans to offer buttons to alumni and parents of students and to sell them in downtown Mankato. The Students for Status effort, a spontaneous movement that grew out of the homecoming hoopla, certainly helped advertise the university status effort.

In advance of the scheduled board meeting, the Mankato State Faculty Association and the American Association of University Professors jointly sponsored two public panel discussions to consider university status. Most of the speakers, who included Robert A. Smith, head of the history section in the Social Studies Division, and Theodore L. Nydahl, head of that division, emphasized that a university, unlike a college, was expected to contribute to knowledge by doing research as well as teaching. Although they believed research contributed to knowledge, they opined that even if Mankato State became a university, research should be a supplement to its traditional teaching role. Clem Thompson, who taught health and physical education, said that "in many ways . . . Mankato State is already a university." He was challenged by H. Harold Hartzler, professor of physics, who thought that the heavy teaching load at Mankato State left "little time for research."[187]

Hartzler's point was shared by many faculty members. At that time, the usual faculty teaching assignment was 16 hours weekly, which generally consisted of four four-credit courses with often more than 200 students. Under these circumstances, only the most dedicated faculty researchers made time for researching and writing. But, sometimes forward-looking administrators such as Theodore L. Nydahl arranged schedules that permitted researchers to have blocks of time.

When Crawford reported to the board on November 16, 1964, about Mankato State's desire for university status, he was accompanied by some faculty members and students. Some of them were spectators, but four of them—John Hodowanic, Jean Beard, president of the Mankato chapter of the American Association of University Professors, Robert A. Smith, professor of history, and Mark Korting, a Mankato State student from Franklin, Minnesota—made presentations.

Hodowanic's statement of some 6,000 words, which he read to the board, was Mankato State's most comprehensive case. He emphasized the college's rapid growth and the upgrading of faculty credentials with 112 who had earned doctorates compared to only seven at the end of World War II. As justification for Mankato State being made Minnesota's second university, Hodowanic cited the *Minneapolis Star Tribune* poll of April 21, 1963 and the need for more university training including engineering. The entire state, Hodowanic insisted, would benefit from a second university that was authorized to offer doctor's degrees. Regarding governance for the second university, Hodowanic concluded: "If a university were created at Mankato, it would want to remain financially responsible to the Legislature. It would be happy to remain as a member of the family under the present governing Board, or any new board of higher education, which the Legislature might choose to create."[188]

Beard distributed copies of four resolutions made by the Mankato chapter of the American Association of University Professors. They included: "We believe that the best interests of the people of Minnesota will be served by the establishment of more than one state university to serve as a focus for the advancement of knowledge."[189]

Smith, who was then serving as president of Mankato State's faculty association, emphasized faculty support for university status. Following the panel discussions sponsored by the faculty association and the campus AAUP chapter, the two organizations polled the faculty by secret ballot on the question of whether or not faculty members wanted to encourage university status. Of the 375 who were eligible to vote 253 voted yes and only seven voted no.

Korting thought that Mankato State students deserved the same opportunity as those in Wisconsin, where the legislature had recently converted its state colleges into universities. Further, he stated: That the Mankato students feel that the name 'university' is not enough, but they want all the things that go with that name, such as additional allocations of money and the expanding of programs . . . ."

In the ensuing discussion, board members agreed there were two possibilities regarding university status. One would be to seek legislation that would make it possible for any of the state colleges to become a university. The other would be to seek university status only for Mankato State. Although board members did not specifically say so, the context of their discussion was that the State College Board would determine either option. They never considered the possibility that Mankato State could be made a university with its own board of trustees. Since the board concurred that Mankato State was the closest to possible university status, it resolved to have Crawford report at its December meeting on the academic areas that Mankato State would designate for advanced degrees in the event it was made a university.

When he appeared at the board's December 19 meeting, Crawford was accompanied by Winston W. Benson, professor of political science, and Robert A. Smith. Crawford and Benson identified professional education as the most likely field for doctoral study. But, Smith recommended several subject matter areas. He thought history, biology and the Division of Health and Physical Education were all qualified to offer advanced graduate work.[190]

F. Kelton Gage, the board member from Mankato, was convinced that Mankato State "has reached a level where serious consideration of University status is warranted . . . ." Therefore, he moved that the board seek legislative authority to use its discretion in designating that status. Gage's motion was seconded and provoked considerable discussion. But the board refused to accept it.

Then Bevington Reed, the recently appointed board chancellor and Mankato State's former academic dean, suggested a broader motion. It stipulated "that the Board would endorse the idea that permissive legislation be requested which would authorize the Board to give university status to such institutions under its jurisdiction as meet criteria to be developed by the State College Board . . . ." Reed's motion was accepted with only one dissenting vote.

But the board did not consider seeking such "permissive legislation" from the 1965 legislature. Therefore, Imm, true to his intention after the 1963 failure, renewed his effort to gain university status for Mankato State College.

In their 1965 university status bill, Imm and Roy Schulz, his House co-sponsor, acknowledged the name change made in the 1963 legislature and the State College Board's assertion of authority. Their brief bill, which was introduced in both the House and the Senate on February 10, first stipulated that: "The Minnesota State University as the successor to the Mankato State College is hereby established at Mankato." Then it provided that: "The operation and management of the Minnesota State University shall be under the state college board or its successor . . . ."[191]

The proposed law authorized Minnesota State University to "confer such honors, degrees, and diplomas as may be deemed appropriate . . . ." But, it could not award degrees in law, medicine, dentistry, agriculture, and veterinary medicine. This provision was obviously intended to allay opposition from the University of Minnesota.

Probably because of anticipated opposition from the other state colleges, the bill included the possibility of them becoming universities. It provided that: "The state college board may establish criteria governing the conferring of university status upon any state college under its jurisdiction; and when it is of the opinion that any such college shall be granted university status it may make recommendations to the legislature in connection therewith."

Soon after Imm and Schulz announced their intention to introduce the bill, University of Minnesota President O. Meredith Wilson objected, because he did not think Mankato State was ready for university status. Before it became a university, he admonished, Mankato State should have a large and well-established master's degree program.[192]

Sharper criticism came from Arthur Naftalin, who was then the Minneapolis mayor. Naftalin thought that Mankato State should not be made a university simply because it was large. Identifying his alma mater, the University of Minnesota, as being at the "'top level of major world universities," he insisted that Mankato State was not in its class.[193]

Imm and other status supporters must have been very pleased by articles in the *Minneapolis Tribune*. Miriam Alburn of the editorial page staff wrote a series of three articles— "Why the 'University Delay' at Mankato?," "Growth of Mankato College Spurs 'U' Hopes," and "Legislators to Decide: Is State Ready for Second University." While, the articles helped advertise Mankato State's case for university status, they also included coverage of opposition to the proposal.[194]

Additionally, the newspaper published the results of another Minnesota Poll titled "Majority Favor 'U' Status for Mankato." The poll of an unspecified number of adult Minnesotans asked for responses to three questions.[195]

Respondents were first asked: "Some people in the Mankato area of southwestern Minnesota would like to see the state college there expanded to become a new state university. What would you say are the main reasons in favor of establishing a state university at Mankato?" The three commonest answers were "relieving overcrowding at the University of Minnesota, 'U' too large" (30 percent), "don't know" (26 percent) and "need a university located in southern Minnesota" (20 percent).

On the second question "What do you think would be the main reasons against it?", the main responses were "don't know," (29 percent), "no reasons against it" (27 percent) and "increase taxes, would cost too much" (23 percent). Only 3 percent answered "would

Pony express rider arriving in St. Paul, 1965

MSC students supporting the "Me for U" petition in St. Paul, 1965

reduce the quality of education, spread resources too think, reduce status of 'U.'"

The third question was: "Do you think you would or would not like to see a new university at Mankato—or don't you much care?" The percentages for would like it, would not like it, don't care and other or no opinion were respectively 52, 8, 35 and 5. Interestingly, the percentages for southern Minnesota and the Twin Cities were nearly identical. But, for northern Minnesota they were 34, 14, 46 and 6.

Students for Status organized the bill's most enthusiastic and demonstrative support. On Saturday night, January 9, 1965, it sponsored a dance with rock and roll music by Al and the Untouchables band. The unspecified dance hall was decorated with "streamers hung from the ceiling with rows of "Me for U' buttons attached to them."[196]

Then, the next month the group delivered petitions and letters to the state capitol by a pony express. It obtained nearly 4,000 signatures to a petition that read: "Whereas: current educational facilities in urban parts of the State of Minnesota are inadequate in providing university level education for the students and future citizens of this state: Whereas: students frequently seek advanced degrees outside of the State of Minnesota because of the lack of university level institutions in this state: Whereas: future growth of the State of Minnesota is dependent on the professionally trained and highly educated, and currently the expansion of Mankato State College is a manifestation of the need to stimulate Minnesota development through higher education; therefore: be it resolved that under-signed do petition the Legislature of the State of Minnesota to enact legislation causing Mankato State College to become a university known

Landkamer's Gift Shop advertisement,
*College Reporter* 26 April 1966

as the University of Southern Minnesota or some other appropriate title."[197]

On Monday morning, February 15, when the temperature was nine below zero, the pony express rider left Mankato State bearing the petitions and about 400 letters. He switched horses about every 10 miles until he reached Jordan, his overnight stay. On Tuesday, as scheduled, he reached the state capitol on his eighth horse at 3 p.m. where he presented the petitions and letters to Imm, Schulz and Anderson on the capitol steps. The event attracted a crowd of some 200 people, including some Mankato State students who had traveled by a bus and car convoy. Mike Eliseuson, a Mankato State student, filmed the student meeting with the Mankato legislators. Students for Status obtained the desired publicity when the film was used as the basis for coverage by three Twin Cities television stations that night.[198]

The pony express stunt was the acme of student euphoria over possible university status. But, it apparently did not convert any opponents. On March 18 Imm wrote to E. E. Popp, president of the State Bank of Vernon Center, that: "We have arrived at the point now of having hearings on the bill in both the House and Senate. Sentiment in favor of the bill has grown considerably since I made the proposal two years ago. We are in hopes of passing the bill this time although we realize and are experiencing a terrific opposition to it."[199]

Imm had good reason to be wary of the bill's prospects. As the session neared its mandated end the *College Reporter* featured a story titled "Proposed University Status Bill Suffers Fatal Setback in House." The House State and Junior College Committee had approved the bill. But its opponents managed to have it sent to the House Civil Administration Committee instead of the Appropriations Committee, the usual direct path to a floor vote. While the bill was languishing in the House Civil Administration Committee, the State College Board voted to oppose it.[200]

Following the House and board actions, Imm conceded that the university status bill was dead for the 1965 session and that he was looking forward to re-introducing it in 1967. After Crawford resigned Imm reassured status supporters that a change in the Mankato State presidency would have no effect on the university status drive.[201]

In the interim between the 1965 and 1967 legislative sessions, interest in university status was kept alive by such things as a Landkamer's Gift Shop ad for a glass bottom pewter mug that urged readers to "Be The First! Here's Looking at You! Bottoms Up . . . Whatever your toast, be the first to have a 'University of Southern Minnesota' Mug'". . . .[202]

But, the long campaign to gain university status for Mankato State College suffered a serious blow when Imm was defeated in his 1966 re-election bid. His forced retirement from public life and opposition from the State College Board effectively ended the first phase of Mankato State's university status quest.

## Crawford's Resignation and Legacy

Crawford submitted his resignation to the State College Board on September 7, 1965. His announcement took the Mankato State faculty and students by surprise. Crawford had been planning to resign for nearly two years, but he was a very private person who rarely revealed his intentions. Crawford explained that he had resigned to accept the position of professor and chairman of Florida Atlantic University's secondary education department. The move would benefit him monetarily and also free him from the stresses of being the administrator of a large college. Crawford's Florida salary was slightly less than the $18,000 he was earning as Mankato State president. But, Florida's retirement system was better. Consequently, Crawford reasoned that if he taught eight years until Florida's mandatory retirement age of 70 his retirement income would be "substantially more" than if he continued in Minnesota until his reached its mandatory retirement age of 68.[203]

Despite Crawford's explanation, the overwhelming faculty consensus was that he had resigned because Mankato State had simply grown too large for his micro-managing style. Habitually, Crawford insisted on being the final voice in all decisions including such things as authorizing leave for a faculty member to participate in a professional conference.

In retrospect, be it from the perspective of 1965 or 2018, Crawford presided over the most revolutionary period of change in the institution's history. The enrollment increased about 13-

fold and the size of the faculty, which was approximately 400 in Crawford's last year, was nearly 10 times larger than it was at the start of his administration. During Crawford's tenure the campus was transformed from a small one to a large one with two campuses. Construction on the new Highland Campus, especially, symbolized unprecedented growth.

Although physical growth was the most obvious feature during Crawford's administration, the college also experienced significant programmatic and academic challenges. The advent of such new programs as business, nursing and graduate studies and the discontinuance of the diploma program for rural school teachers fundamentally changed the college's nature and mission. The reorganization of 1964 not only reflected the rapid growth of programs, but streamlined school and departmental administration.

With regard to academics, a revised grading system was put into effect beginning with the 1958-1959 academic year. Until then the college used the system that dated to the normal school of assigning grades A through E. The E grade represented failure. With respect to honor points this was a 3.0 system with three honor points for every hour of A, two for each hour of B, one for each hour of C and none for D or E. The new marking system of A through F created the 4.0 maximum grade point average. Each credit of A, B, C, D and F grades earned respectively 4, 3, 2, 1 and 0 honor points.[204]

The college's rapid enrollment increases caused some to assume that academic standards were sacrificed on the altar of growth. But, at the very time enrollment was booming the most, many students were dismissed because of poor performances. Crawford reported that at the end of the 1965 winter term "academic dismissal notices were sent to over 600 who had not maintained the required grade point average." About a sixth of them were permitted to continue for another quarter after they appealed because of extenuating circumstances. But, Crawford noted: "However, 500 were not retained and were dropped. Not all of the people dropped were lower achievement level ability students. Many were those who simply did not put forth the required time and effort, or who had too many outside interests, including outside employment. This kind of procedure does serve notice on the student body as a whole, that they must produce and achieve if they are to remain with us."[205]

After Crawford retired from Florida Atlantic in 1972, he continued to live in Boca Raton, Florida. He died at his home there on March 13, 1996.[206]

In eulogizing Crawford, *Free Press* columnist Ken Berg observed that he was: "Staid, conservative, thrifty, terse, authoritarian—sometimes. Disarmingly genuine, quietly warm, trustworthy—always."[207]

# 5

# HIGHLAND CAMPUS EXPANSION AND CONSOLIDATION, 1965-1979

From the close of the Crawford administration until near the end of campus consolidation in 1979, Mankato State's history featured the relatively short presidential administrations of James F. Nickerson (1966-1973) and Douglas R. Moore (1974-1978) and the service of three short term acting presidents: Melvin G. Scarlett (September 1965-July 1, 1966), Kent G. Alm (July 1, 1973-March 17, 1974 and Edward R. McMahon (August 1, 1978-January 19, 1979).

The highlights of the Nickerson administration were an enrollment boom and bust and the anti-Vietnam War protests and the initiation of affirmative action policies. During Moore's presidency, university status was achieved and the hilltop consolidation of the Valley and Highland campuses was nearly completed.

## Forming the Nickerson Administration

After Crawford retired in September 1965, Melvin G. Scarlett served as acting president until July 1, 1966. During Scarlett's brief tenure the governing board established the precedent that acting presidents could not be considered for the presidency. Thus, the board launched a national search for Crawford's replacement. On March 19, 1966, it announced the selection of James F. Nickerson, the 55-year-old vice-president of academic affairs at North Dakota State University.[1]

A native of Gretna, Nebraska, Nickerson earned his bachelor's degree from Nebraska Wesleyan University. Subsequently, he taught in Nebraska and New York public schools before earning a master's degree in music from Columbia University. He completed his doctorate in educational psychology and psychology at the University of Minnesota. From 1953, when he finished his doctor's degree, until 1964, when he accepted the North Dakota State University vice-presidency, he taught at the University of Kansas, conducted research for the U. S. Navy in San Diego, California, and served as a faculty member and dean at Montana State University.

During his first year at Mankato State, Nickerson acted to assemble his administrative team. Soon after Nickerson started on July 1, 1966, Scarlett

President James F. Nickerson, 1970

resigned his academic dean's position to become president of Farmington State College in Maine, the successor of the normal school where George Gage had been principal before being named the first principal of the Mankato Normal School. Rather than fill Scarlett's position Nickerson assigned the academic affairs duties to Meredith Freeman, who continued to serve as the assistant academic dean.[2]

Nickerson's first major step in forming his own administration was the appointment of Kent G. Alm in May 1967 to the newly created position of vice president for academic affairs. Alm, who was then the assistant dean of the College of Education at the University of North Dakota, had earned a Ph.D. in school administration and higher education at the University of North Dakota. Before becoming a university administrator he had taught in South Dakota and California high schools for seven years and had worked as a consultant for several organizations, including the U. S. Office of Education and the American Schools of Central America and Mexico.[3]

Alm, who later wrote that Mankato State at the time of his appointment had an administrative structure befitting a high school, and Nickerson concluded that an assistant vice president for academic affairs should be added. Brendan J. McDonald, who had recently completed his Ph.D. in higher education at Michigan State University, was selected for that position.[4]

McDonald, born and reared in Regina, Saskatchewan, Canada, graduated from St. Cloud State College in 1954. After completing his master's at the University of Minnesota he was employed as St. Cloud State's registrar, 1958-1965. He left that position to pursue his doctorate at Michigan State University. To fulfill the internship requirement for his Ph.D., he worked as a researcher in the summer and fall of 1966 on a University of North Dakota study of statewide education directed by Alm.[5]

To complete his administrative reorganization, Nickerson, with board approval, decided Mankato State should also have vice presidents for administrative affairs and student affairs. In early July 1967, 36- year-old Merlin G. Duncan was named vice president for administrative affairs. A native of Lansing, Michigan, Duncan had earned all of his degrees, including a Ph.D. in higher education and administration, from Michigan State University. His previous experience included serving as the University of North Dakota's coordinator of institute services.[6]

Within a year of Duncan's appointment, Nickerson and the State College Board decided that the complexities of administering administrative affairs required an assistant vice president. Dr. Ronald E. Eick, who was then heading the Education Department at Wittenberg University in Ohio, was chosen for the position. Like Duncan, Eick was a Ph.D. graduate from Michigan State University.[7]

Nickerson's administrative team was fully assembled when David N. Hess was appointed vice president for student services effective July 1, 1968. This third vice presidency replaced the dean of students position. It was created by Nickerson and the State College Board after Mankato State's Dean of Student Services Norbert K. Baumgart resigned because he was named president of Northern State College in Aberdeen, South Dakota.[8]

Hess, 42-years-old at the time of his appointment, had been added to the Mankato State faculty in January 1968 as the director of field services and program development. A Michigan native, he earned his bachelor's degree from the University of Michigan and an M.A. and Ph.D. from Michigan State University. His doctoral dissertation was titled "Person-Centered Higher Education."

Hess had a variety of pre-Mankato State work experiences. He had served as a missionary teacher in Brazil, taught in a Michigan private school and most recently was the director of student educational services and assistant provost at West Virginia University.

## The Nature of the Initial Nickerson Administration

Any administration—be it of an academic institution or any governmental unit—is invariably first compared to its immediate predecessor and ultimately, in the long range historical view, to its successors. As Nickerson was assembling his administrative team, Crawford was the logical model for recent yesterdays.

The faculty and townspeople who were well-acquainted with Crawford soon noticed that the new administration was sharply different. The reserved Crawford had some of the same characteristics that had caused President Calvin Coolidge to become famed as "Silent Cal."

But Nickerson and his administrative cohorts were collectively outgoing. Their central message was an advocacy of change and innovation. There is widespread acceptance of the adage that change is the only constant in history. But over time change occurs at different paces. Much of it is evolutionary, but history is replete with advocates of rapid or revolutionary change.

Anyone concerned with education—including teachers, administrators and government officials—certainly recognizes that part of their work entails planning for an uncertain future. Collectively, they must have anticipatory senses of future demographics as well as likely economic and social trends. Hence, college curriculums have to be continually adjusted to meet society's current and presumed future needs.

It is only natural that various constituencies disagree over the pace of change. Veteran faculty members, especially, tend to think that gradual adaptations to changing times is the most desirable pattern. Collectively, they tend to resist rapid changes to what they had a hand in creating. However, new administrators, who oftentimes come in from the outside, have a perspective unburdened by institutional tradition.

Don Glines, 1968

Those who laud innovation invariably run the risk of seeming to be overly critical of traditional practices. Consequently, when Nickerson and his team advocated some sharp changes, many senior faculty members—especially those who dated to the teachers college era—were at least apprehensive and sometimes even hostile.

Drastically changing the nature of Wilson Campus School was the Nickerson administration's most dramatic innovation. In the summer of 1968 the administration announced that Donald E. Glines had been employed as the Wilson principal.

The 38-year-old Glines, a native of Glendale, California, had earned his bachelor's  degree from Springfield College in Massachusetts and both his M.A. and Ph.D. degrees in education from the University of Oregon. Perhaps the most telltale preview of his likely administration was that he had been employed by the states of Missouri and South Dakota as a consultant in innovative education.[9]

Shortly before classes opened in September 1968, Glines announced the practical application of innovation to Wilson. His 60 identified innovative steps revolutionized the school. It was transformed into a non-traditional institution that emphasized innovation and experimentation. Assuming that traditional schools generally failed to adequately educate students, Glines decreed that Wilson would emphasize individualized learning based on a learning how to learn concept. Each student was required to develop a study plan in consultation with a faculty advisor.  The heart of each plan was that each student would study a topic from an interdisciplinary perspective. So, for example, rather than taking such subject matter courses as English, speech, history and civics, the student would use elements of all of them in studying a topic such as the women's suffrage movement. The learning methods would include research, field trips and consultations with advisors.

In the belief that education should be stimulating, Glines banned such conventional practices as teacher-delivered lectures. In this regard, he was

Elementary students at Wilson Campus School, 1969

quoted as having stated: "We are putting monkeys, boa constrictors and plants in the school. These are the things that are exciting—not books and teachers."[10]

Likewise, such traditional practices as scheduled class periods and mandatory attendance were abolished. Students were free to plan their own days. If they chose, they could sit in a lounge all day or just not show up. This seeming lack of discipline was intended to cause students to become responsible for their own actions. Theoretically, those who chose not to study would realize at some point that they were not making progress on their study project.

The new Wilson method abolished the assignment of all conventional letter grades and the customary progression through grade levels. F grades were eliminated in the belief that all students would ultimately succeed. The abolishment of all traditional passing grades and honor recognitions was intended to eliminate such traditional practices as working for a grade.

Outside of the academic sphere, Wilson students experienced unprecedented social freedoms. The dress code was abolished. Students would decide for themselves if they wanted to wear shorts or be barefooted.[11]

As expected, the reactions to the Wilson changes ranged from glee to dismay. Some students who had experienced difficulties in conventional school settings welcomed the changes. But those wedded to traditional education methods deplored them.

Traditionally, the various model or laboratory schools that dated to the origins of the normal school were administratively placed within the institution's professional education administration. Thus, the pre-Glines Wilson Campus School was a unit within the School of Education, which was headed by Dean John A. Johnson.

Johnson, a veteran educator who had started at Mankato State in 1948, was possibly not consulted in advance about the changes wrought by Glines. He did not approve of them, which caused the administration to remove the Wilson Campus School from the School of Education and place it under the administrative jurisdiction of the assistant vice president for academic affairs.[12]

## Major Events During the Nickerson Administration

Much of the Nickerson administration was concerned with such routine matters as concluding the Highland Campus building boom and beautifying the new campus. But, the administration is best-remembered for the contentious events associated with opposition to the Vietnam War.

## Campus Construction and Mall Development

The Highland Campus building boom, started during the Crawford administration, was continued during Nickerson's presidency, when five more buildings were added. Nickerson inherited four projects—Memorial Library, Performing Arts Building, Centennial Student Union Building and Morris Hall—from the Crawford era. The fifth, Trafton Hall, was first proposed during Melvin G. Scarlett's tenure as acting president. Other than completing the buildings, the Nickerson administration sharply improved the Highland Campus ambience by creating the mall and the adjacent park-like fountain area.

## Memorial Library

By the time Lincoln Library was only four years old, it was rapidly becoming inadequate to meet the demands of Mankato State's burgeoning enrollment and Highland Campus development. So, in 1962 the Crawford Administration decided to seek state funding for a new, greatly enlarged Highland Campus library.[13]

With Val Imm leading the way, the 1963 legislature appropriated $1.7 million to construct the first phase the new library and $850,000 to build about half of the second phase. The first phase was to be a two-story building with a full unfinished basement. The second phase specified basement completion, a third story and extension of the west sides of all four levels. The projected total cost of both phases was $3.4 million.[14]

In June 1965, the Robert W. Carlstrom Construction Company of Mankato, the phase one general contractor, excavated the basement and starting pouring concrete. At that time it was estimated that the first phase alone would provide 140,000 square feet, or more than double the size of Lincoln Library.

After 15 months the Carlstrom Company was making such good progress that the first phase completion date was projected to be January 1967. But, because of unanticipated delays in equipping the building, the state architect refused to release it. Then in June 1967, all of Mankato's building contractors were stalled for at least four weeks by a strike called by the Mankato Carpenters Local.[15]

Everyone concerned, including head librarian Jack O'Bar, President Nickerson, faculty and students, hoped the library's move to the Highland Campus would be completed by the opening of Fall 1967 classes. But, moving 170,000 volumes and many tons of furnishings proved to be a two-month process. The crated books, furniture and equipment were hauled by the Ben Deike Transportation Company of Mankato. Placing the books in proper call

LIBRARY BUILDING · MANKATO STATE COLLEGE. MANKATO, MINNESOTA
A. J. NELSON STATE ARCHITECT
ELLERBE ARCHITECTS                          SAINT PAUL & ROCHESTER MINNESOTA

Architectural drawing of Memorial Library, circa 1965

Minnesota Room, circa 1975

number order in their new home kept 20 librarians, eight classified staff and 10 to 15 student workers busy for a month. Finally, the move was completed and the Highland campus library was opened on October 2, 1967.[16]

The second phase work was completed by the opening of the Fall 1968 term. The temporary western walls were removed and the building was extended about 40 feet. The basement was completed, furnished and occupied. The Minnesota Room (renamed the Marilyn J. Lass Center for Minnesota Studies in 1994), which O'Bar regarded as the library's showplace, was finished with carpeting and walnut paneling.[17]

The library also featured approximately 300 study carrels, which were located on the perimeters of most of the sides in the basement, second floor and third floor. The carrels, a new concept to Mankato State, were intended to provide individual study spaces for faculty and students. Each of them measured about four-feet square and featured a built-in desk surface, book shelves, light and chair.[18]

At O'Bar's insistence the library was adorned with a unique directional marker. Like many who have moved to Mankato, he had difficulty with downtown directions and especially could not understand why North Mankato was so named when it appeared to be west of downtown Mankato. Resolving to have one spot in Mankato where the cardinal directions were evident, O'Bar had a colored circular design showing the four directions inlaid in the second-floor tiled floor about 20 feet from the head of the stairway. Since 1992, when the library was enlarged and remodeled, the O'Bar guide has been covered by carpet.

The Highland Campus library was officially named Memorial Library soon after the completion of its first phase. In approving the name, the State College Board accepted the recommendation of the Mankato State naming committee. The name was selected to perpetuate the memory of military service rendered by Mankato State students and faculty over the years. At its same meeting the board also renamed Lincoln Library to Lincoln Hall, even though it continued to be used as a branch library primarily for the School of Business.[19]

## Performing Arts Building

During its planning and construction phases the Performing Arts Building was usually known as the Speech-Music Building. But, since it was intended for the music and theatre arts departments, it more aptly should have been identified as the Music-Theatre Building.

Preliminary planning for the building was started in 1960 by Theodore Paul, Jr., familiarly known throughout the campus and community as "Ted," the cordial, gregarious Paul had earned a well-deserved reputation as an outstanding play director and producer since his addition to the faculty in 1950.[20]

Acting on the recommendation of the State College Board, the 1963 legislature appropriated $1.5 million to construct the building. But that amount proved to be inadequate. The state architects who designed the

Performing Arts Building, circa 1970

building estimated it would cost $17 per square foot. But the total of all low bids came in at $23 per square foot, or $170,485 more than the appropriation. The Eric A. Carlstrom Construction Co. of Mankato submitted the lowest bid for general construction. Other low bidders were All City Electric Co., Ebert Plumbing and Heating for the mechanical and ventilation work and Gust Lagerquist and Sons for elevator installation.[21]

Once it became apparent that re-bidding would not result in any saving, the legislature agreed to appropriate an additional $300,000 in 1965. This brought the total allocation to $1.8 million.[22]

Like the library, construction on the Speech-Music Building was started in June 1965 and slowed by the same things that affected the library. In November 1965, campus planner Ira Johnson estimated the building would be completed by January 1967. He later revised his estimates to the spring of 1967 and then that year's summer session. But when the carpenters' strike delayed the opening until the opening of the Fall 1967 term, Paul was forced to conduct his summer theatre in a large leaky tent with a small stage on the grounds west of the building.[23]

Especially as compared to the nearby dormitories that resembled oversized boxes, the new speech-music building was an esthetic marvel. Its west side or main entry was adorned with stately Kasota stone columns at the front of a long porch. The rear of the porch consisted of glass walls placed in front of an expansive lobby. Functionally, the building featured a 500-seat theatre, a 350-seat recital hall, dressing rooms, equipment space and some faculty offices on its upper level. The lower level, a half story below the top floor, had a dozen practice rooms for music students, faculty offices and several classrooms.[24]

During construction, the building was sometimes called the new home for the performing arts. The campus building naming committee decided and the State College Board agreed that the structure should be named the Performing Arts Center in recognition of its main function.[25]

Performing Arts Center auditorium/theatre, 1968

## Centennial Student Union

Mankato State's first student union was a single, usually crowded and smoke-filled room on the Administration Building's first floor. Its activities were restricted to serving coffee and snacks. The union's inadequacies caused Ron Barron, a *College Reporter* writer to suggest that the third floor of Lincoln Library should be devoted to union use.[26]

In the fall of 1962 a 13-student Union Committee began planning for a Highland Campus union building. The committee approved the ultimate construction of a three-phase building, which was to be located at the western edge of the flat land just south of the power plant. The first phase was to be started as soon as possible and after it was completed the second phase was to be started within five years. The committee estimated that the first phase would cost about $1,250,000, of which only $57,130 had been raised from a $5 quarterly fee per student that had been first levied in the spring 1961 term. The committee recognized that its recommendations had to be approved by the Student Senate, President Crawford and the State College Board.[27]

Board approval was delayed by more than three years because of insufficient funding. In November 1965, Richard A. Hammel, the board's architect, announced that accumulated student fees would pay for only 15 percent of the estimated construction cost. He asserted that the remainder would have to be financed by a board authorized bond sale. The bonds would be retired through the collection of future student fees. After receiving legislative authorization, the board, on December 9, 1965, approved the bond sale.[28]

At its March 1966 meeting the board approved the $2,327,954 budget for building phase one. The major expenditures were for the low-bid contractors. They included general construction to the George E. Carlstrom Construction Co., electrical work to Hoffman Electric of Minneapolis, Schwickert Co. of Mankato for all mechanical and ventilation work and St. Cloud Restaurant Supply for kitchen equipment installation. Other significant costs were for the fees of the consulting and project architects and for site construction.[29]

By the time bids were let the consulting architects and campus planner Ira Johnson had decided that the union building would be erected south of the library and directly across the street from the planned classroom building that became Morris Hall. May

Construction of phase 1 of the Centennial Student Union building, 1966

20, 1966, when construction started, was designated Union Recognition Day. It featured a recognition ceremony in Blakeslee Stadium as well as a street dance, art exhibit and folk music concert.[30]

Initially, the union's general contractor made good progress. By early November the basement and most of the exterior work on the two-story building had been completed.[31]

But the same carpenters' strike that delayed work on the library and speech-music building affected the union. Consequently, the union was not opened until Friday, October 27, 1967, the day before the Homecoming Ball was held in its second floor ballroom.[32]

The three level (basement, first floor and second floor) first phase had a total area of about 100,000 square feet. Its showplace feature was the second story multi-use ballroom that could be used for dances, banquets, lectures, concerts, film programs and meetings. Comprising 12,000 square feet, it could be easily converted into three rooms by closing sliding walls. But most daily use of the union was concentrated in the first floor's food service area.[33]

Unfortunately, some union patrons did not appreciate the new facility. Only about six weeks after the union was opened, assistant manager James Zwickey reported widespread theft and vandalism. Some culprits stole ashtrays, coffee cups, billiard cues and tops from cigarette urns. Zwickey further noted that: "Sofas have been torn, burnt, and soaked with coke. Two carpets have also been burnt, and cigarettes are commonly butted on the floors and bulletin boards." Zwickey felt compelled to remind *Reporter* readers that repairs would have to be financed by student funds.[34]

For some reason, union management did not observe the building's grand opening until Friday, May 3, 1968. The evening program featured talks by Kent Alm, representing President Nickerson and Norbert Baumgart, the dean of students, and a fireworks display.[35]

As early as January 1967, nine months before it was completed, the union board was calling the building the Centennial Student Union. They chose this name because of an erroneous campus tradition that the institution had been founded in 1867. The naming committee endorsed the union board's choice and it was subsequently made official by the State College Board on December 18, 1967.[36]

During the Nickerson administration a second phase of the Centennial Student Union was planned, financed and constructed. This addition of 60,000 square feet was nearly two-thirds the size of the original building. Like the first phase it had a full basement, a ground floor and a second floor. By the opening of the Fall 1971 term, the Nels Johnson Construction Company of Winona, which had been awarded the $2,185,000 general construction contract, had completed the basement and part of the first floor. At that time, campus planner Ira Johnson anticipated that the building should be completed by the start of the next fall term.[37]

But, during the summer of 1972, the work was delayed by a nearly six-week long lockout of union laborers by the Johnson Company. So by late September, the bookstore on the ground floor was the only completely finished area. Roy Lashway, the Centennial Student Union director, expected that the bowling alley in the basement and the second-floor offices of the *Reporter* and Student Senate would be open within a few days.[38]

Lashway also said the 350-seat auditorium would have its "grand opening" on October 10, even if it was not completed. The auditorium seats had not

Students in first floor Centennial Student Union Lounge, 1969

been manufactured yet, so rows of temporary chairs would have to be used.

The second phase's grand opening, which marked the project's official completion, was held on January 17, 1973. The basement level featured a 12-lane bowling alley and billiards and table tennis facilities. Most of the ground floor space was occupied by the bookstore and auditorium. The new second floor area had offices for the Student Senate and college publications including the *Reporter* and the literary magazine *Medicine Jug*.[39]

## Morris Hall

After Armstrong Hall was opened, the Crawford administration became increasingly anxious to shift more classes to the Highland Campus. Therefore, it planned to add a small classroom just south of Armstrong.

The State College Board endorsed the proposal and the 1965 legislature appropriated $650,000 for construction. In November 1965, Richard Hammel, the board's architect, visited campus to confer with Acting President Scarlett and campus planner Ira Johnson about constructing the classroom and the union building.[40]

It took about a year to complete the competitive bidding process and the awarding of contracts for the classroom building. On November 29, 1966, the *College Reporter* announced that the general construction contract had been awarded to the Robert W. Carlstrom Co. The two other major contracts also went to Mankato companies. Schwickert Plumbing and Heating agreed to do the mechanical and ventilation work and Mankato Electric Company got the electrical contract. The building's lone elevator was to be installed by the Montgomery Elevator Company of Moline, Illinois.[41]

Once the contracts were awarded, construction proceeded rapidly. Within a few days the Carlstrom Company was excavating the basement. By late October 1967, when the exterior work was nearly completed, Building 47, as it was identified on the architectural plan, was expected to be completed the following spring.[42]

The building was intended to be the first phase of a much larger structure. Building 47 was to be a two-story structure with an unfinished basement whose floor was covered with sand. The contemplated second phase was to consist of basement completion, the extension of the east side and the addition of a third story.

Building 47 somewhat resembled the neighboring English-Education Building. It was a boxlike brick structure with some use of Kasota stone and featured an overhang of the first floor and recessed windows.

Although the building was intended for the use of the history and political science departments, it was

Morris Hall, postcard, circa 1968

also designed to enable more students to take all their classes on the Highland Campus. Consequently, in addition to classrooms and office space, it included three laboratories for biology, chemistry and physics classes. The classrooms included two auditoriums with stages and inclined floors that seated about 200 each. The seven other classrooms each had room for about 60 students. The joint first floor History and Political Science Office had individual offices for departmental leaders, a shared clerical pool section and a conference room. Some 30 individual faculty offices were placed on the perimeters of the second floor's south, west and north sides. The original plans specified that these offices would be eight-feet square, the same size of those in the English-Education Building. But, since numerous faculty members were dissatisfied with those cramped quarters, the Building 47 offices were enlarged to nine-feet square.

The history and political science departments did not move en masse into the building until just prior to the start of the Fall 1968 term. But, each of the departments moved several faculty members into the building and began teaching classes there the preceding spring.

On December 18, 1967, as part of its renaming of most campus buildings, the State College Board officially renamed Building 47 to Morris Hall. The name was recommended by the campus naming committee to recognize the long service of Albert B. Morris from 1919 -1956. Morris, who joined the faculty as a history instructor, also held the distinction of being the institution's first registrar.[43]

Interestingly, at the same meeting the board decreed that the Administration Building on the Valley Campus would be officially named Old Main. This action was an endorsement of a name that had been used colloquially since the mid-1950s. In a way it seems strange to refer to a building that was barely 30 years old as "old." But, for college-age students, nostalgic feelings for the past usually occur about a generation after the event.

## Trafton Science Center

In February 1966, Mankato State requested that the legislative building commission in its recommendations to the 1967 legislature include $4.6 million for a Science Building, which was to be located east of Armstrong Hall. The multi-story structure would have separate wings for the laboratories of its three components—the chemical, physical and biological sciences. The building was intended to help serve the 12,500 students projected for 1972.[44]

The State College Board included the science building appropriation in its request to the 1967 legislature. The lawmakers endorsed the concept by appropriating $250,000 in planning funds.[45]

That development was an encouraging sign that the building might be fully funded by the 1969 legislature. On November 9, 1967, when the Legislative Building Commission met in the Centennial Student Union, Nickerson requested $7,350,000 for the science building. He pointed out that construction of the building was essential to achieve a self-contained Highland Campus. But he also admonished the commission that delays were costly.

Chemistry lab in Trafton Science Center, circa 1980

Lecture hall in Trafton Science Center, 1975

Because of inflation his requested amount was considerably higher than the one first submitted to the 1967 legislature.[46]

Influenced by rapidly rising enrollments, the 1969 legislature funded construction of the science building to the extent of $9,550,000. Continuing inflation and building enlargement were the main factors in sharply raising costs from Nickerson's request of November 1967.[47]

Construction of the Science Building was started during the summer of 1970. By September 22, 1971, Ira Johnson opined that it might be completed by the following spring. But his estimate proved to be too optimistic. The Biology, Chemistry, Physics, Mathematics and Environmental Studies departments did not start using the Science Building until Fall 1972. However by late September some of laboratory equipment had still not arrived. The Science Building occupation caused some remodeling in Nichols Hall whose space vacated by the sciences and mathematics was assigned to art, business administration, business education, home economics and nursing.[48]

Originally known simply as the Science Building, the new structure, which was the college's largest building and the largest science building in the state college system, was renamed Trafton Science Center in honor of Gilbert H. Trafton, the most pre-eminent scientist and first prolific author in institutional history. President Nickerson announced the renaming on March 2, 1973, after the State College Board accepted the recommendation of a faculty-student-administrator-alumni committee.[49]

The formal dedication of Trafton Science Center occurred on October 12, 1973. In connection with it, the Biology, Chemistry, Physics and Mathematics departments sponsored a series of talks by nationally recognized experts in their respective fields over a four-day period. The featured speaker was Joseph Kerwin, a scientist who had been a pilot on the first National Aeronautics

Trafton Science Center, circa 1975

and Space Administration (NASA) Skylab Mission the preceding spring. Other presenters included Grace Murray Hopper, a renowned mathematician in the computer science field, Robert H. Dicke, who had served as the chairman of Princeton University's Physics Department, and Efriam Racker, the Albert Einstein Professor of Biochemistry and Molecular Biology at Cornell University.[50]

## Mall Development

Like any new construction zone, the Highland Campus, at the time Memorial Library's first phase and the Centennial Student Union were completed, was a rather ugly place. It featured inadequate outdoor lighting, few sidewalks, rather heavy vehicle traffic and a dearth of trees, shrubs and other plantings. Duane W. Heuer, a *College Reporter* writer, saw it "as an aesthetic's nightmare; a vast wasteland of stone and steel . . ."[51]

Campus planner Ira Johnson was certainly aware of the problem, but obviously any beautification could not be done until after construction. Typically, there was a delay because campus improvements relating to the grounds had to have special funding. In November 1967, Johnson conferred with political science faculty members Robert Barrett and Truman Wood, geographer James Goff and Mankato city engineer Ken Surprenant. They agreed that a mall should be developed on that portion of Ellis Avenue that ran between Nelson Hall, Armstrong Hall and the soon-to-be Morris Hall on the east and Memorial Library and the Centennial Student Union on the west. The mall as a pedestrian-only place was immediately established by blocking off the affected part of Ellis Avenue.[52]

Surfacing the mall and erecting large planters for shrubbery and flowers was undertaken in 1971 and not completed until the summer of the next year. The $130,000 project was done by the R-Lee Construction Company of the Twin Cities.[53]

Development of the area between the union and the library was seen as a natural extension of the planned mall. By late January 1968, the administration had decided that this space should be first adorned with a fountain. At that time the New York City's World Fair of 1964-65, which had lost money, was selling off fair property and even entire

Highland campus with new campus mall, circa 1974

The fountain as originally installed, 1969

The fountain with above-ground pump, circa 1974

The fountain and campus mall, circa 1976

exhibits. Apparently, the fair's management prepared and circulated a catalog of sale items. Mankato State used an electric company as its agent in purchasing fountain equipment that had been used at the fair.[54]

Johnson, in consultation with Bert Burns, Geography Department chairman, H. Roger Smith, assistant professor of geography, and artist-in-residence Arnold Grüter, had the fountain installed in 1969. The fountain's pool area, 71-feet in diameter, was excavated about 80 feet west of the sidewalk running along the west side of Ellis Avenue. Engineering for the project was quite complex. The fountain was designed to create a spiral effect with stationary water jets. Its water flow was controlled by a wind sensor on the union building's roof.[55]

Although the fountain originated with the New York World's Fair, it would be fallacious to assume that there was one at the fair that looked exactly like it. Rather, the Mankato State fountain was only part of a much larger fountain complex that was built next to the fair's 12-story Unisphere, which symbolized the globe.

Unfortunately, the fountain, which was intended as a centerpiece in campus beautification, soon became an eyesore. Its original underground pump malfunctioned, in part, because it was clogged by trash including t-shirts. By the time the adjoining mall was completed, the fountain was inoperative and its surrounding area was overgrown with weeds.[56]

Ira Johnson got the fountain running again by having an above-ground pump installed. But, since it was unattractive, he decided to have it topped with a sculptured piece. The 23-foot high steel sculpture, which cost $1,600, was installed in May, 1975. Its original design was done by William E. Richmond, a Mankato State art instructor in the early 1970s. But Minneapolis architect Roger Johnson adapted and finalized Richmond's idea. Although the sculpture looked like a piece of rusted metal, Johnson explained that it was made of corten steel, which would gradually change to a copper brown color after about six months of use.[57]

In the long run, the fountain has given the campus a unique decor and proven to be a significant tourist attraction. Hundreds of students and campus visitors have photographed it or used it as a backdrop for pictures.

## Confusion Over the Centennial Observance

The Mankato Normal School, the first phase of Minnesota State University, Mankato, was founded in 1868. But for nearly a third of its history, the erroneous date of 1867 was accepted and publicized as the institution's actual founding.

Some historical background is needed to understand this confusion. In 1866 the Minnesota legislature authorized the creation of the second state normal school at Mankato and the third state normal school at St. Cloud provided that each of the communities donated $5,000 to the state before the schools could be founded. The law also specified that if the money was not raised within three years the normal school sites could be moved to other communities. After Mankato failed to get $5,000 in contributions promptly, Daniel Buck, a Mankato representative, convinced the legislature by an act of February 18, 1867 to authorize Mankato to issue and sell bonds to meet its $5,000 obligation. The bond plan was successful. On July 15, 1868, when the State Normal School Board met in Mankato, Buck presented it with $5,000. Board members selected a normal school site at the same meeting and appointed a three-man prudential committee to start the school as soon as practicable. The first Mankato Normal School classes were held on October 7, 1868, in the basement of Mankato's Methodist Episcopal Church.[58]

As the normal school aged and then evolved into a teachers college in 1921, its various administrators and faculty always considered October 7, 1868 as its founding date. The first homecoming, which was observed in 1928, was scheduled for October 26-27 during the month in which the institution noted its 60th birthday. In 1938 President Frank D. McElroy chose October 7 as the day for valley fieldhouse ground breaking ceremonies, because it was the institution's 70th birthday. In 1943, on the occasion of the 75th anniversary, the college sponsored public

A PROUD PAST
A PROMISING FUTURE

100

A CAROUSEL
OF
COMMEMORATION

MANKATO STATE COLLEGE
CENTENNIAL YEAR 1967-1968

Mankato State College, Centennial Celebration program, 1967

Window cling,
Mankato State College centennial,
1967

College seal as adopted in 1971

programs and tours during the week in which October 7 fell.

Until 1947 all those associated with the institution's history correctly claimed that it was founded in 1868. Then the 1947-1948 *Mankato State Teachers College Catalog*, in reporting on the college's "historical development", contained the statement: "The institution which today is Mankato State Teachers College was founded by legislative enactment in the year 1867; actual classes did not get underway, however, until the fall of 1868."[59] This statement was repeated verbatim in subsequent catalogs. But, it had been changed by 1961. The 1961-1962 catalog contained a listing of "historical briefs" rather than a description of historical development. Its first fact was "1867: Founded as Mankato State Normal School."[60] Whoever first wrote about the purported 1867 founding apparently just accepted some word-of-mouth misinformation. The 1867 legislature did not do anything that could be construed as the founding of the Mankato State Normal School.

Throughout this period of reiterating an error, the wrong founding date became part of the college's tradition. Constant reiteration of any error bestows it with undeserved veracity. The wrong founding date of 1867 was well-entrenched by the time Mankato State College observed its centennial. So, the student union building, whose first phase was opened in October 1967, was named the Centennial Student Union and the 1967 homecoming marked the end of the college's supposed first century 1867-1967. As a result of the centennial observance the 1867 date was incorporated in the college's letterhead and seal. The seal, in turn, was featured on all official college regalia and publications. So hundreds of t-shirt and sweatshirt wearers and the annual catalogs advertised the wrong founding date.[61]

The development and perpetuation of the erroneous 1867 founding tradition is quite puzzling, because there was some scholarship that should have raised doubts about it. In 1954, Sexton Larson, the first degree earner in Mankato State's new Master of Science program, completed a thesis titled "The Organization and Early Development of Mankato State Normal School 1867-1871." Anyone who only looked at the title would logically conclude that the normal school had been founded in 1867. But Larson's text did not substantiate that assumption. He correctly summarized the 1866 and 1867 laws and the actual founding of the school in 1868. Apparently, Larson used 1867 in his title, because it conformed with campus usage. Despite its misleading title the Larson thesis should have caused those interested in Mankato State's history to wonder about the correct founding date.

Those who are concerned with writing factually correct history are well-advised to remember that if there are two versions of something they both cannot be correct. But they could both be wrong, or one could be correct and the other wrong. In such a situation, the only obvious recourse is to do further research. However, there was no apparent reason to do so until after University Archives was organized in 1979.

During the eve of campus consolidation in 1979, Professor of History

William E. Lass, who was then directing the Southern Minnesota Historical Center, suggested to President Margaret R. Preska that the university should act to save important historical records when the Valley Campus was closed. She concurred and University Archives was started as an adjunct of the historical center.

Once University Archives was formed, it was necessary to establish a chronology of the institution's history. Research in such primary records as the legislative acts of 1866 and 1867 and verbatim copies of the meeting minutes of the State Normal School Board proved conclusively that the Mankato State Normal School was founded in 1868 and that there was no factual basis for claiming that it had been founded in 1867.

This finding was included in Debra L. Anderson's 1987 Master of Arts thesis "Mankato State Normal School: The Foundation Years, 1868-1880." However, the committee created to observe Mankato State's presumed 125th anniversary in 1992 ignored the thesis and perpetuated the mythical 1867 founding date.

This action prompted Lass to conclude that the best prospect for correcting the founding date error was to expose it publicly. Consequently, on January 21, 1993, he presented a lecture titled "Mankato State: From Normal School to University" in the Douglas R. Moore Faculty Research Lecture Series. Among other things he pointed out that the 1867 founding tradition was wrong and that the institution had actually been established the next year. The lecture prompted President Richard R. Rush to ask Lass for proof that 1868 was the correct founding date. After considering the Lass report, which contained attachments of verbatim primary sources, Rush decided that the institution was founded in 1868 and accordingly ordered its use.

## Background of the Vietnam War Student Protests

The Nickerson administration lasted for seven years. But its most memorable events occurred during the course of three weeks. For a week in May 1970, and about two in May 1972, the campus and Mankato community were shocked by massive anti-Vietnam War demonstrations. The protests resulted from widespread disillusionment with an aspect of American foreign policy that dated to 1950, when during the administration of President Harry S. Truman, the first American military advisers were sent to French Indo-China.

From 1887-1954, France controlled the country of French Indo-China, which included three principal ethnicities—Vietnamese, Cambodian and Laotian. Both 20th-century world wars aroused ethnic nationalism. The quest for a Vietnamese nation was particularly stimulated by opposition to the Japanese occupation during World War II. After the war the Vietnamese, under the leadership of Ho Chi Minh, a Communist, fought and finally decisively defeated French forces at the Battle of Dien Bien Phu on May 7, 1954.

Shortly before that engagement a number of nations including the United States, China, France and the newly formed Democratic Republic of Vietnam had agreed to meet at Geneva, Switzerland, to negotiate settlements of the wars in Korea and Vietnam. By the Geneva Accords, they recognized the independence from France of three new nations—Vietnam, Cambodia and Laos. But, because of the sharp differences between Vietnamese Communists and non-Communists, Vietnam was divided at the seventeenth parallel north into North Vietnam (Communist) and South Vietnam.

Although South Vietnam was officially non-Communist, it had an active Communist Party that sought national unification. Beginning in 1960, that party called itself the National Liberation Front, but it came to be better known to Americans as the Viet Cong, the name used by the government of South Vietnam. Initially, the Communists believed that unification could be achieved politically, but in 1959 it had begun emphasizing a military solution.

By the time the two Vietnams were formed, Cold War concerns dominated American foreign policy. Faced with what seemed to be the dire threat of international Communism, the United States had committed itself to the containment doctrine of restricting Communism to its present range. The administration of President Dwight D. Eisenhower (January 20, 1953- January 20, 1961) was alarmed

## Arnoldus J. Grüter: Artist-in-Residence

Arnoldus J. Grüter (September 12, 1930-August 31, 2015) holds the unique distinction of being the only artist-in-residence in Mankato State's 150-year history. A native of Amsterdam, The Netherlands, the youthful Grüter experienced the German conquest and occupation of his country during World War II.

In 1960, seven years after migrating to Winnipeg, Manitoba, Canada, Grüter earned a diploma from the University of Manitoba Teachers College. Subsequently, he was awarded a Bachelor of Fine Arts degree from the University of Manitoba's School of Fine Arts in 1966. Two years later he completed a Master of Arts degree at Sir George Williams University in Montreal.

By the time he finished his formal education, Grüter had established a regional reputation as an artist in Manitoba and neighboring North Dakota. His first one-man show attracted the attention of Ronald Barnes, an administrator at the University of North Dakota. Barnes, in turn, recommended Grüter to Kent Alm, Mankato State's first vice president for academic affairs.

In 1968 Alm, who was very interested in making the Highland Campus more attractive, arranged to have Grüter employed as Mankato State's artist-in-residence. Alm, a persistent advocate of innovation, never considered placing Grüter in the Art Department. Years later he wrote that: "The Art Department had its feathers ruffed over his appointment. It was not consulted, and, in

Arnoldus J. Grüter demonstrating to students in his Centennial Student Union studio, 1969

retrospect, should have been."

As artist-in-residence, Grüter was expected to not only produce works of art, but to relate art to the lay public. His first studio in the northeast corner of the Centennial Student Union's first floor was highly visible from the building's interior and exterior. This inviting, open location helped prompt numerous students, faculty members and others to stop in and talk with Grüter about his work and experiences. Grüter estimated that he sometimes had 150 visitors a day.

Grüter was artist-in-residence from the fall of 1968 to June 1980. His position was fulltime until 1976, when, because of budget cuts, it was reduced to part-time. His part-time appointments were funded by the Centennial Student Union management, which regarded his work as a significant contribution to student life. Especially when employed part-time, Grüter supplemented his income by selling his art works at regional shows and by marketing some of his custom made furniture. Finally, after 12 years the artist-in-residence position had to be eliminated, because there was no funding for even a part-time position.

In keeping with Alm's original expectation, many of Grüter's paintings and sculptures were displayed in the Centennial Student Union art gallery. But, his most visible works were two pieces between the union building and Memorial Library. The largest, most-talked-about and most enduring was

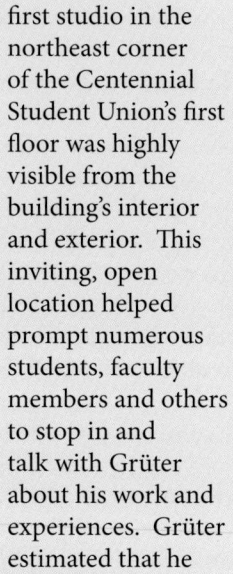

named "Waves" by Grüter, although many viewers called it Lips. In was primarily funded by a donation from Mrs. Doris Berger to perpetuate the memory of her husband Jerry, a Mankato State alum who had been killed in an industrial accident. But, Mankato State's Research and Development Foundation also contributed to its production and installation. This massive, red-painted, steel structure, which is 12 feet long, 10.5 feet high and weighs 2,000 pounds, was installed in late spring 1971. It was produced from Grüter's model by the Jones Sheet Metal Company of Mankato. It symbolizes the persistent action and force of both ocean waves and an institution of higher learning.

"Waves" on campus mall, 2015

Grüter carved his other fountain area sculpture on-site from a block of black polyurethane foam. He gave it the Latin name "Chthonic," which he explained meant original in German and organic in English. "Chthonic" had an unfortunate and ultimately disastrous history. It was vandalized in 1980 and had to be repaired. Finally, it was removed in the fall of 2016, because it was irreparably damaged by an insect infestation and deterioration of its concrete base.

After leaving his artist-in-residence position, Grüter earned a Master of Science degree in Counseling Psychology from Mankato State University (1983) and a Ph.D. from The Fielding Institute of Santa Barbara, California (1989). He worked as a psychologist for the St. Peter State Security Hospital, 1986-1996.

(Alm's narrative in Nickerson, *Out of Chaos*, 43. Arnoldus J. Grüter file in University Archives; *College Reporter*, 05 November 1981, 8; *Mankato State College Today* 1 (Winter 1969), 10-11, 3 (Fall 1971), cover, [2].)

"Chthonic" 1970

about the prospect of the domino effect, by which successive nations would supposedly fall to the inexorable international march of Communism.

Consequently, acting on the recommendations of its Central Intelligence Agency (CIA), the Eisenhower administration assisted South Vietnam with both advisers and foreign aid. By late 1959, there were 900 American military advisers in South Vietnam.

The Democratic administration of John F. Kennedy (January 20, 1961-November 22, 1963) expanded the nation's commitment to South Vietnam. By the time of Kennedy's assassination, there were 16,300 American military personnel in South Vietnam. But significantly, they were still non-combat advisers.

Lyndon F. Johnson, Kennedy's vice president, succeeded Kennedy and then was overwhelming elected to his own term in 1964. The Johnson administration was marked by a dramatic increase of armed forces committed to the war in Vietnam and an upsurge of widespread American opposition to the war. The key watershed event was the Gulf of Tonkin Resolution, which was approved by Congress on August 7, 1964. The joint resolution authorized the president to use military force in Vietnam without a formal declaration of war.

Armed with the Gulf of Tonkin Resolution, Johnson quickly escalated the commitment of American troops to fight the Viet Cong in South Vietnam. The first heavy consignment of combat troops reached Vietnam in March 1965; by the end of the year American forces numbered 184,300. This escalation thrust the war into the national consciousness and prompted antiwar demonstrations.

By October 1967, the American military force in Vietnam numbered 485,000. Perhaps more significantly, by that time 16,021 Americans had been killed in action. For the first time in the nation's history, televised news allowed Americans to see live battlefield action and the almost daily featuring of American casualties. Increasing opposition to the war was clear from opinion polls. According to Gallup polls, the percentage of Americans who agreed with the war dropped from 61 percent in August 1965 to 48 percent in December 1967.

Because of the strong antiwar movement in his own party, Johnson, on March 31, 1968 announced that he would not seek re-election. Subsequently, the Democrats nominated Vice President Hubert H. Humphrey, whose presidential campaign urged continuing the war. This hawkish stance alienated thousands of anti-war Democrats. Humphrey narrowly lost the general election to Republican Richard M. Nixon, who had served for two terms as vice-president during Eisenhower's presidency.

In February 1969, the month after Nixon's inauguration, a Gallup poll showed the percentage of Americans who agreed with the war had dropped to less than 40%. By May 1971, when the last poll was conducted, pro-war percentage had plunged to its all-time low of 28%.

Nixon, ever the pragmatist, tried both peace and war strategies. As part of his Vietnamization policy, Nixon decided to gradually withdraw American troops and cause South Vietnam to assume more responsibility. From April to October 1969, the American military presence was reduced from 543,000 to 475,200. On February 20, 1970, Henry Kissinger, Nixon's national security adviser, began secret peace talks in Paris with a North Vietnamese envoy.

But, on April 30, 1970, the United States invaded neighboring Cambodia to sever North Vietnamese supply lines. This sudden military escalation caused a sharp reaction by anti-war elements on hundreds of college and university campuses throughout the nation, including Mankato State. Millions of people nationwide felt betrayed by Nixon, who had continually pledged to end the war during his presidential campaign.[62]

## Mankato State Protests in 1970

For four successive days starting on Tuesday, May 5, large numbers of Mankato State College students engaged in anti-war protests. Their immediate triggering event was the Kent State University incident in Ohio, where national guardsmen called out by the governor shot and killed four students and wounded nine. Like dozens of campuses nationwide, Kent State students protested Nixon's decision to extend the war into Cambodia.[63]

# MSC participates in strike

By PAT BANZ
Reporter Staff Writer

A crowd of nearly 3,000 gathered on the highland campus mall yesterday afternoon for a teach-in supporting the nationwide student strike in protest of the Indochina war.

President James F. Nickerson addressed the crowd first, and said he offered his highest praise to the students who conducted the peaceful march through downtown Mankato, which was highlighted by a sit-in at the post office Wednesday.

NICKERSON ALSO COMPLEMENTED the Mankato police for "reading the marchers right. When you have large crowds your dealing with dynamite," he said. "We have to stay within sufficient control or we'll lose the whole thing."

A student striker demanded to know if the faculty was going to strike with the students, but was told this was against the Minnesota State Law.

Gene Kramer, one of two students who was sleeping in the mock Vietnamese huts built in the mall that was set fire to Wednesday night said, "I discovered we have a Vietnam right here in Mankato.-"

KRAMER TOLD THE crowd that "whoever was guilty of the act had the mind of those we're fighting against. The ones in the war are in for the money and are the one who are trying to screw us up."

Students collected an estimated $250,—almost $60 more than needed, to adopt a Vietnamese child, during the teach-in.

Seven faculty members, a church pastor and a city businessman also spoke at the teach-in expressing their disapproval of President Nixon's recent move of American troops into Cambodia.

CHARLES MUNDALE, political science instructor, was among those who spoke. He answered the question of why demonstrations were taking place and what good they would do. "This countries ass is in the ditch. You don't work on the Sabboth when your ass is in the ditch."

One person interrupted the teach-in twice, asking

## mankato state
## REPORTER

VOL. 43  NO. 80          MANKATO, MINN.          Friday, May 8, 1970

MARCHERS making their way down front street as they protest the Nixon policy in Cambodia and the incident at Kent State University.

*Photo by Bob Stevens*

*Reporter* 8 May 1970

News of the Kent State shootings, which occurred on Monday, May 4, during the noon hour (Eastern time), spread over the Mankato State campuses that afternoon and evening. In response, protest organizers persuaded the Student Senate to act like many other campuses and call for a student strike.[64]

The proposed general class strike never occurred. Instead, during the afternoon of Tuesday, May 5, some students assembled in the student union to hear the Reverend John Fry, a visiting Presbyterian minister from South Chicago, Illinois, denounce the war. At Fry's talk someone announced that there would be protest march to the Mankato post office, the site of the Blue Earth County draft board, that night just after dark.

The protesters, some 300 strong, marched from the Highland Campus to their final assembly point in front of Old Main. Then, while holding burning torches, they went down the Jackson Street Hill to the post office.

Some of them apparently hoped they could force their way into the building and destroy draft records. However, Abbas Kessel, a Mankato State faculty member from the Political Science Department, dissuaded them. Speaking from the top of one of the post office's South Second Street entry stairways, Kessel insisted that the anti-war movement could be effective only through peaceful protests.

Kessel's appeal mollified most of his listeners. But, before leaving the post office site, some of the group burned effigies of Nixon and Vice President Spiro Agnew. Additionally, some projectile throwers broke two holes in a second-story window of the draft board's space and a U. S. Navy recruitment van parked in the bus depot lot just south of the post office was damaged by a Molotov cocktail.

Since they could not get into the locked post office, the protesters decided they would be more disruptive if they blocked traffic at the corner of Front and Main streets, the busiest downtown intersection. For more than an hour the demonstrators halted traffic by standing, sitting and, in some instances, laying in the intersection. But, one determined motorcyclist got through by driving his machine over the legs of a prostrate demonstrator, who was slightly injured.

The protestors ended their blockade a half hour before midnight. On their return to campus, they marched to within a block of the National Guard Armory on North Second Street. Someone broke off from the group and threw a Molotov cocktail against side of the armory. But the building was not damaged.

Interestingly, the Mankato police, who were certainly aware of the demonstrations, boycotted them. Evidently, they concluded their presence would only provoke a violent response.

The events of May 5 proved to have the greatest potential to incite violence. The next afternoon students assembled in the fountain area on the Highland Campus to listen to faculty and student speakers and to argue with each other. The May 6 crowd of some 2,100 was treated to Kessel's reading of an anti-war letter he had written to Nixon. Judging by the coverage of the *Mankato State Reporter*, there was a diversity of opinions in the assembled masses. There was an anti-war element, a group that supported the war as a deterrent to Communism, and a large contingent that was generally apathetic but curious enough to be attracted to a very large meeting.[65]

After the campus rally about three-quarters of the crowd marched to the post office. Since postal employees locked the building and the protestors were not inclined to break in, they assembled on the building's Jackson Street side and listened to various anti-war speakers. City hall was located across Jackson Street from the post office. Some of the invited "establishment" speakers included Mayor Cliff Adams, who professed to be "against war."[66]

The next day, an even larger crowd, which the *College Reporter* estimated at "nearly 3,000" and the *Mankato Free Press* reported as "nearly 2,000,"

Bomb threat evacuation outside Armstrong Hall, 1971 *Katonian*

assembled on the mall for a "teach-in." During the three-hour affair, which started at 12:30 P.M., Nickerson and other speakers, including political science faculty members Abbas Kessel, Charles Mundale, Scott Shrewsbury and Truman Wood, spoke to the assemblage. Nickerson commended the protesting students for their peaceful conduct during the downtown marches and demonstrations.[67]

The last demonstration of the week occurred on Friday, May 8, when about 600 students in very hot, humid conditions marched from the Highland Campus to the Mankato High School (the present-day Mankato West High School). The procession's leaders bore a simulated coffin, a cross fashioned from tree limbs and a half-lowered American flag to symbolize the nation's Vietnam War casualties. They were inspired by a fallacious story that some 50 high school students had been disciplined for skipping classes to participate in the campus demonstrations. But when they neared their destination, they stopped short of entering the grounds. The *Mankato State Reporter* noted that: "Reaction to the non-violent demonstrations were mixed, and among those were these comments by two Mankato High School administrators: One said, "'Here come the hippies,' while another remarked, 'What a bunch of nuts to go marching on a hot day like today.'"[68]

After the high school march there were no more mass demonstrations, because some of the most avid protestors left campus to participate in anti-war demonstrations in St. Paul and Washington, D. C. Nonetheless, student angst was further stimulated by the killing of two students and the wounding of 12 more at Jackson State, a black college in Mississippi, on Friday, May 15. The incident resulted from the action of city police assisted by the Mississippi Highway Patrol to control a campus disturbance unrelated to anti-war protests. But, because of its close proximity to the Kent State killings, many students nationwide saw it as another effort by "the establishment" to assert their control.[69]

Although attendance at the Mankato State protests was impressive, the vast majority of students did not participate in the protest rallies. For the academic year 1969-1970, the college had an on-campus enrollment of 12,592 students (11,105 undergraduate and 1,487 graduate).[70]

The motivation of the protestors was multi-faceted. Some were inspired by opposition to the draft. There were also Vietnam War veterans who reacted against the seeming futility of the war. Some religious people saw the war as an immoral transgression. Some black students and their supporters condemned the war, because compared to the overall population, a disproportionate number of black men were drafted and served in Vietnam. Lastly, the protests occurred in a general milieu of widespread resistance to the majority culture by advocates of women's, minority and student rights.

Although the largest and most vocal protests were confined to several days, concern with potential violence persisted. Bomb threats of classroom buildings were commonplace. The erstwhile bombers invariably selected nice, sunny picnic-type days, which could be something like a high school skip day. Bomb threats were so frequent that they lost their impact. At first, buildings were routinely evacuated. But, as the threats escalated, the administration requested that the faculty simply announce the threat and give students who were concerned about their safety the option of leaving. Usually, everyone decided to stay.

About a week after the mass protests were over, the campus was riled by reaction to the Jackson State incident. The Black Student Union on May 18 persuaded the Student Senate to adopt a resolution condemning the Jackson State killings. It read; "'Be it resolved that the Student Senate condemns the action taken by the U. S. government in the assassination of two black students at Jackson State on May 14, 1970, and the wounding of seven others.'"[71] The Jackson State incident occurred shortly after midnight on May 15 and the federal government was not involved.

Although some senators were reluctant to support the resolution because Mankato State had only 60 black students, the Senate agreed to endorse the Black Student Union's call for a class strike and seek some type of amnesty for students who engaged in it.[72]

The amnesty plan, which was offered to all students, was originated by the Student Senate, supported by Nickerson and approved by the Faculty Senate. Its three options were: (1) students who negotiated an incomplete with an instructor could have a completion extension beyond the next term they enrolled; (2) students could request that an instructor assign them the grade

# War protest marches on

## ★ Cool march prevails in hot weather

**By RICK HUGG**
**Managing Editor**

Silence marked the memorial march of 600 Mankato State students Friday afternoon as they marched from upper campus to the High School and back to the campus as the wave of protest continued on this campus.

A simulated black coffin, representing those that have died in America and abroad because of the Vietnamese conflict, was carried at the head of the procession, as was a cross constructed from tree limbs and a half lowered American flag. A somber and dedicated atmosphere seemed to prevail as few words were spoken during the march which lasted one hour and 25 minutes. Those that did speak did it infrequently and in low tones.

**THE DESTINATION** of the marchers, after going through downtown Mankato, was the Mankato High School. Approximately 50 high school students were disciplined for skipping classes Wednesday in order to join the protest held at the college. Friday's marchers wanted to give sympathetic high schoolers the opportunity to join the march at least symbolically, because state law prevented actual participation.

Reactions to the non-violent demonstration were mixed, and among them were these comments by two Mankato High School administrators: One said, "Here come the hippies," while another remarked, "What a bunch of nuts to go marching on a hot day like today."

The peaceful column which stretched out over two blocks got noticeably tired in the humid heat of mid-day as they walked up the hill at the end of the demonstration. The regimentation of five people to a row became lax, and occasionally a few marchers would leave the column.

**CAMPUS MINISTERS** led the demonstrators in a memorial service, dedicated to the deaths of the war victims, when the march was over. The service was held beside a shallow grave dug between Armstrong and Morris Halls with the audience participating in readings and prayers.

The afternoon's demonstration ended as the marchers filed silently past the lowered coffin, each dropping a handful of dirt on its cover.

STUDENTS WERE ASKED TO REMEMBER THE TRAGIC EVENT at Kent State University which contributed to the eruption of last week's demonstrations at Mankato State.

## ★ Big rally in D.C.

*EDITOR'S NOTE: Among the delegation sent to Washington, D. C., from Mankato State to the anti-war protest this weekend were six staff members of the Reporter. This story was sent back by telephone, relating Saturday's events in the national capital as seen by these reporters.*

Approximately 75-100,000 people gathered peacefully at the White House in Washington, D. C. Saturday in the largest single anti-war protest demonstration since President Nixon sent troops into Cambodia.

The march climaxed two days of non-violent demonstration aimed at showing President Nixon how the nation felt concerning his handling of the Indochinese war and the killing of four students at Kent State by National Guardsmen.

**THE PROTESTERS** began pouring into the nation's capital when the National Student Association called for a nation-wide strike to begin last Tuesday.

Protesters were housed and fed free at the various universities around the city.

Coordinators of the demonstration included actress Jane Fonda, David Dellinger, a member of the Chicago 7, the National Student Association president and the New Mobilization Committee to End the War in Vietnam.

**WEEKEND ACTIVITIES** included a rally Friday night at the Washington Monument where demonstrators watched President Nixon's press conference on television. The demonstrators were not receptive to the President's remarks. Halfway through the speech, four members of the Chicago Seven trampled the television set and draped it with the new Yippie flag.

(Continued on page 8)

## mankato state REPORTER

VOL. 43  NO. 81　　　MANKATO, MINN.　　　Monday, May 11, 1970

## 50 high schoolers given reprimands for joining protest

**By HENRY FISCHER**
**Assistant News Editor**

Mankato High School was accused of threatening the right to freedom of dissent last week as about 50 students were placed on detention for cutting classes to attend rallies on campus.

Mervale Wolverton, principal, expressed his views on the issue and disagrees entirely with the claim.

**HE SYMPATHIZES** deeply with the families of the Kent Six. "Most thinking people knew a year and a half ago or more that something like this was going to happen," he said.

At Mankato High no general assembly was called, nor was a teach-in set up, primarily because he felt need for it was insufficient to call out 1,500 students.

"At every level we have social studies classes where one day a
(Continued on page 8)

## Barrett to head new institute

Appointment of Dr. Robert A. Barrett as director of Mankato State's newly created Institute for Urban Studies was announced Friday by President James F. Nickerson.

With the appointment, Barret indicated he will resign as chairman of the political science department effective Sept. 1.

**THE INSTITUTE** — Mankato State's first—will permit and promote interdisciplinary study efforts between the specialized academic departments, said Dr. Kent G. Alm, vice president for academic affairs.

The creation of the institute will allow Barrett to devote full time attention to the college's urban studies program which he helped establish five years ago.

Since his appointment as department chairman in August 1966, Barrett has handled both departmental and urban studies center matters.

**THE URBAN STUDIES** program is an indisciplinary curriculum providing training for careers in management and planning with public agencies and private consulting firms. Mankato State is the only institution in the state to offer both bachelors and masters degrees in urban studies.

The political scientist who has devoted much of his time in the past five years to urban studies projects said he is making the move at this time because the growing program needs a full time director.

"It has developed to the point where the program doesn't have the capability of sustaining and continuing anything for the future," explained Barrett.

**"WITHOUT INSTITUTE STATUS** and a director we would be limited in the number of link-ups and innovations we would like to see the next few years."

Under Barrett's guidance the urban studies center has developed a comprehensive program offering academic training, continuing research and community services.

The new Urban Studies Institute, which was approved by the College Curriculum Committee last month, will continue its instructional, service and research activities both on and off campus, said Barrett. The institute—a full member of Council of University

**DR. ROBERT A. BARRETT**
. . . to direct new institute

Institutes for Urban Affairs—will be the only one in the Midwest offering the complete range of activities.

As in the past, the program will rely on 17 other departments for instructors and coordinated classes. Participating departments are political science, sociology, geography, health, recreation, home economics, nursing, art, biology, economics, business administration, English, history, industrial arts, mathematics, philosophy and special education.

Barrett, the institute's only regular staff member, will also be teaching as a professor of political science.

**ENROLLMENT** in Mankato State's program has increased rapidly since the bachelors degree was authorized in January 1966 and the masters degree was approved in October of the following year, said Barrett.

Current estimates include 75 undergraduate and 25 graduate degree majors. The curriculum has also increased to the point where 35 per cent of the non-general education courses in departments such as political science are used largely by the urban studies students, he added.

## ★ Protest at State Capital

A crowd of 68,000 people, announced as the largest of its kind in Minnesota's history, gathered peacefully on the lawn of the State Capital building in St. Paul Saturday to protest United States involvement in Southeast Asia.

Demonstrators numbering 10,000 collected in the pouring rain at noon at the University of Minnesota campus in Minneapolis, and began the 12-mile journey to the capital. As the weather cleared up as sympathizers from colleges along the route and other citizens

joined the initial group, swelling its ranks far beyond the estimates given by most news media in their reports of the event.

**COMPOSED OF STUDENTS** from colleges throughout the state, including Mankato, middle-aged and elderly people in addition to children, the well-organized protest was conducted without any trouble as numerous volunteer student parade marshalls and city police were on hand to discourage any faction from disrupting the order of the march.

Several students from Mankato State were scattered throughout the huge gathering, which reportedly stretched out over two-miles at one point. Posters and banners identified delegations from most of the colleges in the state as well as others from North and South Dakota.

Excellent organization was evident as the volunteer student marshalls walked along the edge of the march, preventing leg-weary students from trampling grass and
(Continued on page 8)

*Reporter* 11 May 1970

they had accumulated to the May 29 drop deadline (23 days later than the originally scheduled drop deadline); and (3) students could drop any course by the deadline. Since these options mostly benefitted all students who were performing poorly they were seen by many faculty members as an ill-advised relaxation of academic standards.

## The 1972 Mankato State Anti-War Protests

Between the springs of 1970 and 1972 the only notable Mankato State activity concerned with the Vietnam War occurred in November 1971. On October 27, 1971, the Student Senate considered the possibility of endorsing participation in a national student strike that had been called for November 3. The Senate, which then included several 1970 protesters, decided not to endorse the strike call. Subsequently the Student Mobilization Committee organized a teach-in about the war.[73]

The four-hour program was held in the Centennial Student Union on November 3. In keeping with its purpose of providing information about the war, the teach-in featured eight half-hour presentations. Six of them were by Mankato State faculty members. Michael Fagin, director of the Minority Groups Study Center, spoke on "Racism and the War." "The Psychological Effects of the War on Veterans" was addressed by John Anderson, a former army medic and spokesman for Vietnam Veterans Against the War. Robert Idso, another member of Vietnam Veterans Against the War, spoke about the disastrous effect of the war on Vietnamese civilians. Art Levin of journalism talked about "Mass Media and the War." The topics of Mike Scullin, sociology, and Ronald Yezzi, philosophy, were respectively "Culture of Vietnam" and "Morality of the War." Lewis H. Croce, history, provided "Historical Perspectives on the Vietnam War" and James Goff, geography, spoke about "Effect of War on Natural Resources."

In April and May 1972, Mankato State and dozens of other American colleges and universities experienced another round of anti-Vietnam War demonstrations. The protests were triggered by Nixon's decision to escalate the war. On April 14, the United States, after a four-year lull, resumed aerial bombing of Hanoi, North Vietnam's capital and largest city, and the port city of Haiphong. Then the U. S. Navy followed up this action by laying mines in the Haiphong harbor and other North Vietnamese waters beginning on May 9.[74]

Nixon, in his nationally televised May 8 speech, justified these actions as a way of forcing the North Vietnamese to resume peace negotiations. Furthermore, he insisted his decisions were a necessary response to a new North Vietnamese offensive against South Vietnam.

Nixon's actions re-aroused fears of another troop buildup supported by reactivation of the draft. Although the draft was still in effect,

## SMC sponsors teach-in

"Our ground troops are coming out, but the bombs are still dropping and the Vietnamese are still dying. Are we going to be satisfied with that kind of 'peace'?," asked Vicky Bolton, co-chairman of the Student Mobilization Committee.

SMC is sponsoring a four hour teach-in today on specific aspects of the war in Southeast Asia. "Everyone has heard general speeches, so we decided to have each speaker discuss the specific topic he is most familiar with," said Bolton.

Site of the teach-in is the first floor lounge of the Union, where SMC will also be signing up students who want to ride buses to Saturday's anti-war demonstration in Minneapolis. The schedule for the teach-in is as follows:

| | | |
|---|---|---|
| 10 a.m. | Racism and the war | Minority Groups Studies Center |
| 10:30 a.m. | Psychological effects of the war on veterans | John Anderson, former medic |
| 11 a.m. | Mass media and the war | Art Levin, journalism |
| 11:30 a.m. | Culture of Vietnam | Mike Scullin, sociology |
| 12 noon | Morality of the war | Ronald Yezzi, philosophy |
| 12:30 p.m. | Vietnam Veterans Against the War | |
| 1 p.m. | Historical Perspectives | Lewis Croce, history |
| 1:30 p.m. | Effect of war on natural environment | James Goff, geography |

*Daily Reporter* 3 November 1971

Mitchell Goodman,
*Daily Reporter* 24 May 1972

it was inactive at the time. Those drafted by the lottery of February 2, 1972, were never called to active duty.[75]

Obviously, there were similarities between the 1970 and 1972 Mankato State protests. But a new and very significant factor in 1972 was the campus presence of Mitchell Goodman. A self-described radical, Goodman, a novelist and poet in his late 40s, was nationally known for being part of the Boston Five. In 1968, along with three of the four other schemers including the famous pediatrician Dr. Benjamin Spock, Goodman was convicted in a federal court of conspiracy for organizing draft resistance. His two-year jail sentence, like those of his co-defendants, was overturned because of a legal technicality and the government decided not to conduct a re-trial.[76]

Goodman was hired by Mankato State for the spring 1972 term to fill a quaint position named the Chair of Ideas. The chair was created because of some student agitation over C. Barclay Kuhn, who taught political science on a one-year, fixed term appointment during the academic year 1968-1969. The fixed-term appointment was just what its name implied: a terminal appointment with no possibility of renewal or extension. But, the enterprising Kuhn, who obviously did not feel bound by legal niceties, told his students that he had been "fired."[77]

Some of them immediately moved to save him. According to Larry Spencer, a student activist, Kuhn had an "unorthodox teaching style" and was "steeped in a tradition of [Herbert] Marcuse and [Karl] Marx, seasoned with excess use of marijuana and drugs."[78]

But Nickerson correctly insisted that there was no vacant faculty position that Kuhn could fill. However, Kuhn's student champions responded with the demand that the college should create a chair of ideas supported by student funds allocated by the Student Senate. Naturally, they wanted Kuhn to fill the chair.[79]

Establishing the chair required the approval of the Student Senate, Faculty Senate and the administration. Since the Faculty Senate did not finally act until June 6, 1969, the implementation of the process to fill the chair could not occur before the Fall 1969 term.

By the time the chair committee was finally formed, Kuhn had left campus. So student interest was no longer primarily concerned with saving him. The chair committee was to be constituted of five student "regents" elected by the student body, two faculty members appointed by the Faculty Senate and an eighth member appointed by Nickerson. Only 265 students, or less than two percent of the student body, were interested enough to vote for the regents on Tuesday, October 14, 1969.[80]

The need to replace some regents later in the year and the process of nominating and selecting a chair recipient delayed the filling of the Chair of Ideas until well into the Fall 1970 term. Finally, in early October, the *Reporter* announced that: "Al Huang, a noted master of the Tai Chi dance and a popular guest at last spring's Fine Arts Festival, has been selected to fill the 'Chair of Ideas' this quarter."[81]

Huang proved to be just what he was expected to be—an apolitical artist. His main responsibilities were to arrange choreography for drama productions, work with the student dance group Orchesis and teach a Tai Chi class for students and the public.

After Huang's term the Chair of Ideas was vacant until Goodman's selection for the spring 1972 term. The student regents, who were Goodman's strongest supporters, were attracted to him because of his anti-war activities. Others, including Nickerson, evidently thought that hiring Goodman, which was done in early fall, 1971, posed no risk. The Nixon Administration was then continuing to reduce the American military presence in Vietnam and was negotiating peace with North Vietnam.[82]

Goodman's specific duties were to teach a writing class for the English Department, participate in the Writers Workshop, a non-credit creative writing program that had been initiated in Fall 1971, and teach a political science class that dealt with the meaning of America. Curiously, both of his regular classes were held in the former health services building (the one-time Avoca House) at the corner of South Fifth and Jackson streets. Although this site was only a block from Nickerson's office in Old Main, it was quite isolated from the Highland Campus, the hub of most student activity.

Goodman's presence was well-publicized by the *Reporter*, but his April 10 reception in the Centennial Student Union's south ballroom drew only 18 people. However, because of Nixon's expansion of the Vietnam War, Goodman soon attracted much more attention as the most strident advocate of shutting down the college.

# N.S.A. strike set today

## *Strike schedule*

7:30-9:30  Guerrilla Theatre at High Schools

10:00-2:00  Voter Registration in CSU lobby
Speakers  (11:00-2:00)

11:00  Introduction Paul Caffrey, Peter Dahm, Mark Halverson, Larry Spencer, Student Senate President
John Anderson, Bob Corbett, VVAW-Vets for Peace
Mayor Vern Lundin
Rita  Gallagher, Women's Liberation

12:00 Dr. and Mrs. Cobb Faculty
Mrs. Rieke, 70 year old peace-nik from W. W. II.

12:30  Brian Wells, John Foster, Mankato Citizens for Peace

1:00  Wallace McLaughlin, Director-Minn. Valley Action Council

1:15  Dick Wigley

1:30  Abbas Kessel, Faculty Musicians (10:00-2:00)

10:00  Colleen Kahill

11:00  Zeke Smith

12:00  City Mouse

1:00  Chicken Lips
All Day Draft Counseling I-301
McElroy Phone 389-6449, Joint - 387-6779

*Daily Reporter* 21 April 1972

Mankato State's 1972 anti-war protests were tripped off by a call for nationwide protests, which were to be held on Friday, April 21. Two days in advance, student agitators met to organize a Mankato State strike. Both the student and faculty senates promptly supported the strike, because they were influenced by minority opinions. However most of the student body and faculty favored a business-as-usual approach.[83]

But disruption on the strike day proved to be quite effective, because some protesters poured liquid tear gas on the stairways of Armstrong Hall, Morris Hall and Old Main. This action not only forced the cancellation of numerous classes but greatly concerned Nickerson, a strong advocate of non-violent protests. Subsequently, Nickerson, along with Mankato mayor Vernard Lundin and Goodman, met with an estimated 400 students in the Centennial Student Union. In their remarks to the crowd, both Nickerson and Lundin expressed sympathy and support for non-violent protests. But Goodman admonished that a strike did not go far enough. He thought a stronger anti-war message could be delivered by a "teach-in" involving both students and faculty.

After the strike day meeting, protest activities lulled for almost two weeks until they were resumed on Wednesday, May 3. This second phase, which lasted nearly two weeks, featured some sabotage at the college and in the community and protests at the Mankato post office, U. S. Highway 169 in North Mankato, the downtown Front-Main intersection and Old Main.

The movement against the draft board office in the post office on the evening of May 3 was preceded by a Highland Campus mall rally. About 100 anti-war protestors bearing flaming torches marched to the post office where some anti-draft protesters had maintained a vigil since the April 21 strike day.[84]

The protesters were much more active on May 4. They first held a noon rally on the Highland Campus mall prior to dedicating a stone memorial to perpetuate the legacy of the Kent State and Jackson State incidents of two years before. Then a considerable part of the approximately 800-1,000 rally attendees marched to the post office with the intention of demonstrating against the draft.

Accompanied by Goodman, some of them forced their way into the second-floor draft board office. Goodman insisted that they had the right to be there because they were taxpayers. Goodman's belief was supported by Brian Wells, a student who had spent time in prison because of a draft evasion conviction. Goodman and Wells wanted to meet with draft board members, but none were available. Meanwhile, other students sat on the post office's first floor. All of the protesters carefully avoided physical confrontations. They vacated the building shortly before the announced closing time of 5:30 P.M.

The post office demonstration seemingly satisfied the protesters. But they were re-aroused by Nixon's announcement about the mining of North Vietnamese ports and other waters. On Monday evening, May 8, as soon as

Students on Hwy 169, 9 May 1972. Image courtesy of Don Olson.

Nixon's speech was over, Goodman went to the Centennial Student Union where he helped organize a noon rally followed by a protest march for the next day.[85]

Some unidentified agitators acted before the rally. At about 4 A.M. on Tuesday morning the Blue Earth County-Mankato Law Enforcement Center on South Front Street, which was then under construction, was rocked by a violent explosion. County and city officials estimated the cost of repairing the damage at $250,000 to $300,000.

Six hours later a called-in bomb threat caused the administration to order a two-hour evacuation of Old Main. While that was occurring some saboteurs tried to halt Highland Campus classes by pouring liquid solder in the locks of over a hundred classroom doors. College maintenance personnel promptly began drilling the locks out so classrooms could be used. The discovery of six Molotov cocktails in a construction area behind the Centennial Student Union indicated the campus mischief-makers had ambitions beyond damaging locks.

More property damage by unidentified persons occurred on the morning of May 10. Using dynamite, they destroyed a five-ton dump truck and damaged several other vehicles in the military compound near the Army Reserve building at the junction of highways 169 and 60, four miles southwest of Mankato. Inspectors also found that unexploded dynamite sticks had been placed in adjacent vehicles.

At the May 9 rally, Goodman not only urged a college shutdown, but stressed that blockading traffic was the most effective way of involving the public in anti-war protests. In

President Nickerson urging students to disband, 9 May 1972. Image courtesy of Don Olson.

One of many rallies held on the campus mall, 1972.
Image courtesy of *Mankato Free Press*

response, an estimated 2,000 student protesters left campus at 1 P.M. and marched downtown. Most of them staged a sit-in at the Main-Front intersection where they remained all afternoon. But perhaps a tenth of the group crossed the Main Street bridge to interfere with Highway 169 traffic on the North Mankato side of the Minnesota River. They blockaded the four-lane highway near its overpass of Belgrade Avenue, downtown North Mankato's main street. Their stand-in, sit-in, lay-in, which lasted about three hours, backed up traffic, which in turn caused the state highway patrol and the Nicollet County sheriff to rush patrolmen, deputies and squad cars to the scene.

Nickerson, who hurried to the site, was given the opportunity to persuade the blockaders to disband. After he appealed three times to no avail, the law enforcement officers moved in. Using mace, tear gas and batons, they repelled the retreating protesters. Some of the vanquished responded by throwing bottles and stones.

Meanwhile, the larger protest group was staging a peaceful sit-in at the Main-Front intersection. Kessel, who reprised his non-violent advocacy of two years before, was apparently mainly responsible for calming passions. Significantly, the Mankato police refrained from acting against the intersection demonstrators.

Protest organizers resumed their agitation the next day (Wednesday, May 10) with a Highland Campus mall noontime rally. The demonstration attracted some 3,000 protesters and spectators, including some Gustavus Adolphus College students from St. Peter. Nickerson and Frank Barth, the Gustavus president, urged protesters to act peaceably. Following the rally about two-thirds of the crowd marched down Val Imm Drive and briefly interfered with downtown traffic.

At seven on Thursday morning, May 11, 175 students left campus on buses provided by the college to demonstrate in Washington, D. C. Any hope that their departure might break the protest momentum was dashed within a few hours when about 60 antiwar demonstrators barricaded themselves in Old Main.[86]

Their occupation turned violent when an unidentified, fearful college employee asked the Mankato police to intervene. That afternoon about 30 Mankato policemen forced their way into the entrances that were barricaded with office desks, chairs and other furniture. Wielding batons they swept through the building and forced the protesters out in about half an hour. Meanwhile, about 50 protesters outside the building were trying to force their way in. But, they were repelled by mace sprayed by the police. As an added show of force, 70 state highway patrolmen in 20 cars as well as deputy sheriffs from Blue Earth, Nicollet and Waseca stayed outside the building.

Protest agitators seized on this seeming establishment over-reaction to call for another rally. That evening an estimated crowd of 4,000 assembled on the Highland Campus mall. Unlike earlier rallies, this one attracted an unusually high number of townspeople. Circumstantial evidence suggests that Nickerson and city officials believed it was necessary to assure protesters that there was not a city-college plot to squelch their movement by force. Nickerson told the group that he had not called the police to Old Main and City Manager William A. Bassett explained: "We don't come up here unless the president or someone calls us. This afternoon we were led to believe some people felt their lives were in danger." Several other community members tried to assuage protest resentment that they too thought the war was unjust and unnecessary. A combination of the

One of two occupations of Old Main, 1972.
Image courtesy of the *Mankato Free Press.*

## Abbas Kessel: A Voice for Peace

Abbas Kessel (1918-September 26, 1987) taught political science at Mankato State, 1966-1985. He is primarily remembered for his crucial role in defusing tensions during Mankato's anti-Vietnam War demonstrations in 1970 and 1972.

Kessel was born of humble origins in Tehran, Iran. His father was a minor tax collector and his mother was an illiterate housewife. Kessel's parents did not register his birth until he was about seven years old. For some unknown reason, they identified only the birth year on the certificate.

In 1935, when he was about 17 years old, Kessel was awarded a scholarship to study engineering in Great Britain. In July 1939, he completed his undergraduate degree at the University of Birmingham. That event coincided with his legalization as a British citizen.

Kessel returned to Iran in 1940, where he subsequently worked as an engineer for the Anglo-Iranian Oil Company (1940-1941) and as an administrator in the Iranian government's construction office (1942-1946). In 1946 he decided to continue his engineering studies at the University of California, Berkeley, where he earned a master's degree. In 1951 he completed a second master's in engineering from the Illinois Institute of Technology in Chicago.

Kessel decided to make an abrupt career change by studying political science at the University of Chicago, where he earned his Ph. D. in 1956. He worked briefly in the Chicago Department of Planning before becoming a teacher at the University of Chicago Downtown College. While teaching in Chicago he became an American citizen in 1964.

At Mankato State, Kessel's well-deserved

Abbas Kessel, May 9, 1972

reputation as a peace advocate was established during the anti-Vietnam War protests in May 1970. His most dramatic action occurred on Tuesday night, May 5, when he addressed student protestors at Mankato's downtown post office. His call to refrain from violent actions set the tone for ensuing demonstrations

Well-acquainted with the peaceful protests led by Mahatma Gandhi and Martin Luther King, Jr., Kessel stressed non-violence as the most effective protest tool, because it tended to preclude an escalation of tensions. Kessel's effectiveness was apparently due, in part, to his own overt criticism of America's intervention in Southeast Asia.

The next two afternoons after his post office performance, Kessel spoke to hundreds of students on the campus mall. Eyewitness Sindie Lind, an English major, thought "the important aspect of this experience is that the students listened to him and heeded his words. Only very minor damages were done, thanks to Dr. Kessel."

Kessel's response to the 1970 demonstrations established him as the institution's main peace advocate and foreign policy critic. His reputation was reinforced two years later when he acted as the soothing voice in the principal Main-Front street intersection sit-in. His efforts stimulated interest in pacifism as a societal ideal and led directly to the college's establishment of a Peace Studies minor.

On the occasion of Kessel's retirement in 1985, Scott Shrewsbury, chairman of the Political Science Department, extolled Kessel's contributions to promoting peace and progressive environmental practices. In announcing the establishment of an annual Kessel Lecture Series, Shrewsbury observed that: "Kessel could be counted on to serve as our conscience and our guide in ethical matters and was bravely always visible up front in the defense of justice, truth, and goodness . . . the series will be our way of reminding ourselves, the campus and the community of the impact that Kessel has had on all of us."

Kessel's legacy has been perpetuated by the Kessel Institute for the Study of Peace and Change. Since Kessel's retirement it has featured annual presentations by speakers who shared some of Kessel's advocacies.

Personally, Kessel was a short, slight man who habitually wore a brown suit that seemed to be about two sizes too large for him. He exuded gentleness and found great satisfaction in tending the flower garden in the front yard of his home near the Valley Campus.

In 1984 Kessel married Dr. Ruth Miner. They had first become acquainted during their Chicago graduate school days. After retiring, Kessel joined Miner, who was teaching at the University of Wisconsin-Whitewater. (Abbas Kessel file in University Archives; Shrewsbury quotation in Kessel information at http://sbs.mnsu.edu/goverrment/sprograms/kessel.html Lind quotation in *College Reporter*, 25 May 1970, 2.)

rally and Nickerson's announcement of a class dropping/withdrawal policy comparable to that of 1970 had the desired effect of cooling passions.

But a relatively small contingent felt compelled to continue protesting. The next day, Friday, May 12, about 75 of them re-occupied Old Main with the announced intention of staying for at least the weekend. However, without bedding and food service, an extended occupation was not feasible. Some of them left the next morning and others straggled out over the weekend. Finally, at 8 A.M. Monday morning, the 25, that the *Mankato Free Press* described as "weary and hungry," vacated Old Main. Throughout the occupation either Nickerson or some member of his "crisis cabinet" stayed in the building to maintain contact with the protesters.

Goodman was not involved in the Old Main incidents. He was then secluded, because of threats to his life. Goodman's advocacy of traffic disruptions alienated Nickerson, Kessel and other community supporters of peaceful demonstrations. But some Mankatoans had absolutely no tolerance for what they perceived to be an Eastern troublemaker. Nickerson and Marc Karson, chairman of the Political Science Department, became very concerned about Goodman's safety when they heard stories that some irate barflies had threatened to "dismember" him. After the Highway 169 blockade, Karson, accompanied by Mankato city councilman Herb Mocol, toured downtown bars to allay resentment of Goodman. Goodman was concerned about his own safety, but he also complained that Nickerson and Karson were exaggerating the death threats in order to force him to voluntarily leave Mankato.

Goodman not only stayed, but arranged to have the last word, at least to his own satisfaction. On Tuesday evening, May 23, he reviewed his Chair of Ideas experience before a Centennial Student Union audience of 200 people. His conclusion was that it was terrible. He complained that the college emphasized the "mechanical process" of teaching information rather than stressing such human values as "'mercy, kindness, generosity, tenderness, care and concern.'" He thought the community reaction to him was a type of "hysteria" in a "witch trial atmosphere" where he was portrayed as a "devil." *The Free Press*, he charged had "misrepresented" him.[87]

The next day, in a letter to the *Reporter* editor, he lauded his own determination and dedication to the cause. He proclaimed: "I'm still here, in spite of the ugly terror tactics used by the head of the Political Science Department [Marc Karson] and by the President of the College to frighten me away. And yes, I'm still calling for acts of civil disobedience, if for no other reason than to help people overcome the sense of helplessness that corrodes the spirit and reduces us to something less than men and women."[88]

Perhaps as an act of defiance, Goodman organized a protest rally that was held two days after his speech. In addition to Goodman, its presenters included three well-known anti-establishment protesters—Brian Webster, Connie Beckley and Frank Joyce—who Goodman had invited to the campus. At the afternoon mall rally on May 25, Webster, a draft resister and an editor of *Win* magazine, deplored society's condemnation of the draft resistance movement. Beckley, who represented *Liberation*, a publication devoted to the Women's Liberation movement, stressed the inhumane aspects of the Vietnam War. Joyce, who had been affiliated with the Chicago Seven, the principal organizers of the disruption of the 1968 Democratic National Convention in Chicago, glorified civil disobedience as a necessary solution to society's ills.[89]

Despite the importation of outside talent, the rally attracted only 200 spectators. A persistent rain may have caused some to stay away. Furthermore, some previous protesters had apparently either dropped classes or withdrawn from school. Whatever the reason, the zeal that prompted the massive turnouts of two weeks earlier was gone. A post-rally part of the crowd, reacting to a rumor that Kato Engineering had war materials contracts, marched to the downtown business. They met with company officers, who apparently convinced them that the firm's business was to manufacture electric generators.

During his Chair of Ideas residency, Goodman had more on his mind than teaching responsibilities and anti-war agitation. When he was in Mankato, Goodman had been married to the poet Denise Levertov for more than 23 years. Levertov's first biographer described their relationship as an "open marriage." Furthermore, they had discussed separating as early as 1970. Under these circumstances it is not at all surprising that Levertov did not accompany Goodman to Mankato.[90]

While in Mankato, Goodman began dating Sandra "Sandy" Gregor, a 20-year old Mankato State sophomore from Wayzata. Gregor, who was enrolled in the Experimental College Program, wrote byline articles for the *Reporter* and participated in the dance group Orchesis. Her fascination with alternatives to traditional college teaching was no doubt one of the reasons she was attracted to Goodman, who was highly critical of conventional curriculums.[91]

Kent State – Jackson State Memorial, circa 1980

Judging by later developments, Goodman and Gregor started a serious relationship during the spring 1972 term. Goodman returned to Boston at the quarter's end and Gregor joined him there several months later. Although Levertov was upset by the "Gregor affair," she did not request a divorce until August 1974 and it was not finalized until December 2, 1975, their 26th wedding anniversary. In the divorce settlement, Goodman got a farmhouse in Maine where he and Gregor later lived. Goodman and Gregor got married in 1980 and their only child, a son, was born soon thereafter.[92]

## The Legacy of the Vietnam War Protests

During the 1972 anti-war protests the likelihood of ending America's participation in the Vietnam War seemed to be elusive and distant. But once they resumed their Paris negotiations, the United States and North Vietnam soon agreed to end the war by the Paris Peace Accords, which they concluded on January 27, 1973. This peace treaty ended American fighting in the war, but proved to be a license for North Vietnam and the Viet Cong to expand their war against South Vietnam. Saigon, the capital of South Vietnam, was occupied by North Vietnamese and Viet Cong troops on April 30, 1975.[93]

The 1970 and 1972 anti-war protests left a deep impression on Mankato State's psyche. Participants sensed that they were engaged in unusual acts that they hoped would be remembered far into the future. The history of the protests has been perpetuated by two campus monuments, a book compiled by Nickerson and the peace studies program.

The Kent State-Jackson State monument was dedicated to the students who were killed on those two campuses in May 1970. The St. Cloud granite monument, placed on the east side of the Highland Campus mall between Armstrong and Morris halls, was dedicated on May 4, 1972, as part of that day's protest agenda. Goodman spoke at the dedication, which capped a long campaign to have the monument produced, erected and dedicated.[94]

The monument's principal planners were students Mark Halverson and Dan Quillin. They

Vietnam memorial, circa 1983

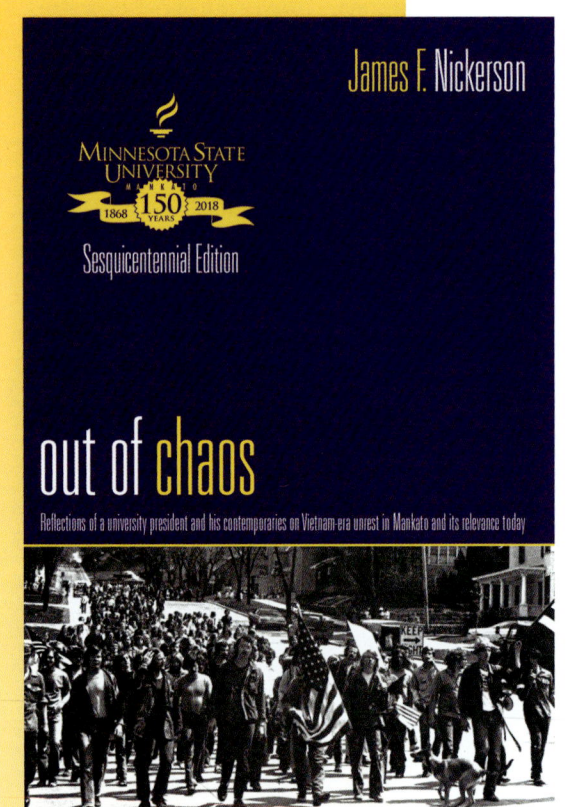

*Out of Chaos* by James F. Nickerson, Sesquicentennial Edition, 2017

originally aspired to dedicate the monument on May 4, 1971, the first anniversary of the Kent State incident. But their prolonged endeavors must have seemed like a tragicomedy. The inscriber of the first version somehow managed to misspell buried. Replacing it could not be done before the first Kent State anniversary. Then the second version was accidentally ruined while standing in the Student Senate office. Finally, a third and correct monument was ready to be placed and dedicated on the second anniversary of the Kent State incident. The inscription of the tombstone-like monument proclaimed that "Hate, war, poverty, and racism are buried here." While conceding that those words were "wishful thinking," Halverson observed that they nonetheless identified the reasons for the Kent State and Jackson State shootings.

During its Veterans Week observance in November 1982, the Mankato State University Veterans Club first considered the possibility of erecting a second campus monument about the Vietnam War. They were inspired by the dedication of the Vietnam Veterans Memorial in Washington, D. C. on November 13, 1982, and their belief that Mankato State should have a monument that provided a different perspective on the war.[95]

Over the winter of 1982-82, the club sponsored a contest for the monument's design and raised funds to purchase a piece of fashioned granite and have it inscribed. After receiving six design entries, the club decided to accept the design submitted by student Mark Dragan and the inscription suggested by student John Domcier. The top of the monument featured a dove with an olive branch in its mouth and an upright rifle imbedded in the ground by its bayonet and a helmet on its butt end. They were separated by a gap and crack. Paul Schroder, spokesman for the Veterans Club, explained that these features symbolized the dichotomous national moods that existed during the war. The stone was inscribed on three levels below the slanted top that had the dove, gap-crack and rifle. In descending order, the inscriptions read VIETNAM, FOR THOSE WHO FOUGHT FOR IT, FREEDOM HAS A TASTE THE PROTECTED WILL NEVER KNOW, 1959 — 1975. The club raised $2,490 to purchase the stone and have it inscribed through donations from Mankato's American Legion and Veterans of Foreign Wars clubs and various on-campus events.

After the club made arrangements with the university's administration, the monument was placed on the mall side (east) of Memorial Library. Congressman Tim Penny was the featured speaker at the monument's dedication on May 30—Memorial Day—1983. Claire Faust, vice president of administrative affairs, represented Mankato State University.

Mankato State may be the nation's only institution of higher learning that has monuments representing dual aspects of the Vietnam War. But, proving that unique distinction would require a survey that is beyond the pale of this history.

After resigning from Mankato State University in 1973, Nickerson spent most of the next decade directing the Servicemen's Opportunity Colleges Consortium. This program, which was under the auspices of the Department of Defense, was devoted to coordinating educational opportunities for servicemen in the nation's college and universities. Nickerson's work with the

## Ruth M. Schellberg: Women's Physical Education Leader

Ruth M. Schellberg (22 July 1912-13 October 2004) played a key role in developing the women's physical education program at Mankato State. A native of Omaha, Nebraska, she completed her undergraduate degree in physical education at the University of Nebraska-Lincoln in 1934. Then she taught physical education at the Nebraska City High School for two years. In that position she pioneered a Camp Fire Girls program for blind girls.

With the intention of becoming a college instructor, Schellberg earned a master's degree in physical education from New York University, 1936-37, with an emphasis on camp leadership training. In the 1937-38 academic year she had a temporary appointment at the University of Minnesota.

Ruth M. Schellberg, circa 1985

Schellberg taught women's physical education at Macalester College in St. Paul, 1938-46. In that position she continued her passion for canoeing by offering it as a college sport. When the editors of *Life*, a nationally circulated illustrated weekly, were informed that Macalester was the only Minnesota higher education institution offering canoeing, they decided to do a story on Schellberg's novel program. The article, published in the July 14, 1941, issue, was intended to help promote Minnesota tourism.

In 1946 Schellberg was appointed an assistant professor in physical education at Mankato State Teachers College. She regarded this move as professional advancement, because the college offered a major in physical education. But after two years she left Mankato State to complete her doctorate at New York University. When she was working on her dissertation, "Evaluation of the Camping Program of Camp Fire Girls in Terms of the Characteristics and Needs of Girls 7-17," Schellberg accepted a position at the University of Nebraska-Lincoln.

But, in 1952 she returned to Mankato State, whose location facilitated trips to her beloved Boundary Waters Canoe Area (BWCA) in northeastern Minnesota. Another attraction was

that she was named to lead the newly formed Women's Physical Education Department.

Schellberg remained at Mankato State until she retired in 1974. During her time she influenced the transition of women's sports from intramural to varsity status. This development presaged the 1972 start of Title IX, a federal mandate that began a drive to achieve equality in women's and men's sports. She also initiated a program of offering academic credit for participation in BWCA expeditions. As a participating leader, she transported and paddled her own canoe. Her canoe-topped SUV was a familiar sight on Mankato streets whenever she was about to undertake another BWCA expedition.

After Schellberg retired from teaching, she continued leading trips to the BWCA until she was at least 83 years old. Over the years she had canoed in the area about 90 times.

As part of its campus consolidation plan, which was initiated soon after Schellberg retired, Mankato State had Highland Arena North constructed. In 1991 the women's gymnasium in this addition was named Schellberg Gymnasium. Ten years before achieving this honor, Schellberg had been named to the Mankato State Athletic Hall of Fame.

Schellberg's long, active career made her an internationally recognized leader in the development of women's sports and rights. In 1993 at its Melbourne, Australia, meeting the International Association of Physical Education and Sport for Girls and Women recognized Schellberg as the recipient of the Dorothy Sears Ainsworth Award.

(Schellberg, Ruth M. Papers, 1937-2000, Southern Minnesota Historical Center, Minnesota State University, Mankato; Diane LeBlanc and Allys Swanson, *Playing for Equity: Oral Histories of Women Leaders in the Early Years of Title IX* (Jefferson, NC: McFarland & Co., 2016; *Mankato State Today* 5 (1974), 6; 16:1 (Winter 1985), [7].

Woman working on her industrial education mini-course, 1973.

consortium was recognized in 1981 when he was awarded the Secretary of Defense Medal for outstanding public service.[96]

After retiring to Minnesota, Nickerson first lived in rural Elysian and then moved to Old Main Village in Mankato. In about 2001, Nickerson began working on a book about his experiences and those of other participants during Mankato State's anti-Vietnam War protests.

The result was *Out of Chaos: Reflections of a University President and His Contemporaries on Vietnam Era Unrest in Mankato and Its Relevance Today,* which was published by the Minnesota State University, Mankato Foundation in 2006. A Sesquicentennial Edition was published by the Foundation in 2017. This second edition includes a very helpful index and a three-page Foreword by Monika Antonelli, outreach librarian and Common Read Committee Chair.

Readers will immediately notice that Nickerson was more compiler than author. The Sesquicentennial Edition has 202 pages. The parts written by Nickerson are the same as those in the original edition. They consist of a three-page Introduction, a one-page Acknowledgements and seven pages of Reflections.

The bulk of the book is 134 pages of Contributions and a 28-page Chronology of Vietnam War Era events compiled by Suzanne Bunkers in May 2006, when she was a professor of English at Mankato State University, Mankato.

Through meetings and individual contacts, Nickerson solicited narratives by 51 contributors including faculty members, administrators, students and townspeople, who had been either participants or eyewitnesses of the protests. Collectively, they are a very useful source of history. But they generally reflect the anti-war viewpoint. No one has attempted to write a complete, objective historical monograph of Mankato State during the Vietnam Era.

When he was working on *Out of Chaos,* Nickerson also intended to write his memoirs. But he did not complete that project before his death on March 6, 2009.[97]

The formation of a Peace Studies Center or Institute was first suggested by an Ad Hoc College-Community Committee of Concern during the May 1972 protests. The committee consisted of community representatives David Boyce and C. Donald Bond, student leaders Dan Quillin and Larry Spencer and college faculty and staff members David Hess, John Hodowanic, Abbas Kessel, Charles Mundale, Roy L. Lashway and Clarence R. Perisho. The original goal was soon changed to the creation of a Peace Studies minor in the School of Arts and Science.[98]

English Professor John Foster, an ardent pacifist, served as the first coordinator of the Peace Studies Program. Other than offering courses, Peace Studies sponsored outside speakers in cooperation with other departments. In February 1975, Foster reported that much of the initial enthusiasm for peace studies had ebbed. Only one student had graduated with a Peace Studies minor and only one other was pursuing it.

When Foster retired at the end of the 1975-76 academic year he was replaced by Ronald Yezzi of the Philosophy Department. Yezzi subsequently coordinated Peace Studies until the discontinuation of the program in 1980.

## The Enrollment Decline Shock

Although the anti-war protests were the most dramatic events of Nickerson's administration, the most consequential event in terms of economic impact and institutional growth was the enrollment decline that first became evident in the Fall 1971 term.

During Nickerson's first four years, enrollment continued the Crawford era pattern of increasing each year. This trend caused Nickerson to assume that it would continue to increase rapidly well into the future. In a "state of the college" address to faculty and students on January 17, 1968, he predicted that enrollment would surpass 20,000 by 1980.[99]

At the start of the Fall 1969 term, enrollment was expected to surpass 14,000. But for the 1969-1970 academic year it fell short with a total of 13,902. This number consisted of 10,968 on-campus undergraduate students, 1,520 on-campus graduate students and 1,414 off-campus students.[100]

Total enrollment for the next year was 13,232. This was low enough to have some negative economic repercussions. Customarily, the institution publicized its head count enrollment, which was its preferred way of advertising progress. But, the head count was not used as the basis of state funding. Allocations were based on full-time equivalent students (also known as FTEs). The number of FTEs for undergraduates was determined by totaling the enrolled credit hours and dividing that by 15, the equivalent of a full-time load. The total number of graduate hours was divided by 10.[101]

At a general faculty meeting on December 9, 1971, Alm announced that credit hour production had declined by 611 FTEs. This resulted in a loss of $580,000 from the college's budget. Tentative calculations indicated that as many as 36.4 faculty and 12 classified employee positions would have to be eliminated the following year.[102]

### 1972-73 FACULTY ALLOCATIONS

| SCHOOL OF ARTS & SCIENCES | 1971-72 Allocations | Adjustments | 1972-73 Allocations |
|---|---|---|---|
| Art | 22.00 | 0 | 22.00 |
| Biology | 23.54 | -1.04 | 22.50 |
| Chemistry | 18.00 | -1 | 17.00 |
| Dental A & H | 1.00 | 0 | 1.00 |
| English | 40.32 | -4.32 | 36.00 |
| Foreign Lang. | 13.00 | -2 | 11.00 |
| Geography | 18.33 | 0 | 18.33 |
| History | 21.47 | -1.97 | 19.50 |
| Journalism | 3.00 | 0 | 3.00 |
| Mathematics | 34.50 | -3 | 31.50 |
| Music | 24.41 | -1.00 | 23.41 |
| Philosophy | 5.20 | 0 | 5.20 |
| Physics | 14.00 | -2.00 | 12.00 |
| Political Science | 19.41 | 0 | 19.41 |
| Sociology | 22.87 | + .63 | 23.50 |
| Speech | 22.09 | -2.09 | 20.00 |
| Exp. Group | 7.74 | -1.74 | 6.00 |
| **SCHOOL OF BUSINESS** | | | |
| Accounting | 12.00 | -1.00 | 11.00 |
| Bus. Adm. | 33.48 | + .02 | 33.50 |
| Economics | 18.00 | -2.00 | 16.00 |
| **SCHOOL OF EDUCATION** | | | |
| Audio-Visual | 3.00 | 0 | 3.00 |
| Business Ed. | 9.00 | -1.00 | 8.00 |
| Ed. Adm. | 7.07 | -1.07 | 6.00 |
| Elem. Ed. | 15.00 | -1.00 | 14.00 |
| Ed. Psych. | 15.00 | 0 | 15.00 |
| Home Economics | 9.25 | +1.00 | 10.25 |
| Industrial Arts | 9.00 | -1.00 | 8.00 |
| Library Science | 5.00 | 0 | 5.00 |
| Psychology | 15.86 | +1.14 | 17.00 |
| Sec. & Found. | 22.96 | - .96 | 22.00 |
| Special Ed. | 3.63 | 0 | 3.63 |
| Wilson Campus | 35.50 | -1.70 | 33.80 |
| **SCHOOL OF HPER** | | | |
| Health | 11.20 | +1.00 | 12.20 |
| Phy. Ed. | 35.20 | -2.00 | 33.20 |
| Recreation | 2.00 | +1.00 | 3.00 |
| **DIVISION OF NURSING** | 6.73 | +1.00 | 7.73 |
| **SPECIAL ALLOCATIONS** | | | |
| Urban Studies | 1.00 | +3.00 | 4.00 |
| Environmental Studies | 0.00 | +3.00 | 3.00 |
| Institutional Research | | +1.00 | 1.00 |
| **TOTALS** | 545.26 | -17.40 (Net) | 527.86 |

Total Reductions 30.19
Total Additions 12.79

*Daily Reporter* 1 March 1972

The news shocked the faculty. With the exception of a few professors who had experienced the enrollment doldrums of the Great Depression and World War II, the faculty had been added during a time of spectacular growth. Thus, they were not mentally prepared for a decline. The immediate reaction to the proposed cuts was a college-wide effort to stimulate off-campus enrollment by aggressively adding extended campus courses and starting a mini-course program. Mini-courses were one-credit courses on a special topic that was not already in the curriculum. Typically, they were scheduled as night classes over the span of several weeks. Mini-course instructors donated their time in an effort to ameliorate the effect of the pending cuts. By March 1972 Nickerson estimated that the mini-courses had saved three to four faculty positions. Additionally, there was an increase in on-campus enrollment for the winter term of the 1971-1972 academic year.[103]

On March 1, 1972, the Nickerson administration announced that the faculty cuts had been reduced to 30.19 positions. But, the faculty was surprised to learn that 13 new faculty positions would be added. Thus, the size of the faculty was reduced by slightly more than 17 positions, but the holders of the 30.19 positions would be terminated. The administration insisted that this "programmatic change" was necessary to reduce overstaffed programs and add faculty to new and expanding programs.

The Faculty Senate certainly understood the rationale for programmatic changes, but many senators thought it was more important to save the positions of current faculty members. At the Faculty Senate meeting of March 8, Carl Lofy, assistant vice-president for academic affairs, defended the administration's position. But, the Senate finally passed a motion censuring the administration. The censure motion resulted in a 12-12 tie, which was decided by the pro-vote of Charles Mundale, the Senate chairman. The vote, which did not cause the administration to change its plan, tended to exacerbate administration-faculty differences. But anyone who entertained thoughts that the new dark age was over soon learned otherwise.[104]

The staffing crisis worsened in the Fall 1972 term when the administration determined that on-campus head count enrollment was down 9.64 percent compared to the preceding fall. This amounted to a 6.5 percent decrease in FTEs, which meant that an estimated 78 positions would have to be cut from the approximately 600 faculty members over the course of the next two years.[105]

As the administration was developing its two-year personnel plan, it calculated the FTEs generated by each department and school. This study showed that the greatest enrollment decline had occurred in the School of Arts and Sciences. Consequently, its was to be reduced by 59.16 faculty positions. Other planned cuts were 9.5 positions in the School of Business, 4.5 in the School of Health and Physical Education and 9.9 in administration and support.[106]

The administration's reduction plan developed in consultation with the Faculty Senate, established a process for faculty cuts. Following a "last hired, first fired" policy, non-tenured faculty were to be cut first. If this was not sufficient, tenured faculty members could be terminated after their department/program had been assigned a new staffing limit.

The two-year faculty reduction plan originated in the Fall 1973 term coincided with the advent of planning to consolidate the Valley and Highland campuses. Consequently, Gary M. Andrew and Duane Grande, consultants for a consolidation study released in January 1975, categorized all departments/programs as growing, stable or declining. For the School of Arts and Science the growing units were Biology, Computer Science, Environmental Studies, Mass Communications, Minority Studies and Urban Studies. The school's stable departments were Art, Chemistry, Dental Assisting, Mathematics, Music, Philosophy, Physics, Political Science, Sociology, Speech and Theatre; its declining departments were English, Foreign Languages, Geography, History and Speech Pathology. An accompanying "Position Allocation" table showed that from 1972-73 to 1974-75 the heaviest reductions were in the school's declining units. English had been reduced from 35.67 to 23.67 positions, Foreign Languages from 11.50 to 8.0, Geography from 19 to 15, and History from 19.50 to 14. Speech Pathology had four positions in both years.[107]

The college's other schools fared much better than Arts and Science. From 1972-73 to 1974-75 Education gained five position, Business lost 5.5 and Health, Physical Education and Recreation lost four. Within

# Nickerson announces presidency resignation

by Diane Nelsen
Daily Reporter Senior Staff Writer

"Seven years in a contemporary college presidency is a long time. I have decided to submit my resignation as president of Mankato State College effective July 1."

Speaking before an assembly of approximately 600 students, faculty, and administrators, Dr. James F. Nickerson thus regretfully and quietly ended his career as president of MSC.

The atmosphere at the Performing Arts Center was grim as the 62-year-old president said he must "slow down from the impossible pace of the presidency...to protect my own health and take up work that does not make such a long term continuous drain on one's energies."

HE STRESSED THAT, although the recent health problem (a tumor in his throat), still exists it is improving. "There is no serious threat to my health."

Opportunities for short term assignments in research, special studies, legislative work, as a consultant, or in teaching were future career opportunities Nickerson said he was considering.

He expressed hope that he could work in Minnesota, maybe at MSC, and that his home will remain in Mankato.

"In no way do I turn my back on Mankato State or on you, its faculty, staff and students."

ADDRESSING THE tumulous problems MSC has encountered in recent years, Nickerson said:

"...as an institution we need all the support and loyalty we can muster. But I've given it seven years—seven rewarding years, and, in my judgement, not only do I need a change, but the college needs a change."

Nickerson praised the college faculty for taking significant steps to adjust the institution to the changing needs and expectations of this area, and the students for constructive testing of the faculty, the administration, and the community.

"YOU HAVE ESTABLISHED yourselves as a social force and a strong voice in the community, the college, and in legislative halls."

"This is the essence of college for the '70's. The unseen changes ahead may bring even more painful times to higher education. There is no way to stop change. What will happen will happen. But this means that as faculty and as students we must keep as objective as we can in assessing the social forces which will shape the college and indeed our own careers and lives."

"This we must do to avoid the chaos, the disruption and the loss of purpose which could ensue. We must seek that objectivity and detachment in our everyday decisions to save that part of higher education which is desperately needed to solve our problems."

IN A HIGHLY EMOTIONAL tone, Nickerson concluded his short speech.

"I have often said that a president of a college or a university or any other large organization for that matter, has probably done all he can do in five years. I have stayed two years more than the five. I have enjoyed all seven years and am proud of my association with MSC. It has been one of the highlights of my career. I regret its termination and thank you for the experience."

After Nickerson hurried off-stage, the entire assembly stood and applauded. Many misty eyes could be seen in the crowded theater. See page three.

JAMES F. NICKERSON                    photo by Darryl Tjaden

*Daily Reporter* 4 May 1973

Physical Education and Recreation, its Division of Nursing was identified as growing. But, even though it had a "waiting list of over 100 qualified students" it could not be expanded due to inadequate funding.

Understandably, there was a lot of anguish as the two-year reduction plan was implemented from 1972-1974. Generally, those departments that lost faculty were reduced to their 1968-69 size.

At the time of the reductions there was a tendency among the faculty to attribute the losses to the end of the Vietnam War. According to that scenario, a surge in draft-dodging enrollees artificially swelled the college's ranks, and once the draft was ended they left school. Although this is an interesting premise, it has never been substantiated. Rather, studies of student demographics show that the enrollment drop, which affected all of the state colleges to varying degrees, was primarily caused by a decrease in the number of high school graduates. Furthermore, it was proven that the state colleges were attracting a somewhat smaller percentage of high school graduates.

The enrollment crisis cast a pall over the last part of the Nickerson administration and certainly made the president's job more stressful. On May 21, 1973, Nickerson submitted his resignation effective July 1 to the State College Board. His resignation letter included a statement he had made to the Mankato State faculty on May 3, when he announced his intention to resign. In it, he commented: "No one knows better than I that our problems are great and that as an institution we need all the support and loyalty we can muster. But I have given it seven years—seven rewarding years—and in my judgment, not only I need a change but I believe the college needs a change. Thus my decision to resign as President."[108]

## From Nickerson to Moore

On the very day the State College Board accepted Nickerson's resignation, it named Alm acting president effective July 1 with the stipulation that his position could never become permanent. Then it developed and approved the process for selecting a permanent president. This involved screening of all applicants by committees including Mankato State faculty, classified staff and students.

The search attracted 222 applicants, which were winnowed down to four finalists—Helen Edmonds, distinguished professor of history, North Carolina Central University; Douglas R. Moore, executive vice president and dean, Metropolitan State College (St. Paul); Margaret R. Preska, chairperson of the faculty, La Verne College, La Verne, California; and James Rosser, associate vice chancellor for academic affairs, University of Kansas. But, Rosser withdrew the day before the board conducted interviews at its May 22, 1974, meeting.[109]

Immediately after completing the interviews each board member cast a written ballot. The tally was six votes for Moore, three for Preska and none for Edmonds. The board then decided to cast a unanimous vote for Moore.

A native of Texas, the 45-year-old Moore had earned a Bachelor of Science degree from Texas Wesleyan College (Fort Worth), a divinity degree from the Boston University School of Theology, and a Ph.D. in psychology and counseling from Boston University. After serving as a Methodist minister in Massachusetts and Texas, he began his higher education career in 1964 as the dean of students at Southwestern College (a United Methodist Church college in Winfield, Kansas.) After leaving Southwestern in July 1967, Moore worked for four years as the dean and then the provost of Callison College, an innovative international relations college of the University of the Pacific (Stockton, California). In September 1971, he was named executive vice president and dean of the new Metropolitan State College.[110]

## Overview of the Douglas R. Moore Presidency

Moore started at Mankato State on Monday, March 18, 1974. Before arriving he decided that the president's office in Old Main restricted his opportunities to interact with students and faculty. Approximately three-quarters of all classes then were held on the Highland Campus. So Moore arranged to also have a Highland Campus office by renting space in the Centennial Student Union.[111]

In contrast to the extrovertish Nickerson, who seemed to legitimately enjoy meeting and greeting students, faculty and townspeople, Moore was quite reclusive. His greatest satisfaction appeared to be smoking his pipe, which was in his mouth almost as much as his teeth. Moore's incessant pipe-smoking provoked much interest and some criticism, because Mankato State was then in the early stages of an anti-tobacco campaign. Although smoking was permitted, some departments had banned it at their meetings.

Moore's first major task was to assemble his administrative team. In August 1974, he announced the major changes. Carl Lofy, who had served as the assistant vice president for academic affairs since 1971, was named the acting vice-president for academic affairs. Edward R. McMahon, who had been the assistant vice president for academic administration since 1973, was assigned to the president's office. His principal duties were budget development, personnel planning and the operation of computer services. Dean Trauger was selected to manage the business office. The combination of McMahon and Trauger was to perform all of the duties of the former vice president for administrative affairs. After Merlin Duncan, the original holder of that position, resigned in 1968, he was replaced by Robert Hopper, who, in turn, resigned in May 1974. In addition to these changes, Moore reassigned Kent Alm from day-to-day management. Alm was to principally work with the Department of Administration in planning for possible campus consolidation.[112]

President Douglas Moore on top of the Gage Center, 1974

Typically, administrations are characterized by a relatively high degree of fluidity. Moore's was no exception. At its February meeting in 1975 the State College Board named Margaret R. Preska vice-president of academic affairs. This move prompted Lofy to announce that he would not serve in the academic affairs office after the start of the Fall 1975 term. In late March, 1975, Moore announced that Alm's position of executive vice president would be eliminated no later than September 1. This was tantamount to a dismissal, because Moore did not offer Alm another position in his administration. In mid-June Alm was selected to direct the Center for Planned Change in the National Center for Higher Education in Washington, D. C. In July 1978, he was named North Dakota's state higher education commissioner.[113]

Moore's presidency, which lasted until July 27, 1978, was a continuation of Mankato State's time of troubles. Enrollment generally stabilized after the shocking faculty reduction, 1972-74. But, there appeared to be no chance that the institution would ever recoup those losses. Generally, faculty positions lost to death, retirement or resignation were not filled.[114]

Enrollment stagnation during Moore's term resulted in tighter budgets, which in turn, forced Moore to make some hard decisions. In November 1968, Mankato State had switched from the Northern States College Conference to the North Central Conference. The change was to be effective for the 1969-1970 year for all sports other than basketball and football. Basketball was to be phased in as scheduling permitted and football competition would start with the 1972 season. Like the men's varsity coaches and many students, the Nickerson administration thought the new conference provided a higher level of competition and more prestige. The general campus belief was that this move was initiated by Nickerson, but actually it had been promoted by coaches and students for about a decade. The Nickerson administration did herald the move as a major achievement and hired John Coatta, the former University of Wisconsin-Madison football coach, to lead the football team.[115]

Moore's complaint about North Central affiliation was that it was too costly, primarily because football, its principal revenue producing sport, was also its most expensive. North Central allowed all member institutions to offer 45 "full-ride" football scholarships. But, Mankato State was able to fund only 27 in 1975. When the program was re-assessed in 1976, the institution projected that it could fund only 16 scholarships for 1977. This projected dire shortfall caused President Moore, athletic director Roy B. Moore, football coach John Coatta and some football players to question the advisability of continuing football. Moore was particularly influenced by some players who favored cancelling the 1976 season so they would become eligible to transfer to other institutions. Therefore, much to the disappointment of some boosters, Moore cancelled the season. He had no other option, because Mankato State had to support women's intercollegiate athletics. Equal treatment of men's and women's programs in terms of the number of sports offered was required by Title IX, a federal government mandate.[116]

Moore's critics seemed to think that the cancellation of the football season was part of his plan to downsize the institution. For example, Jim Anderson, a Mankato businessman, accused Moore of having said that his goal was to reduce Mankato State to 7,200 students. Anderson did not present any substantiation. But, shortly after Moore's June 14, 1978, announcement that he was resigning, because he had been appointed president of Redlands University (Redlands, California) effective August 1, Moore stated that one of the principal reasons for this move was that he would be more comfortable in a smaller institution where he would know all of the faculty. He said, in essence, that Mankato State was too big and too complex for him.[117]

Moore also used his exit interview as an opportunity to criticize what he saw as the formality of collective bargaining that, he opined, tended to estrange a president and the faculty. The legislature authorized collective bargaining in 1971. But, the first two-year master contract between the IFO/MEA (Minnesota Education Association) and the State University Board, which began July 1, 1975, was not approved until March 8, 1976. The process was delayed by contention over selecting the bargaining agent for the state colleges/universities faculties and numerous meet and confer sessions between the IFO/MEA and board representatives to decide such issues as a salary schedule and terms of employment.[118]

The embarrassment of cancelling the 1976 football season had immediate repercussions. Mankato State could not continue in North Central, because it required all member schools to offer both football and basketball. Therefore, Mankato State decided to apply for membership in its pre-1970 conference. While Mankato State was in North Central, the former Northern States Conference had added Southwest State at Marshall, the University of Minnesota-Morris, the University of Minnesota-Duluth and Michigan Technological University to its membership of the Minnesota state colleges at Bemidji, Moorhead, St. Cloud and Winona and Northern Michigan University, and evolved into the Northern Intercollegiate Conference. In November, 1976, Mankato State University formally applied to re-join it. The Northern Intercollegiate Conference re-admitted Mankato State effective with the fall of 1977; Mankato State had already scheduled the 1977 football schedule with non-conference teams, so they did not resume conference play until 1978. [119]

Mankato State's and the nation's concern with implementing Title IX grew out of the same milieu that had triggered the affirmative action movement. The federal Civil Rights Act of 1964 and subsequent executive orders and congressional clarifications banned discrimination against women and racial minorities (including people with Hispanic surnames) with respect to hiring, retention and salaries. In 1972 the State College Board developed and implemented a salary equity policy. Then it adopted rules requiring all of the colleges to appoint affirmative action officers, who, among other things had to approve position applications. Judith Mans, Moore's executive assistant, served as

# REPORTER

MANKATO STATE UNIVERSITY REPORTER

Vol. 47, No. 210. Wednesday August 11, 1976

## Title IX: MSU 'can easily comply'

Title IX of the Educational Amendments of 1972 prohibits discrimination on the basis of sex in any educational program or activity receiving general financial assistance by way of grant, contract or loan.

*Peggy Barker*

The responsibility, for equal employment and educational opportunities at Mankato State rests with President Douglas Moore who

designated Vice President Margaret Preska as Equal Opportunity Officer with responsibility for promoting and encouraging programs that meet the University's equal opportunity goals.

The Federal Government set a deadline for the self-evaluation of University policies and practices pertinent to admission of students, treatment of students, employment of faculty, and employment of non-academic personnel. Peggy Barker, a 1975 graduate of MSU, was appointed to conduct the study and make recommendations for modification and remediation.

Each academic school division was given a set of questions to answer concerning policies of admission, current operating procedure (as applicable to students), and various forms and publications used by each school or division, and the departments within it.

Separate questionaires concerning student employment were distributed to every department and office on campus with focus on hiring practices and possible sex-based distinctions.

Barker sees athletics as the biggest thorn in Mankato's pocket.

"Men have gotten all the pie and the women the crumbs in athletics," she said. "But, the athletic leadership has indicated a willingness to work and coordinate efforts to reduce the

disparity between what's offered to men and what's offered to women."

Male athletes, the study reports, have an edge over women when it comes to facilities. The men's program is housed in Highland Arena, on upper campus, and the women are currently in the Valley Physical Education (VPE) building. This will be changed with campus consolidation. "But the status quo in terms of buildings is not at issue," Barker said. "The issue involves the facilities offered within the buildings."

The men have team locker rooms—the women do not.

Highland Arena contains equipment rooms for men's athletics. If the women move out of VPE they will not have adequate equipment storage.

Men have time and space allotted each team for practice and competition from 3 to 6 p.m.—women from 5 to 6 p.m.

Amount of publicity given to sports is another area the report lists as needing modification. Press guides, programs and other literature are prepared for men's teams, while little is done for the women's teams.

"Scholarships," Barker reported, "have been a very obvious area of discrimination. During the 1975-76 academic year, 83 male athletes were receiving scholarships. Until now, no scholarship money has ever been made available to women athletes."

For the upcoming year two scholarships have been awarded in the men's basketball program; an equal amount of money has been made available to the women's athletic program.

The women's program received a financial boost in 1975-76 when the Legislature made a special allocation of $35,833 to the program. With this allotment, women's funding reached a level comparable to mens. However, there is no guarantee that this funding will continue. If not, Barker recommends that "the men's program be cut in some area(s) in order to maintain comparability between the men's and women's programs."

Also to concur with the spirit of Title IX certain forms and literature used by the School of Health, Physical Education and Recreation will need revision (to eliminate generic terms or references to one sex over another).

Communication, or lack of it, was cited by Barker as at the root of the athletic problems. "It is recognized that leadership changes are currently being experienced," Barker said. But this fact only augments the necessity of good communication."

She recommends establishment of a system of goals and priorities developed and distributed between the staffs. "Because the next three years will entail reorganization and revamping of the entire athletic program," Barker advised, "it would behove the 2 staffs to work together as closely as possible, in order to prevent further misunderstanding and difficulty.

The remainder of the report indicated that MSU can easily comply with the Title IX requirements, Barker said. **Title IX to 4**

*Reporter* 11 August 1976

Mankato State's first affirmative action officer.[120]

Aside from its concerns with budgetary shortages, conference affiliation, affirmative action and Title IX, the Moore administration featured the achievement of university status, changing of the university's mascot and campus consolidation. Moore, like everyone else on campus, was essentially a spectator of the university status movement that was primarily a legislative issue. But he played the lead role in changing mascots and assisted in the development of campus consolidation.

## Achievement of University Status

The first noteworthy event of Moore's administration was the achievement of university status effective August 1, 1975. This attainment capped a 15-year

F. Kelton Gage,
1965 *Katonian*

quest. Although the drive for university status featured continuity, it had two distinct phases. During the Crawford presidency, when State Senator Val Imm championed university status, the principal aim was to convert Mankato State College to the University of Southern Minnesota. But after Crawford's retirement in 1965 and Imm's 1966 defeat in his bid for another four-year term, the university status effort was directed by the State College Board. Rather than work for something unique to Mankato State, the board developed policies that created opportunities for some of Mankato State's sister institutions to also be designated state universities.

During the first few years of the Nickerson presidency, university status continued to be advocated by Senator F. Kelton Gage, a Mankato attorney who succeeded Imm. Gage, who had served on the State College Board, 1960-64, professed to have particular insight into the board's role in seeking university status. His strategy was to work for university status through the board, which was consistent with Nickerson's stance.[121]

In 1970, the State College Board had Dr. David Sweet, its vice-chancellor for academic affairs, conduct a university status study. In his report of November 23, Sweet recommended a way of converting some of the state colleges into universities. Scrupulously avoiding direct competition with the University of Minnesota, Sweet recommended the creation of Doctor of Arts and Doctor of Education degrees. Such practitioner degrees, he advised, would not conflict with the University's Ph.D. degree, which emphasized original research. Sweet concluded that the board should ask the legislature to appropriate $250,000 to start doctoral programs at some of its colleges. Only those colleges that established doctoral degree programs would be considered for university status by the board. Given the situation at that time, only Mankato State and St. Cloud State were likely to develop doctoral programs. In 1967 Mankato State received legislative authorization to offer a Sixth Year (i.e. Specialist Degree, or a year beyond a master's) and St. Cloud was in the process of designing such a degree. Otherwise, Sweet thought that some of the existing state colleges might want to retain their traditional designation and continue their undergraduate emphasis.[122]

On December 4, 1970, the State College Board approved Sweet's proposals. It decided to ask the 1971 legislature for authority to convert one or more of the existing colleges into universities and for $250,000 to launch a doctoral program at such designated institutions. Additionally, the board decided to request legislative authority to rename the Minnesota State College System to the Minnesota State College and University System and to designate, where necessary, new names for the individual institutions. [123]

Nickerson, who was present at the meeting, was enthusiastic about the recommendations, because he evidently presumed Mankato State would be one of the colleges converted into a university. But Robert DuFresne, president of Winona State, came out strongly in favor of a systems approach—make all of the colleges universities even if some of them were not ready. Robert Decker, president of Bemidji State, was apprehensive, because he thought the existing system did not have enough support for even a bachelor's level program.[124]

Gage led the legislative effort to achieve the board's recommendations about university status. On March 11, 1971, he introduced a Senate bill to make Mankato State and St. Cloud State universities, and, if that status was granted, to authorize them to offer doctoral degrees.[125]

By a vote of 38-28 the Senate rejected Gage's bill on April 14. But Gage was able to revive the bill by agreeing to two amendments. The first would have required the approval of university status by the Higher Education Coordinating Commission (HECC) and the second stipulated that no college could become a university unless it had a specialist or doctoral program. The strategy worked. The Senate without debate on April 20 approved the amended bill 43-23.[126]

After the Senate's action, the House considered a companion bill that had been introduced by Representative C. A. "Gus" Johnson (Mankato) and Representative Rodney Searle (Waseca). Johnson was a lawyer and Searle a farmer and Mankato State alum. The House Higher Education Committee by a 13-11 vote approved the bill, but only after stipulating that any of the state colleges was eligible for university status if they met criteria to be established by the committee.[127]

The committee's action caused university supporters to become more optimistic. But the session expired before the House could consider the bill and the House did not re-visit the issue during the legislature's special session. The progress made in 1971 augured well for the legalization of university status when the next legislature met in 1973.[128]

In 1973 the introduction of university status bills was delayed until April 12, when the end of the legislative session was only five-and-a-half weeks away. This late start may have been caused by a turnover in Mankato area legislators. When Gage decided to retire from the Senate, he was succeeded by Arnulf Ueland, a Mankato lumber merchant. Gus Johnson, who had represented Mankato-North Mankato in the House, was defeated by David Cummiskey, a Mankato State student, in the 1972 election. Cummiskey, who had been an anti-war activist, benefitted from strong student support.[129]

The companion university designation bills introduced by Cummiskey and Ueland sought legislative authorization to re-designate to universities those colleges that offered at least a specialist degree. Rather than act on them and some other proposed legislation, the legislature decided that any 1973 proposal would automatically be considered when the legislature convened again in January 1974, the beginning of its practice of holding annual rather than biennial sessions.

When the 1974 legislature considered the university designation bill it made a very significant change from the Cummiskey and Ueland bills. Rather than restrict university status to only those institutions that offered a specialist degree, it decided that any change should be system-wide. Representative Russell Stanton of the Marshall area was one of the most vocal supporters of

# Cummiskey elected

For what may be the first time in Mankato's history, a student has been elected to a position on the city council.

David Cummiskey, the 21 year-old political science major, out polled his 74 year-old opponent Kyle Matteson for the fourth ward council position.

Cummiskey relaxed at the home of his parents, Dr. and Mrs. Cletus Cummiskey at 221 Lincoln Street, after taking inn the returns, and spoke of his campaign.

"I COULDN'T HAVE won without the students," he said, "and I couldn't have won without the townspeople."

The young councilman-elect had kind words for the tenor of the campaign, and for his opponent.

"It was mild and very clean," he said, "I'm really grateful for that. Had he wanted to, Mr. Matteson could have made me look very bad...bearded hippy and that sort of thing."

CUMMISKEY had finished second in the Sept. 15 primary election, receiving 130 votes less than Matteson in that contest.

Cummiskey, along with some 20 to 25 well wishers and campaign workers, sipped beer, ate pretzels, and talked of future plans for Mankato.

Throughout the campaign, he had said that communications between the council and the citizenry had broken down. He had said that he wanted to give students a voice that had often been ignored by the council.

THERE ARE MORE than 1,000 students in Cummiskey's ward, which he feels amounts to a two-third students to one-third townspeople ratio.

He hopes to close the gap between Mankato State students and city affairs by appointing students to various council commissions.

He also said that he would work to ease zoning requirements so that the Highland area basement apartments "closed down by Housing inspectors" recently, might be re-opened.

Cummiskey and his wife, Joyce, a teacher in Waterville, live at 631 South Second Street.

*Reporter* 4 November 1970

Unveiling of new Mankato State University sign, August 1, 1975

this change. He liked the idea of Southwest State College, which had been started only seven years before and offered only undergraduate courses, becoming a university. Stanton's proposal provoked the criticism that renaming all the colleges to universities would be nothing more than a cosmetic name change. But it was nonetheless a shrewd political move. Changing all of the colleges to universities attracted constituencies, which were reluctant to support something that benefitted only Mankato State and St. Cloud State.[130]

However, despite its broadened appeal, the 1974 university status bill failed. It was approved by the House, but voted down in the Senate. The strongest support came from Republicans in rural Minnesota and the opposition was mainly from metropolitan and Mesabi Iron Range Democratic-Farmer-Labor legislators. The *Mankato Free Press* calculated that legislators who were University of Minnesota graduates were the bill's most influential opponents.[131]

After the 1974 setback, university designation supporters correctly sensed that momentum was on their side and their best tactic was to strive until they succeeded. In running for re-election, Cummiskey promoted himself as a champion of university status. But, in somewhat of a surprise, he was defeated by Ronald Evans, a former Blue Earth County commissioner. The change was not locally significant, because Evans proved to be a strong university status supporter.[132]

Two versions of a university status bill, usually identified as the Pehler and McCauley bills, were introduced in the 1975 legislature. Representative James Pehler of St. Cloud sought authorization for the State College Board to bestow university status on those colleges that had graduate programs. But Representative Maurice J. McCauley of Winona countered with a bill that called for the re-designation of all seven state colleges to universities. The state college system had been expanded by the addition of Southwest State (Marshall) in 1967 and Metropolitan State (St. Paul) in 1971. Metropolitan State, the brainchild of State College Board Chancellor G. Theodore Mitau, was an innovative institution that Mitau championed as a "university without walls." It was designed to appeal to non-traditional students who could be granted college credit for work experience.[133]

Everyone concerned recognized that solely on programmatic grounds, Mankato State and St. Cloud State had many graduate programs and were more deserving of university status than Southwest and Metro. But, as the session continued the McCauley bill became more popular. In early March, Mitau, speaking for himself rather than the State College Board, strongly endorsed it. He evidently reasoned that the best case for university status could be made by comparing Minnesota to Wisconsin. In 1971 the Wisconsin legislature incorporated all of the former state colleges into the University of Wisconsin system and re-designated them as universities with names, such as University of Wisconsin-La Crosse. Following this action the states of Minnesota and Wisconsin agreed to tuition reciprocity, which enabled a Minnesota student to attend a Wisconsin school paying regular in-state tuition.[134]

Winona State, in particular, contended that it was detrimentally affected by tuition reciprocity. Minnesota students who otherwise were inclined to enroll at Winona State, could choose nearby La Crosse and obtain a university degree. Most students, and presumably their parents, believed that a university degree was more prestigious than a college degree and gave them an edge in a competitive job market.

Finally, the 1975 legislature passed the McCauley bill. Its critics, including the *Mankato Free Press*, complained that the act, which was to become effective August 1, 1975, did nothing more than rename each of the seven colleges to a university.[135]

The wording of the act, which was approved on June 4, substantiated the claim that it provided only for a change in names. Its first section stipulated that "the re-designation of the Minnesota state colleges as state universities shall not result in additional fiscal commitments through an expansion of graduate or research programs predicated upon such re-designation."[136]

With regard to renaming, the law stipulated: "The state college board shall obtain the concurrence of each institution in designating the name of that institution and may use only the community or regional name, in conjunction with the phrase 'state university,' in the name of each institution."

After obtaining the consent of the seven presidents, the State University Board on August 20, 1975, re-designated the colleges as follows:

"Bemidji State College shall be known as Bemidji State University

Mankato State College shall be known as Mankato State University

Moorhead State College shall be known as Moorhead State University

Metropolitan State College shall be known as Metropolitan State University

St. Cloud State College shall be known as St. Cloud State University

Southwest State College shall be known as Southwest State University

Winona State College shall be known as Winona State University"[137]

Meanwhile, Moore assumed that Mankato State had actually become Mankato State University on August 1. So, he announced a campus celebration for that day. Proclaiming university status to be a "proud occasion," Moore invited students, faculty and community members to attend an informal "Mankato State University Day Open House" on the Highland Campus Mall from 9:30 A.M.-11:00 A.M.[138] Also, by using the August 1 date, Moore decided that those students who graduated on August 15, 1975, were the first to receive diplomas from Mankato State University.[139]

University status necessitated reorganization of the academic units. The schools, the sub-divisions that had been in place since 1964, had to be replaced by colleges. The outcome of the conversion process, which entailed countless committee meetings and consultations, was first shown in the undergraduate catalog for the 1978-1979 academic year.

The most striking reorganization feature was the division of the previous School of Arts and Science into three colleges—Arts and Humanities, Natural Sciences, Mathematics and Home Economics and Social and Behavioral Sciences. The university's other three colleges were Education, Business and Health, Physical Education and Nursing.

The College of Arts and Humanities was headed by Dean Jane Earley, the third and last dean of the former School of Arts and Science. The college had 15 departments and programs, namely: American Studies, Art, English, Foreign Languages, History, Honors, Humanities, Mass Communications, Music, Open Studies, Peace Studies, Philosophy, Pre-Theology, Scandinavian Studies and Speech and Theatre Arts.[140]

V. Dean Turner was named the acting dean of the College of Natural Sciences, Mathematics and Home Economics. Its seven sub-divisions were Biological Sciences, Chemistry and Geology, the Environmental Studies Institute, Home Economics, Mathematics, Astronomy and Statistics, Medical Technology and Physics and Electronics Engineering Technology.[141]

The College of Social and Behavioral Sciences was administered by Dean Bill R. Webster. Its departments and programs were Earth Science, Geography, International Relations, Law Enforcement, Minority Groups Study Center, Political Science, Pre-law, Psychology, Social Studies, Sociology, Urban and Regional Studies and Women's Studies.[142]

Morgan I. Thomas, who had served as the dean of the School of Business throughout its 14-year history, was named dean of the College of Business. Its departments were Accounting, Business Education, Economics, Business Administration, Computer Science and Industrial Technical Studies.[143]

The College of Education was led by Dean Duane C. Orr. Its components were Children's House, Counseling and Student Personnel, Curriculum and Instruction, Educational Administration, Educational Foundations/Higher Education, Instructional Media and Technology, Special Education, Studies in Educational Alternatives, Experimental Studies, Studies in Experiential Education and Vocational Rehabilitation Counseling.[144]

Donald W. Buchanan was the dean of Health, Physical Education and Nursing. Its academic sub-divisions were Dental Assisting, Dental Hygiene, Health Science, Nursing, Physical Education, Recreation, Parks and Community Education and Speech Pathology and Audiology.[145]

Winston W. Benson, a former professor of political science who had administered the School of Graduate Studies continued as the dean of the College of Graduate Studies. Mankato State offered both specialist (i. e. Sixth Year or a year beyond a master's) and master's degree programs. Specialist degrees could be earned in Curriculum and Instruction, Educational Administration and Media and Technology. There were five master's degree programs, namely: Master of Arts in Teaching, Master of Business Administration, Master of Music, Master of Arts and Master of Science. Most of the academic departments offered both the Master of Arts and the Master of Science. The main distinction between them was that the Master of Arts did not require any professional education courses whereas one-fifth of the credits in the Master of Science had to be earned from professional education offerings.[146]

Other than the seven college deans, the university's central administration included the following: Douglas R. Moore, president; Judith Mans, assistant to the president; Margaret R. Preska, vice president for academic affairs; Carl Lofy, vice-president for student services; Edward R. McMahon, vice president for resource management; Ira Johnson, facilities management officer; Andrew Een, assistant vice president for academic affairs; Claire Faust, assistant vice president for academic affairs and director of planning/research/evaluation; Dale Carrison, director of libraries-media; and Melba Leichsenring, associate dean for nursing.[147]

## From Indians to Mavericks

On January 18, 1977, President Moore announced that Mankato State's nickname would be changed from Indians to Mavericks. His decision capped a spirited campaign to discontinue the Indians label that had been in place since 1935.[148]

The first noteworthy campus criticism of stereotyping Indian culture occurred in May 1968, when the Native American Association objected to the presence of an Indian statue in the Centennial Student Union. Dubbed "Goldfeather" by the *Reporter*, this cigar store Indian had been loaned to the college by Hormel estate heirs. The association announced that it would stage an all-day sit-in on May 4 to force the statue's removal. This protest against the symbolic portrayal of American Indians as bloodthirsty, pagan savages, did not prompt the union's administration to remove Goldfeather. Several students responded to this inaction by spiriting the statue away. They took it on a tour of Mankato bars before showing it in various southern Minnesota and northern Iowa towns. Mysteriously, after about a month-long absence, Goldfeather re-appeared in the union at 10:30 P.M. on June 5. More than three months later, the *Reporter* noted that "Goldfeather is currently locked up by the administration."[149]

The Goldfeather incident was a local reflection of national developments. American Indians were affected by the 1960s civil rights movement that, among many other things, emphasized the African heritage of America's blacks. In that same spirit, American Indians rebelled against the ways they were perceived, portrayed and treated by the dominant white culture. In 1968 some Anishinaabe (traditionally called Chippewa) leaders in Minneapolis, including Dennis Banks and Clyde Bellecourt, organized the American Indian Movement (AIM). AIM was soon recognized as the country's main Indian advocacy organization. It was primarily dedicated to working for the civil rights of urban Indians. This rebellion against assimilation into the white people's world included an effort to instill Indian pride by reviving original tribal names and forcing the discontinuation of white-imposed stereotypes. Thus, for example, AIM urged that the tribal designation Sioux, which was concocted by Euro-Americans, be replaced by Dakota, Nakota and Lakota, the names the tribe's three divisions called themselves prior to white contact. AIM's principal complaint about stereotypes was the portrayal of Indians as tomahawk-wielding savages. Consequently, Mankato State and all other colleges and universities that had Indian mascots were targeted by AIM sympathizers.[150]

The Mankato State Student Senate first considered the Indian mascot issue on September 19, 1971. It decided to form a committee to study the continued use of the Indian mascot. Senate president Larry Spencer opined that such a committee was necessary because the Indian symbol might be racist. It is likely that the Senate's action was inspired by Indian students at Stanford University, whose efforts to force the discontinuation of the Stanford Indians was then being publicized nationally. In 1972 Stanford became the nation's first institution of higher learning to drop its Indian nickname in favor of Cardinals. But Cardinals, which was a reference to the color rather than the bird, proved to be confusing. So in 1981 the Stanford president decided the official name was Cardinal.[151]

The Mankato State Student Senate's action ignited a controversy about the Indians future. Michael Scullin, assistant professor of anthropology, helped set the tone of the debate by observing: "The symbol of Mankato State College's athletic teams is a figure so heinous that it is truly remarkable that it has survived this long. . . . Should anyone doubt that this cretinous representation of an Indian is offensive I would suggest—ask an Indian."[152]

Scullin's position was supported by alums Barry Blackhawk and Clair St. Arnaud, who as students, had organized the college's first Indian club in 1966. Blackhawk and St. Arnaud evidently advised the campus Native Americans Club in 1971. Club spokeswoman Carol Littlewolf thought the mascot should be changed and phased out of use, because it displayed "a terrible, unjust and dehumanizing" image of the American Indian.[153]

However, college administrators concerned with intercollegiate athletics defended the Indians nickname. In speaking at a Student Senate meeting, Athletic Director James R. "Bob" Otto, the college's former football coach, claimed the mascot "depicts and shows everything we want to show...a brave, courageous, feisty individual going out to do battle to defend a cause."[154]

Otto was supported by Roy B. Moore, dean of the School of Health, Physical Education and Recreation. Moore, who was apparently trying to reinforce his image as Mankato State's Ogden Nash, wrote a poem which opened as:[155]

"For thirty-five years the Mankato teams
Have striven to rise to the best of their dreams,
And the name they bore through all of this stress
Was Indians! Indians! As they strove for success.

Full loud were their chants as their victories came.
'Indians! Indians!' was the shout at each game.
Respect for the Redman continued to grow,

## Georgene Brock: Director of Women's Athletics

Georgene Brock (15 June 1937-   ), who taught, coached and administered at Mankato State for 34 years,  served as the institution's first and only women's athletics director. Born in Phoenix, Arizona, Brock earned a Bachelor of Arts degree in physical education from Arizona State University. She then taught in Arizona junior and senior high schools before completing her Master of Arts degree at the University of New Mexico.

In 1964, when Brock started teaching women's physical education at Mankato State, the college had only a women's intramural athletics program. During her first year, Brock organized and coached bowling, the institution's first women's varsity sport. The varsity program was expanded rapidly in the next decade. Swimming, gymnastics and track and field were added in 1965. Two years later basketball and volleyball were started and tennis, cross country and softball were begun respectively in 1971, 1972 and 1974.

While continuing to coach bowling, Brock was chosen as the first volleyball coach. In 1970 and 1971 her teams qualified for and participated in national championship tournaments.

In addition to coaching and teaching, Brock served as Mankato State's Director of Women's Athletics from 1970 until her retirement in 1998. In that role she led the evolution of women's sports from a grossly underfunded activity to one that had as many sports as the men's program. Initially, the only funding for women's sports was small amounts from the intramural program. But the financial situation was improved sharply when the Student Allocations Committee first provided some funding for women's varsity sports in 1971.

Despite this breakthrough, the women's program was literally a poor sister compared to men's athletics. That disparity was gradually eliminated with the advent and implementation of Title IX.  As they were developing varsity sports, Brock and the other Mankato State

Georgene Brock,
circa 1995

women's sports coaches become involved in a national movement to achieve equality with men's sports. This broad-based agitation resulted in the enactment of the federal government's Education Amendments Act in 1972. Its Title IX banned sex discrimination in any educational activity or program that received federal financial aid. Although Title IX did not mention athletics, it was subsequently construed to be a mandate for equal treatment of men's and women's sports.

In keeping with the national movement, Title IX was primarily responsible for achieving equity between women's and men's sports at Mankato State in terms of number of sports offered. But, it also caused the awarding of athletic scholarships for women. By 1983 Mankato State funded the equivalent of 66 full scholarships for women student-athletes.

Because of her pioneering role in elevating the status of women's athletics, Brock received significant honors. In 1986 she was added to Mankato State's Athletic Hall of Fame. Since 1978-79, the annual Georgene Brock Award has been bestowed on the university's "most well-rounded senior female student-athlete." Furthermore, Brock was placed in two conference halls of fame—the North Central Conference in 1996 and the Northern Sun Conference in 2001.

(Brock, Georgene. Oral History Interview, 01 March 2016, Southern Minnesota Historical Center, Minnesota State University, Mankato; Wayne Carlson, "Legendary Spectator," *Today Magazine Online,* 26 October 2011, access by title; Mary C. Haugland, "The History of Women's Intercollegiate Athletics at Mankato State University 1964-1983," Master of Science thesis, Mankato State University, 1984; *Mankato State Today* 17:4 (Fall 1986), 6; Minnesota State Mavericks Hall of Fame (online source, access by title, accessed 22 June 2017;  "History of Title IX-Women Sports Foundation," online source, access by title, accessed 22 June 2017.).

# Emblem change demanded

Bob Otto...
against change

**By MARION STRUZYK**
**Daily Reporter Writer**

A face-lift may be forthcoming regarding MSC's Indian emblem. Yesterday, the Student Senate extended discussion regarding the "mascot" pending committee investigation of viable alternatives.

Coach Bob Otto lead the discussion of the "mascot" voicing athletic department and athletes' viewpoints. "I think it depicts and shows everything we want to show," said Otto.

He added, that the caricature "depicts a brave, courageous, fiesty little individual going out to do battle to defend a cause."

According to Otto, the caricature remains a proud emblem for MSC athletes and adequately symbolizes their fighting roles.

OTTO ADDED that if there was a feeling on part of the Indian groups that the caricature emblem was degrading, it should most certainly be changed.

Carol Littlewolf, acting as spokesman for the Native Americans' Club, said, "the majority of Indians feel the mascot emblem should be changed."

Littlewolf indicated the caricature displays a "terrible, unjust, and dehumanizing" picture of the American Indian. She suggested that the present caricature be "changed and phased out of use."

THE TERM "mascot", said Littlewolf, "should be changed because we believe mascot brings to mind the word animal and we feel that the Indians are not animals . . . We don't want to be viewed as a puppy or a pet."

Littlewolf added the Native Americans Club would have no objections to retaining the use of the term Indians because of its obvious connections with Minnesota and Mankato history.

According to Littlewolf, the club would submit alternative symbols to serve as an emblem for the MSC Indians.

(continued on page 10)

Carol Littlewolf...for

*Daily Reporter* 14 October 1971

For Brave was the image they wanted to show."

Moore correctly assumed that Mankato State's Indian warrior image would be discontinued. But in his introduction to his poem he noted: "His image will soon be gone but we hope the spirit he engendered will stay with us, for it urges courage to face any task, no matter what the odds --. This is the symbol we have followed, and if other aspects have given racial offense, we are sorry. It was never intended."

In the spring of 1972 Mankato State discontinued producing any new materials that bore the offensive image of the warring Indian. But the image did not disappear. Otto and band director Clayton Tiede successfully argued that it was too costly to replace the old athletic and band uniforms before they were worn out. Then the Native American Club considered the design of a new emblem for the Indians nickname. Finally, in January, 1973, the Student Senate approved the emblem developed by the club. It featured a circle with the capital letters MSC placed from above its top to below its bottom. The ends of both an arrow and a calumet projected beyond the circle. The club thought this design was an appropriate symbolic depiction of Indian culture.[156]

The new symbol needed Nickerson's approval before it could be adopted. But he rejected it "because he preferred something "more attention-getting."[157] Nickerson's decision meant that the

Proposed new
emblem (above) and
original emblem (left)

*Mankato Free Press*
1 February 1973

**Maverick chosen for new MSU team name**

The new Mankato State team name will be the "Mavericks," President Douglas Moore announced Tuesday. The name was selected over "Fighting Muskies" and "Lightning" on the basis of phone calls and letters received since the University announced the three final choices last week.

The search for a new school nickname began this fall when Moore decided the school should drop the "Indians" insignia. Several Native American students and faculty had complained that the symbol was detrimental to the image of Native Americans.

*Independent* 19 January 1977

Mavericks logo, 1977

practice of using the Indians nickname would be continued and the offensive symbol of the fighting Indian would not disappear until the old uniforms were retired.[158]

But in the closing months of the Nickerson administration, the mascot representation matter was quietly dropped. After a lull of more than three years, President Douglas R. Moore revived it in the Fall 1976 term.[159] Moore's own family history may have been a factor in his decision. In his public utterances, Moore claimed to have a special understanding of racial discrimination because one of his grandmothers was identified as a Cherokee Indian.

Moore, whose obvious personal preference was for a new mascot and logo, asked the University Relations Office, which was headed by John Hodowanic, "to make recommendations concerning the use of the word 'Indians' and the use of the Indian logo."[160] Jerry Bodelson, assistant dean of the School of Health, Physical Education and Recreation, favored retaining the Indians nickname and developing a new logo. But Jeremy P. Rockman, coordinator of the Native American Studies Program, wanted nothing less than a new nickname and logo. Such an action, Rockman insisted, would be consistent with the emerging national trend of colleges and universities discontinuing any stereotyping of Indian culture. Rockman was supported by the *Independent* that emphasized that "old does not mean right."[161]

Within a month of his initial pronouncement about the athletic teams mascot and logo, Moore removed any ambiguity about his position by clearly stating that Mankato State should adopt a new nickname and logo.[162] Subsequently, students, faculty, alumni and the public were invited to make suggestions. The top three suggestions in alphabetical order were Fighting Muskies, Lightning and Mavericks. By mid-January 1977, Mavericks, which was originally suggested by W. Roy Cook, professor of sociology, had been chosen.[163] There are two versions of how that name was selected. The *Independent* of January 19, 1977, reported it was done "on the basis of phone calls and letters." But on June 30, 1977, the newspaper stated the choice was made by a "ballot box vote of students and faculty."[164]

Cook apparently knew that the word maverick was added to the English language in the late 1860s because of Samuel A. Maverick, a Texas rancher, who refused to brand his cattle. Maverick's motive is not clear, but he may have decided this was an effective way of rustling other unbranded cattle. Maverick also came to mean an independently minded person. When Cook suggested the name, Mankato State University did not have any conference affiliation, which made it a maverick in intercollegiate athletics.[165]

Once the Mavericks nickname was selected, a university committee chaired by Anita Stone, director of university publications, decided to solicit designs for a Mavericks logo. The winning entry was conceived by John Vetter, a Mankato State alum, who was teaching English at Windom. But, the actual drawing featuring capital letters that spelled out MANKATO STATE UNIVERSITY MAVERICKS within a circle, was done by Tracy Hanson, one of Vetter's students.[166]

Stone's committee was concerned because the letters of MAVERICKS showed the image of a horse. So the committee had Barbara Furan, a Lake Crystal artist, re-design MAVERICKS so it had the shape of what was proclaimed to be a steer. However, the animal portrayed on the logo appeared to symbolize aggressiveness, vigor and power characteristic of bulls rather than steers (emasculated male cattle).

After the Mavericks logo was approved by the committee, Moore proclaimed that it would officially go into effect on July 1, 1977. But some sports writers started using the name soon after Moore had announced it in January 1977. As another way of publicizing the new logo, images of it were distributed at the July 4th fireworks display in Blakeslee Stadium.[167]

## Campus Consolidation

Campus consolidation involved three presidents and two acting presidents. Serious consideration of closing the Valley Campus and consolidating all institutional activities on the Highland Campus first occurred in 1973 while Nickerson was still president. Planning was continued during Alm's acting presidency. The development of final plans, funding and the beginning of new Highland Campus buildings was accomplished during the presidency of Douglas R. Moore. New construction proceeded rapidly during the approximate five-month term of Acting President Edward R. McMahon. The consolidation was completed effective with the opening of the Fall 1979 term when Margaret R. Preska was president.

The 1973 Minnesota Legislature appropriated $20,000 to the Department of Administration to have a report done on the feasibility of closing the Valley Campus. Legislators were then convinced that the enrollment boom was over and that there was a good possibility Mankato State could be fit into a single campus. Like other state officers they had also been influenced by the freezing of appropriations made by the 1971 legislature, which had authorized a $3.4 million expansion to Morris Hall. That appropriation was made on the premise that the building needed to be enlarged to accommodate the removal of the geography and sociology departments from the Valley Campus. But an enrollment decline at the state colleges and the University of Minnesota caused the administration of Governor Wendell R. Anderson to freeze the Morris Hall and other state building projects. The legislators were also influenced by the continuing inconveniences of the split campuses, including the need to maintain a Valley Campus library, the separation of men's physical education (Highland Campus) and women's physical education except swimming, tennis and indoor track (Valley Fieldhouse), and scheduling difficulties.[168]

The Department of Administration engaged Gary M. Andrew, M.S. Fisher and William E. Taber, consultants in planning and analysis from Boulder, Colorado, and K. Scott Foster of the Higher Education Coordinating Commission staff to study the feasibility of merging the campuses. By the time these men completed their report in January 1974, the energy crisis caused by the Arab Oil Embargo had sharply increased the cost of operating the inter-campus bus service. Thus, a campus merger was presumed to also have the beneficial effect of reducing operating expenses.[169]

The Arab Oil Embargo of the United States that began on October 17, 1973, was a reaction to American support for Israel during the brief Yom Kippur War (October 06-15, 1973). The United States sent arms to Israel after it was invaded by Egyptian and Syrian forces. This action caused the Arab nations (Algeria, Iraq, Kuwait, Libya, Qatar, Saudi Arabia and the United Arab Emirates) of the Organization of Petroleum Exporting Countries (OPEC) to discontinue shipping oil to the United States.[170]

The Arab Oil Embargo had shocking effects. Because domestic oil production had been declining before it, the United States had become increasingly dependent on OPEC imports. Within a few months after the embargo's start the price of oil quadrupled to $12 a barrel, which caused the retail price of gasoline in the United States to rise from an average of $0.39 in 1973 to $0.53 the following year. The embargo also caused shortages, especially in the non-oil producing states, which resulted in aggravatingly long waits at service stations. Aside from the price increase and shortages, the embargo caused the nation to become very pessimistic about both its short and long range energy prospects. In keeping with national policy, Minnesota's government encouraged energy conservation. This policy caused the State College Board to mandate that the various campuses launch such energy savings programs as closing classrooms over Christmas vacations in order to drastically lower thermostat settings. But Mankato State was unique because of its free inter-campus bus service.

MANKATO STATE

# daily reporter

Vol. 47, No. 67, Friday, Feb. 1, 1974

## HECC approves recommendations

# Lower campus move planned

By LuAnn Johansen
Daily Reporter News Editor

A report recommending that MSC lower campus facilities be moved to Highland Campus was accepted at yesterday's Higher Education Coordinating Commission (HECC) meeting.

The HECC staff recommended several action steps be taken. The first step is to move academic and administrative functions to Highland Campus. The goal of the implementation plan is "maximum utilization of all existing space on Highland Campus."

THE REPORT CONTINUES, "This (plan) should include consideration of dormitory space for rehabilitation to other functions and use of the Wilson Lab School space for collegiate purposes."

"New construction would be considered only for functions that are clearly absent on the Highland Campus after all reasonable efforts to utilize all space regardless of current classifications have been made," the recommendations continued.

The study was done by the HECC with the services of Dr. Gary Andrew and Associates, a Colorado consulting firm which specializes in planning and education. The Minnesota Legislature had ordered the Commissioner of Administration in Minnesota to examine the economics and academic impact of putting MSC on one campus. The commissioner then asked the HECC to conduct the study.

BASED ON ENROLLMENT projections and program participation, the report was written after a series of joint meetings with MSC executive staff members.

The types of space needed were outlined in broad general terms, Dr. Daniel Burton of Campus Planning said. All academic programs on lower campus could be fitted into the upper campus with some remodeling, and excepting certain art studios and physical education facilities, he said.

"Some problems will exist for administration that can't be housed on upper," Burton continued. "But generally it would be cheaper over a period of years to move everything so the bus service can be discontinued and maintenance, administration, and support personnel will be on one campus."

LOWER CAMPUS WILL NOT be lost to the state but will be utilized for other purposes, Burton said.

Additional buildings which may be considered in the move includes a maintenace building to house furniture, equipment and supplies, according to Burton. Some additional space will be needed on upper campus for women's and men's facilities in physical education. The Morris Hall addition may be replanned and built, he said.

"We will continue to study the dorms to see how they can be modified to

photo by Sharon Putnam

THIS AERIAL VIEW of Lower campus will no longer be campus buildings if the HECC recommendations are implemented and the campus is moved to Highland.

meet student demands and determine if Cooper and Searing would be occupied if everything else is on upper campus," Burton explained.

BURTON IS "OPTIMISTIC" about the recommendation and believes it is time to begin planning for the move which he forecasts will take 4-5 years. However, the HECC recommendations will go to the Commissioner of Administration who, unless he has objections, will submit them to the state legislature for the final decision.

Burton termed the report "very convincing" and said it is foolish to continue spending money on two campuses which could be better spent on one.

The study projects declining enrollments from 9,161 in 1974 to 7,081 in 1985. The researchers also estimated the mix of the students as far as graduates and undergraduates, on and off campus and possible distribution to departments.

MSC ACTING PRESIDENT Kent Alm attended yesterday's meeting and said MSC administrators were aware of the report and had been consulted in all phases of the study.

Though the research has been completed, only the preliminary report has been written and a finalized copy will be released in about a week.

*Daily Reporter* 1 February 1974

The first recommendation of the consultants' report submitted to the 1974 legislature was that: "Legislation should be enacted enabling the Valley Campus facilities (with the possible exception of Searing and Cooper dormitories . . .) to be phased out and the activities in these facilities systematically moved to the Highland Campus." The closing of the Valley Campus, the consultants noted, would require both new construction and remodeling on the Highland Campus. Therefore, they recommended that some of the frozen funds for the Morris Hall addition should be used to construct an addition to Highland Arena in order to consolidate men's and women's physical education. Furthermore, a maintenance building should be constructed on the Highland Campus to house such service activities as receiving, supply storage and distribution and mail service. After noting a high dormitory vacancy rate, the consultants believed that if this trend continued, the McElroy G and H wings should be converted into spaces for the college's administration and School of Business. But they advised a new administration/school of business building would be required if dormitory occupancy rebounded.[171]

Inter-campus bus service, circa 1963

While studying the potential Highland Campus space availability, the consultants evaluated the possible closing of the Wilson Campus School. But they concluded that it should be continued, because the school had gained a national reputation for its innovative program. The consultants did report that the national trend was to close laboratory schools unless they served a unique function. In Minnesota, Governor Harold LeVander in 1967 had first questioned the desirability of continuing the laboratory schools. In response, the State College Board decided that it was advisable to continue and improve the schools. However, the board members were apprehensive about continued legislative support for the schools. The Nickerson administration was well aware of these development and apparently saw Glines's innovative program as a way of saving the Wilson School. As a result of a consultant's study conducted in 1970, the State College Board ordered either the closing or phase-out of all laboratory schools except Wilson. The consolidation consultants conceded that there were some possible alternative uses for Wilson, including housing the Art Department and providing more classroom space.[172]

Although the consultants submitted recommendations in their 1974 report, they and the legislators realized that it did not include a plan to merge the campuses. Therefore, the 1974 legislature appropriated $40,000 to "the commissioner of administration for preparation of necessary plans phasing out [the] lower campus at Mankato state college [sic]." These plans, which were to be submitted to the legislature by February 15, 1975, were to include schedules and cost estimates for consolidating Mankato State on the Highland Campus.[173]

The resultant "Plan for Mankato State College Consolidation on Highland Campus (Phase II)" was prepared by Gary M. Andrew and Duane Grande, an architect who worked for the Walter Butler Company of St. Paul. While

Construction of Wigley Administration Building and connection to Morris Hall, circa 1978-1980

conducting their study, Andrew and Grande conferred with the Department of Administration, the Minnesota Higher Education Coordination Commission, the State College Board Office and Mankato State administrators including President Douglas Moore.

Andrew and Grande submitted recommendations about Wilson Campus School, new construction and remodeling of existing Highland Campus buildings. After considering alternatives, including closing Wilson, they concluded that "it should continue to operate in its present facility."[174]

The consolidation plan called for three new buildings. The first would be a 63,700-square-foot addition to Morris Hall that would house the Art Department, Computer Center and radio station, KMSU-FM. The second was a 50,875-square-foot addition to Highland Arena, and the third was a college maintenance building of 61,010 square feet that would house, among other things, physical plant shops, receiving-mailing and storage. The first two buildings were to have "mutual interconnections as well as connections with Morris and Trafton." Andrew and Grande recommended that McElroy H be remodeled for the School of Business and "units of College Administration that have low volumes of traffic."[175]

Before submitting their report to the legislature, Andrew and Grande decided to seek the approval of the State College Board's Budget & Finance Committee. After making several minor changes the committee approved the report on January 16, 1975. The committee noted that the estimated total cost of campus consolidation was $10,922,040.[176]

If the 1975 legislature had funded campus consolidation, the project's anticipated starting and completion dates would have been July 1975 and July 1978. But the cautious legislators decided that the amount derived from the sale of the Valley Campus should be ascertained before they made an appropriation. Consequently, the only action of the 1975 legislature was to authorize the commissioner of administration to sell the Valley Campus buildings. But before any sale could be finalized the commissioner was required to consult with the chairman of the Senate Finance Committee and the chairman of the House Appropriations Committee.[177]

In July 1975, the State College Board Office prepared its building proposal for the 1976 legislature. With respect to Mankato State consolidation, the board requested new construction funds for two Highland Campus buildings—$2,057,

000 for a maintenance building and $3,428,000 for a Morris Hall addition that was to house the Art Department and the Computer Center. Additionally, the board asked for $156,000 to plan an addition to Highland Arena.[178]

In acting on the request the legislature also provided a tentative plan for campus consolidation. It appropriated $3,500,000 in new consolidation funds and authorized the use of an additional $1,800,000 from "previous appropriations" (presumably the 1971 Morris Hall expansion allocation). The major new Highland Campus construction projects were to be the construction and equipping of a "general purpose building" (apparently the Morris Hall addition) and a "maintenance service building."[179]

Significantly, the 1976 legislature's action rejected the consultants' recommendation to continue operating the Wilson Campus School on the Highland Campus. Its consolidation plan specified that the Wilson building was to be remodeled for the Art Department and physical education activities. The campus school would then be relocated to the Valley Campus field house, which would be remodeled by the state at an amount of up to $756,000. The remodeling expense was to be gradually reimbursed to the state by Mankato Independent School District #77, which was expected to negotiate a lease arrangement with Mankato State University. But, the appropriations act of April 20 specified that if the school district did not complete its lease arrangement by June 1, 1976, the Valley Campus field house remodeling would not occur and the State University Board "is instructed to proceed with the consolidation of all programs on the upper campus."

On May 24 the Board of Education of Independent School District No. 77 considered the law's provisions about the possibility of relocating the Wilson School. After citing a State Department of Education opinion that a remodeled Valley Field House would not be an adequate laboratory school, the board by a vote of 6 to 1 declined to enter into a lease arrangement. Thus, the last gasp possibility of salvaging Wilson was lost.[180]

Lastly, the act provided up to $300,000 for the development "of a consolidation plan including the architectural and working drawings of the Highland Campus and the plans for a maintenance services building."

After the 1976 legislature adjourned, Mankato State worked with the Department of Administration to develop a final campus consolidation plan. The last refinements were made over the Christmas break and the details were released in early January, 1977. By way of facilities improvements, the plan specified the construction of four new buildings and the conversion of the Wilson School building into a maintenance building. The new buildings were all in the central core area of the Highland Campus: an addition to Nelson Hall that would interconnect with Armstrong Hall; an extension to the east end of Morris Hall that connected to Armstrong Hall by a second story enclosed passageway; an addition to the north side of Highland Arena that would connect by a second story hallway with the Morris Hall expansion and by a tunnel with Trafton Hall; and an Administration Building attached to the east end of the Centennial Student Union with a connecting second story enclosed passageway to Morris Hall.[181]

The new construction was to accommodate departments and offices that were to be shifted from the Valley Campus. The Nelson Hall addition was for the Art Department. The School of Business was to be moved into the Morris Hall addition. The Highland Arena addition included a gymnasium for women's

State surplus property sale advertisement for Valley Campus, *Mankato Free Press* 1 July 1977

Mankato State University after campus consolidation, circa 1980

sports and offices for physical education faculty. The three-story Administration Building was to house all central administrative offices, institutional research, business office, placement office and registrar's office.

As suggested in the first consultants' report, the Wilson School building was to be remodeled as needed to accommodate all aspects of facilities management including campus maintenance, parking, receiving, mail service and vehicle operations.

Significantly, the final consolidation plan determined that the project was underfunded by $1,600,000. This realization caused Commissioner of Administration Richard L. Brubacher to conclude in early April 1977 that the Valley Campus had to be sold before additional funding could be requested from the 1978 legislature.[182]

Brubacher had started sales preparations in August 1976, by having the Valley Campus appraised by William Cushman of Elmquist and Associates in Roseville, Minnesota. Cushman concluded that the campus was worth $6,400,000 as an educational institution, but that there was no prospect of realizing that possibility. As a non-educational facility, it was worth $1,960,000. Cushman estimated that such an option would require a three-year period during which the property would have to be maintained at state expense. Consequently, he calculated that the state would gain an approximately equal sum if the property was sold immediately for $837,000.

Following the appraisal, the Department of Administrations advertised to sell the Valley Campus as an entity or in parts in the *Wall Street Journal, Minneapolis Star, St. Paul Dispatch* and *Mankato Free Press*. The department received a bid of $701,400 for the entire campus and several bids for parcels.

But, after consulting with the House and Senate committees that dealt with higher education financing, the Department of Administration decided to reject all bids, because they required the Valley Campus to be vacated within 90 days. Consequently, bids were re-advertised with the specification that Mankato State would be permitted to use the Valley Field House, Old Main and Nichols Hall for as much as three years.[183]

The bid opening on July 28, 1977, revealed that Valley Campus Associates, a Mankato group headed by realtor Charles Atwood and developer Arthur Petrie had submitted the only offer for the entire Valley Campus. Its $701,000 bid was nearly triple the total amount proffered by bidders for seven parcels. Under these conditions, the Department of Administration had no choice other than to sell to Valley Campus Associates. The sales agreement specified that the state would retain control of the Valley Field House, Old Main and Nichols Hall for up to three years. All other facilities were to be turned over to the new owners within 90 days.[184]

After the sale of the Valley Campus, the 1978 legislature felt compelled to complete campus consolidation as soon as possible. Consequently, it appropriated an additional $3,600,000 for that purpose.[185]

By the time the final consolidation appropriation had been made the process of converting the former Wilson School had been underway for nearly a year. Soon after the Wilson School was closed at the end of the spring 1977 term, the receiving and mail services were moved in.[186]

Completing campus consolidation proceeded much faster than anticipated. At the time the Valley Campus was sold, the anticipated completion date was Fall, 1980. But the project was done in a year less. Layne Hopkins, the university's acting director of facilities management, attributed this excellent progress to the architects and Adolphson and Peterson, the general contractors. Construction of the four new buildings was started in the spring of 1978 and completed by the opening of the fall term in 1979.[187]

In terms of space, the consolidated campus was 366,331 gross square feet smaller than the combined Valley and Highland campuses. The gross square footage of the five Valley Campus buildings (Valley Field House, Old Main, Old Main Annex (former lab school), Lincoln Hall and Nichols Hall) that had been used for instruction/administration was 513,231. New Highland Campus construction provided 146,900 square feet, namely: Morris Hall Addition (28,800); Highland Arena Addition (52,200); Administration Building (49,400); Nelson Addition (13,300); and Wilson Addition (3,200 for garage and loading dock).[188]

The main saving from campus consolidation was the elimination of the $100,000 per year inter-campus bus service. The cost of the bus service had been approximately doubled because of the energy crisis precipitated by the Arab Oil Embargo. But some other savings were effective by reduced custodial services, whose staffing was based on the physical plant's area.

Although all offices and classes had been moved to the Highland Campus by the beginning of the Fall 1979 term, the university arranged to defer turning over the five Valley Campus buildings to Valley Campus Associates until November 1. Evidently, this agreement was made to give the institution ample time to remove surplus property. But the original removal plans did not include records in the Old Main vault, the former office of the presidents since 1923 and some classrooms in the former campus school. When William E. Lass, director of the Southern Minnesota Historical Center, became aware of this oversight, he obtained authorization from President Preska to survey the Valley Campus and remove appropriate records to the newly formed University Archives. This activity resulted in the retrieval of about 50 linear feet of records. Some of them dated to the institution's foundation as a normal school.

Consolidation ceremonies were delayed until May 5, 1980, to allow time for a naming committee to suggest names for new and remodeled buildings. With Truman Wood, professor of political science, presiding, the dedication program featured a talk by Preska and the recognition of Emma Wiecking, Earle J. Wigley and Gretchen Murphy in connection with naming buildings.[189]

The former Wilson Campus School was renamed to the Wiecking Center

Ron Peterson congratulates Emma Wiecking at the dedication ceremony, 1980

Earle J. Wigley, James Zwickey at dedication ceremony, 1980

Effie Conkling, 1958

in honor of the Wiecking sisters—Anna and Emma. Anna, who died on November 23, 1973, had served on Mankato State's faculty, 1917-1956. Mainly she taught elementary education, but she also served some of the time as the elementary principal of the laboratory school. Emma, who joined the faculty in 1922, was head librarian, 1924-1959.

The administration building was designated as the Wigley Administration Building. Wigley, a graduate of the Mankato State Teachers College, filled various roles during his faculty career, 1933-1970. A former varsity athlete (football, basketball and track) Wigley was a member of the inaugural group that in 1963 was inducted into Mankato State's Athletic Hall of Fame. He successively coached, served as the junior high school principal in the lab school and taught history. "Wig," as he was familiarly known, was one of the best-known faculty members. According to campus tradition he had been a confidante of presidents McElroy and Crawford.

Gretchen Murphy represented her deceased aunt Effie Conkling, the namesake of the new art gallery. Conkling, who taught art, 1926-1958, was the institution's first well-known artist and a key figure in the transition from a small teachers college to a booming state college.

The building naming committee decided that the additions to Highland Arena and Morris Hall should not be named after individuals. The new physical education facility was simply designated as Highland Arena North and the new quarters for the College of Business was deemed to be within Morris Hall.

Today, parts of the former Valley Campus stand as reminders of Mankato State's past. Old Main has been converted into senior citizen apartments named Old Main Village. This $7.8 million dollar project was completed in 1988. Although the main entrance of Old Main Village has been shifted from the west to the south side, its exterior otherwise resembles the building constructed after the 1922 fire. The 1909-1959 lab school, which became known as the Old Main Annex after the start of the Wilson Campus School, was razed after vandals burned most of it in April 1984. Since Valley Campus Associates could find no use for the Valley Field House, it was razed to facilitate the Cherry Street connection with Glenwood Avenue. The Lincoln Library is used as a Blue Earth County office building. The former Nichols Hall has been razed except for its five-story portion, which is the home of VINE Faith in Action, an organization that serves older adults and their caregivers. The exteriors of the Cooper and Searing dormitories have not been altered, but both facilities have been converted into apartment buildings named respectively Colonial Square Apartments and Cherry Ridge Apartments.[190]

One way of looking at history is to think of it as the collective memory of the living. Consequently, perceptions of the past are ever-changing. It is just a matter of time until no one who had a Valley Campus experience remains. When that day arrives, much of the appreciation and understanding derived from personal experiences will be lost. But as long as any of the buildings remain, they will, like tombstones, serve as reminders of historical yesterdays.

Campus consolidation was the most significant happening in Mankato State's history. Over the span of slightly more than two decades the institution was transplanted from a small, crowded Valley Campus with no expansion room to a Highland Campus on the city's outskirts.

# 6

# THE POST-CONSOLIDATION ERA

In the nearly four decades from campus consolidation to 2018, its sesquicentennial year, Minnesota State University, Mankato, has had three long-term presidents and two interim presidents. Margaret R. Preska, president from 1979-1992, was immediately succeeded by John B. Davis, who had an approximate six-month appointment in 1992. Richard R. Rush, president from 1992-2001, was followed by Karen A. Boubel, who served on an interim basis for a year until the start of Richard Davenport's presidency. By the sesquicentennial year, Davenport was tied with Frank D. McElroy as the fourth longest serving president in the institution's history after Charles Cooper, Clarence Crawford and Edward Searing.

The main characteristics of the post-consolidation era were enrollment resurgence, faculty enlargement and realignment, campus expansion, a heavier reliance on private funding and the inevitable aging of campus buildings that led most notably to the razing of the Gage Towers in 2013.

## Preska's Selection and Background

At its open meeting of February 8, 1979, the State University Board chose Margaret R. Preska as the permanent replacement for President Douglas Moore, who had resigned in June 1978 to accept the presidency of Redlands University in California. Edward McMahon, Moore's temporary replacement, resigned when he accepted the position of fiscal vice president at Redlands.[1]

The board's decision was difficult and quite contentious. Preska was finally chosen on the fifth ballot by a 6-4 vote after board member Arnold C. Anderson switched his vote from Brendan McDonald, the president of Kearney State College (Nebraska) and former assistant vice-president for academic affairs in the Nickerson administration, to Preska. This action broke a 5-5 stalemate that had prevailed through the first four ballots.

During their deliberations, board members emphasized the merits of both candidates. Preska was praised for being a skilled professional who had the requisite intellect, vision and experience to be an outstanding leader. McDonald's supporters emphasized his successful presidential experience and the desirability of bringing "fresh blood" to Mankato State.

With the exception of Preska, all of the long-term presidents in the institution's

Margaret R. Preska,
circa 1980

history had started as strangers. But Preska had four years of administrative experience as the vice president for academic affairs. After coming in a close second to Douglas Moore in the 1974 presidential search she was hired by the board to head academic affairs the next year. With a rather remarkable talent for remembering names and faces, she knew most of the faculty by the start of her presidency.

Preska, a native of upstate New York, completed her elementary grades in a one-room country school. She entered the State University of New York at Brockport when she was 15 and graduated summa cum laude four years later with a degree in speech/English and early childhood education. She earned her Master of Arts degree from Pennsylvania State University and her Ph.D. in Russian Studies from Claremont Graduate University of Claremont, California.[2]

Just prior to starting at Mankato State, Preska had taught history and political science at La Verne College (La Verne, California), starting in 1968. Beginning in 1972 she served as the college's academic dean. Before teaching at La Verne, Preska had taught kindergarten for nearly a decade.

## Preska's Central Administration

Early in Preska's administration, all of her central administrators held acting positions. One of her first moves was to name Andrew Een acting vice president for academic affairs. Since starting at Mankato State in 1958, he had served at various times as director of the Wilson Campus School, director of admissions, registrar and most recently as assistant vice president for academic affairs. Preska's other acting administrators were Carl Lofy, vice president for student affairs, H. Dean Trauger, vice president for resource management, Layne Hopkins, director for facilities management, Anita Stone, director of university relations and Judith Mans, executive assistant to the president.[3]

Within days after beginning her presidency, Preska announced her intention to name permanent replacements. For the year beginning with July 1979, she added four new administrators—Philip Kendall, Richard Fisher, Thomas Stark and Joseph Farnham. Then in October 1982, she re-designated Claire Faust from director of administrative affairs to vice president of administrative affairs.

Kendall, 44 years old when he was hired as the vice president for academic affairs in July, 1979, had a varied background. From 1964-1969 he taught history at the University of Maine. While thus engaged, he completed his Ph.D. at Boston University. He worked as the associate director and director for special programs for the New England Board of Higher Education, 1969-1971, before moving to Sangamon State University (Springfield, Illinois). At Sangamon, a new school, he was progressively an associate professor of history, executive assistant to the president, assistant vice president for academic affairs and, just prior to joining Mankato State, dean of public affairs.[4]

An Iowa native, Fisher was in his late thirties when he started at Mankato State University as the vice president for student affairs on October 15, 1979. For the previous six years he had been employed by Marshall University of Huntsville, West Virginia. His last position there was as vice president and dean of student affairs.[5]

Stark was chosen to be the vice president of fiscal affairs in February 1980, after having worked as the District 77 (Mankato-North Mankato) superintendent for six years. He was willing to accept a $2,000 reduction from his superintendent's salary of $40,500 in order to make a career change by shifting to higher education administration.[6]

Stark resigned effective June 30, 1983, because he had accepted the presidency of Winona State University. The search committee selected to seek his replacement had received more than 100 inquiries and 59 formal applications by the June 30 filing deadline. Within the next four weeks they reduced the field to six finalists. After on-campus interviews with the finalists, the committee recommended and Preska accepted the selection of Victor Colway, who was then directing interagency services in the New York State Office of General Services.[7]

Colway, whose Mankato State appointment started on September 15, 1983, had completed his bachelor's and master's degrees in accounting from Syracuse University. Before being employed by the State of New York, he worked for Syracuse University as its comptroller and vice president for business and finance. Colway's interest in joining Mankato State stemmed, in part, because his son

Brian had graduated from the university in 1978.

In February 1989, Colway announced the he was retiring from Minnesota State effective June 30, 1989. His retirement plans were to live in an island home in the St. Lawrence River and teach at a nearby university.[8]

Acting on a search committee recommendation, Preska on June 30, 1980, named Farnham director of community relations, a new position that entailed the administration of development, fundraising, alumni affairs, reprographics and university communications. The position was regarded as the equivalent of a vice presidency, so Farnham was a member of the president's cabinet.[9]

Farnham, who had served as Mankato State's admissions director for one year, had previously been at South Dakota State University in Brookings. While there he taught speech before serving as the assistant dean of student services.

Faust, originally from Iowa, started at Mankato State in 1962 as director of the Wilson Campus School.  Before then he had a varied experience in education. His degrees were a B. A. (1941) from Central College (Pella, Iowa), a M. Ed. (1949) from the University of South Dakota and a Ph. D. (1962) from the University of Iowa. His first experience was to teach mathematics, science and instrumental music at Mondamin, Iowa High School, 1941-44. Later he served as a principal and superintendent in Iowa public schools.[10]

Faust filled several positions at Mankato State. In 1966 he moved from the Wilson Campus School to become the coordinator of programs in school administration. He went on to chair the Department of Educational Administration before Preska, who was then the vice president for academic affairs, chose him to be the assistant vice president for academic affairs in 1976.

In 1990, Preska added to her administrative team by naming Michael Fagin associate vice president for cultural diversity. With his new title, Fagin, who had directed the Minority Groups Study Center since 1970, was to coordinate "the university-wide program affecting curriculum, recruitment of minority students and faculty, minority student services and improvement of the cultural diversity environment on campus."[11]

The five new units within cultural diversity were African American recruiter/coordinator, American Indian recruiter/coordinator, Hispanic American recruiter/coordinator, Asian American recruiter/coordinator and cultural diversity activity coordinator.

Preska's cultural affairs action was prompted by the State University Board. The board's goals for the state university system included doubling minority student enrollment within five years, increasing graduation rates for minority students and expanding the minority experience within the curriculum.

## Enrollment Resurgence during the Preska Administration

By the start of the Preska administration there were indications that Mankato State was slowly recovering from the loss of on-campus students that had plagued the late Nickerson and Moore administrations. After peaking at 12,592 for the Fall 1969 term, on-campus enrollment stood at 10,923 three years later. For the four consecutive fall terms, 1973-1976, it was below 10,000. From a low of 9,042 in 1974 it rose to 10,613 for the Fall 1979 term, which also marked the completion of campus consolidation.[12]

So, with the recent past as their guide, the governing board, university administration and faculty generally assumed that there was a good likelihood of continued modest growth. Furthermore, they thought that the university would

Michael Fagin, 1990

Minority Group Studies Center, 20 Years of Success report, 1990 function well within its new consolidated campus, even though it had 366,331 fewer square feet than the combined space of the previous split campuses. A good perspective on the significance of this loss can be gained by considering that it was far more than the equivalent of the Trafton Science Center's 280,804 square feet.[13]

But, surprisingly, new record enrollments were set during the Preska administration. Sharp annual increases led to a new record 13,103 on-campus students for the Fall 1986 term. For the Fall 1990 term, the on-campus headcount was 14,836 and the university's total, which included off-campus registrants, was 16,526.[14]

Causes of the increased enrollment included some large freshman classes, an uptick in international student registrations and more non-traditional students, who were attracted in part by such innovations as Friday College and Saturday College.

For the Fall 1981 term, Mankato State had the largest freshman enrollment in 12 years. The 2,032 new students amounted to a 9.5 percent increase from the previous fall. Significantly, they included 277 who had graduated in the top tenth of their high school graduating class, 26 valedictorians and 29 salutatorians.[15]

Mankato State had 562 international students during the 1982-1983 academic year. They represented 53 countries. China, which led with 133, was followed by Nigeria (79), Iran (71) and Saudi Arabia (33).[16]

Kuhn Lee, director of the International Student Office, advised all international students. Since he had started as the university's part-time adviser in 1969 when there were only 40 to 50 international students, Lee had witnessed sharp growth. By 1972, when he became the full-time director, there were about 200 international students.[17]

Lee inherited a modest tradition of recruiting international students. When Mankato State's international student program was conceived in 1948 there was a lone student from British Guiana (name changed to Guyana in 1966). In 1959 President Crawford reported there were 30 international students with five each from China, Greece, Iran and South Korea, two each from Japan, Trinidad and Turkey and one each from British Guinea, Columbia, Norway and Panama.

The increase of Mankato State's international students was consistent with a national trend during which many American colleges and universities operated successful international student programs. The reasons for the post-World War II boom in attracting international students were somewhat analogous to those of the great 19th century migration of Europeans to the United States. The main determinants for that great flow of immigrants are commonly identified as push, pull and means of travel. In other words, there had to be something negative about their country that caused people to leave, something positive about their new destination and a convenient way of moving. Nineteenth century migrants were motivated by such things as poor economic or political conditions in their homelands, the speed and convenience of steamship travel and the availability of cheap, fertile land in America. International students were influenced by lack of educational opportunities in their home countries, jet plane travel and the diverse offerings of American colleges and universities.

International Student Office, Kuhn Lee (seated right), 1990

## Campus Expansion during the Preska Administration

Surging enrollment was the main reason for more campus construction during the Preska administration. Three of the eight projects —Wiecking Annex, Pennington Foundation Building and Wissink Hall— were spurred by the urgent need for more classroom space. The expansion of Memorial Library resulted from a combination of continually enlarging collections and the resultant shortage of space for a rapidly increasing number of patrons. The Alumni Foundation Building enabled Mankato State to concentrate service functions such as development and alumni affairs and devote their former spaces to other activities. Construction of the Bell Tower and adjoining alumni plaza was done primarily to enhance campus appearance and serve as memorials for the institution's tradition. The two observatories were vital to the enrichment of astronomy curriculum.

Following in chronological order of construction dates are brief histories of the construction projects.

## Wiecking Annex

Surging enrollment in the 1980s created a need for more classroom space. The addition of at least seven classrooms in Wiecking Center was achieved by relocating such maintenance shops as plumbing, masonry and carpentry to the Wiecking Annex. Planned in 1982 and constructed the next year, the new steel building that cost about $200,000 was funded by the Mankato State University Foundation. This precedent-setting approach was used because no state funding was available and there was an imperative need to add classrooms.[18]

The novel funding arrangement was approved by the state legislature, which, in essence authorized the foundation to lend the amount of the construction costs to the State University Board. The foundation was reimbursed for the construction cost and interest on the advanced capital. The annex became state property when the payments were completed.

The two leading planners of the annex, Claire Faust, director of administrative services, and Thomas Stark, vice president of fiscal affairs, promoted the steel building because it cost much less than a comparably sized brick building. They estimated that a brick structure would cost at least four times more than steel.

## Pennington Foundation Building

The Pennington Foundation Building was constructed in 1986 on the Morris Hall side of Highland Arena. A one-story brick building with four classrooms of about a thousand square feet each, the structure's total cost of $285,000 was funded entirely with private funds that had been donated to the Mankato State University Foundation. As a sign of the changing times, it was the first permanent classroom building erected on any campus in the state university system that had been constructed with private funds. Repayment to the foundation was by the method that had been used with the Wiecking Annex.[19]

Pennington Foundation Building, 1986

Dedicated on December 7, 1987, the building was named for Charles Pennington, a Mankato State alumnus. Pennington, who completed his Bachelor of Education degree at Mankato State Teachers College in 1936, was a football, basketball and track star during his student years. He was inducted into the United States Army in 1942 and subsequently served in Europe, 1943-1946.

In 1952 Pennington founded the Katolight Corporation, a manufacturer and worldwide distributor of electric generators. He served as its president until 1987. While engaged in his business, Pennington was a key leader in promoting fund drives for Mankato State. By way of honors, in 1963 he was named a charter member of the institution's Athletic Hall of Fame and 16 years later he was chosen as the recipient of the Mankato State University Distinguished Alumni Award.

## Alumni Foundation Building

The Alumni Foundation Building was the third campus building constructed by the foundation. Its groundbreaking occurred on November 1, 1988 and it was completed the next year on foundation land just across Warren Street from the eastern edge of the campus. With a square footage of 17,400, the construction cost of the two-story structure was $1,272,906.[20]

Alumni Foundation Building, circa 2007

Since its completion, the Alumni Foundation Building has housed Alumni Affairs, all University Development offices including the foundation and KMSU-FM radio. Like the financial arrangements with the Wiecking Annex and Pennington Hall, the system's governing board leased the Alumni Foundation Building from the Mankato State University Foundation.

The 1989 legislature approved the lease arrangement. It stipulated: "The legislature estimates that $150,000 each year will be spent at Mankato State University for payment of a lease for the Warren Street Building. The appropriation must be discontinued upon expiration of the lease or subsequent lease. The current lease expires in 1993, but may be renegotiated to expire in 2013."[21]

## Standeford Observatory

On May 1, 1982, President Preska dedicated a new campus observatory, which had been moved recently to the southern edge of the campus. It was named the Standeford Observatory to recognize the pioneering work of Leo V. Standeford in establishing astronomy as a field of study at Mankato State.[22]

Standeford started teaching at Mankato State in 1968, the same year he completed his Ph.D. in astronomy at the University of Illinois. His Mankato State career was ended abruptly when he died on June 15, 1981, in a Rochester hospital after surgery. He was principally responsible for the addition of an astronomy minor and major to the institution's curriculum. To enhance his astronomy teaching, he supervised the construction of the school's first observatory on the roof of Trafton Center. In its new location this dome, which was three meters high, was equipped with a telescope that had been purchased with Faculty Research Grants.[23]

Standeford Observatory, 1982

## Andreas Observatory

Mankato State's astronomy facilities were improved with the completion of the Andreas Observatory in 1990. This structure was erected in a wooded area about a quarter of a mile south of the Standeford Observatory. The astronomy faculty began planning the observatory five years earlier in order to upgrade its observational techniques. In 1986 Mankato State received a $50,000 National Science Foundation Grant, which covered most of the cost of a new 20-inch computer-controlled telescope.[24]

Andreas Observatory, 1990

Mankato businessman Lowell W. Andreas and his wife Nadine donated $230,000 of the $240,000 cost for building the observatory's dome and adjacent facilities building. The dome had a diameter of 18.5 feet; the rectangular one-story building, which contained a control room, chart room, darkroom, instrument room and presentation room, measured 31 by 45 feet.

Andreas, who was destined to become one of Mankato State's principal benefactors, was born in Lisbon, Iowa, on February 22, 1922. He attended Wheaton College and the University of Iowa before serving in the U.S. Army during World War II. After the war he worked for his family's turkey feed business. In 1947 he and his brother Dwayne bought a Mankato soybean processing plant. They expanded it, changed its name to Honeymead and sold it to the Farmer's Union Grain Terminal Exchange in 1964. They used their sales gain to establish the National City Bank in Minneapolis. Then, in 1968, they invested in Archer Daniels, a Minneapolis-based food processing company. Once they controlled its management, they expanded operations. With its new name of Archer Daniels Midland, it became one of the world's largest food processing companies. Andreas retired when he was only 50. In retirement, he maintained Mankato and Florida homes, invested in race horses that competed at Canterbury Downs and generously donated to Mankato State, Mankato's Immanuel-St. Joseph Hospital and many other organizations.[25]

Dr. Margaret R. Preska and Lowell W. Andreas at the dedication for the Andreas Observatory, 1989.

## Wissink Hall

Wissink Hall, the first major post-consolidation classroom, was opened for winter term 1988 classes. It was attached to the northwestern part of Trafton Hall and extended westward to the alley that separated it from Nelson Hall.

The 1984 legislature appropriated $5.4 million to construct the building because of Mankato State's acute instructional facilities shortage. Campus planners customarily used the Bareither formula to calculate the degree to which classrooms were used. None of the other Minnesota state universities had ever reached 100 percent or full usage. But, Mankato State was overused by 20 percent.[26]

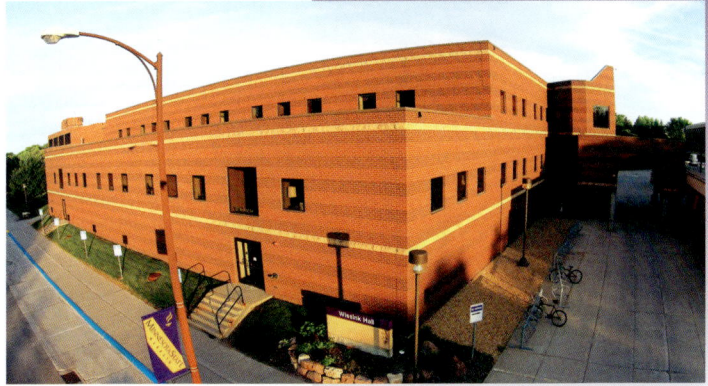

Wissink Hall, 2006

In keeping with the original plan, the state architect designed a building that was to be used by the Computer Science Department, Nursing, and the

Groundbreaking ceremony for
Wissink Hall, 1986

Gerrit M. Wissink,
1964

Melba Leichsenring,
circa 1985

Physics and Mathematics Department. Preska hosted an elaborate ground-breakingceremony on June 5, 1986. Governor Rudy Perpich, who liked to publicize state construction projects, was the principal invited dignitary. He was the first governor to participate in a campus building ceremony since Harold Stassen was featured at the dedication of the Valley Field House in 1939. Preska, Perpich and Bernie Brommer, a State University Board member who represented the board, all spoke. The assemblage of more than 200 people included Mankato Mayor Herb Mocol, State Senator Glen Taylor, State Representative Mark Piepho, Roger Nygaard of the Mankato Chamber of Commerce and John Raulma, who represented the architectural firm. Perpich and Preska led the symbolic groundbreaking in which spades of dirt were excavated from a large M that had been marked on the ground.[27]

Acting on Preska's recommendation, the State University Board approved naming the building after Gerrit M. Wissink and its third floor after Melba Leichsenring. Dedication ceremonies were held on September 20, 1988, when the board met in Mankato. The program included remarks by Preska, Richard Fisher, acting vice president for academic affairs, Rod Searle, president of the Minnesota State University Board and Robert Carothers, chancellor of the Minnesota State University System.[28]

During his 36-year Mankato State career, 1935-1971, Wissink served as a faculty member and administrator. When he was first hired to teach physics at Mankato Teachers College, Wissink had earned a master's and Ph.D. in physics from Iowa State University. After teaching physics for two decades, he was appointed dean of instruction in 1955 by President Crawford. He held that position for four years before being chosen for his eight-year stint as dean of administration.[29]

Leichsenring had served as the dean of the School of Nursing for a decade before her death on January 12, 1987. An Illinois native, Leichsenring earned her bachelor's (1951) and master's (1960) degrees in nursing from Washington University (St. Louis). In 1960 she completed her doctor of education degree in Education Curriculum and Teaching at the Teachers College of Columbia University (New York City). Just before joining Mankato State, Leichsenring had been a professor in the College of Nursing, University of Nebraska-Omaha. Her other experience included teaching at Florida State University and the St. Louis State Hospital.

The building's three floors housed separate functions. The lowest floor featured a 12,000-square-foot computer lab that could accommodate up to 400 users. The second floor had 50 offices for computer science, mathematics and astronomy faculty members and eight classrooms. The three largest classrooms had respectively 117, 84 and 45 seats. The other five each had a capacity of 35. The School of Nursing on the top floor included faculty offices, a simulated hospital ward, a viewing room and a student testing area.[30]

## Memorial Library Remodeling and Expansion

Rapidly increasing enrollment in the early Preska administration caused a shortage of library space as well as classroom space. Memorial Library, which was still a relatively new building, experienced heavier patron use and collection expansion simultaneously. During the 1982-83 academic year, Library Dean Dale Carrison observed that the library was losing about 100 seats a year because of the continuing collection additions. At that rate, he concluded, the library would not have any patron seats left by 1990.[31]

Memorial Library remodeling and expansion, 1991

The looming library crisis caused the Preska administration to propose constructing a library addition.  In the fall of 1982, Mankato State asked the State University Board to request funding for an addition to the legislature. Interestingly, the proposed expansion would have a connection to the Centennial Student Union. Claire Faust, vice president for administrative affairs, cautioned that the expansion was not likely to be funded, because new requests were routinely delayed. Faust was correct. The legislature decided to hold off on library expansion until at least 1985.[32]

But the legislature did not act on the library matter until 1987 when it appropriated planning funds of $623,200. The remodeling and expansion plans were developed by Mankato State in consultation with the state architect and endorsed by the State University Board before being submitted to the 1989 legislature. In its appropriations bill, which was signed by Governor Rudy Perpich on May 30, the legislature appropriated $11,200,000 to "remodel and construct an addition to Memorial Library."[33]

This funding was made, in part, because of a concerted lobbying effort by Mankato State students and alumni. Tim Wierzbicki, former Mankato State Student Senate President who was then serving as State University System Student Association President, reported that the last minute phone campaign that he organized was responsible for gaining legislative support.[34]

Lester Gienart, assistant vice president for facilities planning, noted that the appropriation would permit some remodeling of the original 166,000-square-foot building and enable an 80,000-square-foot addition. He anticipated that the remodeled and enlarged building would be patron-ready by the fall of 1991.

The first phase of remodeling, which was started during the one-week break between the 1990 winter and spring terms, was to remove asbestos, which was used to insulate the study carrels on the library's perimeter. This project, which lasted through the spring term, resulted in the removal of 28 carrels from the basement, 89 from the second floor and 77 from the third floor. While they had proven to be useful to researchers and individuals who wanted a quiet, private study space, many of the carrels that were available for public use had been marred by graffiti and vandalized. This unfortunate experience helped discourage any sentiment to replace the old carrels. Instead, the library's planners opted to construct several new perimeter rooms that

Around the World on the 44th Parallel by Joyce Kozloff, ceramic tile artwork in Memorial Library, circa 1995

could be reserved for study groups and meetings. Other significant remodeling included walling off the library's front and rear entrances, which were relocated to the new addition, and constructing a new conference room at the former site of the second floor circulation desk.[35]

Constructing the west side addition, which got underway in 1990, involved three contractors, who followed the plans developed by the architectural firm of Armstrong, Torseth, Skold and Rydeen, Inc. of Minneapolis. The Knutson Construction Company of Minneapolis was the general contractor. Russ Nelson Electric Company of Ellendale did the electrical work and Schwickert Co. of Mankato did the plumbing and mechanical systems.[36]

The 80,184-square-foot addition, which accounted for nearly a third of the library's total space, was opened on December 6, 1992. But Thomas Peischl, library dean, anticipated it would take several months to have it completely furnished. Some remodeling on the first and second floors of the original library delayed the dedication of the enlarged/remodeled building until November 5, 1992. The dedication program consisted of remarks by Peischl, Julie Reinert, MSSA/Senate president, Myrna Chamberlain, library paraprofessionals, Marilyn J. Lass, library faculty, Richard Crofts, vice president for academic affairs and Richard R. Rush, president.

The cost of the remodeling and expansion amounted to $11.3 million, which included $8.3 million for construction, $2.15 million for architect's fees, testing, inspection and asbestos abatement and $850,000 for furnishings. The total cost was about four times more than that of the original Memorial Library. Much of this sharp increase was caused by the impact of inflation over the intervening 25-year period, which featured four years of ruinous double digit inflation that peaked at 13.5 percent in 1980.[37]

### The Ostrander-Student Memorial Bell Tower

The bell tower, which was completed in 1989, developed out of a student desire to re-capture some of institution's heritage that had been lost with the sale and abandonment of the Valley Campus and its iconic Old Main Building. Originally conceived by the Student Senate, the bell tower was not only intended to improve campus esthetics but was also to symbolize the institution's past, present and future by integrating three building materials—Kasota stone, bricks and glass.[38]

The bell tower idea took a giant step toward reality in the spring of 1987 when alumnus Lloyd B. Ostrander of Chula Vista, California, donated $138,000, or slightly more than half of its estimated $270,000 construction cost. At that time the gift was one of the largest ever received by Mankato State.

Ostrander, an Albert Lea native, completed the two-year program from Mankato State Teachers College in 1927. During his student days he was a center on the football team and a class president. He worked as a depression-era teacher before becoming the director of swimming

Students walking by Ostrander-Student Memorial Bell Tower, 2011 training for all armed forces in the Pacific Theater during World War II. Because of his role in this project, through which an estimated quarter million servicemen were taught to swim, Ostrander was awarded the Medal of Freedom by President Franklin D. Roosevelt. Subsequently, he worked as a United Services Organization (USO) supervisor in the Pacific. After the war, he served as the United Nation's administrator of Tinian Island, located near Saipan. The work that he and his wife completed there won them a Rockefeller Public Service Award. Ostrander's main career was developing apartment houses in California.

Alumni Arch and Plaza, 2013

Construction on the 81-feet-high tower, which was to feature a clock on all four sides did not get underway until September, 1988—a year and a half after the Ostrander gift. By then additional funding has been raised from the Student Services Fund and some other private donations. But, construction was further delayed when the low bid of $285,000 from Kratochivil Construction of New Prague exceeded the available funds. However, the university administration was able to get construction started by re-negotiating a reduced price with Kratochivil and postponing some of the electrical work. Although the tower was completed in 1989, its bells were not installed until shortly before 1990 Homecoming. They were funded by Mildred Ostrander, the widow of Lloyd, who died on September 29, 1987.[39]

In 1991 the Alumni Association launched what it called "the final completion stage" of the tower. This phase entailed constructing a brick patio, walls, benches and installing arches that had been retrieved from the ruins of the former Valley Campus lab school. The most prominent Kasota stone arch had been over the drive-through between Old Main and the lab school. The Alumni Association funded the patio and its accoutrements by selling alumni bricks. The bricks, which could be inscribed with the name of an alum, the graduation year and more, cost from $100 to $500 depending on the number of lines.[40]

## Academic Changes

The main academic changes during the Preska administration were the addition of engineering programs and the restoration of the F grade. Other important developments were the continuing popularity of the construction management program in the Industrial and Technical Studies Department, the Master of Fine Arts program, the major in athletic training and increased growth in computer science and business. The construction management program originated as a cooperative effort of Mankato State and the Associated General Contractors of Minnesota. It provided training in all aspects of construction, including surveying and estimating.[41]

Student studying in dorm room, 1990

Electrical engineering student, 1986

## Engineering Programs

The aim of offering engineering, which was first extensively promoted during the University of Southern Minnesota campaign, was finally realized in 1983 when the legislature funded electrical engineering programs for Mankato State and St. Cloud State. Both institutions were granted $50,000 for each year of the biennium, but the allocated funds had to be matched by non-state funding. If the chairmen of the Senate Finance Committee and the House Appropriations Committee approved, the matches could be donated equipment or supplies.[42]

Dr. George O'Clock, professor of physics and electronic engineering technology, estimated that 30 students who had completed the pre-engineering program could finish the new four-year degree program in two years. Thereafter he anticipated 60 graduates annually.

In early September 1987, Robert Herickhoff, dean of Mankato State's School of Physics, Engineering and Technology, announced that the program had been accredited by the Engineering Accreditation Commission of the American Board for Engineering and Technology. The commission made its decision after a study and campus visit. St. Cloud State's electrical engineering program was also accredited by the commission. Thus, the two state universities joined the University of Minnesota as the state's only institutions with an accredited electrical engineering program.[43]

While the accreditation process for electrical engineering was being conducted, the State University Board approved Mankato State's addition of a bachelor of science degree in mechanical engineering. This program was the state's second. The University of Minnesota was the only other institution that offered mechanical engineering. Herickhoff explained that the addition of the degree would lead to more career choices and an increased supply of mechanical engineers in Minnesota. Mechanical engineers, he thought, were especially important in designing new technology for a variety of industries including food processing and vehicle assembly.[44]

## Restoration of the F Grade

The restoration of the F grade was the most significant change in academic policy during the Preska administration. It was initiated by the 1987-1988 Undergraduate Curriculum Committee, whose faculty representatives were David Abel (Business), Joanne Decker (Health and Physical Education), Winston Grundmeier (Natural Sciences, Mathematics and Home Economics), Wayne Harris (Social and Behavioral Sciences), William E. Lass (Arts and Humanities), Sandra Mitchell (Library) and Edgar Twedt (Education). The committee held monthly sub-meet-and-confer sessions with Philip Kendall, vice president for academic affairs.

When the subject of restoring the F was first broached, Kendall responded that faculty preference was the most important determinant to him. Thus, in the ensuing discussions the committee and Kendall agreed to have the Institutional Research Office in consultation with a Curriculum Committee sub-committee prepare and circulate a preference questionnaire. About four-fifths of the respondents favored restoring the F grade. With this result, the committee at its meeting of April 5, 1988, by a 6 to 1 vote recommended the F restoration. Because of various procedural matters, including consideration at higher meet and confer deliberations, the change first appeared in the university's undergraduate catalog for 1990-1991.[45]

The results of the faculty survey seemed to be surprising to Kendall, who was a relative newcomer to the F grade matter. But, they were hardly surprising to those familiar with faculty concerns and especially to the veteran faculty members who remembered the circumstances of 1971 when the F grade was abolished for undergraduates.

In March 1971, the Nickerson administration, with Ross Alm, director of admissions and brother of Kent Alm, acting as its chief spokesman, strongly supported abolishing the F grade. This endorsement possibly influenced some members of the Undergraduate Curriculum Committee and the Faculty Senate, which also supported the change. However, Roy B. Moore, chairman of the committee, reported that its members approved the change by about the same proportion as a faculty poll, which showed 228 favored it and 149 opposed it.[46]

When the Faculty Senate considered replacing the F grade with the NC (no credit) at its March 10 meeting, Ross Alm explained the rationale for the suggested change. With respect to the F grade, he was quoted as having said: "It does nothing for the student, but something to him. Labeling the student a failure serves no purpose. Therefore, the NC will enable him to make up the course and not be penalized." Some Senate and gallery opponents responded that the change would result in lowering the university's standards. But, in responding obliquely to that contention, Alm insisted that individual instructors could still establish course standards and require their students to meet them. Near the end of a rather contentious meeting, the Faculty Senate by a 14 to 8 vote approved replacing the F for only undergraduate courses with the NC, which would not be calculated in the determination of individual grade point averages (GPAs).

Nickerson approved the change the day after the Faculty Senate's vote. The new NC policy was first published in the college's 1972-1973 catalog. [47]

The recommendation by the Undergraduate Curriculum Committee to reinstate the F grade was an indication of how Mankato State had changed over the course of 17 years. By 1987 all the major components of students, faculty and administration were much more conservative and hence much more likely to regard the F grade as something a student earned, rather than a punishment meted out by an instructor. The overall tendency to be more conservative was a natural reaction to the experimental impulses of the antiwar years. Furthermore, the advent of collective bargaining made the faculty more powerful in academic policy matters. Lastly, faculty thinking had evolved to regarding the NC as a failed policy rather than a noble venture. Generally, the faculty had become increasingly resentful of a system that had the practical effect of making the D a lower grade than the NC, which was assigned to those who earned the equivalent of an F.

Ostensibly, a student who earned an NC had a grade below a D. But, the D was actually a worst grade than the NC. Suppose, for example, that two students had enrolled for a term load of five three-credit courses and that both had earned three hours of A (12 honor points), six hours of B (18 honor points), three hours of C (six honor points), but one had three hours of D (three honor points) and the other three hours of NC. Because the NC did not

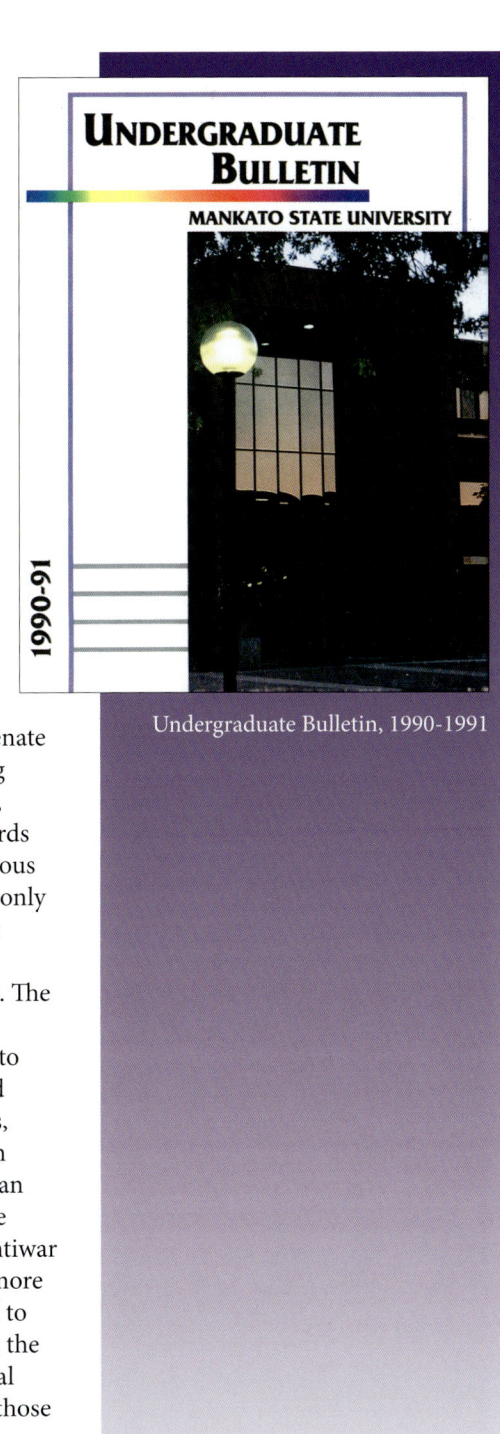

Undergraduate Bulletin, 1990-1991

count in the GPA calculation, the one with the three hours of NC would have a 3.0 GPA, but the D earner would have a 2.6 GPA.

Many students who subsequently applied for admission to programs at other institutions that required minimum GPAs realized that a NC would have been a better grade than a D. Therefore, some of them requested faculty members to change their D to an NC, which, outwardly was a request for a lower grade. The institutional policy on grade changes was clear. They were permitted only in instances of recording errors. Consequently, those who requested a change from a D to an NC as a favor were actually asking faculty members to violate a university policy. The requests for NCs in lieu of Ds seemed to be the faculty's commonest complaint about the no F system, in which, somehow, the lowest possible grade was less detrimental to GPA calculations than the one immediately above it.

## Return to the North Central Conference

The Preska administration's most significant change in Mankato State's intercollegiate athletics program was to quit the Northern Intercollegiate Conference and return to the North Central Conference. The move was prompted by the Northern Intercollegiate Conference's decision to permit all member institutions to grant no more than 24 tuition and fee scholarships in football and nine in basketball. This policy, which was to become effective with the Fall 1981 term, would have reduced Mankato State's scholarship support by nearly two-thirds and barred any scholarships other than football and basketball.[48]

The move was supported by the State University Board as well as student and faculty constituencies and the broader community. Mankato State's athletic department successfully raised private scholarship donations after its representatives made presentations to groups in Mankato as well such area communities as New Ulm, Owatonna, Fairmont, Windom and Worthington.

1987 North Central Conference Football Champions.
Image courtesy of Athletic Communications

At their meeting of April 13-14, 1981, North Central re-admitted Mankato State to the conference, whose other members were then the University of North Dakota, North Dakota State University, the University of South Dakota, South Dakota State University, Augustana College (Sioux Falls, South Dakota), Morningside College (Sioux City, Iowa), the University of Nebraska-Omaha and the University of Northern Colorado (Greeley). The move was to be effective for all sports for the Fall 1981 term, except football in 1983 and basketball in 1983-1984.[49]

Halftime at a football game, 1990

## Major Trends During the Preska Administration

Mankato State's major trends during the Preska administration mirrored those of the other six state universities. New programs and greater diversity were emphasized throughout the system.

A 1988 report on the Minnesota State University System showed major changes in the last decade with respect to enrollment, state funding, nature of faculty, choice of majors and classroom space.

The total number (headcount) of students increased 40 percent from 37,600 to 52,000. By way of comparison, enrollment at the state's private and community colleges grew respectively by 22 percent and 12 percent. But, because part-time attendance had become more common, the state universities gained only 18 percent in fulltime equivalent students. The number of women students rose from 51 percent to 55 percent during the 10 years.[50]

Overall funding increased by 14 percent, but tuition increases were the main reason. State support in terms of inflation adjusted dollars was $150 less per student.

Faculty numbers, which rose from 1,779 to 1,865, did not keep pace with enrollment increases. This limited new hiring led to older, more experienced faculties with fewer assistant professors and more associate and full professors.

There had been a sharp shift in student majors. The greatest gain was in business, with a 30 percent increase. Other significant gainers were science, technology, nursing and engineering, which increased from 15 to 20 percent. The sharpest loss was 29 percent in education majors.

The modest increase of only five percent in instructional space fell far short of providing for the added enrollment. Most of this gain was achieved through remodeling.

A 1991 Mankato State report provided more details about funding trends. Preska reported that for eight of the previous 11 years, state support was less than 50 percent of the university's total budget. For 1990 it was only 42.98 percent. Income from tuition and fees, at 28.3 percent, ranked next. It was followed by grants (12.75 percent); auxiliary services such as residence halls, student union, bookstore administration, student health services, campus computer store, parking operations, athletic camps & leagues, alumni events, and conference and workshop fees, (12.21 percent); sales and services of educational activities such as intercollegiate athletics ticket sales and sponsorships, music and theatre programs ticket sales, and flight training, dental hygiene clinic, and study abroad and field trip fees, (1.57 percent); and other sources, including surplus state property sales, Children's House child care fees, vending commissions, Service Center Revenue from supply room, campus printing and photocopying, postal services and vehicle motor pool, KMSU radio contracts and interest income (2.19. percent).[51]

## Administrative Problems in the Late Preska Administration

Preska's presidency ended on a contentious note. Reduced state funding and faculty dissatisfaction with the administration's response detrimentally affected faculty morale, according to campus IFO leadership. An IFO survey conducted in the summer of 1990 indicated 70 percent of of Mankato State's faculty had low morale. This result prompted the Mankato IFO, led by President Edgar Twedt, to conduct a survey about the performances of Preska, Richard Crofts, vice president of academic affairs,[52] Richard Fisher, vice president of student affairs, Joseph Metro, vice president of university operations, Joseph Farnham, vice president of university advancement, and Dean Trauger, vice president of fiscal affairs.[53]

The survey, which was sent to 622 IFO members, had a 58 percent return rate. It revealed that 58 percent of the respondents disapproved of Preska's performance. Other reported disapproval ratings were 49 percent for Crofts, 44 percent for Fisher and 60 percent for Farnham. The *Reporter*, which had the disapproval percentages on all six administrators, devised a "report card" with an estimated letter grade for each of them. That reckoning produced a D for Preska, C- for Crofts and Fisher, a B for Metro, a C+ for Trauger and an F for Farnham. Other than Preska, Farnham was the most visible administrator. Since his duties included directing university communications, he was thrust into the role of being the bearer of bad news about budget cuts and program reductions.

The Mankato IFO released the survey results on Tuesday, May 28, 1991. Twedt reported that some IFO members had shown them to Preska three days earlier and had given her an opportunity to respond before they went public. Rather than react promptly, Preska chose to ask for a formal meet and confer five days hence. This did not satisfy the IFO, which hurried to publicize the survey.

The issuance of the survey results stirred IFO passions. The very next day the IFO held a special meeting. During a sometimes animated discussion, the faculty members considered various actions including arranging discussions with Preska, doing nothing or casting a no-confidence vote. They decided to go the no-confidence route. By a vote of 76 to 40 they approved a no-confidence in Preska motion.

Twedt explained that "a vote of no-confidence means that the faculty does not trust her in terms of her ability to perform her duties. We don't have confidence that the president can continue as she has." But, he added that the vote was only symbolic, because "they [the university administration and the State University Board] can ignore everything we [the IFO] do. It carries whatever moral strength the faculty may have, it states that the ball is now in the court of the administration."

In explaining the vote to Greg Abbott, a *Free Press* reporter, Twedt attributed it to Preska's failure to consult with the faculty on such matters as university policies and hiring of administrators. But, he also insisted that the no-confidence vote was "conditional," because the IFO was willing to negotiate with Preska to resolve their differences. Twedt said the IFO would present its concerns to Preska and the State University Board by June 30 and give them until September 11 "to give a written, concrete response to those concerns." If the IFO membership was satisfied that Preska and the board sincerely wanted to address its concerns, it could then consider rescinding its no-confidence vote.[54]

Preska's problems were compounded when the *Reporter* editorialized that she should resign. Michael Fibison, the student paper's editor, complained that students had their own complaints about internal bickering and ineffective administration.[55]

Reaction from the State University Board to the IFO action was swift and critical. Board president Rodney Searle of Waseca, a former speaker of the Minnesota House of Representatives and a Mankato State alum, sharply criticized the IFO for going public rather than working with Preska to resolve differences through formal meet and confer sessions. Robert Carothers, chancellor of the state university system, agreed with Searle, but did acknowledge that Mankato State had serious problems that had to be resolved.[56]

In her reaction, Preska suggested that a legislatively imposed budgetary shortfall that necessitated programmatic reductions was the real reason for low faculty morale and the no-confidence vote. Furthermore, she regretted that the IFO chose not to negotiate further with her rather than cast the no-confidence measure.[57]

But, significantly, Preska acknowledged that there was a schism between the faculty and her administration and she declared "that schism must be closed." She proposed to do this by requesting the State University Board to appoint a "special panel" of "distinguished educators" to study her rift with the IFO.[58]

In the fall of 1991, the board complied with Preska's request by naming a three-person panel to study administration-faculty relations at Mankato State. That panel, which was publicly identified as "a Florida consultant to colleges and universities, a retired Massachusetts university president and a Massachusetts university faculty union president" completed its study and report by early December. The critical report, which was publicly released on December 13, acknowledged that Mankato State had serious problems that needed to be addressed. Its specific findings and recommendations were that Mankato State's planning should be "'bottom up, not top down,'" that there "may be a need to redefine the expectations and performance objective of the university's president" and that the "five vice presidents are not perceived as a strongly forged, positive team.'"[59]

The *Reporter* 30 May 1991

Once the State University Board had the panel's report, it negotiated with Preska. The week before the report was made public, Preska announced that she was retiring from her position effective February 1, 1992. Simultaneously, Terrence MacTaggart, chancellor of the state university system, announced that after a year-long sabbatical leave, Preska would serve the system as a "distinguished university professor." In that role she would be assigned to teach and promote scholarship about Russian studies, the area in which she had completed her doctoral degree.[60]

## Interim President John B. Davis

By the time the State University Board released the panel's report, its members had already decided to replace Preska with an interim president who was to have a six-month term. At their January 29 meeting they named 70-year-old John B. Davis as interim president. He was to begin his Mankato State duties on February 10 and serve until a permanent replacement was hired after a nationwide search.[61]

Well before he accepted the Mankato State position, Davis had established a reputation as an administrative rescuer. With a bachelor's degree in history from the University of New Hampshire and both his master's and doctorate in education from Harvard University, Davis had worked as the superintendent of the Minneapolis Public Schools, 1967-1975. As president of Macalester College, 1975-1984, he was credited with solving its financial problems. His reputation as a skillful financial manager was further enhanced by his service as executive director of the Children's Theatre Company and School (Minneapolis), 1984-1986, and interim president of the Minneapolis College of Art and Design, 1989-1990.

Davis's appointment was strongly endorsed by The *Free Press*, which opined: "The only negative thing to say about Mankato State University's interim president is that he won't be in the running as permanent president." The writer conjectured that Davis would get the institution "headed in the right direction," which would enable his permanent successor to deal with its problems.[62]

Davis subsequently served about six and half months while the search committee for a permanent president completed its process with the hiring of Richard R. Rush, who was to start September 1. When Davis hosted his good-bye reception on August 19, he was praised for successfully carrying out his caretaker role. Richard Crofts, vice president for academic affairs, said: "We're all very, very grateful . . . I think he brought us a great deal of stability. He calmed the anxieties as we were searching for a new president." Edgar Twedt, who had served as the president of Mankato State's IFO during the late Preska administration before becoming statewide IFO president, stated: "I have a great deal of respect for him, personally and professionally . . . I think the university is richer for having him here."[63]

## The Hiring of President Richard R. Rush

On June 2, 1992, the State University Board, after the search committee had reduced the field of applicants to five finalists, unanimously chose Richard R. Rush as the new president of Mankato State University.[64]

Rush, whose undergraduate education concentrated on English, philosophy and the Classics, earned a bachelor's degree from Gonzaga University of Spokane, Washington. He completed both his M.A. and Ph.D. degrees in English literature at the University of California, Los Angeles.

The board was particularly impressed by Rush's role in converting San Diego State's North County Branch into the University of California, San Marcos. Before starting his administrative career in 1984, Rush was an associate professor of English at San Diego State University. Rush served for five years as dean of the North County Branch. After the University of California, San Marcos was officially started in 1989, he was its executive vice president and professor of English literature until he accepted his Mankato State post.

## Rush Administration

Rush, who started at Mankato State on September 1, 1992, worked with holdover central administrators for several months. Then, in January 1993, he reorganized his administrative team. Richard Crofts, vice president for academic affairs, was to retain his position until July, when he was to be assigned an unspecified position in the university. Joseph Farnham, vice president for university relations, was re-assigned to the task of preparing a long-term marketing plan for the institution. He was immediately replaced by Paul Hustoles, the chairman of the Theatre Arts Department, who began his duties as interim vice president for university relations on February 1, 1993. Richard Fisher, vice president for student affairs, was to stay on the university's payroll until the end of the 1993-94 academic year, because he had previously been granted a sabbatical for that time.[65]

## New Administrators in the Rush Administration

After national searches, Mankato State hired two new vice presidents who started in the fall of 1993: Lewis Jones, the vice president for academic affairs, and Margaret Healy, the vice present for student affairs. The rest of Rush's administrative team then consisted of Joe Metro, vice president for university operations, Dean Trauger, vice president for fiscal affairs, Hustoles, interim vice president for university advancement and Kathy Trauger, assistant to the president.[66]

Jones had earned an M.A. in American History and African-American History from North Carolina Central University and a Ph.D. in Education Policy Analysis and Higher Education Administration from the University of Iowa. He had prior administrative experience at Central Connecticut State University, the University of Cincinnati, the University of California, Santa Barbara and the College of Wooster. [67]

Healy, who earned a B.S. in physical education from St. Cloud State in 1969, completed her M.A. in college union management, student personnel and counseling from the University of Iowa in 1971. In 1983 she earned her Ph.D. in research and evaluation and professional studies in education from Iowa State University. Her experience included student affairs positions at Rhode Island College and Fontbonne College (St. Louis).[68]

The affable Jones, who held get-acquainted meetings with numerous academic departments, had an uneventful first year. But his second and last one was another matter.

By the time Jones started at Mankato State, the State University System and its individual institutions had about a decade-long tradition of exhorting faculty members to become more productive researchers and scholars. But other than expanding a faculty research fund for each campus from which individuals could apply for small grants, the universities seemed to mostly be paying lip service to research and scholarship. Faculties quickly perceived that with respect to such things as the granting of tenure and promotion, there seemed to be no significant distinction between faculty who authored books and scholarly articles and those who did not.

Consequently, many faculty members were shocked when Jones refused to recommend tenure or promotion to some faculty in the spring of 1994 on the grounds that they had not done adequate research and writing. Some of the aggrieved faculty insisted that Jones should have taken into account such extenuating circumstances as their departmental administrative duties that did

Richard R. Rush,
circa 1992

Lewis Jones,
1993

Margaret Healy,
circa 1993

Karen A. Boubel,
circa 2002

not allow any time for scholarship. Furthermore, it appeared that Jones was initiating unprecedented standards.[69]

During the discontent some of those who complained about Jones' action wondered if he actually had the scholarly record he had claimed on his application vita. Obtaining his vita was easy, because some faculty members who had served on the search committee had retained copies. After verifying that some of Jones' claims were false, the affected faculty members complained to President Rush that Jones was holding them to a standard that he had not met himself.

The three principal charges against Jones were that a book he had listed in the early 1980s as being "in press" had not been published, that a journal article he listed as "published" had only been submitted and that he falsely claimed to be an editorial advisor for another journal from 1985 to the present, when, in fact, the periodical had ceased publication in 1988. Jones tried to dismiss these charges as well as some typos as "nit-picking," but Rush felt obliged to hire a private investigator to determine the accuracy of Jones' claims. Apparently, the investigator, who spent more than a week on campus, confirmed that Jones' resume, as charged, contained errors.

On July 20, 1995, *The Free Press* reported that "Jones to Leave MSU." Technically, his special one-year assignment to Minnesota State Colleges and Universities (MnSCU), the recently created governing board for the state's public universities (other than the University of Minnesota), community colleges and technical colleges, was not a dismissal. Rather, Rush characterized it as a negotiation to which all parties, including Jones, agreed. So, in other words, Jones, when faced with what seemed to be likely dismissal from Mankato State, was retained within the system for one year. This maneuver was as much for the benefit of the university and the governing board as Jones, because it satisfied the legal requirements of timely notice.

After completing his MnSCU assignment in 1996, Jones served as an administrator at several different colleges—including his July 2015 appointment as chief academic officer and academic dean of Goddard College (Plainfield, Vermont). His brief biography on the Goddard website does not mention his Mankato State administrative position. Rather it states: "As a college professor, he taught philosophy of education, policy and history, as well as urban planning and development, at Mankato State University, Cal State San Bernardino, Central Connecticut State University at New Britain and the University of Louisville."[70]

After Jones' departure, Rush selected Duane Orr, the dean of the College of Education, to serve as interim vice president for academic affairs from September 1995 to the end of the academic year...[71]

During Orr's brief term, a search committee chaired by Jane F. Earley, dean of the College of Arts and Humanities, conducted a national search for an academic vice president. By late April 1996, Earley announced that the committee had winnowed the numerous applicants to six finalists—three women and three men. The finalists, all of whom were to be invited for on-campus interviews, did not include anyone currently employed by Mankato State.

On May 17, Rush announced the appointment of Dr. Karen A. Boubel, who was scheduled to assume her new position in July. Boubel, whose most recent position was Dean of the College of Arts and Communications, University of Wisconsin-Whitewater, had impressive credentials. She earned her bachelor's degree from the University of Wisconsin-Superior and her

Master of Music and Ph.D. in Music Theory from the University of Wisconsin-Madison. After teaching at UW-Whitewater for seven years, she was named Associate Dean, College of the Arts in 1985. She served in that position for four years until she was named Dean of the College of Arts and Humanities.[72]

## New Campus Construction During the Rush Administration

Three major construction projects were completed during the Rush administration. Phase III of the Centennial Student Union was opened in 1999. Both the Andreas Theatre, which is connected to the Performing Arts Center for the Performing Arts, and the Taylor Center, a major addition to the athletics/physical education complex, were finished in 2000.

Additionally, Myers Field House was razed and construction of its replacement was commenced and significant additions were made to the utilities plant.

## Centennial Student Union Phase III

The expansion of the student union beyond Phase II was first proposed in 1987 by the Mankato State Student Association (MSSA), the Centennial Student Union Board and union director James Zwickey. Their $12 million proposal called for building expansion, the construction of a new south entrance and the erection of a glass atrium over the courtyard. This ambitious project was rejected and in 1989 a $4 million expansion on the west end of Phase II was approved. But such developments as the transition from the Preska to the Rush administration and the switch of state university governance from the State University Board to Minnesota State Colleges and Universities (MnSCU) delayed ground breaking until May 14, 1998.[73]

Phase III of the Centennial Student Union is home to many student service offices including the LGBT Center (2012).

Met Com, the expansion's general contractor, proceeded rapidly. The exterior work was completed in 1998 and by February 1999, room walls were being constructed. In late June Director of Student Life Henry Morris reported that the project, which was running 45 to 60 days ahead of schedule, would be completed by the opening of the Fall Semester.[74]

Phase III, which added about 30,000 square feet at a final cost of $5 million, increased the Centennial Student Union's total space to slightly more than 200,000 square feet. Even before the expansion, Mankato State had the largest student union building in the state university system. But the addition of Phase III made it about 35,000 square feet larger than the next largest, at St. Cloud State. Various clubs and organizations began moving into Phase III in August 1999. The addition was officially opened at a Ribbon-cutting ceremony on November 12, 1999.

Entrance to Andreas Theatre,
circa 2001

*Talley's Folly* performance in Andreas
Theatre, 2018. Image courtesy of the
Department of Theatre and Dance.

## Andreas Theatre

In December 1995 Lowell Andreas and his wife Nadine donated $1.4 million to Mankato State to help fund the construction of a new on-campus theatre. At that time, it was the largest donation ever received by the university. Since the estimated cost of the theatre was $2.8 million, the donors stipulated that before ground could be broken the institution would have to match their grant by private donations. Rush immediately announced that he was confident the matching amount could be raised within two and a half years. But, he also revealed that the construction would require legislative approval, because state law stipulated that it was necessary in order to build any privately funded structure on a college campus. On May 20, 1997, Governor Arnie H. Carlson signed an act that specified: "The board of trustees of the Minnesota State Colleges and Universities may accept money from the Mankato State University Foundation to construct a black box theater on the Mankato State University campus. The board shall supervise the construction as provided in Minnesota Statutes, section 136F.64."[75]

Paul J. Hustoles, chairman of the Theatre Arts Department, said the new "black box" theatre would fill a long-felt need. It would be used primarily for student directed plays, which would not attract as many spectators as the productions staged in the Ted Paul Theatre. Hustoles suggested that plays in the Andreas Theatre would be Mankato State's version of off-Broadway. Black box theatres, named after the color of their walls, facilitated experimentation with avant-garde productions. Prior to the Andreas Theatre, the Theatre Arts Department had operated a black box theatre in several Mankato venues including the old Carnegie Art Center on South Broad Street and the Belle Mar Mall on the east side of town. In stressing the importance of concentrating all university theatre productions on campus, Hustoles said he was not aware of any other college or university that did not have its black box theater on campus. The Andreases were apparently influenced to make their donation because Mankato State's theatre department, which featured 14 productions that drew 40,000 spectators annually, was one of the nation's most successful.

By June 3, 1998, when ceremonial ground-breaking ceremonies were held for the Andreas Theatre, hundreds of private donors had matched the Andreas gift. Much of this support came from the nearly 200 "Andreas Angels," who had each donated at least $500.[76]

Because of cost overruns amounting to $700,000, the grand opening of the Andreas Theatre was delayed until May 2000. The Andreases contributed another $300,000 and the remainder was raised through private donations. The theatre's opening coincided with the 50th anniversary of Theodore Paul's first season as the leader of theatre arts at the Mankato State Teachers College. Paul, who had developed the institution's outstanding theatre tradition, returned to campus to direct Angel Street, the last play he had directed before his retirement in December 1980.[77]

The Andreas Theatre has an area of 19,469 square feet. In addition to its 200-seat, 60-by-70 foot theatre, it houses two studios (dance and movement and scenic and costume design), dressing rooms, graduate assistant offices, a concession area and a green room (i. e. waiting room and lounge for performers).[78]

## Taylor Center

The Taylor Center was an outgrowth of Campaign MSU, a drive to raise $35 million in private donations to fund improvements to the university's physical facilities and academic programs. In October 1997, businessman and alum Glen Taylor, after extensive consultation with President Rush, decided to donate $8 million for a new academic and recreation building that would also be the new home for the university's admissions office.[79]

Subsequently, the building's planners concluded that it would cost $16.5 million. By the time ground was broken on May 5, 1999, the additional $8.5 million had been raised by three major gifts and numerous others. Taylor increased his total donation to $9.2 million—the largest donation ever made in the Minnesota State Colleges and Universities system. William Bresnan's donation of $2.5 million was earmarked to complete the Bresnan Arena within the Taylor Center. Pepsi Cola of Mankato donated slightly more than $2.25 million for the Taylor Center and made additional contributions for programs and scholarships. The university reciprocated by granting the company exclusive campus beverage rights for 10 years.[80]

By the time he made his donation, Taylor was probably Mankato State's most renowned alum. Taylor was born on April 20, 1941 in Springfield, Minnesota, and grew up on a farm in nearby Comfrey. He graduated from Comfrey High School in 1959 and completed his B. S. in mathematics, physics and social studies at Mankato State College three years later. In 1978 he earned an MBA from the Harvard Business School.[81]

During and after his undergraduate degree, Taylor worked for Carlson Wedding Service (later Carlson Craft), a family-owned North Mankato printing service. Taylor bought the company when Bill Carlson retired in 1975 and soon expanded it into the Taylor Corporation, which acquired printing and electronics businesses around the world.

While enlarging his company, Taylor, a progressive Republican, also served as a Minnesota State Senator for nine years (January 6, 1981-February 3, 1990). For two of those years (January 9, 1985-January 5, 1987) he was the Senate's minority leader. By the time he made his donation to Mankato State, Taylor had gained additional prominence by purchasing the majority ownership of the Minnesota Timberwolves, a Minneapolis-based professional basketball team.

Bresnan's business career, like Taylor's, was another Minnesota

Taylor Center at night with view of Brock/Otto Hall of Champions, 2013

Bresnan Arena, 2012

Commencement, 2008

Women's volleyball competes in the Bresnan Arena, 2009.
Image courtesy of Athletic Communications.

success story. A native of Madison Lake, Bresnan completed a two-year program in television and radio repair at Mankato Technical School (now South Central College). In 1958, at the age of 25, Bresnan, in partnership with fellow engineer Joseph Poire, built the Mankato cable system. They branched out to Rochester, where their success attracted the attention of California entrepreneur Jack Kent Cooke. In 1968, after he had purchased the Rochester company and several others, Cooke made Bresnan president of his merged cable business. By 1974, when Cooke sold out to Westinghouse, the company had a million customers.[82]

Once he completed his association with Cooke, Bresnan formed his own company, which became known as Bresnan Communications in 1984. When Bresnan donated to the Taylor Center project, his company was one of the principal cable television providers in Michigan's Upper Peninsula, Minnesota, Wisconsin, Mississippi and Georgia and had international operations in Chile and Poland.

Aside from the three large donations, perhaps as much as $1.7 million was contributed by alumni and community supporters. The alumni of the men's and women's varsity sports were especially important in this drive. Each sport was headed by a captain, who coordinated contacts with hundreds of alumni.[83]

On April 12, 1999, the Minnesota State University, Mankato Foundation received legislative authorization to build the Taylor Center. The law signed by Governor Carlson described the center as "a multipurpose facility for athletics and related academic programs." The brief act specified that the MnSCU board was to determine site selection and approve the design and that the foundation had to donate the building to the state.[84]

Despite its size and complexity, the Taylor Center was constructed rapidly by Ellerbe Becket, a Minneapolis-based general contractor. Its public grand opening ceremonies were held in conjunction with Homecoming weekend, October 13-15, 2000. Numerous guests were treated to a tour of the showcase building whose most distinctive features were the Hall of Champions, a curved front lobby with display cases containing exhibits of athletic and academic achievements, and the Bresnan Arena. The 4,800-seat facility, which had a drop-down floor, was the new home for basketball, volleyball and wrestling competition and commencement exercises.[85]

When the Taylor Center was under construction its estimated cost was revised upward to $16.5 million. But, the university's Facilities Management Office later concluded that the final cost of the 142,951 square-foot structure was $18,410,174.[86]

Constructing the Taylor Center was made possible by the success of Campaign MSU. Rush launched the campaign after he had a study done by Grenzebach Glier & Associates, a Chicago-based consulting firm that had concluded the University might be able to raise $35 over five years provided it educated its likely donors on the present state of public higher education. A common public perception was that public universities did not need private support, because they were fully funded by state legislatures. Donors like Taylor and Bresnan knew better. But many had to be convinced that its pressing building needs could not be met without private funding. Rush's goal for Campaign MSU exceeded expectations. When the campaign closed on June 30, 2002, it exceeded $38.9 million.[87]

The imperative to raise private funds was caused by reduced legislative appropriations, which had become evident during the Preska administration. In 1996, Minnesota's Department of Finance reported that higher education funding had declined by 20 percent since 1987. When the Department of Finance issued its findings, Mankato State was getting only 40 percent of its $104 million annual budget from state appropriations, a decline of five percent from 10 years earlier. The institution's other revenue sources were student tuition and fees (29 percent), auxiliary services (16 percent), federal and state grants/aid (13 percent) and private support (2 percent).[88]

## Myers Field House

The planning, funding and building of the Taylor Center was part of the Rush administration's master plan that also assessed the status of three adjacent sports and recreational facilities. The field house (renamed to Myers Field House in 1991), Highland Center and the arena (renamed to Otto Arena in 1991) were all showing the effects of 35 years of hard use.

The Rush administration's decision, which was supported by the MnSCU Board of Trustees, was to replace Myers Field House and renovate Highland Center and Otto Arena. Although they were obviously related, the three projects were respectively identified as Phase I, Phase II and Phase III of the sports and recreational facilities overhaul. This approach enabled the administration and the trustees to make a separate request for legislative funding of each phase. Experience had shown that the legislature was much more receptive to piecemeal funding than committing future legislatures to a project's total cost.

Funding for the Myers Field House replacement, whose final total cost was $10,288,152, was provided by the 1998 and 2000 legislatures. Because the original bids exceeded the appropriations and had to be re-let, the old building was not razed until early spring 2000. On April 20, 2000, President Rush led the groundbreaking ceremony for the replacement building. At that time the anticipated completion date was July 2001.[89]

Construction did not proceed as rapidly as planned. When Rush left the university in June 2001, campus officials and the general contractor, Met-Con of Faribault, Minnesota, thought the building would be completed by September 1. But it was not done until November.[90]

With an area of 82,308 square feet, the somewhat enlarged new field house features a 200-meter, eight-lane track. Additionally, the area within the track accommodates four courts for basketball, volleyball, tennis and badminton as well as wintertime practice space for the baseball and softball teams.[91]

As the home of the Minnesota State track and field teams, the new Myers Field House, which has room for 1,000 spectators, was the site of the 2008 and 2012 Division II Indoor Track & Field championship meets. As the premier facility in its conferences, it was also

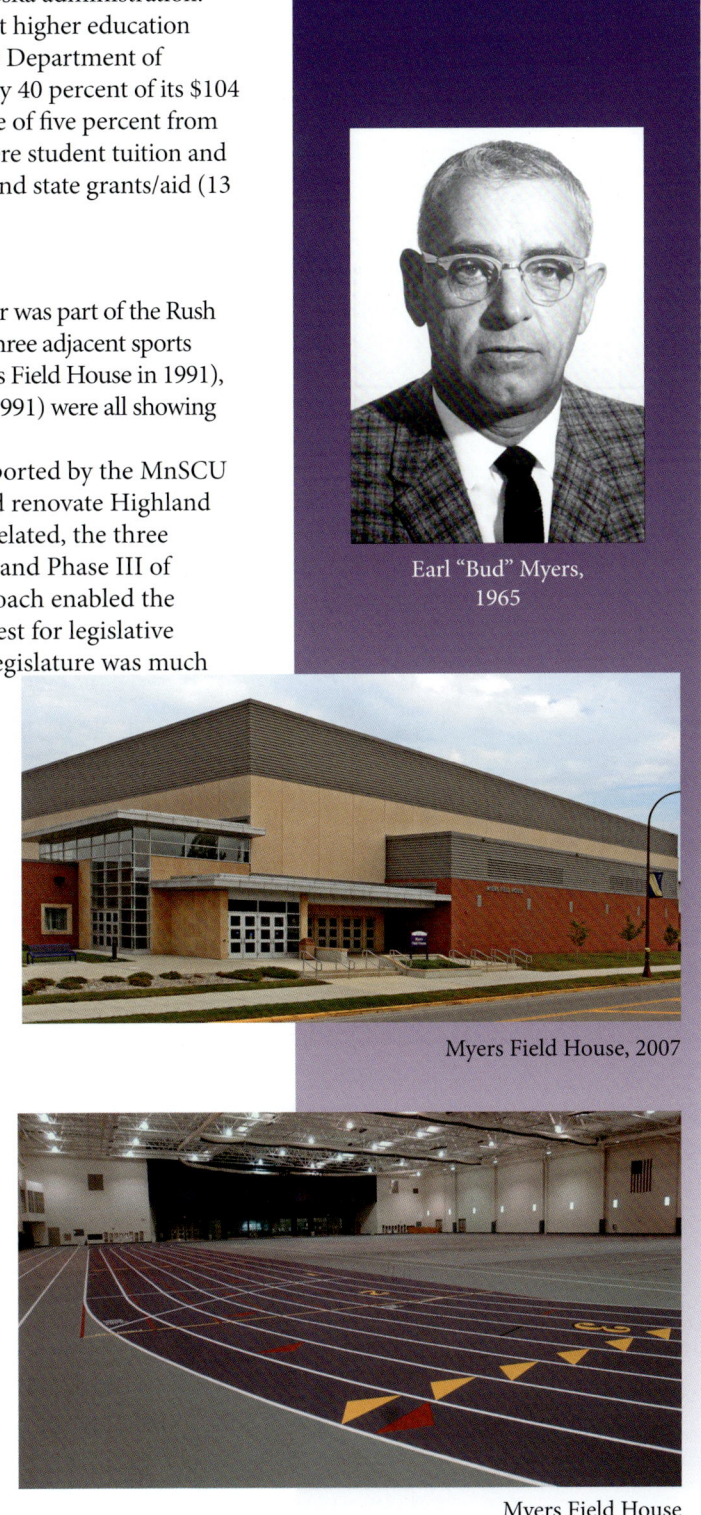

Earl "Bud" Myers, 1965

Myers Field House, 2007

Myers Field House

used for the North Central Conference Indoor Championship Meet in 2002, 2004, 2006 and 2008 and that of the Northern Sun Intercollegiate Conference in six of the eight years between 2010-2017.

Both the new field house and the building it replaced were named to perpetuate the memory of Earl "Bud" Myers, who began coaching track and field and cross country at Mankato State in 1948. After a quarter century, Myers gave up his track and field duties but continued coaching cross country for another six years until he retired in 1979. His track and field teams won 21 conference championships and his cross country squads participated in 23 national championship meets. Myers died on October 15, 1982, a year after he was inducted into the Mankato State Hall of Fame.[92]

## Utilities Plant Changes

The utilities plant was improved by the completion of a central chiller system and the installation of a generator to provide backup electrical power. In 1992 the university administration decided to replace individual building air conditioning with a central chiller source. The change was prompted by the desire to have a more efficient system. Each air-conditioned building had a cooler tower, whose water had to be inspected daily. A central system, in which all inspection was done at the main plant, saved time and was more reliable. Another contributing factor to the change was that the building units were fast approaching the end of their anticipated duration. So the administration decided a change to a central system was preferable to replacing the individual units.[93]

The central chilling system was completed in three stages over a five-year period. A 1,000-ton chiller was installed in 1994; a 1,200-ton chiller, which cost $145,000 was added in 1998 and the third, a 1,000-ton unit, was added the next year. All were placed in the new chiller plant, which was constructed next to the original power plant. The central chiller system entailed circulating chilled water through chiller water lines buried underground. As the buildings were cooled, the heated water was recirculated back to the chiller plant, where it was re-chilled and re-circulated. Minnesota State University, Mankato engineers calculated that the central chiller system had the capacity of more than a thousand typical window air conditioners.

Any central chilling system had to have accompanying cooling towers. When the university was converting to central chilling, it added three cooling towers to its utilities plant.

## Organizational Changes During the Rush Administration

During Rush's presidency there were three significant changes that altered the structure and image of the university. Two of them—the creation of the Minnesota State Colleges and Universities System (MnSCU) and the conversion from the quarter to the semester system— resulted from legislative action. But the third—renaming Mankato State University to Minnesota State University, Mankato —was initiated by Rush.

Historically, Minnesota developed four governing systems for its colleges and universities. The first was the University of Minnesota's Board of Regents, the second was the board of the system that evolved from normal schools to state universities, the third was the board of the community colleges and the fourth was the board for the technical colleges.

During the 1980s some legislators began chaffing at the inconvenience of budget requests from four systems. Legally, they were constitutionally limited with regard to their control over the University of Minnesota. But the idea of merging the seven state universities, 21 community colleges and 21 technical colleges under one board was appealing. In 1991, Senate Majority Leader Roger Moe, a DFLer from the Red River valley, proposed such a merger. He insisted, that among other things, it would facilitate the adoption of a universal academic year calendar and hence make transferring easier and would result in a cost saving in the long run. After some bickering between the Senate and House over the precise wording of a merger bill the 1991 legislature approved it with the stipulation that the merger would take effect June 1, 1995.[94]

Although some legislators wanted to negate the 1991 act, planning for the merger continued. The 1995 legislature reconsidered the merger act in order to resolve some differences about the duties and powers of the new board of trustees. Much of the Higher Education Act, which was approved by Governor Arne Carlson on May 24, 1995, was concerned with the creation of the Minnesota State Colleges and Universities system. Henceforth, 1995 was regarded as the official date of MnSCU's founding.[95]

Among many other things the 1995 law detailed MnSCU's member institutions and proposed budgets for its three divisions—state universities, state community colleges and state technical colleges. The law specified that: "the [sic]following are designated as the Minnesota state colleges and universities: the community colleges located at Austin, Bloomington, Brainerd, Brooklyn Park, Cloquet, Coon Rapids, Ely, Fergus Falls, Grand Rapids, Hibbing, International Falls, Inver Grove Heights, Minneapolis, Rochester, Thief River Falls, Virginia, White Bear Lake, Willmar and Worthington; the community college centers located at Cambridge and Duluth; the state universities located at Bemidji, Mankato, Marshall, Moorhead, St. Cloud, Winona, and the Twin Cities metropolitan area; and the technical colleges located at Alexandria, Albert Lea, Anoka, Austin, Bemidji, Brainerd, Brooklyn Park. Canby, Detroit Lakes, Duluth, East Grand Forks, Eden Prairie, Eveleth, Faribault, Granite Falls, Hibbing, Hutchinson, Jackson, Minneapolis, Mahtomedi, Moorhead, North Mankato, Pine City, Pipestone, Red Wing, Rochester, Rosemount, St. Cloud, St. Paul, Staples, Thief River Falls, Wadena, Willmar, and Winona."[96]

With respect to the annual budgets, the legislature estimated that the instructional expenditures would be $214,536,000 for the technical colleges, $145,565,000 for the community colleges and $253,612,000 for the state universities. The estimated non-instructional costs for the technical colleges were $17,231,000 the first year and $16,937,000 the second, for the community colleges, $10,349,000 each year and for the state universities, $14,573,000 each year.[97]

The 15-member Board of Trustees was in the process of employing a permanent chancellor when the 1995 act was being considered in the legislature. On June 12, it hired Dr. Judith Eaton, whose administration began on August 15. In her first year, she sharply reduced the office staff from 210 to 110 and with the board's approval consolidated 28 community and technical colleges into 11 dual-mission community-technical colleges.[98]

Regarding the semester system, the 1995 legislature passed an act that stipulated: "The board of trustees of the Minnesota state colleges and universities shall convert, and the board of regents of the University of Minnesota is requested to convert, to the semester system by the 1998-1999 academic year."[99]

The initiative for this change came mainly from the legislature, which believed that the semester system allowed more time for classes, because it reduced the number of registration periods over a nine-month period from three to two.

Another appeal of the semester system was that it was dominant in higher education. Nationally, more than 70 percent of all colleges and universities used it. All of the public colleges and universities in the adjoining states of North Dakota, South Dakota, Iowa and Wisconsin were on it. Thus, converting to the semester system would be especially beneficial for transfer students, who had been inconvenienced by the sharply different calendars of quarters and semesters.[100]

The Minnesota State University, Mankato faculty enthusiastically supported the semester conversion. Most of them had earned their degrees under the semester system and had never really adjusted to the quarter

Ad in the *Reporter* about semester conversion, 11 February 1997

Logo for the new name was revealed in April 1999

system. The greatest single advantage of the semester system, they believed, was that it would facilitate the completion of term papers and other long-range projects.

In the process of converting to the semester system, faculty and administrators in academic affairs had to deal with approximately 5,200 courses. The spadework was done by the curriculum committees of the various academic departments. Some courses were dropped, others were combined. The credits of all courses had to be adjusted to the semester system. In such adjustments the guiding principle was that any four-year degree required 192 credits under the quarter system and 128 under the semester system.[101]

When the semester system went into effect in the Fall 1998 semester, its greatest inconvenience was for the students who were partway through their degree program. The naming of the first and second semesters to fall and spring eliminated winter from the academic calendar. This was accomplished by naming the first one after its starting season and the second one after its ending season.

On September 18, 1998, early in the university's first term on the semester system, the MnSCU Board of Trustees officially changed the name of Mankato State University to Minnesota State University, Mankato. The change was to take effect immediately, but the trustees recognized that it would take some time for the university to re-identify itself by using the new name in all letterhead, publications and news releases.[102]

Rush, who had strongly agitated for the change, immediately proclaimed that: "This is a significant step forward for our University. . . . The new name will help us better accomplish our mission as one of the premier higher education institutions in this state and region."

Rush thought it was especially important to have Minnesota as part of the university's name, because it would provide greater visibility over a broader area.

| NEWS IN MINUTES | MEDLEY | SPORTS |
|---|---|---|
| Alcohol involved in deaths of Mankato teens. **Page 3** | Donald Morrill defines "mind dumps." **Page 11** | Mitchell tallies 202 receiving yards in Mav loss. **Page 15** |

MINNESOTA → MANKATO STATE UNIVERSITY, MANKATO

# REPORTER

THE STUDENT NEWSPAPER OF MINNESOTA STATE UNIVERSITY, MANKATO

ADVERTISING 389-5451     TUESDAY, SEPTEMBER 22, 1998     NEWSROOM 389-1776

# It's official: MSU takes on new meaning

**BY Gillia Jewison**
Editor-in-Chief

Same place, new name.
Mankato State University changed its name to Minnesota State University, Mankato Friday after the Minnesota State Colleges and Universities Board of Trustees unanimously approved the name change.

Other MnSCU state university presidents have voiced their approval of the Mankato name change, but have not said whether they plan to follow Mankato's lead.
The name change will apparently be a catalyst for the university, giving MSU a chance to establish an image that will take us into the 21st century, according to the university's stance on the subject.

**Campus organizations, departments will adjust slowly, but surely**

**BY Gillia Jewison**
Editor-in-Chief

While the Minnesota State University, Mankato name may

forms and the softball uniforms in the spring.
The University Bookstore may have a bit more urgency in the time frame for change.

The *Reporter* was quick to switch its masthead to reflect the name change.
22 September 1998

He noted that: "Our research shows the public perception is that universities with state names have more credibility than those with city names."

Faculty, alumni and students welcomed the change. Many of them had complained to Rush that outside of the state, Mankato was usually not a recognizable name. Indeed, in Kansas and its adjoining states it caused people to think of Mankato, Kansas, a small town in the north central part of the state that had been named after Mankato, Minnesota. Rush intended that including the state name would significantly improve the university's national and even international image.[103]

Despite its official name replete with the comma, some variants of Minnesota State University, Mankato, have come into use. The commonest one is to leave out the comma. But, the use of such names as Minnesota State Mankato or Minnesota State manages to ignore its university status.

## Rush's Resignation

On February 20, 2001, the *Reporter* announced that President Rush was one of three finalists for the presidency of the new California State University Channel Islands. Located just outside Camarillo midway between Santa Barbara and Los Angeles, the institution was scheduled to open in the fall of 2002. So its first president would be tasked with forming an administration and hiring a faculty among many other organizational details. Rush informed the *Reporter* "that they came to me" and that he "had the experience they were looking for."[104]

On March 7, 2001, Rush announced to a standing-room-only crowd in the Centennial Student Ballroom that he had been offered and had accepted the presidency of California State University Channel Islands. "This is an exciting opportunity for me and I'm grateful that the trustees at California State University invited me to do this," he said. Although he was obviously delighted with his new position, Rush had only positive things to say about his experience in Mankato. He concluded by informing the crowd that because he felt obligated to complete some projects his resignation would not occur until June.[105]

Before he left for California, Rush further explained his motivation for taking a new position. The death of his wife Jane in December 1999, was a significant transition to him. She was so closely associated with his work that he felt a need to start over in another setting. Furthermore, the Channel Islands campus location put him within two-hours travel of his two daughters. Without specifically stating that he was somewhat homesick for California, Rush mused that he had grown up there.[106]

With respect to Minnesota State University, Mankato, Rush's greatest satisfactions were the private fundraising campaign that led to the completion of the Taylor Center, Bresnan Arena and the Andreas Theatre and his pleasant association with numerous students. In his interview with the *Reporter*, Rush did not mention his persistent campaign to change the image of Mankato State by convincing the governing board to approve the name change to Minnesota State University, Mankato.

Not surprisingly, Rush had a highly successful career at Channel Islands. When Rush announced in August 2015, that he was retiring at the end of the 2015-16 academic year, Timothy P. White, chancellor of the California State University, observed: "President Rush will forever be memorialized for his role in establishing and building the reputation of our newest campus. He is leaving a lasting and living legacy of academic excellence that not only made CSU Channel Islands the campus of choice for high school seniors and community college transfer students in Ventura County but also across the state." Lauding Rush's "character, charisma and passion for students and learning," White noted Rush's contributions in building the academic program, winning federal grants, expanding outreach and working with the business community to assure that the curriculum was relevant to its needs.[107]

## Interim President Karen Boubel

On April 18, 2001, the MnSCU Board appointed Karen Boubel the interim president of Minnesota State University, Mankato. This was done with the clear understanding that she would only serve in the interim between Rush's departure and the beginning of his successor's term and would not be a candidate for the permanent position.[108]

Richard Davenport,
2016

Scott R. Olson,
circa 2005

Marilyn J. Wells,
2013

Boubel served as interim president for slightly more than a year between Rush's departure and the beginning of Richard Davenport's presidency on July 1, 2002. After Davenport's arrival she reverted to her former position of vice president for academic affairs for a year. Effective with the Fall 2003 semester, she was designated a professor of music with a full-time teaching assignment. For the four years prior to her retirement in 2014, Boubel directed Musicorum, a Mankato based choir.[109]

### Hiring of President Richard Davenport

On February 22, 2002, after a national search, the MnSCU Board of Trustees appointed Davenport, then the provost and vice president for academic affairs at Central Michigan University, president of Minnesota State University, Mankato. Davenport's earned degrees were a B.A. in speech and hearing disorders from the University of Nebraska, Kearney, an M.S. in speech and hearing science from Colorado State University and a Ph.D. in higher education administration from Iowa State University.[110]

From 1970-86, Davenport had three teaching appointments. He taught at Iowa State for seven years before serving as an assistant professor in speech science, pathology and audiology at St. Cloud State University, 1977-1980. Davenport directed and taught, 1980-1986, in the Winona Tri-College/University Cooperative Program in Communications Disorders. This program included Winona State University, St. Mary's University and the College of St. Teresa.

Davenport entered administration when he joined Western State College of Colorado (Gunnison) in 1986. During his four years there he worked as dean of the graduate school and associate vice president for academic affairs. At Central Michigan, 1990-2002, Davenport was a full professor and held several administrative posts culminating in his promotion to provost and vice president for academic affairs.

Davenport explained that he had several other opportunities to become a university president, but that he had a particular affinity for Mankato and Minnesota. In addition to spending much of his youth at his grandparents' Worthington home, his Winona and St. Cloud experiences accounted for nine years of his professional career. Furthermore, he was attracted by the excellent reputation and opportunities for development at Minnesota State University, Mankato.[111]

In his address to a crowd of faculty, staff and students at the start of his first academic year, Davenport elaborated his main priorities for Minnesota State University, Mankato. Because student academic success was paramount, it would be necessary to strive for increased funding for university improvements, including technology upgrades and campus renovation projects.[112]

### Academic Affairs Administration During the Davenport Administration

Shortly after the end of the 2002-2003 academic year, Davenport made a significant move in shaping his own administration with the appointment of Scott R. Olson as vice president for academic affairs. Olson, a native of suburban Minneapolis, had earned all three of his degrees from Northwestern University (Evanston, Illinois). His B.A. was in European Intellectual History and both his M.A. and Ph.D. were in Radio-Television-Film.[113]

In his first position at Central Connecticut State University, Olson taught in the Department of Communication and served as assistant to the dean of the college of Arts and Humanities. Later he worked as the dean of the College of Communication, Information and Media at Ball State University and interim vice chancellor for academic and student affairs for MnSCU.

In 2005 Olson was thrust into a two-month stint as acting president when Davenport underwent and recuperated from kidney transplant surgery. Effective in September 2007, Olson's title was changed to provost and vice president for academic affairs. The MnSCU board's decision to add provost to the title of each university's second ranking administrator was part of a nationwide trend.[114]

On May 16, 2012, the MnSCU Board of Trustees appointed Olson the 15th president of Winona State University. He thus became the third Winona State president who had prior experience at Minnesota State University, Mankato and its organizational predecessors: Robert A. DuFresne, Winona State's president, 1967-1977, had taught education at Mankato State, 1959-1963; Thomas F. Stark served as Winona State's president from 1983 until he died from a heart attack five years later.[115]

On April 4, 2013, Davenport announced that effective July 22, Marilyn J. Wells would be the provost and senior vice president for academic affairs. She replaced Linda Baer, who had served as vice president for academic affairs since July 17, 2012. Wells was then the vice provost and graduate dean at East Stroudsburg University (Pennsylvania), a position she had held for five years.[116]

Wells, the first member of her family to attend college, had earned four degrees. She completed her bachelor's in home economics from Indiana University of Pennsylvania in 1980. Her two masters' degrees in health education (1987) and public health (1991) were earned at East Stroudsburg. Her doctoral degree in health education was from Southern Illinois University.

Prior to joining East Stroudsburg, Wells had held a number of public health and higher education positions. They included directing health management strategies at the Center for Health Information/Managed Care Resources in Chesapeake, Virginia and serving as the chair and professor in the Department of Health, Physical Education & Recreation at Hampton University (Hampton, Virginia).

Staffing of academic affairs was bolstered in 2015 by the addition of Robert Fleischman as associate provost. Fleischman, who began at Minnesota State University, Mankato on July 13, had more than two decades of service at East Stroudsburg University. Prior to that he had worked for nine years as a lawyer. During four of them he was a partner in a New York City firm.[117]

Fleischman's academic training was a bachelor's in political science from the University of Michigan, a master's in sport management from the University of Massachusetts at Amherst and doctorate of education in educational theory and practice from Binghamton University (New York). Furthermore, he had completed a juris doctorate from the Hofstra University School of Law.

Fleischman had a varied experience at East Stroudsburg. Before being named the dean of the College of Business and Management, he was a key developer of the sport management program. In addition to teaching undergraduate and graduate courses, he played a key role in enhancing the undergraduate program and developing two master's degree programs.

## Campus Expansion During the Davenport Administration

Like the preceding Preska and Rush administrations, the Davenport administration significantly expanded the post-consolidation campus. Davenport era changes have featured construction of two classroom buildings (Ford Hall and the Clinical Sciences Building), two residence halls (Sears and Preska), the University Dining Center, the Center for Renewable Energy and utilities plant expansion. Additionally, extensive remodeling/renovation has been completed on the Centennial Student Union, Highland Center and the Otto Recreation Center. Other physical plant changes were the razing of the Gage Towers dormitories and the renaming of the Performing Arts Center to the Earley Center for Performing Arts.

## Ford Hall

Construction on Ford Hall, a 67,000-square-foot, $32.5 million addition to Trafton Hall, was started in September 2006 and completed prior to its dedication on September 11, 2008. As the new home for the Chemistry and Geology Department, the hall was appropriately named after Leonard A. Ford, the institution's most famous chemistry professor.[118]

Leonard A. Ford,
1964

Ford Hall, 2014

Southern Minnesota Regional Science
Fair in Highland Arena, 1983

Center of Renewable Energy, 2011

A native of Parkers Prairie, Minnesota, Ford earned his bachelor's degree from Gustavus Adolphus College and his M.S. and Ph.D. from the University of Iowa. Before joining the Mankato State Teachers College faculty in 1939, Ford taught chemistry at several high schools as well as Sioux Falls College and the University of Iowa.

During his teaching career at Mankato State, which was ended by his sudden death on October 27, 1967, Ford popularized chemistry among students and the public. In 1950 he started the Mankato State's Science Fair, which grew into one of the institution's most important outreach programs. Ford's book, *Chemical Magic*, which promoted the joys and instructional values of chemical experimentation, was first published in 1959.  It was subsequently used by thousands of high school and college students.

Other than teaching, Ford chaired the Division of Science and Mathematics for some years. As a strong advocate of science and mathematics studies, Ford helped promote the addition of nursing and dental programs and worked to add an engineering program during the abortive campaign for the University of Southern Minnesota.

 Ford Hall was designed to be a state-of-the-art building with respect to energy saving. Among other things, it featured a rotary heat exchange that reduced heating and cooling costs by an estimated 15 percent and exhaust fans that ran only when necessary, which substantially reduced mechanical costs. The building's unique landscaping ambience featured a rock garden with specimens from throughout the state.

## Center of Renewable Energy

With President Davenport presiding, ground breaking for the Center of Renewable Energy Building was held on November 13, 2009. Located west of Wiecking Center, the 6,300-square-foot facility, which cost $1.8 million, was dedicated on September 23, 2010.[119]

The building contained two laboratories. Approximately three-fourths of its space was allocated to the Center for Automotive Research; the remainder was used by the International Renewable Energy Technology Institute. The Center for Automotive Research, which had been previously housed in Nelson Hall, was dedicated to studying alternative energies for wheeled vehicles, including solar power. The energy technology institute was primarily concerned with the development and use of renewable energies. Both units also facilitated student and faculty research regarding emissions and the efficiency of engines as well as residential and commercial heating systems.

## Clinical Sciences Building

Funding for the Clinical Sciences Building, which opened on January 9, 2017, was provided by the 2014 state bonding act. Minnesota State University, Mankato's $25.8 million request for the facility was included in MnSCU's $155.9 million request for 24 system projects. But Governor Mark Dayton did not include the Clinical Sciences Building in his initial recommendation of January 15, 2014.[120]

Dayton's decision caused Davenport

to work with MnSCU Chancellor Steven Rosenstone to persuade the legislature to include the Clinical Sciences Building in its bonding act. Davenport was confident Dayton would agree with the legislature's decision.

The Davenport-Rosenstone strategy of lobbying selected legislators worked. The Minnesota Jobs bill that Dayton signed on May 20, 2014, included the requested amount for the Clinical Sciences Building. Davenport publicly thanked Dayton and senators Kathy Sheran (DFL-Mankato) and Julie Rosen (Rep.-Fairmont) as well as representatives Kathy Brynaert (DFL-Mankato), Tony Cornish (Rep.-Vernon Center), Robert Gunther (Rep.-Fairmont) and Clark Johnson (DFL-North Mankato).

Clinical Sciences Building, 2017

Ground breaking for the Clinical Sciences Building occurred on September 26, 2014. But, for some unexplained reason, Shaw Lundquist, the St. Paul-based general contractor, did not start site preparation until January 26, 2015. As of July 10, 2016, when construction was running about two months behind schedule, Paul Corcoran, the university's planning and construction director, anticipated it would be completed by late October.[121]

The building was opened for the spring Semester, 2017, which began on January 9. Ten days later Davenport presided at the ribbon-cutting ceremony. In addition to Davenport, remarks were made by Bob Hoffman, board trustee, Kristine Retherford, dean, College of Allied Health and Nursing, Colleen Royle, assistant professor, School of Nursing and Kellie Metzger, a student in the Communications Disorder Program.[122]

The complete cost of the three-story, 79,131-square-foot building was determined to be $28.883 million. This amount included a $2.065 million design cost and $1 million to add a basement, which was unfinished when the building was dedicated.

Unlike most of the brick-covered campus buildings, much of the Clinical Sciences Building featured a Kasota stone exterior. To connect it to the rest of the campus the building has a tunnel connection with Ford Hall. University planners opted for this feature instead of an elevated hallway in order preserve the integrity of the Ostrander Bell Tower view. Internally, the Clinical Sciences Building has features that greatly facilitate the needs of its three occupants— the School of Nursing and the departments of Dental Hygiene and Speech, Hearing & Rehabilitation Services.[123]

Maverick Family Nursing Simulation Center, 2017

## Julia A. Sears Residence Community

The Julia A. Sears Residence Community was opened for the start of the Fall 2008 semester. Located on the longtime soccer practice field south of the utilities plant complex, Sears was the university's first new dormitory since the completion of Gage B in 1966.

The construction of Sears, which got underway in 2007, was caused by the decision that Gage Towers would have to be razed in the

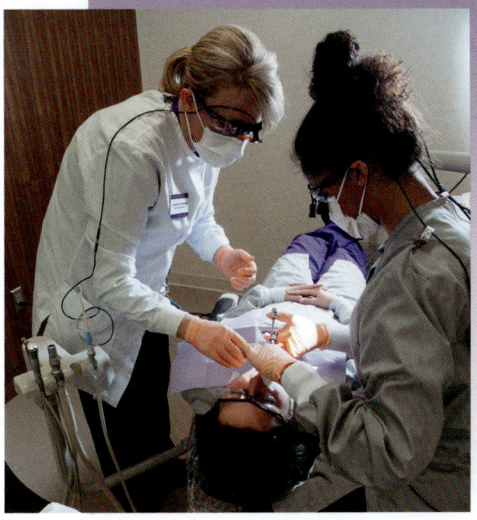
Dental Hygiene, 2017

Julia A. Sears Residence
Community, 2016

short-range future. In 2003, the university determined that the towers were not wearing well. Elevator service was variously slow, erratic or non-existent. Additionally, the plumbing and windows needed to be replaced. The estimated renovation cost of $28.8 million were prohibitive to the point of causing university officials to decide the best option was to build new dormitories closer to the campus core. When the towers were constructed, there was no great concern with the hazards of pedestrian traffic to the classrooms. But the popularization of the Stadium Road route for both university and community vehicle traffic made the Stadium Road-Ellis Avenue intersection, despite its traffic signals, a sometimes risky crossing.[124]

The artfully designed four-story Sears building, which cost $31,009,085 and was finished with brick and Kasota stone, comprised 150,275 square feet. With 608 beds, it could serve about as many students as one of the Gage Towers. Its interior design was based on various surveys of student preferences. Cynthia L. Janney, the university's director of residential life, observed that: "After years of asking students what they would like in the dorms, I think we have made something they will like."[125]

The building's design architect was the Ayers/Saint/Gross firm of Baltimore, Maryland. But it arranged with Bentz, Thompson, Rietow of Minnesota to supervise the construction as the architect of record. Knutson Construction erected the building.

Julia A. Sears Residence
Community Room, 2018

In the Sears semi-suite layout, which was new to campus, two rooms with two occupants each shared an interconnecting full bathroom. This was a marked improvement over Gage, which featured double occupancy rooms and a floor bathroom that served as many as 50 residents. The 10-foot high ceilings, two feet higher than Gage, added much needed storage space. Furthermore, Sears featured central air conditioning with individual unit controls and coed units on all floors.

The most serious drawback of the new dorm was that it did not have its own cafeteria. Any of its residents who chose to eat in Carkowski Commons had to endure sometimes unpleasant wintertime walks.

The Sears building was a hit with the Minnesota Vikings players, who began using it in 2010 during their 45th consecutive summer training camp on campus. Players were particularly appreciative of the semi-suites and the central air conditioning. Their former quarters in Gage A featured window unit air conditioners that were added for the duration of the training camps.[126]

## Margaret R. Preska Residence Community

The completion and opening of the Margaret R. Preska Residence community in 2012 was the second phase of preparing for the impending loss of Gage Towers.

President Davenport presided at the building's groundbreaking ceremony on September 23, 2010. The building was designed by Cannon Design of Chicago and its architect of record was Studio Five of Minneapolis. Met-Con Companies (Faribault and Mankato) was the construction contractor. After construction was well underway the naming ceremony featuring the building's namesake and former president, Margaret R. Preska, was held in the Performing Arts Center on September 22, 2011.[127]

The Preska residence project consisted of constructing a new building with a brick, Kasota stone and glass exterior and then combining it with the adjacent I Wing of the McElroy Residence Community. The building, which cost $29,925,000, had an area of 118,954 square feet, which provided a semi-suite arrangement. About a third of that space was in the former McElroy I dormitory. Its semi-suite arrangement, like that of Sears, provided housing for its approximately 500 residents as well as ground-floor space for the offices of the New Student and Family programs. Like Sears, Preska featured individually controlled air conditioning and heating.[128]

With the opening of the Preska Residence Community for Fall 2012, the university closed Gage Towers. To provide more student housing, the university had leased the privately owned Stadium Heights Community the preceding March. An eight-building complex located off Stadium Road and Heron Drive about a mile from the campus core, Stadium Hills had accommodations for about 400 residents.  It featured three-, four- and five-person apartments. The apartments had central air-conditioning, cable and both wired and wireless internet; each building was coed, but each apartment was single gender. The university's Office of Residential Life still manages the Stadium Heights Community, whose residents can use a free campus shuttle service.[129]

Margaret R. Preska Residence Community, 2013

## Demolition of Gage Towers

During the 2012-2013 school year, the abandoned Gage Towers were fenced off preparatory to their destruction the following summer. Once news of the scheduled razing spread, the university was deluged with requests for mementoes by many of the nearly 50,000 former Gage residents. Jen Myers, the university's interim director of Alumni Relations and Special Events, reported: "One guy wanted the back of his old desk. Somebody else wanted the corkboard. We've had requests for mirrors, garbage cans, [and] nearly anything you can think of."[130]

Alumni interest prompted Donald Seymour, the architect charged with clearing the building, to encourage the university to advertise sales. The sale of mailboxes was particularly successful. A resident of 30 years ago wanted the numbered box that he had used then.

The main task in preparing the buildings for destruction was the systematic removal of hazardous material. After that was completed, the towers were scheduled for destruction on Saturday, June 29, 2013. An estimated crowd of

Mailboxes before removal from Gage Towers, 2013

Gage Towers demolition, 2013

5,000-6,000 spectators witnessed the implosion. Many of them crowded onto Stadium Road, where they stood behind a fence placed 1,000 feet from the towers. Others got prime viewing spots from the top rows of Blakeslee Stadium or by standing atop the baseball field's dugouts. Additionally, an unspecified number, who wanted to avoid crowds and traffic, drove to the highest points on the rural roads south of campus or to such places as the Lookout Drive Hill above North Mankato. At precisely 9:30 a.m., as scheduled, strategically placed dynamite charges were ignited. It took only 12.23 seconds for the buildings to buckle and collapse into a giant rubble pile beneath a huge dust cloud and to dramatically lower the highest point on the Mankato skyline.[131]

As planned, most of the rubble was ground into material that was used to build a parking lot on the Gage site.

University Dining Center, 2017

## University Dining Center

The University Dining Center, which was first considered in 2008, was opened for the start of the spring 2017 semester. Building it became imperative with the construction of the Sears and Preska residence communities and the closing of Gage Towers. As hundreds of dormitory residents were shifted to the campus core, the inadequacies of Carkowski Commons, the original food services building, became apparent. By the Fall 2012 semester, Carkowski, which was designed for 1,800 patrons was actually forced to serve over three thousand after the closing of Gage Towers and its cafeteria. This overcrowding caused long lines and numerous complaints about poor service. After a study determined that Carkowski could not cost effectively be renovated to serve the new need, the university decided it had to be replaced with a new facility nearby.[132]

Designing the new food services center commenced in 2013. On May 15, 2015, President Davenport presided at the obligatory ceremonial groundbreaking. Construction got underway the next month. The building's design architect was Ayers/Saint/Gross of Baltimore and its architect of record

was Bentz, Thompson and Rietow of Minneapolis. The McGough Company (Minneapolis) was the general contractor.[133]

The eye-catching $25,176,442 University Dining Center with its south-facing glass exterior, which permits use of much natural light, has an area of 60,614 square feet.  This capacity facilitates service to its 3,000 customers. The center was opened for the winter 2017 semester with food service provided by Sodexo, the contracted vendor, and was dedicated on February 2, 2017, in a ceremony featuring presentations by President Davenport and Cynthia Janney, director of residential life.[134]

Inside University Dining Center, 2017

## Utilities Plant Expansion

Minnesota State University, Mankato buys its electricity from a utility company. But, it had to have its own generators to provide backup power capable of operating emergency lights, exit signs and fire alarms during power outages. In 2005 campus utilities were upgraded by the construction of a Generation Building equipped with three additional diesel-fueled Caterpilllar generators. This improvement, which provided full backup for all of the campus electrical needs, qualified the university for reduced charges from its regular electricity supplier.[135]

## Centennial Student Union Remodeling

The Centennial Student Union was extensively remodeled from February 2004 to September 2005. Design and construction of the $11 million project, which affected about a third of the union's space and increased its area by 8,200 square feet, was performed by Paulsen Architects (Mankato).[136]

The most striking change was to much of the building's southern exterior where the previous brick covering was replaced by glass. This glass front featured a tower-like structure above the new wide entry and glass walls extending

Centennial Student Union, 2014

Hearth Room in Centennial
Student Union, 2016

Jazzman's Café & Bakery is on
the first floor of the Centennial
Student Union, 2016

well west of it. This modernistic look was intended to call attention to the emerging theme that the front of the campus was on its south side.

The glass front influenced key aspects of interior remodeling. A lower level area, previously used as a television room, was converted into the Hearth Room. This new reception area, which featured a 16-by-5-foot fireplace, benefitted from the natural light provided by its exterior glass wall. Its openness was accentuated by a wide Kasota stone stairway, the connection to the first floor. A similar stairway was installed from near the south entry to the second floor's ballroom area.

Most of the other interior changes affected the union's original Phase I. The food service center was completely redone and three new vendors — Chick-fil-A, Taco Bell Express and Sub Generation — were added. The capacity of the adjacent dining area was increased from 350 to 500 patrons. The dining facilities and the bordering lounge sections were equipped with new furniture. Lastly, a long service counter for the Campus Hub was added near the entrance from the Wigley Administration Building.

## Highland Center Renovation

The Highland Center renovation, Phase II of the plan originated in the Rush administration, was completed early in Davenport's administration. Most of the work was done during the interim presidency of Karen A. Boubel, but Davenport had the honor of leading the ribbon-cutting ceremony on Saturday, October 12, 2002.[137]

The $5-million project entailed major changes to Highland Center's north side and interior. The new north side featured a rotunda near the indoor entrance to the Myers Field House, which served as a commons area, and a remodeled hallway that led to Highland North and the Otto Recreation Center. Other changes included adding four classrooms, conference rooms, locker rooms, an equipment issue room as well as offices for faculty members in the departments of Intercollegiate Athletics, Recreational Sports and Human Performance.

## Otto Recreation Center

In the winter of 2000, several months before construction was begun on the Myers Field House, President Rush lobbied area legislators to obtain Phase III funding for Otto Arena renovation and related projects. The 2000 legislature did not fund the projects. But, after the request was renewed eight members of the House Capital Improvements Committee visited campus in September, 2001, to hear presentations from university officials and students about the pressing need to fund Phase III. The committee was obviously impressed, because the 2002 legislature included $8.4 million for the Phase III work in its state facilities bonding bill.

Otto Recreation Center, 2016

But Governor Jesse Ventura line-item vetoed that and a number of other provisions. Ventura's action had only the effect of delaying the funding for a year. In 2003 Governor Tim Pawlenty approved full funding of the Phase III request.[138]

The renovation of the original Highland Arena was started in May 2004. Heymann Construction of New Ulm, the general contractor, completed it only days before its formal opening on Saturday, October 1, 2005 during the annual Homecoming.[139]

Converting the former home of the varsity basketball teams into a recreation center entailed major changes to the building's structure and accommodations. The main structural changes were to replace the flooring, including the sub-floor, and to install spacious ground-level windows, which enhanced natural lighting. More natural lighting was achieved by installing opaque glass windows at the highest level of the exterior walls. Removal of the stands allowed space for three basketball/volleyball courts that would be used for physical education classes, intramural competition and other recreational activities. A first-floor weight room further enhanced recreational activities. A lounge section equipped with big screen television sets was added to the building's north section. The arena's most striking feature was a gigantic, purple M that extended from floor to ceiling on the center's east end. Other than extolling school pride, it contained conduits that made the newly installed central air conditioning more efficient.

The building's second level featured a three-lane jogging/walking track and 40 Tech/Rec machines. The machines were bikes and treadmills equipped with computers, keyboards and monitors.

With the completion of the renovations the building's name was changed to Otto Recreation Center from Otto Arena, which had been used for 14 years. In the summer of 1991, Highland Arena was renamed to Otto Arena to recognize the key role of James R. "Bob" Otto in the institution's history.[140]

A native of Fort Dodge, Iowa, Otto played football at the University of Iowa, 1939-41. During his 30 years at Mankato State, 1953-83, Otto worked primarily as the football coach and athletic director. In 17 years of coaching, his teams won five conference championships. He served as athletic director from 1970 until he retired in 1983. Otto's many honors included being chosen for the Mankato State and Northern Intercollegiate Conference halls of fame. He died on November 9, 1993.

## Earley Center for the Performing Arts

The dedication ceremony for the newly named Earley Center for the Performing Arts was held on Saturday, November 12, 2011. President Davenport recommended the name change to recognize and honor the long, distinguished career of Jane F. Earley as the dean of the College of Arts and Humanities.[141]

Earley, who had earned a Ph.D. from Northwestern University, started in 1969 at the then Mankato State College as an assistant professor of English. Like many junior faculty members she was designated for termination during the trying times of the early to mid-1970s. But she was selected as the assistant dean

James R. "Bob" Otto, 1960

Otto Recreation Center basketball court, 2016

Otto Recreation Center, 2005

Jane F. Earley,
2011

Pillars and Ellis Avenue Gateway,
2011

of the School of Arts and Sciences in 1974 to replace the retiring Elias J. Halling. She was promoted to associate dean, Halling's last designation, the next year and was named acting dean in 1976 when Dean Elwood B. Earle resigned to accept another position. As a result of university reorganization in 1977, Earley was chosen as the dean of the College of Arts and Humanities, one of the three colleges formed out of the previous School of Arts and Sciences.

Earley, who served as dean until her retirement in 2009 (except for one year when she was the acting academic vice president), earned the unique distinction of being the first woman dean of an academic college in the institution's history.

In addition to her normal administrative duties, Earley actively participated in state and national organizations. Her numerous activities included serving on the Minnesota Humanities Commission and the Minnesota News Council and serving as the president of the nationwide Council of Arts and Sciences for a term.

The dedication ceremony included presentations by the Concert Choir, directed by David Dickau, and pianist David Viscoli, greetings from Brett Anderson, representing the MnSCU Board, remarks by Davenport and comments by Earley and the placement of a plaque in the building's lobby.

## Landscape Changes

The campus landscape has been changed significantly by the Pillars and a pedestrian passageway that connects the Centennial Student Union and Memorial Library.

The Pillars, located near the southwest corner of Otto Recreation Center at the intersection of Ellis Avenue and Stadium Road, were erected in 2007. Anyone expecting to see actual physical pillars will be disappointed. Sculptor Steven Woodward of St. Paul explained that he chose the name pillars because the students were the pillars of the institution. He chose to portray various academic subjects by embedding eight large, horizontal slabs of Kasota stone in a graded dirt slope facing Ellis Avenue.[142]

Those rectangular blocks etched with the names THEATRE, PHYSICS, LITERATURE, ASTRONOMY and HISTORY are upright, but the PHILOSOPHY and GEOLOGY slabs are upside down and one is nameless. This arrangement, Woodward explained, symbolized the different ways of looking at things in an academic environment. Some things could be better approached, he mused, by standing them on their head; the nameless piece, he explained, stood for open studies. Judging by spectator comments, Woodward accomplished his aim of causing people to think about the meaning and purpose of a university.

The $65,000 cost of the Pillars came out of the funds allocated for Otto Arena renovation. The Pillars project was part of the overall plan to accustom people to the idea that the south side of the campus was the front of the university. Prior to consolidation, when most traffic approached the Highland Campus via Val Imm Drive, the south side appeared to be the rear of the campus. But such projects as the completion of the Wigley Administration Building in 1979 and the hard-topping of Stoltzman Road through the Indian Creek Slough in 1986 helped re-orient the southern campus approach to the designated Ellis Avenue Entry.

After campus consolidation left Memorial Library as a west side outlier the idea of connecting the Centennial Student Union and Memorial Library became more popular. Interest seemed to peak on boreal winter days when the wind was howling out of the northwest. An interconnection was seriously considered when Mankato began planning for the library addition during the Preska administration, but it was not accomplished until 2013.

Whenever the passageway was contemplated, most people seemed to envision a ground-level, enclosed hallway. But, when the Davenport administration decided to act, it opted for a below ground level connection, which was designed by representatives of the four contractors—Leo A. Daley, EDR Ltd., Brennan Construction of Mankato and American Engineering Testing.[143]

Rather than build a true tunnel that would have been completely underground, the contractors decided to construct a tunnel under the sidewalks and buildings at both ends and otherwise build a hallway that let in natural light. They accomplished this by excavating a small amphitheater on the passageway's windowed west side. Although the excavation was necessary to get natural lighting, the amphitheater also provided a venue for events such as performances and social gatherings.

The project, which entailed 1,680 square feet at a total cost of $1,241,125, got underway on May 13, 2013. Despite being delayed somewhat by heavy rains, its completion was marked by a dedication on November 13. At the dedication Davenport remarked that he had first become seriously interested in the project three years earlier when a disabled student expressed concern about getting to the library in the winter.

At the time of the dedication, the administration anticipated a rather heavy use of the passageway. Daily visitor estimates for the union and library were respectively 9,500 and 5,000.

Memorial Library and pedestrian connection, 2015

Interior of pedestrian connection, 2017

## Intercollegiate Athletics Conference Change

The crisis precipitated by the demise of the North Central Conference caused Minnesota State University, Mankato to return to the Northern Sun Intercollegiate Conference in 2008.[144]

The North Central Conference, which was formed in 1922, disbanded because most of its non-Minnesota institutions decided to compete at the National Collegiate Athletics Association's (NCAA) Division I level instead of their traditional Division II. The exodus began in 2003 with the withdrawal of the University of Northern Colorado. A more serious blow occurred the next year with the withdrawal of North Dakota State and South Dakota State, both of which had been charter members. In the summer of 2006 the University of North Dakota announced that it was quitting the conference. On November 29, 2006, the same day the University of South Dakota announced

Maverick Golf Team, 2009 NSIC Champions. Image courtesy of Athletic Communications

its decision to compete in Division I, the North Central conference revealed that it would cease operating effective July 1, 2008.

The dissolution of the North Central Conference caused Minnesota State University, Mankato as well as St. Cloud State and the University of Minnesota Duluth to rejoin the Northern Sun Intercollegiate Conference, which had been so-named in 1979. The genesis of the Northern Sun was the Northern Teachers Athletic Conference, which was formed in 1932.[145]

The 16-member Northern Sun Intercollegiate Conference, with institutions in Minnesota, North Dakota, South Dakota, Iowa and Nebraska, sponsors eight men's and 10 women's sports. But only Minnesota State Mankato, Augustana University and Minot State actually field teams in all the men's sports—baseball, basketball, cross country, football, golf], track & field indoor, track & field outdoor and wrestling. In addition to Minnesota State University, Mankato, Augustana, Minnesota State University, Moorhead, St. Cloud State and Sioux Falls University have the women's sports of basketball, cross country, golf, soccer, softball, swimming & diving tennis, track & field indoor, track & field outdoor and volleyball.

## Hockey Competition

Both the men's and women's teams at Minnesota State University, Mankato compete in Division I hockey. Only selected institutions in the North Central Conference and the Northern Sun Conference had hockey teams, which competed in specifically designated hockey conferences.

The men's team has been competing in the Division I Western Collegiate Hockey Association since 1999, when the varsity program was 30 years old. During the era of Coach Don Brose, 1969-1983 and 1984-2000, when it competed variously as an independent or as a Division II or III team, Mankato State gained national recognition. The Mavericks were the Division II national tournament runner-up in 1979 and won the national tournament the following year.[146]

The advent of Division I hockey brought big time sports to Minnesota State University, Mankato. WCHA competition against such in-state rivals as the University of Minnesota, St. Cloud State, University of Minnesota Duluth and Bemidji State University attracted much public interest and publicity.

But this WCHA competition was detrimentally affected by two 2013 realignments: Minnesota had to compete in the Big 10 after hockey was added as a conference sport, and St. Cloud and Duluth joined the newly formed

Maverick soccer, 2009

Women's hockey, 2009

2017-18 Men's Hockey Team
Image courtesy of Athletic Communications.

National Collegiate Hockey Conference. As a result, Minnesota's five Division I hockey teams now compete in three difference conferences. Women's hockey has been a varsity sport since its inaugural year, 1998-99. Like the men's team, it plays its home games at the municipal Verizon Wireless Center, which has a seating capacity of 5,280, in downtown Mankato.[147]

## The Advent of Doctoral Degree Programs

The idea that Mankato State should offer doctoral degrees was first advanced in the mid-1960s during the abortive campaign for the University of Southern Minnesota. At that time, proponents were considering Ph.D. degrees in such fields as history that would require research on an original topic. The thought of the state universities offering doctorates was kept alive over the years, but legislatures were leery of authorizing degrees that would compete with the research mission of the University of Minnesota. For example, when the possibility of offering doctorates was advanced by MnSCU in 1999, the legislature refused to authorize it. Rather, in the Higher Education Appropriations Act the lawmakers stipulated that: "During the biennium, neither the board [MnSCU trustee] nor campuses shall plan or develop doctoral level programs or degrees until after they have received the recommendation of the house and senate committees on education, finance and ways and means."[148]

Six years later when legislators re-considered the offering of doctoral degree programs by the state universities, they clearly distinguished between the missions of those institutions and the University of Minnesota. In their Higher Education Appropriations Act, they first specified that: "The state universities shall offer undergraduate and graduate instruction through the master's degree, including specialist certificates in the liberal arts and sciences and professional education, and may offer applied doctoral programs in education, business, psychology, physical therapy, audiology, and nursing . . ." The very next sentence read: "The University of Minnesota shall offer undergraduate, graduate, and professional instruction through the doctoral degree, and shall be the primary state supported academic agency for research and extension services."[149]

By 2009 Minnesota State University, Mankato had developed and obtained MnSCU approval for applied doctoral degrees in three of the areas—education, nursing and psychology— authorized by the 2005 law. The Doctor of Education (Ed.D.) was available in both Counselor Education and Supervision and Educational Leadership. The other two degrees were the Doctor in Nursing Practice (DNP) and the Doctor of Psychology.[150]

Through the 2017 calendar year, Minnesota State University, Mankato had awarded 75 doctor's degrees. Forty-five of them were in education, 17 in nursing and 13 in psychology.[151]

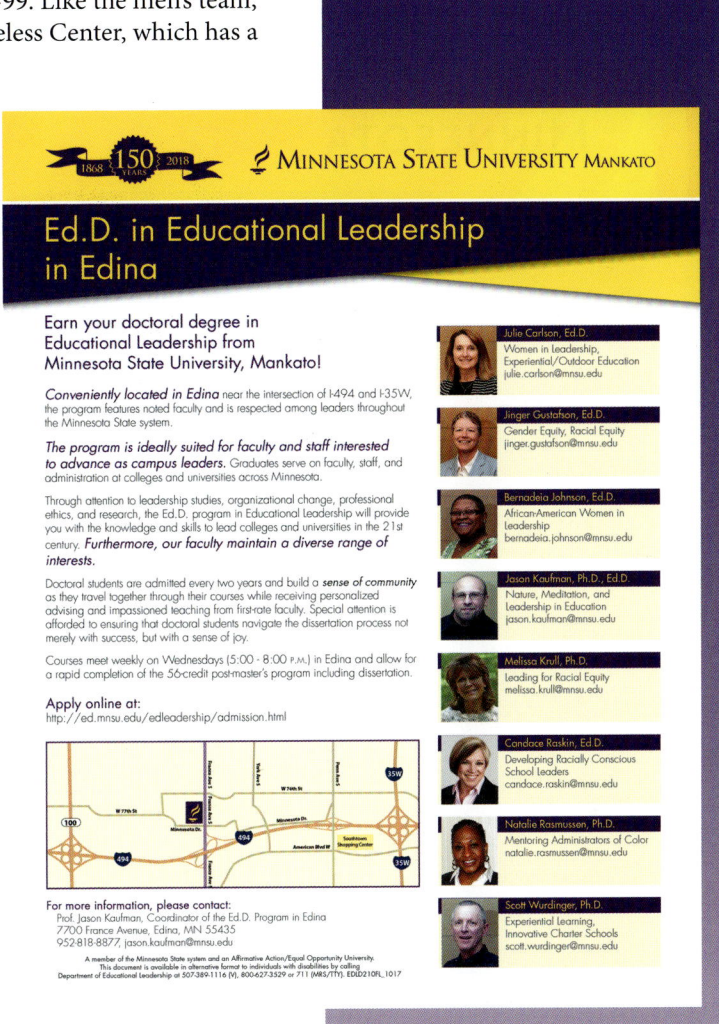

Educational Leadership, 2017

Minnesota State logo, 2017

## Rebranding MnSCU to Minnesota State

On April 19, 2016, the MnSCU Board of Trustees considered a consultant's recommendation that their system's nickname be changed from MnSCU to Minnesota State, which would have a new logo. The proposal was strongly supported by Chancellor Steven Rosenstone, who reported that surveys had shown that various constituencies including the public and students did not know what MnSCU meant. Many thought it was the acronym for all public and private colleges and universities in the state and others believed it was only the name of the system's office.[152]

Although she favored the proposal, Noelle Hawton, MnSCU's chief marketing and communications officer, thought the name Minnesota State might detrimentally affect those institutions, such as Minnesota State University, Mankato and Minnesota State University Moorhead, that had been using the Minnesota State label since 1998. President Richard Davenport opined that the change would not disadvantage his institution, which had a well-established identity as well a distinctive marketing tagline —Big ideas. Real-world thinking. But Richard Rush, the former president who led the effort to rename Mankato State University to Minnesota State University, Mankato, doubted that the name Minnesota State would lead to a clear understanding of the system's composition. The proposal's most vocal opponent was MnSCU trustee Bob Hoffman of Waseca, a former Minnesota State University, Mankato administrator who thought the proposal was nothing more than a "solution in search of a problem."

As judged by the *Free Press* coverage, the proposed change was very unpopular in the Mankato area, where opponents thought it was much too costly as well as potentially damaging to the image of Minnesota State University, Mankato. MnSCU had already paid public-relations firm Padilla CRT $272,000 to survey perceptions of MnSCU and had committed an additional $345,000 for additional research on the rebranding effort. Those students interviewed by the *Free Press* thought marketing the system by the nickname Minnesota State would only cause confusion because that name was already popularly used to describe Minnesota State University, Mankato. Furthermore, some critics believed the name Minnesota State was too reminiscent of the fictional Minnesota State in the former ABC-TV sit-com "Coach." Many Minnesotans would have been happier if the make-believe university, which hardly qualified as higher education, had been named after some other state.

Publicity about the Minnesota State proposal did not cause any of the MnSCU trustees to change their positions. When the board took its final vote on June 21, 2016, only Hoffman opposed the rebranding. Hawton, who was particularly enthusiastic about the change, thought it would more effectively publicize the member institutions and increase enrollment.

Less than two years is too brief to determine if MnSCU accomplished its purpose of better educating its constituencies by rebranding its system as Minnesota State—a name that apparently needs to be explained. An online search for Minnesota State brings up the heading Minnesota State Colleges and Universities. Under that heading one will find the name Minnesota State and its logo (a star above a capital M). Then if one clicks on "About Minnesota State," its mission statement mentions "The Minnesota State Colleges and Universities system . . . ." So, the singular Minnesota State and the plural Minnesota State Colleges and Universities are synonymous. Thus, the 2016 change amounted to a retention of the legal name Minnesota State Colleges and Universities and the replacement of the branding acronym MnSCU with Minnesota State.

## End of the Vikings Era

In July 2017 the Minnesota Vikings announced that their upcoming August training camp at Minnesota State University, Mankato would end an era that started in 1966. A National Football League expansion team, the Vikings, were organized in 1960 and began playing the next year in Metropolitan Stadium in Bloomington. Bemidji State College was the site of the team's first five training camps. But the Vikings switched to Mankato State College in 1966 in part because of its excellent facilities, but also to better serve its numerous metropolitan area fans who preferred a training site within relatively convenient commuter distances.[153]

Viking Training Camp at Mankato State University, Mankato, 1991

Over the decades, as Mankato State evolved from Mankato State College to Mankato State University and Minnesota State University, Mankato, the Vikings training camps became part of the institution's tradition. The 52 consecutive summer camps attracted numerous out-of-town visitors and boosted, in particular, the local restaurant, hotel/motel and service station businesses. As many as 60,000 annual visitors added as much as $5 million to the local economy.

Minnesota State University, Mankato benefitted economically by renting dormitory rooms and practice facilities and providing food service for the Vikings. But, in the long run, the intangible benefit of advertising the institution to people who may not have seen it otherwise was probably of more value. There is no doubt that the training camps were a significant factor in promoting Minnesota State University, Mankato as well as the community of Mankato.

The Vikings ended their last Mankato training camp with a final night practice in Blakeslee Stadium on Saturday, August 5, 2017. Henceforth, they had decided to use their newly constructed facilities in the Twin Cities suburb of Eagan. Their departure prompted President Davenport to observe that the Vikings had been associated with Mankato for more than a third of its entire history.

# Distinguished Faculty Scholars

Its increased emphasis in promoting faculty research and writing caused the Davenport Administration to establish a Distinguished Faculty Scholars Award Program. The guidelines for the awards, which were first granted in 2008, specify: (1) That up to three awards will be made each year; (2) each recipient receives a recognition plaque and $5,000 for research support and/or professional development; (3) award recipients will also be granted $4,000 from their respective deans to support research-related activities; and (4) award winners and nominees will be announced every March and recognized at an annual luncheon.

Only full-time tenured faculty members who hold the rank of professor and have at least eight years of service at Minnesota State Mankato are eligible for the award. Nominees must have at least a national reputation in their respective fields.

Award recipients are selected by the Faculty Research Committee and the Center for Excellence in Scholarship and Research. All awards are granted on the basis of outstanding professional achievements in artistic, historical, literary, philosophical, scientific and technical fields. The selection criteria in priority order are: (1) Quality of the nominee's scholarly or creative achievements, with an emphasis on originality, imagination and innovation; (2) impact on the nominee's discipline of field of study; (3) national and international scholarly reputation; (4) contribution to undergraduate and/or graduate education, and (5) contributions to the university, profession and wider community.

For the period 2008-2017 the following 30 faculty members have been designated Distinguished Faculty Scholars.

## 2008:

### Dr. Suzanne L. Bunkers,
### Department of English.

Suzanne L. Bunkers, an Iowa native, earned her B.A. in English education (1972) and M.A. in English Literature (1974) at Iowa State University. In 1980, the same year she began teaching at what was then Mankato State University, she completed her Ph.D. in English at the University of Wisconsin-Madison. Her doctoral dissertation about Katherine Anne Porter, the essayist, short story writer and novelist, who won both the Pulitzer Prize and the National Book Award in 1966, was titled "Katherine Anne Porter: A Re-assessment."

During her Minnesota State University, Mankato teaching career, which lasted until she retired in 2011, Bunkers established an outstanding record because of her research and writing on women's diaries and personal journal writing. These aspects of scholarship contributed significantly to the emerging field of New Social History that emphasized the importance of everyday lives and experiences as opposed to the traditional emphasis on political history and big events.

Between 1981 and 2001 Bunkers authored, co-authored and edited eight books. Her most renowned book is *In Search of Susanna* (Iowa City: University of Iowa Press, 1996). This partially autobiographical history covers the period from the Luxembourg origins of Bunkers' ancestors to her own life as a teacher and writer. In her edited works, which include *The Diary of Caroline Seabury, 1854-1863* (Madison: University of Wisconsin Press, 1991) and *"All Will Yet Be Well": The Diary of Sarah Gillespie Huftalen, 1873-1952,* Bunkers wrote detailed introductions and prepared copious explanatory notes. In addition to her books, Bunkers has written several dozen articles that were published in a variety of scholarly journals.

(Sources: Distinguished Faculty Scholar Awards, online source, access by title. Bunkers, Suzanne L. in World Cat. Guide to the Suzanne Bunkers Papers, University of Iowa Libraries, online source. Porter, Katherine Anne in *Wikipedia*. Bunkers, Suzanne folder, University Advancement Collection, 1939-ongoing, University Archives.)

### Dr. David Dickau,
### Department of Music.

David Dickau, a nationally famed choral conductor and composer, began serving as director of Choral Activities at Minnesota State University, Mankato in 1991. He had graduated from the University of Southern California with a Bachelor of Music degree in 1975. His graduate degrees were a Master of Music, Northwestern University, 1979 and a Doctor of Musical Arts from the University of Southern California.

His work at Minnesota State University, Mankato has included conducting the Concert Choir and Chamber Singers and teaching conducting and composition. A number of Dickau's numerous compositions, including *A House Carol and Life Has Loveliness to Sell* have been published by Santa Barbara Music Publishing, Inc.

Additionally, Dickau has been commissioned to write compositions for special events. For example, his "View from the Air" premiered at Little Falls, Minnesota, on August 16, 1997 during the celebration of the 70th anniversary of Charles Lindbergh's trans-Atlantic flight.

Dickau has been a very active member of the American Choral Director's Association. He served as its Repertoire and Standards Chair, 1987-1991, American Choral Director's Association. He served as its Repertoire and Standards Chair, 1987-1991, presented at its national and regional conferences and was president of the Minnesota chapter for a term.

(Sources: Distinguished Faculty Scholar Awards, online source, access by title. Dickau, David vita, dean's office, College of Arts and Humanities, Minnesota State University, Mankato. David Dickau: Bio & Choral Music Santa Barbara Music Publishing, Inc., online source, access by title. David C. Dickau— Choral Conductor, Choral Composer, Choral Clinician —Home, online source, access by title. Dickau, David folder, University Advancement Collection, 1939-ongoing, University Archives.)

### Dr. James E. Robertson,
### Department of Sociology and Corrections.

James E. Robertson, who joined the Minnesota State University, Mankato faculty in 1980, completed a B.A. with a history major (1972) at the University of Washington (Seattle), a M.A. with a corrections major at California State University, Sacramento (1974) and a J.D. (Juris Doctor) at Washington University (St. Louis) in 1975. In 1988 he earned his second law degree—a Diploma in Law from Oxford University (Keble College), Oxford, England. Just prior to starting at Minnesota State University, Mankato, he was employed as a research specialist at the Center for the Study of Law and Society, University of California, Berkeley.

With his background in criminology and law, Robertson was well-prepared to research and write about various aspects of the criminal justice system. His scholarship resulted in more than 50 articles that were published in such journals as the *Journal of Criminal Law and Criminology, Criminal Justice Review* and the *Correctional Law Review.*

His works, which have been consulted by judges, lawyers and legal researchers, have resulted in changes to prisoner rights policies. Furthermore, he contributed to scholarship by serving for some years as the editor-in-chief of the *Criminal Law Bulletin* and the contributing editor of *Criminal Law Bulletin.*

Robertson retired from the university in May 2017.

(Sources: Distinguished Faculty Scholar Awards, online source, access by title. James E. Robertson folder, University Advancement Collection, 1939-ongoing, University Archives. James E. Robertson file, College of Social and Behavioral Sciences, Minnesota State University, Mankato.)

## 2009:

### Dr. John Janc,
### Department of Modern Languages.

John Janc, who began teaching French at Minnesota State University, Mankato in 1979, studied French language and literature while earning five degrees. He earned a B.A. from the University of Wisconsin-Eau Claire in 1967 and a M.A. from the University of Michigan the next year. In 1974 he was awarded a Master of Arts in Comparative Literature from the University of Wisconsin-Madison. He earned a doctoral degree from the Universite La Sorbonne Nouvelle, Paris in 1977 and a Ph.D. from the University of Wisconsin-Madison in 1981.

Janc had a distinguished career as a teacher and scholar during his tenure at the university until his retirement in 2010. His teaching was recognized by two prestigious awards. In 1986 the French government made him a knight in the Ordre des Palmes Academiques, the highest recognition it granted to teachers who contributed significantly to French education and the prestige of French culture. Janc's qualifications included his organization and administration of Mankato State's annual Summer Study in France program. In 1988 he was one of only 30 professors selected as State Professor of the Year by the Council for the Advancement and Support of Education (CASE).

Janc's French language scholarship included preparing new editions of several plays written by the noted French dramatist Victor Hugo that were published by the University Press of America (Lanham, Maryland). They were *Les Deux Trouvailles de Gallus* (1983), *Torquemada* (1989) and *Marion de Lorme* (2013).

(Sources: Distinguished Faculty Scholar Awards, online source, access by title. Janc, John J. folder, University Advancement Collection, 1939-ongoing, University Archives. John J. Janc, American language educator. Online source, access by title.)

### Professor Richard L. Robbins,
### Department of English.

Richard L. Robbins joined the Minnesota State University, Mankato faculty in 1984 after earning a B.A. degree from San Diego State University, California (1975) and an M.F.A. in creative writing from the University of Montana (1979).

As the longtime director of the university's creative writing program, Robbins created and administered the annual Good Thunder Writing Series. This significant event, which has featured nationally known authors, has proven to be the English Department's most visible beyond-the-classroom activity.

Poetry has been Robbins' own creative writing. His poems have been published in six books, namely: *The Invisible Wedding: Poems* (Columbia: University of Missouri Press, 1984), *Famous Persons We Have Known: Poems* (Spokane: Eastern University Washington Press, 2000), *The Untested Hand* (Omaha: Backwaters Press, 2008), *Radioactive City* (Pittsburgh: Bellday Books, 2009), *Other Americas* (Janesville, Minn.: Blueroad Press, 2010) and *Body Turn to Rain: New & Selected Poems* (Spokane: Lynx House Press, 2017). His poetry has also been published in such journals as the *Colorado Review* and *Creative Arts Journal.*

Because of his writing, Robbins has won several major awards. They include the Robert H. Winner Memorial Award in the annual contest sponsored by the Poetry Society of America (1988), a $20,000 fellowship from the National Endowment for the Arts (1992) and a McKnight Artist Fellowship for Writers (1997).

(Sources: Distinguished Faculty Scholar Awards, online source, access by title. Robbins, Richard L. folder, University Advancement Collection, 1939-ongoing, University Archives.)

### Professor Richard Terrill,
### Department of English.

Richard Terrill, a creative writing professor who began his Minnesota State University, Mankato career in 1990, earned his B.A. (1975) from the University of Wisconsin-Eau Claire, his M.F.A. (1978) in creative writing from the University of Arizona and his M.A. (1989) from the University of Michigan. Among his many contributions to the university, Terrill established the Writers Bloc, a monthly public forum that provided students with an opportunity to read their writings.

An accomplished writer, Terrill wrote both poetry and prose. His two collections of poetry—*Coming Late to Rachmaninoff: Poems* (2003) and *Almost Dark: Poems* (2010) were published by the University of Tampa Press (Florida).

Terrill's three prose books concerned recent Chinese history and jazz music. *Saturday Night in Baoding: A China Memoir* (Fayetteville: University of Arkansas Press, 1990) emphasized his own experiences as a Fulbright scholar in China. *The Cross and the Red Star: John Foster Travels to the Eighth Route Army* (St. Paul: Asian Pacific Foundation, 1994) describes the experiences of John Foster, who, in 1934, carried a shipment of medical supplies behind Japanese lines to the Eighth Route Army (Communist). Foster, who later taught English at Mankato for more than two decades, worked in China for 15 years in the 1930s and 1940s. A jazz saxophonist himself, Terrill wrote *Fakebook: Improvisations on a Journey Back to Jazz* (New York: Limelight Editions, 2000.)

Terrill won many honors, including three Fulbright scholarships (China, Korea and Poland). In 2004 *Coming Late to Rachmanioff* won the Minnesota Book Award for poetry. *Saturday Night in Baoding* was the winner of an Associated Writing Programs Award.

Terrill retired in 2017.

(Sources: Distinguished Faculty Scholar Awards, online source, access by title. Terrill, Richard in *Wikipedia*. Terrill, Richard in World Cat. Terrill, Richard folder, University Advancement Collection, 1939-ongoing, University Archives.)

## 2010:

### Dr. Steven M. Buechler,
### Department of Sociology and Corrections.

Steven M. Buechler, who joined the Minnesota State University, Mankato faculty in 1986, earned both his B.A. (1973) and M.A. (1975) from the University of Wisconsin-Milwaukee. In 1982 he completed his Ph.D. at the State University of New York at Stony Brook. His dissertation title was "Social Change and Movement Transformation: The Deradicalization of the Illinois Women's Rights/Suffrage Movement, 1850-1920."

During his Mankato career, which ended with his retirement in May 2017, Buechler was one of the institution's most productive scholars. His seven books included *The Transformation of the Woman Suffrage Movement: The Case for Illinois: 1850-1920* (New Brunswick, NJ: Rutgers University Press, 1986), *Social Movements in Advanced Capitalism: The Political Economy and Cultural Construction of Social Activism* (New York: Oxford University Press, 2000) and *Critical Sociology* (Boulder, CO: Paradigm Press, 1st ed., 2008, 2nd ed., 2014.)

Buechler also had 25 articles and chapters published in various scholarly journals and books. His articles appeared in such journals as *The Sociological Quarterly and Teaching Sociology*.

(Sources: Distinguished Faculty Scholar Awards, online source, access by title. Buechler, Steven M. folder, University Advancement Collection, 1939-ongoing, University Archives. Buechler, Steven, M. file, College of Social and Behavioral Sciences, Minnesota State University, Mankato.)

### Dr. Daniel Cronn-Mills,
### Department of Speech Communications.

A native of Lake Crystal, Minnesota, Daniel Cronn-Mills earned his B.A. (1987) and M.A. (1989) from then Mankato State University. He joined the faculty of his alma mater in 1992. In 1995 he completed his Ph.D. in Communications Studies at the University of Nebraska-Lincoln. His dissertation was titled "A Social Construction of Reality Evident in the Discourse of Jehovah's Witnesses."

In addition to teaching, his career at Minnesota State University, Mankato has included directing intercollegiate forensics, research and writing. In 1997, Cronn-Mills was recognized as the Outstanding New Teacher of the Year by the Central States Communication Association.

As director of Maverick Forensics, Cronn-Mills developed it into one of the nation's leading programs, which facilitated the recruitment of talented students who were seeking careers as forensic coaches and teachers.

Cronn-Mills' first book was based on his doctoral dissertation. *A Qualitative Analysis of the Jehovah's Witnesses: The Rhetoric, Reality and Religion in the Watchtower Society* was published in 1999 by the E. Mellen Press of Lewiston, New York. Additionally, he co-authored *Religious Misperceptions: The Case of Muslims and Christians in France and Britain* (New York: Hampton Press, 2011) and *Understanding Communication Research Methods: A Theoretical and Practical Approach* (New York: Routledge, 2015).

(Sources: Distinguished Faculty Scholar Awards, online source, access by title. Cronn-Mills, Daniel folder, University Advancement Collection, 1939-ongoing, University Archives. Cronn-Mills, Daniel in World Cat.)

### Professor Brian L. Frink,
### Department of Art.

Brian L. Frink, who started at Minnesota State University, Mankato, in 1989 earned his Bachelor of Fine Arts from Illinois State University, Normal in 1979. He then lived in New York City for five years, where he frequented the city's numerous galleries and studios while working as a carpenter and electrician. After returning to the Midwest, he earned a Master of Fine Arts degree in art from the University of Wisconsin-Madison (1988).

At Minnesota State University, Mankato Frink has regularly taught painting and drawing and established an outstanding reputation as a painter. He uses an encaustic process in which oil paint is mixed with hot wax. This creates images that feature a sense of depth.

Frink's paintings have been displayed in many Midwestern galleries and added to private collections. His reputation and work have been recognized by some prestigious awards, including a $5,000 grant from the Wisconsin State Arts Board (1990), a McKnight Foundation Fellowship (1992), a $20,000 fellowship from the National Endowment for the Arts (1992) and a $6,000 grant from the Minnesota State Arts Board (1995.)

(Sources: Distinguished Faculty Scholar Awards, online source, access by title. Frink, Brian L. folder, University Advancement Collection, 1939-ongoing, University Archives.)

## 2011:

### Dr. Michael D. Bentley,
### Department of Biological Sciences.

Before joining the Minnesota State University, Minnesota faculty in 1989, Bentley had been awarded three degrees. In 1968 he graduated from Central Michigan University with a B.S. in Biology. The next year he completed his M.S. in Biology at the University of Minnesota. In 1983 he was awarded his Ph.D. in Veterinary Anatomy by the University of Minnesota. His dissertation topic was "The Kidney of the Mongolian Gerbil (*Mariones unguiculatus*):

Morphology and Effect of Antidurectic Hormone on the Collecting Duct System."

For the six years prior to joining the University, Bentley was employed as a research fellow (1983-86), research associate (1986-88) and special project associate (1988-89) in the Department of Biophysics and Physiology, Mayo Foundation and Medical School, Rochester, Minnesota.

Bentley has had a distinguished career as a teacher and researcher. He has mentored many undergraduate students who conduct research and present at the Undergraduate Research Symposium and the National Conference for Undergraduate Research.

Bentley's research emphasizes the use of imaging technology to study organs and tissue with particular reference to the vascular structure of kidneys. His findings have been published in leading professional journals such as the *American Journal of Pathology* and *Kidney International* (official journal of the International Society of Nephrology).

(Sources: Distinguished Faculty Scholar Awards, online source, access by title. Bentley, Michael D. folder, University Advancement Collection, 1939-ongoing, University Archives. Articles in the Minnesota State University, Mankato website, namely: "Dr. Bentley's Selected Publications," "Michael Bentley," "Dr. Michael Bentley: 2017 Mentor of the Year," and "Dr. Bentley's Research Projects.")

### Dr. Martin Mitchell,
### Department of Geography.

Martin Mitchell, who started teaching at Minnesota State University, Mankato in 1993, earned his B.A. in Geography at California State University, Chico (1984) and his M.A. in Geography from the University of Georgia two years later. In 1993 he completed his Ph.D. in Geography at the University of Illinois at Champaign-Urbana. His dissertation topic was "Changes in Landscape Form and Function in the Sacramento-San Joaquin Delta, California: 1920-1993."

At the university, Mitchell has served as department chair for several terms, taught a variety of courses including Climatology, Water Resources, Computer Assisted Cartography and Environmental Regulations, advised more than two dozen graduate students who have completed alternate plan papers or theses and has engaged in research and writing.

With research interests in climate change, American landscapes and historical geography, Mitchell has authored some two dozen articles through 2016 about a variety of topics including "Southern Minnesota: An Evolving Alternative Energy Frontier" (*Journal of Geography and Geology* 5:3, 2013) and "Deadwood, South Dakota: Place and Setting Combine with Gambling and Preservation" (*Focus*, 51:2, 2008). In 2012 his autobiographical book *Back at the Ranch: Growing up in the American West* was published by Beavers

Pond Press of Minneapolis.

Mitchell has also presented many papers at professional geography conferences and served as a consultant for the Minnesota Department of Natural Resources and the U. S. National Park Service, Jewel Cave National Monument, Custer, South Dakota.

(Sources: Distinguished Faculty Scholar Awards, online source, access by title. Mitchell, Martin file, in College of Social and Behavioral Sciences, Minnesota State University, Mankato.)

### Dr. Stephen J. Stoynoff, Department of English.

Stephen J. Stoynoff joined the Minnesota State University, Mankato English Department faculty in 1996. He completed his bachelor's degree in environmental science in 1976 at Willamette University (Salem, Oregon) and his master's in English Education at Portland State University eight years later. In 1990 he earned his Doctor of Education degree from the University of Oregon (Eugene). His dissertation topic was "English Language Proficiency and Study Strategies as Determinants of Academic Success for International Students in U. S. Universities." Prior to joining Minnesota State University, Mankato, he taught at Oregon State University, Central Washington University and Lewis and Clark College (Portland, Oregon).

Stoynoff's teaching and scholarship at Mankato were primarily concerned with teaching English to speakers of other languages. His books *The Handbook of Funding Opportunities in the Field of TESOL* [Teachers of English to Speakers of Other Languages] (1998) and *ESOL* [English Speakers of Other Languages] *Tests and Testing: A Resource for Teachers and Administrators* (2005) were both published in Alexandria, Virginia, by Teachers of English to Speakers of Other Languages, Inc. Additionally, he authored chapters and/or articles for at least five other books.

Stoynoff moved from teaching to administration in August 2013 when he was appointed Interim Dean of International Affairs. In June 2015, he was named Dean of Global Education, a newly created position. In these positions he successfully helped recruit hundreds of international students for Minnesota State University, Mankato. In 2018, he was named the Interim Associate Vice President for Research and Graduate Studies.

(Sources: Distinguished Faculty Scholar Awards, online source, access by title. Stoynoff, Stephen J. in World Cat. The following articles in the Minnesota State University, Mankato website: "Stephen Stoynoff Biography," "Stephen Stoynoff Appointed Interim Dean of International Affairs," and "Stephen Stoynoff Named Dean of Global Education".)

### 2012:

### Dr. Daniel D. Houlihan, Department of Psychology.

Daniel D. Houlihan earned two degrees from Mankato State University— a B.S. in Psychology (1979) and a M.A. in Clinical Psychology (1983). In 1989 he completed his Ph.D. in School Psychology at the University of Utah. He started teaching at Minnesota State University, Mankato in September 1987.

He has established an enviable record as a teacher, scholar and director. Before shifting to the School Psychology Doctoral Program (which he directs), Houlihan taught primarily in the Clinical Psychology master's program.

Houlihan's main research interests are behavior disorders, autism, compliance and anxiety disorders. He has authored or co-authored more than 70 articles in such professional journals as the *Journal of Applied Behavior Analysis* and the *Journal of Behavior Therapy and Experimental Psychiatry*. Furthermore, he has served on the editorial boards of seven peer-reviewed journals such as the *International Journal of Psychological Studies and Behavior Therapy*.

In 2013 Houlihan received the Distinguished Alumni Harold J. Fitterer Service Award from the Minnesota State University, Mankato Alumni Association.

(Sources: Distinguished Faculty Scholar Awards, online source, access by title. Houlihan, Daniel D. folder, University Advancement Collection, 1939-ongoing, University Archives. The following articles in the Minnesota State University, Mankato website: "Daniel Houlihan," "Daniel Houlihan, Ph. D." and "Elysian's Daniel Houlihan Receives Distinguished Alumni Award.")

### Dr. Paul J. Hustoles, Department of Theatre and Dance.

Paul J. Hustoles, who joined the Minnesota State University, Mankato faculty in 1985, earned his B.F.A. from Wayne State University (Detroit) in 1973 and completed his M.A. in acting/directing from the University of Michigan the next year. In 1984 he was awarded his Ph.D. from Texas Tech University. His dissertation was titled "Musical Theatre Directing: A Generic Approach." Prior to joining the university he had taught and served as theatre director at Tarkio College (Tarkio, Missouri) 1977-83 and taught undergraduate and graduate classes and managed the University Theatres at the University of Mississippi, 1984-85.

As chair of the Department of Theatre and Dance, Hustoles has established an outstanding reputation. By 2013, he had directed 196 plays and musicals. In 2011 he directed The Odyssey, which was one of four collegiate productions to be performed at the Kennedy Center for Festival 44. Extremely active in professional organizations, he has chaired Region V (Minnesota, North Dakota, South Dakota, Nebraska, Kansas, Iowa and Missouri) of the Kennedy Center American College Theatre Festival and directed the Irene Ryan Evening of Scenes at the Kennedy Center in Washington, D. C. In 1998 he received the Region V Gold Medallion of Excellence Award in Theatre.

Other than his teaching and directing, Hustoles has twice served the university as the Interim Director of University Advancement. His first stint of 15 months (February 1993-May 1994) was during the Richard Rush administration. His second, in the Richard Davenport administration, extended from November 2015 to April 2016. Additionally, he is co-chair (with Kent Stanley, Vice President of University Advancement) of the University's Sesquicentennial Observance Committee, which has been planning and coordinating all activities leading up to the institution's 150th anniversary.

(Sources: Distinguished Faculty Scholar Awards, online source, access by title. Hustoles, Paul J. folder, University Advancement Collection, 1939-ongoing, University Archives. The following articles in the Minnesota State University, Mankato website: "Mankato State University Professor Paul J. Hustoles Honored for Lifetime Achievement," 02 February 1999; "Paul J. Hustoles Biography College of Arts and Humanities, Minnesota State University, Mankato" and "Kent Stanley Named Vice President for University Advancement.")

### Dr. Christopher T. Ruhland,
### Department of Biological Sciences.

Christopher T. Ruhland, who joined the Minnesota State University, Mankato faculty in 2001, earned his B.S. (1992) from Wheeling Jesuit University (Wheeling, West Virginia) and his M.S. (1995) from West Virginia University. He was awarded his Ph.D. by Arizona State University in 2001. His dissertation topic was "Effects of Ultraviolet-B Radiation on Phenylpropanoids and Growth of Vascular Plants in Antarctica."

His courses are Plant Biology, Advanced Field Ecology, Global Change Biology, Plant Physiology, Plant Biotechnology and General Biology. Much of his research has been on the impact of global warming. Since 1995 he has worked periodically with a team in Antarctica that is examining the effects of rapid climate change on carbon and nitrogen cycling. This work has been funded by The National Science Foundation's Office of Polar Programs. He has also researched the effects of ozone depletion on crop plants. This research has been supported by grants from the U. S. Department of Energy.

Ruhland's list of "Selected Publications" shows that for the period 1996-2017 he authored or co-authored 29 articles that were published in a number of scholarly journals including *Global Change Biology, Polar Biology and Photochemistry and Photobiology.*

(Sources: Distinguished Faculty Scholar Awards, online source, access by title. The following articles in the Minnesota State University, Mankato website: "Dr. Christopher T. Ruhland," "Dr. Ruhland's Research Projects," "Dr. Ruhland's Selected Publications," and "Dr. Christopher Ruhland's Lab." Ruhland vita which he sent to William E. Lass, 16 January 2018.)

## 2013:

### Dr. Russell L. Palma,
### Department of Physics and Astronomy.

Russell L. Palma, who joined the Minnesota State University, Mankato faculty in 2004, earned his B.S. in astrophysics from the University of Indiana (1974) and his M.S. (1978) and Ph.D. (1981) in space physics and astronomy from Rice University. His previous experience included 24 years in the Department of Physics at Sam Houston State University.

His research in the fields of astronomy, cosmochemistry and extraterrestrial materials, emphasizes using ultra-high vacuum mass spectrometry to measure gases in extraterrestrial materials obtained from such things as lunar materials, meteorites and interplanetary dust particles. As part of a team of NASA scientists from the United States, Germany and Japan, and with the assistance of Jacob Simones, a Minnesota State University, Mankato student, Palma played a significant role in the discovery of a new comet-borne mineral that has been named Brownleeite.

Palma also served as senior research associate at Texas A&M University and the University of California, San Diego. He has participated in the research of international scientific consortia that have studied samples from NASA's Genesis and Stardust Missions.

A widely recognized scholar in his field, Palma co-authored 50 articles about various aspects of astronomy. Half of them have been published since his arrival at Minnesota State University, Mankato. Most of the articles were published in such professional journals as *Science, Lunar and Planetary Science and Meteorics & Planetary Science*." Palma announced his retirement in 2018.

(Sources: Distinguished Faculty Scholar Awards, online source, access by title. The following articles in the Minnesota State University, Mankato website: "Russell Palma," "Russ Palma, Student Jacob Simones Help Discover New Mineral from Tail of Comet," and "Astronomy Faculty Member Russell Palma Had Key Role in Discovery of New Comet-borne Mineral." Palma vita which he sent to William E. Lass, 16 January 2018.)

**Dr. David Viscoli,
Department of Music.**

David Viscoli, a pianist, joined the Minnesota State University, Mankato faculty in 1999. He earned his Bachelor of Music degree in Applied Piano at the University of Texas at Austin in 1987 and both his Master of Music (1989) and Doctor of Musical Arts (1989) at the University of Southern California.

He has performed extensively as a piano soloist and chamber musician at various locales in the United States, Canada, Central America, Europe and Asia. His most noteworthy performances include guest artist recitals at the National Theatre in Panama City, Panama, the National University of the Arts and the Japanese Embassy in Taiwan, Chung-Ang University in Korea and the Palais Corbelli in Vienna, Austria. He has performed at such major universities and academies as the University of Texas at Austin, University of Washington, University of Oregon, Ohio State University, University of Iowa, University of California at Santa Barbara, Interlochen Arts Academy (Michigan) and Idyllwild Arts Academy (California). Closer to home, he has performed with principal members of the Minnesota Orchestra and the St. Paul Chamber Orchestra.

Viscoli has won awards in national and international piano competitions, including the Los Angeles Liszt Competition, the Carmel Music Society Piano Competition and the Joanna Hodges International Piano Competition.

(Sources: Distinguished Faculty Scholar Awards, online source, access by title. David Viscoli vita in dean's office, College of Arts and Humanities, Minnesota State University Mankato. The following articles in the Minnesota State University, Mankato website: "David Viscoli," and "David Viscoli Biography College of Arts and Humanities, Minnesota State University, Mankato.")

**Dr. Dennis D. Waskul,
Department of Sociology and Corrections.**

Dennis Waskul, who joined the Minnesota State University, Mankato faculty in 2004, earned his B.A. in Sociology from the University of Minnesota Morris in 1990 and his M. A. in Sociology from Mankato State two years later. The topic of his Master's thesis was "Removal Reflection and Reaggregation: A Sociological Analysis of the Experiences of a Camp Staff." In 1997 he completed his Ph.D. in Sociology at Oklahoma State University (Stillwater.)

Waskul's teaching specialties are Human Sexualities, Social Psychology, Popular Culture and Ethnography. A very active researcher and writer, he is the sole author of two books, the co-author of two others and a chapter contributor to 14 more.

His *Self-games and Body Play: Personhood in Online Chat and Cybersex* was published in 2003 by Peter Lang of New York City and *Ghostly Encounters: The Hauntings of Everyday Life* was published in Philadelphia by the Temple University Press in 2016. His co-authored books (with Phillip Vannini) are *Body Embodiment: Symbolic Interaction and the Sociology of the Body* (Hampshire, England: Aldershot; Burlington, VT: Ashgate, 2006) and *The Senses in Self, Society and Culture: A Sociology of the Senses* (New York: Routledge, 2012). Additionally, he has authored or co-authored 19 scholarly journal articles and 17 book chapters.

(Sources: Waskul, Dennis D. vita, in dean's office, College of Social and Behavioral Sciences, Minnesota State University, Mankato. Distinguished Faculty Scholar Awards, online source, access by title. The following articles in the Minnesota State University, Mankato website: "Dennis Waskul" and "Dennis Waskul Ph.D."; Waskul, Dennis D. in World Cat.)

## 2014:

**Dr. Kimberly E. Contag,
Department of World Languages and Cultures.**

Kimberly E. Contag, who joined the Minnesota State University, Mankato faculty in 1992, earned her M.A. and Ph.D. degrees from the University of Minnesota. She completed her master's thesis "Humorous Function of Jokes and Hoaxes in Don Quijote" in 1983. Her doctoral dissertation (1989) was titled "The Nature and Function of Burlesque: The Ideology of Mockery in Golden Age Spanish Literature."

Contag's main publication is her book *Mockery in Spanish Golden Age Literature: Analysis of Burlesque Representation* (Lanham, MD: University Press of America, 1996). She has also written parts of several other books including *Cross-disciplinary Essays on Don Quixote: The Minnesota Conference Celebrating the 400th Anniversary of Its Publication* (Lewiston, NY: Edwin Mellen Press, 2007.) She has also authored a number of journal articles and introductions and translated several published works.

In addition to her Minnesota State University, Mankato teaching, Contag has taught at the State University in Cuenca, Ecuador, the University of Minnesota, Carleton College and the University of Oklahoma. At Oklahoma she received the Cecil W. Woods Memorial Award for Excellence in Teaching foreign languages. As the recipient of two Fulbright awards, she taught in Spain (1986-87) and Ecuador (1986).

Contag served twice as a Minnesota State University, Mankato administrator. In 2009-10, she was the interim assistant vice president for undergraduate studies and in 2014-16 the interim dean of the College of Arts and Humanities.

(Sources: Distinguished Faculty Scholar Awards, online source, access by title. Contag, Contag, Kimberly vita in dean's, office, College of Arts and Humanities, Minnesota State University Mankato. Contag, Elizabeth E. in World Cat.)

### Professor Mika Negishi Laidlaw, Department of Art.

Mika Laidlaw, a native of Kobe, Honshu, Japan, earned her B.A. in Studio Art from Southern Illinois University at Edwardsville in 1994. She worked the next three years as a ceramic apprentice at Akishino Pottery in Nara (City) near Kobe. In 2000 she completed her Master of Fine Arts degree in ceramics at Kansas State University. She was hired by Minnesota State University, Mankato in 2003. She was promoted to associate professor in 2009 and full professor four years later.

Her work as an outstanding ceramics artist has been widely recognized. Her numerous awards include the McKnight Award for Ceramic Artists in 2001, 2006 and 2011 and a Summer Artist Residence at the Archie Bray Foundation for Ceramic Art in 2003. She was recognized as an Emerging Artist at the annual conference of the National Council on Education for the Ceramic Arts in 2004.

Laidlaw's art has been shown in more than a hundred solo or joint exhibitions, which were held nationally and abroad in Japan, Taiwan, Korea and Spain. Her work has been displayed in two dozen publications and she has presented numerous workshops nationwide.

(Sources: Distinguished Faculty Scholar Awards, online source, access by title. Laidlaw, Mika Negishi vita, in dean's office, College of Arts and Humanities, Minnesota State University, Mankato.)

### Dr. Gwen Westerman, Department of English.

Gwen Westerman, a member of the Minnesota State University, Mankato faculty since 1991, earned her B.A. and M.A. degrees in English from Oklahoma State University and her Ph.D. in English from the University of Kansas (1994). Her doctoral dissertation was titled "Bridging the Gap between Designers and Users: Identification, Persuasion, and Rhetorical Community in Computer-Human Interaction Design."

An enrolled member of the Sisseton-Wahpeton Dakota Oyate, Westerman is fluent in the Dakota language. She has established an excellent reputation in three fields—history, poetry and art. Her historical scholarship has emphasized Dakota history and culture. Her award-winning book *Mni Sota Makoce: The Land of the Dakota* (Bruce White co-author) (St. Paul: Minnesota Historical Society Press, 2012) won

a Minnesota Book Award (Minnesota History Category) in 2013 and a Hognander Foundation Minnesota History Award in 2014. In 2013, Westerman received the Leadership in American History Award from the American Association for State and Local History.

Her book *Follow the Blackbirds*, a collection of poetry in Dakota and English that is a heartfelt appreciation of the past, present and future of the Dakota people, was published by Michigan State University Press. During the period 2007-12, Westerman's poetry was also published in the *Yellow Medicine Review, Water-Stone Review* and *Natural Bridge*.

Westerman's art has been exhibited at the James J. Hill House Gallery (St. Paul) and the Hillstrom Art Gallery (Gustavus Adolphus College, St. Peter, Minnesota). She has also exhibited at All My Relations Gallery (an Indian Arts organization in St. Paul). Additionally, her art is in the permanent collections of the Minnesota Historical Society, the University Art Galleries of the University of South Dakota and on the Pine Ridge Reservation (Oglala Lakota, South Dakota).

(Sources: Distinguished Faculty Scholar Awards, online source, access by title. Westerman, Gwen in *Wikipedia*. Westerman, Gwen in World Cat. Westerman, Gwen, email to William E. Lass, 03 October 2017.)

## 2015:

### Dr. Rebecca Bates, Professor of Computer Science and Integrated Engineering.

Rebecca Bates, who joined the Minnesota State University, Mankato faculty in 2002, earned a B.S. in biomedical engineering and an M.S. in electrical engineering from Boston University. She completed her Ph.D. in electrical engineering from the University of Washington.

At Minnesota State University, Mankato, Bates has served as the principal administrator of two National Science Foundation MAX (Mentored Academic Experience) Scholar Programs. Both the $500,000 2006 grant and the $600,000 2012 grant provided scholarships for Science, Technology, Engineering and Mathematics students. The purposes of these grants were to increase the number of under-represented students, to improve student retention, to attract non-traditional students and to partner with community colleges to promote and provide educational opportunities.

Widely recognized in her field, Bates spent the academic year 2011-12 as an American Association for the Advancement of Science Policy Fellow in the Division of Engineering Education & Centers at the National Science

Foundation. From August 2009 through May 2010 she was a Fulbright scholar at the University of Sao Paulo in Brazil. Her project had the two-fold purpose of developing a Portuguese spoken-language interface for handheld devices that support public health-care workers and collecting narratives of women who have succeeded in engineering or computer science in order to encourage more women and girls to seek careers in those fields.

Bates has been actively involved in engineering associations. In 2014-15 she served as the division director of the Engineering Ethics Division of the American Society for Engineering Education and has also been division program chair for its national conference and a delegate to its Diversity Committee. Additionally, she is a senior member of the Association for Computing Machinery.

(Sources: Distinguished Faculty Scholar Awards, online source, access by title. The following articles in the Minnesota State University, Mankato website: "Minnesota State Receives $500,000 NSF Grant for Scholarships," 27 September 2006; "MAX Scholar Program Receives $600,000 from National Science Foundation," 13 February 2012 and "Faculty Member Rebecca Bates Wins Fulbright to Study in Brazil.")

### Professor Elizabeth Miller,
### Department of Art.

Elizabeth Miller joined the Minnesota State University, Mankato faculty in 2005 after completing a Bachelor of Fine Arts in Painting from the Rhode Island School of Design in 1999 and a Master of Fine Arts in Drawing and Painting from the University of Minnesota in 2005.

She introduced installation art to the University. This specialty has contributed significantly to the Art Department's tradition of innovativeness.

Miller has been extremely active in practicing her craft. Her work has been exhibited in 22 solo exhibitions and 26 two to three artist exhibitions. Her display sites include galleries in Minneapolis, St. Paul, Denver, New York City and London.

Widely recognized in her field, Miller has received a number of grants and fellowships including a McKnight Foundation Fellowship, a Joan Mitchell Foundation Grant and three grants from the Minnesota State Arts Board.

(Source: Distinguished Faculty Scholar Awards, online source, access by title. Miller, Elizabeth vita, in dean's office, College of Arts and Humanities, Minnesota State University, Mankato.)

### Dr. Daniel Sachau,
### Department of Psychology.

Daniel Sachau earned three degrees from the University of Utah. He completed his first master's in Economics in 1983 and his second in Social Psychology three years later. In 1990 he was awarded his Ph.D. in Social Psychology, a year after he joined the Mankato State University faculty.

From 2003 to the present (2017), Sachau has served as the director of the graduate program in Industrial/Organizational Psychology. Mainly because of his efforts, the program has become the nation's top ranking master's program in Industrial/Organization Psychology.

Sachau has compiled an impressive record in research and writing. He has authored or co-authored approximately 50 articles in professional journals. His work has appeared in such well-known scholarly journals as *Environment and Behavior, American Psychologist* and *Teaching of Psychology*. Within his specialization of Social Psychology, Sachau has particular research interest in job satisfaction, employee motivation, self-presentation strategies and sport psychology.

(Sources: Distinguished Faculty Scholar Awards, online source, access by title. Daniel Sachau file, College of Social and Behavioral Sciences, Minnesota State University, Mankato.)

## 2016:

### Dr. Paul Force-Emery Mackie,
### Department of Social Work.

Paul Force-Emery Mackie, who joined the Minnesota State University, Mankato faculty in 2004 earned a B.S. from Northern Michigan University, a Master of Social Work degree from the George Warren Brown School of Washington University (St. Louis) and a Ph.D. from the University of Denver. His doctoral dissertation "Job Satisfaction and Burnout Among Rural and Urban Social Workers" was completed in 2005. His major publication is *Practicing Rural Social Work* (Chicago: Lyceum Books, Inc., 2016) with co-authors Kimberly Zammit and Michelle Alvarez.

Because of his specialty in rural social and behavioral health issues, Mackie has advised members of Congress, Minnesota state legislators, federal agency administrators and the Rosalynn Carter Symposium on Public Health Policy. His ongoing research is concentrated on the development and implementation of strategies to sustain and further develop a strong rural behavioral health work force.

As a prominent leader in his field, Mackie has served as the president of the National Association for Rural Mental Health. Additionally, he has been the chief consulting editor and manager of the *Journal for Rural Mental Health* and a peer reviewer for the professional periodicals *Journal of Contemporary Rural Social Work and Advances in Social Work*.

(Sources: Distinguished Faculty Scholar Awards, online source, access by title. Mackie, Paul Force-Emery in World Cat Discovery, online source.)

### Dr. Robert Pettitt,
**Department of Human Performance.**

Robert Pettitt, who joined the Minnesota State University, Mankato faculty in 2008 earned a Master of Science degree (1998) from the University of Wisconsin-La Crosse and a Ph.D. from the University of Utah (2004). His doctoral dissertation was titled "Surrogate Measures for Monitoring Responses to Heavy Exercises."

Pettitt was a very active researcher and writer during his career at the university. His textbook *Exercise Physiology: Laboratory Manual* was published by Kendall Hunt of Dubuque, Iowa, in 2009. He also wrote more than 50 articles that were published in various peer-reviewed journals, including the *International Journal of Sport Physiology and Performance* and the *International Journal of Sports Medicine.*

As a Certified Athletic Trainer with the National Athletic Trainers' Association and a Certified Strength & Conditioning Specialist with the National Strength and Conditioning Association, Pettitt has developed new procedures for exercise testing.

Pettitt left the university in August 2017.

(Sources: Distinguished Faculty Scholar Awards, online source, access by title. Pettitt, Robert in World Cat Discovery, online source. William E. Lass, telephone conversation with Kim Krueger, office coordinator, Department of Human Performance, 25 September 2017.)

### Dr. Fei Yuan,
**Department of Geography.**

Fei Yuan began her faculty appointment at Minnesota State University, Mankato in 2005. In 1994 she completed her B.S. in geography with a computer science minor at East China Normal University (Shanghai). Her graduate geography degrees are a master's (2003) and a Ph.D. from the University of Minnesota. Her doctoral concentration was in natural resources and management with an emphasis on remote sensing.

Her teaching has been mainly concerned with remote sensing, the Global Information System (GIS) and regional geography. She helped create the Geography Department's undergraduate and graduate GIS certificate programs.

An active scholar, Yuan has co-authored over two dozen peer-reviewed articles in professional journals. They include "Long Term Land Use and Land Cover Changes Affected by the Conservation Reserve Program Along the Minnesota River Basin" in the *Journal of Geography and Geology* and "Comparison of Various Spectral Analytical Techniques for Impervious Surface Estimation Using Landsat Imagery" in *Photogrammetric Engineering and Remote Sensing.*

She has shared her expertise with the broader community by serving on the board of the Minnesota GIS/LIS Consortium, reviewing papers for some 30 journals and evaluating grant proposals.

(Sources: Distinguished Faculty Scholar Awards, online source, access by title. Yuan, Fei vita, in dean's office, College of Social and Behavioral Sciences, Minnesota State University, Mankato, "Mapping Out a Future," Graduate School Research, Minnesota State University, Mankato, Winter, 2009. The following articles in the Minnesota State University, Mankato website: "Fei Yuan" and "Professor Fei Yuan.")

## 2017:

### Dr. Jeffrey A. Buchanan,
**Department of Psychology.**

Jeffrey A. Buchanan, who joined the Minnesota State University, Mankato faculty in 2004, earned his undergraduate degree from the University of Northern Iowa (1995), his master's from Mankato State University (1997) and his Ph.D. from the University of Nevada at Reno (2004). His dissertation title was "Generalization of the Effects of a Cognitive-Behavioral Intervention for Family Caregivers of Individuals with Dementia."

Buchanan's teaching and research specialty is geropsychology. The American Psychological Association defines "Clinical Geropsychology" as the application of "the knowledge and methods of psychology to understanding and helping older persons and their families to maintain well-being, overcome problems and achieve maximum potential during later life." His particular interests are developing restraint-free interventions for managing behavior problems in persons with dementia, investigating the impact of caregiver verbal instructions to persons with dementia, studying the impact of Elderspeak on older adults, developing and evaluating memory enhancement techniques for those afflicted with dementia and determining practical applications of the Theory of Gerotrancendence.

A productive scholar, Buchanan has co-authored over three dozen articles in professional journals or book chapters. The articles include "The Role of Behavior Analysis in the Rehabilitation of Persons with Dementia" in *Behavior Therapy* and "Implications of Skinner's Verbal Behavior for Studying Dementia" in the *Journal of Speech-Language Pathology and Applied Behavior Analysis.*

(Sources: Distinguished Faculty Scholar Awards, online source, access by title. Buchanan, Jeffrey A., vita, in dean's office, College of Social and Behavioral Sciences, Minnesota State University, Mankato. The following article in the Minnesota State University, Mankato website: "Jeffrey Buchanan Ph. D." "Clinical Geropsychology" in *Wikipedia*.)

### Dr. Paul Eskridge,
### Department of Physics and Astronomy.

Paul Eskridge, who started at Minnesota State University, Mankato in 2001, earned three degrees in astronomy. They were: B.S., California Institute of Technology (1982), M.S. University of Washington (1984) and Ph.D., University of Washington, 1987. His dissertation title was, "Global Properties of the Sculptor and Fornax Dwarf Elliptical Galaxies."

Eskridge's research specialty is Extragalactic Astronomy. More specifically, he has done research and writing about multi-wave lengths of late-type galaxies, polar-ring galaxies, dwarf galaxies and star formation in early galaxies. At Mankato he teaches courses in astronomy and works with the campus observatories.

His many writings include 33 authored or co-authored articles in scholarly journals including *The Astronomical Journal* and *The Astrophysical Journal*. They include such topics as "The Global Luminosity Function of the Sculptor Dwarf Elliptical Galaxy" and "Arm Structure in Anemic Spiral Galaxies."

(Sources: Distinguished Faculty Scholar Awards, online source, access by title. "Dr. Paul Eskridge," in the Minnesota State University, Mankato website.)

### Dr. John W. Seymour,
### Department of Counseling and Student Personnel.

John W. Seymour began his Minnesota State University, Mankato career in 2001 as an assistant professor in the Counseling and Student Personnel Department. He was promoted to associate professor in 2006 and full professor in 2011.

His undergraduate degree was a B.A. in Sociology and Religion from Houston Baptist University (Houston, Texas) in 1975. In 1978, he completed a Master of Divinity at the Southern Baptist Theological Seminary (Louisville, Kentucky) and five years later earned a M.A. in Family Therapy and Psychology from the University of Houston at Clear Lake. In 2000 he finished his Ph.D. in counseling at Texas A&M University.

Seymour has held leadership roles in professional organizations. At the national level they include the American Association for Marriage and Family Therapy and the Association for Play Therapy. Since 2006 he has held a succession of gubernatorial appointments to the Minnesota Board of Marriage and Family Therapy. He has served variously as its chairman, vice chairman and member of its personnel, credentials, continuing education and rules revision committees.

An active researcher and writer, Seymour had authored or co-authored nearly three dozen scholarly journal articles or articles that were published in reference-type books. His journal articles include "Digital Dilemma: Play Therapy and Online Social Networking," that appeared in *Play Therapy*. For articles in books, he wrote, for example "History of Psychotherapy Integration and Related Research," pp. 3-19 in *Integrative Play Therapy* by A. A. Drewes, S. C. Bratton and C. E. Schaefer, eds. (New York: John Wiley, 2011).

(Sources: Distinguished Faculty Scholar Awards, online source, access by title. Seymour, John W. vita. Emailed by John W. Seymour to William E. Lass, 25 October 2017.)

## Minnesota State University, Mankato in Its Sesquicentennial Year

Customarily, organizations, societies, governments, academic institutions and other entities observe such seeming watershed events as centennials, sesquicentennials, bicentennials and millennia. But a 23rd or 144th anniversary does not attract much attention. Undoubtedly, the future generations of Minnesota State University, Mankato students, administrators, faculty, staff and alumni, who will observe such events as the university's bicentennial, will have questions about the nature of the institution at its sesquicentennial mark. Perhaps, the following will help them better understand their past.

Stomper, President Davenport and MSSA President Faical Rayani with a 150th wrapped City of Mankato bus, 2017.

## Staffing

The university's basic personnel components are the administration, faculty and support staff. For the fiscal year 2018 (July 1, 2017-June 30, 2018) the headcount of all employees was 1,738, which was the equivalent of 1,416 fulltime positions.[154]

President Richard Davenport is assisted by six vice presidents. In January 2018 they were: Marilyn J. Wells, Provost and Senior Vice President, David P. Jones, Student Affairs and Enrollment Management, Richard J. Straka, Finance & Administration, Kent Stanley, University Advancement and Mark Johnson, Information Technology Solutions (includes computer services). Johnson was also the Interim Vice President of Strategic Business, Education and Regional Partnerships.[155]

The Academic Affairs Division has Associate Provost Robert P. Fleischman, Interim Associate Vice President for Research and Graduate Studies Stephen Stoynoff, Assistant Vice President for Institutional Research, Planning and Assessment Lynn D. Akey, Assistant Vice President for Undergraduate Education Ginger L. Zierdt and ten deans. The deans and their positions are Kristine Retherford, College of Allied Health and Nursing; Matt Cecil, College of Arts and Humanities; Brenda Flannery, College of Business; Jean Haar, College of Education; Brian Martensen, College of Science, Engineering and Technology; Maria Bevacqua, Interim Dean, College of Social and Behavioral Sciences; Joan Roca, Library Services; Henry Morris, Institutional Diversity; Anne Dahlmann, Interim Dean of Global Education and Thomas Norman, University Extended Education.

The number of faculty positions has remained relatively constant in recent years. For the 2016-2017 academic year, there were 587.1 faculty positions assigned to instruction, 52.0 to non-instruction including chairpersons, directors and librarians and 11.6 for research. Four years earlier the respective numbers were 581.3, 47.2 and 11.8.[156]

Twin Cities Engineering classroom at Normandale Partnership Center, 2015

Armstrong Hall classroom, 2015

Morris Hall classroom, 2015

Students outside the Centennial Student Union, 2016

More precise information about the nature of the faculty is contained in a report that covers the 2015-2016 academic year. For that time there were 329 tenured faculty, 122 with probationary appointments, 71 with fixed term appointments, 368 adjunct, 3 non-tenure track and 285 teaching assistants. The grand total of instructional personnel was 1,178. All of the adjuncts and graduate assistants were part-time employees.[157]

For fiscal year 2018 the university had 543 classified staff, which amounted to 480 fulltime positions. The 190 different clerical and office workers, the equivalent of 165 fulltime positions, was the largest classified staff group. They, as well as the employees in the maintenance, service and technical units, were represented in collective bargaining by the American Federation of State, County and Municipal Employees (AFSCME), the nation's largest trade union of professional employees. More than a hundred classified staff including accountants and the information technology workers were represented by the Minnesota Association of Professional Employees (MAPE). Like the IFO, the faculty's bargaining agent, AFSCME and MAPE negotiate two-year master contracts with Minnesota Management and Budget. All master contracts are subject to legislative review and approval.[158]

## Enrollment

The headcount enrollment for the Fall 2017 semester was 14,712, which consisted of 12,775 undergraduate students and 1,937 graduate students. By way of comparison, the enrollment for the most recent preceding fall semesters were 15,409 (13,461 undergraduate; 1,948 graduate) in 2013; 15,376 (13,388 undergraduate; 1,988 graduate) in 2014; 15,193 (13,188 undergraduate; 2,005) in 2015; and 15,110 (13,155 undergraduate; 1,955 graduate) in 2016.[159]

The Fall 2017 students were from many states and countries. A good perspective on their origins can be derived by considering that the top ranked six states were Minnesota (11,137), Wisconsin (840), South Dakota (297), Iowa (245), Illinois (129) and North Dakota (63).

Within Minnesota, the enrollment statistics show the significance of the Twin Cities Metropolitan Area. Four of the topmost counties are in the metro area. The five ranking counties, with enrollment indicated parenthetically, were: Hennepin (1,539), Dakota (976), Blue Earth (790), Scott (741) and Anoka (552)

The Minnesota State system regularly monitors the annual enrollments of all of its institutions. The report that was released in January 2018, shows that the entire system enrollment had declined 17 percent since the 2010-11 academic year and that over half of the system's institutions were operating at a loss. The five percent enrollment decline of Minnesota State University, Mankato and its accompanying income decline, were deemed to be manageable. But system officials cautioned that statewide enrollment would drop another two percent in the next biennium. Furthermore, they noted there was no prospect of a quick recovery, because of Minnesota's low unemployment rate and a declining number of young adults.[160]

Students on the campus mall, 2014

## Global Student Program

International student enrollment has increased sharply in recent years. In Fall 2010 there were 564 international students. For Fall 2017 the enrollment was 1,338 (about 9.2 percent of the institutional total) from 89 countries. The top 10 countries were Nepal (164), South Korea (122), Kuwait (94), Saudi Arabia (90), India (80), Nigeria (68), Ivory Coast (65), Japan (65), Ethiopia (63) and Bangladesh (60).[161]

Most of the international student are attracted to Minnesota State University, Mankato because of family, friends and internet information. Seventy percent of them are funded by their families or themselves, 20 percent are supported by either the United States government or their home country and the remaining 10 percent get financial aid from a partner institution in their home countries. Approximately 90 percent of the students are seeking degrees from Minnesota State University, Mankato and the remainder are non-degree students, who typically engage in year-long study.

The university has at least one partner institution in Australia, Austria, China, Costa Rica, Ecuador, Egypt, Finland, France, Germany, Ghana, Greece, India, Ivory Coast, Japan, Kuwait, Mexico, Netherlands, Northern Ireland, Norway, Qatar, South Korea, Russia, Scotland, South Africa, Spain and Sweden. Each partnership arrangement provides for tuition reciprocity by which international students and Mankato students who attend each other's university pay tuition to their home institution.

The increasing significance of international student enrollment has led to some recent administrative changes. In August 2013, Stephen J. Stoynoff, who taught English as a second language in the English Department, was appointed interim dean of international affairs by President Davenport. In June 2015, Davenport appointed Stoynoff as Dean of Global

2017-2018 Circle K International club a Recognized Student Organization (RSO)

Students by the Fountain, 2014

Education, a newly created position.

Global Education has three divisions—the Kearney Center for International Student Services, Center for Education Abroad and Away and Center for English Language Programs. The Kearney Center administers all aspects of the international student program. The Center for Education Abroad and Away administers various programs that are usually a semester or two long, except for programs led by Minnesota State University, Mankato faculty that typically run 10-14 days. Its principal functions are faculty-led programs, exchange programs with partner institutions, programs involving student study at a non-partner institution and the National Student Exchange Program by which Mankato students study at another higher education institution in the United States.

For the Fall 2017 term, approximately 300 Minnesota State University, Mankato students were either studying abroad or at an institution in the United States. Their commonest foreign destinations were Australia, Austria, Belize, Germany, Netherlands, South Korea, Spain and the United Kingdom.

## Big ideas. Real-world thinking

Minnesota State University, Mankato has used its popular tagline, Big ideas. Real-world thinking, since 2009. The idea for a unique slogan that would portray the essence of the university's mission resulted from an effort spearheaded by Jeff Iseminger, who served as assistant vice president and associate vice president in University Advancement.[162]

With the encouragement and support of President Davenport and other administrators, Iseminger, the university's Integrated Marketing team and Forte Consulting of the Twin Cities developed the tagline. Their decision to use Big ideas. Real-world thinking. instead of any of the other seven possibilities was based on extensive market research including professionally managed telephone surveys of 1,000 Twin Cities households and meetings with focus groups of high school students, alumni and major donors.

The tagline was chosen because big ideas, which represented research, distinguished the university from the two-year colleges; real-world thinking, represented applied research. Iseminger believes that "this research-based tagline and the marketing in which it's been used over the years have helped Minnesota State Mankato differentiate itself in a memorable, engaging way within a hyper-competitive marketplace."

# NOTES

## Chapter One

[1] Robert B. Downs, *Horace Mann: Champion of Public Schools* (New York: Twayne Publishers, 1974), 28-30.

[2] Here and the four paragraphs below see Frederick M. Binder, "Carter, James Gordon," *American National Biography*, vol. 4 (New York: Oxford University Press, 1999), 487-488 and Edward L. Lach, Jr., "Mann, Horace," *American National Biography*, vol. 14, 424-427.

[3] *Ibid.*; C[lyde] O[rvall] Ruggles, *Historical Sketch and Notes: Winona State Normal School, 1860-1910...*([St. Paul]: Minnesota Normal School Board., 1910), 12.

[4] Here and the following paragraph. Downs, *Horace Mann*, 87, 96.

[5] Here and the paragraph below Fred F. Harcleroad, H. Bradley Sagen and C. Theodore Molen, Jr., *The Developing State Colleges and Universities: Historical Background, Current Status, and Future Plans* (Iowa City: The American College Testing Program, 1969) , 14-19.

[6] Here and the paragraph below, *Mankato Normal School Catalog*, 1878-79, 17; norma in on-line Latin-English Dictionary; Harcleroad, Sagen and Molen, *Developing State Colleges and Universities*, 14-19.

[7] Minnesota Territory, *Laws*, 1849, 41.

[8] R.W. Murchie and M. E. Jarchow, *Population Trends in Minnesota* (University of Minnesota Agricultural Experiment Station, Bulletin 32, May 1936), 7; Edward Duffield Neill, *The History of Minnesota from the Earliest French Explorations to the Present Time* ( 4th ed,; Minneapolis: Minnesota Historical Company,1882), 569.

[9] William E. Lass, *Minnesota: A History* (2d. ed.; New York: W. W. Norton & Co., 1998), 108-12, 120.

[10] Thomas Hughes, *History of Blue Earth County* (Chicago: Middle West Publishing Co., [1909]; (L[afayette] G. M. Fletcher, "The Public Schools," *Mankato: Its First Fifty Years 1852-1902* (Mankato: Free Press Printing Co., 1903), 62-63.

[11] William Watts Folwell, *A History of Minnesota*, vol. 1 (St. Paul: Minnesota Historical Society, 1921), 261.

[12] *Ibid.*, vol. 4 (1930), 65.

[13] R[obert] A. DuFresne, *Winona State University: A History of One Hundred Twenty-Five Years* (Winona: Winona State University, 1985), 21. On Winona boosterism, see: William E. Lass, "'Utterly Blind, Stupid and Absurd:' Minnesota Press Reaction to the Capital Removal Attempt," *Minnesota History* 63 (Fall 2013): 281-93.

[14] DuFresne, *Winona State University*, 18; "Peckham, Joseph," in Warren Upham and Rose Barteau Dunlap, comps., *Minnesota Biographies* 1655-1912, in *Collections of the Minnesota Historical Society*, vol.14 (St. Paul, 1912), 585.

[15] Here and the three paragraphs below see Minnesota, *General Laws*, 1858, Ch. 69.

[16] Folwell, *Minnesota*, vol. 1, 363.

[17] Here and the paragraph below State Normal School Board Minutes,16 August 1859, typed copy in Minnesota State University, Mankato Archives. Original in Minnesota Historical Society, St. Paul; DuFresne, *Winona State University*, 23.

[18] Ruggles, Winona State Normal School, 60; DuFresne, *Winona State University*, 66.

[19] *Mankato: Its First Fifty Years*, 188-90; Hughes, *Blue Earth County*, 291.

[20] Minnesota, *General Laws*, 1860, Ch. 81; 1865, Ch. 12.

[21] Minnesota, *General Statutes*, 1866, Ch. 37.

[22] For the historic value of the dollar see the online source Consumer Price Index (Estimate) 1800-; *Mankato Weekly Record*, 11 August 1866.

[23] Minnesota, *Special Laws*, 1867, Ch. 61.

[24] Minnesota, *Executive Documents*, 1869, 197; Normal School Board Minutes, 24 June 1868.

[25] Here and the paragraph below, Normal Board Minutes, 16 July 1868; *Mankato Weekly Record*, 18 July 1868.

[26] Gage, George M. Research File, Minnesota State University, Mankato Archives; *Mankato: Its First Fifty Years*, 219; Richard P. Mallett, *University of Maine at Farmington: A Study in Educational Change* (1864-1974), (Freeport, ME: Bond Wheelwright Co., 1974), 4, 22, 33.

[27] Minnesota, *Executive Documents*, 1868, 613; Minnesota, *Special Laws*, 1868, Ch. 27.

[28] Hughes, *Blue Earth County*, 166: For the impact of steamboating on Mankato see Thomas Hughes, "A History of Steamboating on the Minnesota River," *Collections of the Minnesota Historical Society*, vol. 10, pt. 1 (St. Paul, 1905), 131-63.

[29] U. S. Census Office, *Population of the United States in 1860*, 255; *Compendium of the Ninth Census*, June 1, 1870, 230.

[30] Here and the paragraph below *Compendium of the Ninth Census*, 750-51.

[31] *Mankato Weekly Record*, 05 October 1867; Fletcher, "Schools of Mankato," in *Mankato: Its First Fifty Years*, 67. (The present-day Union School Building on South Broad Street between Mulberry and Plum streets is at the site of the original school, which was razed in 1918. This replacement for the first Union School, constructed in 1919, was also named Union School. *Mankato Daily Review*, 23 October 1918, 6; 20 May 1919, 1; *Mankato Daily Free Press*, 23 October 1918, 6, 06 November 1919, 2.)

[32] Minnesota, *Executive Documents*, 1868, 221.

[33] Mankato Normal School Prudential Committee Minutes, 05 September 1868, Minnesota State University, Mankato Archives; *Mankato Weekly Record*, 12 September, 10 October 1868.

[34] *Mankato Weekly Record*, 10, 31 October 1868; Prudential Committee Minutes, 26 October 1868.

[35] Minnesota, *Executive Documents*, 1868, 222.

[36] Here and the paragraph below *Ibid.*, 220, 223,225.

[37] *Mankato Weekly Record*, 03 April 1869.

[38] Normal School Board Minutes, 08 April 1869; *Mankato Weekly Record*, 10 April 1869; Minnesota, *Executive Documents*, 1869, 412.

[39] Prudential Committee Minutes, 03 May 1869; *Mankato Weekly Record*, 08 May 1869.

[40] *Mankato Weekly Record*, 15, 28 May, 19 June 1869.

[41] *Mankato Union*, 25 June 1869.

[42] Old Main Cornerstone Box Collection, Minnesota State University, Mankato Archives.

[43] *Mankato Union*, 25 June 1869.

[44] *Mankato Weekly Record*, 29 January 1870.

[45] *Mankato Weekly Review*, 01 March 1870.

[46] *Mankato Union*, 03 June 1870.

[47] *Ibid.*, 01 July 1870.

[48] *Mankato Weekly Union*, 05 August 1870.

[49] Minnesota, *Executive Documents*, 1870, 355.

[50] Here and the paragraph below *Mankato Weekly Record*, 29 January 1870 and *Mankato Weekly Review*, 15 February 1870.

[51] Here and the paragraph below Minnesota, *Executive Documents*, 1868, 1970, 355; *Mankato Weekly Union*, 26 August 1870.

[52] William Dodsworth Willard, "Reminiscences, 1856-1952," 8, Southern Minnesota Historical Center, Memorial Library, Minnesota State University, Mankato.

[53] *Mankato Weekly Record*, 12 September 1868.

[54] Minnesota, *Executive Documents*, 1869, 90-91.

[55] *Ibid.*, 1868, 223, 1872, vol. 2, 264.

[56] *Ibid.*, 1870, 353-54. For similar profiles of Mankato Normal School students, 1871-1880, see Debra L. Anderson, "Mankato State Normal School: The Foundation Years,1868-1880, unp. M. A. thesis (Mankato State University, 1987), 204-21.

[57] Minnesota, *Executive Documents*, 1868, 223; *Mankato Weekly Union*, 11 August 1871; *Mankato: Its First Fifty Years*, 214.

[58] *Mankato Weekly Union*, 21, 28 June 1872.

[59] Sears, Julia A. Research File, Minnesota State University, Mankato Archives.

[60] Minnesota, *Executive Documents*, 1872, vol. 2, 261.

[61] *Ibid.*, 238.

[62] *Ibid.*, 261.

[63] *Ibid.*, 265

[64] *Ibid.*, 1872, 31.

[65] *Mankato Weekly Review*, 25 September 1873.

[66] Minnesota, *General Laws*, 1873, Ch. 2.

[67] *Mankato Weekly Record*, 15 March, 05 April 1873.

[68] Normal School Board Minutes, 03 June 1873; *Mankato Weekly Review*, 10 June 1873.

[69] Normal School Board Minutes, 22 July 1873.

[70] ." "John, D. D. Rev. David Clark[e]," *Mankato: Its First Fifty Years*, 245-46; John, David Clarke Research File, Minnesota State University, Mankato Archives.

[71] Normal School Board Minutes, 22 July 1873.

[72] *Mankato Weekly Review*, 10 June 1873.

[73] *Ibid.*, 09, 23 September 1873; *Mankato Weekly Record*, 27 September 1873.

[74] *Normal School Board Minutes*, 04 September 1873.

[75] Minnesota, *Executive Documents*, 1873, vol. 2, 890-91.

[76] *Mankato Weekly Review*, 16 September 1873; *Mankato Weekly Record*, 27 September 1873.

[77] For the verbatim text of the petition and the identity of its signers see State Normal School Board Minutes, 12 November 1873, in University Archives.

[78] Here and the paragraph below Minnesota, *Executive Documents*, 1873, vol.2, 891; *Mankato Weekly Record*, 20 September 1873.

[79] State Normal School Board Minutes, 12 November 1873; *Mankato Weekly Review*, 18 November 1873.

[80] State Normal School Board Minutes, 04 December 1873; *Mankato Weekly Review*, 30 December 1873. This article of about 1,800 words includes a verbatim copy of the Grievance Committee's report.

[81] *Mankato Union*, 02 January 1874.

[82] Here and the paragraph below George E. Warner and Charles M. Foote, eds., *History of the Minnesota Valley*…(Minneapolis: North Star Publishing Co., 1882), 597; *Mankato Union,* 27 February 1874.

[83] *Mankato Weekly Review*, 24 March 1874.

[84] For a comprehensive history of Sears' life, see Joan Forssmark Pengilly, "The First Female President of a Co-educational Public Institution of Higher Learning: An Historical Examination of the Presidential Tenure of Julia Ann Sears, 1872-1873," (unp. Ph. D. dissertation, University of Akron, 1995).

[85] *Ibid.*, 16-17.

[86] *Ibid.*, 13.

[87] A[lfred] L[eland] Crabb, "A Most Remarkable Woman," *Peabody Journal of Education* 46 (November, 1968), 139-41.

[88] *Mankato Weekly Record*, 03 January 1874; *Mankato Union*, 02 January 1874; *Mankato Review*, 31 March 1874.

[89] Gage, George M. Research File, Minnesota State University, Mankato Archives.

[90] Here and the two paragraphs, below Lass, *Minnesota*, 200. For a scholarly biography of Donnelly see Martin Ridge, *Ignatius Donnelly: Portrait of a Politician* (Chicago: University of Chicago Press, 1962.

[91] For detailed coverage of the Donnelly closure bill debate see *Mankato Weekly Record*, 24, 31 January 1874; *Mankato Weekly Review*, 13, 20 January, 10, 17, 24 February 1874; *Mankato Union*, 13, 20 February 1874.

[92] *Mankato Weekly Review*, 18 November 1873.

[93] Minnesota, *Executive Documents*, 1873, 892.

[94] Here and the paragraph below *Ibid.*, 1874, vol. 2, 114-15.

[95] *Ibid.*, 1874, vol. 1, 10; *Mankato Normal School Catalog*, 1877-78, 15.

[96] *Mankato Weekly Record*, 28 August 1875; Minnesota, *Executive Documents*, 1875, vol.2, 250.

[97] Minnesota, *Executive Documents*, 1875, vol.2, 250.

[98] *Mankato Weekly Record*, 16, 23 June 1877; Minnesota, *Executive Documents*, 1877, vol.2, 206.

[99] Minnesota, *Executive Documents*, 1877, vol.2, 206.

[100] *Mankato Weekly Union*, 16 November 1877.

[101] *Ibid.*, 23 November 1877.

[102] *Mankato Weekly Review*, 08 August 1875.

[103] *Mankato Weekly Record*, 04 September 1875.

[104] Minnesota, *Executive Documents*, 1873, vol. 2, 893.

[105] *Ibid.*, 1876, vol. 1, 445.

[106] Here and the two paragraphs below. *Ibid.*, 1877, vol. 2, 62, 204-05; *Mankato Normal School Catalog*, 1877-78, 17.

[107] Here and the two paragraphs below Minnesota, *Executive Documents*, 1877, vol. 2, 35, 65-66.

[108] *Ibid.*, 1877, vol. 2, 205.

[109] *Ibid.*, 1878, vol. 2, 272.

[110] *Mankato Weekly Review*, 11 December 1877.

[111] David W. Johnson, *Hamline University: A History* (St. Paul: North Central Publishing Co., 1980), 17.

[112] *Mankato Normal School Catalog*, 1879-80, 18.

[113] Johnson, *Hamline University*, 23.

[114] John, David Clarke Research File, University Archives, Minnesota State University, Mankato; *Mankato: Its First Fifty Years*, 1852-1902 (Mankato: Free Press Printing Co., 1903, 245-46; World Cat bibliographical search.

## Chapter Two

[1] Here and the paragraph below Searing, Edward Research File, University Archives; Mankato: *Its First Fifty Years,* 302-03.

[2] Bibliographical search in World Cat Discovery; Edward Searing, *The First Six Books of Virgil's Aeneid*, New York: A. S. Barnes and Co., 1874.

[3] Minnesota, *Executive Documents*, 1880, vol. 2, 464.

[4] Normal School Board Minutes, 11 May 1880; *Mankato Weekly Review*, 18 May 1880.

[5] Minnesota, *Executive Documents*, 1880, vol. 2, 464.

[6] Here and the paragraph below *Mankato Weekly Review*, 08 June 1880.

[7] *Ibid.*, 15 June 1880.

[8] *Ibid.*, 08 June 1880; Minnesota, *Executive Documents*, 1880, vol. 1, 10; Minnesota, *General Laws*, 1881, Ch.178.

[9] *Mankato Weekly Review* 22 June 1880; Minnesota, *Executive Documents*, 1880, vol. 2, 464; "James, James A." in Upham and Dunlap, *Minnesota Biographies*, 368.

[10] *Mankato Normal School Catalog*, 1880-81, 10-13; Minnesota, *Executive Documents*, 1886, vol. 3, 42.

[11] R. W. Murchie and M. E. Jarchow, *Population Trends in Minnesota* (University of Minnesota Department of Agriculture Bulletin 327, May 1936), 7, 98; U. S. Census Office, *Statistics of the Population of the United States, 1880*, 224; *Population*, Part 1, 1890 census, 216.

[12] *Mankato Normal School Catalog*, 1880-81, 19, 25.

[13] *Minnesota, General Laws*, 1881, Ch. 190.

[14] State Normal School Board Minutes, 09 May 1882.

[15] Here and the three paragraphs below Minnesota, *Executive Documents*, 1882, vol. 2, 722, 767.

[16] Minnesota, *Executive Documents*, 1880, vol. 2, 481-82.

[17] Minnesota, *Executive Documents*, 1882, vol. 2, 722-23, 767-68; Minnesota, *General Laws*, 1883, Ch. 169.

[18] State Normal School Board Minutes, 05 June 1883.

[19] Here and the three paragraphs below Minnesota, *Executive Documents*, 1884, vol. 2, 115-17.

[20] Minnesota, *Executive Documents*, 1884, vol. 2, 149.

[21] Ibid.; 1886, vol. 3, 99-103; 1890, vol. 2, 507-09; Hughes, *Blue Earth County*, 194: For a scholarly biographical sketch of Bell see: Bruce, Robert V., "Bell, Alexander Graham," *American National Biography* 2: 496-500 (New York: Oxford University Press, 1999).

[22] Here and the two paragraphs below Minnesota, *Executive Documents*, 1884, vol. 2, 121.

[23] Here and the paragraph below *Ibid.*, 1888, vol. 2, 1122.

[24] *Ibid.*, 1129: Minnesota, *Legislative Manual*, 1891 (2d. ed., 1891), 344. For detailed history of the Moorhead Normal School see Clarence A. Glasrud, *The Moorhead Normal School* (Moorhead, MN: Moorhead State University, 1987).

[25] Minnesota, *Executive Documents*, 1890, vol. 2, 464.

[26] *Ibid.*, 511.

[27] *Ibid.*, 464; *Mankato Normal Catalog* 1888-89, 33.

[28] Here and the paragraph below *Minnesota, Executive Documents*, 1890, vol.2, 464.

[29] Minnesota, *General Laws*, 1893, Ch. 241 (p.391).

[30] *Mankato Weekly Review*, 16 May 1893.

[31] *Mankato Weekly Review*, 21 August 1894; "Baker, Gen. James H." in *Mankato Its First Fifty Years*, 169-72; "Pope, Edmund M." in Upham and Dunlap, *Minnesota Biographies*, 608.

[32] *Hughes, Blue Earth County*, 194, 205; *Mankato Free Press*. 23 March 1944, 11 (article on retiring custodian Andrew Carlson, who recalled that wood was the heating fuel when he started working at the Mankato Normal School in 1899.)

[33] The earliest extant issue of *The Student* identified as number 1 of volume 2 was published in October 1899. Files of *The Student* and *The Mankatonian* are in University Archives and digitized copies are on-line: https://arch.lib.mnsu.edu.

[34] *The Mankatonian*, April 1892, 15-16.

[35] *Ibid.*, September 1892, 13.

[36] *Mankato Normal Catalog,* 1885-86, 42.

[37] *The Student*, December, 1890, 13.

[38] *The Mankatonian*, September, 1891, 17.

[39] *Ibid.*, November, 1892, 16.

[40] *Ibid.*, December, 1898, 10.

[41] Hughes, *Blue Earth County*, 212; *Mankato Free Press*, 17 May 1968, 3A.

[42] *Mankato Normal Catalog*, 1880-1881, 13; 1885-1886, 24.

[43] These enrollment figures are from Searing's "Annual Report of the President, June 1898," Typescript in University Archives. A table of the enrollment of the Mankato Normal School and its successors, 1868-1967 is in Donald B. Youel, *Mankato State College: An Interpretative Essay* (Mankato: Mankato State College, May 1968), 65  Youel's totals exclude the preparatory department and the Model School/Practice School/Campus School enrollments.

[44] Here and the two paragraphs, below Minnesota, *Executive Documents*, 1896, vol. 2, 413.

[45] Searing's report for year ending June 24, 1898, in *Tenth Biennial Report of the Superintendent of Public Instruction State of Minnesota for the School Years Ending July 31, 1897 and 1898* (St.  Paul: Pioneer Press Co., 1899). *Mankato Free Press*, 11 June 1897. For further information about faculty service periods see the inserted dates on the 1880-1881 and 1897-1898 faculty information. These dates are all from Youel, *Mankato State College*, 123-40. Youel erroneously lists Agnes H. Ford and Agnes H. Rowe as different persons.

[46] Consumer Price Index (Estimate) 1800- (Online source can be accessed by this title,)

[47] *Mankato Normal Catalog*, 1880-1881, 4 (faculty listing); Normal School Board Minutes, 11 May 1880 (salaries); Youel, *Mankato State College*, 123-40 (years of service).

[48] *Mankato Normal Catalog*, 1897-1898, 4-5 (faculty listing); Normal School Board Minutes, 01 June 1897 (salaries); Youel, *Mankato State College*, 123-40 (years of service).

[49] *Mankato Normal Catalog*, 1879-1880, 18.

[50] Normal School Board Minutes, 10 May 1882. The closing date of the fall 1882 term is unclear. The Normal School Board minutes, inaccurately list a March date and no end of term date could be found in the *Mankato Normal Catalog* or the *Mankato Weekly Review* for that time period.

[51] Here and the paragraph below *Mankato Normal Catalog*, 1884-1885, 24-25.

[52] *Mankato Normal Catalog*, 1885-1886, 24.

[53] *Ibid.*

[54] *Biographical Directory and Condensed History Alumni Association State Normal School, Mankato, Minn., 1870-1880* (Mankato: *Free Press* Co., 1891), 54-58.

[55] Sanford Niles, "The Common Schools," in John N. Greer, *The History of Education in Minnesota* (Washington: Government Printing Office, 1902), 29

[56] *Mankato Normal Catalog*, 1891-1892, 50.

[57] Normal School Board Minutes, 26 April 1895; *Mankato Normal Catalog*, 1895-1896, 11.

[58] A. W. Rankin, "High Schools," in Greer, *History of Education in Minnesota*, 76.

[59] Here and the paragraph below *Ibid.*, 73-77; Folwell, *History of Minnesota*, vol. 4, 75; Minnesota, *Executive Documents*, 1878, vol. 2, 51-53.

[60] Minnesota, *Executive Documents*, 1882, vol. 2, 234; 1890, vol. 2, 579-80; *Tenth Biennial Report of the Superintendent of Public Instruction*, 1899, 4.

[61] Mankato Normal School Commencement Program, 23 June 1899, in Minnesota State University, Mankato Archives.

[62] Here and the paragraph below Minnesota, *Executive Documents*, 1896, vol. 2, 411.

[63] Here and the four paragraphs below, *Tenth Biennial Report of the Superintendent of Public Instruction*, 5, 67-73.

[64] Here and below *The Mankatonian*, November, 1898; Normal School Board Minutes, 22 December 1898.

[65] Here and the paragraph below *The Mankatonian*, October, 1899, 19; *Mankato Daily Free Press*, 25 October 1899; *Mankato Daily Review*, 25 October 1899; *Daily Reporter* (Mankato State College), 23 September 1971; 22 June 1981 (Mankato State University).

[66] Normal Board Minutes, 07 December 1898.

[67] Minnesota, *Executive Documents*, 1892, vol. 4, 418.

[68] Normal Board Minutes, 07 December 1898.

[69] Harriet Beale, "The Early Life of Mr. Cooper," *School Progress* (Mankato State Teachers College), January, 1935, 3.

[70] *Ibid.*, 3-6; *The Mankatonian*, January, 1899, 1-2; *Mankato: Its First Fifty Years*, 200; Cooper, Charles H., Research File, University Archives, Minnesota State University, Mankato.

[71] Here and the paragraph below *The Mankatonian*, January, 1899, 1.

[72] *Minnesota, Executive Documents*, 1900, vol. 3, 531.

[73] *Ibid.*, 1902, vol. 1, 823-24.

[74] *Ibid.*, 1900, vol. 3, 556.

[75] *Ibid.*, 1902, vol. 1, 824.

[76] *Ibid.*, 1900, vol. 3, 558.

[77] Minnesota, *Legislative Manual*, 1905, 252.

[78] Normal Board Minutes, 18 February 1903; 18 June 1906.

[79] *Ibid.*, 18 June 1906; Mankato Daily Review, 19 June 1906.

[80] *The Mankatonian*, 01 May 1907, 19.

[81] *Fifteenth Biennial Report of the Superintendent of Public Instruction of Minnesota*, 1907-1908, 89.

[82] *Ibid.*, 61-62.

[83] *Ibid.*, 90.

[84] Here and the four paragraphs below *Mankato Daily Review*, 08 February 1909, 2; *The Mankatonian*, February 1909, 3-5.

[85] *Sixteenth Biennial Report of the Superintendent of Public Instruction…for the School Years 1909 and 1910*, 61.

[86] *Mankato Daily Review*, 24 April 1912, 1.

[87] Normal Board Minutes, 08 August 1911.

[88] Here and the paragraph below Folwell, *History of Minnesota*, vol. 3 (1926), 262, 287.

[89] *Mankato Daily Review*, 24 April 1912, 1.

[90] *Mankato Daily Free Press*, 06 May 1912, 1.

[91] *Ibid.*, 13 June 1913, 2.

[92] *Ibid.*, 19 February 1913, 1.

[93] Here and the two paragraphs below *Mankato Daily Free Press*, 13 June 1913, 2.

[94] Cooper, Charles H., "Annual Report of the President, 1912-1913," typescript, Minnesota State University, Mankato Archives, 2.

[95] Cooper, Charles H., "Annual Report of the President,1911-1912," Typescript in Minnesota State University, Mankato Archives; *Mankato Daily Free Press*, 11 March 1913, 1; Normal School Board Minutes, 07 July 1913.

[96] Cooper, "Annual Report, 1910-1911."

[97] *Ibid.; M. S. N. Normal 1916* (pages are unnumbered).

[98] *The Mankatonian*, December, 1911, 28.

[99] *Senior Annual M. S. N. 1914* (pages are unnumbered).

[100] Cooper, "Annual Report, 1915-1916."

[101] *M. S. N. Annual 1916.*

[102] *Mankato Normal Catalog*, 1899-1900, 5-6; Normal Board Minutes, 09 June 1899, 219-20.

[103] Bohannon, Eugene W. File, University of Minnesota Duluth Archives.

[104] Mark C. Bartusis, ed., *Northern State University: The First Century 1901-2000* (Aberdeen, SD: Northern State University Press, 2001), 18-35.

[105] Cooper, "Annual Report, 1911-1912"; Youel, *Mankato State College*, 129.

[106] Cooper, "Annual Report 1911-1912,"; Arthur O. Lee, "Paternalistic President: Manfred W., Deputy of Bemidji State College," *Minnesota History* 42 (Spring 1971), 179.

[107] Cooper, "Annual Report, 1916-1917,"; Lee," "Paternalistic President," 179.

[108] Cooper, "Annual Report, 1916-1917."

[109] *Fifteenth Biennial Report of the Superintendent of Public Instruction*, 90.

[110] *Mankato Normal Catalog*, 1910-1911, 5.

[111] Here and the paragraph below, David B. Danbom, "Rural Education Reform and the Country Life Movement, 1900-1920," *Agricultural History* 53 (April 1979), 462-74.

[112] Cooper, "Annual Report, 1910-1911."

[113] *Mankato Normal Catalog*, 1911-1912, 5; Youel, *Mankato State College*, 126, 140.

[114] Here and the paragraph below Cooper, "Annual Report, 1912-1913."

[115] Here and the paragraph below Cooper, "Annual Report, 1910-1911; 1913-1914."

[116] Cooper, "Annual Report, 1913-1914"; *M. S. N. Annual 1916*; Youel, M*ankato State College*, 128.

[117] *Fifteenth Biennial Report of the Superintendent of Public Instruction*, 90.

[118] Normal Board Minutes, 07 May 1918.

[119] *Ibid.; M. S. N. Annual 1916.*

[120] Here and the two paragraphs below, *Mankato Normal Catalog*, 1919-1920, 6-9.

[121] Here and the paragraph below Normal Board Minutes, 13 April 1920.

[122] Consumer Price Index (Estimate) 1800-

[123] Normal Board Minutes, 13 April 1920.

[124] *Ibid.*, 09 June 1901.

[125] *Ibid.; Mankato Normal Catalog*, 1900-1901, 8.

[126] *Mankato Normal Catalog*, 1900-1901, 8.

[127] Cooper, "Annual Report, 1910-1911".

[128] Otto Welton Snarr, *The Education of Teachers in the Middle States: An Historical Study of the Professional Education of Public School Teachers as a State Function* (Chicago: University of Chicago, 1945), 254.

[129] Normal Board Minutes, 13 August 1912.

[130] *Ibid.*, 02 October 1912.

[131] *Minneapolis Morning Tribune*, 03 October 1912, 9. The coverage in the *Mankato Daily Review*, 03 October 1912, was almost identical to that of the *Tribune*. The articles were probably done by the same writer and placed on a wire service.

[132] *Minneapolis Morning Tribune*, 03 October 1912, 9.

[133] Normal Board Minutes, 02 October 1912.

[134] *Mankato Normal Catalog*, 1912-1913, 14.

[135] Normal Board Minutes, 30 November 1912.

[136] *Ibid.*

[137] *Ibid.*, 09 November 1915.

[138] *Mankato Normal Catalog*, 1916-1917, 16-17.

[139] Minnesota Department of Education, *Nineteenth Biennial Report*, 1915-1916, 31.

[140] Theodore Christianson, *Minnesota the Land of Sky-Tinted Waters: A History of the State and Its People*, vol. 2 (Chicago: American Historical Society, 1935), 322-23.

[141] Minnesota Department of Education, *Nineteenth Biennial Report*, 36.

[142] U. S. Bureau of the Census, *Historical Statistics of the United States: Colonial Times to 1970*, pt. 2 (Washington: GPO, 1975), 716; Christianson, *Land of Sky-Tinted Waters*, 2:375.

[143] Normal School Board Minutes, 12 June 1915

[144] Virginia Brainard Kunz, *Muskets to Missiles: A Military History of Minnesota* (St. Paul: Minnesota Statehood Centennial Commission, 1958), 157.

[145] Here and the four paragraphs below Christianson, *Sky-Tinted Waters*, 2: 396-403.

[146] Minnesota, Department of Education, *Twentieth Biennial Report*, 1917-1918, 24

[147] *Ibid.*, 23.

[148] *Ibid.*, 36.

[149] *Ibid*, 38.

[150] *Ibid.*, 40.

[151] *Ibid.*, 48.

[152] Cooper, "Annual Report," 1917-1918; 1918-1919.

[153] "The First Seventy-Five Years," *School Progress* 25 (January 1944), 12.

[154] Cooper, "Annual Report, 1917-1918," *Mankato Daily Review*, 05 June 1918, 6; Mrs. Lafayette G. M. Fletcher, "Early Days in the Mankato State Normal School," in Otto Welton Snarr Research Notes, 1918-1939, Southern Minnesota Historical Center, Minnesota State University, Mankato.

[155] Philip D. Jordan, *The People's Health: A History of Public Health in Minnesota to 1948* (St. Paul: Minnesota Historical Society, 1953), 412.

[156] *Minneapolis Morning Tribune*, 12 October 1918, 1.

[157] *Ibid.*, 19 October 1918, 8; *Mankato Daily Review*, 26 October 1918, 1.

[158] *Mankato Daily Review*, 26 October 1918.

[159] Cooper, "Annual Report," 1918-1919.

[160] Normal School Board Minutes, 12 November 1918.

[161] Jordan, *People's Health*, 415.

[162] Minnesota Department of Education, *First Report of the State Board of Education and Twenty-first Biennial Report of the Department of Education*, 1919-1920, 8.

[163] *Ibid.*, 20.

[164] Normal Board Minutes, 25 January 1921.

[165] Minnesota, *Session Laws*, 1921, Ch. 260.

## Chapter 3

[1] Here and the paragraph below *Mankato State Teachers College Catalog*, 1921-1922, 4-7.

[2] *Ibid.*, 8-9.

[3] *Ibid.*, 26.

[4] Here and the paragraph below Minnesota Department of Education, *Nineteenth Biennial Report*, 1915-1916, 33.

[5] Minnesota, Department of Education, *Second Report of the State Board of Education and Twenty-second Biennial Report of the Department of Education*, 1921-1922, 42, 62, 65; Minnesota, Department of Education, *First Report of the State Board of Education and Twenty-first Biennial Report of the Department of Education*,1919-1920, 23; for personal memories of high school trained rural teacher, see Clarence A. Glasrud, *Moorhead State Teachers College* (1921-1957), (Moorhead: Moorhead State University, 1990), 4-5.

[6] *Mankato State Teachers College Catalog*, 1921-1922, 26; Minnesota Department of Education, *Second Report…*, 64.

[7] *Mankato State Teachers College Catalog*, 1921-1922, 10.

[8] Normal School Board Minutes, 11 February 1919.

[9] Minnesota, *Session Laws*, 1919, Ch. 466, Sec. 2; *Mankato State Teachers College Catalog*, 1921-1922, 30.

[10] Here and the paragraph below Normal School Board Minutes, 26 April 1921; *Mankato Free Press*, 27 April 1921, l.

[11] Cooper, "Annual Report," 1920-1921, Minnesota State University, Mankato Archives; *Mankato State Teachers College Catalog*, 1920-1921, 1, 1921-1922, 30.

[12] Here and the three paragraphs below *Mankato State Teachers College Catalog*, 1921-1922, 30-31.

[13] *Ibid.*

[14] Youel, *Mankato State College*, 65.

[15] Here and the paragraph below, *Mankato State College Catalog*, 1921-1922, 46.

[16] Here and the four paragraphs below *Mankato Free Press*, 06 February 1922, 1; 17 May 1968, 18A.

[17] Teachers College Board Minutes, 15 February 1922.

[18] *Mankato Free Press*, 06, 1, 07 February 1922, 3; 17 May 1968, 18A; *College Reporter*, 07 March 1968, 3.

[19] *College Reporter*, 29 May 1958, 6B.

[20] *Mankato Free Press*, 06 February 1922, 1.

[21] Class schedules for Spring, Summer, Fall 1922 and Winter, Spring, Summer 1923, in Minnesota State University, Mankato Archives; *Mankato Free Press*, 06 December 1922, 1; for a brief history of the Episcopal Church see: Thomas L. Moir, *History of St. John's Episcopal Church Mankato, Minnesota* (Mankato: Privately printed, February, 1966).

[22] *Mankato Free Press*, 07 May 1922, 3.

[23] *Ibid.*, 06 February 1922, 4.

[24] *Ibid.*, 11 February 1922, 1.

[25] *Ibid.*, 07 February 1922, 9.

[26] *College Reporter*, 23 September 1971, 15.

[27] Teachers College Board Minutes, 06 February, 24 October 1922.

[28] *Mankato Free Press*, 06 February 1922, 4.

[29] *Ibid.*; "For Future Generations: The Legacy of Blue Earth County Historical Society's Founders," T*he Blue Earth County Historian* 22 (Spring 2016): 12.

[30] *Mankato Free Press*, 06 February 1922, 4; Teachers College Board Minutes, 06 February 1922.

[31] Teachers College Board Minutes, 06 February 1922.

[32] *Ibid.*, 15 February 1922; *Mankato Free Press*, 07 February 1922, 3.

[33] State Teachers College Board Minutes, 15 February, 16 March, 11 April 1922.

[34] *Ibid.*, 11 April, 20 June 1922; *Mankato Free Press*, 24 April 1923, 1.

[35] Teachers College Board Minutes, 11 April 1922.

[36] *Ibid.*, 05 December 1922; DuFresne, *Winona State University*, 170-73.

[37] Minnesota, Session Laws, 1923, Ch. 58, Sec. 1.

[38] *The Katonian*, 1923, 14.

[39] Here and the paragraph below *Mankato Free Press*, 24 April 1923, 1.

[40] Minnesota Department of Education, *Third Report of the State Board of Education and Twenty-third Biennial Report of the Department of Education*, 1923-1924, 154.

[41] *Mankato Free Press*, 04 April 1924, 7, 01 March 1939, 5.

[42] *Ibid.*, 01 March 1939, 5.

[43] Here and the paragraph below *Ibid.*, 09 April 1924, 1.

[44] Teachers College Board Minutes, 10 January 1922.

[45] *Ibid.*, 26 March 1925.

[46] Here and the paragraph below *Ibid.*, 05 May 1925.

[47] *Mankato State Catalog*, 1921-1922, 26; 1926-1927, 31.

[48] Mankato State Teachers College commencement programs, 07 June 1928 and 06 June 1929, Minnesota State University, Mankato Archives.

[49] For further biographical information on Aurit, see Aurit, Val H. file in Minnesota State University, Mankato Archives.

[50] Teachers College Board Minutes, 04 December 1928.

[51] Here and the paragraph below *Ibid.*, 10 May 1929.

[52] *Ibid.*, 23 September 1939.

[53] Here and the paragraph below *Ibid.*, 08 April 1930.

[54] Here and the paragraph below *Mankato Free Press*, 11 February 1929, 1.

[55] Here and the paragraph below *School Spirit*, 19 May 1930, 1.

[56] *Ibid.*, 02 June 1930, 1.

[57] *Ibid.*, 28 September 1932, 3; *Katonian*, 1933, 114, 1934, 20; Class schedules, 1930-34, Minnesota State University, Mankato Archives.

[58] *Mankato Free Press*, 13 September 1934, 1.

[59] Teachers College Board Minutes, 18 August 1930.

[60] Here and the three paragraphs below *Mankato Free Press*, 18 August 1930, 1, 08 December 1954, 1.

[61] *Mankato Free Press*, 06 September 1928, 10; 07 September 1928, 14, 17 May 1968, 13B; *Atlas of Mankato, Minnesota Compiled from Public Records and Plats and Public Surveys . . .* (Mankato: M. H. Haynes, 1910). (For additional coverage of Lewis Field see *Katonian*, 1926, article titled "School Spirit" on unnumbered page, *Among Ourselves*, 08 December 1926, 1; *School Spirit*, 08 November 1929, 1, 3; 14 October 1931, 1; 28 September 1932, 3, 14 October 1932, 1.

[62] State Teachers College Board Minutes, 17 August 1928; Minnesota, *Session Laws*, 1929, Ch. 288, Sec. 6.

[63] Deed Record No. 127, pp. 481-82, 485, 494, 564, 571, 586, 595, 598-99, 603, 609-11, and 622, Recorders Office, Blue Earth County Courthouse, Mankato.

[64] Minnesota, *Session Laws*, 1931, Ch. 411, Sec. 7.3.

[65] *School Spirit*, 08 May 1933, 2.

[66] *Ibid.*, 08 May 1931, 1.

[67] *Ibid.*, 28 September 1932, 3.

[68] *Ibid.*, 06 April 1933, 3.

[69] *Ibid.*, 06 October 1933, 1.

[70] *Mankato Free Press*, 17 April 1940, 1.

[71] Minnesota, *Session Laws*, 1937, Ch. 385, Sec. 3; Minnesota, *Legislative Manual*, 1935, 160; Christianson, *Minnesota: The Land of Sky-Tinted Waters*, 2:447-51.

[72] Teachers College Board Minutes, 14 September 1937; *College Reporter*, 04 February 1938, 5.

[73] Here and the two paragraph below *Mankato Free Press*, 06 November 1937, 7; *College Reporter*, 12 November 1937, 1

[73] Teachers College Board Minutes, 14 December 1937; list of vouchers for land owned by the State of Minnesota on the Mankato State Teachers College campus, Administrative Services Collection, Minnesota State University, Mankato Archives.

[75] *College Reporter*, 04 February 1938, 5; State Teachers College Board Minutes, 08 March 1938, Minnesota State University, Mankato Archives, *Mankato Free Press*, 09 March 1938, 17.

[76] *Mankato Free Press*, 16 August 1938, 7, 19 July 1939, 7; T[heodore] L. Nydahl, "Alterations in the Physical Plant Under President McElroy," *School Progress* 27 (May 1946), 9.

[77] Here and the four paragraphs below *College Reporter*, 14 October 1938, 1.

[78] *Mankato Free Press*, 17 October 1938, 5.

[79] *Ibid.*, 26 October 1938, 4, 16 December 1938, 4; *College Reporter*, 06 October 1939, 1.

[80] *Mankato Free Press*, 19 July 1939, 7; *College Reporter*, 06 December 1940, 1.

[81] *College Reporter*, 29 September 1939, 1.

[82] Here and the paragraph below *Mankato News*, 23 March 1940, 1.

[83] *Ibid.*, 18 April 1940, 1; *Mankato Free Press*, 17 April 1940, 11.

[84] Here and the two paragraphs below *Mankato Free Press*, 09 January 1940, 8.

[85] *School Progress* 27 (May 1946), 10.

[86] *College Reporter*, 06 December 1940, 1; Photograph of terraced hillside, online source (http://cornerstone.lib.mnsu.ed/aerial_1959_HxG/1261)

[87] *College Reporter*, 09 January 1942, 1, 11 May 1945, 3; William E. Lass, terraced hillside inspections, 15 July, 29 November 2016.

[88] *Among Ourselves*, 23 March, 19 October 1926, 1.

[89] *College Spirit*, 04 September 1934, 2.

[90] *College Reporter*, 03 September 1935, 1.

[91] *Katonian*, 1927, 63.

[92] *Ibid.*, 54.

[93] "The First Seventy-Five Years: An Informal History of Mankato State Teachers College," *School Progress* 25 (January 1944), 15.

[94] *Ibid.*, 52-53; *Mankato State Teachers College Catalog*, 1926-1927, 27.

[95] *Katonian*, 1927, 51, 58, 1930, 104.

[96] "First Seventy-Five Years", 15.

[97] Youel, *Mankato State College*, 130; *College Spirit*, 04 September 1934, 3; *Mankato Free Press*, 17 May 1968, 16A.

[98] *Katonian*, 1923, 103, 108.

[99] *Ibid.*, 1924, 93, 1927, 65; Mankato State Teachers College Athletics pamphlet [1931], in Mankato State University, Mankato archives 26, folder 24 (University Athletics. Collection, 1925-ongoing); "America's Lost Colleges/Duluth Junior College http://www.lostcolleges.com/ Accessed 15 October 2016.

[100] *Katonian*, 1928, 75.

[101] *Ibid.*, 1933, 40, 87; *Mankato Free Press*, 01 October 1932, 10.

[102] *Katonian*, 1925, pages unnumbered; 1929, 72; *Mankato Free Press*, 29 October 1928, 11.

[103] *Katonian*, 1930, 71, 82.

[104] *Among Ourselves*, 08 December 1926, 1; *Mankato Free Press*, 31 October 1927, 6; *Katonian*, 1931, [69].

[105] *Among Ourselves*, 18 November 1926, 1; *Mankato Free Press*, 31 October 1927, 6; Alumni Dinner Program, October 26, 1929, in Homecoming Papers Collection, Collection 19, box 1; *Katonian*, 1930, 75, 1931, [69].

[106] *College Spirit*, 11 October 1934, 5.

[107] *Ibid.*, 11 April 1935, 6.

[108] *College Reporter*, 30 March 1950, 3.

[109] Track and field artifacts, Accession 2016-48, University Archives.

[110] P. 4.

[111] *Katonian*, 1936, 84.

[112] *Ibid.*, 1929, 78.

[113] *Ibid.*, 1922, 92, 94; 1924, 103; 1929, 78; Youel, *Mankato State College*, 133, 135.

[114] *Katonian*, 1927, 79.

[115] Here and the four paragraphs below *Mankato State Teachers College Catalog*, 1930-1931, 3-8.

[116] *Ibid.*, 4; *Katonian*, 1934, 18.

[117] Here and the paragraph below *Katonian*, 1933, 17; *Mankato State Teachers College Catalog*, 1930-1931, 5.

[118] *Mankato State Teachers College Catalog*, 1933-1934, 8; *Katonian*, 1934, 17.

[119] Here and the paragraph below Lass, *Minnesota*, 227; Theodore C. Blegen, *Minnesota: A History of the State*, (Minneapolis: University of Minnesota, 1963), 537.

[120] For the verbatim text of the act that created the Department of Administration see Minnesota, *Session Laws*, 1939, Ch. 431. For a brief description of the Department of Administration see Minnesota, *Legislative Manual*, 1949, 137.

[121] T. Harry Williams, Richard N. Current and Frank Freidel, *A History of the United States [Since 1865]* (New York: Alfred A. Knopf, 1960), 127.

[122] Here and the paragraph below: Minnesota, *Session Laws,* 1939, Ch. 441.

[123] *Mankato State Teachers College Catalog*, 1944-1945, vii-xiii.

[124] "North Central Association of Colleges and Schools," in *Wikipedia*, an online encyclopedia.

[125] *Mankato State Teachers College Catalog*, 1930-1931, 3-8.

[126] Mankato State Teachers College, Staff Meeting Minutes, 11 February 1932, Minnesota State University, Mankato Archives.

[127] Here and the paragraph below *Mankato State Teachers College Catalog*, 1938-1939, 43-51, 53-80, 1939-1940, 19-20, 86-88.

[128] Edwin H. Cates, *A Centennial History of St. Cloud State College* (Minneapolis: Dillon Press, 1968), 197.

[129] Ibid.; Jean Talbot, "Winona State College: First State Normal School 1860 Winona State College 1960," *Quarterly Bulletin of Winona State College* (August 1959), 38; DuFresne, *Winona State University*, 231; Mankato State Teachers College staff meeting minutes, 08 February 1939, in Minnesota State University, Mankato Archives.

[130] Cates, *Centennial History of St. Cloud State College*, 198; *Mankato News*, 11 April 1940, 1; *Mankato Free Press*, 10 April 1940, 11.

[131] *College Reporter*, 15 May 1942, 1.

[132] *Ibid.*, 17 March 1944, 1; Copy of constitution in Minnesota State University, Mankato Archives.

[133] Here and the two paragraphs below State Teachers College Board Minutes, 12 December 1939.

[134] Here and the four paragraphs below see "Report to the Board of Review of the Commission on Institutions of Higher Education North Central Association of Colleges and Secondary Schools" by Oldfather and Latham in Records of 1940 North Central Accreditation, Minnesota State University, Mankato Archives.

[135] State Teachers College Board Minutes, 11 June 1940; Cates, *Centennial History of St. Cloud State College*, 200.

[136] Compiled from data in *Mankato State Teachers College Catalog*, 1941-1942, vii-xi.

[137] Here and the two paragraphs below Maurice L. Farrell, ed., *The Dow Jones Averages 1885-1970* [New York]: Dow Jones & Co., 1972, pages unnumbered, book consists of daily reports arranged chronologically; Kimberly Amadeo, "Black Thursday 1929: What Happened and What Caused It," updated August 05, 2016, online source, access by title.

[138] Consumer Price Index (Estimate), 1800-

[139] Infoplease, "Employment & Unemployment Statistics," online source, access by title.

[140] *Mankato Free Press*, 31 December 1929, 15; 31 December 1931, 13.

[141] *Ibid.*; Consumer Price Index (Estimate), 1800-

[142] State Teachers College Board Minutes, 25 April 1932.

[143] *Ibid.*, 10 June 1932.

[144] *Ibid.*, 25 April 1932; 10 May 1933.

[145] *Ibid.*, 10 May 1935; 27 July 1937.

[146] Minnesota, *Session Laws*, 1933, Ch. 294.

[147] *Ibid.*; State College Board Minutes, 01 May 1933.

[148] Mankato State Catalog, 1933-1934, 17; Consumer Price Index (Estimate), 1800-

[149] *Mankato State Catalog*, 1935-1936, 22.

[150] "Essay: The Federal Emergency Relief Administration," online source, access by title.

[151] Here and the paragraph below Report of "State Teachers College, Mankato Minnesota, May 20, 1934," in Frank D. McElroy records, Minnesota State University Archives; *Mankato State Catalog*, 1933-1934, 62.

[152] "National Youth Administration," in *Wikipedia*, the online encyclopedia.

[153] Frank D. McElroy, "Mankato State Teachers College: A Report of Progress and of Present Status," November 30, 1938, 31-34, in McElroy records, Mankato State University Archives.

[154] For more information on specific aspects of World War II see Spencer C. Tucker, ed., *Encyclopedia of World War II: A Political, Social, and Military History*, 5 vols. (Santa Barbara, CA: ABC-CLIO, 2005.

[155] For the history of the World War II home front see: Susan Hartmann, *The Home Front and Beyond: American Women in the 1940s* (Boston: Twayne Publishers, 1982) and Richard Polenberg, *War and Society: The United States, 1941-1945* (Philadelphia: Lippincott, 1972.)

156 U. S. Bureau of the Census, *Sixteenth Census of the United States*, 1940: *Population*, Vol. 1, 535; Kunz, *Muskets to Missiles*, 182.

157 Here and the paragraph below Enrollment Statistics, Institutional Research Records, Mankato State University Archives, Collection 1, Box 26.

158 *Mankato State Teachers College Catalog*, 1943-1944, 5.

159 Minnesota State Teachers College Board Minutes, 08 December 1942; Minnesota, *Session Laws*, 1943, Ch. 519; Diane R. Tuinstra, "Mankato State Teachers College during World War II," (unp. Master of Arts thesis), Mankato State University, 1994, 39.

160 Tuinstra, "Mankato State Teachers College," 40; Minnesota State Teachers College Board Minutes, 12 October 1944.

161 "Civilian Pilot Training Program," in *Wikipedia*, the online encyclopedia; *Mankato State Teachers College Catalog*, 1944-1945, 4. Tuinstra, "Mankato State Teachers College," 60-62.

162 "Civilian Pilot Training Program," in *Wikipedia*; Tuinstra, "Mankato State Teachers College," 65.

163 Here and the paragraph below, V. R. Cardozier, *Colleges and Universities in World War II* (Westport, CT: Praeger Publishers, 1993), 156; Tuinstra, "Mankato State Teachers College," 65-72. *Mankato State Teachers College Catalog*, 1943-1944, 6.

164 Cardozier, *Colleges and Universities in World War II*, 157.

165 *Mankato State Teachers College Catalog*, 1943-1944, 6.

166 *Katonian*, 1943, pages unnumbered.

167 *Mankato Free Press*, 10 October 1952, 8.

168 State Teachers College Board Minutes, 23 August 1943.

169 *Mankato Free Press*, 02 October 1943, 5; *Katonian*, 1945, 61: "Arthur Edgar Morgan," in *Wikipedia*, the online encyclopedia.

170 Youel, *Mankato State College*, 138; Otto Welton Snarr, Research Notes, 1938-1939, Southern Minnesota Historical Center, Minnesota State University, Mankato.

171 *Mankato Free Press*, 02 October, 5, 07 October, 3, 08 October, 1, 1943; Will Durant, in *Wikipedia*.

172 *Mankato Free Press*, 08 October 1943, 1.

173 *Mankato Free Press*, 02 October, 7, 04 October, 7, 05 October, 9, 06 October, 11, 07 October, 13 and 08 October 1943, 9. Xerox copies of Hook's articles are in Minnesota State University, Mankato Archives.

174 *Mankato State Teachers College Catalog*, 1946-1947, vii-xii, 35, 47, 59, 67, 75 and 87.

175 *Ibid.*, 1930-1931, 3-8.

176 *Ibid.*, 60; "Summary of Annual Attendance," Institutional Research Records, Mankato State University Archives, Collection 1, Box 26.

177 *Mankato Free Press*, 08 December 1954, 1; *College Reporter*, 16 December 1954, 1.

## Chapter 4

1 Here and the paragraph below see: Minnesota State Teachers College Board Minutes, 05 March 1946; *College Reporter*, 22 March 1946, 1; "Crawford, Clarence Leonard," *Who's Who in America*, vol.33 (1964-1965), Chicago: Marquis-Who's Who, 1965); *Mankato Teachers College Catalog*, 1946-1947, viii.

2 *Youel*, Mankato State College, 65.

3 *Ibid.*

4 U. S. Bureau of the Census, 1990: *Census of Population and Housing*, 26.

5 United States GDP Annual Growth Rate, 1948-2016," online source, access by title. Accessed 14 May 2017.

6 *Historical Statistics of the United States: Colonial Times to 1970*, Part 1, 383.

7 Here and the paragraph below, "G.I. Bill," in *Wikipedia*; Table of G. I. and Rehab Enrollment, 1945-49 and Table of Enrollment, 1938-48, both in Institutional Research Records, University Archives.

8 Joseph Anthony Amato and John Radzilowski, *A New College on the Prairie: Southwest State University's First Twenty-five Years, 1967-1992* (Longmont CO: Crossings Press, 1991), 26.

9 "Mankato, Minnesota," in *Wikipedia*.

10 Class schedules Fall 1946, Fall 1949 and Winter 1950-51, in Class Schedule Collection, University Archives.

11 *Mankato Free Press*, 14 March 1946, 9.

12 On the false Crawford tradition, see: Marcia Baer, ed., *Those Barracks Babies* (Mankato: Alumni Affairs Office, Mankato State University, 1990), 2, and *College Reporter*, 15 September 1994, 11.

13 State Teachers College Board Minutes, 05 March 1945.

14 *Ibid.*, 08 March 1947.

15 *Mankato Free Press*, 14 March 1946, 9.

16 Here and the two paragraphs below see Baer, *Barracks Babies*, 2.

17 *Ibid.*, 3-4.

18 Minnesota, Session Laws, 1949, Ch. 742, Sec. 3, Subd. 2; State Teachers College Board Minutes, 21 June, 23-24 August 1949; *Atlas of*

*Mankato, Minnesota*, 6.

[19] Here and the three paragraphs below see: *Mankato Free Press*, 10 October 1952, 1, 6; Photographs of Searing Hall, Minnesota State University, Mankato Archives.

[20] Here and the two paragraphs below see: *College Reporter*, 09 October, 1, 16 October 1952, 1; *Mankato State College Today* 13:4 (1982), 1; *Minnesota Legislative Manual*, 1955, 118.

[21] Minnesota, *Session Laws*, 1955, Ch. 715, Sec. 1.

[22] *College Reporter*, 01 March 1956, 1.

[23] *Ibid.*, 26 April 1956, 1. The general construction contract was for $549,740 and the other contracts were in the amounts of mechanical ($145,700), electrical ($56,450) and elevator ($21,381).

[24] *Ibid.*, 20 June 1956, 4; 27 September 1956, 1.

[25] *Ibid.*, 25 July 1957, 1, 16 September 1957 1, 29 May 1958, 2B, and 16 September 1958, 1.

[26] State College Board Minutes, 20 November 1959.

[27] Minnesota, Session Laws, 1951, Ch. 2, Sec. 5.

[28] Here and the paragraphs below see: *College Reporter*, 14 August 1953, 1.

[29] Here and the two paragraphs below see: *College Reporter*, 24 September 1953, 5; 10 February 1955, 2; 13 October 1955, 4.

[30] State College Board Minutes, 20 November 1959.

[31] State Teachers College Board Minutes, 20 June 1944; *Mankato Free Press*, 19 July 1941, 1.

[32] Minnesota, Session Laws, 1947, Ch. 636, Sect. 1, Subd. 4; *Mankato Free Press*, 04 July 1947, 7; C. L. Crawford to Val Imm, 11 March 1947, John R. Snow, president Board of Education of the City of Mankato to Imm, 10 April 1947 and Imm to Snow, 25 April 1947, all in Imm, Val Papers, Southern Minnesota Historical Center.

[33] *Mankato Free Press*, 04 July 1947, 7.

[34] *Ibid.*, 01 August 1947, 7.

[35] Here and the paragraph below *Ibid.*, 01 November 1947, 7.

[36] *Ibid.*, 11 November 1947, 11.

[37] *Minnesota, Session Laws*, 1949, Ch. 742, Sec. 4; *Mankato Free Press,* 09 April 1951, 9.

[38] *Minneapolis Sunday Tribune*, 24 June 1951, 7. The general construction contract was for $847,000 and the heating and electric contracts were respectively for $173,000 and $68,000.

[39] Here and the two paragraphs below see *Ibid.*; *Mankato Free Press,* 10 October 1952, 7, 25 June 1953, 1.

[40] *Mankato Free Press*, 25 June 1953, 1, 11; *College Reporter*, 14 August 1953, 4.

[41] Minnesota, *Session Laws*, 1957, Ch. 2, Sec. 2, Subd. 29.

[42] Here and the three paragraphs below see *College Reporter,* 06 November 1958, 1, 13 November 1958, 1, 07 May 1959, 1, 29 January 1960, 1, 11 March 1960, 1, 21 June 1960, 1 and 14 September 1960, 1. The general construction contract amount was $794,870.

[43] State College Board Minutes, 18 December 1967.

[44] Here and the paragraph below, *Mankato Free Press*, 10 September 1938, 9.

[45] *Ibid.*, 15 September 1938, 7.

[46] *Mankato State Teachers College Catalog*, 1935, 5.

[47] State Teachers College Board Minutes, 22 September 1954.

[48] *Minnesota, Session Laws*, 1955, Ch. 855, Sec. 4, Subd. 3; Photograph of Victorian style homes, Mankato State University Archives, Identifier: MSUrepository.615.MSU-UA-309-10453, msu10453.

[49] *College Reporter*, 25 July 1957, 1, 16 September 1957, 1.

[50] Here and the two paragraphs below see: *Ibid.*, 16 September 1958, 1; 07 May 1959, 5.

[51] *Ibid.*, 07 May 1959, 5; *Mankato State Teachers College Catalog*, 1953-54, vii.

[52] *College Reporter*, 09 August 1961, 1.

[53] State College Board Minutes, 20 November 1959.

[54] For this and the following eight paragraphs about the meeting see: State Teachers College Board Minutes, 05 November 1938.

[55] *Ibid.*, 23 September 1939.

[56] For a description of the B. E. and B. S. requirements, see respectively: *Mankato State Teachers College Catalog*, 1938-1939, 16 and *Mankato State Teachers College Catalog*, 1940-1941, 12-13.

[57] *College Reporter*, 27 October 1939, 1, 24 November 1939, 1.

[58] Here and the two paragraphs below see: State Teachers College Board Minutes, 06 July 1944.

[59] Here and the paragraph below see: *Ibid.*, 14 May, 27 August 1945.

[60] Here and the paragraph below see: *Ibid.*, 12 August 1946.

[61] *College Reporter*, 05 June 1947, 1.

[62] Val Imm to Frank D. McElroy, 11 February 1947, Val Imm Papers, Southern Minnesota Historical Center, Mankato State University,

Mankato; Stanford Lehmberg and Ann M. Pflaum, *The University of Minnesota, 1945-2000* (Minneapolis: *University of Minnesota Press*, 2001), 60.

[63] See, for example, Richard L. McKown to Imm, 24 March 1947, Imm Papers.

[64] Magnus to Imm, 16 March 1947, Imm Papers.

[65] Stewart to Imm, 19 February 1947 and Imm to Stewart, 21 March 1947, both in Imm Papers.

[66] Stewart to Almen, 05 April 1947, Imm Papers.

[67] Imm to Stewart, ca. 10 April 1947, Imm Papers.

[68] Imm to Schellberg, 25 April 1947, Imm Papers.

[69] Lehmberg and Pflaum, *University of Minnesota*, 60.

[70] State Teachers College Board Minutes, 30 August 1948.

[71] Here and the paragraph below *Ibid.*, 09 November 1948.

[72] *Ibid.*, 19 May 1949.

[73] Minnesota, *Session Laws*, 1957, Ch. 576.

[74] *Mankato Teachers College Catalog*, 1954-1955, 34, 1955-1956, 105. (Covers only nursing.)

[75] Youel, Mankato State College, 65.

[76] *Mankato Teachers College Catalog*, 1946-1947, 59-64, 67-69; 1956-1957, 92-95, 111, 113-115.

[77] Commencement programs, 03 June 1946, 01 June 1956, Commencement Program Collection, University Archives.

[78] Stanley Hall, "History of Common Schools in Blue Earth County," Master of Arts in Teaching thesis, (Mankato State College, 1973), 50.

[79] Commencement program, 01 December 1960, University Archives.

[80] *College Reporter*, 02 May 1957,1 and 11 October 1957, 1.

[81] Minnesota, *Session Laws*, Extra Session, 1957, Ch. 2, Sec. 2, Subd. 29.

[82] *College Reporter*, 25 July 1957, 1.

[83] Here and the five paragraphs below see: *Mankato Free Press*, 13 September 1957, 1-2.

[84] State College Board Minutes, 26 September 1958.

[85] Copy of letter from Hammel to Naftalin, 26 September 1957, in Crawford, Clarence L., Incoming correspondence, 1957, University Archives. All of the 171.5 acres were located in Section 19 of Township 108, Range 26, Mankato Township.

[86] Here and the two paragraphs below see: State College Board Minutes, 26 September 1958.

[87] *Ibid.*, 20 November 1959.

[88] *College Reporter*, 12 December 1957, 2.

[89] *Ibid.*, 24 July 1958, 1.

[90] *Ibid.*, 18 June 1959, 1.

[91] *Ibid.*, 12 November 1959, 2.

[92] *Ibid.*, 26 January 1960, 3.

[93] State College Board Minutes, 20 November 1959.

[94] Here and the two paragraphs below see State College Board Minutes, 30 June 1958. The general construction contract was for $1,452,163. The mechanical contract was $309,900 and the electrical contract was $142,112.

[95] *College Reporter*, 24 July 1958, 1, 15 January 1959, 2.

[96] Here and the two paragraphs below see *Mankato State Catalog*, 1959-1960, [253] and Crawford reports to the State College Board, 10 November 1959 and 08 February 1960, in University Archives.

[97] *College Reporter*, 12 July 1962, 2; State College Board Minutes, 20 November 1959.

[98] State College Board Minutes, 20 November 1959.

[99] *Ibid.*, 10 July 1959.

[100] Here and the paragraph below see Ibid., 29 October, 20 November 1959. The general construction contract was for $1,677,432. The other two contracts were $181,682 for electrical and $338,200 for plumbing.

[101] *College Reporter*, 07 July 1961, 3.

[102] State College Board Minutes, 25 April 1963; *Mankato Free Press*, August 1963, 13. The general construction contract was for $798,250. The mechanical contractor bid $166,590 and the electric contract was $82,196.

[103] College R*eporter*, 26 September 1963, 1, 28 July 1964, 1.

[104] *Ibid.*, 24 September 1964, 1; Crawford Report to the State College Board, 23 October 1964, University Archives.

[105] *College Reporter*, 24 September 1964, 1.

[106] State College Board Minutes, 15 June 1964. The low bid for the general construction contract was $1,699,300. The electrical contract was $188,657 and the mechanical contract was $378,000.

[107] *College Reporter*, 24 September 1964, 1.

[108] *Ibid.*, 25 May 1965, 2.

[109] State College Board Minutes, 02 August 1965, 17-18; *College Reporter*, 10 August 1965, 1.

[110] Here and the paragraph below, see *College Reporter*, 14 October 1965, 2.

[111] *Mankato Free Press*, 15 August 1964, 9.

[112] *College Reporter*, 18 May 1965, 1.

[113] *Ibid.*, 01 June 1960, 1, 14 September 1960, 3.

[114] *Mankato Free Press,* 14 October 1960, 11. The general construction bid was for The largest plumbing, heating, automatic controls and thermal insulation contract was for $255,000. The electrical work bid was $158,000.

[115] *College Reporter,* 27 September 1961, 1. Crawford evidently meant that the gymnasium-auditorium could seat 7,000 for such programs as commencement exercises when the basketball floor could be used for seating.

[116] *Ibid.*, 10 May 1961, 1; 19 September 1962, 1, 27 September 1962, 4, 7; 07 February 1963, 4, 07 July 1963, 1.)

[117] *Ibid.*,28 February 1963, 5, 24 September 1963, 1; 26 September 1963, 1.

[118] *Ibid.*, 28 March 1963, 1. The general construction contract was $125,375. The mechanical and electrical contracts were $11,460 and $13,340 respectively.

[119] *Mankato Free Press*, 28 October 1960, 13. The general construction contract was $513,000 and the lowest electrical and mechanical work bids were $97,796 and $129,800 respectively.

[120] *College Reporter*, 15 May 1961, 1; Class schedule, Fall 1962. Class Schedule Collection, University Archives.

[121] Building Floor Plans —Minnesota State University, Mankato, online source, access by title.

[122] Minnesota, *Session Laws*, Extra Session, 1961, Ch.72, Sec. 1, Subd. 25; College Reporter, 27 September 1961, 1.

[123] *Mankato Free Press*, 19 August 1964, 24; 26 February 1965, 4A; 15 June 1967, 15; *College Reporter*, 29 January 1969, 5.

[124] Crawford report to the State College Board, 23 October 1964, University Archives.

[125] *College Reporter*, 20 October 1964, 2.

[126] *Mankato Free Press*, 22 September 1964, 19, 26 February 1965, 4A.

[127] *College Reporter,* 03 November 1966, 2.

[128] State College Board Minutes, 18 December 1967.

[129] *Katonian*, 1933, 17; *Mankato State Teachers College Catalog*, 1933-1934, 8; Youel, Mankato State College, 134.

[130] *Mankato State Teachers College Catalog*, 1941-1942, viii; Youel, *Mankato State College*, 123.

[131] Here and the paragraph below *College Reporter,* 29 September 1964, 1.

[132] Here and the paragraph below see *Mankato Free Press*, 22 October 1960, 7, *Mankato Free Press,* 23 February 1962, sect. C, 10; Interview of Steven Ardolf, chief engineer, Minnesota State University, Mankato, by William E. Lass during Ardolf-led tour of Utilities Building and tunnels, 21 April 2017. Hereinafter cited as Ardolf Tour. The general construction contract was for $72,630. The lowest bids for the electrical and mechanical works were respectively $91,927 and $197,150.

[133] *College Reporter*, 12 May 1964, 3; *Mankato Free Press*, 26 February 1965, 4A; Crawford report to State College Board, 01 March 1965, University Archives; Ardolf Tour.

[134] Here and the paragraph below see *Mankato State Teachers College Catalog*, 1947-1948, vii, 1950-1951, vii.

[135] Here and the paragraph below see *College Reporter*, 24 September 1959, 1.

[136] *College Reporter,* 12 July 1961, 1, 28 September 1961, 1, 19 September 1962, 10, and 19 May 1964, 1.

[137] *Ibid.*, 04 March 1965, 1.

[138] *Mankato State College Catalog*, 1965-1966, 116-17.

[139] Roy Benjamin Moore, *Chronicle of Athletics Control: A History of Administration of Intercollegiate Athletics at Mankato State University 1890s-1980s* (Mankato: College of Health Physical Education and Nursing, Mankato State University, 1989), 12.

[140] *Mankato State Teachers College Catalog,* 1949-1950, 33, 1955-1956, 105.

[141] Complied from *Mankato State Catalogs,* 1946-1964.

[142] *Mankato State College Catalog*, 1964-1965, 73.

[143] *Ibid.*, 34.

[144] Here and the two paragraphs below see; *Mankato State College Catalog*, 1965-1966, 35, 79 and 86.

[145] Here and the two paragraphs below see; *Ibid.*, 101, 104-05 and 111.

[146] "Churchill Delivers Iron Curtain Speech," online source, access by title. Accessed 16 January 2016.

[147] Here and the paragraph below, "Timeline of Events in the Cold War," from the on-line encyclopedia *Wikipedia*, access by title, accessed 16 January 2017.

[148] "Federal Civil Defense Administration," from the on-line encyclopedia *Wikipedia*, access by title, accessed 16 January 2017.

[149] Here and the three paragraphs below see Minnesota, *Session Laws*, 1951, Ch. 694; "Civil Defense in Minnesota, 1950-1974," in *MNOPEDIA*, an online encyclopedia, access by title, accessed 16 January 2017.

[150] Here and the paragraph below *College Reporter*, 20 June 1956, 4.

[151] Here and the paragraph below *Mankato Free Press*, 21 July, 1, 23 July, 1, 7 1956.

[152] Here and the paragraph below *Ibid.*, 04, 05 May 1960, p. 1 and 13 respectively; *College Reporter*, 05 May 1960, 3.

[153] "Civil Defense in Minnesota, 1950-1974,"

[154] *College Reporter*, 28 February 1963, 1; For an illustration of the civil defense logo see "Federal Civil Defense Administration," in *Wikipedia*; State College Board Minutes, 11 January 1963.

[155] *Mankato Free Press*, 19 December 1968, 25.

[156] Here and the paragraph below see "C-ration" from *Wikipedia*, access by title, accessed 16 January 2017.

[157] "Timeline of Events in the Cold War," and "Civil Defense in Minnesota."

[158] *College Reporter,* 21 June 1960, 2.

[159] *Mankato Free Press*, 13 September 1957, 2.

[160] *College Reporter*, 07 December 1960, 1.

[161] *Ibid.*, 07 March 1961, 1-2.

[162] *Ibid.*, 18 April 1961, 5.

[163] *Ibid.*, 23 March 1961, 2.

[164] *Ibid.*, 11 May 1961, 2.

[165] *Ibid.*, 11 April 1962, 6.

[166] *Mankato Free Press*, 18 December 1962, 1.

[167] Here and the two paragraphs below see College *Reporter*, 22 January 1963, 1.

[168] University of Minnesota *Daily* article reprinted in *College Reporter*, 24 January 1963, 2.

[169] State College Board Minutes, 17 December 1962.

[170] *College Reporter*, 19 February 1963, 2.

[171] Press release, 13 February [1963], Imm Papers; *College Reporter*, 21 February 1963, 1.

[172] Here and the two paragraphs below, see: Copy of "An Act to change the name of the Mankato State College to the University of Southern Minnesota and to strike from the Minnesota Statutes the name of Mankato State College to conform to said change," Imm Papers.

[173] Memorandum to "Chairman and members of the Committee," ca. 15 February 1963, Imm Papers.

[174] *College Reporter*, 21 February 1963, 1.

[175] See, for example, P. M. Ferguson, Jr., to Senator Robert H. Dunlap, 14 March 1963 and Everett E. Collin to Leonard Ford, 18 April 1963, both in Imm Papers.

[176] Here and the paragraph below *Minneapolis Sunday Tribune*, 21 April 1963, Editorial—Feature and Business Section, 3.

[177] ."Alumni Legislative Newsletter from the Minnesota Alumni Association," University of Minnesota, 29 April 1963, copy in Imm Papers.

[178] Here and the paragraph below see: Final printed copy of bill, in Imm papers: Minnesota, *Senate Journal*, 1963, 304, 1061-62, 1301-02, 1312, and 2556; *College Reporter,* 23 April 1963, 1.

[179] Crawford to Imm, 23 May 1963, Imm Papers.

[180] *St. Paul Pioneer Press*, 09 November 1963, 9 *Mankato Free Press*, 09 November 1963, 3.

[181] State College Board Minutes, 19 September 1964.

[182] *College Reporter,* 08 October 1964, 1.

[183] *Ibid.*, 15 October 1964, 1.

[184] *Ibid.*, 13 October, 2, 20 October, 2, 1964.

[185] *Ibid.*, 27 October 1964, 1-2.

[186] *Ibid.* 12 November 1964, 1.

[187] *Ibid.*, 05 November 1964, 1.

[188] Statement titled "Possible University Status at Mankato," presented to Minnesota State College Board by John Hodowanic, attached to board minutes of 16 November 1964.

[189] Here and the three paragraphs below State College Board Minutes, 16 November 1964.

[190] Here and the two paragraphs below State College Board Minutes, 19 December 1964.

[191] Here and the two paragraphs below see: Copy of "A Bill for an Act Establishing the Minnesota State University at Mankato Under the State College Board," in Imm Papers.

[192] *Mankato Free Press*, 22 December 1964, 11.

[193] *College Reporter*, 21 January 1965, 1.

[194] *Minneapolis Tribune*, 06 January, 5; 07 January, 4 and 08 January, 4, 1965.

[195] Here and the three paragraphs below *Ibid.*, 31 January 1965, 16A.

[196] *College Reporter*, 14 January 1965, 1.

[197] *Ibid.*, 11 February 1965, 1.

[198] *Ibid.*, 18 February, 1 and 23 February 1965, 1.

[199] Imm to Popp, 18 March 1965, Imm Papers.

[200] *College Reporter*, 04 May, 1, 13 May, 1, 1965.

[201] *Ibid.*, 18 May, 1, 23 September, 1, 1965.

[202] *Ibid.*, 26 April 1966, 3.

203 *College Reporter,* 17 September 1965, 1.

204 *Mankato State College Catalog,* 1957-1958, 29-30, 1958-1959, 32-33.

205 Crawford report to the State College Board, 14 June 1965, University Archives.

206 *Mankato Free Press,* 16 March 1996, 14.

207 *Ibid.,* 29 March 1996, 11.

# Chapter 5

1 Here the paragraph below, *College Reporter,* 08 March 1966, 1; State College Board Minutes, 19 March 1966.

2 State College Board Minutes, 05 August 1966.

3 *Ibid.,* 08 May 1967.

4 Alm's narrative in James F. Nickerson, *Out of Chaos: Reflections of a University President and His Contemporaries on Vietnam Era Unrest in Mankato and Its Relevance Today* (Mankato: Minnesota State University, Mankato Foundation, Sesquicentennial ed., 2017), 42; *College Reporter,* 20 June 1967, 1.

5 McDonald vita in Brendan John McDonald file, University Archives.

6 *Mankato Free Press,* 06 July 1967, 11.

7 *Ibid.,* 05 June 1968, 18.

8 Here and the two paragraphs below *College Reporter,* 04 June 1968, 1; Hess vita in David N. Hess file, University Archives.

9 Glines vita in Donald E. Glines file, University Archives.

10 *College Reporter,* 24 September 1969, 17.

11 University Archives has an extensive holding of Wilson Campus School records. Particularly significant coverage of the Glines changes is described in the *College Reporter,* 05 August 1969, 6, 20 January 1971, 5, 24 June 1971, 2 and 28 February 1984, 10.

12 Alm's narrative in Nickerson, *Out of Chaos,* 43.

13 For a good summary of the problems resulting from insufficient library space see an article by Bob Swanson in the *Mankato Free Press,* 07 August 1964, 9.

14 Here and the paragraph below, *College Reporter,* 20 July 1965, 1; *Mankato Free Press,* 28 July 1965, 15.

15 *College Reporter,* 22 September 1966, 1; 20 June 1967, 1.

16 *Mankato Free Press,* 02 October 1967, 17.

17 *Ibid.,* 24 February 1967, 11A; *College Reporter,* 23 September 1968, 25.

18 *College Reporter,* 15 November 1966, 2;

19 State College Board Minutes, 18 December 1967.

20 *College Reporter,* 17 October 1967, 1: *Mankato State Catalog,* 1953-54, xiii.

21 *College Reporter,* 06 October 1964, 1. The lowest bid for general construction was $1,127,000. The other low bids were $156,800 for electric and $352,400 for the mechanical and ventilation work. Elevator installation was $34,285.

22 *Ibid.,* 19 July 1966, 3.

23 *Ibid.,* 22 September 1966, 1.; 11 April 1967, 1; 01 August 1967, 1.

24 *Ibid.,* 01 March 1966, 1; *Mankato Free Press,* 20 September 1967, 6.

25 State College Board Minutes, 18 December 1967.

26 *College Reporter,* 16 November 1960, 2.

27 *Ibid.,* 23 October 1962, 5.

28 *Ibid.,* 23 November 1965, 1; 09 December 1965, 5.

29 Specific contract amounts were: $1,139,400 for general construction, $196,820 for electrical work, $369,168 for all mechanical and ventilation work and $179,129 for kitchen equipment installation. Other significant costs were $113,076.42 for the fees of the consulting and project architects and $113,076.42 for site construction. State College Board Minutes, 19 March 1966.

30 *College Reporter,* 19 May 1966, 1.

31 *Ibid.,* 08 November 1966, 1.

32 *Ibid.,* 28 September 1967, 1; 12 October 1967, 1.

33 *Ibid.,* 07 March 1967, 4; 06 April 1967, 4.

34 *Ibid.,* 12 December 1967, 3.

35 *Ibid.,* 02 May 1968, 1.

36 *Ibid.,* 19 January 1967, 4; State College Board Minutes, 18 December 1967.

37 *College Reporter,* 22 September 1971, 1.

38 Here and the paragraph below, *Ibid.,* 25 September 1972, 3.

39 *Ibid.,* 04 January 1973, 4.

40 *Ibid.,* 04 November 1965, 1.

[41] *Ibid.*, 29 November 1966, 1.

[42] Here and the three paragraphs below *Ibid.*, 01 December 1966, 1; 31 October 1967, 1.

[43] State College Board Minutes, 18 December 1967.

[44] *College Reporter*, 22 February, 1966, 1.

[45] *Ibid.*, 27 June 1967, 1.

[46] *Mankato Free Press*, 10 November 1967, 9.

[47] *College Reporter*, 04 June 1969, 2

[48] Here and the paragraph below see: *Ibid.*, 22 September 1971, 1; 25 September 1972, 3.

[49] *Ibid.*, 02 March 1973, 3; *Mankato State College Today* 4 (Winter 1973), [3]. Also, see biographical sketch of Trafton in Chapter 3.

[50] *Mankato State College Today* 4 (Summer 1973), [7]; *College Reporter*, 27 September 1973, 6; 11 October 1973, 3; *Mankato Free Press*, 13 October 1973, 1.

[51] *College Reporter*, 25 January 1968, 2.

[52] *Ibid.*, 16 November 1967, 16; 25 January 1968, 2.

[53] *Ibid.*, 22 September 1971, 1; *Mankato State College Today* 4 (Fall 1972), [7].

[54] *College Reporter*, 25 January 1968, 2.

[55] Here and the paragraph below *Ibid.*, 20 September 1969, 2; 24 September 1969, 1; Elizabeth Broman, "1964: Fountains, Fireworks, Fifty Years Ago — A World's Fair," online source, access by title.

[56] *College Reporter,* 22 September 1971, 1

[57] Ibid., 15 May 1975, 1.

[58] See Chapter 1 for more detail about these events.

[59] *Mankato State Teachers College Catalog*, 1947-1948, 1.

[60] *Mankato State College Catalog*, 1961-1962, 8.

[61] *Mankato Free Press*, 26 October 1967, 9; *Mankato State College Today* (Fall 1971), [16].

[62] The principal sources for the background of the Vietnam War student protests are: James P. Smith, "Vietnam Remembered: Minnesotans and the Vietnam War." *Roots* 19 (Spring 1991); "Opposition to United States Involvement in the Vietnam War," *Wikipedia* (online source, access by title, and George C. Herring, *America's Longest War: The United States and Vietnam, 1950-1975* (Boston: McGraw-Hill, 2002).

[63] "Kent State Shootings," in *Wikipedia*, online source, accessed 20 June 2017.

[64] Here and the eight paragraphs below *College Reporter*, 08 May 1970, 1; *Mankato Free Press*, 06 May 1970, 1-2.

[65] *College Reporter*, 08 May 1970, 4.

[66] *Mankato Free Press,* 07 May 1970, 19.

[67] *College Reporter*, 08 May 1970, 2; *Mankato Free Press*, 08 May 1970, 9.

[68] *Ibid.*, 11 May 1970, 1. On the rumor about the high school students see *Mankato Free Press*, 09 May 1970, 11.

[69] "Jackson State Killings," in *Wikipedia*, online source, accessed 21 June 2017.

[70] Faust, *Mankato State University*, 34.

[71] *College Reporter*, 20 May 1970, 1.

[72] Here and the paragraph below, *Ibid.*, 20 May 1970, 1; 22 May 1970, 1; Mankato State College, Spring, 1972 class schedule, University Archives.

[73] Here and the paragraph below *College Reporter*, 28 October 1971, 9; 03 November 1971, 3 and 05 November 1971, 5. Suzanne Bunkers incorrectly identified the teach-in as having occurred on November 3, 1972. (Nickerson, *Out of Chaos*, 23.)

[74] "Mining of Haiphong Harbor," Vietnam War.net Online source access by title. Accessed 22 June 2017.

[75] "Vietnam War Draft," online source, access by title. Accessed 22 June 2017.

[76] "Mitchell Goodman," in *Wikipedia*, online source, access by title. Accessed 22 June 2017. The Boston Five members who were convicted with Goodman were Spock, the Reverend William Sloane Coffin, the Yale University chaplain, and Michael Ferber, a Harvard University graduate student. Marcus Raskin, the fifth defendant, was not convicted.

[77] *College Reporter*, 25 April 1969, 1.

[78] Nickerson, *Out of Chaos*, 153.

[79] *Katonian*, 1971, 48.

[80] *College Reporter*, 15 October 1969, 1.

[81] Here and the paragraph below *Ibid.*, 02 October 1970, 1. For detailed coverage of the Chair of Ideas, see the Chair of Ideas File in University Archives, which consists mainly of *Reporter* articles.

[82] Here and the two paragraphs below *College Reporter*, 28 September 1971, 5; 19 January 1972, 7; 07 April 1972, 1, 3; and, 11 April 1972, 3.

[83] Here and the paragraph below *Ibid.*, 20 April 1972, 3- 4; 24 April 1972, 3, 14.

[84] Here and the two paragraphs below *Ibid.*, 04 May 1972, 1 and 05 May 1972, 3.

[85] Here and the seven paragraphs below *Mankato Free Press*, 09 May 1972, 15, 10 May 1972, 1, 21-22.

[86] Here the four paragraphs below *Minneapolis Tribune*, 12 May 1972, 1A; *Mankato Free Press*, 15 May 1972, 7A.

[87] *College Reporter*, 24 May 1972, 1.

[88] *Ibid.*, 19.

[89] Here and the paragraph below *Ibid.*, 26 May 1972, 3.

[90] Dana Greene, *Denise Levertov: A Poet's Life* (Urbana: University of Illinois Press, 2012), 116-17.

[91] Ibid., 118; *Mankato State College Campus Directory 1970-71*, 20; *Mankato State College Katonian*, 1971, 169, 232-33.

[92] Greene, *Levertov*, 118-19; For information on Goodman and Gregor after their marriage see Goodman sketch in *Wikipedia*. Goodman died on February 1, 1997. For his obituary in the *New York Times* see "Mitchell Goodman, Antiwar Protest Leader, Dies at 73." (Online source. Access by title.) Gregor's life span was 04 February 1952-08 October 2009. Her obituary can be accessed at the online subscription source ObituatyData.com

[93] "Paris Peace Accords," in *Wikipedia*, accessed 04 August 2017.

[94] Here and the paragraph below, Nickerson, *Out of Chaos*, 93, 123-24; *College Reporter*, 05 May 1972, 3.

[95] Here and the two paragraphs below *College Reporter*, 05 May 1983, 8; 08 June 1983, 1; 04 October 1983, 10; *Mankato Free Press*, 31 May 1983, 1.

[96] Nickerson, *Out of Chaos*, [183].          -`

[97] *Ibid., Mankato Free Press*, 07 March 2009, A1.

[98] Here and the two paragraphs below see *College Reporter*. 09 May 1972, 9; 31 May 1972, 2; 21 February 1973, 2; 28 March 1973, 6; 24 February 1975, 7; *University Reporter*, 20 April 1976; The last description of the Peace Studies minor was printed in the 1979-1980 undergraduate bulletin, p. 50.

[99] *Mankato Free Press*, 18 January 1968, 13.

[100] *College Reporter*, 22 September 1969, 1; History of enrollment statistical table, attached to email from Jerold J. Oman, research specialist, Institutional Research, Planning & Assessment Office to Daardi Sizemore Mixon, university archivist, 11 November 2016. Copy in University Archives.

[101] Oman to Daardi Sizemore Mixon, 11 November 2016.

[102] *College Reporter*, 10 December 1977, 1.

[103] Here and the paragraph below *Mankato Free Press*, 01 March 1972, 27.

[104] *Ibid.*, 09 March 1972, 1.

[105] *Mankato State College Today* 4 (Fall 1972), [5]; *Mankato Free Press*, 17 October 1972, 1.

[106] *Mankato Free Press*, 14 November 1972, 1.

[107] Here and the paragraph below Gary M. Andrew and Duane Grande, "Plan for Mankato State College Consolidation on Highland Campus (Phase II)," January, 1975, 2-11 and 2-12.

[108] State College Board Minutes, 21 May 1973.

[109] Here and the paragraph below *Ibid.*, 22 May 1974.

[110] Moore vita in Moore, Douglas R. File, University Archives; *Mankato State College Today* 5 (1974), 3.

[111] *College Reporter*, 20 March 1974, 3.

[112] Mankato State College, Informational Services news release, 21 August 1974, Moore File.

[113] Mankato State College news release, 04 March 1975, in Carl Lofy file, Minnesota State University Archives; *Mankato Free Press*, 31 March 1975, 1, 11 June 1975, 19, 19 July 1978, 12.

[114] Mankato State University New Bureau release, 18 July 1978, in Moore file.

[115] *College Reporter*, 25 November 1968, 7; Moore, *Chronicle of Athletics Control*, 61-64.

[116] *Mankato State University Today* 7:2 (1976), 2. See also information on Title IX in this chapter's Brock, Georgene sketch.

[117] *Mankato Free Press*, 26 May 1977, 29; Mankato State University, News Bureau release, 14 June 1978, Moore File; *University Reporter*, 13 September 1978, 3.

[118] *Ibid.*, G. Theodore Mitau, *Minnesota's Colleges of Opportunity: From Normal Schools to Teachers College and State University System — A Century of Academic Change in Minnesota* (n.p.: Alumni Associations of the Minnesota State University System, March, 1977), 75-76, 96-97.

[119] *Mankato State University Today*, 8:1 (1976), 2; 8:2 (1977), 5.

[120] For the development of an affirmative action policy by the State College Board see its minutes of 22 February, 29 May and 18 August 1972 and Mitau, *Minnesota's Colleges of Opportunity*, 63.

[121] *College Reporter*, 29 September 1966, 1; 23 February 1967, 1.

[122] *Ibid.*, 25 November 1970, 1.

[123] Here and the paragraph below *Mankato Free Press*, 05 December 1970, 13; *College Reporter*, 07 December 1970, 1; and, State College Board minutes, 04 December 1970.

[124] *Mankato Free Press*, 05 December 1970, 13; *College Reporter*, 07 December 1970, 1.

[125] *College, Reporter*, 12 March 1971, 3.

[126] *Ibid.*, 19 April 1971, 1; 21 April 1971, 1.

[127] *Ibid.*, 21 April 1971, 2; 11 May 1971, 1.

[128] *Ibid.*, 24 May 1971, 2; 27 May 1971, 1, 2.

[129] Here and the paragraph below *Ibid.*, 12 April 1973, 3; 13 April 1973, 8.

[130] *College Reporter*, 05 March 1974, 8; 24 April 1974, 8.

[131] *Ibid.*, 28 March 1974, 8; *Mankato Free Press*, 15 March 1974, 16.

[132] *College Reporter*, 22 October 1974, 7; 06 November 1974, 1; 11 November 1974, 4; 10 January 1975, 1.

[133] *Ibid.*, 06 March 1975, 1; Joseph A. Amato and John Radzilowski, *A New College on the Prairie: Southwest State University's First Twenty-Five Years, 1967-1992* (Longmont CO: Crossings Press, 1991), 26; Mitau, *Minnesota's Colleges of Opportunity*, 63-64.

[134] Here and the paragraph below *College Reporter*, 06 March 1975, 1; 12 February 1975, 1.

[135] *Mankato Free Press*, 03 June 1975, 8.

[136] Here and the paragraph below Minnesota, *Session Laws*, 1975, Ch. 321.

[137] State University Board Minutes, 20 August 1975.

[138] *College Reporter*, 30 July 1975, 1.

[139] *University Reporter*, 13 August 1975, 3.

[140] *The 1978-1979 Bulletin of Mankato State University: Undergraduate Course Offerings*, 34.

[141] *Ibid.*, 104.

[142] *Ibid.*, 126.

[143] *Ibid.*, 58.

[144] *Ibid.*, 78.

[145] *Ibid.*, 88.

[146] *The 1978-1979 Bulletin of Mankato State University: Graduate Course Offerings*, 7.

[147] *1978-1979 Bulletin of Mankato State University: Undergraduate Course Offerings*, [1].

[148] *University Independent*, 19 January 1977, 2.

[149] *College Reporter*, 30 April 1968, 1; 23 September 1968, 3A.

[150] Regarding the formation and activities of AIM see "American Indian Movement," *Wikipedia*, access by title, accessed 31 July 2017 and William T. Hagen, *American Indians* (Rev. ed.; Chicago: University of Chicago Press, 1979), 171-72.

[151] *College Reporter*, 22 September 1971, 24; "Stanford Cardinal," in *Wikipedia*, online source, access by title. Accessed 08 July 2017.

[152] *College Reporter*, 27 September 1971, 5.

[153] *Ibid.*, 11 October 1971, 5; 14 October 1971, 1.

[154] *Ibid.*, 14 October 1971, 1.

[155] *Ibid.*, 26 October 1971, 1.

[156] *Ibid.*, 30 January 1973, 1. For an illustration of the traditional Indian warrior logo and its suggested replacement see *Mankato Free Press*, 01 February 1973, 15.

[157] *Mankato Free Press*, 01 February 1973, 15.

[158] *Ibid.*

[159] *University Independent*, 06 October 1976, 1.

[160] *Ibid.*

[161] *Ibid.*, 12 October 1976, 2. The *University Independent* was the name of the school newspaper from 21 September 1976-19 May 1977 at which time it returned to the *Reporter*.

[162] *Ibid.*, 10 November 1976, 1.

[163] *Ibid.*, 30 June 1977, 1.

[164] *Ibid.*, 19 January 1977, 2.; 30 June 1977, 7.

[165] For biographical information on Samuel A. Maverick see: Carl H. Moneyhon," Maverick, Samuel Augustus," *American National Biography*, Vol. 14 (New York: Oxford University Press, 1999) and MAVERICK, SAMUEL AUGUSTUS. The Handbook of Texas Online. For the evolution of maverick as a common name, see: *Oxford English Dictionary: The Definitive Record of the English Language* (Oxford, England: Oxford University Press, 2017).

[166] Here and the paragraph below *University Independent*, 30 June 1977, 1.

[167] *Mankato State Today* 8:3 (1977), 5; *University Independent*, 07 July 1977, 2.

[168] Minnesota, *Session Laws*, 1973, Ch. 778, Sec. 4 (2); *Mankato State College Today* 5 (1975), 4; *Mankato Free Press*, 11 February 1974, 14; Moore, *Chronicle of Athletic Control*, 58.

[169] "A Study to Determine the Need for the Valley (Lower) Campus Mankato State College Mankato, Minnesota," January 1974, title page and preface.

[170] Here and the paragraph below "1973 Oil Crisis," in *Wikipedia*, access by title, accessed 10 July 2017; U. S. Office of Energy Efficiency & Renewable Energy, "Fact #915: March 7, 2016 Average Historical Annual Gasoline Pump Price, 1929-2015," online source, access by title, accessed 10 July 2017.

[171] "Study to Determine the Need for Valley Campus", 1-1, 1-2, 6-6 and 6-7.

[172] *Ibid*, 6-6.; State College Board Minutes, 04 February 1967; 11 May 1970.

[173] Minnesota, *Session Laws*, 1974, Ch. 516, Sec. 3.

[174] Andrew and Grande, "Plan for Mankato State College Consolidation on Highland Campus (Phase II)," 1-4.

[175] *Ibid.*, 1-4, 1-5.

[176] State College Board Minutes, 17 January 1975, Appendix VI.

[177] Minnesota, *Session Laws*, 1975, Ch. 433, Sec. 3.

[178] G. Theodore Mitau, chancellor, State College System to Norbert Arnold, chairman, Senate Finance Committee, 15 July 1975. Attached to board minutes, 20 August 1975.

[179] Here and the paragraph below Minnesota, *Session Laws*, 1976, Ch. 348, Sec. 4, Subd. 5.

[180] "Factors Related to Future Wilson School Funding and Facilities," in Wilson Campus School, Closing of Wilson Campus School Correspondence, Miscellaneous, 1974-1976, University Archives Collection 307, Box 7, Folder 1.

[181] Here and the two paragraphs below *University Independent*, 04 January 1977, 1; *Mankato State Today* 8:2 (1977), 5; 8:3 (1977), 9.

[182] Here and the two paragraphs below Richard L. Brubacher to Roger D. Moe, state senator, and Fred C. Norton, state representative, 06 April 1977. Attached to memo of 07 April 1977 from Edward R. McMahon, vice president for resource management, Mankato State University to John Hodowanic, Ira Johnson, Carl Lofy, Judith Mans, Douglas Moore and Margaret Preska, in Campus Consolidation File, Academic Affairs Records, Mankato State Archives Collection 14, Box 37, Folder 1.

[183] *Ibid., University Reporter*, 07 July 1977, 1.

[184] *University Reporter*, 04 August 1977, 2; 11 August 1977, 1.

[185] Minnesota, *Session Laws*, 1978, Ch. 792, Sec. 9, Subd. 3.

[186] On the closing of Wilson Campus School see: *Mankato Free Press*, 26 May 1977, 19; *University Independent*, 21 April 1977, 1.

[187] *Mankato State Today* 10:2 (1979), 3.

[188] Here and the paragraph below "Reduction Projections for the Campus Consolidation," attached to McMahon to Winston Benson, *et. al.*, 18 July 1978, in Campus Consolidation File, Academic Affairs Records, Mankato State Archives Collection 14.

[189] Here and the three paragraphs below *Mankato State Today* 11:3 (1980), [4]; *Mankato Free Press*, 13 May 1963, 17; 08 June 1979, 18. For an obituary of Anna Wiecking see *Mankato Free Press*, 23 November 1973, 11.

[190] On the creation of Old Main Village see: *Today at Mankato State University* 19:4 (Fall 1988), 8. On the burning and subsequent razing of the old lab school see: *Mankato Free Press*, 18 April 1984, 1; *Mankato State University Reporter*, 17 April 1984, 1.

## Chapter 6

[1] Here and the two paragraphs below, see: *Reporter*, 09 February 1979. 1.

[2] Here and the paragraph below, see: *Mankato State Today* 10:1 (1979), 3.

[3] *Mankato Free Press*, 19 February 1979, 28.

[4] *Ibid.*, 27 June 1979, 2.

[5] *Ibid.*, 09 July 1979, 2.

[6] *Ibid.*

[7] Here and the paragraph below, see: *Reporter*, 20 July, 2, 27 July, 1, 10 August, 1983, 1; Victor Colway file, University Archives.

[8] Mankato State University News Service release, 27 February 1989, in Colway file, University Archives.

[9] Here and the paragraph below, see: *Reporter*, 02 July 1980, 1.

[10] Here and the paragraph below *Mankato Free Press*, 16 October 1982, 5; Faust, Claire file, in University Archives. For an obituary of Faust see *Mankato Free Press*, 09 February 2010, 1.

[11] Here and the two paragraphs below see: *Today at Mankato State University* 21 (Fall 1990), 4.

[12] Claire E. Faust, *Mankato State University: The Second Century: The First Twenty-Five Years 1968-1992: An Interpretive Essay*, ([Mankato: Mankato State University, 1993], 34.)

[13] "Reduction Projections for the Campus Consolidation," attached to Edward McMahon to Winston Benson, *et. al.*, 18 July 1978, in Campus Consolidation File, Academic Affairs Records, Mankato State Archives Collection 14; Trafton Science Center in Buildings, Mankato State University, Mankato, online source.

[14] Faust, *Mankato State University*, 34.

[15] *Today* 12: 1 (1981), [2].

[16] *Ibid.* 14 (Summer 1983), 3.

[17] Here and the paragraph below, see: *Ibid.* 20 (Spring 1989), 15 and Clarence L. Crawford, Report to the State College Board, 10 November 1959, in University Archives.

[18] Here and the two paragraphs below, see: *Reporter*, 06 April, 1 and 28 September 1982, 3; Faust, Mankato State University, 66-67; and, "Wiecking Center," in Buildings, Facilities Management-Minnesota State University, Mankato, online source.

[19] Here and the two paragraphs below, see: *Today at Mankato State University* 19 (Winter 1988), 1; *Reporter*, 18 August 1966, 3.

[20] Here and the paragraph below, see: "Alumni Foundation Building," in Buildings, Facilities Management-Minnesota State University,

Mankato; *Today at Mankato State University*, 20 (Spring 1989), 13.

21 Minnesota, *Session Laws*, 1989, ch. 293, Sec. 5, Subd. 1.

22 Here and the paragraph below, see: *Mankato State Today* 14: 1 (1983), 7; *Reporter*, 24 June 1981, 3.

23 For additional information about Standeford Observatory, including its re-location in 2006 and its various telescopes, see: Standeford Observatory —Facilities—Physics and Astronomy, online source.

24 Here and the paragraph below, see: *Today at Mankato State University* 20 (Fall 1989), 13; Andreas Observatory—Facilities—Physics and Astronomy, online source.

25 For a lengthy interview with Andreas, see: *Connect Business Magazine* (July 2002). His obituary was published in the *Mankato Free Press*, 06 April 2009, A1.

26 *Mankato State Today* 15 (Summer 1984), 7.

27 *Ibid.* 17 (Summer 1986), 1; *Reporter*, 11 June 1986, 1.

28 Wissink Hall dedication ceremony program, in Wissink Hall file, University Archives.

29 Here and the paragraph, below see: *Mankato State Today* 19 (Summer 1988), 14; *Reporter*, 06 September 1935, 1; *Mankato Free Press*, 13 January 1987, 10; Melba Leichsening file, University Archives.

30 Mankato State University News Service release, 19 May 1988, Wissink Hall file, University Archives.

31 *Reporter*, 21 April 1983, 3.

32 *Ibid.*, 09 November 1982, 7, 21 April 1983, 3.

33 Minnesota, *Session Laws*, 1987, Ch. 400, Sec. 19, Subd. 3, 1989, Ch. 300, Art. 1, Subd. 3.

34 Here and the paragraph below, see: *Today* 20 (Summer 1989), 1.

35 *Ibid.*, 21 (Spring 1990), 16.

36 Here and the paragraph below, see: *Reporter*, 09 December 1992, 4; "Memorial Library Dedication and Mankato See University's 125th Anniversary Celebration, November 5, 1991," in Library Services Collection, 1911-ongoing, University Archives Collection 167.

37 Consumer Price Index, 1800- (The article "Buildings Facilities Management" on the Minnesota State University, Mankato website shows the total cost of the original Memorial Library and the remodeling/addition as $14,090,749.)

38 Here and the two paragraphs below, see: *Mankato State Today* 18 (Summer 1987), 1, 19 (Winter, 1988), 12.

39 *Reporter*, 27 September 1988, 2; *Today* 19 (Winter 1988), 12, 22 (Winter 1991), 1.

40 *Today* 22 (Winter 1991), 1.

41 *Ibid.* 14 (Fall 1983), 4.

42 Here and the paragraph below, see: Minnesota, *Session Laws*, 1983, Ch. 258, Sec 4, Subd. 2; *Today* 14 (Fall 1983), [7].

43 *Ibid.*, 19 (Winter 1988, 1.

44 *Ibid.*, 18 (Winter 1987), [16].

45 Mankato State University Undergraduate Curriculum Committee Minutes, 10 November 1987, 02 February, 05 April 1988, in Academic Affairs Office Records, University Archives; *Mankato State University Undergraduate Bulletin*, 1990-91, 15.

46 Here and the paragraph below, see: *Daily Reporter*, 11 March 1971, 1.

47 *Ibid.*, 12 March 1971; *The 1972-1973 Bulletin of Mankato State College*, 20.

48 Here and the paragraph below, see: *Today* 12:2 (1981), 4.

49 *Ibid.*, and 12:3 (1981), 8.

50 Here and the four paragraphs below, see: *Reporter*, 22 September 1988, 1.

51 *Today* 22 (Fall 1991), 13. Steve W. Smith, vice president for budget & business services, Minnesota State University Mankato, email to William E. Lass, 20 November 2017.

52 Crofts was the permanent replacement of Philip Kendall, who resigned abruptly on February 1, 1988. There was considerable faculty and student concern about Kendall's sudden termination, because the Preska administration failed to give a clear explanation. Preska herself stated that Kendall had resigned for personal reasons. John Winkworth, director of institutional research, opined that Kendall resigned because he was experiencing respiratory problems. Neither version explains why Kendall vacated his office over a weekend and was assigned the official status as on leave. Kendall refused to comment publicly, but he did tell a number of faculty members that he had been fired, because of his sometimes acrimonious relations with the chancellor's office of the State University System. Kendall had been quite vocal in criticizing what he saw as the St. Paul bureaucracy. Fisher served as Kendall's temporary replacement until Crofts was hired. (*Reporter*, 02 February 1988, 1; Mankato State University Newsweekly, 08 February 1988.)

53 For this and the four paragraphs below, see: *Reporter*, 30 May 1991, 1.

54 *Mankato Free Press*, 30 May 1991, 1.

55 *Minneapolis Star Tribune*, 31 May 1991, 1B.

56 *Ibid., Mankato Free Press*, 31 May 1991, 13.

57 *Minneapolis Star Tribune*, 31 May 1991, 1B., 05 June 1991, 3Be.

58 *Ibid.*, 05 June 1991, 3Be.

59 *Mankato Free Press*, 14 December 1991, 9.

[60] *Ibid., Reporter*, 09 January 1992, 1; *Today* 23 (Winter 1992), 1.

[61] Here and the paragraph below, see: *Mankato Free Press*, 30 January, 1, 20 August, 2, 1992; *Today at Mankato State University* 23 (Spring 1992), 1, 13.

[62] *Mankato Free Press*, 04 February 1992, 2.

[63] *Ibid.*, 20 August 1992, 2.

[64] Here and the two paragraphs below, see: *Today* 23 (Summer 1992), 13 and "University of California, San Marcos" in *Wikipedia*

[65] *Mankato Free Press*, 30 January 1993, 13.

[66] *Today* 23 (Fall 1993), 3.

[67] *Ibid.; Mankato Free Press*, 20 July 1995, 1; "Lewis Jones Goddard College," online site, access by title, accessed 25 October 2017.

[68] *Today* 23 (Fall 1993), 3.

[69] Here and the three paragraphs below see: *Mankato Free Press*, 10 June, 1, 20 July 1995, 1.

[70] "Lewis Jones, Goddard College. For additional information on Jones see the online articles "Goddard Defends Hiring of Dean With a Past No Confidence Vote" and Goddard Announces the Appointment of New Chief Academic Officer."

[71] Here and the paragraph below, see: *Mankato Free Press*, 25 April 1996, 17.

[72] Boubel, Karen A., candidate profile [1996] and Mankato State University news release, 17 May, 1996, both in Boubel, Karen A. Records, University Archives.

[73] *Reporter*, 21 May 1998, 1.

[74] Here and the paragraph below, see: *Ibid.*, 02 February 1999, 2 and 23 June 1999, 1, 16 November 1999, 1.; Minnesota State University, Mankato Buildings.

[75] Here and the paragraph below, see: *Mankato Free Press*, 12 December 1995, 1; "The Black Box Andreas Theatre; A New Jewel for the MSU Theatre Arts Department," *Today* 26 (Spring 1996), 10; *Minnesota, Session Laws*, 1997, Ch. 183, Art. 3, subd. 6; *Reporter*, 29 August 2000, sec. 2, p. 1.

[76] *Today* (Fall 1998), 12.

[77] *Ibid.* (Fall 2000), 7.

[78] Minnesota State University, Mankato Buildings, online source.

[79] *Today* (Fall 2002), 23.

[80] *Ibid.* (Spring-Summer 1999), 6.

[81] Here and the two paragraphs below, see: "Glen Taylor' in *Wikipedia*.

[82] Here and the paragraph below, see: "William Bresnan" and "Bresnan Communications" in *Wikipedia* and Daniel Vance, "William J. Bresnan" in *Connect Business Magazine* ((January 2001).

[83] *Today* (Spring, 1998), 10-11.

[84] Minnesota, *Session Laws*, 1999, Ch. 34.

[85] *Today* (Spring-Summer, 1999) 6; Pfingston, Todd, compiler, Facts about Student Athletic Facility Construction —Taylor Center and Phases I-III, in University Archives.

[86] *Ibid.*; Minnesota State University Mankato Buildings, online source.

[87] *Today* (Fall 2002), 23.

[88] *Ibid.*, (Winter, 1996), 15.

[89] Minnesota, *Session Laws*, 1998, Ch. 404, Sec. 3., Subd. 2 and 10; 2000, Ch. 1492, Art. 1, Sect. 3, Subd. 3; *Reporter*, 14 October 1999, 1; 25 April 2000, 2.

[90] *Reporter*, 11 September 2001, 7; 24 January 2002, 3; Pfingston, comp., Facts about Student Athletic Facility Construction.

[91] Here and the paragraph below, see: Minnesota State University, Mankato Buildings; *Reporter*, 24 January 2002. 3; "Myers Field House," Statement prepared by Paul Allan, sports information director, n. d., Minnesota State University, Mankato, copy in possession of William E. Lass.

[92] *Mankato Free Press*, 14 September 1991, 16 and Allan statement.

[93] Here and the two paragraphs below, see: "Minnesota State University, Mankato/Engaged in Thermodynamics," online source, access by title. Refrigeration ton is the standard way of measuring heat transfer. A refrigeration ton is the heat transfer resulting from the melting of a short ton (i.e. 2,000 pounds) of pure ice in 24 hours. "Ton of Refrigeration," *Wikipedia*. "Cooling Tower/Engaged in Thermodynamics," online sources, access by title; "Cooling tower" in *Wikipedia*.

[94] "Minnesota State History and Background," online source, search by title.

[95] *Ibid.*, Minnesota, *Session Laws*, 1995, Ch. 212,

[96] *Ibid.*, Ch. 212, Art. 4, Sec. 14.

[97] *Ibid.*, Art. 1, Subd. 2 and 3.

[98] "Minnesota State History and Background."

[99] Minnesota, *Session Laws*, 1995, Ch. 212, Art. 2, Sec. 4, Subd. 1.

[100] *Today* (Spring 1997), 10.

[101] *Ibid.*

[102] Here and the two paragraphs below *Reporter*, 22 September 1998, 1.

[103] *Today* (Fall 2000), 18.

[104] *Reporter*, 20 February 2001, 1; "California State University Channel Islands," *Wikipedia.*

[105] *Reporter*, 8 March 2001, 1.

[106] Here and the paragraph below, see: *Ibid.*, 29 March 2001, 1.

[107] "CI President Richard Rush to Retire," online article, access by title.

[108] *Reporter*, 19 April 2001, 1.

[109] "Musicorum/About Us," online source, access by title.

[110] Here and the two paragraphs, below, see: "About the President—Office of the President, Minnesota State," online source, access by title.

[111] *Today* 4 (Fall 2002), 17-20.

[112] *Reporter*, 27 August 2002, 1.

[113] Here the paragraph below, see: *Reporter*, 25 January 2007, 1; "President Scott R. Olson," online source, access by title.

[114] *Today* 6 (Spring 2005), 16-19; *Reporter*, 25 January 2007, 1.

[115] *Reporter*, 19 April 2012, 5; "President Scott R. Olson;" "Past WSU Presidents—Winona State University," online sources, access by titles

[116] Here and the two paragraphs below, see: "New Provost and Senior Vice President for Academic Affairs," (Minnesota State University, Mankato Media Relations Office News Release, 4-4-2013). Online source, access by title. Baer's administrative experience included having served as the senior vice president and interim president of Bemidji State University and as the senior vice chancellor of academic and student affairs for MnSCU. ("Linda Baer Appointed Interim Vice President for Academic and Student Affairs," Minnesota State University, Mankato news release, 10 July 2012. Online source, access by title.)

[117] Here and the two paragraphs below, see: "University Welcomes Associate Provost Robert Fleischman," Minnesota State University, Mankato Media Relations Office, 7-13-2013. Online source, access by title.

[118] Here and the three paragraphs below, see: "New Leonard A. Ford Hall to Be Dedicated Sept. 11," Minnesota State University, Mankato Media Relations Office News Release, 2008-09-10. Online source, access by title; *College Reporter*, 31 October 1967, 1.

[119] Here and the paragraph below, see: *Reporter*, 17 November 2009, 14 September 2010, 1; 28 September 2010, 1 and Minnesota State University, Mankato Buildings.

[120] Here and the two paragraphs below, see: "Clinical Sciences Building Bonding Request," Minnesota State University Media Relations News Release, 1-15-2014 and "Funding for New Clinical Sciences Building Signed into Law by Governor," Minnesota State University, Mankato Media Relations Office News Release, 5-20-2014. Online sources, access by titles.

[121] "University Breaks Ground on Clinical Sciences Building," *Mankato Free Press*, 9-27-2014 (online source); "Clinical Sciences Building Construction Phase to Begin," Minnesota State University, Mankato Media Relations Office Announcement, 1-22-2015 (Online) and "MSU's Clinical Science Building Behind Schedule," 10 July 2016, online source.

[122] Here and the paragraph below, see: "Clinical Sciences Ribbon-Cutting Ceremony Set for Jan.19," Minnesota State University, Mankato Media Relations Office News Release, 1-18-2017, online source.

[123] *Today* 18 (Winter 2017), 22.

[124] *Reporter*, 21 September 2010, 1; 24 April 2012, 3.

[125] Here and the three paragraphs below, see: *Reporter*, 28 August 2008, 5; Cynthia L. Janney email to William E. Lass, 31 January 2018; and Buildings Facilities Management—Minnesota State University, Mankato.

[126] *Reporter*, 30 July 2010, 15.

[127] *Reporter*, 21 September 2010, 1; 27 September 2011, 5; Janney to Lass, 31 January 2018.

[128] *Reporter*, 27 September 2011, 5; Buildings Facilities Management—Minnesota State University, Mankato.

[129] Here and the paragraph, below: *Reporter*, 15 March 2012, 5; "Stadium Heights Community, Minnesota State University, Mankato," online source, access by title.

[130] Here and the paragraph below, see: *Reporter*, 07 March 2013, 1.

[131] Here and the paragraphs below, see: *Reporter*, 24 April 2012, 3, 8; 25 April 2012, 5; 07 March 2013, 18 April 2013, 1, 07 November 2013, 1; *Today* (Fall 2013), 6-11; *Mankato Free Press*, 13 June 2013, B1. 27 June 2013, 1 and 30 June 2013, A1, A6 and B4.

[132] "Construction New University Dining Center Location," Minnesota State University, Mankato, online source, access by title.

[133] "May 15: Ceremonial Groundbreaking Held for New Dining Hall," Minnesota State University, Mankato Media Relations Office Press Release, 5-14-2015, online source; Janney to Lass, 31 January 2018.

[134] *Today* 18 (Winter 2017), 23; Dedication program brochure, University Archives; Janney to Lass, 31 January 2018.

[135] Minnesota State University, Mankato/Engaged in Thermodynamics, online source, access by title.

[136] Here and the three paragraphs below, see: *Reporter*, 31 August 2004, 1; 20 January 2006, 6 and 13 April 2006, 2.

[137] Here and the paragraph below, see: *Reporter*, 29 August 2002, 1; 15 October 2002, 1; Minnesota State University, Mankato Buildings.

[138] *Reporter.* 01 February 2000, 1; 18 September 2001, 1; 12 June 2002, 1 11 June 2003, 1; Minnesota, *Session Laws*, 2002, Ch. 393, Sec. 1,

Subd. 13; 2003, Ch. 20, Art. 1, Sec.3, Subd. 8.

[139] Here and the two paragraphs below, see: *Reporter*, 02 September 2004, 1; 11 June 2003, 1; 30 August 2005, 1; 04 October 2005, 5; *Today* 7 (Winter 2006), 16-19.

[140] Here and the paragraph below, see: *Mankato Free Press*, 14 September 1991, 16; 08 November 1993, 7, 09 November 1993, 12; Minnesota State University, Mankato Buildings; Pfingston, comp., Facts about Student Athletic Facility Construction.

[141] Here and the four paragraphs below, see: Earley, Jane F. File, University Archives.

[142] Here and the two paragraphs below, see: *Reporter*, 28 August 2007, A1; 01 September 2009, 1.

[143] Here and the three paragraphs below, see: "Minnesota State University, Mankato, Pedestrian Connection," online source, access by title; *Mankato Free Press*, 14 November 2013, B1.

[144] Here and the paragraph below, see; "North Central Conference," *Wikipedia*.

[145] Here and the paragraph below, see: "Northern Sun Intercollegiate Conference," *Wikipedia*.

[146] Here and the two paragraphs below, see: "Minnesota State Mavericks Men's Ice Hockey," *Wikipedia*.

[147] "Minnesota State Mavericks Women's Ice hockey," *Wikipedia*.

[148] Minnesota, *Session Laws*, 1999, Ch. 214, Art. 1, Sect. 3, Subd. 2.

[149] *Ibid.*, 2005, Ch. 107, Art. 2, Subd. 1(4) and (5).

[150] For details on these degrees, see: Minnesota State University, Mankato, *2009-2011 Graduate Studies Bulletin*, 7, 32, 39, 92 and 103; Minnesota State University, Mankato, College of Graduate Studies and Research, Doctoral Programs, online source.

[151] Jerry Oman, research specialist, Institutional Research, Planning and Assessment, email to Daardi Sizemore Mixon, 13 September 2017.

[152] Here and the three paragraphs below, see *Mankato Free Press*, 21 April 2016, A2, 26 April 2016, A4 and 23 June 2016, B1; *Minneapolis Star Tribune*, 28 April 2016, A10 and 22 June 2015, B2. For information on the TV program Coach, see "Coach (TV series)" in *Wikipedia*.

[153] Here and the three paragraphs below, see: *Mankato Free Press*, O5 August 2017, A1, D1; *Minneapolis Star Tribune*, 08 August 2017, A2; Minnesota Vikings in *Wikipedia*.

[154] Employee Salary Summary, FY 2018, Minnesota State University, Mankato, copy in University Archives.

[155] Here and the paragraph below, see: "Organizational charts—Administration—Minnesota State University," online source, access by title.

[156] Jerry Oman, research specialist, Institutional Research, Planning and Assessment, email to William E. Lass, 16 November 2017.

[157] Institutional Research, Planning and Assessment, University Data Summary, 02 February 2017.

[158] Employee Salary Summary, FY 2018, Minnesota State University, Mankato; American Federation of State County and Municipal Employees in *Wikipedia*; Minnesota Association of Professional Employees in *Wikipedia*; Minnesota State University Mankato, Bargaining Units & Personnel Plans, online source, access by title.

[159] Here and the two paragraphs below: Oman to Daardi Sizemore Mixon, 13 September 2017 and email to William E. Lass, 16 November 2017.

[160] *Mankato Free Press*, 26 January 2018, B1

[161] Here and the five paragraphs below, Cheryl C. Azarbod, administrative assistant, Global Education, email to Daardi Sizemore Mixon, 01 September 2017 and email to William E. Lass, 17 November 2017.

[162] Here and the two paragraphs below, see; Jeff Iseminger email to William E. Lass, 25 February 2018.

# APPENDIX A

## HISTORY OF MINNESOTA STATE UNIVERSITY, MANKATO ATHLETIC TEAMS, COACHES, AND ATHLETIC AFFILIATIONS

### Compiled by Paul Allan, Associate Director of Athletics, January 2018

Minnesota State University, Mankato has had various athletic teams dating back to 1922. Although the earliest teams were all for men, in 1965, the first women's teams were added as well. Now known as the Mavericks, the teams have had several other names as wells, including "Peds," which is short for "Pedagogs."

Today, there are more than 600 student-athletes at Minnesota State University, Mankato who compete in one of the following sports: NCAA Division I men's and women's hockey (Western Collegiate Hockey Association); NCAA Division II (Northern Sun Intercollegiate Conference) men's baseball, basketball, cross country, football, golf, track and wrestling; and NCAA Division II women's basketball, cross country, golf, soccer, softball, swimming, tennis, track and volleyball.

In addition to their successes in their chosen sport, these student-athletes are also successful students. At the end of the Fall 2017 semester, student-athletes had an overall combined GPA of 3.22 with 238 on the Dean's List. More than 65.3% of the student-athletes earned at least a 3.00 GPA this semester, an increase of 0.9% over the 2016 fall semester.

## Conferences
1923: Little 10
1932: Minnesota Northern Teachers College Conference
1957: Northern State Conference
1969: North Central Conference
1978: Northern Intercollegiate Conference
1982: North Central Conference
2008: Northern Sun Intercollegiate Conference

## Other Affiliations
National Association of Intercollegiate Athletics (NAIA) (1952-1960)
National Collegiate Athletics Association (NCAA) (1952-present)
Western Collegiate Hockey Association (WCHA) (1999-present)

## Men's Sports

**Baseball (1935-1941; 1945-present)**
**Coaches:**
Emmett Lowery (1935-1936)
C.P. Blakeslee (1936-1940)
Francis Mulroney (1940-1941)
C.P. Blakeslee (1945-1949)
Quinn Constanz (1949-1952)
Jim Witham (1952-1954)
John Naughton (1954-1955)
Jim Witham (1955-1956)
Bill Morris (1956-1961)
Herb Jones (1961-1963)
Jean McCarthy (1963-1976)
Dean Bowyer (1976-2008)
Matt Magers (2008-present)

**Basketball (1921-present)**
**Coaches:**
Hugh Jameson (1922-1923)
C.P. Blakeslee (1924-1939)
Jim Clark (1939-1944)
Jim Witham (1945-1954)
Bob Otto (1954-1955)
Jim Witham (1955-1956)
Bill Morris (1956-1967)
Art Ollrich (1967-1969)
Red Severson (1969-1973)
Butch Raymond (1973-1984)
Dan McCarrell (1984-2001)
Matt Margenthaler (2001-present)

**Cross Country (1956-present)**
**Coaches:**
Earl Myers (1956-1979)
Mark Schuck (1979-2013)
Loren Ahonen (2013-2016)
Chris Rombough (2016-present)

**Football (1922-1943; 1946-present)**
**Coaches:**
Hugh Jameson (1922-1924)
C.P. Blakeslee (1924-1932)
Fred Just (1932-1933)
C.P. Blakeslee (1933-1935)
Emmett Lowery (1935-1936)
Jim Carter (1936-1939)
Jim Clark (1939-1943; 1946-1949)

Earl Myers (1949-1953)
Bob Otto (1953-1970)
John Coatta (1970-1976)
Al Sandona (1977-1981)
Dan Runkle (1981-2002)
Clarence Holly (2002-2004)
Jeff Jamrog (2004-2008)
Todd Hoffner (2008-2012)
Aaron Keen (2012-2014)
Todd Hoffner (2014-present)

**Golf (1950-present)**
**Coaches:**
C.P. Blakeslee (1950-1965)
Wayne Samuelson (1965-1967)
Jack Amann (1967-1981)
Bill Griffiths (1981-1984)
Rummy Macias (1984-1988)
Jerry Carpenter (1988-1996)
Mark Clouse (1996-2003)
Mike Zinni (2003-2009)
Geoff Klein (2009-2014)
Bryant Black (2014-present)

**Gymnastics (1930-1973)**
**Coaches:**
C.P. Blakeslee (1930-1936)
Bob Weech (1936-1938)
Russ Simondet (1936-1940)
C.P. Blakeslee (1940-1962)
Don Langdon (1962-1965)
Warren Rolek (1965-1969)
Bill Holmes (1969-1973)

**Hockey (1969-present)**
**Coaches:**
Don Brose (1969-1983)
Brad Reeves (1983-1984)
Don Brose (1984-2000)
Troy Jutting (2000-2012)
Mike Hastings (2012-present)

**Swimming (1963-2011)**
**Coaches:**
Don Robinson (1963-1978)
Seemann Baugh (1978-1982)
Phil Rhoade (1982-2003)

Libor Janek (2003-2004)
Nate Owens (2004-2011)

**Tennis (1939-2011)**
**Coaches:**
G.M. Wissink (1939-1947)
Laroy Zell (1947-1949)
Paul Waldorf (1949-1965)
Jim Karabetsos (1965-1966)
Paul Waldorf (1966-1977)
Steve Luke (1977-1980)
Roger Boyer (1980-1984)
Dave Pettingill (1984-1986)
Tim Nothwehr (1986-1987)
Mark Parrott (1987-1989)
Garth Weiss (1989-1991)
Dan McLaughlin (1991-1993)
Jeff Johnson (1993-1994)
Jerry Cook (1994-1998)
Todd Scott (1998-2004)
Phil Brauer (2004-2011)

**Track (1925-present)**
**Coaches:**
C.P. Blakeslee (1925-1940)
Jim Clark (1940-1949)
Earl Myers (1949-1973)
Chuck Petersen (1973-1988)
Mark Schuck (1988-1989)
Lee Loewen (1989-1990)
Li Li (1990-1994)
Mark Schuck (1994-1995)
Bart Gray (1995-2000)
Mark Schuck (2000-2013)
Jim Dilling (2013-2017)

**Wrestling (1950-present)**
**Coaches:**
Rummy Macias (1950-1980)
Chris Sones (1980-1981)
Rummy Macias (1981-1988)
Gary Rushing (1988-1993)
Jim Makovsky (1993-present)

## Women's Sports

**Basketball (1966-present)**
Coaches:
Mary Willerscheidt (1966-1985)
Sarah Novak (1985-1989)
Susan Buntin (1989)
Joan Anderson (1989-1997)
Paula Buscher ( 1997-1998)
Ann Walker (1999-2003)
Lori Fish (2004-2008)
Pam Gohl (2008-2012)
Emilee Thiesse (2012-present)

**Bowling (2004-2011)**
Coaches:
George Cejka (2004-2006
Chad Oakes (2006-2009)
Shane Drahota (2009-2011)

**Cross Country (1972-present)**
Coaches:
Mary Willerscheidt (1972-1973)
Pat Hale (1973-1977)
Peter Thompson (1977-1978)
Jerry Salek (1978-1986)
Greg Schmidt (1986-1987)
Donna Tiegs Ricks (1987-1993)
Beth Sullivan (1993-1995)
Bart Gray (1995-2000)
Jen Behrens Blue (2000-present)

**Golf (1970-present)**
Coaches:
Jane Roberts (1970-1977)
Lois Mussett (1977-1986)
Sarah Novak (1986-1988)
Nick Campa (1988-2004)
John Marston (2004-2006)
Nick Campa (2006-present)

**Gymnastics (1965-1984)**
Coaches:
Vi Holbrook (1965-1968)
Sue Parkins (1968-1969)
Vi Holbrook (1969-1970)
Sally Hokanson (1970-1971)
Vi Holbrook (1971-1974)
Evie Hawkins (1974-1980)
Kristi Anderson (1980-1982)
Loren Christianson (1982-1984)

**Hockey (1998-present)**
Coaches:
Todd Carroll (1998-2001)
Jeff Vizenor (2001-2010)
Eric Means (2010-2015)
John Harrington (2015-present)

**Soccer (1995-present)**
Coaches:
Michelle VanAtta (1995-1996)
Chris Miskec (1996-2008)
Peter McGahey (2008-2013)
Brian Bahl (2013-present)

**Softball (1974-present)**
Coaches:
Pat Hale (1974-1980)
Kim Culligan (1980-1982)
Rosie Stallman (1982-1984)
Lori Meyer (1984-present)

**Swimming (1965-present)**
Coaches:
Lois Mussett (1965-1974)
Sally Cox (1974-1976)
Ken Brown (1976-1977)
Charles Reichert (1977-1978)
Carol Leahy (1978-1980)
Melissa Ward (1980-1982)
Phil Rhoade (1982-2003)

**Tennis (1970-present)**
Coaches:
Georgene Brock (1970-1983)
Peg Hayes (1983-1987)
Kathy Peterson (1987-1989)
Marilyn Rosenau (1989-1990)
Pam Schubbe (1990-1993)
Ibdul Idi (1993-1994)
Jerry Cook (1994-1998)
Todd Scott (1998-2002)
Shaun Sava (2002-2003)
Phil Brauer (2003-2011)
Christie Williams (2011-2016
Sofia Espana Perez
(2016-present)

**Track (1965-present)**
Coaches:
Vi Holbrook (1965-1967)
Mary Willerscheidt (1967-1975)
Iris Kimura (1975-1977)
Peter Thompson (1977-1978)
Jerry Salek (1978-1985)
Sandy Hoover (1985-1987)
Donna Tieg Ricks (1987-1993)
Beth Sullivan (1993-1995)
Bart Gray (1995-2000)
Jen Behrens/Stefanie Kelly
(2000-2002)
Jen Behrens Blue (2002-2016)
Jim Dilling (2016-2017)

**Volleyball (1967-present)**
Coaches:
Georgene Brock (1967-1980)
Pat Wagner (1980-1982)
Rosie Stallman (1982-1985)
Mary Willerscheidt (1985-1986)
Marge Burkett (1986-1998)
Doug Tully (1998-2005)
Dennis Amundson (2005-2015)
Lori Wollmuth (2015-present)

## Athletic Directors

Hugh Jameson (1922-1924)
C.P. Blakeslee (1924-1938)
Jim Clark (1938-1952)
Roy B. Moore (1952-1964)
John Hodapp (1964-1968)
Georgene Brock (1965-1998)*
Richard Koppenhaver (1968-1970)
J. Robert Otto (1970-1983)
Jack Taylor (1983-1985)
Mark Schuck (1985-1986)
Ron Wellman (1986-1987
Mark Schuck (1987-1988)
Don Amiot (1988-2002)
Kevin Buisman (2002-present)

*From 1965-1998 women's athletics was separate from men's and had its own athletic director. The two programs were combined for the 1998-1999 season under one athletic director.

# APPENDIX B

## CONSUMER PRICE INDEX

Value of the U. S. Dollar from 1868 to 2015 in 2017 Dollars

| Dollar of | Value in 2017 | Dollar of | Value in 2017 |
|---|---|---|---|
| 1868 | $18.38 | 1945 | $13.59 |
| 1870 | $19.34 | 1950 | $10.17 |
| 1875 | $22.28 | 1955 | $9.14 |
| 1880 | $25.36 | 1960 | $8.27 |
| 1885 | $27.24 | 1965 | $7.77 |
| 1890 | $27.24 | 1970 | $6.30 |
| 1895 | $29.42 | 1975 | $4.55 |
| 1900 | $29.42 | 1980 | $2.97 |
| 1905 | $27.24 | 1985 | $2.28 |
| 1910 | $26.26 | 1990 | $1.87 |
| 1915 | $24.19 | 1995 | $1.61 |
| 1920 | $12.22 | 2000 | $1.42 |
| 1925 | $13.95 | 2005 | $1.25 |
| 1930 | $14.65 | 2010 | $1.12 |
| 1935 | $17.85 | 2015 | $1.03 |
| 1940 | $17.47 | | |

Source: Consumer Price Index (Estimate) 1800- (Online source. Access by title.)

# BIBLIOGRAPHY

**Books:**

Amato, Joseph Anthony and John Radzilowski, *A New College on the Prairie: Southwest State University's First Twenty-five Years, 1967-1992.* Longmont, CO: Crossings Press, 1991.

*Atlas of Mankato, Minnesota Compiled from Public Records and Plats and Public Surveys . . . .* Mankato: M. H. Haynes, 1910.

Baer, Marcia, ed. *Those Barracks Babies.* Mankato: Alumni Affairs Office, Mankato State University, 1990.

Bartusis, Mark C., ed. *Northern State University: The First Century 1901-2000.* Aberdeen, SD: Northern State University Press, 2001.

*Biographical Directory and Condensed History Alumni Association State Normal School, Mankato, Minn., 1870-1880.* Mankato: Free Press Co., 1891.

Blegen, Theodore C. *Minnesota: A History of the State.* Minneapolis: University of Minnesota, 1963.

Cardozier, V. R. *Colleges and Universities in World War II.* Westport, CT: Praeger Publishers, 1993.

Cates, Edwin H. *A Centennial History of St. Cloud State College.* Minneapolis: Dillon Press, 1968.

Downs, Robert B. *Horace Mann: Champion of the Public Schools.* New York: Twayne Publishers, 1974.

DuFresene, Robert A., *Winona State University: A History of One Hundred Twenty-five Years.* Winona, MN: Winona State University, 1985

Christianson, Theodore. *Minnesota the Land of Sky-Tinted Waters: A History of the State and Its People.* Vol. 2. Chicago: American Historical Society, 1935.

Farrell, Maurice L., ed., *The Dow Jones Averages 1885-1970* ([New York]: Dow Jones & Co., 1972.

Faust, Claire E. *Mankato State University: The Second Century: The First Twenty-Five Years 1968-1992: An Interpretative Essay.* [Mankato: Mankato State University, 1993].

Folwell, William Watts. *A History of Minnesota.* 4 vols. St. Paul: Minnesota Historical Society, 1921-1930.

Glasrud, Clarence A. *The Moorhead Normal School.* Moorhead, MN: Moorhead State University, 1987.

_____. *Moorhead State Teachers College (1921-1957).* Moorhead: Moorhead State University, 1990.

Greene, Dana. *Denise Lervertov: A Poet's Life.* Urbana, IL: University of Illinois Press, 2012.

Hagen, William T. *American Indians.* Rev. ed. Chicago: University of Chicago Press, 1979.

Harcleroad, Fred F., H. Bradley Sagen, and C. Theodore Molen, Jr. *The Developing State Colleges and Universities: Historical Background, Current Status, and Future Plans.* Iowa City, Iowa: The American College Testing Program, 1969.

Hartmann, Susan. *The Home Front and Beyond: American Women in the 1940s.* Boston: Twayne Publishers, 1982.

Herring, George C. *America's Longest War: The United States and Vietnam, 1950-1975.* Boston: McGraw-Hill, 2002.

Hughes, Thomas. *History of Blue Earth County.* Chicago: Middle West Publishing Co., [1909].

Johnson, David W. *Hamline University: A History.* St. Paul: North Central Publishing Co., 1980.

Jordan, Philip D. *The People's Health: A History of Public Health in Minnesota to 1948.* St. Paul: Minnesota Historical Society, 1953.

Kunz, Virginia Brainard. *Muskets to Missiles: A Military History of Minnesota.* St. Paul: Minnesota Statehood Centennial Commission, 1958.

Lass, William E. *Minnesota: A History.* 2d ed. New York: W. W. Norton & Co., 1998.

LeBlanc, Diane and Allys Swanson. *Playing for Equity: Oral Histories of Women Leaders in the Early Years of Title IX.* Jefferson, NC: McFarland & Co., 2016.

Lehmberg, Stanford and Ann M. Pflaum. *The University of Minnesota, 1945-2000.* Minneapolis: University of Minnesota Press, 2001.

Mallett, Richard P. *University of Maine at Farmington: A Study of Educational Change (1864-1974).* Freeport, ME: Bond Wheelwright Co., 1974.

Mitau, G. Theodore. *Minnesota's Colleges of Opportunity: From Normal Schools to Teachers College and State University System — A Century of Academic Change in Minnesota.* n. p.: Alumni Associations of the Minnesota State University System, March, 1977.

Moir, Thomas L. *History of St. John's Episcopal Church Mankato, Minnesota.* Mankato: Privately printed, February, 1966.

Moore, Roy Benjamin. *Chronicle of Athletics Control: A History of Administration of Intercollegiate Athletics at Mankato State University 1890s-1980s.* Mankato: College of Health Physical Education and Nursing, Mankato State University, 1989.

Murchie, R. W. and M. E. Jarchow. *Population Trends in Minnesota.* University of Minnesota Agricultural Experiment Station. Bulletin 32. May 1936.

Neill, Edward Duffield. *The History of Minnesota from the Earliest French Explorations to the Present Time.* 4th ed. Minneapolis: Minnesota Historical Co., 1882.

Nickerson, James F. *Out of Chaos: Reflections of a University President and His Contemporaries On Vietnam Era Unrest in Mankato and Its Relevance Today.* Sesquicentennial ed. Mankato: Minnesota State University, Mankato Foundation, 2017.

Polenberg, Richard. *War and Society: The United States, 1941-1945.* Philadelphia: Lippincott, 1972.

Ridge, Martin. *Ignatius Donnelly: Portrait of a Politician.* Chicago: University of Chicago Press, 1962.

Ruggles, Clyde Orvall. *Historical Sketch and Notes: Winona State Normal School, 1860-1910.* [St. Paul]: Minnesota Normal School Board, 1910.

Snarr, Otto Welton. *The Education of Teachers in the Middle States: An Historical Study of the Professional Education of Public School Teachers as a State Function.* Chicago: University of Chicago, 1945.

Searing, Edward. *The First Six Books of Virgil's Aeneid.* New York: A. S. Barnes & Co., 1874.

Stevens, Hiram F. *History of the Bench and Bar of Minnesota.* Vol. 1. Minneapolis: Legal Publishing and Engraving Co., 1904.

Tucker, Spencer C., ed., *Encyclopedia of World War II: A Political, Social, and Military History,* 5 vols. Santa Barbara, CA: ABC-CLIO, 2005.

University of Minnesota. *General Alumni Catalogue,* 1916.

Upham, Warren and Rose Barteau Dunlap, comps. *Minnesota Biographies 1655-1912.* Vol. 14 *Collections of the Minnesota Historical Society.* St. Paul, 1912.

Warner, George E. and Charles M. Foote, eds. *History of the Minnesota Valley . . . .* Minneapolis: North Star Publishing Co., 1882.

Williams, T. Harry, Richard N. Current and Frank Freidel, *A History of the United States [Since 1865].* New York: Alfred A. Knopf, 1960.

Youel, Donald B. *Mankato State College: An Interpretative Essay.* Mankato: Mankato State College, May 1968.

## Articles and Chapters:

Beale, Harriet. "The Early Life of Mr. Cooper." *School Progress* (Mankato State Teachers College), January 1935.

Binder, Frederick M. "Carter, James Gordon." *American National Biography.* Vol. 4. New York: Oxford University Press, 1999.

Bruce, Robert V. "Bell, Alexander Graham." *American National Biography,* Vol. 2. New York: Oxford University Press, 1999.

Crabb, Alfred Leland. "A Most Remarkable Woman." *Peabody Journal of Education* 46 (November 1968): 139-41.

Danbom, David B. "Rural Education Reform and the Country Life Movement, 1900-1920." *Agricultural History* 53 (April 1979): 462-74.

Fletcher, Lafayette G. M. "The Public Schools." *Mankato: Its First Fifty Years.* Mankato: Free Press Printing Co., 1903.

"For Future Generations: The Legacy of Blue Earth County Historical Society's Founders," *The Blue Earth County Historian* 22 (Spring 2016).

Hughes, Thomas. "A History of Steamboating on the Minnesota River." *Collections of the Minnesota Historical Society,* vol. 10, pt. 1. (St. Paul, 1905):1 31-63.

"John, D. D. Rev. David Clark[e]." *Mankato: Its First Fifty Years.* Mankato: Free Press Publishing Co., 1903.

Lach, Edward L., Jr. "Mann, Horace." *American National Biography.* Vol. 14. New York: Oxford University Press, 1999.

Lass, William E. "Histories of the U. S.-Dakota War of 1862: A Review." *Minnesota History* 63 (Summer 2012): 44-57.

_____. "'Utterly Blind, Stupid and Absurd:' Minnesota Press Reaction to the Capital Removal Attempt." *Minnesota History* 63 (Fall 2013): 281-93.

Lee, Arthur O. "Paternalistic President: Manfred W. Deputy of Bemidji State College." *Minnesota History* 42 (Spring 1971): 178-85.

"MAVERICK, SAMUEL AUGUSTUS." *The Handbook of Texas Online.*

"McCleary, James Thompson." *Biographical Directory of the United States Congress 1774-2005.* Washington: Government Printing Office, 2005.

Moneyhon, Carl H. "Maverick, Samuel Augustus." *American National Biography,* vol. 14. New York: Oxford University Press, 1999.

Niles, Sanford. "The Common Schools." In Greer, John N. *The History of Education in Minnesota.* Washington: Government Printing Office, 1902.

Oxford English Dictionary: T*he Definitive Record of the English Language.* Oxford, England: Oxford University Press, 2017.

Rankin, A. W. "High Schools." In Greer, John N. *The History of Education in Minnesota.* Washington: Government Printing Office, 1902.

Smith, James P. "Vietnam Remembered: Minnesotans and the Vietnam War." *Roots 19* Spring 1991.

Talbot, Jean. "Winona State College: First State Normal School 1860 Winona State College 1960," *Quarterly Bulletin of Winona State College,* August 1959.

## Institutional Publications

"The First Seventy-Five Years an Informal History of Mankato State Teachers College." *School Progress* 25. January 1944.

*Katonian,* 1921-1945, 1971.

*Mankato Normal School Catalog,* 1877-1921.

*Mankato State Teachers College Catalog,* 1922-1957.

*Mankato State College Catalog,* 1957-1975.

*Mankato State University Graduate Bulletin,* 1978-1979.

*Mankato State University Undergraduate Bulletin,* 1978-1979.

*The Mankatonian,* 1891-1913.

*Mankato State University Newsweekly,* 1988.

*M. S. N. Normal 1916.*

Nydahl, Theodore L. "Alterations in the Physical Plant Under President McElroy," *School Progress* 27 (May 1946).

*Senior Annual M. S. N. 1914.*

*The Student,* 1888-1891.

*Today* (Alumni Affairs Newsletter), 1982-2017.

## Minnesota Government Documents

*Executive Documents,* 1868-1902. (These volumes include reports from the various branches of state government including the State Normal School Board and the Superintendent of Public Instruction.)

*Fifteenth Biennial Report of the Superintendent of Public Instruction of Minnesota,* 1907-1908.

*General Laws,* 1860, 1866, 1873, 1881, 1883, 1893.

*General Statutes,* 1866.

*Legislative Manual,* 1877, 1879, 1891,1893, 1905, 1935, 1949, 1955.

Minnesota Department of Education. *First Report of the State Board of Education and Twenty-First Biennial Report of the Department of Education,* 1919-1920.

_____. *Nineteenth Biennial Report,* 1915-1916.

_____. *Twentieth Biennial Report,* 1917-1918.

_____. *Second Report of the State Board of Education and Twenty-second Biennial Report of the Department of Education,* 1921-1922.

_____. *Third Report of the State Board of Education and Twenty-third Biennial Report of the Department of Education,* 1923-1924.

*Minnesota Territory. Laws,* 1849.

*Minnesota. Senate Journal,* 1963.

_____. *Sixteenth Biennial Report of the Superintendent of Public Instruction . . . for the School Years 1909 and 1910.*

_____. *Session Laws,* 1919, 1921, 1923 1929, 1931, 1933, 1937, 1939, 1943, 1947, 1949, 1951, 1955, 1957, 1961, 1973-1976, 1978, 1983, 1987, 1988, 1989, 1995, 1997, 1998, 1999, 2002, 2005.

_____. *Special Laws,* 1867, 1868.

*Tenth Biennial Report of the Superintendent of Public Instruction State of Minnesota for the School Years Ending July 31, 1897 and 1898.* St. Paul: Pioneer Press Co., 1899.

## Newspapers

*Among Ourselves* (Mankato State Teachers College), 1926.

*College Spirit* (Mankato State Teachers College), 1934-1935.

*The Free Press,* 1897, 1899, 1905, 1912-1913, 1918-1919, 1921-1924, 1927-1932, 1934, 1937-1939, 1940, 1943, 1946-1947, 1951-1954, 1956-1957, 1960, 1962-1965, 1967-1968, 1970-1975, 1977-1979, 1981-1984 1987, 1991-1993, 1995-1996, 2009-2010, 2013, 2016-2018.

*Mankato Weekly Record,* 1866-1877.

*Mankato Daily Review,* 1899, 1906, 1909, 1912, 1918, 1919.

*Mankato News,* 1940.

*Mankato Weekly Review,* 1870-1894.

*Mankato Union,* 1869-1877.

*Minneapolis Morning Tribune,* 1912, 1918.

*Minneapolis Star Tribune,* 1991, 2016-2017.

*Minneapolis Sunday Tribune,* 1951, 1963.

*Minneapolis Tribune,* 1965, 1972.

*Reporter* (Mankato State Teachers College, Mankato State College, Mankato State University, Minnesota State University, Mankato), 1935, 1937, 1938, 1939-1940, 1942, 1944, 1946-1953, 1955-1978, 1980-1984, 1986, 1988, 1991-1992, 1994, 1998, 2000-2002 and 2004-2014.

*St. Paul Pioneer Press,* 1963.

*School Spirit* (Mankato State Teachers College), 1929-1933.

*Tacoma News Tribune,* 1967.

*University Independent* (Mankato State University), 1976-1977. (The Reporter was renamed the Independent, 21 September1976-19 May 1977.)

## Archival Records

(Unless otherwise indicated all collections are from the University Archives at Minnesota State University, Mankato.)

Academic Affairs. Collection, 1916-ongoing. MSU Archives Collection 14
   Campus Consolidation "Report to the Board of Review of the Commission on Institutions of Higher Education North Central Association of Colleges and Secondary Schools" by Oldfather and Latham

Administrative Services. Collection, 1901-1993. MSU Archives Collection 170
   Andrew, Gary M. and Duane Grande. "Plan for Mankato State College Consolidation on *Highland Campus (Phase II)*. January, 1975
   List of vouchers for land owned by the State of Minnesota on the Mankato State Teachers College campus "A Study to Determine the Need for the Valley (Lower) Campus Mankato State College Mankato, Minnesota." January 1974

Bohannon, Eugene W. Research File. University of Minnesota Duluth Archives.

Commencement. Collection, 1870-ongoing. MSU Archives Collection 46

Directories, Collection, 1927-ongoing. MSU Archives Collection 149

Employee Salary Summary, FY 2018, Minnesota State University, Mankato. https://www.mnsu.edu/hr/publicinfo/publicinfo.html   Online Source

Faculty Governance. Collection, 1868-ongoing.  MSU Archives Collection 36 Inter-Faculty Organization. 1944 constitution. Staff Meeting Minutes, 1932, 1939.

Homecoming Papers. Collection, 1928-ongoing.  MSU Archives Collection 19
   Alumni Dinner Program, October 26, 1929

Institutional Research. Collection, 1921-ongoing. MSU Archives Collection 16
   Enrollment Statistics
   Summary of Annual Attendance

Institutional Research, Planning and Assessment, University Data Summary, http://www.mnsu.edu/instres/annualreports/ Online Source 02 February 2017.

Library Services. Collection, 1911-ongoing.  MSU Archives Collection 167

Miller, George J, 1880-1973. Collection, 1865-1988. MSU Archives Collection 302

Old Main Cornerstone. Collection, 1869-1969. MSU Archives Collection 22

Oman, Jerry. Research specialist, Institutional Research, Planning and Assessment.
    Email to Daardi Sizemore Mixon, university archivist, 13 September 2017.
    History of Enrollment Statistical Table. Attached to email from Jerold J. Oman to Daardi Sizemore Mixon, university archivist, 11 November 2017.
    Email to William E. Lass, 17 November 2017.

Pfingston, Todd, comp., Facts about Student Athletic Facility Construction —Taylor Center and Phases I-III, in University Archives.

President's Office. Collection, 1867-ongoing.  MSU Archives Collection 13
    Cooper, Charles H. Annual reports, 1910-1911, 1911-1912, 1912-1913,  1913-1914, 1915-1916, 1917-1918, 1918-1919, 1920-1921
    Crawford, Clarence L. Correspondence and reports McElroy, Frank D. "Mankato State Teachers College: A Report of Progress and of Present Status," November 30, 1938.
    _____. Report of "State Teachers College, Mankato Minnesota, May 20, 1934."

Registrar's Office. Collection, 1870-Ongoing. MSU Archives Collection 100 Class Schedules Series

State University System/Minnesota State. Collection, 1859-Ongoing.  MSU Archives Collection 10
    State Normal School Board Minutes, 1859-1921
    State Teachers College Board Minutes, 1921-1957
    State College Board Minutes, 1957-1975
    State University Board Minutes, 1975-1995

University General Records. Collection, 1868-Ongoing.  MSU Archives Collection 12
    Mankato Normal School Prudential Committee Minutes, 1868-1873

University Archives Research Files
    Aurit, Val H.
    Boubel, Karen A.
    Colway, Victor
    Chair of Ideas
    Cooper, Charles H.
    Earley, Jane F.
    Faust, Claire E.
    Gage, George M.
    Glines, Donald E.
    Hess, David N.
    John, David Clarke
    Leichsenring, Melba
    McDonald, Brendan John
    Moore, Douglas R.
    Morris, Gretchen S.
    Searing, Edward
    Sears, Julia A.
    Trafton, Gilbert H.
    Wagen, Alma D.
    Wissink Hall

University Athletics Collection, 1925-ongoing. MSU Archives Collection 26
    Mankato State Teachers College.  Athletics pamphlet [1931]
    Track and field artifacts, Accession 2016-48.

Wagen, Alma D. Records. University of Minnesota Archives, Minneapolis.

Wilson Campus School, Collection, 1917-2002. MSU Archives Collection 307
    "Factors Related to Future Wilson School Funding and Facilities." Wilson Campus School, Closing of Wilson Campus School Correspondence, Miscellaneous, 1974-1976.

## Manuscripts

(Unless otherwise indicated all collections are from the Southern Minnesota Historical Center at Minnesota State University, Mankato.)

Brock, Georgene, 1937-. Oral History Interview, 2016. SMHC Manuscript Collection 254

Imm, Val, 1893 - 1981. Papers, 1932 - 1974. SMHC Manuscript Collection 153

Schellberg, Ruth M. 1912-. Collection, 1937-2000. SMHC Manuscript Collection 225

Snarr, Otto Welton, 1866-1966. Collection, 1857-1968. SMHC Manuscript Collection 122. Fletcher, Mrs. L. G. M. "Early Days in the Mankato State Normal School."

Willard, William Dodsworth, 1867 - 1952. Reminiscences, 1856 - 1952. SMHC Manuscript Collection 121

## U. S. Government Documents

U. S. Census Bureau. *Historical Statistics of the United States: Colonial Times to 1970.* Pt.2. Washington: GPO, 1975.

Census Office. *Population of the United States in 1860.*

_____. *Statistics of the Population of the United States,* 1880.

_____. *Population,* Pt. 1, 1890.

_____. *Compendium of the Ninth Census,* 1870.

U. S. Bureau of the Census, *Sixteenth Census of the United States, 1940: Population,* Vol. 1.
_____, 1990. *Census of Population and Housing.*

## Unpublished Theses and Dissertations

Anderson, Debra L. "Mankato State Normal School: The Foundation Years, 1868-1880." M.A. Thesis. Mankato State University, 1987.

Giebel, Arnie. "The Development of Mankato Normal School from 1877-1890." M.S. Thesis, Mankato State Teachers College, 1956.

Grev, Julian Richard. "Mankato State College 1890 through 1900." M.S. Thesis, Mankato State College, 1964.

Hall, Stanley. "History of Common Schools in Blue Earth County." Master of Arts in Teaching Thesis, Mankato State College, 1973.

Haugland, Mary C. "The History of Women's Intercollegiate Athletics at Mankato State University 1964-1983." M.S. Thesis, Mankato State University, 1984.

Larson, Sexton. "The Organization and Early Development of Mankato State Normal School 1867-1871." M.S. Thesis. Mankato State Teachers College, 1954.

Pengilly, Joan Forssmark. "The First Female President of a Co-educational Public Institution of Higher Learning: An Historical Examination of the Presidential Tenure of Julia Ann Sears, 1872-1873." Ph.D. dissertation. University of Akron, 1995.

Tuinstra, Diane R. "Mankato State Teachers College during World War II." M.A. Thesis. Mankato State University, 1994.

## Other

"About the President—Office of the President, Minnesota State." Online source.

Amadeo, Kimberly. "Black Thursday 1929: What Happened and What Caused It," updated August 05, 2016, online source, access by title.

"American Federation of State County and Municipal Employees." *Wikipedia.*

"American Indian Movement." *Wikipedia.*

"America's Lost Colleges/Duluth Junior College" http://www.lostcolleges.com/ Accessed 15 October 2016.

Ardolf, Steven. Interview of Ardolf, chief engineer of Minnesota State University, Mankato, by William E. Lass, 21 April 2017.

"Arthur Edgar Morgan." *Wikipedia.*

Azarbod, Cheryl C. Administrative assistant, Global Education. Email to Daardi Sizemore Mixon, 01 September 2017.

_____. Email to William E. Lass, 17 November 2017.

"Bresnan Communications." *Wikipedia.*

Broman, Elizabeth. "1964: Fountains, Fireworks, Fifty Years Ago — A World's Fair." Online source.

"Buildings, Facilities Management- Mankato State University, Mankato." Online source.

Carlson, Wayne. "Legendary Spectator." *Today Magazine Online,* 26 October 2011.

"Ceremonial Groundbreaking Held for New Dining Hall." Minnesota State University, Mankato Media Relations Office Press Release, 5-14-2015. Online source.

"CI President Richard Rush to Retire." Online article.

"C-Ration." *Wikipedia.*

"Churchill Delivers Iron Curtain Speech." Online source. Access by title.

"Civil Defense in Minnesota, 1950-1974," in MNOPEDIA, an online encyclopedia.

"Civilian Pilot Training Program." *Wikipedia.*

"Clinical Sciences Building Bonding Request." Minnesota State University Media Relations News Release, 1-15-2014. Online source.

"Clinical Sciences Building Construction Phase to Begin." Minnesota State University, Mankato Media Relations Office Announcement, 1-22-2015. Online source.

"Clinical Sciences Ribbon-Cutting Ceremony Set for Jan. 19." Minnesota State University, Mankato Media Relations Office News Release, 1-18-2017. Online source.

"Coach (TV series)" in *Wikipedia*.

"Construction New University Dining Center Location." Minnesota State University, Mankato. Online source.

Consumer Price Index (Estimate) 1800- Online source. Access by title.

"Cooling tower." *Wikipedia*.

"Cooling Tower/Engaged in Thermodynamics." Online source.

Crawford, Clarence Leonard. *Who's Who in America,* vol. 33 (1964-1965). Chicago: Marquis-Who's Who, 1965.

Deed Record No. 127. Recorder's Office, Blue Earth County Courthouse, Mankato.

"Employment & Unemployment Statistics," *Infoplease*. Online source,

"Essay: The Federal Emergency Relief Administration." Online source. Access by title.

"Federal Civil Defense Administration." *Wikipedia*.

"Funding for New Clinical Sciences Building Signed into Law by Governor." Minnesota State University, Mankato Media Relations Office News Release, 5-20-2014. Online source.

"G. I. Bill." *Wikipedia*.

"Glen Taylor." *Wikipedia*.

"Goddard Announces the Appointment of New Chief Academic Officer." Online source.

"Goddard Defends Hiring of Dean With a Past No Confidence Vote." Online source.

"History of Title IX-Women Sports Foundation." Online source.

Iseminger, Jeff. Email to William E. Lass, 25 February 2018.

"Jackson State Killings." *Wikipedia*.

Janney, Cynthia L. Email to William E. Lass, 31 January 2018.

John, David Clarke. World Cat bibliographical search.

"Kent State Shootings." *Wikipedia*.

"Lewis Jones Goddard College." Online source.

"Linda Baer Appointed Interim Vice President for Academic and Student Affairs." Minnesota State University, Mankato news release, 10 July 2012. Online source.

McCleary, James Thompson. World Cat bibliographical search.

"Mankato, Minnesota." *Wikipedia*.

Miller, George J World Cat bibliographical search.

*"Mining of Haiphong Harbor."* Vietnam.net. Online Source.

"Minnesota Association of Professional Employees." *Wikipedia*.

"Minnesota Legislative Reference Library: Legislators Past & Present." Online Source.

*Minnesota Normal Schools Quarterly Journal 1*. October 1915.

"Minnesota State Mavericks Hall of Fame." Online source.

"Minnesota State Mavericks Men's Ice Hockey." *Wikipedia*.

"Minnesota State Mavericks Women's Ice hockey." *Wikipedia*.

"Minnesota State University Mankato, Bargaining Units & Personnel Plans." Online source.

"Minnesota State University, Mankato, College of Graduate Studies and Research, Doctoral Programs". Online source.

"Minnesota State University, Mankato/Engaged in Thermodynamics." Online source.

"Minnesota State University, Mankato, Pedestrian Connection." Online source

"Minnesota Vikings." *Wikipedia.*

"Mitchell Goodman." *Wikipedia.*

"Mitchell Goodman, Antiwar Protest Leader, Dies at 73." *New York Times* obituary. Online source.

"MSU's Clinical Science Building Behind Schedule." 10 July 2016. Online source.

"Musicorum/About Us." Online source.

"New Leonard A. Ford Hall to Be Dedicated Sept. 11." Minnesota State University, Mankato Media Relations Office News Release, 2008-09-10. Online source.

"New Provost and Senior Vice President for Academic Affairs." Minnesota State University, Mankato Media Relations Office News Release, 4-4-2013. Online source.

"1973 Oil Crisis." *Wikipedia.*

"North Central Association of Colleges and Schools." in *Wikipedia.*

"North Central Conference." *Wikipedia.*

"Northern Sun Intercollegiate Conference," *Wikipedia.*

"Opposition to United States Involvement in the Vietnam War." *Wikipedia.*

"Organizational charts—Administration—Minnesota State University." Online source.

"Paris Peace Accord." *Wikipedia.*

"Past WSU Presidents—Winona State University." Online source.

"President Scott R. Olson." Online source.

Searing, Edward. World Cat bibliographical search.

Smith, Steve W. Assistant vice president for budget and business services, Email to William E. Lass, 20 November 2017.

"Stadium Heights Community, Minnesota State University, Mankato." Online source.

"Standeford Observatory—Facilities—Physics and Astronomy." Online source.

"Stanford Cardinal." *Wikipedia.*

Terraced hillside photograph, online source http://cornerstone.lib.mnsu.ed/aerial_1959_HxG/1261) He died on December 7, 1954. (2s, 1941-1945 Polenberg, ember 7, 1954. (ticipated in several fraternal clubs and unsuccessfull

"Timeline of Events in the Cold War." *Wikipedia*

"Ton of Refrigeration," *Wikipedia.*

Trafton, Gilbert. World Cat bibliographical search.

"United States GDP Annual Growth Rate, 1948-2016." Online source. Access by title.

U. S. Office of Energy Efficiency & Renewable Energy. "Fact #915: March 7, 2016, Average Historical Annual Gasoline Pump Price, 1929-2015." Online source.

"University of California, San Marcos." *Wikipedia.*

University Dining Center dedication program brochure, University Archives.

"University Welcomes Associate Provost Robert Fleischman." Minnesota State University, Mankato Media Relations Office, 7-13-2013. Online source.

Vance Daniel. "William J. Bresnan". *Connect Business Magazine* (January 2001).

"Vietnam War Draft." Online source.

"Will Durant." *Wikipedia.*

"William Bresnan." *Wikipedia.*

# INDEX

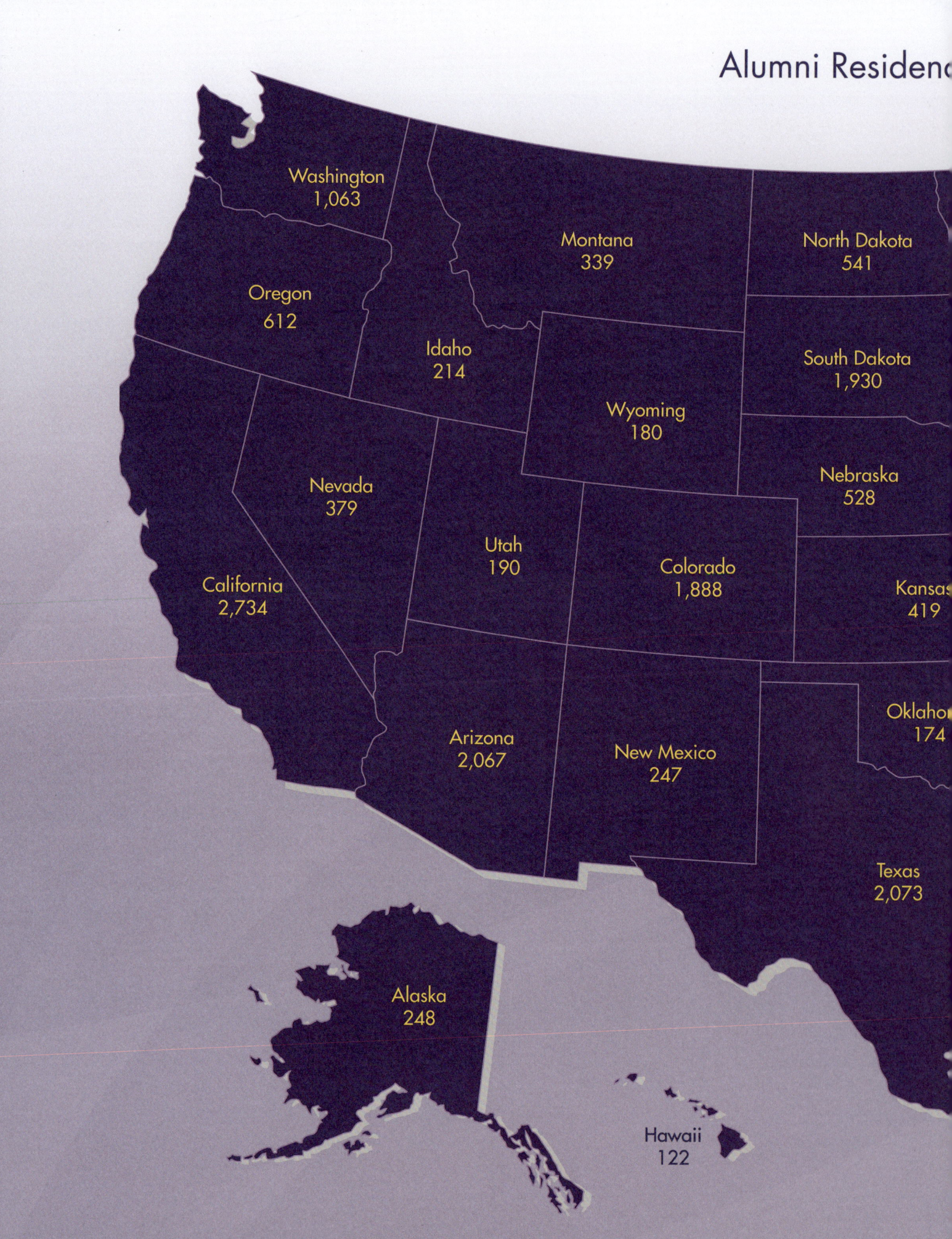

Alumni Residen

Washington
1,063

Montana
339

North Dakota
541

Oregon
612

Idaho
214

South Dakota
1,930

Wyoming
180

Nebraska
528

Nevada
379

Utah
190

Colorado
1,888

Kansas
419

California
2,734

Arizona
2,067

New Mexico
247

Oklahoma
174

Texas
2,073

Alaska
248

Hawaii
122